Translations and Annotations
of
Choral Repertoire

Translations Compiled
by

Ron Jeffers

Edited and Annotated
by

Gordon Paine

Volume II: German Texts

***earthsongs**, 220 nw 29th street, corvallis, oregon 97330*

Acknowledgments

This project has been facilitated by several people to whom I owe a great debt of thanks. In the first place my gratitude goes to my partner Ron Jeffers for inviting me to join him in this experience and for his unflagging efforts to assist me in research and writing. Lee Gilbert of the German faculty at California State University Fullerton gave generously of his time and expertise and was especially helpful with older texts. Joe Arnold and Preston Stedman were of great help when I was incapacitated for some time, and Ute Kreyssig was most kind in finding last-minute bibliographic information. I am also most grateful to the administration of California State University Fullerton for the opportunity to take a research sabbatical and to the inter-library loan and circulation staffs at my university, who have always been most helpful with my arcane requests. To Helmuth Rilling go my thanks for teaching me how to think about music, and I am most grateful to Helmuth and his wife Martina for their hospitality and access to their library. Finally and most specially, my appreciation goes to my beloved wife Sherry for her endless patience, love, kindness, and support through a most challenging year.

Gordon Paine

A book such as this is the result of many people working together to produce a reference work that will be of real service to the entire choral community, that vital group of conductors, teachers, and students, professional and amateur choristers, and avid listeners. Certain individuals deserve special mention and thanks, and first among those would have to be Gordon Paine, whose linguistic sensitivity and musical expertise have improved every page of this book. The reference librarians and the Inter-Library Loan departments at the Valley Library at Oregon State University, the Knight Library at the University of Oregon, and the libraries at the University of California Berkeley were always generous with their time and assistance. Sabbatical leave from Oregon State University provided invaluable, uninterrupted time. Allen Crowell, Rodney Eichenberger, and their graduate choral conducting students assisted with the selection of texts to be included. Joseph Byrd and Lynn Doss were particularly helpful in generating the list of selected settings of the German texts. My *earthsongs* co-workers kept things running smoothly while I was working, especially Twila Hunsaker and Stephanie Mehlenbacher. Each member of my family—Becky, Alan, and Robin—was personally supportive and understanding—always. And finally there were many members of the choral community that were encouraging, eager, and patient to have Volume II appear. Thank you all very, very much.

Ron Jeffers

Editor's Note to Second Edition with Corrections

The printing plates from the second edition of 2000 having been damaged by use and time, it was necessary to produce new plates for a reprinting in 2011. This presented the occasion to incorporate corrections that I have been stockpiling in the hope that such an opportunity might arise.

Gordon Paine

TABLE OF CONTENTS

INTRODUCTION

GERMAN TEXTS

BACH, JOHANN SEBASTIAN (1685–1750)

Cantatas

Motets

BEETHOVEN, LUDWIG VAN (1770–1827)

BRAHMS, JOHANNES (1833-1897)

HYMNS

CAROLS

CANONS

APPENDICES

Introduction

EDITORIAL NOTES

"In the beginning was the word...."

The composers of song are inspired by words, words sacred and secular, joyous and mournful, words beautiful in their own euphony. The experience of studying and singing vocal music is thus incomplete unless both performers and audience understand the meaning of what is being sung. And it is even better when all understand something more about the text, its background, the poet, and the composer's relationship to the words. Reaching such an understanding is a challenge in one's native language and is vastly more difficult in a foreign tongue.

The task we have attempted in this volume is to assist the reader, whether a conductor, singer, or interested amateur, to better comprehend the rich repertoire of choral music in German, and we hope, to develop an appreciation for the texts to which that repertoire is set. To this end we have provided translations, both literal and in relatively idiomatic English, for a great many choral compositions. In addition we have supplied an annotation to each text that can be read by or to a choir and can provide a basis for program notes to inform audiences. We have also provided a glossary, rudimentary assistance with pronunciation, and an index to additional works set to the texts we present here. It is our hope that these tools will enrich the musical lives of those who use them.

The German Texts

Presentation

The German text in the left-hand column is the text the composer set to music, complete with any additions, omissions, and adaptations by the composer. The punctuation of the original poem usually has been restored, however. In some cases, text omitted by the composer is shown in square brackets; in others it is presented and discussed in the annotation.

We expect that a reader usually will come to this work looking for a translation to a specific composition and will have access to a score. Score study will show how the composer treated the text in terms of repetition and rearrangement of words, simultaneous overlay of successive phrases, etc. For this reason we do not address these matters in the presentation of the German texts, though they may be discussed in the annotation.

On the other hand, we presume that readers will not have easy access to a historical or critical version of the original text, and that they therefore will have no knowledge of what the composer might have changed. We therefore provide a list of *Variants* so that the reader can see what the poet actually wrote. The words shown in roman type are those used by the composer; those in italics are from the original source. When the variant substantially changes the meaning of the composer's text, a translation is provided.

One of the challenges of this project has been to communicate what the texts *mean* as well as what they *say*. The two are often divergent, as German and English have different idioms, and poetry involves the artistic and sometimes purposely vague use of language. To this end, the word-for-word translations in the left column are rather literal, while the block translations in the right column may be freer.

The understanding of German poetry, particularly older texts, is a challenge to a non-native speaker or reader, as poets will freely change word order, use imprecise words, paint images that defy translation, and omit word endings that define grammatical function. Such obfuscation is sometimes unintentional, resulting from a need to reduce the number of syllables in a line or to create a rhyme or a specific accentual pattern. Often, however, it is artistically motivated—either as a virtuosic, poetic use of language or as an invitation to the readers to find their own meaning. Our translations may therefore differ in some significant respects from translations by others. Nonetheless, we trust that they will enable the readers both to find their way and enjoy the journey.

2

Sources of Text—as Set to Music

The version of the text as set by the composer was ascertained from critical editions and reference works. When no critical source was available, an octavo edition was used.

Biblical Texts. The numbering of chapters and verses is that of the Revised Standard Version, which may differ from the numbering of the Luther Bible, particularly in the Psalms.

Works of J.S. Bach. Texts to the works of Bach have been taken from Werner Neumann, ed., *Sämtliche von Johann Sebastian Bach vertonte Texte* (Leipzig: VEB deutscher Verlag für Musik, 1974).

Works of Johannes Brahms. Brahms's texts have been taken from Gustav Ophüls, ed., *Brahms-Texte* (Ebenhausen bei München: Langwiesche-Brandt, 1983). Occasional errors have been tacitly corrected.

Canons. Fritz Jode's *Der Kanon: ein Singbuch für alle* (Wolfenbüttel: Möseler, 1959) has served as the source for all canon texts.

Sources of Text—as Originally Written

The source for the original text is shown under *Source* at the end of the translation. By "original" we mean the text as written by its author, before any modifications by composers or others. In the case of original poetry, the specific sources used by the composers (particularly Brahms) have been employed if known and available. Collected-works editions were used in most other cases. Where no "source" is shown, none was found.

Biblical Texts. No "source" has been shown for most of the Biblical texts because it is usually impossible to determine which version of the Bible the composer used. For this reason as well, no "variants" are shown. The annotation will include discussion of any significant deviations from the Luther Bibles available to the editors.

Hymns. The sources for the hymns vary widely in nature. Whenever possible, a facsimile or a modern critical edition of an early source was used (e.g., Luther, Nicolai, Fleming, Spee).

Philipp Wackernagel's compendium *Das deutsche Kirchenlied von der ältesten Zeit bis zu Anfang des 17. Jahrhunderts* (Wackernagel, 1964) provided the texts for several chorales from before 1600 (Eber, Geletzki, Hembold, Reusner, Ringwaldt, Schneegaß, Weiße). Other hymns could be found only in editions from the time of Bach, and several could be located only in modern hymnals.

Many chorales have undergone numerous generations of revision over the centuries, some of which parted ways with the original and some of which were intended to return to it. Because it is usually impossible to know what version of a hymn a specific composer used, it is also impossible to know what changes he might have made personally.

Koran. Quotations from the Koran are from M.H. Shakir, trans. *Holy Qur'an = [al-Qur'an al-hakim]* (1st U.S. ed. Elmhurst, NY: Tahrike Tarsile Qur'an, 1982).

Editing

Some challenges have arisen from the vast time span covered by the texts, as well as changes in the German language:

- Punctuation was either sparse or completely absent until well into the seventeenth century. The hymns of Luther, for example, were often punctuated only with a period at the end of each "sentence," which might include a whole paragraph as we understand it today.

- Spelling and vocabulary have evolved through time, and many older texts may be difficult to read today.

A passage from Luther's hymn "Mitten wir im Leben sind" illustrates both problems:

Luther 1967	EKG 1953
Mitten wyr ym leben sind	Mitten wir im Leben sind
mit den tod umbfangen	mit dem Tod umfangen.
Wen suchen wyr der hulffe thu	Wen suchen wir, der Hilfe tu,
das wyr gnad erlangen	daß wir Gnad erlangen?
Das bistu Herr alleyne	Das bist du, Herr, alleine.
uns rewet unser missethat	Uns reuet unsre Missetat,
die dich Herr erzurnet hat	die dich, Herr, erzürnet hat.

We have adopted the following conventions to deal with these issues:

Hymns. Hymns (chorales) are presented in the earliest form for which the editors had a reliable source, with spelling and punctuation tacitly modernized. The punctuation in the *Evangelisches Kirchengesangbuch* of 1953 (*EKG*) has been adopted in most cases; the *EKG* has also served as the principal source for modernized forms of obsolete words. To preserve the original meter of the text, words have been modernized only when the modern form is of the same number of syllables as the form used by the composer.

Other Works. Punctuation is usually shown as in the cited literary source; spelling has been tacitly modernized.

The Translations

Untranslated Words

German sentences often contain words that are not normally translated into English. These include words of emphasis (e.g., *doch, ja, wohl*), reflexive pronouns (e.g., *sich, mich*), or on occasion, definite articles (e.g., *der, die, das*). In addition, many German verbs have separable prefixes that are moved to the end of the clause in which they appear (e.g., *ein-gehen, ab-fallen*). These are omitted in the word-for-word translations, and a dash (—) is shown in their place.

Will mir der Satan widersprechen,	Sehet mich an:
wants to me — Satan oppose,	**Look at me —:**

In English the pronoun "it" can serve as the subject of a sentence, even though it has no antecedent, in constructions such as "it is raining." The same construction exists in German, but sometimes "es" (it) will precede the verb, and the actual subject will follow it. In this volume, when the German and English are analogous, "es" is translated; when "es" anticipates the actual subject, it is not translated.

Es regnet	Es bebet das Gesträuche
it is raining	**— tremble the bushes**

Compounds

Many individual German words, particularly articles, require translation by two or more words in English. Occasionally the converse is true. In such cases, the corresponding texts are centered on each other without special emphasis:

und dem Manne des Weg	vor diesmal schlichten.
and to the man whose way	**for this time settle.**

German also allows compound words to be formed by combining two or more "simple" words, sometimes with a hyphen, sometimes without. When there is no simple English equivalent, these are translated literally, with hyphens separating the individual words in English.

Freudenbecher	Leimruten-Arglist
joy-cup	**Bird-lime's-malice**

Implied Words

German texts, particularly poetic, are often less precise than their English equivalents, requiring the interpolation into the English of words, especially auxiliary verbs, that are implied in German. These are shown in square brackets.

Daß mich mein Jesus nicht vergessen.
that me my Jesus not [has] forgotten.

Deviations from Word-for-Word Translation

The obvious purpose of the word-for-word translations is to show word-for-word meaning. Sometimes, however, particularly in the case of idioms, word-for-word translation yields more confusion than enlightenment:

Das glaub ich, mir ist wohl zumute,
that believe I, to me is well [untranslatable]

In these cases, a cluster of words will be translated with another cluster, enclosed by hyphens.

Das glaub ich, mir ist wohl zumute,
that believe I, –I am in good spirits– ,

Inclusive Language

All of the German texts presented here utilize masculine nouns and pronouns when referring to people in general. These have been translated in gender-neutral form whenever this could be done without distorting meaning or making the translation awkward.

Annotations

Our goal has been to provide what we believe is both important and interesting information. At the same time, we have attempted to bring to the reader material, particularly quotations, that would be difficult for non-German-speaking readers to access. The length, depth, and focus of the annotations thus varies widely, and an unknown text may receive a longer, more detailed discussion than a familiar one.

Texts from the Bible are annotated briefly or not at all, since both general and denomination-specific Biblical exegeses are commonly available. Nonetheless, we have usually annotated those texts that have been created by a composer's selective choice of verses, often from many different places in the Bible. The *Concordia Self-Study Commentary* (Roehrs and Franzmann 1979) is especially helpful in understanding the Bible from a Lutheran perspective.

When a particular poet was responsible for a number of different texts in this collection, a minimal amount of basic information, such as dates, is repeated in most or all of the appropriate annotations. On the other hand, the editors have avoided restating the same information in detail each time. For this reason it would be profitable to peruse several if not all of the annotations for a given poet's works, even if the reader is exploring just a single text.

Biblical Texts

An English translation of a text from any foreign-langue Bible often differs significantly from the same text in a familiar English version. For this reason, the right-column translations of Biblical texts are derived from the German in the left column rather than from an English-language Bible. Other Biblical quotations are from the Standard Revised Version unless taken from the editors' translation.

References and Bibliography

Quoted works are cited for the most part parenthetically within the text. The information supplied—author/editor, year of publication, volume number (if any), and page number—will enable the reader to find complete bibliographic information in the list of *References*.

Other Bibliography includes works that were useful in the research for this work but that are not included among the *References*.

THE LUTHER BIBLE

Few people have had as profound an influence on history as the German monk, theologian, scholar, Bible translator, and reformer Martin Luther (1483–1546). A young cleric and professor of scripture in Wittenberg, Germany, he visited Rome on church business in 1510 and was enraged by the corruption he found. This experience sowed the seeds of a discontent that was to fester through the ensuing years and erupt in the first successful challenge to the authority of the Pope and the Roman Catholic Church.

Through his study and contemplation, Luther concluded that the Roman Church had diverged from the Bible in a number of its teachings, and that its error had spawned institutional depravity. Two critical beliefs that evolved through Luther's study were the sovereignty of scripture over the Pope or any other earthly authority, and the idea that forgiveness and salvation stem solely from man's faith and God's grace ("justification by faith") rather than from earthly good works.

In 1517 the Bishop of Mainz unwittingly laid down the gauntlet in front of Luther. In part to pay the Pope for the honor of his appointment, the bishop dispatched emissaries throughout Germany to sell "indulgences," official certifications of forgiveness for sins. To Luther this represented an intolerable violation of both the primacy of scripture and justification by faith. As the emissary approached Wittenberg on October 31, 1517, Luther posted his famous ninety-five theses on the door of the castle church, challenging the Church to examine and reform itself.[1] Instead of contemplating its own sins, the Church persecuted Luther. He was charged with heresy in 1519 and excommunicated in January of 1521; only the protection of Frederick III, the Elector of Saxony, saved him from imprisonment or execution. He had begun his confrontation with Rome as a Catholic eager to see the Church reform itself. Now he was an excommunicant whose work would instead establish a new church and encourage further Protestant rebellions like those of John Calvin in Geneva and Ulrich Zwingli in Zurich.

After his excommunication, Luther began a lifelong campaign to bring the unsullied word of God to the German people. The Scriptures were largely inaccessible to most lay believers, however, because the *Vulgate* (the official Roman Catholic Bible) was written in Latin. This is not to say that German translations were non-existent. A complete German version of the Bible was in circulation in manuscript before the invention of printing and apparently existed in several thousand copies. The year 1466 saw the publication of the first printed high-German translation, which was followed over the next fifty-five years by thirteen more printed versions, all of which, while different in various ways, probably stemmed from a single translation, the origin of which is unknown.

These Bibles were unsatisfactory to Luther both because of the mediocrity of the translations and the fact that they were apparently derived from the Latin Vulgate rather than the original Hebrew and Greek sources. Since the Bible was the word of God, nothing less than the best possible translation would do. Luther decided to undertake the project himself, aided by several trusted assistants. As an extraordinary scholar of the Bible, an accomplished linguist in Greek, Hebrew, and Latin, and a master of German language and rhetoric, Luther was singularly equipped for the task. In late February, 1522, after eleven weeks of concentrated labor, Luther completed his translation of the New Testament, based largely on the Greek *Urtext* by the Dutch theologian Erasmus of Rotterdam in 1519.[2]

In a remarkable response to a Roman Catholic critic entitled "An Open Letter on Translating" (1530), Luther clearly describes the seriousness with which he approached his translation:

> I have continually tried translating in a pure and accurate German. It has happened that I have sometimes searched and inquired about a single word for three or four weeks. . . . To this I can, with good conscience, give witness—that I gave my utmost effort and care and I had no ulterior motives.

> If I, Dr. Luther, had thought that all the Papists together were capable of translating even one passage of Scripture correctly and well, I would have gathered up enough humility to ask for their aid and assistance in translating the New Testament into German. (Luther 1909, 30/2: 632, tr. Gary Mann)[3]

---

[1]On All-Saints Day, November 1, 1999, 482 years and one day after this historical event, the Roman Catholic Church officially accepted justification by faith as necessary for salvation.

[2]Luther did not know, nor was it common knowledge until more than a century later, that in his haste to beat a competitor to press, Erasmus had made critical errors and taken unconscionable shortcuts in establishing his text.

[3]The order of the paragraphs has been reversed, and the original contains considerable intervening text.

Of particular concern to Luther's critics was his commitment to write in "a pure and accurate German" that conveyed to lay people what was intended in a passage, even if the wording of the original was not translated literally. Luther offers a particularly good example:

> For instance, Christ says: "Ex abundatia cordis os loquitur." If I am to follow these asses, they will lay the original before me literally and translate it as: "Out of the abundance of the heart the mouth speaks." Is that speaking with a German tongue? What German could understand something like that? What is this "abundance of the heart?" No German can say that; unless, of course, he was trying to say that someone was altogether too magnanimous, or too courageous, though even that would not yet be correct, as "abundance of the heart" is not German, not any more than "abundance of the house, "abundance of the stove" or "abundance of the bench" is German. But the mother in the home and the common man say this: "What fills the heart overflows the mouth." That is speaking with the proper German tongue of the kind I have tried for, although unfortunately not always successfully. The literal Latin is a great barrier to speaking proper German. (Luther 1909, 30/2: 632, tr. Gary Mann)

In the absence of copyright laws, Luther's New Testament fell prey to counterfeiters and appeared in no fewer than twelve unauthorized printings in the year 1523 alone. Although Luther began his translation of the Old Testament soon after finishing the New Testament, its length and the problems of language presented by the sources absorbed over twelve years of his life. To assure proper understanding of the scriptures, Luther also wrote copious commentaries, sermons, and letters on the Bible. These are preserved in his collected works and have served Lutheran pastors, theologians, and parishioners from Luther's time to the present.

The effect of Luther's translations on composers was no less significant. For the first time, the Bible was available to German-speaking composers in their own language, and also for the first time, the Lutheran vernacular worship service provided an outlet for sacred-music composition in German. Unlike Calvin and some other religious reformers of the day, Luther looked on music as a force for the glorification of God and the edification of man rather than as an earthly evil. He thus set the stage for the flourishing of music in Lutheran churches that was to bring forth such composers as Schütz and Bach.

The Luther Bible includes all the books of the Old and New Testaments as they are known to Catholics and Protestants alike, but his numbering of verses in some books differs from that of the familiar English translations, especially in the Psalms, where he numbered the headings as verse 1; consequently most of the Psalms have one extra verse in the Lutheran translation. This explains why citations provided in German sources will sometimes lead one to the "wrong" text if it is sought in an English Bible.

Luther's Bible also includes several additional books known as the "Apocrypha," which were included in a pre-Christian Greek version of the Hebrew scriptures called the *Septuagint* that was later adopted by the early Christians. The late date of the books of the Apocrypha, c. 275 B.C. to 100 A.D., led to their exclusion from the later Hebrew Bible as well as most Protestant Bibles. However, the complete *Septuagint* has remained in use to the present day in Orthodox churches, and the books of the Apocrypha remain in the Roman Catholic Bible. In addition to the books included by Luther, the Roman Catholic Bible contains the books of 1 Esdras and 2 Esdras.

Like Walt Whitman, Luther could never consider a work complete and finished; with each new publication he corrected and polished his previous work, at the same time expanding and revising his annotations. Subsequent generations of scholars have made their own changes to his Bible, some occasioned by the discovery of better sources than Luther possessed, and others necessitated by changes in the German language. The most recent revision was undertaken from 1957 to 1975.

The term "Luther Bible" is used generically today to denote a German-language Bible of any vintage based on Luther's translation. Although none of Luther's original versions is currently in use in German Lutheran churches, the last version he supervised, the so-called *Biblia germanica* (Luther 1545) is available in both facsimile and modern-type editions. Despite the evolution of language in the intervening centuries, his translation still retains its power and expressiveness.

Luther's complete Bible translation was a model of eloquent and economical expression. It set the standard for German writing in the sixteenth century and resided with the Catechism in a place of honor in countless German homes—often as the sole reading matter. It is no exaggeration to say that the Luther Bible is the single most important and influential publication in the history of the German language. It has affected the history of German in much the same way that the King James translation has influenced English.

THE BOOKS OF THE GERMAN LUTHERAN BIBLE

OLD TESTAMENT (*ALTES TESTAMENT*)

I. The Books of History (*Die Geschichtsbücher*)

Full Name (German)	Full Name (English)	Short Name (German)	Short Name (English)
Das erste Buch Mose	The First Book of Moses	*Genesis*	Genesis
Das zweite Buch Mose	The Second Book of Moses	*Exodus*	Exodus
Das dritte Buch Mose	The Third Book of Moses	*Levitikus*	Leviticus
Das vierte Buch Mose	The Fourth Book of Moses	*Numeri*	Numbers
Das fünfte Buch Mose	The Fifth Book of Moses	*Deuteronomium*	Deuteronomy
Das Buch Josua	The Book of Joshua	*Josua*	Joshua
Das Buch der Richter	The Book of of Judges	*Richter*	Judges
Das Buch Rut[h]	The Book of Ruth	*Rut[h]*	Ruth
Das erste Buch Samuel	The First Book of Samuel	*1. Samuel*	1 Samuel
Das zweite Buch Samuel	The Second Book of Samuel	*2. Samuel*	2 Samuel
Das erste Buch der Königen	The First Book of Kings	*1. Königen*	1 Kings
Das zweite Buch der Königen	The Second Book of Kings	*2. Königen*	2 Kings
Das erste Buch der Chronik	The First Book of Chronicles	*1. Chronik*	1 Chronicles
Das zweite Buch der Chronik	The Second Book of Chronicles	*2. Chronik*	2 Chronicles
Das Buch Esra	The Book of Ezra	*Esra*	Ezra
Das Buch Nehemia	The Book of Nehemiah	*Nehemia*	Nehemiah
Das Buch Est[h]er	The Book of Esther	*Est[h]er*	Esther

II. The Books of Teachings (*Die Lehrbücher*)

Das Buch Hiob (Ijob)	The Book of Job	*Hiob (Ijob)*	Job
Der Psalter	The Psalter (Book of Psalms)	*Psalter*	Psalms
Die Sprüche Salomos	The Sayings of Solomon	*Sprüche (Sprichwörter)*	Proverbs
Der Prediger Salomo	The Preacher Solomon	*Prediger (Kohelet)*	Ecclesiastes
Das Hohelied Salomos	The Song of Solomon	*Hoheslied*	Song of Solomon

III. The Books of the Prophets (*Die prophetischen Bücher*)

Der Prophet Jesaja	The Prophet Isaiah	*Jesaja*	Isaiah
Der Prophet Jeremia	The Prophet Jeremiah	*Jeremia*	Jeremiah
Die Klagelieder Jeremias	The Lamentations of Jeremiah	*Klagelieder*	Lamentations
Der Prophet Hesekiel (Ezechiel)	The Prophet Ezekiel	*Hesekiel (Ezechiel)*	Ezekiel
Der Prophet Daniel	The Prophet Daniel	*Daniel*	Daniel
Der Prophet Hosea	The Prophet Hosea	*Hosea*	Hosea
Der Prophet Joel	The Prophet Joel	*Joel*	Joel
Der Prophet Amos	The Prophet Amos	*Amos*	Amos
Der Prophet Obadja	The Prophet Obadiah	*Obadja*	Obadiah
Der Prophet Jona	The Prophet Jonah	*Jona*	Jonah
Der Prophet Micha	The Prophet Michah	*Micha*	Michah
Der Prophet Nahum	The Prophet Nahum	*Nahum*	Nahum
Der Prophet Habakuk	The Prophet Habakkuk	*Habakuk*	Habakkuk
Der Prophet Zephanja	The Prophet Zephaniah	*Zephanja*	Zephaniah
Der Prophet Haggai	The Prophet Haggai	*Haggai*	Haggai
Der Prophet Sacharja	The Prophet Zechariah	*Sacharja*	Zechariah
Der Prophet Maleachi	The Prophet Malachi	*Maleachi*	Malachi

THE APOCRYPHA (*DIE APOKRYPHEN*)

Full Name (German)	Full Name (English)	Short Name (German)	Short Name (English)
Das Buch Judith	The Book of Judith	*Judith*	Judith
Die Weisheit Salomos	The Wisdom of Solomon	*Weisheit*	Wisdom
Das Buch Tobias	The Book of Tobit	*Tobias*	Tobit
Das Buch Jesus Sirach	The Book of Ecclesiasticus / Wisdom of Sirach	*(Jesus) Sirach*	Ecclesiasticus / Sirach
Das Buch Baruch	The Book of Baruch	*Baruch*	Baruch
Das 1. Buch der Makkabäer	The First Book of the Maccabees	*1. Makkabäer*	1 Maccabees
Das 2. Buch der Makkabäer	The Second Book of the Maccabees	*2. Makkabäer*	2 Maccabees
Stücke zu Esther	Additions to the Book of Esther	—	—
[Additions to the Book of Daniel, given as separate books in the Luther Bible]	Additions to the Book of Daniel	—	—
(1) Geschichte von Susanna und Daniel	(1) The Story of Susanna and Daniel	—	—
(2) Vom Bel zu Babel	(2) From Bel to Babel	—	—
(3) Vom Drachen zu Babel	(3) From the Dragon to Babel	—	—
(4) Das Gebet Asarjas	(4) The Prayer of Azarias	—	—
(5) Der Gesang der drei Männer im Feuerofen	(5) The Song of the Three Men in the Fiery Furnace	—	—
Das Gebet Manasses	The Prayer of Manasseh	—	—

NEW TESTAMENT (*NEUES TESTAMENT*)

I. The Books of History (*Die Geschichtsbücher*)

Full Name (German)	Full Name (English)	Short Name (German)	Short Name (English)
Das Evangelium des Matthäus	The Gospel according to Matthew	*Matthäus*	Matthew
Das Evangelium des Markus	The Gospel according to Mark	*Markus*	Mark
Das Evangelium des Lukas	The Gospel according to Luke	*Lukas*	Luke
Das Evangelium des Johannes	The Gospel according to John	*Johannes*	John
Die Apostelgeschichte des Lukas	The Acts of the Apostles, by Luke	*Apostelgeschichte*	Acts

II. The Books of Teachings (*Die Lehrbücher*)

Der Brief des Paulus an die Römer	The Letter of Paul to the Romans	*Römer*	Romans
Der erste Brief des Paulus an die Korinther	The First Letter of Paul to the Corinthians	*1. Korinther*	1 Corinthians
Der zweite Brief des Paulus an die Korinther	The Second Letter of Paul to the Corinthians	*2. Korinther*	2 Corinthians
Der Brief des Paulus an die Galater	The Letter of Paul to the Galatians	*Galater*	Galatians
Der Brief des Paulus an die Epheser	The Letter of Paul to the Ephesians	*Epheser*	Ephesians
Der Brief des Paulus an die Philipper	The Letter of Paul to the Philippians	*Philipper*	Philippians
Der Brief des Paulus an die Kolosser	The Letter of Paul to the Colossians	*Kolosser*	Colossians
Der erste Brief des Paulus an die Thessalonicher	The First Letter of Paul to the Thessalonians	*1. Thessalonicher*	1 Thessalonians
Der zweite Brief des Paulus an die Thessalonicher	The Second Letter of Paul to the Thessalonians	*2. Thessalonicher*	2 Thessalonians
Der erste Brief des Paulus an Timotheus	The First Letter of Paul to Timothy	*1. Timotheus*	1 Timothy

Full Name (German)	Full Name (English)	Short Name (German)	Short Name (English)
Der zweite Brief des Paulus an Timotheus	The Second Letter of Paul to Timothy	*2. Timotheus*	2 Timothy
Der Brief des Paulus an Titus	The Letter of Paul to Titus	*Titus*	Titus
Der Brief des Paulus an Philemon	The Letter of Paul to Philemon	*Philemon*	Philemon
Der erste Brief des Petrus	The First Letter of Peter	*1. Petrus*	1 Peter
Der zweite Brief des Petrus	The Second Letter of Peter	*2. Petrus*	2 Peter
Der erste Brief des Johannes	The First Letter of John	*1. Johannes*	1 John
Der zweite Brief des Johannes	The Second Letter of John	*2. Johannes*	2 John
Der dritte Brief des Johannes	The Third Letter of John	*3. Johannes*	3 John
Der Brief an die Hebräer	The Letter to the Hebrews	*Hebräer*	Hebrews
Der Brief des Jakobus	The Letter of James	*Jakobus*	James
Der Brief des Judas	The Letter of Jude	*Judas*	Jude

III. The Book of Prophesy (*Das prophetische Buch*)

Die Offenbarung des Johannes	The Revelation of John	*Offenbarung*	Revelation

GERMAN PRONUNCIATION

Although English is a direct descendant of German, the split occurred so long ago that their common elements are confined largely to word roots. Pronunciation is vastly different, and German contains both consonant and vowel sounds not found in English. Conversely, one of the greatest challenges to American English speakers is avoiding sounds foreign to German—the American "l" and "r," and diphthongs.

For these reasons, a brief printed pronunciation guide such as this is of limited usefulness. While it can help the reader understand basic concepts, it can convey neither the subtleties of native pronunciation nor exceptions to the basic rules. How can those who do not speak German obtain additional help?

- Learn IPA and obtain a German-English / English-German dictionary that uses *standard* IPA to demonstrate the pronunciation of every word.

- Review the text with a speaker of German who can demonstrate proper pronunciation and help you polish yours.

Basic Concepts for Singers

- You must usually enunciate with much greater intensity than you would in English. *The great range of articulatory intensity possible in German is a key to artistic performance.*

- Initiate all vowels at the beginnings of words with a glottal stop. German is not a *legato* language; never elide between words as you would in Italian or English.

- Learn what "long" and "short" vowels are and distinguish clearly between them in sound.

- A single vowel (a, e, i, o, u) is never made into a diphthong. *Improperly making diphthongs out of vowels is the single most common problem of German pronunciation for Americans.*

- The vowel "e" at the end of a word (*Sonne*) is neutral, short, unaccented, and bright: [ɛ]. The "e" in an "-en" or "-er" word ending (*singen, Sänger*) is neutral, short, and unaccented, but darker: [ə].

- When singing vowels before double consonants, which are always short:

    (1) Stop the vowel when it precedes doubled plosive consonants (*Götter*), leaving a slight space before the consonants. Even if the vowel is sustained in the music, this makes its "shortness" clear. Think of the consonants as beginning the syllable after the vowel.

    (2) In the case of voiced and sibilant consonants (f, l, m, n, s), shorten the vowel and sustain the consonant slightly (e.g., *Flamme, alleluia*). The length of consonants can be varied for expressive purposes.

    (3) When forming vowels before double, voiced consonants, prepare your mouth position for the consonants. For example, the first vowel of *alleluia* should be formed so that the lips and tongue must move minimally to make the "ll." This will properly color the vowel.

- Practice making the mixed vowels (umlauts) until you can produce them easily and on demand.

- The letter "r" can be flipped once, flipped more than once, or even rolled in singing [ʀ], depending on context: the longer the "r" the more impact it has. A final "r" is never rolled in song, however. A guttural "r" is used is used in speech but not in singing, and a final "r" may sometimes be dropped. *The American "r" does not exist in German.*

- Make the consonant "l" by flipping the tip of your tongue off the alveolar ridge just in back of your top teeth (where the tongue goes to make the consonants "t" and "d"). This produces a tighter and more energetic "l." *The thick American "l" is a sound foreign to German.*

Consonants

A complete explanation of the rules for consonant production would exceed the scope of this guide. Again, a good German-English dictionary will be invaluable in determining how consonants are pronounced in specific circumstances. The single letters d, f, k, m, n, p, and t are pronounced the same in both English and German regardless of location in the word.

The pronunciation of other individual letters may change depending on context:

Letter	Variation in German	Written	Spoken (IPA)
b	Pronounced as [p] at the ends of words; otherwise like English	Gra<u>b</u>	[grap]
c	The letter "c" is not used alone in German ("k" is used instead) except in words of foreign origin, where it is pronounced as in the original language.	–	–
g	Pronounced as [ç] (like the "h" in *huge*) when it is preceded by "i" at the end of a word or syllable; otherwise like English	seli<u>g</u>	[zelIç]
h	Pronounced as in English except before vowels, where it is a silent indicator of a long vowel	fro<u>h</u>	[fro]
s	Pronounced as in English at the end of a word or syllable, but pronounced as [z] otherwise	<u>S</u>amen	[zamən]

Some consonants are always pronounced differently from English:

Letter	Variation in German	Written	Spoken (IPA)
j	Always pronounced like the initial "y" in English (*yes*)	<u>J</u>ammer	[jamər]
l	See "Basic Concepts for Singers."		
q	Always followed by "u" and pronounced like "kv"	<u>Q</u>ual	[kval]
r	See "Basic Concepts for Singers."		
v	Always pronounced like the "f" in English	<u>v</u>on	[fɔn]
w	Always pronounced like the "v" in English	<u>W</u>ohl	[vol]
z	Always pronounced like the "ts" in English	<u>z</u>ag	[tsak]

Finally, some consonant clusters have a characteristic pronunciation:

Letter	Variation in German	Written	Spoken (IPA)
ch	The letters "ch" are always pronounced differently from the sound of "ch" in the word *charm*. Proper pronunciation must be verified with a dictionary. Three variations will be found as shown below:		
ch (1)	[ç], as in the "h" in *huge*.	i<u>ch</u>	[iç]
ch (2)	[x], as in the Scottish *lo<u>ch</u>*	do<u>ch</u>	[dɔx]
ch (3)	[k], when found at the beginning of some foreign words	<u>C</u>herub	[kerup]
ng	Always pronounced like the English *sing*,	si<u>ng</u>en	[ziŋən]
sch	Always pronounced like the English *shine*	<u>Sch</u>ein	[ʃain]
st (1)	When beginning a syllable, [ʃt] as in *bor<u>sch</u>t*	<u>St</u>ein	[ʃtain]
st (2)	When ending a syllable, [st] as in *be<u>st</u>*	For<u>st</u>	[fɔrst]

Vowels

There are three principal ways of thinking about vowel placement and production.

- **Length.** The terms "long" and "short" refer both to the actual duration of the vowel and to its color.

  Vowels are always **long** when:

  (1) followed by "h" (S<u>o</u>hn)

  (2) doubled (S<u>aa</u>l)

  (3) at the end of a syllable (m<u>u</u>-tig)

  (4) preceding an "ß" that is followed by another vowel (Str<u>a</u>ße)

  Vowels are always **short** when followed by a double consonant (H<u>i</u>mmel)

- **Lip or Tongue.** "Lip" vowels are those that are formed primarily through the positioning of the lips, and "tongue" vowels through the positioning of the tongue.

- **Pure or Mixed.** Individual vowels in German without the umlaut (¨) are pure (unmixed). Vowels with an umlaut are said to be "mixed." *In practical terms this means the lips attempt to make one vowel while the tongue attempts to make another.* This is most clearly seen and demonstrated with the two vowels that contrast most in color and perceived location of pronunciation, the extreme closed vowels [i] and [u]. Mixing these vowels yields the long, mixed vowel [y]:

$$[i] \quad > \quad [y] \quad < \quad [u]$$
$$\text{wie} \quad > \quad \text{Tür} \quad < \quad \text{tut}$$

A good technique for teaching the mixed vowels is to position the tongue for one and the lips for the other. This is most effective with [y] and progressively less so as one moves downward in the chart below.

Diphthongs and Glides

German has three principal diphthongs, which are always indicated by two vowels:

[ai] sei, Mai   [au] Haus, hinaus   [ɔɪ] Leuchten, Fräulein

The letters "ie" at the end of a word (*Lilie, Nänie*) indicate an unaccented glide: [jɛ].

German Vowels Summarized

English	German	tongue vowels		mixed vowels			lip vowels	German	English
see	sie	i *(long)*		Übel	y *(long)*	für	u *(long)*	Mut / gut	shoe / groom
hate	geben / spät	e *(long)*		fröhlich	ø *(long)*	höhe	o *(long)*	Sohn / Kron	moan / groan
pit	bitte / ich	ɪ *(short)*		Sünd	ʏ *(short)*	küssen	ʊ *(short)*	und / Mund	book / soot
get	Welt / Gesänge	ɛ *(short)*		Schöpfer / œ / Götter *(short)*		ɔ *(short)*		Wonne / Sonne	caught / fought
alleluia / father	alle / Wagen	(anterior)	a *(short) (long)*			ɑ (posterior)			

Tongue becomes less arched & flatter

Lips become rounder & more closed

Not used in German

13

THE SACRED CANTATAS OF J.S. BACH

Johann Sebastian Bach had performed only minor duties in church music prior to his assuming the position of Cantor at the St. Thomas Church of Leipzig in 1723, a position at which he remained until his death in 1750. Previously, from 1707 to 1723, while employed successively in the cities of Mühlhausen, Weimar, and Cöthen, he had written only twenty-five cantatas known today. In Leipzig, on the other hand, he was expected to produce a cantata performance for every Sunday and feast day. Although he was free to use the works of others, he seems at first to have felt the need to rely on his own compositions. In the first five years of his tenure he was to write nearly all of the cantatas himself—a total of over 250. For reasons not entirely understood, Bach's composition of cantatas dropped off greatly in the late 1720s, and though he continued to use earlier works, only twenty-eight new cantatas are known to exist from the last two decades of his life. Although some 200 sacred cantatas have been preserved, perhaps 100 or so have been lost.

City	Dates Of Tenure	Position	Surviving Cantatas
Arnstadt	1703–06/1707	Organist at Bonifaciuskirche ("Neukirche")	none
Mühlhausen	6/1707–06/1708	Organist at Church of St. Blasius	6–7
Weimar	7/1708–12/1717	Court Organist and *Konzertmeister* (1714-on)	18–19
Cöthen	12/1717–05/1723	*Kappellmeister*	none
Leipzig	5/1723–1750	Cantor of the Thomaskirche and civic Director of Music	175

The cantata in the Lutheran worship service of Bach's time was intended to illuminate the Gospel and Epistle readings for the day. Since these were also the basis for the pastor's sermon, the cantata could be looked on without exaggeration as a second sermon, delivered through the art of music.

Bach's cantatas can be divided into five groups according to their use of Biblical texts, hymns, and contemporary poetry.[4] In roughly chronological order of development, they are:

(1) **Biblical texts alone.** Only a small number of Bach's cantatas are based entirely on Biblical texts; in the present work there is only one, BWV 50.[5]

(2) **Chorale verses alone.** A larger number of cantatas consists entirely of chorale verses. Many of these are from the year 1724, in which Bach concentrated on the use of chorale-based librettos, producing thirty-two cantatas in which the chorale played a larger role than merely closing the cantata. When a composer sets all the verses of a chorale to music, the product is called a "chorale cantata *per omnes versus.*" Three of these, BWV 4, 137 and 192, can be found in this volume.

(3) **Biblical excerpts combined with chorale verses.** More common yet is a blending of these two types of text, in which a chorale typically will open and/or finish the cantata, enclosing Biblical verses and perhaps another hymn verse. Here we have three such works, BWV 38, 106, and 131. On occasion a chorale verse is sung in dialogue or even simultaneously with a Biblical text, adding another layer of meaning to the scripture.

(4) **Biblical and/or chorale verses combined with some original poetry.** The addition of contempory poetry to the traditional libretto of Bible excerpts and/or hymn verses was a late seventeenth-century development. It was a major stylistic change, one in which the librettist brought a contemporary voice to the cantata. It is also the category to which belong the greatest number of the cantatas we have selected for translation. Of the nine examples here, one (BWV 150) weds the Bible with poetry, five combine poetry with chorale verses (BWV 1, 40, 62, 80, and 125), and three (BWV 61, 68, and 79) join all three types of text in a single cantata. The most frequent uses for free poetry were in recitatives and arias, which were usually the most subjective, personal movements. A chorale verse will typically close the cantata, summarizing its message for the congregation.

(5) **Poetry composed specifically to function as a cantata libretto.** This innovation appeared first in the works of Erdmann Neumeister (1671–1756). As was the case in categories 3 and 4, a chorale usually closes the cantata. No examples of this type are included here.

---

[4]This categorization has been adapted from that of James Day (Day 1966: 25–29).

[5] As a one-movement cantata fragment, this work is an exceptional case.

The cantatas from 1714 on—the later Weimar period and the Leipzig years—were strongly influenced by the "reform" cantatas of Neumeister. Neumeister, a fervent Lutheran pastor, poet, and scholar of poetry whose later career was spent in Hamburg, published nine cycles of cantata librettos, each for the entire church year. His first cycle contained librettos:

> made up of Biblical verses and poetic aria texts, occasionally also a chorale. . . . Neumeister's next cycle was radically different. These he specifically called cantatas, and they consisted entirely of madrigalesque poetry for recitative and aria in the form of the Italian secular cantata. . . . Neumeister's fame rests on his combination of these two types of text in the newer mixed cantata, which became standard in the eighteenth century." (Snyder 1980: 155)

Although Bach set only five of Neumeister's cantata librettos (BWV 18, 24, 28, 59, and 61), Neumeister's "reform" cantata type was the basis for the majority of his cantata compositions. It is ironic that the poetry of his cantatas, which was highly original and popular in his day, is perhaps the greatest barrier to modern audiences understanding and enjoying them. Bach scholar and conductor Helmuth Rilling discusses the problem with such clarity and insight that we quote him at length:

> There are three reasons for the strangeness of these texts. In the first place, they constantly associate Biblical ideas together in new ways that presume a thorough knowledge of the Bible. Consider as an example the text of this recitative from cantata BWV 113, which refers in close proximity to no fewer than four different Biblical stories that have nothing whatsoever to do with one another.
>
> > He calls: . . . "Come to the fount of every blessing: I have chosen you as my friends!" With these words, I would come before you like the penitent Publican, and with humble spirit, pray, "Lord, be merciful unto me." O comfort my feeble heart . . . so shall I also from henceforth become, like David and Manassah . . . a child of heaven.
>
> Bach's congregation was probably able immediately to associate the individual key phrases with their corresponding Biblical stories. . . . (Matthew 11: 28, Luke 18: 13, Samuel 12: 13, and Chronicles 33: 12-13). This is unlikely today.
>
> Likewise, Bach presumed a knowledge of the hymns of his day. In the instrumental parts, without words, he often cites chorale melodies within movements possessing totally different texts. His congregation would have recognized these melodies instantly and put them into associative context. As an example, consider cantata BWV 70, *Watch, Pray*. There, in the orchestrally accompanied recitative *Ah, Shall Not This Great Day*, a chorale appears in the trumpet. The trumpet here is intended to be a symbol of the Last Judgment. The meaning of its presence becomes apparent, however, only when one understands that the chorale being played, "It Is Certainly the Time that God's Son Shall Come," announces the event that is to occur immediately before the Judgment of the World. I imagine that Bach's listeners understood this, but would modern listeners?
>
> The second reason why Bach's texts seem so strange and foreign to us is the compressed presentation of extreme images one after another that to us seem strained and often even ridiculous. Take the beginning of cantata BWV 199, for example:
>
> > My heart is swimming in blood because the hatching of my sins makes me a monster in God's holy eyes.
>
> A third and final reason for the disinterest in Bach's cantata texts is the fact that the connections between ideas often seem too simple or even silly. Consider, for example, this aria text from cantata BWV 84. (The naïve, sing-song meter of the German unfortunately does not survive translation.)
>
> > Ich esse mit Freuden mein weniges Brot
> > Und gönne dem Nächsten von Herzen das Seine.
> >
> > With joy I eat my meager bread
> > and from my heart, I grant to my neighbor what is his.

We encounter these problems in the texts to Bach's cantatas and oratorios, just as previous generations of earlier Bach lovers certainly did. On the other hand, there are positive qualities to Bach's cantata texts. This is especially true where they quote the Bible or cite important hymns such as those by Martin Luther— the cantatas *God the Lord Is Sun and Shield* (BWV 79) and *A Mighty Fortress Is Our God* (BWV 80), for example. These texts do not seem alien to us, since the church itself continues to use both their content and their precise wording today, just as it did during Bach's time, and it sees these texts as central expressions of its teachings. Finally, though, I think that the most important quality of these texts is that they touch upon problems—even though often under the surface or through antiquated wording—that affect us just as much as they did the people of the eighteenth century. The beginning of the first recitative in cantata BWV 25—"The entire world is but a hospital"—is irritating only at first, since these words describe a situation of distress that exists today, just as it did in Bach's era.

Of course, these combinations of texts would be of little interest to us if taken alone. But, even with all their issues in terms of content and expression, they are what stimulated Bach to compose. Bach's imagination was ignited by their words, his thinking about musical structure was set in motion by their phrasing, and his ability to construct large architectonic connections was challenged by the goal that such texts provided.[6]

Bach's cantatas represent a monumental musical and theological achievement. He did not merely set sacred words to pretty music for the delectation of the congregation. Rather, he sought out and used every musical means available to him to represent, elucidate, and interpret his text in sound. It is the privilege of subsequent generations to study and continually rediscover the wonders that his works contain.

---

[6]Rilling 1985: 7. The editor of the present volume was the original translator of this article and has used this opportunity to make small improvements to the original translation.

German Texts

Johann Sebastian Bach

Also hat Gott die Welt geliebt, BWV 68
For God so Loved the World
Christiane Mariane von Ziegler

1. Chorus
Salomo Liscow

Also hat Gott die Welt geliebt,
So did God the world love

Daß er uns seinen Sohn gegeben.
that he to us his son has given.

Wer sich im Glauben ihm ergibt,
Whosoever himself in faith to him gives,

Der soll dort ewig bei ihm leben.
he shall there forever with him live.

Wer glaubt, daß Jesus ihm geboren,
Whosoever believes that Jesus for him was born,

Der bleibet ewig unverloren,
he remains eternally unlost,

Und ist kein Leid, das den betrübt,
and is no sorrow that him grieves

Den Gott und auch sein Jesus liebt.
whom God and also his Jesus loves.

For God so loved the world
that he gave us his son.
Whosoever surrenders in faith to him
shall live with him there forever.
Those who believe that Jesus was born for them
will remain eternally unforsaken,
and there is no sorrow that grieves those
who love God and his Jesus.

2. Aria (soprano)
Christiane Mariane von Ziegler

Mein gläubiges Herze,
My believing heart,

Frohlocke, sing, scherze,
rejoice, sing, jest:

Dein Jesus ist da!
your Jesus is here!

Weg Jammer, weg Klagen,
Away lament, away complaint!

Ich will euch nur sagen:
I want to you only say:

Mein Jesus ist nah.
my Jesus is near.

My believing heart,
rejoice, sing, be merry:
your Jesus is here!

Away with laments, away with complaints!
I only want to tell you:
my Jesus is near.

3. Recitative (bass)
Christiane Mariane von Ziegler

Ich bin mit Petro nicht vermessen,
I am with Peter not presumptuous.

Was mich getrost und freudig macht,
What me comforted and joyful makes

Daß mich mein Jesus nicht vergessen.
that me my Jesus not [has] forgotten.

Er kam nicht nur, die Welt zu richten,
He came not only the world to judge;

Nein, nein, er wollte Sünd und Schuld
no, no—he wanted to sin and guilt

Als Mittler zwischen Gott und Mensch
as mediator between God and humanity

für diesmal schlichten.
for this time settle.

I am, like Peter, not presumptuous.
What comforts me and makes me joyful
is that my Jesus has not forgotten me.
He came to the world not only to judge;
no, no—he wanted,
as an intercessor between God and humanity,
to put right for this time the matter of sin and guilt.

4. Aria (bass)
Christiane Mariane von Ziegler

Du bist geboren mir zugute,
You were born –for my benefit–.

Das glaub ich, mir ist wohl zumute,
That believe I; –I am in good spirits–

Weil du für mich genug getan.
because you for me enough [have] done.

Das Rund der Erden mag gleich brechen,
The round of the earth may soon break,

Will mir der Satan widersprechen,
wants to me — Satan oppose,

So bet ich dich, mein Heiland, an.
so pray I to you, my savior —.

You were born for my benefit.
That I believe; I am content
because you have done enough for me.
The earthly globe may soon shatter,
and Satan may want to oppose me:
thus I pray to you, my savior.

5. Chorus
Christiane Mariane von Ziegler

Wer an ihn glaubet,
Whosoever in him believes

der wird nicht gerichtet;
he will not be judged;

wer aber nicht glaubet,
whosoever however not believes

der ist schon gerichtet;
he is already judged,

denn er glaubet nicht an den Namen
for he believes not in the name

des eingebornen Sohnes Gottes.
of the only-begotten son of God.

Whosoever believes in him
will not be judged;
but whosoever does not believe
is already judged,
because this one does not believe in the power[1]
of the only-begotten son of God.

Cantata type:	Bible, chorale, and free poetry
Liturgical usage:	Whit-Monday (the day after Pentecost)
First performance:	May 21, 1725
Epistle:	Acts 10: 42–48
	The conclusion of Peter's sermon to the devout centurion Cornelius, and the baptism of the Gentiles
Gospel:	John 3: 16–21
	God so loved the world that he gave his son

CHRISTIANE Mariane von Ziegler (née Romanus, 1695–1760), a contemporary of Bach in Leipzig, composed the libretto to this joyous cantata. Ziegler was a student of the then-renowned literary figure Johann Christoph Gottsched (1700–1766) and a member of the Deutsche Gesellschaft, a literary society led by Gottsched. In 1728 she published a collection of cantata librettos in the manner of Erdmann Neumeister (see "The Sacred Cantatas of J.S. Bach"), the *Versuch in gebundener Schreib-Art, Teil I* (loosely translated, an "Essay in Poetic Composition, Part 1"), which Bach used as the basis for nine cantatas, including BWV 68. Though her reputation was built in Leipzig, where she won the Gesellschaft's prize for poetry in 1732 and 1734, it extended much further; in 1733 she was selected as the imperial poet laureate by Wittenberg University.

As was customary, the libretto reflects the content of the Epistle and Gospel for the day. Ziegler's libretto called for an appropriate chorale to open the cantata, leaving the choice to the composer. Bach selected the opening verse to "Also hat Gott die Welt geliebt" of Salomo Liscow (1640–1689), a paraphrase and elaboration of John 3: 16, the first verse of the Gospel. Movements 2–5 stem from Ziegler's pen.

The text to the second movement is a simple celebration of the presence of Jesus that led Bach to compose one of his most beautiful arias. Bach alters Ziegler's text in three places, molding it better to the theme of the cantata (belief) and providing a closer textual connection to his ebullient music:

---

[1] Regarding the rendition of the word *Namen* (name) as "power," see footnote 5, p. 37.

Ziegler	Bach
My comforted heart,	My *believing* heart,
rejoice and be merry:	rejoice, *sing*, be merry:
your Jesus is here!	your Jesus is here!
Away with laments and troubles	Away with laments, *away with complaints!*
I only want to tell you:	I only want to tell you:
my Jesus is near.	my Jesus is near.

The following recitative continues the paraphrase of the Gospel begun in the first movement, with the reminder from John 3: 17 that the Christ was sent to save the world, not to condemn it. This also happens to be—not by chance, of course—the message of the Epistle, in which Paul is sent by God to convert and baptize a Roman centurion and his household. Once again, Bach makes some changes to Ziegler's libretto, bringing the meter of line 3 into accord with that of line 1 and cutting a line that must have seemed to be a digression between lines 5 and 6 (see *Variants*). His final change, in the last line, from Ziegler's "*fully* put right the matter of sin and guilt" to "put right *for this time* the matter of sin and guilt" may refer to the First vs. the Second Coming.

The fourth movement, an aria, draws together the themes of the preceding movements, declaring the speaker's faith and praying for God's protection from evil. For the closing movement, Ziegler provided a continuation of the Gospel, John 3: 18, in which the Christian, perhaps a bit distracted by the beautiful music and comforting texts, is reminded that eternal damnation is the consequence of a lack of faith in Jesus as the Christ.

Source: Ziegler 1728: 262. Facsimile in Neumann 1974: 363

Variants: (Bach = roman, Ziegler = *italic*)

Stanza 2, line 1: Mein gläubiges (my believing) = *Getröstetes* (comforted)
        line 2: sing (sing) = *und* (and)
        line 4: weg Klagen (away complaints) = *und Plagen* (and troubles)
Stanza 3, line 3: daß mich mein Jesus nicht vergesssen (that my Jesus has not forgotten me) = *Ist, daß mein Heiland mich ohnmöglich kann vergessen* (Is the fact that it is impossible for my savior to forget me)
        line 5a: Bach omits *Durch die besondre Lieb und Huld* (through special love and grace)
        line 6: diesmal (this time) = *völlig* (fully)
Stanza 4, line 2: ich (I) = *es* (it)

Aus der Tiefen rufe ich, Herr, zu dir, BWV 131
Out of the Depths I Cry to You
Librettist unknown

1. Chorus
Psalm 130: 1, 2

Aus der Tiefen rufe ich, Herr, zu dir.
From the depths call I, Lord, to you.

Herr, höre meine Stimme,
Lord, hear my voice;

laß deine Ohren merken
let your ears attend

auf die Stimme meines Flehens!
to the voice of my supplication!

Out of the depths I cry to you, O Lord.
Lord, hear my voice;
let your ears attend
to the voice of my supplication.

2. Aria (bass) and Chorale (soprano)
Aria: Psalm 130: 3, 4; chorale by Bartolomäus Ringwaldt

Aria

So du willst, Herr, Sünde zurechnen,
If you want, Lord, sin to ascribe,

Herr, wer wird bestehen?
Lord, who will stand?

Aria

If you, Lord, were to note iniquities,
Lord, who could escape your scrutiny?

Chorale

Erbarm dich mein in solcher Last,
Pity — me in such distress;

Nimm sie aus meinem Herzen,
take it from my heart,

Dieweil du sie gebüßet hast
since you it atoned have

Am Holz mit Todesschmerzen,
on the wood with death's pains

Denn bei dir ist die Vergebung,
For with you is — forgiveness,

daß man dich fürchte.
that one you fear.

Auf daß ich nicht mit großem Weh
so that I neither with great woe

In meinen Sünden untergeh,
in my sins perish

Noch ewiglich verzage.
nor forever despair.

Chorale

Have mercy on me in such distress;
take the burden from my heart,
for you have atoned for it
on the cross with death's pains

For with you is forgiveness,
that we may fear you.

so that I with great sadness
may neither perish from my sins
nor forever despair.

> **Source** (chorale): Wackernagel 1964, 4: 1028
> **Variants:** (Bach = roman, Wackernagel = *italics*)
> Line 4: mit = *in*   Line 5: mit = *für*

3. Chorus
Psalm 130: 5

Ich harre des Herrn,
I wait for the Lord;

meine Seele harret,
my soul waits,

und ich hoffe auf sein Wort.
and I trust in his word.

I wait for the Lord;
my soul waits,
and I trust in his word.

4. Aria (tenor) and Chorale (alto)
Aria: Psalm 130: 6a; chorale by Bartolomäus Ringwaldt

Aria

Meine Seele wartet auf den Herrn
My soul waits for the Lord

von einer Morgenwache
from one morning watch

bis zu der andern.
–until– the other.

Chorale

Und weil ich denn in meinem Sinn,
And since I then in my mind,

Wie ich zuvor geklaget,
as I before lamented,

Auch ein betrübter Sünder bin,
also a troubled sinner am

Den sein Gewissen naget,
whom his conscience gnaws,

Und wollte gern im Blute dein
and want very much in blood your

Von Sünden abgewaschen sein,
from sins washed be,

Wie David und Manasse.
like David and Manasseh.

Aria

My soul waits for the Lord
from one morning watch
to the next.

Chorale

And since in my mind,
as I have long lamented,
I, too, am a troubled sinner
who is gnawed by his conscience,
and I want very much to be cleansed
from sinfulness with your blood,
like David and Manasseh.

> **Source** (chorale): Wackernagel 1964, 4: 1028
> **Variants:** (Bach = roman, Wackernagel = *italic*)
> Line 5: wollte gern = *gerne möcht*
> Line 6: abgewaschen = *absolvieret*

21

5. Chorus
Psalm 130: 7, 8

Israel, hoffe auf den Herrn;
Israel, trust in the Lord;

denn bei dem Herrn ist die Gnade
for with the Lord is — grace

und viel Erlösung bei ihm.
and much redemption with him.

Und er wird Israel erlösen
And he will Israel redeem

aus allen seinen Sünden.
from all its sins.

Israel, trust in the Lord;
for with the Lord there is mercy
and plentiful redemption.
And he will redeem Israel
from all its iniquities.

Cantata type:	Bible and chorale
Liturgical usage:	Times of penitence
First performance:	May or June, 1707
Epistle:	—
Gospel:	—

*I*N this work we have what is likely Bach's earliest cantata, a fact that is reflected in the choice of the Bible and hymns as the basis for the libretto (see "The Sacred Cantatas of J.S. Bach"). A notation at the close of the lost original score suggested that the libretto may have been conceived by Georg Christian Eilmar, the Archdeacon of Mühlhausen, where Bach began employment as organist in June, 1707. Containing text from neither a Gospel nor Epistle, the cantata is not tied to a particular day of the church year, although it is clearly penitential. It may well have been written in commemoration of a great fire that destroyed a large portion of Mühlhausen and left many of its residents homeless shortly before Bach's took up residence there.

The way in which the two types of texts are combined is both beautiful and sophisticated. Each of the five movements is based on successive verses of Psalm 130, which is presented in its entirety. The chorus sings the odd-numbered movements, thus opening and closing the cantata. These choral presentations frame two arias, both duets, in which one voice sings the Biblical text while the other sings a complementary verse (2 and 5, respectively) from the Lenten hymn "Herr Jesu Christ, du höchstes Gut" (1588) (*EKG*: 167) by Bartolomäus Ringwaldt (1530–1599). The obscure reference in verse 5 of the hymn (movement 4) to being "cleansed from sinfulness like David and Manasseh" pertains to the story in 2 Chronicles 33 of King Manasseh, who ignored the Lord and experienced his wrath by being conquered and led away in chains by the Assyrians. Thereafter "he humbled himself greatly before the God of his fathers" and was restored to his throne (2 Chronicles 33: 12–13).

While the Bible provides the principal text, the hymn supplies a personal response to it. This device appears frequently in Bach's cantatas, motets, and Passions, and creates an often profound and penetrating confrontation with the theology that neither text could achieve alone.

Aus tiefer Not schrei ich zu dir
In Deep Distress I Cry to You
Librettist unknown

1. Chorus
Martin Luther

Aus tiefer Not schrei ich zu dir,
From deep distress cry I to you:

Herr Gott, erhör mein Rufen;
Lord God, hear my cries;

dein gnädig Ohr neig her zu mir
your gracious ear incline here to me

und meiner Bitt sie öffne!
and to my request them open!

Denn so du willst das sehen an,
For as you want to that consider —,

was Sünd und Unrecht ist getan,
what sin and injustice has been done,

wer kann, Herr, vor dir bleiben?
who can, Lord, before you remain?

In deep distress I cry to you:
Lord God, hear my cries;
incline your gracious ear to me
and open it to my request!
For if you choose to consider
what sin and injustice have been done,
Lord, who can withstand your scrutiny?

2. Recitative (alto)
Author unknown

In   Jesu   Gnade   wird   allein
In   Jesus's   grace   will   alone

Der   Trost   vor   uns   und   die   Vergebung   sein,
the   comfort   for   us   and   the   forgiveness   be,

Weil   durch   des   Satans   Trug   und   List
because through — Satan's deceit and cunning,

Der   Menschen   ganzes   Leben
—   humanity's   whole   life

Vor   Gott   ein   Sündengreuel   ist.
before God   a horror of sins   is.

Was   könnte   nun
What   could   now

Die   Geistesfreudigkeit   zu   unserm   Beten   geben,
the   spirit's joy   to   our   prayer   give,

Wo   Jesu   Geist   und   Wort
where   Jesus's   spirit   and   word

     nicht   neue   Wunder   tun?
     indeed   new   wonders   do?

In Jesus's grace alone will be
our comfort and forgiveness,
for because of Satan's deceit and cunning,
humanity's whole existence
is a sinful horror before God.
What could now
bring a joyful spirit to our prayer,
where Jesus's spirit and words
    create new wonders?

3. Aria (tenor)
Author unknown

Ich   höre   mitten   in   den   Leiden
I   hear   amidst   the   suffering

Ein   Trostwort,   so   mein   Jesus   spricht.
a   comfort-word, that   my   Jesus   speaks.

Drum,   o   geängstigtes   Gemüte,
Therefore, o   anguished   soul,

Vertraue   deines   Gottes   Güte,
trust   your   God's goodness.

Sein   Wort   besteht   und   fehlet   nicht,
His   word   remains   and   fails   not;

Sein   Trost   wird   niemals   von   dir   scheiden!
his   comfort   will   never   from   you   depart!

I hear amidst the suffering
a word of comfort that my Jesus speaks.
Therefore, O anguished soul,
trust in your God's goodness.
His word remains and fails not;
his comfort will never depart from you!

4. Recitative (soprano)
Author unknown

Ach!
Alas!

Daß   mein   Glaube   noch   so   schwach,
that   my   faith   still   so   weak,

Und   daß   ich   mein   Vertrauen
and   that   I   my   trust

Auf   feuchtem   Grunde   muß   erbauen!
on   moist   ground   must   build!

Wie   ofte   müssen   neue   Zeichen
How   often   must   new   signs

Mein   Herz   erweichen!
my   heart   soften?

Alas!
that my faith is still so weak,
and that I must build my trust
on soggy ground!
How often must new signs
soften my heart?

Wie? kennst du deinen Helfer nicht,
What? know you your helper not,

Der nur ein einzig Trostwort spricht,
who only a single comfort-word speaks,

Und gleich erscheint,
and instantly appears,

Eh deine Schwachheit es vermeint,
before your frailty it imagines,

Die Rettungsstunde.
the salvation-hour.

Vertraue nur der Allmachtshand
Trust only the Almighty's hand

und seiner Wahrheit Munde!
and his truthful mouth!

What? Do you not know your helper,
who speaks only a single comforting word,
and instantly there appears,
before your weakness imagines it,
the hour of salvation?
Trust only in the hand of the Almighty
and his truthful sayings!

5. Aria (soprano/alto/bass trio)
Author unknown

Wenn meine Trübsal als mit Ketten
When my misery, as with chains,

Ein Unglück an dem andern hält,
one misfortune to the other binds,

So wird mich doch mein Heil erretten,
indeed will me — my salvation rescue,

Daß alles plötzlich von mir fällt.
that all suddenly from me fall.

Wie bald erscheint des Trostes Morgen
How soon appears — consolation's morning

Auf diese Nacht der Not und Sorgen!
upon this night of need and sorrow!

Even though my misery, as if with chains,
binds one misfortune to the next,
my savior will surely rescue me,
and all fetters will suddenly fall from me.
How soon appears consolation's morning
after this night of need and sorrow!

6. Chorale
Martin Luther

Ob bei uns ist der Sünden viel,
If with us is of the sins much,

Bei Gott ist viel mehr Gnade;
with God is much more grace;

Sein Hand zu helfen hat kein Ziel,
his hand to help has no end,

Wie groß auch sei der Schade.
how great also be the wrong.

Er ist allein der gute Hirt,
He is alone the good shepherd

Der Israel erlösen wird
who Israel save will

Aus seinen Sünden allen.
from its sins all.

Even if we are guilty of many sins,
with God there is much more grace;
his helping hand has no end,
however great the wrong.
He alone is the good shepherd
who will save Israel
from all its sins.

Cantata type:	Chorale and free poetry
Liturgical usage:	Twenty-first Sunday after Trinity
First performance:	October 29, 1724
Epistle:	Ephesians 6: 10–17
	The arming of the spirit
Gospel:	John 4: 47–54
	Jesus heals the nobleman's son

MARTIN Luther's 1523 hymn of the same name,* based on Psalm 130, provides the framework for Bach's cantata. The unknown librettist begins and ends the cantata with Luther's opening and closing verses. Movements 2, 3, and 5 paraphrase Luther's verses 2, 3, and 4, binding the cantata even more closely to the chorale. The only movement not derived directly from the hymn is no. 4, a recitative that relates to the Gospel for the day, a story of faith and trust rewarded.

Christ lag in Todes Banden, BWV 4

Christ Lay in Death's Bonds

Martin Luther

1. Sinfonia

2. Chorus

Christ lag in Todes Banden
Christ lay in death's bonds,

Für unsre Sünd gegeben,
for our sins given.

Er ist wieder erstanden
He has again risen

Und hat uns bracht das Leben;
and has us brought — life;

Des wir sollen fröhlich sein,
for this we shall joyful be,

Gott loben und ihm dankbar sein,
God praise, and to him thankful be,

Und singen Halleluja,
and sing Hallelujah.

Halleluja!
Hallelujah!

Christ lay in death's bonds,
sacrificed for our sins.
He has risen again
and brought us life;
therefore we shall be joyful,
praise God, and be thankful to him,
and sing Hallelujah.
Hallelujah!

3. Aria (soprano/alto)

Den Tod niemand zwingen kunnt
— death no one subdue could

Bei allen Menschenkindern,
among all humans.

Das macht' alles unsre Sünd,
This does all our sin;

Kein Unschuld war zu finden.
no innocence was to be found.

Davon kam der Tod so bald
Therefore came — death so soon,

Und nahm über uns Gewalt,
and seized over us power,

Hielt uns in seinem Reich gefangen.
held us in his realm captive.

Halleluja!
Hallelujah!

No one among all mortals
could conquer death.
Our sin causes all this;
no innocence was to be found.
Therefore death came so soon,
seized power over us, and
held us captive in his realm.
Hallelujah!

4. Aria (tenor)

Jesus Christus, Gottes Sohn,
Jesus Christ, God's son,

An unser Statt ist kommen
in our stead has come

Und hat die Sünde weggetan,
and has — sin taken away.

Damit dem Tod genommen
Thereby — death taken

All sein Recht und sein Gewalt,
all his privilege and his power.

Da bleibet nichts denn Tods Gestalt,
There remains nothing but death's image;

Den Stach'l hat er verloren.
the sting has it lost.

Halleluja!
Hallelujah!

Jesus Christ, the Son of God,
has come in our stead
and taken away our sin.
Thereby he has taken from death
all its dominion and power.
Nothing remains but death's mere form;
it has lost its sting.
Hallelujah!

5. Chorus

Es war ein wunderlicher Krieg,
It was a strange war,

Da Tod und Leben rungen,
when death and life wrestled:

Das Leben behielt den Sieg,
— life retained the victory;

Es hat den Tod verschlungen.
it has — death devoured.

Die Schrift hat verkündigt das,
The scripture has made known this,

Wie ein Tod den andern fraß,
how one death the other consumed;

Ein Spott aus dem Tod ist worden.
a mockery of — death has become.

Halleluja!
Hallelujah!

It was a strange war
when life and death struggled:
life retained the victory;
it has devoured death.
The scripture has proclaimed this,
how one death consumed the other;
death has become a mockery.
Hallelujah!

6. Aria (bass)

Hier ist das rechte Osterlamm,
Here is the true Paschal Lamb

Davon hat Gott geboten,
of which has God commanded;

Das ist hoch an des Kreuzes Stamm,
that has high on the cross's stem,

In heißer Lieb gebraten,
in hot love roasted.

Das Blut zeichnet unsre Tür,
The blood marks our door,

Das hält der Glaub dem Tode für,
that holds — faith — death before;

Der Würger kann uns nicht mehr schaden.
the slayer can us no more harm.

Halleluja!
Hallelujah!

Here is the true Paschal Lamb
whom God has offered;
he is high on the stem of the cross,
roasted in burning love.
His blood marks our door, and
faith holds this up before death;
the slayer can harm us no more.
Hallelujah!

7. Duet (soprano/tenor)

So feiern wir das hohe Fest
Therefore celebrate we the high feast

Mit Herzensfreud und Wonne,
with heart's joy and delight

Das uns der Herre scheinen läßt,
that to us the Lord shine lets.

Er ist selber die Sonne,
He is himself the sun,

Der durch seiner Gnade Glanz
who through his grace's splendor

Erleuchtet unsre Herzen ganz,
illuminates our hearts wholly;

Der Sünden Nacht ist verschwunden.
the sin's night has vanished.

Halleluja!
Hallelujah!

Therefore we celebrate the high feast
with joyous heart and great delight
that the Lord allows to shine upon us.
He is himself the sun,
who through the splendor of his grace
wholly illumines our hearts;
the night of sin has vanished.
Hallelujah!

8. Chorale

Wir essen und leben wohl
We   eat   and live well

In   rechten   Osterfladen,
on the   true   Passover bread;

Der alte Sauerteig nicht soll
the old sourdough not shall

Sein   bei dem Wort der Gnaden,
exist beside the word of   grace.

Christus will die Koste sein
Christ   will the food be

Und speisen die Seel allein,
and   feed   the soul alone;

Der Glaub will keins andern leben.
— faith will no   other live.

Halleluja!
Hallelujah!

We eat and live well
on the true Passover bread;
the old leaven shall not exist
beside the word of grace.
Christ desires to be the food
that alone will feed the soul;
faith wants to live on no other.
Hallelujah!

Cantata type:	Chorale cantata *per omnes versus*
Liturgical usage:	Easter Sunday
First performance:	Probably April 24, 1707 or Easter, 1708
Epistle:	1 Corinthians 5: 6–8 Christ the Easter Lamb
Gospel:	Mark 16: 1–8 Resurrection

*B*ACH scholar Alfred Dürr dates this cantata as most likely from 1707 or 1708, but in any case before 1714. If it was first performed on Easter, 1707, probably as Bach's audition piece for the organist position at the Bonifaciuskirche in Mühlhausen, it would be his very first cantata.

Bach wrote only three surviving Easter cantatas, BWV 4, 31, and 249. Cantatas 31 and 249 have joyous Easter texts and festive orchestrations including three trumpets and timpani. BWV 4 presents the starkest contrast. It is set austerely and archaically for strings with doubled violas. In structure it is a seventeenth-century-style chorale cantata *per omnes versus*—a chorale cantata in which all verses are set in sequence. Luther himself penned the poetry in 1524, a year in which he published fifteen of his thirty-six chorales. The text itself is discussed in this volume under Luther's hymn of the same name.*[2]

Luther ended verse 1 with an "alleluia" that Bach gave to all the other verses as well. His idea may have been borrowed from a historical antecedent. Precedents are found in the repetition of "Kyrie eleison" in "Christ ist erstanden," as well as in the "halleluja" that ends each line in the Easter hymn "Surrexit Christus hodie" which was known in German well before the time of Luther.[3]

Like other German composers of the early sixteenth century, Luther was not particularly concerned about the congruity of musical and textual stress when he wrote the text and melody to this chorale. In fact, bar lines were nonexistent, and meter in the modern sense was unknown. Nonetheless, the text itself naturally creates a meter through its accentual pattern. The first verse as written by Luther illustrates the "normal" textual accents of the poem within its seven lines of seven syllables, plus "alleluia." For simplicity, this is expressed in terms of a 4/4 meter, with its alternating strong and weak beats:

	4	1	2	3	4	1	2	3	
1	Christ	lag´	in	To´ - des-	ban´ - den,				*7 syllables, with anacrusis*
2	Für	uns´ - re	Sünd´ ge -	ge´ - ben,					*ditto*
3	Der´	ist	wie´- der	er -	stan´- den				*ditto*
4	Und	hat´	uns	bracht´ das	Le´ - ben.				*ditto*
5		Des´	wir	sol´ - len	fröh´- lich	sein,			*7 syllables, beginning on strong beat*
6	Gott	lo´ - ben	und	dank´- bar	sein				*7 syllables, with anacrusis*
7	Und	sing´- en	al´ - le -	lu´ - ia.					*ditto*
8		Al - le -	lu´ - ia.						

---

[2]The final word of the cantata title appears in the literature interchangeably as "Todesbanden" and "Todes Banden." The meaning is identical. The latter is used here following Neumann 1974.

[3]"Erstanden ist der heilig Christ," *EKG:* 78.

The pattern is simple. Four lines of seven syllables beginning with an upbeat comprise the first half. The second half is introduced by a single line of seven syllables that begins with an accent; this is followed by two lines like those in the first part, and then the final "alleluia." Even the first verse contains irregularities, however; the accentuation of line 3 is "wrong" until the penultimate syllable, and in line 7 *dankbar* falls on the "wrong" beat. These were obviously of no consequence to Luther. He nonetheless provided eight notes for each line (save line 5, with seven), which required the performers to slur two notes on a single syllable, thereafter effecting restoration of the accentual pattern.

Unlike Luther, Bach wrote in a period in which musical accent was regular and metrical. The incongruity of Luther's musical and textual accent thus presented Bach with a problem that he solved by adding and subtracting syllables as needed.

The list below of variants between Bach and Luther contains sixteen items. It is interesting to note that eleven of the sixteen arose from Bach's efforts to regularize accent.

Source:	Luther 1967: 14	
Variants:		(Bach = roman, Luther = *italic*)
	Verse 1, line 2:	Er = *Der*
	line 6:	ihm dankbar sein = *dankbar sein*
	Verse 2, line 7:	in seinem Reich = *in seim Reich*
	Verse 3, line 3:	weggetan = *abgetan*
	line 7:	Stach'l = *Stachel*
	Verse 4, line 1:	wunderlicher = *wunderlich*
	line 3:	Das Leben da behielt den Sieg = *Das Leben behielt den Sieg*
	Verse 5, line 1:	rechte = *recht*
	line 2:	hat Gott = *Gott hat*
	line 3:	Das ist hoch an des Kreuzes Stamm = *Das ist an des Kreuzes Stamm*
	line 6:	Tode = *Tod*
	line 7:	nicht mehr schaden (injure no more) = *nicht rühren* (not touch)
	Verse 6, line 1:	das hohe = *das hoch*
	line 3:	Herre = *Herr*
	line 5:	Gnade = *Gnaden*
	line 7:	verschwunden (disappeared) = *vergangen* (gone)

Ein feste Burg ist unser Gott, BWV 80
A Mighty Fortress Is Our God
Salomo Franck, J.S. Bach (?)

1. Chorus
Martin Luther

Ein feste Burg ist unser Gott,
A firm fortress is our God,

Ein gute Wehr und Waffen;
a good bulwark and weapon;

Er hilft uns frei aus aller Not,
he helps us free from all misery

Die uns jetzt hat betroffen.
that us now has affected.

Der alte böse Feind,
The old evil foe:

Mit Ernst er's jetzt meint,
with seriousness he it now intends.

Groß Macht und viel List
Great power and much cunning

Sein grausam Rüstung ist,
his cruel armament is;

Auf Erd ist nicht seinsgleichen.
on earth is not his equal.

A mighty fortress is our God,
a strong bulwark and weapon;
he sets us free from all the misery
that has now beset us.
The ancient, evil foe:
grave is his intent.
Vast power and cunning
are his cruel weapons;
on earth he has no equal.

28

2. Aria (bass) and Chorale (soprano)
Author of aria unknown; chorale by Martin Luther

Aria

Alles,   was von Gott geboren,
Everyone that from God is born

Ist zum Siegen auserkoren.
is for victory chosen.

Chorale

Mit unsrer Macht ist nichts getan,
With our power is nothing done;

Wir sind gar bald verloren.
we are very soon lost.

Es streit' vor uns der rechte Mann,
— fights for us, the just man

Den Gott selbst hat erkoren.
whom God himself has chosen.

Wer bei Christi   Blutpanier
Who by Christ's blood banner

In der Taufe   Treu geschworen,
in — baptism loyalty has sworn

Siegt   im Geiste für und für.
triumphs in the spirit   forever.

Fragst du,   wer er ist?
Ask   you, who he is?

Er heißt Jesus Christ,
He is called Jesus Christ,

Der Herre Zebaoth,
the Lord Sabaoth,

Und ist kein andrer Gott,
and is no other God.

Das Feld muß er behalten.
The field must he retain.

Alles,   was von Gott geboren,
Everyone that from God is born

Ist zum Siegen auserkoren.
is for victory chosen.

Aria

*Everyone who is born of God
is chosen for victory.*

Chorale

With our own power, nothing is accomplished;
we will very soon be lost.
The just man fights for us,
the one whom God himself has chosen.

*He who has sworn allegiance in baptism
to Christ's bloodstained banner
triumphs in the spirit forevermore.*

Do you ask who he is?
His is called Jesus Christ,
the Lord of Sabaoth,
and there is no other God;
master of all he must remain.

*Everyone who is born of God
is chosen for victory.*

3. Recitative (bass)
Author unknown

Erwäge doch, Kind Gottes, die so große Liebe,
Ponder —,   child of God, the so great love

Da Jesus sich
that Jesus —

Mit seinem Blute dir verschriebe,
with his blood to you has pledged,

Wormit er dich
with which he you

Zum Kriege wider Satans Heer und wider
for war against Satan's army and against

Welt und Sünde
world and sin

Geworben hat!
enlisted has!

Ponder well, child of God, the great love
that Jesus
has pledged to you with his blood,
with which he,
for war against Satan's army and against
the world and sin,
has enlisted you!

Gib   nicht in deiner Seele
Yield not in your soul

Dem Satan und den Lastern statt!
to   Satan and the   vice   —!

Laß nicht dein Herz,
Let not your heart,

Den Himmel Gottes auf der Erden,
the heaven of God on the earth,

Zur Wüste werden!
into desert become!

Bereue deine Schuld   mit   Schmerz,
Repent your   guilt through pain,

Daß Christi Geist mit dir sich fest   verbinde!
that Christ's spirit with you — firmly might unite!

Yield not your soul
to Satan and depravity!
Let not your heart,
God's kingdom on earth,
become like a wasteland!
Repent your guilt through pain,
that Christ's spirit might firmly unite with you!

4. Aria (soprano)
Author unknown

Komm in mein Herzenshaus,
Come into my   heart's house,

Herr Jesu, mein Verlangen!
Lord Jesus, my   longing!

Treib Welt und Satan aus
Drive world and Satan out

Und laß dein Bild in mir erneuert prangen!
and let your image in me   anew   shine!

Weg,   schnöder Sündengraus!
Away, despicable sin-horror!

Komm in mein Herzenshaus,
Come into my   heart's house,

Herr Jesu, mein Verlangen!
Lord Jesus, my   longing!

Come into the house of my heart,
Lord Jesus, my longing!
Drive the world and Satan out
and let your image shine anew in me!
Away, despicable horror of sin!
Come into the house of my heart,
Lord Jesus, my longing!

5. Chorale
Martin Luther

Und wenn die Welt voll Teufel   wär
And   if the world full of devils were

Und wollten   uns verschlingen,
and wanted to us   devour,

So fürchten wir uns nicht so sehr,
so fear   we — not so much,

Es soll uns doch gelingen.
 –we shall still succeed–.

Der Fürst dieser Welt,
The prince of this world,

Wie   saur   er sich stellt,
how difficult he — poses,

Tut er uns doch nicht,
does he to us —   not.

Das macht, er ist gericht',
That means, he is judged;

Ein Wörtchen kann ihn fällen.
a   little word can him fell.

And if the world were full of devils
who wanted to devour us,
we would not be too frightened,
for we shall still succeed.
The prince of this world,
however troublesome he seems,
does us no harm.
That means he is doomed;
a mere word can fell him.

6. Recitative (tenor)
Author unknown

So stehe dann bei Christi blutgefärbten Fahne,
Thus may you stand then by Christ's blood-colored banner

O Seele, fest
O soul, firmly

Und glaube, daß dein Haupt dich nicht verläßt,
and believe, that your head you not abandons

Ja, daß sein Sieg
Yea, that his victory

Auch dir den Weg zu deiner Krone bahne!
also for you the way to your crown may prepare!

Tritt freudig an den Krieg!
March gladly into the war!

Wirst du nur Gottes Wort
Will you only God's Word

So hören als bewahren,
so hear as preserve,

So wird der Feind gezwungen auszufahren,
then will the foe be forced to leave,

Dein Heiland bleibt dein Hort!
your savior remains your shield!

May you thus stand firmly by Christ's
bloodstained banner, O soul,
and trust that your head abandons you not—
yea, that his victory
may also prepare the way for you to your crown!
March gladly into war!
If you will only hear
and preserve God's word,
then the foe will be forced to leave,
and your savior will remain your shield!

7. Aria (alto/tenor)
Author unknown

Wie selig sind doch die,
How blessed are — those

die Gott im Munde tragen,
who God in the mouth carry;

Doch selger ist das Herz,
yet more blessed is the heart

das ihn im Glauben trägt!
that him in faith keeps!

Es bleibet unbesiegt
It remains unconquered

und kann die Feinde schlagen
and can the foes defeat

Und wird zuletzt gekrönt,
and will ultimately be crowned

wenn es den Tod erlegt.
when it — death slays.

How very blessed are those
who have God in their speech;
still more blessed is the heart
that keeps him in faith!
The heart remains unconquered
and can defeat the foes
and will ultimately be crowned
when it slays death.

8. Chorale
Martin Luther

Das Wort sie sollen lassen stahn
The word they shall let stand

Und kein' Dank dazu haben.
and no thanks for it have.

Er ist bei uns wohl auf dem Plan
He is with us surely on the battlefield,

Mit seinem Geist und Gaben.
with his spirit and gifts.

Nehmen sie uns den Leib,
Take they from us the body,

Gut, Ehr, Kind und Weib,
goods, honor, child, and wife,

Laß fahren dahin,
let go thither;

Sie habens kein' Gewinn;
they have no gain.

Das Reich muß uns doch bleiben.
the kingdom must for us — remain.

They shall allow the word to stand
and receive no thanks for it.
He is surely with us on the field of battle,
along with the Spirit and its gifts.
If they take from us our body,
goods, honor, child, and wife,
let them go;
they gain no victory from that,
for the kingdom is ours forever.

Cantata type:	Chorale and free poetry
Liturgical usage:	Reformation
First performance:	1732 / 1735?
Epistle:	2 Thessalonians 2: 3–8
	Steadfastness against the enemy
Gospel:	Revelation 14: 6–8
	Admonition to fear God

*T*HE occasion for which Bach wrote the present version of this cantata is unknown, as is when it was first performed. W. Murray Young (1989: 95) echoes W. Gillies Whittaker (1959, 1: 221) in assigning it to the 200th anniversary celebration of the Augsburg Confession in 1730.[4] The scholarship of Alfred Dürr (1971: 578), however, suggests Reformation Sunday in or about the year 1735, while the *Bach Compendium* (Wolff and Schulze 1985–: 777) places the first performance as late as 1744–1747.

Bach wrote the first version of the cantata (BWV 80a) to a libretto by Salomo Franck (1659–1725) for Oculi Sunday, the fourth Sunday in Lent, of 1715. When Bach moved to Leipzig in 1723 he could not reuse the earlier work, as cantatas were not performed there during Lent. He thus undertook a revision and expansion of the cantata to make it suitable for Reformation Sunday.

Probably because the earlier work already ended with the second verse of Luther's chorale "Ein feste Burg," and the opening movement already contained the same melody, Bach elected to transform it into a chorale cantata by the inclusion of all four of Luther's verses. He thus wrote an opening chorus (80/1) based on Luther's first verse and added the words of the second verse to the chorale melody already present in 80a/1, transforming it into 80/2. For his third, fourth, sixth, and seventh movements he retained 80a/2, 3, 4, and 5, respectively, and for his fifth movement he simply inserted a setting of the chorale, verse 3. The addition of Luther's fourth and final verse as the closing chorale nearly completed the cantata's transformation. All that remained was to make a couple of alterations to Franck's text in order to free it from ties to the readings for Oculi Sunday (see *Variants*).

Bach reused pre-existing musical material in a great many of his works, as long as the music possessed the affect needed in the new composition. In the cantatas, this usually meant retaining the music and replacing the words. The present cantata is one of the few examples in which the original words, written for a completely different purpose, perfectly suited their new function. For further information on the Luther chorale, see the annotation to the hymn "Ein feste Burg."*

Source (mvts. 2–4, 7, 8): Franck 1715: 60. Facsimile in Neumann 1974: 278
Variants: (Bach = roman, Franck = *italic*)

No. 2, line 3 (aria): wer (who) = *was* (what)
line 5 (aria): Geiste (spirit) = *Christo* (Christ)
No. 7, lines 1, 2: Wie selig sind doch die, die Gott im Munde tragen
(How blessed are those who have God in their speech) =
Wie selig ist der Leib, der Jesu dich getragen
(How blessed is the body that brought you to Jesus)
line 4: ihm (him) = *dich* (you)

---

[4]Luther's reforms fomented political intrigues throughout German-speaking Europe in the 1520s. His challenge to Roman Catholic Church doctrine and practice was also a threat to the sovereignty of the Catholic Church as a political entity, and to the authority of the Holy Roman Emperor and his princes. Several attempts were made among German princes at forming alliances based on basic agreement with Luther, but Luther himself resisted such actions on several grounds—among them the fact that there was not yet a confession or statement of faith that fully represented his principles.

The year 1529 and the first half of 1530 saw numerous attempts at the creation of a confession; these were assisted by the publication in 1529 of Luther's Catechism, the first formal statement of Lutheran doctrines. On June 15, 1530 what was to be known as the Augsburg Confession was read at the Diet of Augsburg and was thereafter signed by several princes. It had been revised countless times in response to the political machinations of the preceding year and strongly bore the personal stamps of both Luther and his close colleague Philipp Melanchthon. The creation of the Augsburg Confession became one of great days in history for what was to become the Lutheran Church, a symbol of the triumph of the Reformation.

Gott der Herr ist Sonn und Schild, BWV 79

God the Lord Is Sun and Shield
Librettist unknown

1. Chorus

Psalm 84: 11

Gott der Herr ist Sonn und Schild.
God the Lord is sun and shield.

Der Herr gibt Gnade und Ehre,
The Lord gives grace and glory;

er wird kein Gutes mangeln lassen
he will nothing good lack permit

den Frommen.
to the righteous.

God the Lord is sun and shield.
The Lord gives grace and glory;
he will withhold no good thing
from the righteous.

2. Aria (alto)

Author unknown

Gott ist unsre Sonn und Schild!
God is our sun and shield!

Darum rühmet dessen Güte
Therefore praises his goodness

Unser dankbares Gemüte,
our grateful soul,

Die er für sein Häuflein hegt.
which he for his tiny band preserves.

Denn er will uns ferner schützen,
For he wants to us further protect,

Ob die Feinde Pfeile schnitzen
If the foes arrows carve

Und ein Lästerhund gleich billt.
and a blasphemous dog — barks.

God is our sun and shield!
Therefore our grateful soul
praises his goodness,
which he preserves for his chosen.
For he wants to continue protecting us,
even if our foes sharpen their arrows
and a blasphemous dog howls.

3. Chorale

Martin Rinckart

Nun danket alle Gott
Now thank all God

Mit Herzen, Mund und Händen,
with heart, mouth, and hands,

Der große Dinge tut
who great things does

An uns und allen Enden;
at us and all ends;

Der uns von Mutterleib
who us from womb

Und Kindesbeinen an
and infancy on,

Unzählig viel zugut
incalculably much benefit,

Und noch jetzund getan.
and still now has done.

Let all give thanks to God
with heart, voice, and deeds,
to the one who achieves great things
for us and in all ways;
who from the womb
and childhood on
has done us incalculable good,
and does so even now.

4. Recitative (bass)
Author unknown

Gottlob,   wir wissen
Praise God! We know

Den rechten Weg zur   Seligkeit;
the right path to blessedness;

Denn, Jesu, du hast ihn uns
for, Jesus, you have it to us

durch   dein Wort gewiesen,
through your word shown.

Drum   bleibt dein Name jederzeit gepriesen.
Therefore remains your name always   praised.

Weil aber viele noch
Since but many still

Zu dieser Zeit
at   this time

An fremden Joch
at foreign yoke

Aus   Blindheit ziehen müssen,
out of blindness pull   must,

Ach! so erbarme dich
ah! so   pity

Auch ihrer gnädiglich,
also them mercifully,

Daß sie den rechten Weg erkennen
that they the right way recognize

Und dich bloß ihren   Mittler nennen.
and you only their intercessor call.

Thank God! We know
the proper path to salvation;
for Jesus, you have shown it to us
through your word.
Therefore your name shall always be praised.
But, because at this time many still must,
out of blindness,
bear a foreign yoke,
ah! mercifully pity them also
that they might recognize the proper path
and call you their only intercessor.

5. Aria (soprano/bass)
Author unknown

Gott, ach Gott, verlaß die Deinen
God, O God, forsake — yours

Nimmermehr!
nevermore!

Laß dein Wort uns helle scheinen;
Let your word us brightly shine;

Obgleich sehr
although much

Wider uns die Feinde toben,
against us the foes   rage,

So   soll unser Mund dich loben.
thus shall our mouth you praise.

God, O God, forsake your people
nevermore!
Let your word brightly shine for us;
although our foes rage against us,
still shall our mouths praise you.

6. Chorale
Ludwig Hembold

Erhalt   uns in der Wahrheit,
Preserve us in the   truth,

Gib ewigliche Freiheit,
give eternal freedom,

Zu preisen deinen Namen
to praise your   name

Durch   Jesum Christum. Amen.
through Jesus Christ. Amen.

Preserve us in the truth;
grant us everlasting freedom
to praise your name
through Jesus Christ. Amen.

Cantata type:	Bible, chorale, and free poetry
Liturgical usage:	Reformation
First performance:	Most likely October 31, 1725
Epistle:	2 Thessalonians 2: 3–8
	Steadfastness against the enemy
Gospel:	Revelation 14: 6–8:
	Admonition to fear God

*T*HE readings for Reformation Sunday focus on the fear of God and holding steadfast against the enemy. These themes are nearly absent, however, from the anonymous libretto for Bach's cantata. Instead, the text focuses on praising God. The opening chorus from Psalm 84: 11 provides the reason: God is the "sun and shield," the light and the protector, who will never leave the righteous in need.

The praise begins in the second movement, an aria that echoes the first line of the opening chorus and calls upon the Christian to be grateful for God's protection against the enemy, manifested here as arrow-sharpening soldiers and howling dogs. The chorale that follows, the first verse of Martin Rinckart's "Nun danket alle Gott,"* comes as a surprise, since such homophonic chorale settings customarily closed cantatas but seldom appeared within them. Bach scholar and conductor W. Gillies Whittaker remarks with some justification that the continuation of the cantata is anticlimactic and superfluous, given the overwhelming strength of the first movement and the finality of the chorale. (Whittaker 1959, 2: 208)

In the recitative that follows the chorale, Jesus is again praised, this time for showing the Christian the way to salvation. At the same time, he is implored to reveal himself to the non-believers who "out of blindness bear a foreign yoke." A plea to "forsake your people nevermore!" begins the next movement, an aria that promises to praise God despite tribulation. For the closing movement the librettist used the eighth and final verse of Ludwig Helmbold's 1575 hymn "Nun laßt uns Gott dem Herrn Dank sagen." (*EKG*: 227) First God is entreated to hold the Christian steadfast in truth and to grant him eternal freedom (= salvation). But it is the last two lines of the chorale that make it a perfect choice for this cantata and reveal careful thought on the part of the librettist: The prayer of the first two lines was not uttered for the humanity's comfort, but rather to grant everyone the chance "to praise your name through Jesus Christ."

Source (chorale):   Wackernagel 1964, 4: 647

Gottes Zeit ist die allerbeste Zeit, BWV 106
God's Time Is the Very Best Time.
Librettist unknown

1. Sinfonia

2a. Chorus
Acts 17: 28 (italics), embedded in free poetry; author unknown

Gottes Zeit ist die allerbeste Zeit.
God's time is the very best time.

In ihm leben, weben und sind wir,
In him live, move, and are we,

solange   er will.
as long as   he wills.

In ihm sterben wir zur rechten Zeit,
In him die   we at the right   time,

wenn er will.
when he wills.

God's time is the very best time.
In him we live, move, and have our being,
as long as he wills.
In him we die at the appointed time,
whenever he wills.

2b. Arioso (tenor)
Psalm 90: 12

Ach, Herr, lehre uns bedenken,
O   Lord, teach us to ponder,

daß wir sterben müssen,
that we   die   must,

auf daß wir klug werden.
so that we wise become.

O Lord, teach us to ponder
the fact that we must die,
so that we may become wise.

2c. Aria (bass)

Isaiah 38: 1

Bestelle dein Haus;
Prepare your house;

denn du wirst sterben
for you will die

und nicht lebendig bleiben!
and not alive remain!

Set your house in order!
For you will die
and not remain alive.

2d. Chorus and Arioso (soprano)

Chorus: Ecclesiastes 14: 17; Arioso: Revelation 22: 20b

Chorus
Es ist der alte Bund:
It is the old law:

Arioso
Mensch, du mußt sterben!
mortal, you must die!

Ja, komm, Herr Jesu!
Yes, come, Lord Jesus!

Chorus
It is the old law:
mortal, you must perish!

Arioso
Yes, come, Lord Jesus!

3a. Aria (alto)

Psalm 31: 5

In deine Hände befehl ich meinen Geist;
Into your hands commend I my spirit;

du hast mich erlöset, Herr,
you have me redeemed, Lord,

du getreuer Gott.
you faithful God.

Into your hands I commend my spirit;
you have redeemed me, Lord,
you faithful God.

3b. Arioso (bass) and Chorale (alto)

Arioso: Luke 23: 43b; chorale by Martin Luther

Arioso

Heute, wirst du mit mir im Paradies sein.
Today, will you with me in Paradise be.

Chorale

Mit Fried und Freud ich fahr dahin
With peace and joy I go thither

In Gottes Willen,
in God's will,

Getrost ist mir mein Herz und Sinn,
comforted is me my heart and mind,

Sanft und stille.
calm, and quiet.

Wie Gott mir verheißen hat:
As God to me promised has:

Der Tod ist mein Schlaf worden.
— death has my sleep become.

Arioso

Today you will be with me in Paradise.

Chorale

In peace and joy I depart,
according to God's will;
my heart and mind are comforted,
calm, and still.
As God has promised me,
death has become my sleep.

4. Chorus
Adam Reusner

Glorie, Lob, Ehr und Herrlichkeit
Glory, praise, honor, and majesty

Sei dir, Gott Vater und Sohn bereit',
be for you, God Father and Son prepared,

Dem Heilgen Geist mit Namen!
to the Holy Spirit with name!

Die göttlich Kraft
The divine strength

Mach uns sieghaft
makes us victorious

Durch Jesum Christum, Amen.
through Jesus Christ, Amen.

Glory, praise, honor, and majesty
be given to you, God the Father,
Son, and Holy Spirit with your power!
The divine strength
makes us victorious
through Jesus Christ, Amen.

Cantata type:	Bible and chorales with a few lines of free poetry
Liturgical usage:	Funeral
First performance:	Fall, 1707
Epistle:	—
Gospel:	—

Source (chorale): Wackernagel 1964, 3: 133
Variant: Line 2: "dir" is absent in the original

*L*IKE BWV 4, 131, and 150, "Gottes Zeit" is one of the earliest cantatas—possibly the second or third. The text, consisting almost entirely of Bible verses and chorales, is stylistically typical of the early cantatas; later Bach made much more use of free poetry. The work was undoubtedly written for a funeral. This is immediately clear from the text and is also suggested by the archaic instrumentation of two recorders, two gambas, and continuo—an ensemble unique in Bach's works. Alfred Dürr (1971: 611), the scholar most responsible for dating Bach's cantatas, believes it probable that the funeral in question was that of Bach's uncle Tobias Lämmerhirt, who died on August 10, 1707. The recorder was traditionally the instrument of the shepherd, and it would have been poetically fitting to use recorders in this case (*Lämmerhirt* = shepherd of the lambs).

The first vocal movement, which follows the opening instrumental sinfonia, consists of four sections, each of which is given a distinctive musical setting. The first section contains the only free poetry. It begins with the confident optimism often found in Lutheran funeral texts of this period: God's time—for life and then death—is serenely declared to be "the best time." Words from Acts 17: 28, "In him we live, move, and have our being," appear in the second line and are balanced by the parallelism of the fourth line, "In him we die at the appointed time."

The next three sections constitute a reflection on death, seen through words from three books of the Old Testament. The reader is first reminded that death inevitably comes to all and then he is exhorted to be prepared for it, for it is the Law of the Old Covenant. But as the Law is recited in archaic musical style by the altos, a lone soprano—the voice of the departed spirit or the faithful Christian—calls for the coming of Jesus.

In the third movement, it is clear that the soprano's text was intended to function as a pivot, turning the cantata from the Old Testament to the New. Although the opening section is a setting of a Psalm, its first words are also the last words of Jesus on the cross (Luke 23: 46b): "Into your hands I commend my spirit." The second section of this movement unites an earlier utterance of the crucified Jesus ("today you will be with me in paradise") with the first verse of Luther's chorale "Mit Fried und Freud ich fahr dahin,"* a poetic interpretation of the Song of Simeon. The Christian is thus able to depart in peace because he has been promised union with Jesus in paradise.

The cantata closes with verse 7 of a chorale by Adam Reusner (c. 1496–c. 1576) "In dich hab ich gehoffet, Herr" (In You Have I Trusted, Lord, 1533).[5] This verse, with its doxology and declaration of victory over death through the power of Jesus Christ, also provides the closing "amen," which Bach sets to ascending sixteenth-note melismas. While this could be seen as a purely musical decision, it surely had symbolic meaning as well. Such melismas had been used by composers since the sixteenth century as musical symbols for life—which is precisely what the text promises.

---

[5] Line 3, literally "to the Holy Spirit with name," has a deeper meaning. The word "name" "denotes the person and his power. 'In the name of the Lord' = (It comes to pass through the) power of the Lord. . . ." (Stapel 1950: 243) Thus the phrase in question means "to the Holy Spirit with his power."

Lobe den Herren, den mächtigen König der Ehren, BWV 137

Praise to the Lord, the Mighty King of Glory

Joachim Neander

1. Chorus

Lobe den Herren, den mächtigen König der Ehren,
Praise to the Lord, the mighty king of glory,

Meine geliebete Seele, das ist mein Begehren.
my beloved soul, that is my desire.

Kommet zu Hauf,
Come together

Psalter und Harfe, wacht auf!
psaltery and harp, awake!

Lasset die Musicam hören.
Let [us] the music hear.

Praise to the Lord, the mighty king of glory;
my beloved soul, that is my desire.
Come together;
psaltery and harp, awake!
Let the music be heard!

2. Aria (alto)

Lobe den Herren, der alles so herrlich regieret,
Praise to the Lord, who all so gloriously rules,

Der dich auf Adelers Fittichen sicher geführet,
who you on eagle's wings safely has led,

Der dich erhält,
who you preserves,

Wie es dir selber gefällt;
as it you yourself pleases;

Hast du nicht dieses verspüret?
have you not this perceived?

Praise to the Lord, who rules so gloriously over all,
who has led you safely on eagle's wings,
who preserves you,
as it pleases you.
Have you not perceived this?

3. Aria (soprano/bass)

Lobe den Herren, der künstlich und fein dich bereitet,
Praise the Lord, who artfully and finely you prepares,

Der dir Gesundheit verliehen, dich freundlich geleitet.
who to you health has given, you kindly led.

In wieviel Not
In how much distress

Hat nicht der gnädige Gott
has indeed the merciful God

über dir Flügel gebreitet!
over you wings spread!

Praise the Lord, who artfully and finely prepares you,
who has given you health and kindly led you.
In how many times of distress
has the merciful God indeed
spread his wings over you!

4. Aria (tenor)

Lobe den Herren, der deinen Stand sichtbar gesegnet,
Praise to the Lord, who your state visibly blessed,

Der aus dem Himmel mit Strömen der Liebe geregnet;
who from the heaven with streams of love rained.

Denke dran,
Think of that,

Was der Allmächtige kann,
what the Almighty can do,

Der dir mit Liebe begegnet.
who you with love meets.

Praise to the Lord, who has visibly blessed your state,
who has rained streams of love from the heavens.
Consider
what the Almighty can do,
he who meets you with such love.

5. Chorale

Lobe   den Herren; was in mir ist, lobe den Namen!
Praise to the Lord; what in me is, praise the name!

Alles, was Odem hat, lobe mit Abrahams Samen!
All   that breath has, praise with Abraham's seed!

Er ist dein Licht,
He is your light;

Seele, vergiß es ja nicht;
soul, forget it — not!

Lobende   schließe mit Amen.
Those who praise, conclude with Amen.

Praise to the Lord; all within me praise his name!
All that has breath, praise with Abraham's seed!
He is your light;
O soul, forget it not!
Those who praise the Lord, close with Amen!

Cantata type:	Chorale cantata *per omnes versus*
Liturgical usage:	Twelfth Sunday after Trinity
First performance:	August 19, 1725
Epistle:	2 Corinthians 3: 4–11
	New vs. Old Covenant: the written code kills, but the spirit gives life
Gospel:	Mark 7: 31–37
	The healing of the deaf and dumb man

*T*HE long stretch of Sundays after the feast of Trinity—in certain years up to twenty seven—has always presented pastors and church musicians with both problems and opportunities. On one hand, most lack the strong thematic focus of many other Sundays of the church year; on the other hand, this is an opportunity to use general texts that are not directly connected with a specific feast. Such is the case with the present cantata.

The Epistle and Gospel for this Sunday have little in common except that they both present opportunities to praise God. Second Corinthians 3: 4–11 contrasts the Old and New Covenants, providing reason to praise God for his gift of salvation through Jesus. The healing of the deaf and dumb man in Mark 7: 31–37 is one of the many miracles of Jesus—further grounds for the praise of God.

For this Sunday in August, 1725, Bach could have composed a musical exegesis of either of these texts, the result of which might have been more somber than he desired at the moment. Instead, he chose simply to praise God through Joachim Neander's vigorous and joyous chorale from 1680, "Lobe den Herren, den mächtigen König der Ehren,"* all five verses of which he set to music.

Source: Neander 1700: 42
Variant:
(Bach = roman, Neander = *italic*)
Verse 1, line 3: zu Hauf = *zuhauf*
Verse 4, line 3: dran = *daran.* (In this context, Bach seems to have wanted to use a specific motive that required the contraction.)

Mit Fried und Freud ich fahr dahin, BWV 125
In Peace and Joy I now Depart
Librettist unknown

1. Chorus
Martin Luther

Mit   Fried und Freud ich fahr dahin
With peace and joy I   go thither

In Gottes Willen;
in God's will.

Getrost ist mir mein Herz und Sinn,
Consoled is —   my heart and mind,

Sanft und stille;
calm, and still;

Wie Gott mir verheißen hat,
as God me promised has,

Der Tod ist mein Schlaf worden.
— death has my   sleep become.

In peace and joy I now depart
according to God's will.
My heart and mind are comforted,
calm, and still;
as God has promised me,
death has become my sleep.

2. Aria (alto)
Author unknown

Ich will auch mit gebrochnen Augen
I want also with broken eyes

Nach dir, mein treuer Heiland, sehn.
to you, my faithful savior, look.

Wenngleich des Leibes Bau zerbricht,
When even the body's form breaks,

Doch fällt mein Herz und Hoffen nicht.
yet fall my heart and hope not.

Mein Jesus sieht auf mich im Sterben
My Jesus looks on me in dying

Und lässet mir kein Leid geschehn.
and lets to me no harm happen.

I want, even with blinded eyes,
to look to you, my faithful savior.
Even if my body breaks,
my heart and hope fail not.
My Jesus watches over me in dying
and lets no harm come to me.

3. Recitative and Chorale (bass)
Author of recitative unknown; chorale by Martin Luther

Recitative

O Wunder, daß ein Herz
Oh wonder, that a heart

Vor der dem Fleisch verhaßten Gruft
before the to the flesh hated tomb

und gar des Todes Schmerz
and even — death's pain

Sich nicht entsetzet!
— not is terrified!

Recitative

Oh miracle, that one's heart
is not terrified
before the flesh's hated tomb
and even death's suffering!

Chorale

Das macht Christus, wahr' Gottes Sohn,
That does Christ, truly God's son,

Der treue Heiland,
the faithful Savior,

Der auf dem Sterbebette schon
who on the deathbed already

Mit Himmelssüßigkeit den Geist ergötzet,
with heaven's sweetness the spirit delights,

Den du mich, Herr, hast sehen lan,
whom you me, Lord, has see let,

Da in erfüllter Zeit ein Glaubensarm
when in fulfilled time a faith-arm

das Heil des Herrn umfinge;
the salvation of the Lord may embrace;

Und machst bekannt,
and made known,

Von dem erhabnen Gott, dem Schöpfer aller Dinge,
of the exalted God, the creator of all things,

Daß er sei das Leben und Heil,
that he might be the life and salvation

Der Menschen Trost und Teil,
the people's comfort and portion,

Ihr Retter vom Verderben
their savior from corruption.

Im Tod und auch im Sterben.
in death and also in dying.

Chorale

This Christ has done, God's true son,
the faithful Savior,

The one who already is at the deathbed
delights the spirit with heaven's sweetness,

whom you, Lord, have let me see

when at the final hour an arm of faith
may embrace the salvation of the Lord;

and made known to me,

from the exalted God, the creator of all things,

so that he might be my life and salvation

humanity's comfort and portion,
its savior from corruption.

in death and also in dying.

4. Aria (tenor/bass duet)
Author unknown

Ein unbegreiflich Licht erfüllt
An incomprehensible light fills

   den ganzen Kreis der Erden.
   the whole circle of the earth.

Es schallet kräftig fort und fort
It sounds strongly on and on

Ein höchst erwünscht Verheißungswort:
a most highly desired promise-word:

Wer glaubt, soll selig werden.
who believes, shall blessed become.

An incomprehensible light fills
the whole sphere of the earth.
It echoes strongly on and on,
a most highly desired promise:
whosoever believes shall be blest.

5. Recitative (alto)
Author unknown

O unerschöpfter Schatz der Güte,
O unexhausted store of goodness

So sich uns Menschen aufgetan:
that itself to us people has disclosed:

   es wird der Welt,
   it will be for the world,

So Zorn und Fluch auf sich geladen,
so wrath and plague on itself has burdened,

Ein Stuhl der Gnaden
a chair of grace

Und Siegeszeichen aufgestellt,
and victory sign set up,

Und jedes gläubige Gemüte
and every faithful soul

Wird in sein Gnadenreich geladen.
will into his grace-kingdom be invited.

O unexhausted store of goodness
that is revealed to us mortals:
one day the world,
which has burdened itself with wrath and plagues,
will receive a throne of grace
and a sign of victory,
and every faithful soul
will be summoned into his kingdom of grace.

6. Chorale
Martin Luther

Er ist das Heil und selig Licht
He is the salvation and blessed light

Für die Heiden,
for the Gentiles,

Zu erleuchten, die dich kennen nicht,
to enlighten those you know not,

Und zu weiden.
and to nurture.

Er ist deins Volks Israel
He is your people's Israel

Der Preis, Ehr, Freud und Wonne.
the reward, glory, joy, and bliss.

He is the salvation and blessed light
for the Gentiles,
to enlighten those who know you not
and to nurture them.
He is, to your people Israel,
the reward, glory, joy, and bliss.

Cantata type:	Chorale and free poetry
Liturgical usage:	Purification (British: *Candlemas*; German: *Mariae Reinigung*)
First performance:	February 2, 1725
Epistle:	Malachai 3: 1–4
	The Lord shall come to his temple
Gospel:	Luke 2: 22–32
	Simeon sees the child Jesus in the temple

DURING Bach's second year of service in Leipzig he continued the practice he had established in his first year of composing a new cantata for most Sundays and feast days of the church year. In this year, however, he concentrated on "chorale cantatas," works based on Lutheran hymns. "Mit Fried und Freud" is an example of a chorale cantata in which the hymn is presented along with free poetry composed expressly to serve as part of a cantata libretto. (BWV 80, "Ein feste Burg,"* is an example of the same type.)

Luther's 1524 hymn "Mit Fried und Freud ich fahr dahin"* is a versification of the Gospel for the Purification of the Virgin Mary: the story of Simeon's encounter with the baby Jesus at his presentation in the Temple, and his Messianic prophesy. It was thus a perfect choice for this day's cantata libretto. One must go back a few verses in Luke 2 to understand the connection between these two events. The story of Jesus's birth in Luke 2: 1–20 is followed immediately by a discussion of the things done by Mary and Joseph to observe the law and customs of the Jews, symbolically showing Jesus to be subject to the Old Covenant Law that he was to supplant through his death and resurrection. The familiar ceremonies were the circumcision on the eighth day and the presentation in the Temple, which was customarily accompanied by a "sacrifice," a payment of five shekels.

Less known today is the custom of "purification" of the mother. After the birth of a male child, the mother was considered unclean for seven days and had to remain at home for a further thirty three; on the fortieth day a purification sacrifice had to be offered (Leviticus 12: 1–8). This is described in Luke 2: 24. (Guthrie et al. 1970: 893) The Feast of the Purification is the celebration of this event. Although the Purification is less of a festival in the Lutheran Church than in the Roman Catholic Church, it was still a major event in Bach's time, for the celebration of which he wrote seven cantatas (BWV 82, 83, 125, 157, 158, 161, and 200).

The present cantata begins with the opening verse of the chorale. In the following aria the singer, representing the pious Christian, pledges loyalty to the Savior through the trials of life. The third movement combines the second verse of the chorale with free poetry that expresses Simeon's thoughts on his approaching death and his faith in God. Verse 3 of the chorale is omitted, but the librettist presents it by proxy through an aria and recitative that touch on its ideas. The cantata closes with the fourth and final verse of the chorale.

Source:	Neumann 1974: 156
Variant:	(Bach = roman, Luther = *italic*)
	No. 3: Im Tod und auch im Sterben (in death and also in dying)
	= *In Not und Sterben* (in troubles and death)

Nach dir, Herr, verlanget mich, BWV 150
For You, O Lord, I Long
Librettist unknown

1. Sinfonia

2. Chorus
Psalm 25: 1–2

Nach dir, Herr, verlanget mich.
For you, Lord, long I.

Mein Gott, ich hoffe auf dich.
My God, I rely on you.

Laß mich nicht zuschanden werden,
Let me not confounded become,

daß sich meine Feinde
that — my foes

nicht freuen über mich.
not exult over me.

For you, O Lord, I long.
My God, I trust in you.
Let me not be confounded,
so that my foes
will not exult over me.

3. Aria (soprano)
Author unknown

Doch bin und bleibe ich vergnügt,
Yet am and remain I content,

Obgleich hier zeitlich toben
although here on earth rage

Kreuz, Sturm und andre Proben,
cross, storm and other trials—

Tod, Höll und was sich fügt.
death, hell and what comes to pass.

Ob Unfall schlägt den treuen Knecht,
If misfortune strikes the faithful servant,

Recht ist und bleibet ewig Recht.
right is and remains eternally right.

I am and remain content,
even though here on earth
the cross, storms, and other trials rage—
death, hell, and whatever else comes to pass.
Even if misfortune strikes the faithful servant,
right is right and remains forever right.

4. Chorus

Psalm 25: 5

Leite mich in deiner Wahrheit und lehre mich;
Lead me in your   truth and teach me,

denn du bist der Gott,   der mir hilft,
for   you are the God, who me helps,

täglich harre ich dein.
daily   wait   I for you.

Lead me in your truth and teach me,
for you are the God who saves me;
daily I wait for you.

5. Trio (alto/tenor/bass)

Author unknown

Zedern müssen von den Winden
Cedars must from the   winds

Oft   viel Ungemach empfinden,
often much hardship   suffer,

Oftmals werden sie verkehrt.
often   are they upturned.

Rat   und Tat auf Gott gestellet,
Counsel and deed on God based,

Achtet nicht, was   widerbellet,
heed   not,   what barks against [it]

Denn sein Wort ganz   anders   lehrt.
For   his word totally differently teaches.

Cedars must often suffer
much hardship from the winds;
many times they are upturned.
When counsel and deed are founded upon God,
heed not what howls against them,
for his word teaches very differently.

6. Chorus

Psalm 25: 15

Meine Augen sehen   stets   zu dem Herrn;
My   eyes   look constantly to the Lord;

denn er wird meinen Fuß
for   he will my   foot

aus   dem Netze ziehen.
out of the   net   pluck.

My eyes look constantly to the Lord,
for he will pluck my foot
from the net.

7. Chorus

Author unknown

Meine Tage in dem Leide
My   days in — suffering

Endet Gott   dennoch zur Freude;
ends God nevertheless to   joy;

Christen   auf den Dornenwegen
Christians on the   thorny paths

Führen Himmels   Kraft   und Segen.
carry   heaven's strength and blessing.

Bleibet Gott mein treuer   Schutz,
Remains God my faithful protector;

Achte ich nicht Menschentrutz;
heed I   not humanity's defiance;

Christus, der uns steht   zur Seiten,
Christ,   who us stands at the side,

Hilft mir täglich sieghaft   streiten.
helps me daily victoriously to fight.

My days of suffering
God turns to joy.
Christians on the thorny paths
carry heaven's strength and blessing.
God remains my faithful protector;
I heed not humanity's defiance.
Christ, who stands beside us,
helps me daily to fight victoriously.

Cantata type:	Bible and free poetry
Liturgical usage:	various
First performance:	1708
Epistle:	—
Gospel:	—

CANTATA 150 is unusual among Bach's early cantatas in its use of free poetry for three of its movements. It is typical, however, in its employment of Bible verses for the remaining four. All of the Biblical citations, on which the even-numbered movements are based, are taken from Psalm 25, which the librettist carefully excerpted for statements of trust in God.

Bach just as carefully chose musical ideas that symbolized his text. The sinfonia and the opening vocal movement (no. 2) are both based on the chromatic outline of a fourth, the so-called "lamento bass," which is found as early as Monteverdi as a representation of anguish, pain, and longing. (The most familiar example is the chaconne bass to the "Crucifixus" of the B-minor Mass.) Movement 3, "Lead me in your truth . . . ," is characterized by a scale that continuously ascends through the voices and then the violins for over three octaves, a musical synonym in German ("scale" = *Leiter*) for the verb "to lead" (= *leiten*). The last of the Biblical movements, no. 6, repeats its opening text ("My eyes look constantly to the Lord") several times with an unchanging accompanimental figuration in the strings, in clear symbolism of the steadfastness described in the Psalm.

The poetry of movements 3 and 5 teaches that faith and trust conquer adversity. The latter is particularly pictorial in its image of the cedars bending before the winds, painted by the continuous sixteenths in the continuo. The closing movement has a rather unimaginative text, which teaches one last time that "Christ . . . helps me daily to fight victoriously" through the travails of the world. Bach's musical symbolism in this movement is not directed toward individual words, but rather to the concept of faith, which he symbolizes by the steadfast repetition of a chaconne bass.

Nun danket alle Gott, BWV 192
Let All Give Thanks to God
Martin Rinckart

1. Chorus

Nun danket alle Gott
Now thank all God

Mit Herzen, Mund und Händen,
with heart, mouth, and hands,

Der große Dinge tut
who great things does

An uns und allen Enden;
at us and all ends;

Der uns von Mutterleib
who us from womb

Und Kindesbeinen an
and infancy on,

Unzählig viel zugut
incalculably much benefit

Und noch jetzund getan.
and still now has done.

Let all give thanks to God
with heart, voice, and deeds,
to the one who does great things
for us and in all ways;
who from the womb
and childhood on
has done us incalculable good
and does so even now.

2. Duet (soprano/bass)

Der ewig reiche Gott
The eternally rich God

Woll uns bei unserm Leben
may to us in our life

Ein immer fröhlich Herz
an always joyful heart

Und edlen Frieden geben
and genuine peace give

Und uns in seiner Gnad
and us in his grace

Erhalten fort und fort
preserve forever

Und uns aus aller Not
and us from all distress

Erlösen hier und dort.
deliver here and there.

May the ever-bounteous God
give us throughout our life
an ever-joyful heart
and genuine peace,
and in his grace
preserve us forever and ever,
and from all distress
deliver us here and there.

3. Chorus

Lob, Ehr und Preis sei Gott, **Praise, honor and glory be to God,**	Praise, honor, and glory be to God, to the Father, and to the Son,
Dem Vater und dem Sohne **to the father and to the son**	and to him who is the same as both on heaven's high throne,
Und dem, der beiden gleich **and to him, who both the same**	to God the Three-in-One, as he was in the beginning
Im hohen Himmelsthrone, **on the high heavenly throne,**	and is and shall be now and evermore.
Dem dreieinigen Gott, **to the three-in-one God,**	
Als der ursprünglich war **as he originally was**	
Und ist und bleiben wird **and is and remain will**	
Jetzund und immerdar. **now and evermore.**	

Cantata type:	Chorale cantata *per omnes versus*
Liturgical usage:	unknown, possibly Reformation
First performance:	October 31, 1730
Epistle:	—
Gospel:	—

ALL three verses of Martin Rinckart's 1636 chorale of the same name* provided Bach with his text. He used the version of the hymn from the *Neu Leipziger Gesangbuch* of 1682, the closing verse of which Neumann (1974: 192) states differed from the original. The editors were unable to obtain the hymn in its original form for comparison.

Nun ist das Heil und die Kraft, BWV 50
Now Have Come the Salvation and Strength
Revelation 12: 10

Chorus

Nun ist das Heil und die Kraft **Now has the salvation and the strength**	Now have come the salvation and strength, the kingdom and might
und das Reich und die Macht **and the kingdom and the might**	of our God and of his Christ, for he is cast down, he who
unsers Gottes seines Christus worden, **of our God [and] of his Christ come,**	accused them day and night before God.
weil der verworfen ist, der sie **for he cast down is, who them**	
verklagete Tag und Nacht vor Gott. **accused day and night before God.**	

THIS brilliant, 136-measure choral setting is all that is left of what was probably the opening movement to a complete cantata for the Feast of St. Michael. The text, from Revelation 12: 10, comes from St. John's fourth revelation, in which the church of the Christ is unsuccessfully attacked by the forces of evil, the latter represented by a dragon who engages in battle with St. Michael and his angels. After the dragon and his minions are vanquished and cast down from heaven, John hears a "loud voice in heaven" that declares the triumphant words of this movement.

The work, which survives only in sources from after Bach's time, is an eight-part, double-choir fugue, the like of which exists nowhere else in Bach's cantatas. Also unusual is the fact that there are never more than five contrapuntally independent parts. These facts and others have led American Bach scholar William H. Scheide to conclude that *Nun ist das Heil* was originally written for a single, five-part choir, in which form Scheide and Reinhold Kubik have reconstructed and published the work (Scheide 1982).

Nun komm, der Heiden Heiland, BWV 61

Now Come, Savior of the Gentiles
Erdmann Neumeister

1. Chorus

Martin Luther

Nun komm, der Heiden Heiland,
Now come, the Gentiles' savior,

Der Jungfrauen Kind erkannt,
of the Virgin child recognized,

Des sich wundert alle Welt,
so that — marvels all world

Gott solch Geburt ihm bestellt.
God such birth for him ordained.

Now come, savior of the Gentiles,
you who are known as the Virgin's child,
so that the whole world marvels
that God ordained for him such a birth.

2. Recitative (tenor)

Erdmann Neumeister

Der Heiland ist gekommen,
The savior has come,

Hat unser armes Fleisch und Blut
has our feeble flesh and blood

An sich genommen
on himself taken

Und nimmet uns zu Blutsverwandten an.
and taken us as blood relations —.

O allerhöchstes Gut,
O very best goodness,

Was hast du nicht an uns getan?
what have you not for us done?

Was tust du nicht
What do you not

Noch täglich an den Deinen?
still daily for — yours?

Du kömmst und läßt dein Licht
You come and let your light

Mit vollem Segen scheinen.
with full blessing shine.

The savior has come;
he has taken on himself
our feeble flesh and blood
and accepted us as his blood relations.
O supreme goodness,
what have you not done for us?
What do you not still do
daily for your people?
You come and let your light
shine with your full blessing.

3. Aria (alto)

Erdmann Neumeister

Komm, Jesu, komm zu deiner Kirche
Come, Jesu, come to your church

Und gib ein selig neues Jahr!
and give a blessed new year!

Beförde deines Namens Ehre,
Promote your name's honor,

Erhalte die gesunde Lehre
uphold the wholesome doctrine

Und segne Kanzel und Altar!
and bless pulpit and altar!

Komm, Jesu, komm zu deiner Kirche
Come, Jesu, come to your church

Und gib ein selig neues Jahr!
and give a blessed new year!

Come, Jesus, come to your church
and grant us a blessed new year.
May you increase the honor of your name,
uphold wholesome doctrine,
and bless the pulpit and the altar.
Come, Jesus, come to your church
and grant us a blessed new year.

4. Recitative (bass)
Revelation 3: 20

Siehe, ich stehe vor der Tür
Behold, I stand before the door

und klopfe an.
and knock —.

So jemand meine Stimme hören wird
If anyone my voice hear will

und die Tür auftun,
and the door open,

zu dem werde ich eingehen
to him will I enter

und das Abendmahl mit ihm halten
and the evening meal with him take

und er mit mir.
and he with me.

Behold, I stand at the door and knock.
If anyone will hear my voice
and open the door,
I will enter into him
and take communion with him,
and he with me.

5. Aria (soprano)
Erdmann Neumeister

Öffne dich, mein ganzes Herze,
Open yourself, my whole heart—

Jesus kommt und ziehet ein.
Jesus comes and moves in —.

Bin ich gleich nur Staub und Erde,
Am I although only dust and earth,

Will er mich doch nicht verschmähn,
will he me — not disdain,

Seine Lust an mir zu sehn,
his delight in me to see,

Daß ich seine Wohnung werde.
that I his dwelling might become.

O wie selig werd' ich sein!
O how happy will I be!

Öffne dich, mein ganzes Herze,
Open yourself, my whole heart—

Jesus kömmt und ziehet ein.
Jesus comes and moves in —.

Open yourself, my whole heart—
Jesus comes and enters in.
Although I am only ashes and dust,
he will not disdain
to see his delight filling my heart,
so that I might become his dwelling.
O how happy I will be!
Open yourself, my whole heart—
Jesus comes and enters in.

6. Chorale
Philipp Nicolai

Amen, amen!
Amen, amen!

Komm, du schöne Freudenkrone,
Come, you beautiful joy crown,

bleib nicht lange!
tarry not long!

Deiner wart ich mit Verlangen.
You wait for I with longing.

Amen, amen!
Come, you beautiful crown of joy,
do not delay!
I wait for you with longing.

Cantata type:	Bible, chorales, free poetry
Liturgical usage:	Advent 1
First performance:	December 2, 1714
Epistle:	Romans 13: 11–14: Our salvation is near
Gospel:	Matthew 21: 1-9 The entry of Jesus into Jerusalem

*I*N the opening years of the eighteenth century Erdmann Neumeister (1671–1756), a Hamburg minister, theologian, and poet, published nine cycles of cantata texts for the complete church year. His early librettos were a combination of Biblical texts, madrigalesque poetry, and chorale verses. (See "The Sacred Cantatas of J.S. Bach.") This is precisely the type of text found in "Nun komm der Heiden Heiland," the second of Bach's five settings of Neumeister cantata librettos.

Neumeister's opening chorus and closing chorale are both based on hymns. The first movement, one of Bach's rare settings for chorus in the form of a French overture, has as its text the first verse of Luther's hymn "Nun komm der Heiden Heiland."* The choice of the French overture is symbolic; the form was devised for the court of the Sun King, Louis IV, and is used here to usher in the solemn entrance of another king, the king of heaven. (Note that the Gospel is the story of the entry of Jesus into Jerusalem, which itself is symbolic of the second coming of the Messiah.) The majestic opening and closing sections utilize lines 1, 2, and 4 of the hymn, respectively, while the third line ("at whom the world marvels") provides the basis for the brisker middle section.

The first and last movements enclose two recitative-aria pairs. Neumeister wrote the poetry for the first pair, a declaration of Christ's mortal incarnation and an invitation for him to "come to his church." The second pair begins with a remarkable setting of Revelation 3: 20. Here Jesus stands at the door and knocks (pizzicato strings), inviting the faithful to open the door—i.e., their hearts. The aria, by Neumeister, is the Christian's appeal to her heart to open itself and let the Savior enter—i.e., like the previous aria, to "come into his church."

Bach closes with an unusual, utterly un-hymnlike setting of the final four lines of Philipp Nicolai's "Wie schön leuchtet der Morgenstern,"* a chorale for Epiphany. The first words, "amen, amen," sound out of place—the "amen" customarily appears at the end—until one contemplates their meaning in context. The "amen" in the hymn, meaning "so be it!", is immediately preceded by the confident declaration that God will "accept me into Paradise; for this I clap my hands." The "amen" is thus a prayer for the fulfillment of this declaration. In the cantata, the "amen" is, once again, a prayer for fulfillment, this time of the soprano's immediately preceding plea, "open yourself, my whole heart—Jesus comes and enters in."

One can only speculate at Bach's reasons for the two small changes he made to Neumeister's libretto (*Variants*, below). In the first case, the text indeed trips off the tongue more easily if Neumeister's "selbst" is omitted. In the second case, the meaning and the number of syllables are unchanged, making one wonder whether the sound of the word *Staub* was not more onomatopoetic to Bach than the librettist's *Asch*.

Source: Neumeister 1717: 8
Variants: (Bach = roman, Neumeister = *italic*)
No. 2, line 4: uns zu (us as) = *uns selbst zu* (us ourselves as)
No. 5, line 3: Staub (dust) = *Asch* (ashes)

Nun komm, der Heiden Heiland, BWV 62
Now Come, Savior of the Gentiles

1. Chorus
Martin Luther

Nun komm, der Heiden Heiland,
Now come, the Gentiles' savior,

Der Jungfrauen Kind erkannt,
of the Virgin child recognized,

Des sich wundert alle Welt,
so that — marvels all world

Gott solch Geburt ihm bestellt.
God such birth for him ordained.

Now come, savior of the Gentiles,
you who are known as the Virgin's child,
so that the whole world marvels
that God ordained for him such a birth.

2. Aria (tenor)
Author unknown

Bewundert, o Menschen, dies große Geheimnis:
Marvel, O mortals, this great mystery:

Der höchste Beherrscher erscheinet der Welt.
the highest ruler appears to the world.

Hier werden die Schätze des Himmels entdecket,
Here are the treasures of heaven discovered,

Hier wird uns ein göttliches Manna bestellt,
here is for us a divine manna prepared.

O Wunder! die Keuschheit wird gar nicht beflecket.
O miracle! — Chastity is -not at all- defiled.

Marvel, O mortals, at this great mystery:
the supreme ruler appears to the world.
Here the treasures of heaven are discovered,
here a divine manna is prepared for us.
O miracle! Chastity is not defiled.

3. Recitative (bass)
Author unknown

So geht aus Gottes Herrlichkeit und Thron
Thus goes from God's majesty and throne

Sein eingeborner Sohn.
his only-begotten son.

Der Held aus Juda bricht herein,
The hero from Judah rushes in,

Den Weg mit Freudigkeit zu laufen
the way with gladness to walk

Und uns Gefallne zu erkaufen.
and us fallen ones to redeem.

O heller Glanz, o wunderbarer Segensschein!
O shining splendor, o wonderful blessing-light!

Thus from God's majesty and throne
proceeds his only-begotten son.
The hero from Judah rushes in
to run his course gladly
and to redeem us fallen souls.
O shining splendor, O wondrous light of blessing!

4. Aria (bass)
Author unknown

Streite, siege, starker Held!
Fight, be victorious, strong hero!

Sei vor uns im Fleische kräftig!
Be for us in the flesh strong!

Sei geschäftig,
Be zealous,

Das Vermögen in uns Schwachen
the powers in us weak ones

Stark zu machen!
strong to make!

Fight, be victorious, strong hero!
Be strong in the flesh for us!
Be zealous,
empower us weak ones,
make us strong!

5. Recitative (soprano/alto duet)
Author unknown

Wir ehren diese Herrlichkeit
We honor this majesty

Und nahen nun zu deiner Krippen
and approach now to your crib

Und preisen mit erfreuten Lippen,
and praise with joyful lips

Was du uns zubereit';
what you for us prepared.

Die Dunkelheit verstört' uns nicht
The darkness troubles us not;

Und sahen dein unendlich Licht.
and saw your unending light.

We honor this majesty
and now approach your crib
and praise with joyful lips
what you have prepared for us.
The darkness troubles us not;
we have seen your unending light.

6. Chorale
Martin Luther

Lob sei Gott, dem Vater, ton,
Praise be God, the Father given,

Lob sei Gott, sein'm eingen Sohn,
Praise be God, his only son,

Lob sei Gott, dem Heilgen Geist,
Praise be God, the Holy Spirit,

Immer und in Ewigkeit!
always and in eternity!

Praise be given to God the Father,
praise be to God, his only son,
praise be to God, the Holy Spirit,
always and eternally!

Cantata type:	Chorale and free poetry
Liturgical usage:	Advent 1
First performance:	December 3, 1724
Epistle:	Romans 13: 11–14:
	Our salvation is near
Gospel:	Matthew 21: 1–9
	The entry of Jesus into Jerusalem

LIKE its better-known namesake cantata BWV 61, this cantata is for the first Sunday of Advent. Also like that cantata, the present work consists of two recitative-aria pairs (in this case, however, aria-recitative), surrounded by opening and closing hymn verses. Both works also begin with the first verse of Martin Luther's 1523 Advent chorale "Nun komm, der Heiden Heiland."* Here, however, the parallels end. Whereas BWV 61 parted ways with the hymn after the opening verse, BWV 62 begins and ends with Luther's parallel verses, and paraphrases the remaining six verses in the four interior movements. The free paraphrases by the unknown librettist transform Luther's rather austere words into the more emotional personal language popular in Bach's time.

Luther's second and third verses are treated in the first aria. His focus was on the two intertwined miracles of the Incarnation (verse 2) and the Virgin Birth (verse 3). The librettist, however, devotes four lines to the former, and just one to the latter. He also ignores the miracle of a mortal giving birth to God, and instead expresses wonder at the fact that "chastity is not defiled." The following recitative condenses the content of Luther's verses 4 and 5 into a single movement: God came to earth for the salvation of humanity through his preordained sacrifice. Once again, the librettist could not resist closing with an ecstatic exclamation that would have been utterly foreign to Luther: "O shining splendor! O wondrous light of blessing!"

The next two movements, an aria and recitative, reformulate Luther's verses 6 and 7 but stay quite close to their content. In the aria, Jesus is exhorted to fight the battle and bring victory to sinful mortals (= Luther's "sick flesh"). The aria brings us to the manger scene, which ends with the same imagery of light and radiance (= salvation) that Luther used. Luther's eighth and final verse, a doxology, provides the text for the closing chorale.

Wachet auf, ruft uns die Stimme, BWV 140
"Awake," the Voices Call to Us

1. Chorus
Philipp Nicolai

"Wachet auf," ruft uns die Stimme
"Wake up," call to us the voices

Der Wächter sehr hoch auf der Zinne,
of the watchmen very high on the battlement.

"Wach auf, du Stadt Jerusalem!
"Wake up, you city Jerusalem.

Mitternacht heißt diese Stunde";
Midnight is called this hour!"

Sie rufen uns mit hellem Munde:
They call us, with bright voices:

"Wo seid ihr klugen Jungfrauen?
"Where are you wise virgins?

Wohl auf, der Bräutgam kömmt;
Cheer up, the bridegroom is coming.

Steht auf, die Lampen nehmt!
Get up, the lamps take!

Allelujah!
Hallelujah!

Macht euch bereit
Make yourself ready

Zu der Hochzeit,
for the wedding;

Ihr müsset ihm entgegen gehn!"
you must him –go to meet–!"

"Awake," call the voices of the watchmen
from the high battle tower.
"Awake, you city of Jerusalem!
This is the midnight hour!"
They call to us, with ringing voices:
"Where are you, wise virgins?
Cheer up; the bridegroom is coming.
Rise up; take your lamps!
Hallelujah!
Prepare yourself
for the wedding;
you must go to meet him!"

2. Recitative (tenor)
Author unknown

Er kommt, er kommt,
He comes, he comes,

Der Bräutgam kommt!
the bridegroom comes!

Ihr Töchter Zions, kommt heraus,
You daughters of Zion, come out;

Sein Ausgang eilet aus der Höhe
his departure hurries from the highest

In euer Mutter Haus.
into your mother's house.

Der Bräutgam kommt, der einem Rehe
The bridegroom comes, who a deer

Und jungen Hirsche gleich
and young stag like,

Auf denen Hügeln springt
on the hills springs

Und euch das Mahl der Hochzeit bringt.
and to you the meal of the wedding brings.

Wacht auf, ermuntert euch!
Wake up, rouse yourselves,

Den Bräutgam zu empfangen!
the bridegroom to receive!

Dort, sehet, kommt er hergegangen.
There, see, comes he walking thence.

He is coming, he is coming,
the bridegroom is coming!
You daughters of Zion, come forth;
he journeys quickly from on high
into your mother's house.
The bridegroom is coming, who like a deer
and a young stag,
leaps upon the hills
and brings you the wedding feast.
Wake up, rouse yourselves
to welcome the bridegroom!
There, see, he is coming here.

3. Aria (soprano/bass duet)
Author unknown

Die Seele

Wenn kömmst du,[6] mein Heil?
When come you, my savior?

Jesus

Ich komme, dein Teil.
I come, your portion.

Ich warte mit brennendem Öle.
I wait with burning oil.

Eröffne den Saal
Open the hall

Ich öffne den Saal
I open the hall

Zum himmlischen Mahl
for the heavenly meal

Zum himmlischen Mahl
for the heavenly meal

Komm, Jesu!
Come, Jesus!

Ich komme; komm, liebliche Seele!
I come; come, sweet soul!

The Spirit

When are you coming, my savior?

Jesus

I am coming, your portion.

I am waiting with burning oil.
Open the hall

I am opening the hall

for the heavenly banquet.

for the heavenly banquet.

Come, Jesus!

I am coming; come, sweet soul.

---

[6] The spelling "wenn" and the subjunctive verb "kömmst" are antiquated; the phrase is customarily rendered in the indicative "Wann kommst du."

4. Chorale
Philipp Nicolai

Zion hört die Wächter singen;
Zion hears the watchmen singing;

Das Herz tut ihr vor Freuden springen,
the heart does her for joy leap;

Sie wachet und steht eilend auf.
she awakens and gets hurriedly up.

Ihr Freund kommt vom Himmel prächtig,
Her friend comes from heaven glorious,

Von Gnaden stark, von Wahrheit mächtig,
of grace strong, of truth mighty;

Ihr Licht wird hell, ihr Stern geht auf.
her light becomes bright, her star rises.

Nun komm, du werte Kron,
Now come, you worthy crown,

Herr Jesu, Gottes Sohn!
Lord Jesus, God's son!

Hosianna!
Hosanna!

Wir folgen all
We follow all

Zum Freudensaal
to the hall of joy

Und halten mit das Abendmahl.
and –partake of– the communion.

Zion hears the watchmen singing;
her heart leaps for joy;
she awakens and quickly rises.
Her friend comes from heaven's glory,
strong in grace, mighty in truth;
her light brightens, her star rises.
Now come, you worthy crown,
Lord Jesus, God's son!
Hosanna!
We all will follow
to the banquet hall
and take communion together.

5. Recitative (bass)
Author unknown

So geh herein zu mir,
So go within to me,

Du mir erwählte Braut!
you my chosen bride!

Ich habe mich mit dir
I have myself with you

Von Ewigkeit vertraut.
from eternity betrothed.

Dich will ich auf mein Herz,
You want I on my heart,

Auf meinem Arm gleich wie ein Siegel setzen
on my arm just like a seal to set

Und dein betrübtes Aug ergötzen.
and your sorrowful eye to delight.

Vergiß, o Seele, nun
Forget, O soul, now

Die Angst, den Schmerz,
the fear, the pain,

Den du erdulden müssen;
that you suffer had to;

Auf meiner Linken sollst du ruhn,
on my left shall you rest,

Und meine Rechte soll dich küssen.
and my right shall you kiss.

So come within to me,
you, my chosen bride!
I have betrothed myself to you
since the beginning of time.
I want you set as a seal
upon my heart and my arm;
I want to delight your sorrowful eye.
Forget now, O soul,
the fear and the pain
that you had to suffer;
on my left side you shall rest,
and my right shall kiss you.

6. Aria (soprano/bass duet)
Author unknown

Die Seele

Mein Freund ist mein,
My friend is mine,

Jesus

Und ich bin sein,
and I am his;

Jesus *und die Seele*

Die Liebe soll nichts scheiden.
— love shall nothing separate.

Die Seele

Ich will mit dir in Himmels Rosen weiden,
I will with you in heaven's roses graze,

Jesus

Du sollst mit mir in Himmels Rosen weiden,
You shall with me in heaven's roses graze,

Jesus *und die Seele*

Da Freude die Fülle, da Wonne wird sein.
where joy the fullness, where bliss will be.

The Spirit
My friend is mine,

Jesus
and I am his;

Jesus *and the Spirit*
nothing shall separate this love.

The Spirit
I will feed on heaven's roses with you,

Jesus
You shall feed with me on heaven's roses,

Jesus *and the Spirit*
where abundant joy and bliss will be found.

7. Chorale
Philipp Nicolai

Gloria sei dir gesungen
Glory be to you sung

Mit Menschen- und englischen Zungen,
with mortal and angelic tongues,

Mit Harfen und Zimbeln schon.
with harps and cymbals beautiful.

Von zwölf Perlen sind die Pforten,
Of twelve pearls are the portals;

An deiner Stadt sind wir Konsorten
in your city are we consorts

Der Engel hoch um deinen Thron.
of the angels high around your throne.

Kein Aug hat je gespürt,
No eye has ever perceived,

Kein Ohr hat je gehört
no ear has ever heard

Solche Freude.
such joy.

Des sind wir froh,
Of that are we glad,

Io! io!
io! io!

Ewig *in dulci jubilo.*
Eternally with sweet rejoicing.

Glory be sung to you
with mortal and angelic voices, and
with beautiful harps and cymbals.
Your gates are made of twelve pearls;
in your city we are consorts
of the angels high around your throne.
No eye has ever seen,
no ear has ever heard
such joy.
Therefore we are glad,
io! io!
Ever *in dulci jubilo.*

Cantata type:	Chorale and free poetry
Liturgical usage:	Twenty-seventh Sunday after Trinity
First performance:	November 25, 1731
Epistle:	1 Thessalonians 5: 1–11 Being prepared for the Second Coming and the Last Judgment
Gospel:	Matthew 25: 1–13 The parable of the wise and foolish virgins

THIS, one of the most beloved of Bach's cantatas, is based on the chorale of the same name by Philipp Nicolai (1556–1608).* The chorale itself is based on the story of the wise and foolish virgins, related in the Gospel for the day. The moral of that scripture, the need for the Christian to be prepared for the Second Coming and the Last Judgment, is stated without art or artifice in the Epistle reading.

The unknown librettist constructed this cantata using the three verses of the chorale as pillars, between which he placed two recitative-aria pairs that contain numerous references to the Song of Songs. The first recitative, given to the tenor, who traditionally functions as the Evangelist, joyously exhorts the Christian to welcome Christ, the bridegroom. The following aria is structured as a dramatic dialogue between Jesus and the Christian spirit, who with her "burning oil" is to be compared to the wise virgins of the parable. The spirit speaks of her yearning for the coming of Jesus, who assures her that he is coming to "the heavenly banquet." Following the middle verse of the chorale, the recitative is given to the bass, the traditional voice of Jesus. Now he speaks to the Christian soul, inviting union, which is consummated in the accompanying aria, another dramatic dialogue between Jesus and the spirit. Nicolai's third verse concludes the cantata with the same sense of joy and fulfillment that it imparted to his hymn.

Source (chorales):   Nicolai 1963: 412. Quotation marks have been added for clarity in verse 1.
Variant: (Bach = roman, Nicolai = *italic*)
                                 Verse 3, line 5:   wir sind Konsorten = *sind wir Konsorten*

Wie schön leuchtet der Morgenstern, BWV 1
How Beautifully Shines the Morning Star
Librettist unknown

1. Chorus
Philipp Nicolai

Wie   schön   leuchtet der Morgenstern
How beautifully shines   the   morning star,

Voll   Gnad und Wahrheit von dem Herrn,
full of grace and   truth from the Lord,

Die süße Wurzel   Jesse!
the sweet   root   [of] Isaiah.

Du Sohn Davids aus   Jakobs Stamm,
You son of David from Jacob's stem,

Mein König und mein Bräutigam,
my   king and my   bridegroom,

Hast mir mein Herz   besessen,
has   me my heart   possessed—

Lieblich,
lovely,

Freundlich,
friendly,

Schön   und herrlich,
beautiful and glorious,

groß und ehrlich,
great and honest,

reich von Gaben,
rich   in   gifts,

Hoch und sehr prächtig erhaben.
highly and very splendidly exalted.

How beautifully shines the morning star,
full of grace and truth from the Lord,
the sweet root of Isaiah.
You, David's son from Jacob's lineage,
my king and my bridegroom,
you have possessed my heart—
lovely,
friendly,
beautiful and glorious,
great and righteous,
rich in blessings,
high and magnificently exalted.

2. Recitative (tenor)
Author unknown

Du wahrer Gottes und Marien Sohn,
You true   God's and Mary's son,

Du König derer Auserwählten,
you king, of the   chosen,

Wie süß ist uns dies Lebenswort,
how sweet is for us this life-word,

Nach dem die ersten Väter   schon
by   which the first fathers already

So   Jahr' als Tage zählten,
both years and days numbered

Das Gabriel mit Freuden dort
that Gabriel with joys   there

In Bethlehem verheißen!
in Bethlehem promised!

You true son of God and Mary,
you king of the elect,
how sweet for us is this word of life,
by which the first patriarchs
numbered both the years and the days
that Gabriel promised with joy
there in Bethlehem.

O Süßigkeit, o Himmelsbrot,
O sweetness, O heavenly bread,

Das weder Grab, Gefahr, noch Tod
which neither grave, danger, nor death

Aus unsern Herzen reißen.
from our hearts tear.

O sweetness, O heavenly bread,
which grave, danger and death
cannot tear from our hearts.

3. Aria (soprano)
Author unknown

Erfüllet, ihr himmlischen göttlichen Flammen,
Fill, you heavenly, divine flames,

Die nach euch verlangende gläubige Brust!
the for you longing, believing breast!

Die Seelen empfinden die kräftigsten Triebe
The souls feel the strongest urges

Der brünstigsten Liebe
of impassioned love

Und schmecken auf Erden die himmlische Lust.
and savor on earth the heavenly desire.

Fill, you heavenly, divine flames,
the faithful heart that longs for you!
The souls feel the strongest impulses
of impassioned love
and savor heavenly desire on earth.

4. Recitative (bass)
Author unknown

Ein irdscher Glanz, ein leiblich Licht
An earthly brightness, a worldly light

Rührt meine Seele nicht;
touches my soul not;

Ein Freudenschein ist mir von Gott entstanden,
A joyful radiance has me from God arisen,

Denn ein vollkommnes Gut,
for a perfect treasure,

Des Heilands Leib und Blut,
the Savior's body and blood,

Ist zur Erquickung da.
is for refreshment there.

So muß uns ja
So must us indeed

Der überreiche Segen,
the abundant blessing,

Der uns von Ewigkeit bestimmt
which for us from eternity ordained

Und unser Glaube zu sich nimmt,
and our faith accepts,

Zum Dank und Preis bewegen.
to thanks and praise move.

No earthly gleam, no worldly light
touches my soul;
a joyful radiance from God has arisen
because a perfect treasure,
the Savior's body and blood,
is there for refreshment.
Thus, indeed,
the abundant blessing,
which was ordained for us forever
and which our faith accepts,
must move us to gratitude and praise.

5. Aria (tenor)
Author unknown

Unser Mund und Ton der Saiten
Our mouth and sound of the strings

Sollen dir
should for you

für und für
always

Dank und Opfer zubereiten.
thanks and sacrifice prepare.

Herz und Sinnen sind erhoben,
Heart and mind are uplifted

Lebenslang
lifelong

mit Gesang,
with song,

Großer König, dich zu loben.
great king, you to praise.

Our voice and the sounding strings
shall prepare gratitude and sacrifice
for you
for evermore.
Heart and mind are uplifted
lifelong
with song,
great king, to praise you.

6. Chorale
Philipp Nicolai

Wie bin ich doch so herzlich froh,
How am I — so sincerely glad

Daß mein Schatz ist das A und O,
that my beloved is the A[lpha] and O[mega],

Der Anfang und das Ende;
the beginning and the end.

Er wird mich doch zu seinem Preis
He will me — to his praise

Aufnehmen in das Paradeis,
take into — paradise,

Des klopf ich in die Hände.
about which clap I –my hands–.

Amen!
Amen!

Amen!
Amen!

Komm, du schöne Freudenkrone,
Come you beautiful joy-crown;

Bleib nicht lange,
remain not long.

Deiner wart ich mit Verlangen.
You await I with longing.

I am so sincerely glad
that my beloved is the A and O,
the beginning and the end!
He will, to his praise,
take me into Paradise;
for this, I clap my hands.
Amen!
Amen!
Come, you beautiful crown of joy;
tarry not too long.
I await you with longing.

Cantata type:	Chorale and free poetry
Liturgical usage:	Annunciation (March 25)
First performance:	March 25, 1725
Epistle:	Isaiah 7: 10–16 Prophecy of the Messiah's birth (included in cantata)
Gospel:	Luke 1: 26–38: The angel Gabriel reveals to Mary the coming birth of Jesus

Source (chorales): Nicolai 1963: 409

MANY of Bach's cantatas have come down to us with no record of the librettist's name, the present work among them. The opening and closing movements are settings of the first and seventh (final) stanzas of Philipp Nicolai's 1599 chorale of the same name.* Free poetry is used for the four inner movements of the libretto, but as in cantatas BWV 62 ("Nun komm der Heiden Heiland"*) and BWV 80 ("Ein feste Burg ist unser Gott"*), that poetry serves to paraphrase the hymn into contemporary language. Although the hymn was principally used for Epiphany, it was also sung in Bach's time for the related Feast of the Annunciation, for which he wrote this cantata. Bach scholar Alfred Dürr expresses an unusual admiration for the libretto:

> All in all, it may be said that the poet sensitively captures the sincerity and fervor that characterizes Nicolai's poem and has made his songs a lasting treasure of the Lutheran Church, and that he has produced meaningful and engaging, if not brilliant, poetry. (Dürr 1971: 547, tr. ed.)

Notable as well is the degree to which the librettist preserved the literary tone of his model. His task was perhaps lightened by the original itself, which was strikingly personal for the late sixteenth century, but quite at home in the Germany of a hundred-twenty-five years later.

The inner movements of the cantata consist of two recitative-aria pairs. In the first pair the librettist reworked Nicolai's second and third stanzas, preserving the hymnist's imagery of the Gospel as nourishment to the faithful and the flame as a symbol of God's love. Nicolai's fourth and fifth stanzas are paraphrased in the second recitative. The fifth stanza is only tangentially referred to, however, perhaps because the librettist wanted to avoid its bride/bridegroom imagery. Bach's librettist reworked Nicolai's sixth and penultimate stanza in his second aria. Once again, the bride/bridegroom symbolism disappears, but the strings still sound in praise of the "great king."

Der Geist hilft unsrer Schwachheit auf, BWV 226
The Spirit Helps Our Weakness

1. Double Chorus
Romans 8: 26

Der Geist hilft unsrer Schwachheit auf,
The Spirit helps our weakness —,

denn wir wissen nicht
for we know not

was wir beten sollen,
what we pray should,

wie sich's gebühret;
how — it is proper;

sondern der Geist selbst
but the Spirit itself

vertritt uns aufs beste,
represents us –in the best way–

mit unaussprechlichem Seufzen.
with inexpressible sighing.

The Spirit helps our weakness,
for we know not
what we should pray,
nor how we ought to pray;
but the Spirit
pleads for us in the best possible way,
with inexpressible sighing.

2. Chorus
Romans 8: 27

Der aber die Herzen forschet,
He but the hearts searches,

der weiß, was des Geistes Sinn sei;
he knows what the Spirit's thinking is;

denn er vertritt die Heiligen
for he represents the saints

nach dem, das Gott gefället.
–according to the way– it God pleases.

But he who searches our hearts
knows the mind and thinking of the Spirit;
for the Spirit intercedes for the saints,
according to God's pleasure.

3. Chorale
Martin Luther

Du heilige Brunst, süßer Trost,
You holy fire, sweet consolation,

Nun hilf uns, fröhlich und getrost
now help us, joyful and consoled,

In deinem Dienst beständig bleiben,
in your service steadfast to remain;

Die Trübsal uns nicht abtreiben.
the affliction us not drive away.

O Herr, durch dein Kraft uns bereit
O Lord, by your power us prepare

Und stärk des Fleisches Blödigkeit,
and strengthen the flesh's timidity,

Daß wir hie ritterlich ringen,
that we here gallantly struggle

Durch Tod und Leben zu dir dringen.
through death and life to you reach.

Alleluia, Alleluia.
Alleluia, Alleluia.

You holy fire, sweet consolation,
now help us, joyful and consoled,
to remain steadfast in your service;
let affliction not drive us away.
O Lord, prepare us by your power
and strengthen our feeble flesh,
so that we here may gallantly struggle
through death and life to reach you.
Alleluia, Alleluia.

Source (chorale):   Luther 1967: 2
Variant: (Bach = roman, Luther = *italic*)
        No. 3, line 3:   deinem = *deim*

ALTHOUGH five of Bach's seven motets were likely written for funerals, only in the case of "Der Geist hilft" is the actual occasion known. The present motet was written for the funeral of St. Thomas School Rector Johann Heinrich Ernesti on October 20, 1729. Bach's instrumental parts, which survive, included the first movement but not the closing chorale. This suggests that the latter might have been performed at graveside, where there would have been no instruments.

The latter portion of Romans, chapter 8 deals with life after death under the New Covenant. This scripture provided Bach with the Biblical verses for the motet "Jesu, meine Freude" and it also supplied the text (verses 26–27) for the body of the present motet.

The third, penultimate verse of Martin Luther's Pentecost hymn "Komm heiliger Geist, Herre Gott"* is the basis for the closing chorale, which also uses Luther's melody in the soprano. As in the cantatas, the final chorale serves to summarize the message of the motet. The idea of God's help, which is promised in the verses from Romans and prayed for in the chorale, provides the logical connection between the two texts.

Fürchte dich nicht, ich bin bei dir, BWV 228
Fear not; I Am with You

1. Double Chorus
Isaiah 41: 10

Fürchte dich nicht, ich bin bei dir;
Fear   you not;   I am with you!

weiche nicht, denn ich bin dein Gott!
Yield   not: for I am your God!

Ich stärke   dich, ich helfe dir auch,
I strengthen you, I   help you also,

ich erhalte dich durch   die rechte Hand
I uphold you through the right hand

meiner Gerechtigkeit.
of my   justice.

Fear not; I am with you!
Yield not: for I am your God!
I strengthen you and I also help you;
I uphold you by the right hand
of my righteousness.

2. Chorus and Chorale (soprano)
Isaiah 43: 1; chorale by Paul Gerhardt

Chorus

Fürchte dich nicht, denn ich habe dich erlöset,
Fear   you not,   for I have you redeemed.

ich habe dich bei deinem Namen gerufen,
I have you by   your   name   called.

du bist mein!
You are mine!

Chorus

Fear not, for I have redeemed you.
I have called you by your name.
You are mine!

Chorale (soprano)

Herr, mein Hirt,   Brunn aller Freuden,
Lord, my shepherd, source of all   joys,

Du bist mein, ich bin dein:
You are mine, I am yours:

Niemand kann uns scheiden.
No one   can us separate.

Ich bin dein, weil du dein Leben
I am yours, for you your life

Und dein Blut, mir zugut
And your blood my benefit

In den Tod   gegeben.
In — death has given.

Du bist mein,   weil ich dich fasse,
You are mine, because I you embrace,

Und dich nicht, o mein Licht,
And you not, O my light,

Aus   dem Herzen lasse.
out of the   heart allow.

Laß mich, laß mich hingelangen,
Let me,   let me   arrive,

Wo   du mich, und ich dich
where you me, and I   you

Lieblich werd umfangen.
gently   will   embrace.

Chorale (soprano)

Lord, my shepherd, source of all joys,
you are mine and I am yours:
no one can separate us.
I am yours, for you have given
your life and your blood
in death for my sake.

You are mine, because I embrace you,
and do not allow you, O my light,
out of my heart.
Let me, let me arrive
where you me, and I you,
may gently embrace.

Source (chorale): Gerhardt 1957: 246
Variant: (Bach = roman, Gerhardt = *italic*)
Stanza 2, line 5: wo = *da*

T HOUGH the specific occasion that brought forth this motet is unknown, it may have been composed for the funeral of Susanna Sophie Winckler on February 4, 1726, the sermon for which was based on Isaiah 43: 1–5. A firm connection to the motet is unproven, however. Based on the overlay of a chorale with words from the Bible, which is similar in style to the closing section of the motet "Ich lasse dich nicht," the editors of the *Bach Compendium* posit 1712–13 as another possible time of origin.

The Biblical text is from the second major division of the book of Isaiah, which deals with "the way of salvation through forgiveness"—Isaiah's prophesy of the New Covenant. Many passages here, including those chosen by Bach (41: 10 and 43: 1), counsel the children of Israel not to be afraid, because God will bring deliverance and salvation. Of particular importance to Bach was God's claim on the sinner, "du bist mein" (you are mine), which concludes the second quotation. These words created an intimate link to the two closing verses of the Paul Gerhardt chorale "Warum sollt ich mich denn grämen" (Why Should I Grieve or Worry?, 1653), which addresses God using the same words with which God addressed humanity in Isaiah 43: 1. The power of this combination must have proven irresistible to Bach and may well have led him to use both texts in this motet.

The final section of the work is an extended, imitative setting of God's declaration, "for I have redeemed you; I have called you by name; you are mine." Above this Bach set his chorale, juxtaposing the words of God with the chorale's statement of faith. In an effort to underline the mutual claims of possession of the two texts, he inserted the words "you are mine" into the Biblical quotation some fifteen times before they would normally appear.

The final bars of the motet show yet again Bach's genius in handling his texts. Here he combines the opening words of Isaiah 41:10, "Fear not," with the closing words of Isaiah 43:1, "You are mine," bringing together God's commandment and the reason for it, while uniting for one last time, in all voices, the words of the Bible and those of the chorale.

Ich lasse dich nicht, BWV Anh. 159
I Will Not Let You Go

Double Chorus
Genesis 32: 26b; author of chorale unknown

Bible

Ich lasse dich nicht,
I   let   you   not

du segnest mich denn, mein Jesu!
you bless   me   then, my Jesus!

Chorale

Weil   du mein Gott und Vater bist,
Since you my   God and father are,

dein Kind wirst du verlassen nicht,
your child will you abandon not,

du väterliches Herz.
you fatherly   heart.

Ich bin ein armer Erdenkloß,
I   am   a poor   clay lump:

auf Erden weiß ich keinen Trost.
on earth know I   no   consolation.

Ich dank dir, Christe, Gottes Sohn,
I   thank you, Christ, God's Son,

daß du mich solchs erkennen lan
that you me   such recognize let

durch   dein göttliches Wort;
through your divine   Word;

verleih mir auch Beständigkeit
grant   me   also constancy

zu meiner Seelen Seligkeit!
for my   soul's salvation!

Bible

*I will not let you go
unless you bless me, my Jesus!*

Chorale

For you are my God and father;
you will not abandon your child,
you fatherly heart.
I am but a poor lump of clay;
on earth I know no consolation.

I thank you Christ, God's Son,
that you let me realize this
through your divine Word;
grant me constancy also
for my soul's salvation!

59

Lob Ehr und Preis sei dir gesagt, **Praise, honor and glory be to you said**	Praise, honor, and glory be to you for all your loving kindness,
für alle dein erzeigt Wohltat, **for all your shown good deeds,**	and I humbly ask, let me not be forever banished
und bitt demütiglich, **and I ask humbly,**	from your countenance.
laß mich nicht von dein'm Angesicht **let me not from your countenance**	
verstoßen werden ewiglich. **banished become eternally.**	

Source: Bach 1988

*B*ACH was fond of combining complementary texts from different sources, and his fusions of Biblical texts with chorales are particularly effective. In this motet words from Genesis 32: 26 are layered together with the third verse of the anonymous chorale "Warum betrübst du dich, mein Herz?" (Why Are You Troubled, My Heart?, c. 1560).

The Biblical quotation comes from the story of Jacob's return to Caanan. Jacob, the grandson of Abraham and the son of Isaac, had spent fourteen years in exile, toiling for his father-in-law Laban in return for the privilege of marrying his daughters Leah and Rachel. In a dream, the one God of Abraham came to him and commanded him to return to his homeland. Jacob complied, and while on the journey learned of the approach of an army led by his estranged brother Esau, whom Jacob had fled in fear fourteen years before. By cover of night Jacob sent his family, servants, and animals away across the river Jabbok, where he remained. He was approached by an angel in the form of a man, with whom he did combat through the night. The angel, fearful that Jacob would perish from seeing the face of the Lord in the approaching morning light, crippled him by dislocating his thighbone, but Jacob continued to hold him fast, declaring, "I will not let you go unless you bless me." The angel blessed him and named him "Israel," or "He strives with God," in the place of "Jacob," which means "the deceiver."[7] Thus Jacob began his new life as a servant of God and the father of the nation of Israel.

Bach transplants the Old Testament text into a New Testament context by adding the words "my Jesus" to Jacob's "I will not let you go unless you bless me." The tenacity of Jacob—in Bach's motet the faithful Christian—is reflected in the continual repetition of these few words throughout the entire motet. Likewise, the origin of the text in the story of Jacob's conflict with the angel is reflected both in the double-chorus texture and the fast, imitative polyphony of the closing section. Bach's final creative touch was to superimpose over the "struggle" of the final section the chorale text, which declares the powerlessness of the sinner and looks toward God's promised redemption through Jesus.

Johann Christoph Bach (1642–1703), the son of J.S. Bach's great uncle, was long thought to be the composer of "Ich lasse dich nicht." Recent scholarship by Daniel Melamed, however, has convincingly shown the motet to be by J.S. Bach. It originated during Bach's Weimar period in the years 1712–1713, making it probably his first motet. The concluding chorale is a homophonic, four-part setting of the chorale melody "Warum betrübst du dich, mein Herz?", words from which were used in the first movement. Although the sources provide the music for the closing chorale, they do not provide the words. The chorale was probably added to the motet during Bach's Leipzig years and may be omitted if one wishes to perform the Weimar version. (Melamed 1988) If the chorale is performed, the text offered by Melamed in his edition (Bach 1988), the final two verses of the same hymn, is suitable.

---

[7]Jacob was aptly named. He had successfully conspired with his mother to steal from Esau, the first-born son, his right of inheritance as well as his father's blessing, making of Esau a bitter and destitute enemy.

Jesu, meine Freude, BWV 227

Jesu, My Joy

1. Chorale

Johann Franck

Jesu, meine Freude,
Jesu, my joy,

Meines Herzens Weide,
my heart's pasture,

Jesu, meine Zier,
Jesu, my adornment,

Ach, wie lang, ach lange
ah, how long, ah long

Ist dem Herzen bange
is the heart anxious

Und verlangt nach dir!
and longs after you!

Gottes Lamm, mein Bräutigam,
God's lamb, my bridegroom,

Außer dir soll mir auf Erden
besides you shall to me on earth

Nichts sonst Liebers werden.
nothing else dearer become.

Jesu, my joy,
my heart's delight,
Jesu, my treasure,
how long, ah, how long
my heart is troubled
and longs for you!
God's lamb, my bridgroom,
besides you, nothing else on earth
shall become dearer to me.

2. Chorus

Romans 8: 1, 8: 4b

Es ist nun nichts Verdammliches an denen,
There is now nothing condemnable in them

die in Christo Jesu sind,
who in Christ Jesus are,

die nicht nach dem Fleische wandeln,
who not according to the flesh walk,

sondern nach dem Geist.
but rather according to the spirit.

There is now nothing condemnable in them
who are in Christ Jesus,
who walk not according to the flesh,
but according to the spirit.

3. Chorale

Johann Franck

Unter deinem Schirmen
Under your protection

Bin ich vor den Stürmen
am I from the storms

Aller Feinde frei.
of all foes free.

Laß den Satan wittern,
Let — Satan curse,

Laß den Feind erbittern,
Let the foe become bitter;

Mir steht Jesus bei.
me stands Jesus by.

Ob es jetzt gleich kracht und blitzt,
If it now instantly crashes and flashes,

Ob gleich Sünd und Hölle schrecken:
if instantly sin and hell frighten,

Jesus will mich decken.
Jesus wants me to protect.

Under your protection
I am free from the storms
of all my foes.
Let Satan curse and swear,
let the foe become bitter;
Jesus stands by me.
If a storm suddenly crashes and flashes,
if sin and hell suddenly frighten me,
Jesu wants to protect me.

4. Trio (ssa)

Romans 8: 2

Denn das Gesetz des Geistes,
For the law of the spirit,

der da lebendig machet in Christo Jesu,
which here alive makes in Christ Jesus,

hat mich frei gemacht von dem Gesetz
has me free made from the law

der Sünde und des Todes.
of sin and of death.

For the law of the spirit,
which gives life in Christ Jesus,
has made me free from the law
of sin and death.

5. Chorale

Johann Franck

Trotz dem alten Drachen,
Despite the old dragon,

Trotz des Todesrachen,
despite — death's jaws,

Trotz der Furcht dazu,
despite — fear in addition,

Tobe Welt und springe,
Rage, world, and burst,

Ich steh hier und singe,
I stand here and sing

In gar sichrer Ruh.
in quite secure peace.

Gottes Macht hält mich in acht;
God's might holds me in awe;

Erd und Abgrund muß verstummen,
earth and abyss must become silent,

Ob sie noch so brummen.
If they still so grumble.

Despite the old dragon,
despite death's jaws,
and despite fears as well,
even though the world might rage and burst,
I will stand here and sing
in utterly confident peace.
God's might holds me in awe;
earth and abyss must become silent,
even though they still grumble.

6. Chorus

Romans 8: 9

Ihr aber seid nicht fleischlich, sondern geistlich,
You, however, are not carnal, but spiritual,

so anders Gottes Geist in euch wohnet.
–if indeed– God's spirit in you dwells.

Wer aber Christi Geist nicht hat,
Who but Christ's spirit not has

der ist nicht sein.
he is not his.

You, however, are not carnal, but spiritual,
if indeed God's spirit dwells in you.
But anyone who does not have Christ's spirit
does not belong to him.

7. Chorale

Johann Franck

Weg mit allen Schätzen!
Away with all treasures!

Du bist mein Ergötzen,
You are my delight,

Jesu, meine Lust!
Jesu, my pleasure!

Weg, ihr eitlen Ehren,
Away, you vain honors,

Ich mag euch nicht hören,
I want you not to hear;

Bleibt mir unbewußt!
remain to me unknown!

Elend, Not, Kreuz, Schmach und Tod
Misery, distress, cross, shame and death

Soll mich, ob ich viel muß leiden,
shall me, if I much must suffer,

Nicht von Jesu scheiden.
not from Jesu separate.

Away with all treasures!
You are my delight,
Jesu, my pleasure!
Away, you vain honors,
I do not want to hear you;
remain unknown to me!
Misery, distress, cross, shame and death
shall not, even if I must suffer greatly,
separate me from Jesu.

8. Trio (atb)

Romans 8: 10

So   aber Christus in euch ist,
If however Christ in you is,

so ist der Leib zwar   tot
so is the body indeed dead

um der Sünde willen;
for — sin's sake;

der Geist   aber   ist das Leben
the spirit however is — life

um der Gerechtigkeit willen.
for — righteousness' sake.

But if Christ is in you,
the body is indeed dead
because of sin;
the spirit, however, is alive
because of righteousness.

9. Chorale

Johann Franck

Gute Nacht, o Wesen,
Good night, O existence

Das die Welt   erlesen,
that the world [has] chosen;

Mir gefällst du nicht!
me please you not!

Gute Nacht, ihr Sünden,
Good night, you sins.

Bleibet weit   dahinten,
Stay far away behind;

Kommt nicht mehr ans Licht!
come   not more into light!

Gute Nacht, du Stolz und Pracht!
Good night, you pride and pomp;

Dir sei ganz, du Lasterleben,
to you be utterly, you life of iniquity,

Gute Nacht gegeben!
good night given!

Farewell, O life
that the world has chosen;
you please me not!
Farewell you sins.
Stay far behind me;
come no more into the light!
Farewell pride and pomp;
to you, life of iniquity,
a final farewell be bidden.

10. Chorus

Romans 8: 11

So nun der Geist   des,
If now the spirit of him

der Jesum von den Toten auferwecket hat,
who Jesus from the dead   raised up has

in euch wohnet,
in you dwells,

so wird auch derselbige,
so will also the same

der Jesum von den Toten auferwecket hat,
who Jesus from the dead   raised up has

eure sterbliche Leiber lebendig machen
your   mortal bodies alive   make,

um des willen, daß sein Geist
for the sake that his spirit

in euch wohnet.
in you dwells.

If the spirit of him
who has raised Jesus from the dead
dwells in you,
so will the same one
who has raised Jesus from the dead
bring life to your mortal bodies,
because his spirit
dwells in you.

11. Chorale
Johann Franck

Weicht, ihr Trauergeister!
Yield, you grief-spirits!

Denn mein Freudenmeister,
for my joy-master,

Jesus, tritt herein.
Jesus, enters in.

Denen, die Gott lieben,
Those who God love,

Muß auch ihr Betrüben
must even their sorrows

Lauter Zucker sein.
pure sugar be.

Duld ich schon hier Spott und Hohn,
Endure I even here mockery and scorn,

Dennoch bleibst du auch im Leide,
still remain you even in suffering,

Jesu, meine Freude.
Jesu, my joy.

Give way, you spirits of grief!
for my lord of joy,
Jesus, enters in.
For those who love God,
even their sorrows
must be pure sweetness.
Even if I must endure mockery and scorn,
you still remain, even in suffering,
Jesu, my joy!

Source (chorale): Franck 1674: 91
Variants: (Bach = roman, Franck = *italic*)
No. 3, line 4: wittern (suspect) = *wüttern* (curse)
line 5: Laß den Feind erbittern (Let the foe become bitter) =
Laß die Welt erschüttern (Let the world tremble)
No. 7, line 8: ob ich viel muß = *muß ich gleich viel*
No. 9, lines 7, 8: du = *o*

*A*S is the case with most of Bach's motets, the origins of this work are cloudy. Since no original sources survive, neither paper, ink, nor handwriting can be subjected to the scholarly scrutiny that has provided dates for the great majority of the cantatas. The text, however, yields at least a hint. Just three months after Bach arrived in Leipzig, a memorial service was held on July 18, 1723 for Joanna Maria Kees, the widow of Alderman and Postmaster Johann Jacob Kees. The sermon was based on Romans 8: 11, which is also the concluding scripture of the motet. Had Bach written a work for the occasion, it would likely have been based on that text. Nonetheless, no specific evidence links the motet to this event.

The motet comprises eleven movements—nearly double the number contained in most of Bach's cantatas. The hymn of the same name* provides the structural framework for the motet. It considers various aspects of Jesus as the Messiah (verses 1–3), then it invites the Christian to shed the woes of this life (verses 4, 5). Finally, it welcomes Jesus into the heart.

Bach alternates these chorale stanzas with five verses from Romans 8: 1–11, the portion of Paul's letter that deals with how the Gospel frees man from death:

Movement:	1	2	3	4	5	6	7	8	9	10	11
Chorale:	v. 1		v. 2		v. 3		v. 4		v. 5		v. 6
Bible:		Rom. 8: 1		Rom. 8: 2		Rom. 8: 9		Rom. 8: 10		Rom. 8: 11	

The eloquence of Paul's words alone would have been sufficient for Bach to use this text. In addition, however, Paul wrote so that each verse functions as a self-contained aphorism. This gave Bach the opportunity to break up the Biblical text into short segments that could serve as individual movements. The brilliance of his libretto lies in the alternation of these quotations with the hymn verses, and the way in which they complement each other synergistically.

Komm, Jesu, komm, BWV 229

Come, Jesus, Come
Paul Thymich

Komm, Jesu, komm, mein Leib ist müde,
Come, Jesu, come, my body is weary,

die Kraft verschwind't je mehr und mehr,
the strength vanishes — more and more.

ich sehne mich nach deinem Friede;
I yearn — for your peace;

der saure Weg wird mir zu schwer!
the bitter journey becomes for me too difficult!

Komm, ich will mich dir ergeben;
Come, I want myself to you to submit;

du bist der rechte Weg,
you are the right way,

die Wahrheit und das Leben.
the truth and the life.

Come, Jesus, come. My body is weary;
my strength is vanishing more and more.
I yearn for your peace;
life's bitter journey is becoming too difficult!
Come, I want to give myself to you;
you are the right way,
the truth, and the life.

Drum schließ ich mich in deine Hände
Thus entrust I — into your hands

und sage, Welt, zu guter Nacht!
and say, world, to good night!

Eilt gleich mein Lebenslauf zu Ende,
Hurries now my life's course to end,

ist doch der Geist wohl angebracht.
is yet the spirit well prepared.

Er soll bei seinem Schöpfer schweben,
It shall with his creator hover,

weil Jesus ist und bleibt
because Jesus is and remains

der wahre Weg zum Leben.
the true way to life.

Thus I entrust myself into your hands
and bid the world good night.
My life's journey rushes to its end,
yet the spirit is well prepared.
It shall hover with its creator,
for Jesus is and remains
the true path to life.

Source: Wagner 1697: 328

THE motet "Komm, Jesu, komm" is one of the five Bach motets that may well have been composed for a funeral. Based on the writing of the copyist in the earliest source, who departed Leipzig in 1731 or 1732, the *Bach Compendium* dates the motet prior to that time. Although we do not know the occasion for which Bach wrote his music, this information is preserved with regard to the text. "Komm, Jesu, komm" is taken from an eleven-stanza poem by Paul Thymich (1656–1694), originally written for the September 14, 1684 funeral of Jakob Thomasius, Rector of the St. Thomas School of Leipzig. The Cantor of the Thomasschule at the time, Thomas Seele, set the entire poem to music for the funeral. Two generations later Bach followed Seele into the same position.

For his motet, Bach chose just the first and last stanzas of Thymich's poem, which he set to music in quite different ways. Bach composed the first verse as an elaborate double chorus, in which each line of text is accentuated by his giving it its own, highly individual musical interpretation. By contrast, Bach set the second stanza (Thymich's eleventh) as a four-part, homophonic hymn. A "simple" chorale it is not, however. Perhaps as a parallel to the complexity of the first movement, Bach wrote one his most intricate chorale settings, complete with rhythmic ornamentation, hemiola cadences, and symbolic word painting. Most interesting is the melismatic setting of the word "Jesus," which is followed by similar melismas on "Weg" (path). Thus Bach states in music what the text says in words: "Jesus is and remains the true path to life."

Lobet den Herrn, alle Heiden, BWV 230

Praise the Lord, All You Nations
Psalm 117: 1, 2a, with alleluia

Lobet den Herrn, alle Heiden,
Praise the Lord, all heathen,

und preiset ihn, alle Völker!
and praise him, all people!

Denn seine Gnade und Wahrheit
For his grace and truth

waltet über uns in Ewigkeit.
reign over us for eternity.

Alleluja.
Alleluia!

Praise the Lord, all you nations,
and praise him, all you people.
For his grace and truth
reign over us for evermore.
Alleluia!

FIVE of Bach's seven motets were either demonstrably composed for funerals or are based on texts that suggest such usage. "Lobet den Herrn" is one of the two exceptions. Unfortunately the date and occasion of its composition are unknown, and the earliest surviving source is a print issued by Breitkopf and Härtel in 1821, over seventy years after Bach's death.

The text, a Psalm of praise set by many composers, is brief and contains no strong contrasts of affect. A composer like Bach who wants to employ it in a work of several minutes' length thus faces the challenge of determining how to create interest and variety. Bach solved the problem by treating the second sentence as a reflective, lyric interlude between two bright, joyous sections in faster tempo. In this way it is similar in overall structure to the much longer and more complex motet "Singet dem Herrn ein neues Lied,"* BWV 225.

Singet dem Herrn ein neues Lied, BWV 225

Sing to the Lord a New Song

1. Double Chorus
Psalm 149: 1–3

Singet dem Herrn ein neues Lied;
Sing to the Lord a new song;

die Gemeine der Heiligen sollen ihn loben.
the assembly of the saints shall him praise.

Israel freue sich des, der ihn gemacht hat.
Israel rejoices — in him, who it made has.

Die Kinder Zions sei'n fröhlich über ihrem Könige,
The children of Zion be joyful about their king.

Sie sollen loben seinen Namen im Reihen;
They shall praise his name in the dance;

mit Pauken und mit Harfen
with timbrel and with harps

sollen sie ihm spielen.
shall they to him play.

Sing to the Lord a new song!
The assembly of saints shall praise him.
Let Israel rejoice in its creator.
May the children of Zion be joyful in their king.
They shall praise his name in the dance;
with timbrel and harps
they shall play to him.

2. Chorale (Chorus 2) and Aria (Chorus 1)
Chorale by Johann Gramann; author of *Aria* unknown

Chorale

Wie sich ein Vater erbarmet
As — a father has mercy

    Aria

    Gott nimm dich ferner unser an,
    God take care you further of us —.

Über seine junge Kinderlein,
on his young child,

    Gott nimm dich ferner unser an,
    God take care you further of us —.

So tut der Herr uns allen,
so does the Lord on us all,

    Gott nimm dich ferner unser an,
    God take care you further of us —.

So wir ihn kindlich fürchten rein.
if we him childlike fear genuinely.

    Gott nimm dich ferner unser an,
    God take care you further of us —.

Er kennt das arm Gemächte,
He knows the feeble powers,

    Gott nimm dich ferner unser an,
    God take care you further of us —.

Gott weiß, wir sind nur Staub,
God knows, we are only dust,

    Denn ohne dich ist nichts getan
    For without you is nothing achieved

    Mit allen unsern Sachen.
    in all our affairs.

Gleichwie das Gras vom Rechen,
like as the grass from the rake,

    Gott nimm dich ferner unser an,
    God take care you further of us —.

Ein Blum und fallend Laub.
a flower and falling leaf.

    Denn ohne dich ist nichts getan
    For without you is nothing achieved

    Mit allen unsern Sachen.
    in all our affairs.

Der Wind nur drüber wehet,
The wind only over blows,

    Gott nimm dich ferner unser an,
    God take care you further of us —.

So ist es nicht mehr da,
so is it no more there,

    Drum sei du unser Schirm und Licht,
    Therefore be you our shield and light,

    Und trügt uns unsre Hoffnung nicht,
    and deceive — our hope not,

    So wirst du's ferner machen.
    so will you it continue doing.

Also der Mensch vergehet,
Thus the mortal passes away,

Sein End, das ist ihm nah.
his end, it is to him near.

    Wohl dem, der sich nur steif und fest
    Happy he, who — only rigidly and firmly

    Auf dich und deine Huld verläßt.
    on you and your grace relies.

Chorale

As a father has mercy

    Aria
    God, continue to care for us.

on his young child,

    God, continue to care for us.

so the Lord has mercy on us all,

    God, continue to care for us.

if, like children, we sincerely fear him.

    God, continue to care for us.

He knows our feeble powers;

    God, continue to care for us.

God knows we are but dust,

    For without you, nothing is achieved
    in any of our affairs.

like the grass before the rake,

    God, continue to care for us.

a fading flower, a falling leaf.

    For without you, nothing is achieved
    in any of our affairs.

The wind but blows over it,

    God, continue to care for us!

and it is there no more!

    Therefore be our shield and light,
    and do not disappoint our hope.
    Thus you will continue to do.

Thus we all pass away;
our end is near.

    Happy is the one who steadfastly
    relies on you and your grace!

3. Double Chorus
Psalm 150: 2, 6

Lobet   den Herrn in seinen Taten,
Praise the Lord for his   acts,

lobet   ihn in seiner großen Herrlichkeit!
praise him for his   great   glory!

Alles, was Odem hat,   lobe den Herrn,
All   that breath has praise the Lord.

halleluja!
Hallelujah!

Praise the Lord for his acts,
praise him for his great glory!
Let all that has breath praise the Lord.
Hallelujah!

Source (chorale):	Wackernagel 1964, 3: 822 (no. 969)
Variants (chorale):	(Bach = roman, Wackernagel = *italics*)
	Line 1: Vater (father) = *man* (one)
	Line 6: Gott weiß (God knows) = *er weiß* (he knows)
	Line 10: nicht mehr (no more) = *nimmer* (never)

*F*OR reasons both musical and textual, "Singet dem Herrn" is certainly the most popular of Bach's motets. The first and third movements are from two of the most joyous Psalms of praise, nos. 149 and 150, respectively. Movement 2 consists of texts of two different types that speak with greater eloquence together than separately.

In the second movement Choir 2 sings a chorale verse by Johann Gramman (1487–1541), an opponent of and later convert to Luther's cause who served from 1520 to 1522 as Rector of the St. Thomas School in Leipzig, where Bach was to begin his twenty-seven years service as Cantor almost precisely 200 years later. The Gramman text, the third verse of the hymn "Nun lob mein Seel" from 1530, closely paraphrases Psalm 103: 13–16:[8]

> As a father pities his children, so the Lord pities those who fear him. For he knows our frame; he remembers that we are dust. As for man, his days are like grass; he flourishes like a flower of the field; for the wind passes over it, and it is gone, and its place knows it no more.

This vivid reminder of humanity's mortality is complemented by a poem of unknown origin (an "aria" in Bach's parlance) sung by Choir 1. It contains four messages in its eight lines:

(1) a prayer for God to hold us near,

(2) a humble acknowledgment of his power and our weakness,

(3) an appeal for him to be our "shield and light," and

(4) a blessing on those who cleave to him.

The art of this movement lies the way Bach intersperses lines from his two sources so that the "aria" adds hope to the grave message of the chorale.

"Singet dem Herrn" was written sometime between June, 1726 and April, 1727. The occasion is unknown, but the nature of the second movement suggests a funeral. In English Bibles, Psalm 150 closes with the words "Praise the Lord," which Luther rendered and Bach set as "Halleluja." It is interesting and most poignant that a motet commemorating the end of earthly life should close with the last words of the last Psalm.

---

[8]The first four verses paraphrase the entire Psalm: (1) verses 1–5, (2) verses 6–12, (3) verses 13–16, and (4) verses 17–22. The fifth was added in 1549 by another, unknown author. The metaphor of the dying grass for the frailty of man is familiar from the use in the Brahms *Requiem* of 1 Peter 1: 24, which itself quotes Isaiah 40: 6–8.

Ludwig van Beethoven

Elegischer Gesang, op. 118
Elegiac Song
Author unknown

Sanft wie du lebtest
Gently, as you lived,

hast du vollendet,
have you passed away,

zu heilig für den Schmerz!
too holy for — pain!

Kein Auge wein'
No eye is weeping

ob des himmlischen Geistes Heimkehr.
because of the heavenly spirit's return home.

Sanft wie du lebtest
Gently, as you lived,

ja, hast du vollendet.
yea, have you passed away.

Gently, as you lived,
you have passed away,
too holy to know pain!
No eye is weeping
because of the heavenly spirit's return home.
Gently, as you lived,
yea, thus you have passed away.

BEETHOVEN'S tender "Elegiac Song" was written by an unknown poet (according to Beethoven biographer T. von Frimmel, possibly Ignaz Franz von Castelli [Kinsky 1955: 341]) and may have been produced specifically for Beethoven to set to music. The choral song was composed for a memorial service honoring Baroness Eleonore von Pasqualati on the third anniversary of her death (August 5, 1814) and was dedicated to Baron von Pasqualati.

Fantasie, op. 80
Fantasy
Christoph Kuffner (?)

Schmeichelnd hold und lieblich klingen
Caressingly sweet and lovely sound

Unsers Lebens Harmonien,
our life's harmonies,

Und dem Schönheitssinn entschwingen
and from the sense of beauty arise

Blumen sich, die ewig blühn.
flowers — that eternally blossom.

Caressingly sweet and lovely are the sounds
of our life's harmonies,
and from the sense of beauty spring forth
flowers that bloom eternally.

Fried und Freude gleiten freundlich
Peace and joy glide cheerfully

Wie der Wellen Wechselspiel;
like the waves' interplay;

Was sich drängte rauh und feindlich,
what — pressured roughly and with hostility

Ordnet sich zu Hochgefühl.
settles — into elation.

Peace and joy flow cheerfully
like the interplay of waves;
pressures that were harsh and hostile
are transformed into elation.

Wenn der Töne Zauber walten
When the sounds' magic reigns

Und des Wortes Weihe spricht,
and the word's holiness speaks,

Muss sich Herrliches gestalten,
must — glorious form;

Nacht und Stürme werden Licht.
night and storms become light.

When the magic of sound reigns
and the word's solemnity speaks,
something glorious must appear;
darkness and storms become light.

Äußre Ruhe, innre Wonne
Outer calm, inner bliss

Herrschaft für den Glücklichen.
[are] domain for the happy one.

Doch der Künste Frühlingssonne
But the arts' spring sun

Läßt aus beiden Licht entstehn.
lets from both light emerge.

Outer calm and inner bliss
are the domain of the happy one.
But the spring sun of the arts
causes light to emerge from both.

Großes, das ins Herz gedrungen,
Greatness, that into the heart penetrated,

Blüht dann neu und schön empor,
blossoms then new and beautiful forth,

Hat ein Geist sich aufgeschwungen,
has a spirit — soared upwards,

Hallt ihm stets ein Geisterchor.
resounds for it always a spirits' choir.

Greatness that has penetrated into the heart
then blossoms forth fresh and beautiful;
when a spirit has soared aloft,
a choir of spirits always echoes for it.

Nehmt denn hin, ihr schönen Seelen,
Accept then —, you beautiful souls,

Froh die Gaben schöner Kunst.
gladly the gifts of beautiful art.

Wenn sich Lieb' und Kraft vermählen,
When — love and strength marry,

Lohnt dem Menschen Götter-Gunst.
rewards the mortal gods' favor.

Then, you beautiful souls, gladly accept
the gifts of beautiful art.
When love and strength are united,
God's good will rewards us all.

*B*EETHOVEN composed his "Choral Fantasy" in December 1808 for one of his "Academy" concerts, at which he presented new compositions. Only the choral conclusion of the work was complete for the concert, and Beethoven may well have improvised at the piano before its performance. According to Carl Czerny, Beethoven commissioned the Viennese poet Christoph Kuffner (1780–1846) to write the text at the last minute to the composer's specifications, so that the words would fit the music he had already written.[9] No evidence exists to support this thesis, however. Kuffner was a minor but recognized name in Viennese artistic circles. He had studied voice and violin, and had been acquainted with both Haydn and Mozart. Beethoven composed his *Triumph-Marsch* in C major for a production of Kuffner's tragedy *Tarpeja*, and Schubert set his "Glaube, Hoffnung und Liebe" (D. 955) immediately before the *Schwanengesang* of August–October, 1828.

Unlike the ninth symphony, in which darkness struggles with light, the "Fantasie" contains only light. The text sings the praises of "the spring sun of the arts," particularly music, which causes "light to emerge" from both "outer calm and inner bliss." The poem is naive, with strained rhymes (*Harmonien - Blühn, Wechselspiel - Hochgefühl, Glücklichen - entstehn*), but perhaps its weaknesses do not matter, as the music communicates the composer's joy better than the words.

Symphony No. 9, op. 125

4. O Freunde, nicht diese Töne!

O Friends, Not This Music!

Friedrich von Schiller / Ludwig van Beethoven [?]

O Freunde, nicht diese Töne!
O friends, not these tones!

Sondern laßt uns angenehmere
But let us more pleasant ones

anstimmen, und freudenvollere!
strike up, and more joyful ones!

O friends, not this music!
Let us strike up something more
pleasant and more joyful!

---

[9]See Dagmar Wiese, *Ein Skizzenbuch zur Chorfantasie op. 80 und zu anderen Werken.* Bonn, 1957: 9. Cited in Beethoven 1966: 1.

Freude, schöner Götterfunken,
Joy,   beautiful divine spark,

Tochter   aus   Elysium,
daughter from Elysium:

Wir betreten feuertrunken,
we   enter,   fire-drunk,

Himmlische,   dein Hieligtum.
heavenly one, your sanctuary.

Deine Zauber binden wieder,
Your   magic   binds again

Was die Mode streng geteilt;
what — custom sternly divided;

Alle Menschen werden Brüder,
all   mortals   become brothers

Wo   dein sanfter Flügel weilt.
where your gentle   wing abides.

Wem   der große Wurf   gelungen,
For whom the great throw was successful

Eines Freundes Freund zu sein,
a   friend's   friend to be,

Wer ein holdes Weib errungen,
who a gracious wife   gained,

Mische seinen Jubel   ein!
mix in   his   rejoicing —!

Ja— wer auch nur eine Seele
Yes— who also only one soul

Sein nennt auf dem Erdenrund!
his calls on the   globe!

Und wer's nie gekonnt,   der stehle
And who it never was able, that one steal

Weinend sich   aus   diesem Bund!
weeping — away from this union!

Freude trinken alle Wesen
Joy   drink all creatures

An den Brüsten der Natur;
at   the breasts of nature;

Alle Guten, alle Bösen
all   good, all evil [ones]

Folgen ihrer Rosenspur.
follow its   rose-trail.

Küße   gab sie uns und Reben,
Kisses gave it to us and grapes,

Eine Freund, geprüft im Tod;
a   friend, tested in death;

Wollust ward dem Wurm gegeben,
bliss   was to the worm given,

Und der Cherub steht   vor   Gott.
and the cherub stands before God.

Froh, wie seine Sonnen fliegen
Glad, like his   suns,   fly

Durch des Himmels prächt'gen Plan,
through the heaven's splendid plane.

Laufet, Brüder, eure Bahn,
Go,   brothers, your way,

Freudig, wie ein Held zum Siegen.
joyously, like a hero toward victory.

Joy, you beautiful, divine spark,
daughter from Elysium:
enflamed with passion, heavenly one,
we enter your sanctuary!
Your magic power re-unites
what custom has sternly divided;
all mortals become as kin
wherever your gentle wing abides.

Those who have had the great fortune
to be a friend to a friend,
those who have won a gracious spouse,
should join together in rejoicing!
Yes—all those who also have just one soul
on earth to call their very own!
And those who cannot, may they steal
tearfully away from this company!

All creatures drink joy
at nature's breast;
all, good and evil alike,
follow its rosy path.
Joy gave us kisses and grapes,
a friend, faithful to the end;
even the worm was granted bliss,
and the cherub stands before God.

Gladly, like his suns, fly
through the splendid plane of the firmament.
Thus, comrades, run your course,
joyously, like a hero off to victory.

Seid umschlungen, Millionen.
Be embraced, millions.

Diesen Kuß der ganzen Welt!
This kiss for the whole world!

Brüder— über'm Sternenzelt
Brothers, above the star-tent

Muß ein lieber Vater wohnen.
must a beloved father dwell.

Ihr stürzt nieder, Millionen?
You fall down, millions?

Ahnest du den Schöpfer, Welt?
Sense you the creator, world?

Such ihn über'm Sternenzelt!
Seek him above the star-tent!

Über Sternen muß er wohnen.
Above stars must he dwell.

Be embraced, you millions!
This kiss is for the whole world!
Brothers and sisters—above the starry canopy
a beloved father must surely dwell.

Do you prostrate yourselves, you millions?
Do you sense your creator, world?
Seek him above the canopy of stars!
Above the stars he must surely dwell.

Source: Schiller 1867, 1: 47
Variant:
(Beethoven = roman, Schiller = *italic*)
Stanza 5, line 3: laufet = *wandert*

*J*OHANN Christoph Friedrich Schiller (1759–1805) was raised in a number of south-German cities around Stuttgart. From age 13 to 21 he attended the Karlsschule, a military academy in Stuttgart, graduating as a doctor in 1780. For the next eighteen months he followed in his father's footsteps as an army physician, simultaneously writing dramas and poetry for which he began to acquire some renown.

Neither the army nor Stuttgart was to remain in Schiller's future. A 1781 Mannheim performance of his first, politically sensitive play, written while a pupil at the Karlsschule, got him into hot water with the Duke of Württemberg and forced him to leave Stuttgart. First he went to Mannheim, where opportunity beckoned but faded into penury less than three years later. After two more successful years in Leipzig he moved to Weimar, where he met and befriended Goethe and established a personal and artistic friendship.

Best known among literary scholars as a dramatist and critical thinker, Schiller's fame among musicians lies in a poem entitled "An die Freude" (Ode to Joy), "an essay in secular religion" (Kerman and Tyson 1980: 387) that Beethoven immortalized in the finale to his revolutionary ninth symphony of 1824. The poem originally appeared in the first issue (February, 1786) of *Thalia*,[10] the successor to a failed theatrical magazine of similar name that Schiller had published in Mannheim the previous year. Schiller wrote the poem in honor of his friendship with Christian Gottfried Körner, who invited him to move to Leipzig from Mannheim, opening his door to Schiller at the most difficult juncture in his life. Körner was to remain lifelong a valued critic and friend of the poet.

> As the one late-period Beethoven symphony the Ninth is in a sense retrospective in resuming the "symphonic ideal" which for decades had inspired little music [in Beethoven]; retrospective, too, is the frank echo of revolutionary French cantatas in the choral finale. Yet as a gesture, this finale shows once again Beethoven's uncanny grasp of essences below "the adornments of Art." As Wagner always insisted, words and a choir with soloists to sing them seem to force their way into the symphony in order to make instrumental music fully articulate, to resolve the conflict of the earlier movements with a consummation of unexampled triumph. (Kerman and Tyson 1980: 387)

Nine years before Beethoven, Schubert had set the complete poem as a strophic song—all eight stanzas of eight lines, each followed by a "chorus" of an additional four lines. This tedious type of setting was of no interest to Beethoven, who needed a "custom-built" text for his freer, symphonic context. He thus selected six from among the sixteen sections of Schiller's poem, arranging them according to his own plan.

Beethoven's choices were all from the first half of the poem: stanzas 1, 2, and 3, followed by "choruses" 4, 1, and 3. He arranged his selections to provide two distinct textual sections: the three eight-line stanzas provide an essay on joy and happiness, and the three four-line choruses, distinguished by a different, a-b-b-a rhyme scheme, exhort humanity to acknowledge the divine—by implication the source of all joy. The third chorus, with its penetrating questions, is a fitting choice to conclude the libretto.

Schiller's poem did not provide Beethoven with the introduction he needed, a transition from musical anarchy into the joyful confidence of Schiller's poem. The composer therefore began with three lines, possibly his own, that call upon his "friends" to change their tune to "something more pleasant and joyful." Beethoven's music, of course, obliges gloriously.

---

[10]In Greek, *Thalia* means "the flowering of beauty." The name is that of one of the Graces of Greek mythology, the three sister goddesses of beauty.

Johannes Brahms

Begräbnisgesang, op. 13

Burial Song

Michael Weiße

Nun laßt uns den Leib begraben,
Now let us the body bury,

Bei dem wir kein'n Zweifel haben,
about which we no doubt have

Er werd am letzten Tag aufstehn,
it will on the last day rise up,

Und unverrücklich herfürgehn.
and indomitably go forth.

Now let us bury the body,
which we have no doubt
will rise up on the last day
and indomitably go forth.

Erd ist er und von der Erden
Earth is it and from the earth

Wird auch wieder zu Erd werden,
will also again earth become,

Und von Erden wieder aufstehn,
and from earth again rise up

Wenn Gottes Posaun wird angehn.
when God's trombone will begin.

It is dust and from the dust,
and will also again become dust
and from the dust again rise up
when God's trumpet begins to sound.

Seine Seel lebt ewig in Gott,
His soul lives eternally in God,

Der sie allhier aus seiner Gnad
who it here out of his grace

Von aller Sünd and Missetat
from all sin and misdeed

Durch seinen Bund gefeget hat.
through his covenant purified has.

This soul lives eternally in God,
who, in his mercy,
has cleansed it from all sin and misdeeds
through his covenant.

Sein Arbeit, Trübsal, und Elend
His work, sadness, and misery

Ist kommen zu ein'm guten End.
has come to a good end.

Er hat getragen Christi Joch,
He has borne Christ's yoke,

Ist gestorben und lebet noch.
has died and lives yet.

Toil, sadness, and misery
have come to a good end.
This person has borne Christ's yoke,
has died, and yet lives.

Die Seel, die lebt ohn alle Klag,
The soul, it lives without any complaint;

Der Leib schläft bis am letzten Tag,
the body sleeps until the last day,

An welchem ihn Gott verklären,
on which it God will transfigure

Und der Freuden wird gewähren.
and — joys will grant.

The soul lives without any complaint;
the body sleeps until the judgment day,
when God will transfigure it
and grant many joys.

Hier ist er in Angst gewesen,
Here — he in fear was,

Dort aber wird er genesen,
there however will he be healed

In ewiger Freude und Wonne
in eternal joy and bliss

Leuchten wie die schöne Sonne.
shine like the beautiful sun.

Here this person was in fear;
there, however, this soul will be healed
and shine in eternal joy and bliss
like the beautiful sun.

Nun lassen wir ihn hier schlafen
Now   let   we him here   sleep

Now we leave this body here to sleep
and we all go our many ways.

Und gehn allsamt unser Straßen,
and   go   all   our   paths.

Send us forth with all diligence,
for death will come to us in the same way.

Schicken uns auch mit allem Fleiß,
Dispatch us also with all diligence,

Denn der Tod kommt uns gleicher Weis.
for   — death comes to us the same way.

Source: Weiße 1957: M5
Variants: (Brahms = roman, Weiße = *italic*)
        Stanza 2, line 2: wieder zu Erd = *zu Erd wieder*
        Stanza 5, line 1: Die Seel, die lebt = *Die Seele lebt*
        Stanza 6, line 3: Freude = *Freud*

THE occasion for which Brahms wrote his "Burial Song" of 1858, if there was one, is unknown. It was, however, among his very first choral works, preceded only by the "Ave Maria" for women's chorus, op. 12, of the same year. He took as his text a hymn by Michael Weiße (c. 1488–1534) entitled "Nun laßt uns den Leib begraben" (Now Let Us Bury the Body) from 1519.

Weiße began his ecclesiastical career as a monk in the Catholic Church but left his order in disenchantment. He then joined the "Bohemian Brethren," followers of the early fifteenth-century heretic and martyr Jan Hus, who emphasized simplicity, and a highly disciplined community and congregational life based on that of the early Christians. Weiße was impressed by the writings of Luther and was twice (1522 and 1524) sent as an emissary to him in Wittenberg to explain the tenets of the Brothers, which were largely consonant with those of Luther, but for some beliefs regarding the sacrament of communion. The present hymn was one of the 155 in the *Gesangbuch der böhmischen Brüder* (Hymnbook of the Bohemian Brethren, Jungbunzlau, 1531), all of which were apparently written or translated by Weiße himself. (Julian 1985: 1247) "Nun laßt uns den Leib begraben" is thought to have been adapted from a Czech original. It is the fifth hymn in section "M," which consists of hymns "for those who have fallen."

Weiße's version of the hymn consisted of seven verses of four lines each. Luther prepared an eighth and final verse that beseeches Christ to help the Christian through the travails of life enumerated in the previous stanzas. The tone of the hymn is quite different when Luther's verse is added: The uplifting "to him alone [Christ] be praise, glory, and honor!" is heard as the closing words rather than Weiße's somber "for death comes to us as well." Brahms chose to keep a consistently funereal tone and omitted Luther's final verse.

All three of Brahms's emendations of the original text serve musical purposes; the changes in stanzas 2 and 6, for example, permit him to employ motives that would not be usable with the original text. The reordering of words in stanza 2 moves the word "Erd" into juxtaposition with the verb and toward the end of the sentence, balancing the use of the same word at its beginning.

"Nun laßt uns den Leib begraben" is found in the *EKG* as no. 174; it does not appear in the *LBW*.

Dem dunkeln Schoß der heilgen Erde, o op. 19

To the Dark Womb of the Sacred Earth

Friedrich Schiller

Dem dunkeln Schoß der heilgen Erde
To the dark   womb of the sacred earth

Vertraut der Sämann seine Saat
entrusts the sower his seed

Und hofft, daß sie entkeimen werde
and hopes that they sprout will

Zum Segen, nach des Himmels Rat.
to a blessing according to — heaven's counsel.

To the dark womb of the sacred earth
the sower entrusts the seeds, hoping
that they will sprout forth into a blessing
in accordance with heaven's counsel.

Noch köstlicheren Samen bergen
Still more precious seed shelter

Wir trauernd in der Erde Schoß
we mourning in the earth's womb

Und hofft, daß er aus den Särgen
and hope that it from the coffins

Erblühen soll zu schönerm Los.
blossom shall to better lot.

Grieving, we shelter even more precious seed
in the earth's womb
and trust it shall blossom from the coffins
to find a better fate.

Source: Schiller 1867, 1: 251
Variants:

(Brahms = roman, Schiller = *italics*)

Stanza 1, line 2:   Brahms deletes the original second line, "vertrauen wir
der Hände Tat" (we entrust the works of our hands)

Stanza 1, line 3:   hofft = *hoffen*

BRAHMS'S text is an eight-line excerpt from a four-hundred-twenty-six-line poem entitled *Das Lied von der Glocke* (The Song of the Bell), written in 1799 by Friedrich Schiller (1759–1805). Schiller's work consists of two parallel and alternating tracks—the episodic story of the casting of a bell, and the foundryman's similarly episodic commentary and meditation on life occasioned by the stages of the casting process. A Latin inscription preceeds the poem:

Vivos voco   *Mortuos plango*   *Fulgura frango*
I call the living   I grieve the dead   I shatter the lightning

These lines refer to three of the traditional functions of the bell—calling people to worship, keeping demons away from the unburied dead, and offering protection from the weather. Such inscriptions, known as the *Virtutes* or "moral virtues," had adorned European bells since at least the thirteenth century.[10]

The lines Brahms chose are from the fourth meditation, on the pouring of metal into the mold. Immediately previously, the foundryman had contemplated the charity and tragedy of fire, which he imagined to destroy a town and many of its people. As he poured the molten metal into its earthen form, he turned his thoughts to death and burial—and to the solemn duty of the bell to toll the grave-song.

Brahms selected nine lines from this section of the poem and deleted the second line, "vertrauen wir der Hände Tat" (we entrust the works of our hands). This had the virtues of condensing the text, creating two halves of identical length, and regularizing the rhyme scheme. Both within their full context and as excerpted by Brahms, these lines conceal their actual subject—the burial of the dead—until the last word of the penultimate line, and surprise the reader accordingly.

After living in Goethe's home city of Weimar for a few years, Schiller and Goethe became close friends. In 1815, ten years after Schiller's death, Goethe wrote an "epilog" to *Das Lied von der Glocke*, an addition nearly half again as long as Schiller's poem. (Goethe 1948–, 3: 666)

---

[10]Price 1983: 128. Price (127) offers further background of interest:

It will be seen that in the Middle Ages the church tower bell was not held to be mere metal. With its reception into Christianity through baptism, with its possession of a name, with its mantel of iconography and holy symbols exposed to the powers of the air, . . . and above all with the trust that the whole community had in the effectiveness of these attributes, the bell was regarded as a half-divine being with a personality. It was therefore natural that any inscribed statements of the bell's purpose or power which were cast on it when it was made should be in the first person.

Der 13. Psalm, op. 27

The 13th Psalm

Psalm 13

Herr, wie lange willst du
Lord, how long will you

mein so gar vergessen?
me so totally forget?

Wie lange verbirgst du
How long hide you

dein Antlitz vor mir?
your face from me?

Lord, how long will you
so completely forget me?
How long will you hide
your face from me?

Wie lange soll ich sorgen
How long shall I worry

in meiner Seele, und mich ängsten
in my soul and — be frightened

in meinem Herzen täglich?
in my heart daily?

Wie lange soll sich mein Feind
How long shall himself my foe

über mich erheben?
over me exalt?

How long shall my soul be troubled
and my heart be frightened daily?
How long shall my foes
exalt themselves over me?

Schaue doch und erhöre mich,
Behold — and hear me,

Herr, mein Gott.
Lord, my God.

Erleuchte meine Augen, daß ich
Light my eyes, that I

nicht im Tode entschlafe.
not in death sleep.

Behold and hear me,
Lord, my God!
Light my eyes,
that I might not sleep in death,

Daß nicht mein Feind sich rühme,
That not my foe — boast,

er sei mein mächtig worden,
he –has achieved mastery over me–,

und meine Widersacher sich nicht freuen,
and my adversaries — not rejoice,

daß ich niederliege.
that I am dejected.

that my foe might not boast
that he has prevailed over me,
and my adversaries might not rejoice
that I am dejected.

Ich hoffe aber darauf,
I trust, however, —

daß du so gnädig bist,
that you so merciful are;

mein Herz freuet sich,
my heart rejoices —

daß du so gerne hilfst.
that you so gladly help.

I trust, however,
that you are most merciful;
my heart rejoices
that you so gladly help.

Ich will dem Herrn singen,
I want to the Lord to sing,

daß er so wohl an mir tut.
that he so good to me does.

I want to sing to the Lord,
for he does such good things for me.

ALTHOUGH no record exists of the reason for Brahms's choice of this text, the origin of the motet is thoroughly documented through letters and diary entries. (Kross 1958: 114–115) The twenty-six-year-old composer wrote it on Sunday, August 22, 1859 for the women's choir he had established after his recent move to Hamburg. The rehearsal eight days later was disappointing because of the unexpected vocal challenges of the work—so much so that Brahms reworked the problem spots to make them easier for the voices. The result, the final version, was first rehearsed on September 12, 1859.

DREI GESÄNGE, op. 42
Three Songs

Abendständchen, op. 42, no. 1
Evening Serenade
Clemens Maria Brentano

Hör, es klagt die Flöte wieder,
Listen! — laments the flute again,

Und die kühlen Brunnen rauschen,
and the cool springs murmur.

Golden wehn die Töne nieder,
Golden blow the sounds down;

Stille, stille, laß uns lauschen!
silent, silent, let us listen!

Holdes Bitten, mild Verlangen,
Gracious imploring, gentle longing,

Wie es süß zum Herzen spricht!
how it sweetly to the heart speaks!

Durch die Nacht, die mich umfangen,
Through the night, which me [has] embraced,

Blickt zu mir der Töne Licht.
shines to me the sounds' light.

Listen! The flute laments again,
and the cool springs murmur.
The golden tones waft down;
be still, hush, let us listen!

Gracious imploring, gentle longing,
how sweetly they speak to the heart!
Through the night, which has embraced me,
the light of the music shines.

Source: Brentano 1963–1968, 1: 1063

CLEMENS Maria Brentano (1778–1842) made a name for himself in his late twenties when, along with his friend from Heibelberg Achim von Arnim, he published a collection of folk poetry under the title *Des Knaben Wunderhorn* (The Youth's Magic Horn, 1805–1808). Fewer than ten years later, after composing numerous plays, novels, and a great volume of poetry, he returned to the Catholic faith that he had abandoned in his youth and renounced further writing.

The light and unburdened verses of "Abendständchen" are taken from Brentano's *Singspiel* of November, 1802 entitled *Die lustige Musikanten* (The Merry Musicians), which he wrote in four days while living briefly with with an itinerant theatrical troupe. The poem is sung as a duet between Piast, a blind old man, and his daughter Fabiola. The instructions to the director read, "Fabiola leads the blind Piast with his cane and the boy [a cripple taken in by Pianst] on his arm. In the background a flute is heard, coming ever closer. . . ." (Brentano 1963–1968, 1: 1063, tr. ed.).

2. Vineta, op. 42, no. 2
Vineta
Wilhelm Müller

Aus des Meeres tiefem, tiefem Grunde
From the ocean's deep, deep depths

Klingen Abendglocken, dumpf und matt.
ring evening bells, muffled and faint.

Uns zu geben wunderbare Kunde
To us to give wondrous tidings

Von der schönen, alten Wunderstadt.
of the beautiful, old, wonder city.

In der Fluten Schoß hinabgesunken,
Into the flood's womb sunk down,

Blieben unten ihre Trümmer stehn.
remained below its ruins standing.

Ihre Zinnen lassen goldne Funken
Its battlements let golden sparks

Widerscheinend auf dem Spiegel sehn.
reflecting on the surface be seen.

From the ocean's deepest depths,
evening bells ring, muffled and faint.
They bring us wondrous tidings
of the beautiful, old, miraculous city.

Sunken into the flood's womb,
its ruins remained standing below.
Its battlements cause golden sparks
to be seen reflecting on the surface.

Und der Schiffer, der den Zauberschimmer
And the boatman, who the magical shimmer

Einmal sah im hellen Abendrot,
once saw in the bright sunset,

Nach der selben Stelle schifft er immer,
to the same place sails he always,

Ob auch ringsumher die Klippe droht.
even though also all around the cliffs threaten.

And the boatman, who once saw the magical shimmer
in the evening's bright red glow,
always sails back to the same place,
even though the cliffs threaten all around.

Aus des Herzens tiefem, tiefem Grunde
From the heart's deep, deep depths

Klingt es mir wie Glocken, dumpf und matt.
sounds — to me like bells, muffled and faint.

Ach, sie geben wunderbare Kunde
Ah, they give wondrous tidings

Von der Liebe, die geliebt es hat.
of the love, that loved it has.

From the heart's deepest depths
it sounds to me like bells, muffled and faint.
Ah, they bring wondrous tidings
of the love that it has felt.

Eine schöne Welt ist da versunken,
A beautiful world has there sunk;

Ihre Trümmer blieben unten stehn,
its ruins remained below standing,

Lassen sich als goldne Himmelsfunken
let — like golden, heavenly sparks

Oft im Spiegel meiner Träume sehn.
often in the mirror of my dreams be seen.

A beautiful world has sunk there;
its ruins remained standing below,`
often causing golden, heavenly sparks
to be seen in the mirror of my dreams.

Und dann möcht ich tauchen in die Tiefen,
And then would like I to dive into the depths,

Mich versenken in den Wunderschein,
myself immerse in the wonder-shine;

Und mir ist, als ob mich Engel riefen
and to me is, as if me angels called

In die alte Wunderstadt herein.
into the old wonder-city — .

And then I would like to dive into the depths,
to immerse myself in the wonderful shimmer;
and it feels to me as if angels called me
into the old, miraculous city.

> **Source:** Müller 1838, part 6: 63
>
> **Variant:** (Brahms = roman, Müller = *italic*)
> Stanza 6, line 2: Wunderschein = *Wiederschein* (reflection)

WILHELM Müller (1794–1827) was one of the minor poets of the early nineteenth century whose work was immortalized in Schubert's songs. Müller has a certain pride of place among them, being the author of both *Die schöne Müllerin* and *Die Winterreise*.

"Vineta" comes from a six-part collection of European "folk songs" entitled *Volksharfe* (The Harp of the People), where it is found as no. 52 in part 6.[11] Müller's name is found nowhere in the collection except in the table of contents as the author of two poems, "Vineta" not one of them.[12] From the foreword to vol. 1 it appears that Müller was commissioned to collect a variety of light, "easy-reading" poems for a popular series of anthologies.

The poem is the last of a set of seven supposed to be from the island of Rügen, at the northernmost tip of what was East Germany. Müller provides the following explanation of Vineta's mythology (Müller 1838, part 6: 63, tr. ed.):

> The legend of the ancient, magnificent city of Vineta, located between Pommerania and Rügen prior to its supposed sinking under the sea, increases in poeticism inversely to the actual evidence of it historical existence. The boatmen hear the sounds of its bells coming up from the depths of the sea, and the reflection of its towers on the water's surface is called the *Waseln*, a northern *fata morgana* [mirage].

---

[11]Represented are poems from Germany, Poland, Russia, Greece, Sweden, Denmark, Ireland, England, France, Spain, Slovakia, Bohemia, Estonia, Scotland, Serbia, and Switzerland.

[12]Although a number of poets are cited by name following their poems, Müller's is the only name to be found in any of the six tables of contents.

The image of the "lost city" must have appealed to the romantic in Brahms, just as it did to Debussy ("La cathédral engloutie") and Cowell ("The Tides of the Manaunaun"). And the metaphor for lost love must have made the poem yet more attractive. The last stanza implies that Vineta exerted a fatal, siren-like attraction on seafarers, which Brahms—whether purposely or not—underlined by setting the text for women's chorus.

Darthulas Grabesgesang, op. 42, no. 3
Darthula's Grave Song
"Ossian" (James Macpherson); trans. Johann Gottfried Herder

Mädchen von Kola, du schläfst!
"Maiden of Kola, you are sleeping!"

Um dich schweigen die blauen Ströme Selmas!
Around you are silent the blue streams of Selma!

Sie trauren um dich, den letzten Zweig
They mourn for you, the last branch

Von Thruthils Stamm!
of Truthill's lineage!

Wann erstehst du wieder in deiner Schöne?
When will rise you again in your beauty?

Schönste der Schönen in Erin!
Fairest of the fair in Erin!

Du schläfst im Grabe langen Schlaf,
You are sleeping in the grave long sleep,

Dein Morgenrot ist ferne!
Your dawn is distant!

Nimmer, o nimmer kommt dir die Sonne
Never, oh never comes to you the sun

Weckend an deine Ruhestätte: "Wach auf!
rousing to your resting-place: "Wake up!

Wach auf, Darthula!
Wake up, Darthula!

Frühling ist draußen!
Spring is abroad!"

Die Lüfte säuseln,
"The breeze rustles,

Auf grünen Hügeln, holdseliges Mädchen,
on green hills, loveliest maiden,

Weben die Blumen!
are waving the flowers!

Im Hain wallt sprießendes Laub!"
In the grove flutter budding leaves!"

Auf immer, auf immer so weiche denn, Sonne,
For ever, for ever thus withdraw then, sun,

Dem Mädchen von Kola, sie schläft!
[before] the maiden of Kola; she is sleeping!

Nie ersteht sie wieder in ihrer Schöne!
Never will rise she again in her beauty!

Nie siehst du sie lieblich wandeln mehr.
Never will see you her lovely wander more.

"Daughter of Colla! thou art low!"
[said Cairbar's hundred bards.]
Silence is at the blue streams of Seláma.
Truthill's race have failed.

When wilt thou rise in thy beauty,
first of Erin's maids?
Thy sleep is long in the tomb.
The morning distant far.

The sun shall not come
to thy bed and say, "Awake,
Dar-thulla! awake,
[thou first of women!]
the wind of spring is abroad."

"The flowers shake their heads
on the green hills.
The woods wave their growing leaves."

Retire, O sun!
the daughter of Colla is asleep.
She will not come forth in her beauty.
She will not move in the steps of her loveliness!

James Macpherson

Sources of text: *column 1:* Herder 1975: 263
column 2: Macpherson 1926: 355
Variants: (Brahms = roman, Herder = *italic*)
Stanza 2: der Schönen (of the beautiful) = *der Mädchen* (of the maidens)
Stanza 3: dir (to you) = *mehr* (again)

THE Celtic, Gaelic-speaking peoples of the British Isles, the Irish and Scottish, have a rich cultural history. Their legends, filled with historical mythology and mythological history, have been preserved orally through nearly two millennia, but very little was ever written down. To the Scottish people, it was therefore tantamount to finding the Holy Grail when in 1760 a twenty-four-year-old countryman named James Macpherson (1736–1796) began publishing the previously unknown writings of "Ossian," a legendary third-century Gaelic bard. The Scottish, who were suffering severe repression by their English neighbors to the south, rallied around Ossian as a symbol of their cultural identity and nationalism.

The excitement was also shared by literati all over Europe who had tired of the rationalism and formalized, neoclassic literary styles of the time and saw in Ossian's primitivism both a kindred spirit and a model for emulation. The melancholy and impending tragedy that suffuses the Ossian stories appealed to them, as did the notion of the ancient, "noble savage" who was able to write equally noble poems between battles.

Ossian's influence was particularly strong in pre-romantic Germany:

> Rebelliousness found direction and coherence in a fighting spirit that became the hallmark of a group of writers known as the Sturm und Drang school. These men, who had reached artistic maturity around 1770, were inspired by Shakespeare, Ossian, Young's *Night Thoughts* and *Conjectures on Original Composition*, Rousseau, and, to a lesser extent, Diderot. Theirs was essentially a liberal spirit; they resisted tyrrany, superstitition, and all restrictions on their freedom. Spontaneity was a cardinal virtue among them. They exalted nature, made strong emotion a virtue, and distrusted the artificial.

> Such virtues were codified by the movement's founder and pioneer, Johann Gottfried Herder. . . . Herder believed that ancient folk poetry, Macpherson's discovery of Ossian, and Percy's *Reliques*, should be taken as models for a new German aesthetic. . . . Herder exhorted writers to search for poetic inspiration from within their own national consciousnesses. (deGaetano 1989: 119–120)

Herder set the example by searching out, translating, and publishing a great deal of "folk" poetry from many countries, principally in a collection entitled *Stimmen der Völker in Liedern* (Voices of the People in Songs, 1778). Though he never translated any of the larger Ossian poems[13] in its entirety, he did translate fragments and excerpts, including the version of "Darthulas Grabesgesang" used by Brahms, which appeared with another Ossian excerpt in *Stimmen der Völker in Liedern*.

Herder's songs were originally in Church Latin, Danish, English, French, Greek, Italian, Lapp, Lithuanian, Morlack, Old Norse, Spanish, and Slovakian. Although he certainly did not have command of all these languages and must have published translations by other writers, they are never cited. The translations Herder selected for publication presumably followed his prescription for authenticity:

> . . . The wilder,—that is, more alive—the freer a people is (for this word means nothing more), the more alive, free, sensual, and lyrical must be the treatment of its songs, should it have them! The further a people is removed from an artificial, scientific way of thinking, speaking, and writing, the less should its songs be made for paper and dead print. (Herder's "Correspondence on Ossian and the Songs of Ancient Peoples," quoted in Reisiger 1970: 128, tr. ed.)

This philosophy was the foundation for Herder's blistering 1769 reviews of a German-language translation of Ossian by a Jesuit named M. Denis. While Herder found them beautiful, he also found their Classical Greek hexameter to be hopelessly anachronistic and civilized for a translation of "primitive," third-century prose. (Herder 1967–1968, 4: 320–325; 5: 322–330)

Despite Ossian's literary reception, the odor of a hoax could not be dispelled. The more sober reviewers saw no literary value in the poems if they were not authentic historical documents. Macpherson's credibility was not helped by his life-long refusal to produce the Gaelic manuscripts from which he had made his English "translations." Samuel Johnson openly called the Ossian poems a fraud, and engaged Macpherson in public conflict. The controversy raged until 1805, nine years after Macpherson's death and honorific burial in Westminster Abbey, when the Highland Society of Scotland issued a report that fell short of calling the Ossian poems a fraud but recognized their problems. It was not until the late nineteenth century that more sophisticated Gaelic scholarship showed that the poems could not possibly be original.

By that time, few really cared whether Macpherson's Ossian had truly sung his epics and set them to paper. Fake or not, they had already profoundly affected both the Scottish people and European literature. As early as 1805, Sir Walter Scott, a Scotsman himself, saw the larger picture:

> Rejecting the argument that the poems' importance rested on some narrow vision of Scottish patriotism and noble primitivism, Scott saw in them another significance. He found Macpherson a poet of remarkable strength who was "capable not only of making an enthusiastic impression on every mind susceptible to poetic beauty, but of giving a new tone to poetry throughout all Europe." (deGaetano 1989: 111)

---

[13]The Ossian works are conventionally referred to as "poems," although Macpherson's renderings were in prose.

The poems were translated into at least ten languages during Macpherson's lifetime and into even more thereafter. Herder, Klopstock, Goethe, and Schiller, to name but a few German poets, embraced Ossian and absorbed his influence. The romantic fascination with things primitive and exotic, and with cultural, ethnic, and national identity, whether real or imagined, had been kindled.

In addition to two epics (*Fingal* and *Temora*), Macpherson wrote some twenty smaller-scale Ossianic poems. One of these is *Dar-Thula* (Macpherson 1926: 341), the characters of which overlap in part with those of *Fingal*. The great warrior of *Fingal*, Cathullin, had three nephews who traveled to Ireland as boys at the behest of their father to learn the craft of war. On their arrival they learned of Cuthullin's death. Though very young and having no experience, one of the nephews, Nathos, took command of his uncle's army and confronted Cairbar the Usurper in several battles, which he won. Nathos's army turned against him, however, and fell in with Cairbar. On the way to Ulster after his army's mutiny, Nathos met the maiden Dar-Thula, who happened to be the object of Cairbar's desire. She fell in love with Nathos, foreswore Cairbar, and fled with her new beloved. Their happiness was short, as Cairbar slew Nathos and his brothers the next day. While he taunted Dar-Thula as she mourned over the body of Nathos, she was hit by an arrow and fell upon him, dying with her "hair spread wide on his face."

The text that Brahms chose consists of the penultimate paragraph of the poem, which immediately follows the death scene. The reader will find it interesting to compare Macpherson's original (right-hand column) with Herder's translation, which is loose in the extreme. Herder clearly was not concerned with literal meaning, but rather with achieving in German the same character of narrative that Macpherson had created in English. (Note Herder's omission of two lines, shown in square brackets.) Brahms himself altered his source in two places, making the first more poetic ("Schönste der Schönen") and the second more personal ("kommt dir die Sonne").

DREI MOTETTEN, op. 110
Three Motets

Ich aber bin elend, op. 110, no. 1
But I Am Miserable
Psalm 69: 29a; Exodus 34: 6, 7; Psalm 69: 29b

Ich aber bin elend, und mir ist wehe.
I, however, am miserable, and to me is woe.

But I am miserable and full of woe.

Herr, Herr Gott,
Lord, Lord God,

barmherzig und gnädig und geduldig,
compassionate and gracious and patient

und von großer Gnade und Treue,
and of great mercy and faithfulness,

der du beweisest Gnade in tausend Glied,
who you show mercy in thousand generations

und vergibst Missetat, Übertretung und Sünde,
and forgive misdeeds, trespassing, and sin,

und vor welchem niemand unschuldig ist;
and before whom no one innocent is:

Lord, Lord God,
compassionate, gracious, patient,
and full of endless mercy and constancy,
you who show mercy to a thousand generations
and forgive iniquity, trespasses, and sins,
and before whom no one is innocent:

Gott, Herr Gott, deine Hilfe schütze mich.
God, Lord God, your help protect me.

God, Lord God, may your help protect me.

Variant: Final line: "Herr Gott" is not Biblical

LIKE Bach, Brahms had an affinity for combining words from different sources into an original, coherent, and expressive text. The "Deutsches Requiem"* is a fine example, as is the motet "Warum ist das Licht gegeben,"* and on a smaller scale, the present work. In all three of the compositions cited, Brahms strives to find combinations of text that present a picture of misery, sadness, or affliction, and then hope or resolution. This task often sends him on a journey through the Bible—here to the books of Psalms and Exodus. Psalm 69 gave Brahms a statement of anguish followed by a prayer for salvation, and Exodus 34: 6, 7 provided a hymn of praise and supplication. He united the two by placing the verses from Exodus between the two sentences of the Psalm, in the manner of a Medieval trope.

Ach, arme Welt, op. 110, no. 2

Ah, Poor World

Author unknown

Ach, arme Welt, du trügest mich,
Ah, poor world, you deceive me,

Ja, das bekenn ich eigentlich,
yes, that admit I truthfully,

Und kann dich doch nicht meiden.
and can you still not avoid.

Du falsche Welt, du bist nicht wahr,
You false world, you are not true,

Dein Schein vergeht, das weiß ich zwar,
your luster fades, that know I indeed,

Mit Weh und großem Leiden.
with woe and great suffering.

Dein Ehr, dein Gut, du arme Welt,
Your glory, your wealth, you poor world,

Im Tod, in rechten Nöten fehlt,
in death, in real need is lacking,

Dein Schatz ist eitel falsches Geld,
your treasure is vain, false money,

Des hilf mir, Herr, zum Frieden.
in this help me, Lord, to peace.

Ah, poor world, you deceive me;
yes, I truthfully admit that,
and still I cannot avoid you.

You false world, you are not real;
your luster fades, indeed I know that,
with woe and great suffering.

Your glory and your wealth, you poor world,
are lacking in death and times of real need;
your treasure is vain, false money.
Help me, Lord, to be at peace with this.

AMONG Brahms's last six sacred works (opp. 109 and 110), "Ach arme Welt" stands out as the only one that was not written for double choir, and the only one set in a severe, note-on-note style, which nonetheless befits the austerity of the old, anonymous hymn text. The structure of the hymn presented a compositional problem in that the additional line in verse 3 did not fit the strophic setting of the first two verses. Brahms could have approached this rather unimaginatively by adding an anacrusis in m. 4, foregoing the first statement of the final line (it is stated twice in verses 1 and 2), and inserting the added line in its place. Instead, he added two extra measures after the first line and rewrote the music at the end of that line to bring the composition to a climax. He then returned to his original setting for the last two lines.

Wenn wir in höchsten Nöten sein, op. 110, no. 3

When We Are in Deepest Misery

Paul Eber

Wenn wir in höchsten Nöten sein
When we in deepest misery are

Und wissen nicht, wo aus und ein,
and know not, –what to do–,

Und finden weder Hilf noch Rat,
and find neither help nor counsel,

Ob wir gleich sorgen früh und spät,
whether we — are troubled early and late,

So ist das unser Trost allein,
thus is it our consolation alone

Daß wir zusammen insgemein
that we together commonly

Dich rufen an, o treuer Gott,
you implore —, O faithful God,

Um Rettung aus der Angst und Not.
for rescue from the fear and misery.

When we are in deepest misery
and know not what to do,
and find neither help nor counsel,
whether we are troubled early and late,

our only consolation is
that together we frequently
call on you, O faithful God,
for deliverance from our fear and misery.

Sieh nicht an unser Sünden groß,
Look not at our sins great;

Sprich uns davon aus Gnaden los;
absolve us thus out of mercy —,

Steh uns in unserm Elend bei,
stand by us in our misery —,

Mach uns von aller Trübsal frei;
make us from all sorrow free,

Auf daß von Herzen können wir
so that from heart can we

Nachmals mit Freuden danken dir,
afterwards with joy thank you,

Gehorsam sein nach deinem Wort,
obedient be to your word,

Dich allzeit preisen hier und dort.
you at all times praise here and there.

Consider not our great sins;
absolve us by your mercy,
stand by us in our misery,
and make us free from all sorrow,

so that afterwards, from our hearts,
we may joyfully thank you,
be obedient to your word,
and praise you at all times in all places.

Source:	Wackernagel 1964, 4:6	
Variants:		(Brahms = roman, Wackernagel = *italics*)
	Stanza 1, line 2:	und = *noch*
	Stanza 2, line 1:	das = *dies*
	line 2:	insgemein = *ingemein*
	line 3:	rufen an = *anrufen*
	Stanza 3, line 2:	davon = *derselb*
	line 4:	aller Trübsal = *allen Plagen*

BRAHMS chose Paul Eber's hymn of the same name as the text for this motet. He truncated it, however, by omitting verses 3–5 of the total of seven. He thus joined the opening and closing sentences of the hymn,[14] moving directly from the introductory idea of God's comfort in times of woe to an appeal for mercy, and a final hymn of praise.

Stulken (1981: 364–365) ascribes to Eber (1511–1569), one of the second-generation Lutheran reformers, a position second only to Luther among Wittenberg hymn composers. He was a student of Luther and student, friend, and secretary to Luther's close colleague and fellow-reformer Philipp Melanchthon. Eber received his divinity degree from Wittenberg and thereafter served as professor of Latin and later Physics and the New Testament. In 1558 he was appointed pastor of the city church and superintendent of the district.

"Wenn wir in höchsten Nöten sein" is an adaptation into German of the Latin "In tenebris nostrae et densa caligine mentis"[15] of Joachim Camerarius (1500–1574) of Nuremberg, one of Eber's early teachers and a professor of Greek and Latin at Nuremberg, Tübingen, and Leipzig. The hymn was published in broadsheet form c. 1560 and first appeared in a hymnal in 1566.

Eber's text illustrates the practice of many early Lutheran hymnists, including Luther himself, of eliding one verse to another; in the *Gesangbuch* of 1912, for example, only two of the first six verses end with terminal punctuation. In these cases the hymnists certainly considered their works to be like complete sermons, which were to be understood as a whole. When set to music, however, with the finality of a cadence at the end of each verse, the result can be confusing.

"Wenn wir in höchsten Nöten sein" is no. 282 in the *EKG* and no. 303 in the *LBW*, where it carries the title "When in the Hour of Deepest Need." The text of this hymn varies substantially among the hymnals consulted, and the text in various printed editions of the Brahms composition varies as well. For the present purposes the Carus edition (Brahms 1983) has been chosen to represent Brahms's text.

---

[14]The seven verses of the hymn consist of three sentences, with the first sentence comprising vv. 1–4 and the final sentence consisting of vv. 6–7.

[15]The text appears in Wackernagel 1964, 1: 324.

Brahms

DREI QUARTETTE, *op. 31*
Three Quartets

Wechsellied zum Tanze, op. 31, no. 1
Song of Exchanges at the Dance
Johann Wolfgang von Goethe

Die Gleichgültigen

Komm mit, o Schöne,
Come along, O beautiful one,

    komm mit mir zum Tanze;
    come with me to the dance!

Tanzen gehöret zum festlichen Tag.
Dancing belongs to the festive day.

Bist du mein Schatz nicht,
Are you my sweetheart not,

    so kannst du es werden.
    then can you it become.

Wirst du es nimmer,
become you it never,

    so tanzen wir doch.
    so dance we nevertheless.

Komm mit . . . zum festlichen Tag.

Die Zärtlichen

Ohne dich, Liebste,
Without you darling,

    was wären die Feste?
    what would be the festivals?

Ohne dich, Süße,
Without you sweet one,

    was wäre der Tanz?
    what would be the dance?

Wärst du mein Schatz nicht,
Were you my sweetheart not,

    so möcht ich nicht tanzen,
    then want I not to dance.

Bleibst du es immer
Remain you it always

    ist Leben ein Fest.
    is life a festival.

Ohne dich Liebste . . . was wäre der Tanz?

Die Gleichgültigen

Laß sie nur lieben,
Let them only love,

    und laß du uns tanzen!
    and let you us dance!

Schmachtende Liebe
Languishing love

    vermeidet den Tanz.
    avoids the dance.

Schlingen wir fröhlich
Intertwine we gaily

    den drehenden Reihen,
    the twisting roundelay.

Schleichen die andern
Sneak the others

    zum dämmernden Wald.
    to the dusky forest.

Laß sie nur lieben . . . was wäre der Tanz?

The Indifferent Ones

Come along, you beautiful one,
    come with me to the dance!
Dancing belongs to the festive day.

If you are not my sweetheart,
    then you can become my sweetheart.
Even if you never become my sweetheart,
    we can still dance.

Come along, beautiful one,
    come with me to the dance!
Dancing belongs to the festive day.

The Affectionate Ones

Without you, darling,
    what would the celebration be?
Without you, sweet one,
    what would the dance be?

Were you not my sweetheart,
    then I would not want to dance.
Always be my sweetheart,
    and life will be a celebration!

Without you, darling,
    what would the celebration be?
Without you, sweet one,
what would the dance be?

The Indifferent Ones

Just let them love,
    and you let us dance!
Languishing love
    avoids the dance.

We intertwine gaily
    in the shifting roundlay.
The others sneak off
    to the dusky woods.

Just let them love
    and let us dance!
Languishing love
    avoids the dance.

Die Zärtlichen

Laß sie sich drehen,
Let them — turn around,

    und laß du uns wandeln!
    and let you us wander!

Wandeln der Liebe
Wandering of love

    ist himmlischer Tanz.
    is heavenly dance.

Amor, der nahe,
Amor the close one,

    der höret sie spotten,
    who hears them ridicule,

Rächet sich einmal
Revenges — some time

    und rächet sich bald.
    and revenges — soon.

Laß sie nur drehen . . . ist himmlischer Tanz.

The Affectionate Ones

Let them whirl around
    and you, let us wander!
The wandering of lovers
    is a heavenly dance!

Amor, the intimate one,
    who hears them ridicule,
will take revenge some day,
    and will take it some day soon.

Let them whirl around
    and you let us wander!
The wandering of lovers
    is a heavenly dance!

Source: Goethe 1948–, 1: 24
Variant: (Brahms = roman, Goethe = *italic*)
Stanza 1, line 10: gehöret (belongs) = *verherrlicht* (makes glorious)

GOETHE'S poem, probably dating from the 1780s, provides four vignettes of two couples at a dance. The first couple ("the indifferent ones") is attracted to dancing but not to each other, and the second ("the "affectionate ones") is madly in love and yearning to escape. In their respective second stanzas, the couples mock each other—the "indifferent ones" scoff at their counterparts, saying, "The others sneak off into the dusky woods. Just let them love and let us dance." "The affectionate ones" answer, saying, "Let them whirl around and you, let us wander! The wandering of lovers is a heavenly dance!"

Brahms complements Goethe's poem most effectively through his music. He assigns the role of "the indifferent ones" to the lower, heavier voices (alto and bass) and gives them ponderous lines in the minor mode that perhaps suggest heavy-footed, clumsy dancing. "The affectionate ones," on the other hand, the lighter sopranos and tenors, sing in the major mode and have lovely, lyric lines that soar romantically into the upper range. These musical differences between the two couples paint the contrast between them perhaps better than the words. Brahms had to devise a means to conclude the song, and he decided on the same device that he was to use in "Neckereien." The two couples repeat their final lines, first separately and them simultaneously, with neither having the last word.

At the end of each stanza the dancers repeat its opening four lines. The repeat is identical except in stanza 1, where Goethe replaces "tanzen gehöret zum festlichen Tag" (dancing belongs to the festive day) with "tanzen verherrlicht den festlichen Tag" (dancing makes the festive day more glorious). Possibly because this would have been too tender for "the indifferent ones," Brahms repeated the opening words as Goethe did in the other three stanzas.

Neckereien, op. 31, no. 2
Teasing
Moravian; Josef Wenzig, trans.

Fürwahr, mein Liebchen,
Indeed, my sweetheart,

    ich will nun frein,
    I want to now court,

Ich führ als Weibchen
I introduce as dear wife

    dich bei mir ein,
    you –at my house– —.

Mein wirst du, o Liebchen,
mine will become you, O darling,

    fürwahr du wirst mein,
    indeed you will become mine,

Und wolltest dus
and wanted you it

    auch nicht sein.
    even not to be.

Indeed, my sweetheart, I want to court you,
to introduce you as my dear wife at my house.
You'll be mine, my darling, indeed you will be mine,
even if you don't want to be.

85

So werd ich ein Täubchen
Thus become I a little dove

  von weißer Gestalt,
  of white shape;

Ich will schon entfliehen,
I want to already fly away,

  ich flieg in den Wald.
  I fly into the forest.

Mag dennoch nicht Deine,
Want nevertheless not yours,

  mag dennoch nicht dein,
  want nevertheless not your,

Nicht eine Stunde sein.
not one hour to be.

Then I'll become a little white dove;
I already want to fly away, I want to fly into the forest.
I don't want to be yours, I don't want to be your
  sweetheart,
not for one hour.

Ich hab wohl ein Flintchen,
I have — a flintlock,

  das trifft gar bald,
  that will hit pretty easily;

Ich schieß mir das Täubchen
I shoot me the little dove

  herunter im Wald.
  down in the forest.

Mein wirst du, o Liebchen, führwahr du wirst mein,
Und wolltest dus auch nicht sein.

I have a good little rifle that shoots pretty easily;
I will shoot down the little dove there in the forest.
You'll be mine, my darling, indeed you will be mine,
even if you don't want to be.

So werd ich ein Fischchen,
Thus become I a little fish,

  ein goldener Fisch,
  a golden fish;

Ich will schon entspringen
I will indeed escape

  ins Wasser frisch.
  into the water fresh.

Mag dennoch nicht Deine, mag dennoch nicht dein,
Nicht eine Stunde sein.

Then I'll become a little fish, a golden fish;
I will indeed escape into the fresh water.
I don't want to be yours, I don't want to be your
  sweetheart,
not for one hour.

Ich hab wohl ein Netzchen,
I have — a little net,

  das fischt gar gut,
  that fishes quite well;

Ich fang mir den goldenen
I will catch me the golden

  fisch in der Flut.
  fish in the stream.

Mein wirst du, o Liebchen, führwahr du wirst mein,
Und wolltest dus auch nicht sein.

I have a good little net that fishes quite well;
I'll catch me the golden fish in the stream.
You'll be mine, my darling, indeed you will be mine,
even if you don't want to be.

So werd ich ein Häschen
Thus become I a bunny

  voll Schnelligkeit,
  full of speed,

Und lauf in die Felder,
and run into the field,

  die Felder breit,
  the field wide.

Mag dennoch nicht Deine, mag dennoch nicht dein,
Auch nicht eine Stunde sein.

Then I'll become a bunny, full of speed,
and run off into the field, the wide field.
I don't want to be yours, I don't want to be your
  sweetheart,
not even for one hour.

Ich hab wohl ein Hündchen,
I have — a little dog,

　　gar pfiffig und fein,
　　rather clever and sly,

Das fängt mir das Häschen
that will catch me the bunny

　　im Felde schon ein.
　　in the field surely —.

Mein wirst du, o Liebchen, fühwahr du wirst mein,
Und wolltest dus auch nicht sein.

I have a good little dog, rather clever and sly,
that will surely catch the bunny in the field.
You'll be mine, my darling, indeed you will be
　mine,
even if you don't want to be.

Source:	Wenzig 1830: 72
Variants:	(Brahms = roman, Wenzig = *italics*)
Stanzas 2, 4, 6, line 3:	mag dennoch nicht deine = *mag doch nicht die deine*

LIKE many composers of his era and more than most, Johannes Brahms (1833–1897) was fascinated by folk poetry and music. His works reflect their influence in many ways, but most obviously in his choice of librettos. A collection of Slavic poetry, translated into German by Josef Wenzig (1807–1876) in 1830,[16] provided Brahms with the texts to five of his compositions, including two of his best known choral works, "Neckereien" and "Der Gang zum Liebchen,"* as well as "Verlorene Jugend."* Wenzig's minor fame rests largely on the texts that Brahms set to music, but also on his authorship of the German libretto for Smetana's opera *Dalibor*, which he wrote in 1865–1867.

Brahms was particularly fond of dialogues (see also "Fragen"* and "Wechsellied zum Tanz"*), and "Neckereien" is one of his best. The poem begins with an overconfident suitor expressing his love for a young lady who flirts while spurning his advances. In the second stanza she explains how she will evade him. He then concocts a wild, new plan to win her hand, and she again tells him how she will foil it. In the suitor's portion of the fourth exchange, the seventh and last stanza of the poem, Brahms found a creative way to bring the song to an end. As the suitor declares for the last time that he will have her for his own, she *simultaneously* declares that he will not. The two compete against each other for the rest of the song, which Brahms climaxes with a nearly unplayable piano flourish.

In Wenzig's collection "Neckereien" is entitled "Mein wirst du, o Liebchen," after the refrain that follows the passages for male chorus. Although labeled as being of Moravian origin, it is in the "Bohemian" section of the book.

Der Gang zum Liebchen, op. 31, no. 3

The Walk to the Beloved
Bohemian; Josef Wenzig, trans.

Es glänzt der Mond nieder,
— shines the moon down;

Ich sollte doch wieder
I should — again

Zu meinem Liebchen,
to my belovéd.

Wie mag is ihr gehn?
How may it for her go?

The moon shines down;
I really should return
to my belovéd.
How is it for her?

Ach weh, sie verzaget
Ah woe, she despairs

Und klaget, und klaget,
and laments and laments

Daß sie mich nimmer
that she me never

Im Leben wird sehn!
in life will see.

Alas, she despairs
and bewails and bemoans
that she will never see me
in this life again.

---

[16]*Slawische Volkslieder, übersetzt von Joseph Wenzig*. Halle: Renger, 1830. Ophüls and other sources give the title of this work as *Slowakische Volkslieder*, which is inconsistent with the title on the copy obtained by the editors. The author's first name is spelled differently in various sources.

Es ging der Mond unter, **— went the moon under;**	The moon went down; I hurried very quickly, I hurried so that no one would abduct my belovéd.
Ich elite doch munter, **I hurried — quickly,**	
Und eilte, daß keiner **and hurried, that no one**	
Mein Liebchen entführt. **my belovéd abduct.**	
Ihr Täubchen, o girret, **You little doves, O coo,**	O coo, you little doves, and whir, you gentle breezes, so that no one will abduct my belovéd.
Ihr Lüftchen, o schwirret, **you little breezes, O whir,**	
Daß keiner mein Liebchen, **that no one my belovéd,**	
Mein Liebchen entführt. **my belovéd abduct.**	

Source: Wenzig 1830: 54

*T*HIS work represents Brahms's second choral setting of a text from Josef Wenzig's 1830 collection of Slavic poetry. (See "Neckereien"* and "Verlorene Jugend."*) The poem is simple and straightforward, relating the thoughts of a lover as he walks to his sweetheart under the moonlight. A particularly nice touch in the last stanza is Wenzig's use of the onomatopoetic verbs "girret" (coo) and "schwirret" (whir), which consequently should have emphasized "r"s in performance.

DREI QUARTETTE, op. 64
Three Quartets

An die Heimat, op. 64, no. 1
To My Homeland
C.O. Sternau (Otto Inkermann)

Heimat! **Homeland!**	Homeland! Wonderful-sounding word! As if on feathered wings you draw my heart toward you. Rejoicing, as if I must bring the greeting of each soul to you, step by step I come to you, friendly homeland!
Wunderbar tönendes Wort! **Wonderful sounding word!**	
Wie auf befiederten Schwingen **Like on feathered wings**	
Ziehst du mein Herz zu dir fort. **draw you my heart to you away.**	
Jubelnd, als müßt ich den Gruß **Rejoicing, as if must I the greeting**	
Jeglicher Seele dir bringen, **of each soul to you bring,**	
Trag ich zu dir meinen Fuß, **carry I to you my foot,**	
Freundliche Heimat! **friendly homeland!**	

Heimat!
Homeland!

Bei dem sanft klingenden Ton
With the softly sounding music

Wecken mich alte Gesänge,
awaken me old songs

Die in der Ferne mich flohn;
that in the distant land me escaped;

Rufen mir freudenvoll zu
call to me joyfully —

Heimatlich lockende Klänge,
homeland-like luring sounds,

Du nur allein bist die Ruh,
you only alone are the rest,

Schützende Heimat!
sheltering homeland!

Homeland!
The softly sounding music
of old songs awakens in me
songs I had forgotten in far-off lands.
Beckoning sounds of my homeland
call joyfully to me;
you alone calm me,
sheltering homeland!

Heimat!
Homeland!

Gib mir den Frieden zurück,
Give me the peace back

Den ich im Weiten verloren,
that I in the expanses lost;

Gib mir dein blühendes Glück!
give me your flowering happiness!

Unter den Bäumen am Bach,
Under the trees at the brook

Wo ich vor Zeiten geboren,
where I before times was born,

Gib mir ein schützendes Dach,
give me a sheltering roof,

Liebende Heimat!
loving homeland!

Homeland!
Return to me the peace
that I lost in faraway places;
grant me your bountiful happiness!
Under the trees by the brook
where I was born so long ago,
give me a sheltering roof,
loving homeland!

O TTO Inkermann (1820–1862), better known by his pen-name C.O. Sternau, published this poem in a collection entitled *Mein Orient* (My Orient) in 1840. It was reprinted in his *Gedichte* (Poems) of 1851, the source from which Brahms likely obtained it shortly after its publication.

Brahms's friend and later biographer Max Kalbeck reported that the young composer wrote it into his notebook, as he did any poem that interested him, and indicated that he should set it to music. (Kalbeck 1976, 1: 97) Brahms carried his notebook(s) around with him, waiting for the right experience or emotion to trigger a response to a particular poem, at which time he would compose. Kalbeck writes that the moment of truth arrived for "An Die Heimat" some ten years later, at Christmas of 1863,[17] when melodic ideas materialized for him. Perhaps he was reminded of the second stanza of the poem, in which "the softly sounding music of old songs awakens in me songs I had forgotten of far-off lands." He finished the quartet the following summer.

Brahms had reason to feel the homesickness that is the subject of Sternau's poem. He had spent all of his twenty-nine years in Hamburg and in the previous summer had moved to Vienna, a magnificent city and the home of a thriving artistic life—but it was not *his home*. According to Kalbeck the longing he felt for Christmases past, family, and friends—the "friendly," "sheltering," "loving homeland" of the poem—found expression in this composition. (Kalbeck 1976, 2: 43)

It appears that little is known of C.O. Sternau other than the publication information given above and the fact that he was the author of the libretto to Carl Maria von Weber's opera *Preciosa*.

---

[17]*The New Grove* dates the composition 1862–63. Kalbeck (1976, 1: 98) gives the date of Brahms's melodic inspiration as Christmas, 1863, which would have to be a year late if *The New Grove* is correct.

Der Abend, op. 64, no. 2

Evening

Friedrich Schiller

Senke, strahlender Gott— die Fluren dürsten **Sink, radiant God— the fields thirst**	Let it sink, radiant God—the fields thirst for refreshing dew; the people languish; the steeds are weary— let the chariot sink down!
Nach erquickendem Tau, der Mensch verschmachtet, **for refreshing dew; the people languish;**	
Matter ziehen die Rosse— **weakly pull the steeds—**	
Senke den Wagen hinab! **sink the wagon down!**	
Siehe, wer aus des Meers krystallner Woge **See, who from the sea's crystalline wave**	Behold the one who beckons to you, sweetly smiling, from the sea's crystalline wave! Does your heart recognize her? Faster fly the steeds; Tethys, the divine one, beckons.
Lieblich lächelnd dir winkt! Erkennt dein Herz sie? **sweetly smiling you signals! Know your heart her?**	
Rascher fliegen die Rosse, **Faster fly the steeds;**	
Thetys, die göttliche, winkt. **Tethys, the divine one, beckons.**	
Schnell vom Wagen herab in ihre Arme **Quickly from chariot down into her arms**	The driver leaps quickly from the chariot into her arms. Cupid seizes the reins; the steeds stand still and drink at the cooling stream.
Springt der Führer, den Zaum ergreift Cupido, **leaps the driver. The bridle seizes Cupid;**	
Stille halten die Rosse, **still hold the steeds**	
Trinken die kühlende Flut. **drink the cooling stream.**	
An dem Himmel herauf mit leisen Schritten **On the sky upward with quiet steps**	Ascending in the sky with quiet steps comes the fragrant night; sweet love follows. Rest and love! Phoebus, the loving one, rests.
Kommt die duftende Nacht, ihr folgt die süße Liebe. **comes the fragrant night; it follows — sweet love.**	
Ruhet und liebet! **Rest and love!**	
Phöbus, der liebende, ruht. **Phoebus, the loving one, rests.**	

Source: Schiller 1867, 1: 149

Variant: (Brahms = roman; Schiller = *italics*)

      Stanza 2, line 4:   Thetys = *Thetis*

SCHILLER'S "Der Abend" was written in the fall of 1795 and first appeared in print that winter in the *Musen-Almanach für das Jahr 1796* (Annual Poetical Review for the Year 1796). Schiller noted that it was "nach einem Gemälde" (based on a painting). That may have been so, but there is no hint in the literature as to which painting that might be.

"Der Abend" is an "evening poem," an example of the German romantic love of nature and its rhythms that engendered individual poems and even entire cycles devoted to the seasons and the changing times of day. The poet's picture of a hot summer afternoon cooling into night is couched in Greek mythology and features three personages from the Greek pantheon. Phoebus (Apollo) is pictured as driving the chariot of the sun through the sky, bringing light and—in summer—parching heat to the earth. As the day wanes, the sea goddess Thetys [English = Tethys] (whom Schiller erroneously calls "Thetis" [English = Thetis]),[18] beckons invitingly, and Phoebus spurs his steeds forward, carrying the sun to the sea's horizon. There he leaps into the arms of the goddess while his horses are attended by Cupid, the god of love. As the lovers embrace, the world settles into the sweetness of night.

The amorous lives of the Greek gods were complicated and often in conflict with what would be acceptable among mortals. Here, for example, Schiller has Phoebus, the son of Zeus, consorting with the

---

[18]Thetys [Tethys], known as the "lovely queen of the sea," was the wife of Oceanus, mother of three thousand Oceanids and all the rivers. Thetis [Thetis], a sea goddess, was the daughter of Nereus and Doris and mother of Achilles (see Brahms's "Nänie."*)

goddess who was the object of his father's love. Zeus would not marry her, however, because of a prophesy that their son would exceed Zeus in power.

A bit of confusion also attaches to the question of who should be driving the sun's chariot. The duty of bringing light to the earth rightly belonged to the god of the sun, Helios. With time and the ascendency of Phoebus in popularity, however, the two characters became confused and ultimately amalgamated in mythology.

Fragen, op. 64, no. 3
Questions
Turkish; Georg Friedrich Daumer, trans.

[Ich sprach zum Herzen:]

"Mein liebes Herz, was ist dir?"
"My dear heart, what is you?"

[Es sprach:]

"Ich bin verliebt, das ist mir."
"I am in love, that is me."

"Wie ist dir denn zu Mut?"
"How is to you then to spirit?"

"Ich brenn' in Höllenglut."
"I am burning in hell's fire."

"Erquicket dich kein Schlummer?"
"Refreshes you no slumber?"

"Den litte Qual und Kummer?"
"Who suffered torment and grief?"

"Gelingt kein Widerstand?"
"Succeeds no resistance?"

"Wie doch, bei solchem Brand?"
"How then, with such a fire?"

"Ich hoffe, Zeit wird's wenden."
"I hope, time will it change."

Es wird's der Tod nur enden."
It will it — death only end."

"Was gäbst du, sie zu seh'n?"
"What would give you, her to see?"

"Mich, dich, Welt, Himmelshöh'n."
"Myself, you, world, heaven's heights."

"Du redest ohne Sinn."
"You talk without sense."

"Weil ich in Liebe bin."
"Because I in love am."

"Du mußt vernünftig sein."
"You must rational be."

"Das heißt, so kalt wie Stein."
"That means, as cold as stone."

"Du wirst zu Grunde gehn/gehen."
"You will to ground go."

"Ach, möcht' es bald geschehn/geschehen!"
"Alas, may it soon happen!"

[I said to my heart:]

"My dear heart, what's wrong with you?"

[It said:]

"I'm in love, that's what."

"How do you feel?"

"I'm burning in hell's fire."

"Doesn't sleep refresh you?"

"One who suffered torment and grief?"

"Doesn't resistance help?"

"How can it with such a fire?"

"I hope time will change it."

"Only death will end it."

"What would you give to see her?"

"Myself, you, the world, the heights of heaven."

"You're talking nonsense."

"Because I'm in love."

"You must be reasonable."

"That means as cold as stone."

"You will perish!"

"Ah, may it happen soon!"

Source: Daumer 1855, 1: 248
Variant: The opening words *Mein liebes* do not appear in the original.

JOHANNES Brahms was fond of dialogue texts that permitted him to characterize different singers or groups of singers in contrasting ways. Included in this volume are three such works, "Neckereien," "Wechsellied zum Tanz," and the present song, based on a Turkish poem from an anthology called *Polydora*, assembled and translated by Georg Friedrich Daumer (1800–1875). "Fragen" is unique in that it is an out-of-body dialogue between a lover's head (the objective voice) and his heart (the passionate voice), in which his heart expresses distress at the absence of its love, and his head tries in vain to talk sense into the heart.

Brahms set this text in 1874 as he was working on his second set of *Liebeslieder,** the *Neue Liebeslieder,** op. 65. He had chosen the texts for both sets from Daumer's collection, and the poem "Fragen" had caught his notice but did not fit the format of either *Liebeslieder*. The op. 64 quartets[19] provided an opportunity to use it. For discussion of the texts from *Polydora*, see the annotation the *Liebeslieder* waltzes, op. 52.

The composer faced a challenge in translating the written poem into music for listening. Daumer preceded each statement with a heading telling who was speaking. The poem thus begins, "I said to my heart," and each succeeding line is introduced with "it said" or "I said" in alternation. Clearly this would be too distracting in a musical presentation. Brahms got around the problem by eliminating the headings, beginning the poem with the direct address "My dear heart," and having the two roles represented by different voice parts. He closed with the same device that he had used in "Neckereien" and "Wechsellied zum Tanz," having both parts sing their final lines simultaneously:

> The head: You will perish!
> The heart: Ah, may it happen soon!

This can be read in two ways: either the head and the heart leave their argument unresolved, with both talking and neither listening, or they come together in agreement. Brahms leaves the choice to the listener.

---

[19]Prior to the publication of the op. 64 quartets, Brahms wrote to his publisher, C.F. Peters, that the pieces could be published either as a set or separately, as "it is possible that they occasionally might be sung by a small choir." Thereupon Peters changed the heading "Quartets" to "Quartets—or for small chorus." Brahms wrote back disapprovingly:

> When I wrote so [of chamber-choir performance], I meant that we should take silent notice of the current bad habit of doing everything with more or less poor taste as differently as possible from what the composer wrote. It [the inscription "or for small chorus"] should not be taken as an encouragement, to begin with, to have "Der Abend" or "Die drei Fragenden" [sic] sung by a small choir. The next thing you know they'll be doing my *Liebeslieder* with choir or even with orchestra! (Kalbeck 1976, 3: 32, tr. ed.)

Ein deutsches Requiem, op. 45
A German Requiem

1. Chorus
Matthew 5: 4; Psalm 126: 5–6

Selig   sind, die da Leid tragen,
Blessed are, who — grief bear,

denn sie sollen getröstet werden.
for they shall comforted be.

Die   mit Tränen säen,
Who with tears   sow,

werden mit Freuden ernten.
will   with joys   harvest.

Sie   gehen hin und weinen,
They go   forth and weep,

und tragen edlen Samen,
and   bear precious seeds,

und kommen mit Freuden
and   come with joys,

und bringen ihre Garben.
and   bring their sheaves.

Blessed are those who mourn,
for they shall be comforted.

Those who sow with tears
will reap with joy.
They go forth and weep,
bearing precious seeds,
and return rejoicing,
bringing their sheaves.

2. Chorus
1 Peter 1: 24; James 5: 7, 8a; 1 Peter 1: 25; Isaiah 35: 10

Denn alles Fleisch es ist wie Gras
For   all flesh — is like grass,

und alle Herrlichkeit des Menschen
and all magnificence of   mortals

wie des Grases Blumen.
like the grasses' flowers.

Das Gras ist verdorret
The grass has dried up,

und die Blume abgefallen.
and the flower fallen off.

For all flesh is like the grass,
and all the magnificence of mortals
is like the flowers of the grass.
The grass has withered,
and the flower has fallen away.

So seid nun geduldig, lieben Brüder,
So be now patient,   dear brothers,

bis auf die Zukunft des   Herrn.
until the   future of the Lord.

Siehe,   ein Ackermann wartet
Behold, a husbandman waits

auf die köstliche Frucht der Erde
for the precious fruit of the earth

und ist geduldig darüber, bis er empfahe
and is patient about it until he receives

den Morgenregen und Abendregen.
the morning-rain and evening-rain.

So now be patient, dear friends,
until the life hereafter.
Behold, a husbandman waits
for the precious fruit of the earth
and is patient
until he receives
the early and later rain.

Aber des Herrn Wort bleibet in Ewigkeit.
But the Lord's word remains in eternity.

But the word of the Lord endures forever.

Die Erlöseten des Herrn werden wieder kommen,
The redeemed of the Lord   will   again   come

und gen Zion kommen mit   Jauchzen;
and to Zion come   with shouts of joy;

ewige Freude wird über ihrem Haupte sein;
eternal joy   will upon their head be,

Freude und Wonne werden sie ergreifen
joy   and delight will   them   seize

und Schmerz und Seufzen wird   weg müssen.
and sorrow and sighing will [go] away have to.

The redeemed of the Lord will return
and come to Zion with shouts of joy;
eternal joy will be upon their heads,
joy and delight will overcome them
and sorrow and sighing will have to depart.

93

3. Baritone Solo and Chorus
Psalm 39: 4–7; Wisdom of Solomon 3: 1

Herr, lehre doch mich,
Lord, teach — me,

daß ein Ende mit mir haben muß,
that an end with me have must,

und mein Leben ein Ziel hat,
and my life an end has,

und ich davon muß.
and I away must.

Lord, teach me
that I must have an end,
and that my life has an end,
and that I must pass away.

Siehe, meine Tage sind
Behold, my days are

einer Hand breit vor dir,
a hand wide before you,

und mein Leben ist wie nichts vor dir.
and my life is as nothing before you.

Ach, wie gar nichts sind alle Menschen,
Ah, how –nothing at all– are all mortals,

die doch so sicher leben.
who yet so confidently live.

Behold, my days here
are but a handbreadth before you,
and my life is nothing before you.
Ah, how insignificant all mortals are,
and yet they live so confidently.

Sie gehen daher wie ein Schemen,
They go about like a phantom

und machen ihnen viel vergebliche Unruhe;
and create them much vain unrest;

sie sammeln und wissen nicht
they gather and know not

wer es kriegen wird.
who it receive will.

Nun Herr, wes soll ich mich trösten?
Now Lord, in whom shall I myself comfort?

Ich hoffe auf dich.
I trust in you.

They go about like a phantom
and create so much vain disquiet;
they gather things and know not
who will receive them.
Now, Lord, in whom shall I find consolation?
I trust in you.

Der Gerechten Seelen sind in Gottes Hand,
The righteous' souls are in God's hand,

und keine Qual rühret sie an.
and no torment touches them —.

The souls of the righteous are in God's hands,
and no torment touches them.

4. Chorus
Psalm 84: 1, 2, 4

Wie lieblich sind deine Wohnungen,
How lovely are your dwellings,

Herr Zebaoth!
Lord Sabaoth!

Meine Seele verlanget und sehnet sich
My soul yearns and longs —

nach den Vorhöfen des Herrn;
for the courts of the Lord;

mein Leib und Seele freuen sich
my body and soul rejoice —

in dem lebendigen Gott.
in the living God.

How lovely are your dwellings,
O Lord of Hosts!
My soul yearns and longs
for the courts of the Lord;
my body and soul rejoice
in the living God.

Wohl denen, die in deinem Hause wohnen,
Well-being to those, who in your house dwell,

die loben dich immerdar.
who praise you forever.

Blessed are those who dwell in your house,
those who praise you forever more.

5. Soprano Solo and Chorus
John 16: 22; Isaiah 66: 13; Ecclesiasticus 51: 35

Ihr   habt   nun   Traurigkeit;
You have now   sorrow;

aber ich   will   euch wieder sehen
but   I   want to you   again   see,

und euer Herz   soll   sich   freuen
and your heart shall   —   rejoice,

und eure Freude soll niemand von euch nehmen.
and your joy   shall no one   from you   take.

You now have sorrow;
but I want to see you again,
and your heart shall rejoice,
and no one shall take your joy from you.

Sehet   mich an:
Look at   me   —:

Ich habe eine kleine Zeit Mühe und Arbeit gehabt,
I   have a   brief time toil and labor   had,

und habe großen Trost funden.
and have   great   comfort found.

Look upon me:
I have toiled and labored a brief time,
and now I have found great comfort.

Ich will   euch trösten,
I   want to you comfort,

wie einen seine Mutter   tröstet.
as   one   his   mother comforts.

I want to comfort you,
as one is comforted by his mother.

6. Chorus and Baritone Solo
Hebrews 13: 14; 1 Corinthians 15: 51, 52, 54, 55; Revelation 4: 11

Denn wir haben hie kleine bleibende Statt,
For   we have here no   permanent place,

sondern die   zukünftige suchen wir.
but   the one to come   seek   we.

For here we have no permanent place,
but we seek the one to come.

Siehe,   ich sage euch ein Geheimnis:
Behold, I   tell you   a   mystery:

Wir werden nicht alle entschlafen,
We   will   not all   fall asleep,

wir werden aber   alle verwandelt werden;
we will, however, all   transformed   be;

und   dasselbige plötzlich in einem Augenblick
and the selfsame suddenly in   an   instant,

zu der Zeit der letzten Posaune.
at the time of the last   trombone.

Denn es wird die Posaune schallen
For   —   will the trombone sound,

und die Toten werden auferstehen unverweslich,
and the dead   will   rise up   incorruptible,

und wir werden verwandelt werden.
and we   will   transformed   be.

Dann wird erfüllet werden
Then will fulfilled   be

das Wort, das geschrieben steht:
the word, that written   stands:

Der Tod ist verschlungen in den Sieg.
— death is swallowed up in — victory.

Tod,   wo   ist dein Stachel?
Death, where is your sting?

Hölle, wo   ist dein Sieg?
Hell, where is your victory?

Behold, I tell you a mystery:
we will not all die,
but we will all be transformed,
and transformed suddenly, in an instant,
at the time of the last trumpet.
For the trumpet will sound,
and the dead will rise up incorruptible,
and we will be transformed.
Then will be fulfilled
the word that is written:
"Death is swallowed up in victory.
Death, where is your sting?
Hell, where is your victory?"

Herr, du bist würdig zu nehmen
Lord, you are worthy to receive

Preis und Ehre und Kraft,
praise and honor and might,

denn du hast alle Dinge geschaffen,
for you have all things created,

und durch deinen Willen haben sie
and by your will have they

das Wesen und sind geschaffen.
— being and are created.

Lord, you are worthy to receive
praise and honor and might,
for you have created all things,
and by your will they have
their being and are created.

7. Chorus
Revelation 14: 13

Selig sind die Toten,
Blessed are the dead,

die in dem Herren sterben
who in the Lord die

von nun an.
from now on.

Ja, der Geist spricht,
Yes, the Spirit says

daß sie ruhen von ihrer Arbeit,
that they rest from their labor,

denn ihre Werke folgen ihnen nach.
for their works follow them after.

Blessed are the dead
who die in the Lord
from now on.
Yea, the Spirit says
that they may rest from their labor,
for their works follow after them.

JOHANNES Brahms was highy sensitive to his texts, both in his choice of them and how he set them to music. This skill was surely at its most acute in his choice and combination of verses from the Bible—a particular irony considering that he was not at all conventionally devout and was perhaps agnostic. Heinz Beckler, the author of the essay on Brahms in *The New Grove*, explains his spiritual orientation as follows:

> Brahms was never "religious" in the strict sense of the word, but in the humane sense he was a Christian. The habits which outlasted his childhood included reading from the children's Bible he was given in the year of his birth and from which he compiled the texts for his sacred choral works. He read it constantly; to the end of his life it remained his book of books, and his correspondence is astonishing for its subtle grasp of problems in the scriptures. His personal religious viewpoint was logically thought out, as shown in his confessional *German Requiem*, which suppressed the eschatological objectives of the Christian faith in favor of a pious orientation to this world. "Life steals more from one than does death," he remarked once about himself. K.M. Reintaler tried to persuade him to add an appropriate movement to bring the *Requiem* nearer the spirit of Good Friday; Brahms politely but firmly refused, and the final passages of the work are dominated not by a vision of merciless death but by comfort for those who are left to mourn. (Beckler 1980: 162)

Brahms's choice of texts for the *Requiem* illustrates his intimate knowledge of the Bible. He assembled the libretto himself, taking verses from eleven different Biblical and Apocryphal books, with as many as five passages from four books in a single movement (no. 2). Nonetheless, the disparate verses fit together as if they had been so conceived.

Some of the sacred works of Brahms based on Biblical texts exhibit a particular structure in which a statement of misery, affliction, or sadness is followed by uplifting and comforting words, usually from elsewhere in the Bible. This organization characterizes four of the seven movements in the *Requiem*, nos. 2, 3, 5, and 6. The remaining three movements reflect happiness in the contemplation of heaven (no. 4), and hope and comfort for the living and the dead (nos. 1 and 7, respectively). The resultant structure is symmetrical, built around the fourth movement, the only one completely unburdened by any reference to death.

1	2	3
Selig sind die da Leid tragen.	Denn alles fleisch, es ist wie Gras . . . . *Aber des Herrn Wort bleibet in Ewigkeit.*	Herr, lehre doch mich, daß ein Ende mit mir haben muß . . . . *Der Gerechten Seelen sind in Gottes Hand und keine Qual rühret sie an.*
Blessed are those who mourn.	For all flesh is like the grass . . . . *But the word of the Lord endures forever.*	Lord, teach me that I must have an end . . . . *The souls of the righteous are in the hands of God, and no torment touches them.*

	4	
	Wie lieblich sind deine Wohnungen, Herr Zebaoth!	
	How lovely are your dwellings, O Lord of Hosts!	

5	6	7
Ihr habt nun Traurigkeit . . . . *Ich will euch trösten.*	Denn wir haben hie keine bleibende Statt . . . . *Herr, du bist würdig zu nehmen Preis und Ehre und Kraft.*	Selig sind die Toten.
You now have sorrow . . . . *I want to comfort you.*	For here we have no permanent place . . . . *Lord, you are worthy to receive praise and honor and might.*	Blessed are the dead.

It is unlikely that Brahms had this structure in mind when he started work on the *Requiem* in 1857. Over the next eleven years the work gestated slowly, first as a torso consisting of movements 1–4 and 6 and then in 1866 as the complete work less the fifth movement. The death of Brahms's mother inspired and motivated the composition of the fifth movement, which was added in 1868.

Only once did Brahms find it necessary to change the original text, at "der Gerechten Seelen . . . ." in movement 3. Wisdom 3: 1 reads, "*Aber* der Gerechten Seelen" (*But* the righteous souls), the word "but" referring to the final statement of Wisdom, chapter 2. Brahms needed a different transition, however, in which the "but" would have been nonsensical. He therefore dropped it.

FEST– UND GEDENKSPRÜCHE, op. 109
Festival and Memorial Aphorisms

Unsere Väter, op. 109, no. 1
Our Fathers
Psalm 22: 5, 6; 29: 11

Unsere Väter hofften auf dich;
Our   fathers trusted in you,

und   da   sie hofften, halfst du ihnen aus.
and because they trusted, helped you them out.

Zu dir schrieen sie und wurden errettet;
To you cried they and   were delivered;

sie hofften auf dich und wurden nicht zu Schanden.
they trusted in you and were not   disgraced.

Der Herr wird seinem Volk   Kraft   geben,
The Lord will   his   people strength give;

der Herr wird sein Volk   segnen mit Frieden.
the Lord will   his people bless with peace.

Our fathers trusted in you,
and because they trusted,
you helped them.
They cried to you, and were delivered;
they trusted in you and were not disgraced.

The Lord will give his people strength;
the Lord will bless his people with peace.

Wenn ein starker Gewappneter, op. 109, no. 2
When a Strong, Armed Man
Luke 11: 21, 17b

Wenn ein starker Gewappneter
When a strong, armed man

seinen Palast   bewahret,
his   palace guards,

so bleibet   das Seine   mit Frieden.
so remains –that which is his– in   peace.

Aber, ein jeglich Reich,
But   every   kingdom,

so es mit ihm selbst uneins wird,
if it with   itself   divided becomes,

das   wird   wüste, und ein Haus
that becomes desolate, and one house

fället über das andere.
falls over the other.

When a strong, armed man
guards his palace,
his possessions remain in peace.

But every kingdom,
if it becomes divided against itself,
becomes desolate, and one house
falls upon the other.

Wo ist ein so herrlich Volk, op. 109, no. 3
Where Is there such a Glorious People
Deuteronomy 4: 8, 9

Wo   ist ein so   herrlich Volk,
Where is –such a– glorious people,

zu dem Götter   also   nahe sich tun,
to whom Gods just as close   come

als der Herr, unser Gott,
as the Lord, our God

so oft   wir ihn anrufen.
whenever we him call on.

Where is there such a glorious people,
whose gods come as close to them
as the Lord our God is to us
whenever we call on him?

Hüte	dich	nur
Beware	**—**	**only**

Only beware,
and guard your soul well,
that you do not forget the things
that your eyes have seen,
and that they may not leave your heart
all your life.
And you shall teach this to your children
and your children's children. Amen.

und bewahre deine Seele wohl,
and guard your soul well,

daß du nicht vergessest der Geschichte,
that you not forget the events

die deine Augen gesehen haben,
that your eyes seen have,

und daß sie nicht aus deinem Herzen
and that they not out of your heart

komme alle dein Lebelang.
come all your life long.

Und sollt deinen Kindern
And you shall your children

und Kindeskindern kundtun. Amen.
and children's-children make known. Amen.

*I*N the spring of 1889 Johannes Brahms was working on three Biblical motets for double choir. Although he was not writing them for a commission or a particular occasion, he did have in mind the commemoration of three historical events. As he explained to conductor Hans von Bülow in a letter of May 30, 1889:

> . . . They are three, short, hymn-like sayings for eight-voice, a-cappella choir that are intended for national festival and memorial days, specifically the days of Leipzig [the "Battle of the Nations" in October 1813, in which Napoleon's army was crushed], Sedan [the final defeat of the French in the Franco-Prussian War of 1870–1871], and the coronation of the Kaiser [on January 18, 1871, after the defeat of the French and the declaration of German empire] might be explicitly cited. (Perhaps better not!) (Kross 1958: 435, tr. ed.)

The connection of the motet texts with historical events provides two ways of reading them—Biblically and politically. The first of the motets provides the simple message that God will give strength to those who trust in him. Seen through political spectacles, however, the text appears to single out the Germans as a "chosen people." The second motet is on its face a hymn in praise of strength and unity. If considered in the context of the Battle of Sedan, it becomes a self-congratulatory anthem to German military strength and the unity of the new empire. Rejoicing in God, and passing on knowledge and heritage to future generations is the subject of the third motet. As a commemoration of the Kaiser's crowning, however, the opening words become another arrogant declaration of a "chosen people": "Where is there such a glorious people, whose gods come as close to them as the Lord our God is to us . . . ?"[20]

In summary, the motets are not explicitly political and could have been appropriate for many German civic festivals and observances. On the other hand, however, they can be seen as strongly nationalistic.

Brahms's "perhaps better not" was prescient. His connection of the motets with historical events has provided grist for historians who have been uncomfortable with a work that expressly celebrates three anniversaries of French humiliation, two of them at Teutonic hands.[21]

Brahms himself testified that the motets were in no way bound to specific celebrations. During the summer of 1889, as a result of the quiet diplomacy of Hans von Bülow, Brahms was invited to become an honorary citizen of Hamburg—the city's highest honor. As a token of thanks he dedicated the three double-choir motets to Hamburg Bürgermeister Carl Petersen, a long-time friend, and presented their first performance in Hamburg on September 14, the date he received his honorary citizenship.

---

[20] Compare the opening and closing stanzas of a Christmas carol written during the Third Reich (1942, tr. ed.):

In keinem Volk auf Erden
Ward's noch so Hell und rein.
Wo kann's so Weihnacht werden?
In deinem Volk allein.

In no people upon earth
has such radiance and purity become manifest.
Where can such a Christmas come to be?
In your people alone.

Sein Wort hat deutsche Sprache,
Ist männlich, hart und klar
Deutschland, mein Volk, erwache!
Gott ward dir offenbar!

His [God's] word is spoken in German;
It is masculine, hard, and clear.
Germany, my people, awake!
God has revealed himself to you!

[21]Siegfried Kross, in his book on Brahms's choral music written thirteen years after the end of WWII, explores this subject in some detail and with obvious discomfort. (Kross 1958, 436–437)

FÜNF GESÄNGE, op. 104
Five Songs

Nachtwache [I], op. 104, no. 1
Night Watch [I]
Friedrich Rückert

Leise Töne der Brust
Soft sounds of the breast,

   geweckt vom Odem der Liebe,
   awakened by the breath of love,

Hauchet zitternd hinaus,
breathe trembling forth

   ob sich euch öffen ein Ohr,
   if — to you opens an ear,

Öffen ein liebendes Herz,
opens a loving heart;

   und wenn sich keines euch öffnet,
   and if — none to you opens,

Trag ein Nachtwind euch
bear a night wind you

   seufzend in meines zurück.
   sighing into mine back.

Soft music of the heart,
   awakened by the breath of love,
whisper tremulously
   if an ear opens to you,
or a loving heart;
   and if none should open,
let a night wind bear you,
   sighing, back into mine.

Source: Rückert 1979, 4: 47

Nachtwache [II], op. 104, no. 2
Night Watch [II]
Friedrich Rückert

"Ruhn sie?" rufet das Horn
"Rest they?" calls the horn

   des Wächters drüben aus Westen,
   of the watchman over there from the west;

Und aus Osten das Horn
and from the east the horn

   rufet entgegen: "sie ruhn!"
   calls to meet it: "they rest!"

Hörst du, zagendes Herz,
Hear you, timorous heart,

   die flüsternden Stimmen der Engel?
   the whispering voices of the angels?

Lösche die Lampe getrost,
Extinguish the lamp consoled,

   hülle in Frieden dich ein.
   wrap in peace yourself —.

"Do they rest?" calls the horn
   of the watchman from the west;
and from the east the horn
   answers back: "they rest!"

Do you hear, timorous heart,
   the whispering voices of the angels?
May you extinguish your lamp in consolation
   and wrap yourself in peace.

Source: Rückert 1979, 4: 48

RÜCKERT'S "Nachtwache" poems are part of a vast collection of c. 300 verses entitled "Wanderung," in this case perhaps best translated as "Travel." The first section, from which the present poems are taken, is "Italian Poems," which were inspired by and written during Rückert's trip to Italy in late 1817 and early 1818. The remaining poems are organized into "regions," from the Middle East to China and finally India—places that Rückert (1788–1866) had visited only through literature. The contents of the "fifth region" are in fact translations of Chinese poetry. But because Rückert did not read Chinese, he worked from Latin texts, which were themselves translations. One must wonder whether any traces of the Chinese originals could still be found in the German versions.

The "Nachtwache" poems appear to reflect no specific experience of the Italian journey. Rather, they contemplate thoughts of love, present and lost, that enter the poet's mind in the darkness and loneliness of the night. Brahms set the first and last of Rückert's five "Nachtwache" verses, each of which can stand independently. Poetically, however, the "Nachwache" poems are best considered as a unit, to which the first is an introduction and the fifth a conclusion.

Rückert's fascination with the cultures and literatures of the East was to remain a major focus of his artistic life. This is reflected in the "motto" with which the editor of his complete works begins his biographical sketch (Rückert 1979, 1: vii):

> Mir ist Verse zu machen und künstlich Vers' ein Bedürfnis;
> Fehlt mir ein eigenes Lied, so übersetz' ich mir eins.

> For me, the writing of verse is a necessity, as is artistic poetry;
> should I lack a song of my own, I will simply translate one.

Letztes Glück, op. 104, no. 3
Last Happiness
Max Kalbeck

Leblos   gleitet Blatt   um   Blatt
Lifeless glides leaf after leaf

Still   und traurig von   den   Bäumen;
quietly and sadly from the   trees;

Seines Hoffens nimmer   satt,
of its   hope   never satisfied,

Lebt das Herz   in Frühlingsträumen.
lives the heart in   spring dreams.

Noch verweilt ein Sonnenblick
Still   lingers a   sun-glance

Bei den späten Hagerosen—
at   the   late   wild rose—

Wie bei einem letzten   Glück,
like at   a   last happiness,

Einem süßen, hoffnungslosen.
a   sweet, hopeless one.

Leaf after leaf lifelessly glides
quietly and sadly from the trees;
its hopes never fulfilled,
the heart lives in dreams of spring.

A sunbeam still lingers
on the late wild rose—
as on a last happiness,
sweet and hopeless.

MAX Kalbeck (1850–1921), in his four-volume biography of Brahms (Kalbeck 1976, 140–146), discusses the origins of each of the texts in this opus—with the exception of this work, for which he personally wrote the words. It was published in a collection of Kalbeck's poetry entitled *Nächte* (Nights) in 1877; the *Brahms-Werke-Verzeichnis* indicates, however, that Kalbeck provided it to Brahms in manuscript form.

Kalbeck describes his poem thusly: "The melancholy sorrow of a grey fall day, on which, while the dead leaves softly drop, the final flowers of the human heart attempt a last, hopeless, heavenward bloom . . . ." (Kalbeck 1976, 4: 142, tr. ed.)

This poem darkens yet further the mood set by nos. 1 and 2, and the two poems that follow are among the most bitter, pessimistic verses that Brahms ever set. The entire opus, composed in 1886 and 1888, lies under a pall of dejection and resignation that in one way or another permeates most of the composer's late choral music and indeed, most of his late music of all genres.

Verlorene Jugend, op. 104, no. 4
Lost Youth
Bohemian; Josef Wenzig, trans.

Brausten alle   Berge,
Raged   all mountains,

Sauste   rings der Wald—
stormed around the forest—

Meine jungen Tage,
My   young days,

Wo   sind sie so bald?
where are they so soon?

They raged on the mountains,
stormed around the forest—
days of my youth,
where have they gone so soon?

Jugend, teure Jugend,
Youth, precious youth,

Flohest mir dahin;
fled me away;

O du holde Jugend,
O you sweet youth,

Achtlos war mein Sinn!
careless was my mind!

Ich verlor dich leider,
I lost you unfortunately,

Wie wenn einen Stein
as if a stone

Jemand von sich schleudert
someone from himself throws

In die Flut hinein.
into the stream —.

Wendet sich der Stein auch
Turns — the stone even if

Um in tiefer Flut,
around in deep stream,

Weiß ich, daß die Jugend
know I, that — youth

Doch kein Gleiches tut.
however not same does.

Youth, precious youth,
has fled away.
O sweet youth,
how careless I was!

I lost you, unfortunately,
like a stone
someone tosses away
into the torrent.

Even though the stone
may turn around in the deep stream,
I know that youth
does not do the same.

Source:	Wenzig 1830: 82	
Variants:		(Brahms = roman, Wenzig = *italic*)
	Stanza 1:	brausten (raged) = *sausten* (howled)
	Stanza 2:	flohest (fled) = *welktest* (withered); holde = *liebe*
	Stanza 3:	Wie wenn einen Stein / Jemand von sich schleudert (someone threw) =
		Als ob einen Stein / Ich geworfen hätte (I would have thrown)

WITH the choice of this poem, a Bohemian folk song translated by August Wenzig (1807–1876) in his *Slawische Volkslieder* (Slavic Folk Songs) of 1830, Brahms sinks deeper into the darkness established in the preceding three pieces of op. 64. Here the speaker laments his lost youth and rues his stupidity in not savoring it while he could.

As he did from time to time, Brahms altered the title—originally "Erinnerung an die Jugend" (Recollection of Youth)—and text to fit his own artistic preferences. By substituting "brausten" for "sausten" in the first line he avoided having two adjacent lines begin alike; the other emendations were unnecessary, however, and thus must simply have sounded better to him or brought the poem closer to his own thinking.

Brahms respected his poets but he had no compunctions about changing what did not suit him. Biographer Max Kalbeck reports that he would collect poems in notebooks and would often copy them by hand just to get the feel of them. He would even recopy poems given to him by their authors for the same reason. "Only after he had, so to speak, taken possession of his favorites [by copying them] with his own hand did he consider them to be his property, with which he might do as he pleased as a musician." (Kalbeck 1976, 1: 97, tr. ed.)

Brahms was enamored of folk song and folk poetry throughout his life, and they were a major influence on his vocal compositions. Wenzig's translations stand beside those of Daumer (the *Liebeslieder**) as particularly important in this genre. Brahms set twelve of Wenzig's poems, including four in this volume.[22]

For reasons unknown, probably length, Brahms omitted the original second stanza:

Zeiten, meine Zeiten,　　　Days, my days,
Ich genoß euch nie;　　　I never did enjoy you;
Meine jungen Jahre,　　　years of my youth,
Öd verflossen sie.　　　drearily you slipped away.

Im Herbst, op. 104, no. 5

---

[22]In addition to the present work, "Neckereien," "Der Gang zum Liebchen," and "Sehnsucht."

In Autumn
Klaus Groth

Ernst   ist der   Herbst,
Somber is the   autumn,

Und wenn die Blätter fallen,
and when the leaves fall,

Sinkt auch das Herz zu   trübem   Weh herab.
sinks also the heart to melancholy woe down.

Still   ist die Flur,
Quiet is the field,

Und nach dem Süden wallen
and   to   the south travel

Die Sänger stumm, wie nach dem Grab.
the songsters mute, as   to   the grave.

Bleich ist der   Tag,
Pale   is   the day,

Und blaße Nebel schleiern
and pallid mists   veil

Die Sonne wie   die Herzen ein.
the sun as well as the hearts —.

Früh kommt die Nacht:
Early comes the night,

Denn alle Kräfte feiern,
for   all vigor idles,

Und   tief verschlossen ruht das Sein.
and, deeply enfolded,   rests our being.

Sanft   wird   der Mensch.
Gentle becomes — mortal;

Er sieht die Sonne sinken,
he sees the sun   sink,

Er ahnt des Lebens   wie   des Jahres Schluß.
He senses — life's –as well as– the year's end.

Feucht wird   das Aug,
Moist becomes the eye,

Doch in der Träne   Blinken,
yet in the tears' glistening

Entströmt des Herzens   seligster   Erguß.
streams   the heart's most blissful outpouring.

Somber is the autumn,
and when the leaves fall,
the heart also sinks into melancholy woe.
Quiet is the field,
and southward travel
the silent songsters, as if going to the grave.

Pale is the day,
and pallid mists veil
the sun as well as the hearts.
The night comes early;
then all vigor lies fallow
and our being, enfolded deeply inward, rests.

People become meek;
they see the sun setting and
they foresee the end of life, as well as of the
    year.
Their eyes become moist,
but in the glistening of their tears
streams the heart's most blissful outpouring.

Source: Groth 1956–1960, 5: 50

IN 1860 Klaus Groth (1819–1899) published a large collection of Low German[23] poetry entitled *Quickborn* that is perhaps the era's most important body of literature in that dialect, and it won him lasting renown. Works in Low German had an inherently smaller audience than those in High German, which was more universally understood. Groth probably grasped this limitation on his artistic heritage and produced a body of poetry in High German that he published in 1854 under the title *Hundert Blätter: Paralipomena zum Quickborn* (A Hundred Pages: Addendum to *Quickborn*). It is from this collection that Brahms took the poem "Im Herbst." The composer set ten more Groth poems to music, including one in Low German. The poet and composer were acquainted and shared more than poetry; in the 1880s they were rival suitors of a singer named Hermine Spies.

---

[23]The German language has a rich evolutionary history. Off of its trunk have split many branches that include English, Dutch, Flemish, and several Scandinavian languages. Two of those branches represent forms of German used in the nineteenth century and still employed today: Low and High German. Low German was historically the language of the rural and uneducated; it still survives in numerous regional dialects. High German, the form one learns in school throughout the world, became the dialect of the educated and therefore the language of literature and scholarship. In the nineteenth century the Romantic fascination with folk history brought about an interest in preserving Low German in written as well as spoken form, in part through a literature in Low German. Two of the poets represented in this volume, Groth and Seidl, contributed to this literature—Groth in the *Plattdeutsch* dialect of northern Germany and Seidl in the dialect of lower Austria.

Siegfried Kross, the author of a study of Brahms's choral music, sees this poem, another resigned reflection on life about to end, as an autobiographical expression: "he is no longer setting lyrics to music; here Brahms the man speaks" at the close of an opus that was to be his last in the realm of secular choral music. (Kross 1958: 422, tr. ed.) Kross's later discussion of the poem and its relationship to the composer is insightful:

> The premonition of the impending end of life is certainly not seen here as the experience of parting and as painful mourning, but rather it is portrayed as the fulfillment of life itself. Thus at the end of his body of secular vocal compositions the north-German Brahms stands with his reflections on death, the lonely man who [in his own words] "lived too little on this earth," the embittered man from whom "life stole more than death," who through his art exceeded his mortal loneliness; through the language of music he expressed that death to him signified gain. (Kross 1958: 342, tr. ed.)

Geistliches Lied, op. 30

Sacred Song

Paul Fleming

Laß dich nur nichts nicht dauren
Let yourself only nothing indeed suffer

Mit Trauren,
with grief;

Sei stille;
be still.

Wie Gott es fügt,
As God it ordains,

So sei vergnügt,
so be satisfied,

Mein Wille!
my will!

Was willst du heute sorgen
What want to you today worry

Auf morgen?
for tomorrow?

Der Eine
The one

Steht allem für;
commands all —;

Der gibt auch dir
he gives also you

Das Deine.
— yours.

Sei nur in allem Handel
Be only in all doing

Ohn Wandel,
without change,

Steh feste;
stand firmly.

Was Gott beschleußt,
What God ordains,

Das ist und heißt
that is and signifies

Das Beste.
the best.

Amen.
Amen.

Let nothing ever
grieve you;
be at peace.
Whatever God ordains,
accept it gladly,
my soul!

Why do you want to worry today
about tomorrow?
The One
is lord of all;
he also gives to you
that which is yours.

In all things
be not inconstant;
stand firmly.
Whatever God ordains
is and signifies
the best.
Amen.

Source: Fleming 1965, 1: 244
Variant: Stanza 3: "Amen" does not appear in the original.

*P*AUL Fleming (1609–1640) was a native Saxon who studied at the Thomasschule in Leipzig (1623), where J.S. Bach was to begin serving as Cantor exactly a century later. He studied medicine, fine arts, and philosophy, and earned a Master's degree in poetry in 1632. *The Oxford Companion to German Literature* says of Fleming and his poetry that in his "insistence on transience, vanity, and a stoical resignation, Fleming is a man of his age, but many of his poems have also an immediacy of experience which is uncommon in the poetic writing of the 17th c." (Garland 1976: 229)

Fleming's untitled poem beginning "Laß dich nur nichts," a gentle exhortation to trust in God and accept his will, appeared as the introductory verse, and thus possibly as a sort of heading, in his collection of odes published in 1650. Brahms set it to music at the age of twenty three in 1856, a time at which he was engaged in the study of counterpoint, particularly in old music; perhaps he found this antiquated text to be a fitting subject for such an exercise. The work is based on a double canon at the ninth, a ferociously difficult technical task, especially when the melody is predetermined,[24] and even more so when one considers that this may be the composer's very first choral composition.

The music complements the text in two specific ways that show the depth of Brahms's thought. (Kalbeck 1976, 1: 266) The first is the fact that he writes so as to make clear the "echo" of the two three-syllable lines in each stanza:

	1			2			3	
sei stille	–	*mein Wille*	*der Eine*	–	*das Deine*	*steh feste*	–	*das Beste*
be at peace	–	my soul	the One	–	that which is yours	stand firmly	–	the best

The second is his creation of the musical climax at what is in fact the climactic line of the poem: "The One is in command of all."

The age of the text presents a couple of challenges in translation. In the first line the word "nicht" appears to create a nonsensical double negative: "Let *nothing never* grieve you." Fleming almost certainly intended the word to be understood in quite the opposite sense, which curiously is possible in German: "Let *nothing indeed* grieve you." In the second stanza, the textual climax "Der Eine steht allem für" is meaningless in modern German, but becomes figuratively as well as literally the center of the poem when the word *für* is changed into its modern equivalent, *vor*.

Gesang der Parzen, op. 89
Song of the Fates
Johann Wolfgang von Goethe

Es   fürchte   die Götter
— should fear the gods

Das   Mehschengeschlecht!
the   human race!

Sie   halten   die Herrschaft
They hold   —   dominion

In ewigen   Händen,
in eternal   hands,

Und können sie brauchen,
and can   it   use

Wies ihnen   gefällt.
as it to them is pleasing.

Der fürchte   sie doppelt,
He should fear them   double,

Den je   sie erheben!
whom ever they elevate!

Auf Klippen und Wolken
on   cliffs and clouds

Sind Stühle bereitet
are chairs readied

Um   goldene Tische.
around golden tables.

The human race
should fear the gods.
They hold dominion
in their eternal hands,
and can use it
as they please.

Any whom they exalt
should fear them doubly!
On cliffs and clouds
thrones stand ready
around golden tables.

---

[24]In keeping with his old style of composition, Brahms appears to have based his melody on the hymn "Herr Jesus Christ, du höchtes Gut" (*EKG*: 158), an anonymous chorale first recorded in the city of Chemnitz in 1713.

Erhebet ein Zwist sich,
Comes up a dispute —,

So stürzen die Gäste,
then plunge the guests,

Geschmäht und geschändet
despised and disgraced,

In nächtliche Tiefen
into nocturnal depths,

Und harren vergebens,
and wait for in vain,

Im Finstern gebunden,
in darkness bound,

Gerechten Gerichtes.
[for] just judgment.

Sie aber, sie bleiben
They, however, they remain

In ewigen Festen
in eternal feasts

An goldenen Tischen.
at golden tables.

Sie schreiten vom Berge
They stride from mountain

Zu Bergen hinüber:
to mountains over:

Aus Schlünden der Tiefe
from abysses of the deep

Dampft ihnen der Atem
steams to them the breath

Erstickter Titanen,
of suffocated Titans

Gleich Opfergerüchen,
like sacrificial odors,

Ein leichtes Gewölke.
a light cloud.

Es wenden die Herrscher
— turn the rulers

Ihr segnendes Auge
their blessing eye

Von ganzen Geschlechtern
from entire races,

Und meiden, im Enkel
and avoid, in the grandchild,

Die ehmals geliebten,
the formerly beloved,

Still redenden Züge
silently speaking features

Des Ahnherrn zu sehn.
of the ancestor to see.

So sangen die Parzen;
Thus sang the Fates;

Es horcht der Verbannte
— listened the exiled one

In nächtlichen Höhlen,
in nocturnal caves,

Der Alte, die Lieder,
the old one, the songs,

Denkt Kinder und Enkel
thinks of children and grandchildren,

Und schüttelt das Haupt.
and shakes his head.

If dissension arises,
then the guests are hurled down,
despised and disgraced,
into the nocturnal depths,
and they wait there in vain,
bound in darkness,
for just judgment.

The gods, however, continue
the eternal feasts
at the golden tables.

They stride over mountains
from peak to peak:
from the abysses of the deep
the breath of suffocated Titans
steams up to them
like scents of sacrifices,
a light cloud.

The immortal rulers
avert their blessing-bestowing eyes
from entire races,
and avoid seeing, in the grandchild,
the once-loved,
silently speaking features
of the ancestor.

Thus sang the Fates.
The old, banished one
listens to the songs
in his nocturnal caverns,
thinks of his children and grandchildren,
and shakes his head.

Source: Goethe 1961–1964, 5: 54

*F*ATE was the subject of three of Johannes Brahms's major choral-orchestral compositions, the "Schick-salslied"* (Song of Destiny), the "Rhapsody,"* and the "Gesang der Parzen"* (Song of the Fates). He took his text for the latter work from the poem that closes Act 4 of Johann Wolfgang von Goethe's play *Iphigenie auf Tauris* (Iphigenia in Tauris). Goethe (1749–1832) had initially written the drama in prose in 1779 and he himself played Oreste in the premiere on April 6 of that year. During the years 1786–1787 he revised the work into blank verse. Friedrich Schiller (1759–1805) assisted in the preparation of the second performance. This occurred in the summer of 1802 in the new theater at Bad Lauchstädt, for the opening of which Goethe had written his "Prologue" entitled "Was wir bringen," the source of Brahms's "Warum doch erschallen."*

The characters and the outlines of the story were derived from the homonymous tragedy of Euripides (c. 485–406 B.C.), written c. 414–412 B.C. There, however, the two works part company. The original play was rather formalized and required a *deus ex machina* to provide a happy ending. Goethe's drama, on the other hand, was a study in human morality, honesty, and loyalty, in which the characters had real personalities and tragic conflicts to confront and resolve. Although the language and style were neoclassical (this was the first of Goethe's major works in this style, for which he became renowned), the human aspect of the drama was universal.

The poem tells the story of a young woman named Iphigenia who flees Greece to avoid being offered as a sacrifice. She finds refuge in the land of the barbaric Tauri, ruled by King Thoas, into whose court she is admitted as a priestess of the goddess Diana. Through a series of fateful circumstances Iphigenia finds herself faced with sacrificing her own brother Oreste or betraying Thoas, who had shown her kindness, loyalty, and love. At the end of Act 4 she sinks into desperation, feeling inexorably impelled by fate into an impossible choice. She then recalls a song from her childhood, "The Song of the Three Fates," which expresses the helplessness of mortals before the overwhelming power of destiny. It is this song that Brahms sets without alteration as "The Song of the Fates."

GESÄNGE FÜR FRAUENCHOR, op. 17
Songs for Women's Chorus

Es tönt ein voller Harfenklang, op. 17, no. 1
A Full Harp Sound Resounds
Friedrich Ruperti

Es tönt ein voller Harfenklang,
— **rings a   full   harp sound,**

Den Lieb und Sehnsucht schwellen,
that love and longing   swell;

Er   dringt   zum Herzen tief und bang
it penetrates to the heart deep and fearful

Und läßt das Auge quellen.
and lets the eye overflow.

O rinnet, Tränen, nur   herab,
Oh flow,   tears, only downward;

O schlage, Herz, mit   Beben!
oh beat,   heart, with trembling!

Es sanken Lieb und   Glück   ins   Grab,
— sank love and happiness into the grave;

Verloren ist das Leben!
lost   is —   life!

A full harp sound rings forth,
increasing love and longing;
it pierces deep into the frightened heart
and makes the eyes overflow.

O tears, flow on;
O heart, throb and tremble!
Love and happiness sank into the grave;
life is lost!

*F*RIEDRICH Ruperti (1805–1867) is one of several poets whose works Brahms set but about whom little is known. In 1850 he published a collection of poetry, presumably original, entitled *Dunkles Laub: Jugend-gedichte* (Dark Leaf: Poetry of [my] Youth), from which Brahms took the present poem. Although the editors were unable to locate *Dunkles Laub* or any further information on the poet, two additional Ruperti works surfaced during research. The earlier of these is a pair of long narrative poems published in 1850 under the title *Erzählende Gedichte*; twelve years later he published a collection of translations and adaptations of foreign poetry entitled *Fremde Dichtungen in deutschem Gewande*.

Brahms used Ruperti's poem for the first in his set of four songs for women's voices, horn, and harp. While each of the poems is of a different character and origin, all are laments, the first for lost love, the second for a lost lover, the third for love unexpressed and unrequited, and the last for a slain warrior in a distant time. Brahms chose his instruments to complement the affect of the words: the quickly decaying sound of the harp traditionally represented the transcience of life, and the horn was the instrument of destiny.

Lied von Shakespeare, op. 17, no. 2
Song by Shakespeare
August Wilhelm Schlegel, trans.

Komm herbei, komm herbei, Tod!
Come here, come here, death!

Come away, come away death,
And in sad cypress let me be laid.
Fly away, fly away, breath,
I am slain by a fair cruel maid.

Und versenk in Zypressen den Leib.
And bury in cypresses the body.

Laß mich frei, laß mich frei, Not!
Let me free, let me free, misery.

Mich erschlägt ein holdseliges Weib.
Me slays a lovely woman.

Mit Rosmarin mein Leichenhemd,
With rosemary my shroud,

My shroud of white, stuck all with yew,
Oh prepare it!
My part of death, no one so true
Did share it.

O bestellt es!
oh prepare it!

Ob Lieb ans Herz mir tötlich kommt,
If love to the heart me deadly comes,

Treu hält es.
faithful remains it.

Keine Blum, keine Blum süß
No flower, no flower sweet

Not a flower, not a flower sweet
On my black coffin let there be strown;
Not a friend, not a friend greet
My poor corpse, where my bones shall be
thrown.

Sei gestreut auf den schwärzlichen Sarg.
be strewn on the blackish coffin.

Keine Seel, keine Seel grüß
No soul, no soul greet

Mein Gebein, wo die Erd es verbarg.
my bones, where the earth them concealed.

Um Ach und Weh zu wenden ab,
In order alas and woe to avoid —,

A thousand thousand sighs to save,
Lay me, O where
Sad true love never find my grave,
To weep there.

William Shakespeare

Bergt alleine
bury alone

Mich, wo kein Treuer wall ans Grab
me where no faithful one will come to the grave

Und weine.
and weep.

Source: column 1: Ophüls 1983: 27
         column 2: Shakespeare 1986: 279

SHAKESPEARE'S 1601 comedy *Twelfth Night, or, What You Will* is the source for this lovely, melancholy song of unrequited love couched in sixteenth-century death imagery. The elaborate, contrived, and convention-filled plot hinges on all manner of adventure, misadventure, and deception, with low-comic relief generously thrown into the stew. At the end, protagonists Duke Orsino and Olivia learn lessons of true love from Olivia's brother Sebastian and his sweetheart Viola.

The Duke is introduced in Act 1, scene 1. In the following scene Viola enters, having survived a shipwreck, but now alone and without support after the apparent death of her brother in the same wreck. She contrives to disguise herself as a eunuch to enter the employment of the Duke and avoid becoming a beggar—or worse. In Act 2, scene 4 the Duke engages the disguised Viola in a conversation about love, which he has not found the courage to express to Olivia.

Come hither, boy: if ever thou shalt love,
In the sweet pangs of it remember me;
For such as I am all true lovers are,
Unstaid and skittish in all motions else,
Save in the constant image of the creature
That is beloved.

Orsino then turns to criteria for selecting a wife, the discussion of which is interrupted by the arrival of the court jester Feste, who is commanded to sing and responds with "Come Away, Death."

August Wilhelm Schlegel (1767–1845) was a masterful translator of literature and produced versions of seventeen of Shakespeare's plays between 1797 and 1810. His translation does a remarkable job of preserving the meaning and tone of Shakespeare's original, as well as its rhyme scheme. Schlegel's Shakespeare translations are not included in his complete works (Schlegel 1971) and were unavailable to the editors for comparison with the text as set by Brahms.

Der Gärtner, op. 17, no. 3
The Gardener
Joseph von Eichendorff

Wohin ich geh' und schaue,
Where I go and look,

In Feld und Wald und Tal,
in field and forest and valley,

Vom Berg hinab in die Aue:
from the mountain down to the meadow,

Vielschöne, hohe Fraue,
very beautiful, high woman,

Grüß' ich dich tausendmal.
greet I you a thousand times.

Wherever I go and look,
in field and forest and valley,
from the mountain down to the meadow,
most beautiful, noble lady,
I greet you a thousand times.

In meinem Garten find ich
In my garden find I

Viel Blumen, schön und fein,
many flowers, beautiful and fine;

Viel Kränze wohl draus wind ich
many garlands likely from them weave I

Und tausend Gedanken bind ich
and a thousand thoughts bind I

Und Grüße mit darein.
and greetings –into them– .

In my garden I find
many lovely and delicate flowers;
indeed, I weave many garlands with them
and I bind a thousand thoughts
and greetings into them.

Ihr darf ich keinen reichen,
To her may I none offer;

Sie ist zu hoch und schön,
she is too high and beautiful.

Die müssen alle verbleichen,
They must all fade;

Die Liebe nur ohnegleichen
— love only without equal

Bleibt ewig im Herzen stehn.
remains forever in the heart —.

To her I may offer none of these;
she is too noble and fair.
They must all wither and die;
only love beyond compare
remains forever in the heart.

Ich schein wohl froher Dinge,
I seem — of good mood,

Und schaffe auf und ab,
and work here and there,

Und ob das Herz zerspringe,
and even if the heart bursts,

Ich grabe fort und singe
I dig away and sing

und grab mir bald mein Grab.
and dig me soon my grave.

I seem to be in good spirits,
and I work here and there,
and even if my heart bursts,
I will dig away and sing
and soon will dig my grave.

Source: Eichendorff 1958, 1: 199

EICHENDORFF'S "Der Gärtner" appears in a group of poems entitled "Spring and Love." It is a tale of the almost chivalric, unrequited love of a gardener for an unapproachable noblewoman. The expression is beautiful, but the emotions are objectified and seem distant rather than personal. All of this changes without warning in the last line. By this time the reader has become accustomed to the objectivity of the poem, as well as to its rather sing-song poetic meter. The words "and soon will dig my grave" thus comes as a jolting surprise. Although "Der Gärtner" appears in Eichendorff's *Werke* as an independent poem, it is in fact excerpted from the first act of his novella entitled "Aus dem Leben eines Taugenichts" (From the Life of Good-for-Nothing).

Gesang aus Fingal, *op. 17, no. 4*
Song from Fingal
"Ossian" (James Macpherson); Johann Gottfried Herder, trans.

Wein an den Felsen der brausenden Winde,
Weep on the rocks of the raging winds;

Weine, o Mädchen von Inistore!
weep, O maiden of Inistore!

Beug' über die Wogen dein schönes Haupt,
Bend over the waves your beautiful head,

Lieblicher du als der Geist der Berge,
lovelier [are] you than the spirit of the mountains,

Wenn er am Mittag in einem Sonnenstrahl
when he at noon in a sunbeam

über das Schweigen von Morven fährt.
over the silence of Morven passes.

Er ist gefallen, dein Jüngling liegt darnieder,
He has fallen, your young man lies down there,

Bleich sank er unter Cuthullins Schwert.
pale sank he under Cathullin's sword.

Nimmer wird Mut deinen Liebling mehr reizen,
Never will courage your loved one more rouse,

Das Blut von Königen zu vergießen.
the blood of kings to shed.

Trenar, der liebliche Trenar starb!
Trenar, the lovely Trenar died,

O Mädchen von Inistore!
O maiden of Inistore!

Seine grauen Hunde heulen daheim;
His gray hounds howl at home;

Sie sehn seinen Geist vorüberziehn.
they see his ghost pass by.

Sein Bogen hängt ungespannt in der Halle,
His bow hangs unstrung in the hall,

Nichts regt sich auf der Heide der Rehe.
nothing moves — on the heath of the deer.

Weep on the rocks of the raging winds,
O maid of Inistore!
Bend thy fair head over the waves,
thou lovelier than the ghost of the hills,
when it moves, in a sunbeam at noon
over the silence of Morven!

He is fallen! thy youth is low!
pale beneath the sword of Cathullin!
No more shall valour raise thy love
to match the blood of kings.

Trenar, graceful Trenar died,
O maid of Inistore!
His gray dogs are howling at home!
they see his passing ghost.
His bow is in the hall unstrung.
No sound is in the hill of his hinds!

James Macpherson

Source: *column 1:* Ophüls 1983: 29
column 2: Macpherson 1926: 44

*B*RAHMS set excerpts of two poems by "Ossian," purportedly a third-century Celtic poet. (The story of the controversy surrounding the Ossianic poems is related here in the annotation to Brahms's "Darthulas Grabesgesang," op. 42, no. 3.) *Fingal* was the title of one of the two large-scale Ossian epics and the name of a great Scottish warrior of legend, the father of Ossian. It is set in six "books" (chapters), the first of which is the source for the passage that Brahms set in op. 17, no. 4.

In Book 1 of Macpherson's poem, Fingal sailed with his troops to Ireland to reinforce the army of the Irish general Cuthullin against an invasion by Scandinavians, including troops from Inistore (probably a name for the Orkney Islands). Prior to Fingal's arrival, Cuthullin engaged the enemy in a victorless battle, during which many died including the invader Trenar, the brother to the king of one of the Shetland Islands. Brahms's text deals with the lament of the "maid of Inistore," the daughter of Gorlo, king of the Orkney islands, for Trenar.

Despite the complexity of the underlying story, the song of mourning has a universality that obviously appealed to Brahms. The "maid of Inistore" likely suggested his setting of the poem for women's chorus, and the use of horns, the instruments symbolic of destiny to the German romantics, must have seemed particularly appropriate.

Kross (1958: 92) may be incorrect in attributing the German version of this text to Johann Gottfried Herder (1744–1803), who translated and published other Ossian excerpts. (See "Darthulas Grabesgesang.") The "Gesang aus Fingal" is absent from Herder's collection of folk poetry, *Stimmen der Völker in Liedern* (Herder 1975) and is not found in his collected works (Herder 1967–1968).

In stiller Nacht, o op. 33, no. 42
In the Still Night
Friedrich Spee von Langenfeld, SJ

In stiller Nacht, zur ersten Wacht,
In still night, at the first watch,
Ein Stimm begunnt zu klagen,
a voice began to lament.
Der nächtge Wind hat süß und lind
The night wind has sweetly and gently
Zu mir den Klang getragen.
to me the sound carried.
Von herben Leid und traurigkeit
From bitter suffering and sadness
Ist mir das Herz zerflossen,
is — the heart melted;
Die Blümelein, mit Tränen rein
the flowers, with tears pure
Hab ich sie all begossen.
have I them all moistened.

In the still night, at first watch,
a voice began to lament.
The night wind sweetly and gently
carried the sound to me.
From bitter suffering and sadness
my heart has melted;
I have watered all the flowers
with my pure tears.

Der schöne Mond will untergahn,
The beautiful moon wants to go down,
Für Leid nicht mehr mag scheinen,
because pain not more may shine,
Die Sterne lan ihr glitzen stahn,
The stars let their glitter die;
Mit mir sie wollen weinen.
with me they want to weep.
Kein Vogelsang, noch Freudenklang
No birdsong nor joy-sound
Man höret in den Lüften,
one hears in the air.
Die wilden Tier trauern auch mit mir
The wild animals grieve also with me
In Steinen und in Klüften.
on rocks and in ravines.

The beautiful moon wants to set and
may never rise again because of its pain.
The stars let their twinkle die;
they want to weep with me.
Neither a birdsong nor a sound of joy
can be heard in the air.
The wild animals also grieve with me
on the rocks and in the ravines.

Source:	Spee 1985–, 1: 182	
Variants:		(Brahms = roman, Spee = *italics*
	Stanza 1, line 1:	In stiller Nacht = *Bei stiller Nacht*
	Stanza 1, line 2:	Ein Stimm begunnt zu klagen = *Ein Stimm sich gunt zu klagen*
	Stanza 1, lines 3–8:	The remaining six lines of stanza 1 bear no resemblance to any portion of the Spee poem.
	Stanza 2, line 7:	trauern auch mit mir = *auch trauern mit mir*

*B*RAHMS must have been taken with the devotional poem "Bei stiller Nacht" of the Jesuit Friedrich Spee (1591–1635)—enough so to rework it into a secular text. The original poem of fifteen four-line stanzas began and ended with thoughts that could be either sacred or secular. The intervening text, however, was clearly devotional. Brahms therefore adopted Spee's first two lines with minor alterations, completely rewrote (or had rewritten) the next six lines, and returned to Spee's closing strophe for his last stanza. The result is a secular "night poem" of beauty and melancholy, a seamless mixture of words written more than two centuries apart.

An interesting feature of Brahms's poem is its combination of four of the original, four-line stanzas into two, eight-line stanzas. This was certainly for musical purposes, as he sets the second half of the second stanza to music different from though parallel to the music of the first stanza.

Regarding the author, Friedrich Spee, see the annotation to the hymn "O Heiland, reiß die Himmel auf."

LIEBESLIEDER WALZER, op. 52
Lovesong Waltzes
Georg Friedrich Daumer, trans.

Rede, Mädchen, allzu liebes, op. 52, no. 1 (satb)
Russian

"Rede, Mädchen, allzu liebes,
"Speak, maiden, all too dear,

Das mir in die Brust, die kühle,
who to me into the breast the cool

Hat geschleudert mit dem Blicke
has hurled with the glance

Diese wilden Glutgefühle!"
these wild passionate feelings!"

"Willst du nicht dein Herz erweichen;
"Want you not your heart to soften?

Willst du, eine überfromme,
Want you, a super–pious,

Rasten ohne traute Wonne,
to rest without true delight?

Oder willst du, daß ich komme?"
Or would you that I come?"

"Rasten ohne traute Wonne—
"Rest without true delight—

Nicht so bitter will ich büßen.
not so bitterly want I to suffer.

Komme nur, du schwarzes Auge,
Come only, you dark eye,

Komme, wenn die Sterne grüßen!"
come when the stars greet!"

"Speak, dearest maiden,
you whose glance has hurled
into my cool heart
these wild, passionate feelings!"

"Don't you want to soften your heart?
Do you want, you overly pious one,
to rest without true delight?
Or do you want me to come?"

"Rest without true delight—
I don't want to suffer so bitterly.
Do come, you dark-eyed maid,
come when the stars appear!"

Source: Daumer 1855, 2: 41

Am Gesteine rauscht die Flut, op. 52, no. 2 (satb)
Russian-Polish Dance Song

Am Gesteine rauscht die Flut,
Upon rocks rushes the high tide,

Heftig angetrieben;
vehemently driven.

Wer da nicht zu seufzen weiß,
Who there not to sigh knows

Lernt es unter'm Lieben.
learns it by loving.

Upon the rocks the high tide breaks,
hurled by a mighty force.
The one who knows not how to sigh
learns it by loving.

Source: Daumer 1855, 2: 66

O die Frauen, op. 52, no. 3 (tb)
Russian-Polish Dance Song

O die Frauen, o die Frauen,
Oh the women, oh the women,

Wie sie Wonne tauen!
how they delight bestow!

Wäre lang ein Mönch geworden,
[I] would have long a monk become

Wären nicht die Frauen!
were not the women!

Oh women, oh women,
how they do delight!
I would've become a monk long ago
were it not for women!

Source: Daumer 1855, 2: 72

Wie des Abends schöne Röte, op. 52, no. 4 (sa)

Russian-Polish Dance Song

Wie des Abends schöne Röte
Like the evening's beautiful redness,

Möcht' ich arme Dirne glüh'n,
would like I, poor maiden, to glow;

Einem, Einem zu gefallen,
one, one to please,

Sonder Ende Wonne sprüh'n.
without end delight to shower.

Like the evening's beautiful sunset,
I, poor maid, would like to glow;
I would like to please one and one alone,
to shower her with endless delight.

Source: Daumer 1855, 2: 71

Die grüne Hopfenranke, op. 52, no. 5 (satb)

Russian

Die grüne Hopfenranke,
The green hop-vine

Sie schlängelt auf der Erde hin—
it creeps on the earth toward.

Die junge, schöne Dirne,
The young, beautiful maiden—

So traurig ist ihr Sinn!—
so sorrowful is her heart!

The green hop-vine
creeps toward the ground.
The beautiful young maiden—
so sorrowful is her heart!

Du höre, grüne Ranke!
You listen, green vine,

Was hebst du dich nicht himmelwärts?—
why raise you — not heavenwards?

Du höre, schöne Dirne!
You listen, beautiful maiden,

Was ist so schwer dein Herz?
why is so heavy your heart?

Listen, green vine,
why don't you climb toward the heavens?
Listen, beautiful maiden,
why is your heart so heavy?

Wie höbe sich die Ranke,
How would raise — the vine

Der keine Stütze Kraft verleiht?—
to which no support strength gives?

Wie wäre die Dirne fröhlich,
How would be the maiden happy

Wenn ihr der Liebste weit?—
if her the beloved far away?

How can a vine climb
that has no support for strength?
How could the maiden be happy
if her lover is far away?

Source: Daumer 1855, 2: 49

Ein kleiner, hübscher Vogel, op. 52, no. 6 (satb)

Hungarian

Ein kleiner, hübscher Vogel nahm den Flug
A little, pretty bird took — flight

Zum Garten hin, da gab es Obst genug.
to the garden here, there was — fruit enough.

Wenn ich ein hübscher, kleiner Vogel wär',
If I a pretty, little bird were,

Ich säumte doch, ich täte nicht wie der.
I would delay —; I would do not as he.

A pretty little bird flew
to the garden where fruit was plentiful.
If I were a pretty little bird,
I'd not delay; I'd do just as he did.

Leimruten-Arglist lauert' an dem Ort;
Bird-lime's malice lies in the place;

Der arme Vogel konnte nicht mehr fort.
the poor bird could not more away.

Wenn ich ein hübscher, kleiner Vogel wär',
If I a pretty, little bird were,

Ich säumte doch, ich täte nicht wie der.
I would delay —; I would do not as he.

Treacherous, sticky sap lies in ambush;
the poor bird could not escape.
If I were a pretty little bird,
I'd definitely delay; I'd not do as he did.

Der Vogel kam in eine schöne Hand,
The bird came into a beautiful hand;

Da tat es ihm, dem Glücklichen, nicht and.
there harm — to him, the happy one, not —.

Wenn ich ein hübscher, kleiner Vogel wär',
If I a pretty, little bird were,

Ich säumte nicht, ich täte doch wie der.
I would delay not; I would do — as he.

The bird was freed by a lovely hand;
no harm came to the happy little bird.
If I were a pretty little bird,
I'd not delay; I'd certainly do as he did.

Source: Daumer 1855, 2: 127

Wohl schön bewandt war es vorehe, op. 52, no. 7 (sa)
Polish

Wohl schön bewandt
Really well formed

War es vorehe
was it before,

Mit meinem Leben,
with my life

Mit meiner Liebe;
with my love;

Durch eine Wand,
Through a wall,

Ja, durch zehn Wände,
yea, through ten walls,

Erkannte mich
recognized me

Des Freundes Sehe;
the friend's eye.

Doch jetzo, wehe,
Yet now, alas,

Wenn ich dem Kalten
if I to the cold

Auch noch so dicht
ever so closely

Vor'm Auge stehe,
before eye stand,

Es merkt's sein Auge,
— notices it his eye,

Sein Herze nicht.
his heart not.

How very pleasant
it used to be,
both with my life
and with my love;
through a wall,
even through ten walls,
my friend's eye
noticed me.
Yet now, alas,
even if I stand
eye to eye
with the cold one
his eye, his heart
notice me not.

Source: Daumer 1855, 2: 62

Wenn so lind dein Auge mir, op. 52, no. 8 (satb)
Polish

Wenn so lind dein Auge mir
When so gently your eye on me

und so lieblich schauet—
and so fondly gazes,

Jede letzte Trübe flieht,
every last sorrow flees,

Welche mich umgrauet.
that me troubles.

When your eyes so gently
and so fondly gaze on me,
every last sorrow
that troubles me flies away.

Dieser Liebe schöne Glut,
This love's beautiful glow—

Laß sie nicht verstieben!
let it not die!

Nimmer wird, wie ich, so treu
Never will, as I so faithfully

Dich ein Andrer lieben.
you -another- love.

This beautiful glow of our love—
do not let it die!
Never will another love you
as faithfully as I.

Source: Daumer 1855, 2: 60

Am Donaustrande, da steht ein Haus, op. 52, no. 9 (satb)
Hungarian

Am   Donaustrande, da steht ein Haus,
On the Danube bank, there stands a house,

Da   schaut ein rosiges Mädchen aus.
there gazes a rosy   maiden out.

Das Mädchen, es ist wohl gut   gehegt,
The maiden, she is quite well protected;

Zehn eiserne Riegel sind vor   die Türe gelegt.
ten   iron   bars   are before the door laid.

Zehn eiserne Riegel— das ist ein Spaß;
Ten   iron   bars— that is a joke!

Die   spreng' ich, als wären sie nur von Glas.
these break I,   as   were they only of glass.

On the Danube's bank there stands a house,
and there a rosy maiden gazes out.
The maiden is quite well protected;
ten iron bars block her door.

Ten iron bars—that's a joke!
I'll break them as if they were only glass.
Source: Daumer 1855, 2: 128
Variant: Line 4: *Eiserne* does not appear
in the original.

O wie sanft die Quelle, op. 52, no. 10 (satb)
Russian-Polish Dance Song

O wie sanft die Quelle sich
Oh how gently the stream —

Durch   die   Wiese   windet:
through the meadow winds!

O wie schön, wenn Liebe sich,
Oh how beautiful, when love itself

Zu der Liebe findet!
with the love finds!

Oh how gently the stream
winds through the meadow!
Oh how beautiful when one love
finds itself another!

Source: Daumer 1855, 2: 64

Nein, es ist nicht auszukommen, op. 52, no. 11 (satb)
Polish

Nein, es ist nicht auszukommen
No,   it is not   to get along

Mit den Leuten;
with the people;

Alles   wissen sie so   giftig
everything know they so maliciously

Auszudeuten.
to interpret!

Bin ich heiter, hegen   soll   ich
Am I merry, harbor am said to I

Lose   Triebe;
frivolous desires;

Bin ich still, so heißt's, ich wäre
Am I silent, so means it, I were

Irr aus Liebe.
mad with love.

No, it is impossible to get along
with such people;
they know how to interpret everything
so maliciously!

If I'm merry, I'm said to have
frivolous desires;
if I'm silent, then supposedly I'm
mad with love.

Source: Daumer 1855, 2: 61

Schlosser auf, und mache Schlösser, op. 52, no. 12 (satb)
Russian-Polish Dance Song

Schlosser   auf, und mache Schlösser,
Locksmith come, and make locks,

Schlösser ohne   Zahl!
locks   without number,

Denn   die bösen Mäuler will ich
because the evil mouths want I

Schließen allzumal.
to close   forever!

Locksmith, come and make locks,
innumerable locks,
because I want to close their evil mouths
once and for all!

Source: Daumer 1855, 2: 73

Vögelein durchrauscht die Luft, op. 52, no. 13 (sa)
Russian-Polish Dance Song

Vögelein durchrauscht die Luft,
Little bird rushes through the air

Sucht nach einem Aste;
looking for a branch;

Und das Herz, ein Herz begehrt's,
and the heart— a heart yearns it

Wo es selig raste.
where it blissfully rests.

A little bird rushes through the air
looking for a branch;
and the heart—it yearns for a heart
where it may blissfully rest.

Source: Daumer 1855, 2: 66

Sieh, wie ist die Welle klar, op. 52, no. 14 (satb)
Russian-Polish Dance Song

Sieh, wie ist die Welle klar,
See, how are the waves clear

Blickt der Mond hernieder!
gazes the moon down!

Die du meine Liebe bist,
Who you my love are,

Liebe du mich wieder!
love you me again!

See how the waves are clear
when the moon gazes down!
You who are my love,
love me again!

Source: Daumer 1855, 2: 66

Nachtigall, sie singt so schön, op. 52, no. 15 (satb)
Russian-Polish Dance Song

Nachtigall, sie singt so schön,
Nightingale, she sings so beautifully

Wenn die Sterne funkeln.
when the stars twinkle.

Liebe mich, geliebtes Herz,
Love me, dear heart;

Küsse mich im Dunkeln!
kiss me in the darkness!

The nightingale sings so beautifully
when the stars twinkle.
Love me, dear heart;
kiss me in the darkness!

Source: Daumer 1855, 2: 67

Ein dunkeler Schacht ist Liebe, op. 52, no. 16 (satb)
Hungarian

Ein dunkeler Schacht ist Liebe,
A dark pit is love,

Ein gar zu gefährlicher Bronnen;
a far too dangerous well,

Da fiel ich hinein, ich Armer,
there fell I into, I poor one,

Kann weder hören, noch seh'n.
Can neither hear nor see;

Nur denken an meine Wonnen,
only think of my delight,

Nur stöhnen in meinen Weh'n.
only groan in my misery.

Love is a dark pit,
a far too dangerous well,
and poor me, I fell into it.
Now I can neither hear nor see;
I can only remember my delight,
only groan in my misery.

Source: Daumer 1855, 2: 122

Nicht wandle, mein Licht, op. 52, no. 17 (t)
Hungarian

Nicht wandle, mein Licht, dort außen
Do not wander, my light, there outside

Im Flurbereich!
in the fields!

Die Füße würden dir, die zarten,
–your feet would be–, the delicate,

Zu naß, zu weich.
too wet, too soft.

All überströmt sind dort die Wege,
All flooded are there the roads,

Die Stege dir;
the paths for you—

So überreichlich tränte dorten
so profusely shed tears there

Das Auge mir.
–my eyes–.

Don't wander, my light,
over there in the fields!
Your dainty feet would become
too wet, too soft.

All the roads are flooded there,
all your paths—
so profuse were the tears
that flowed from my eyes.

Source: Daumer 1855, 2: 125

Es bebet das Gesträuche, op. 52, no. 18 (satb)
Hungarian

Es bebet das Gesträuche,
— tremble the bushes,

Gestreift hat es im Fluge
brushed did it in flight

Ein Vögelein.
a little bird.

In gleicher Art erbebet
In same way trembles

Die Seele mir, erschüttert
–my soul–, shaken

Von Liebe, Lust und Leide,
by love, joy, and sorrow,

Gedenkt sie dein.
thinks it of you.

The bushes tremble,
brushed during the flight
of a little bird.
In the same way
my soul trembles; shaken
by love, joy, and sorrow,
it thinks of you.

Source: Daumer 1855, 2: 126

The common people have no love for difficult poets, nor for wine from Pramnos; they cause the eyes to squint and the stomach to cramp. They love the fragrant, the mild, and that which is sweet as nectar.

Aristophanes (tr. ed.)

---

*T*HUS Georg Friedrich Daumer (1800–1875) begins *Polydora: ein Welt-poetisches Liederbuch* (Polydora: a World-Poetic Songbook), his two-volume collection of international poetry, translated into German. The quotation from Aristophanes was more than a formality; it summarized the philosophy behind Daumer's collection and expressed the quality that drew Johannes Brahms to these texts—their directness, simplicity, and universal appeal.

Daumer was a teacher at a Nuremberg *Gymnasium* (high school) who quit to pursue the writing of poetry. He made his name not through original works, but by collecting and translating poems of other cultures, principally eastern European and Middle Eastern. The two-volume *Polydora* of 1855 was his largest-scale work, a collection of "folk" poetry from (vol. 1) China, Madagascar, India, Malaysia, Persia, Egypt, Jewish culture, Arabia, Afghanistan, Turkey, (vol. 2) Russia, Poland, Sicily, Spain, Serbia, Hungary, Latvia, and Lithuania. The anthology was planned to be the foundation of a global collection that never came to fruition. Nonetheless, Daumer did publish other anthologies, principally of Persian and Arabian origin or in imitation of same. Perhaps his most important collection aside from *Polydora* was his 1856 set of translations from the Persian poet Hafis (1320–1389), who had been widely admired and emulated among German literati for nearly a century.[25]

It is not known when Brahms became acquainted with *Polydora*, but biographer Max Kalbeck believes it was in a used-book store, and that Brahms was already familiar with the Hafis/Daumer poetry. It is also not known what stimulated the composer to set the Daumer poems as waltzes. Perhaps his positive experience with the Waltzes of op. 39 and the first Hungarian Dances (composed 1852–1869; no opus number) was an influence, as might have been the graceful Austrian Ländler of Schubert. But Brahms's imagination may also have been piqued by a paragraph in vol. 2 of *Polydora* in which Daumer discusses the dances associated with the "Russian-Polish miniatures" in his anthology:

> Songs in this category belong to the dance entertainments of the named peoples. For example, the more active dances of the Cossacks, which they call *Schäumer* [frothies], *Brauselieder* [bubbly songs], or *Tanzbrauser* [dance-bubbles],[26] certainly had their own words and melodies. Of the same sort are the dance songs sung by Polish peasantry to poems of their own composition.[27] (tr. ed.)

Brahms selected the entirety of op. 52 from the second volume of *Polydora*, placing his accent on Russian, Polish, and Russian-Polish poems (13/18), eight of which Daumer had labeled as "dance songs." A thread ran through all but one of these, as well as two other verses (*Liebeslieder* nos. 2, 4–6, 10, 13–15, 18). As Daumer himself observed in the continuation of the quotation above:

> It is a special characteristic of these poems that they often fall into two parts, the first of which contains some sort of visual image from nature to which the second part adds a social element. The pointed and enlightening analogy is capable of creating very nice effects. (tr. ed.)

Number 2, "Am Gesteine rauscht die Flut," serves as a good example:

Am Gesteine rauscht die Flut,	Upon the rocks the high tide breaks,
Heftig angetrieben;	hurled by a mighty force.
Wer da nicht zu seufzen wieß,	The one who knows not how to sigh
Lernt es unter'm Lieben.	learns it by loving.

These poems—and most of the other *Liebeslieder* as well—also had the virtues of terseness and focus on a single idea—what poets would call an "epigrammatic" character. There is no doubt that these qualities are what attracted Brahms to the Daumer poems, of which he set no fewer than fifty three (thirty five for chorus/quartet and eighteen for soloists), more by far than his settings of any other poet.

> For Brahms Daumer's anthologies were a veritable treasure trove of song texts. Even in Daumer's rather brittle and disjointed original poetry, which suffers noticeably in comparison to his imitations and free translations, Brahms knew how to kindle the hidden spark of genius into a bright flame, and he felt himself most deeply indebted to the poet. (Kalbeck 1976, 2: 137) (tr. ed.)

The debt was so great that in 1872 Brahms visited the aged Daumer in Würzburg to express his thanks. The composer was astonished to encounter a "withered Gnome" (Kalbeck 1976, 2: 137) at the end of life who was blissfully unaware of Brahms or his famous waltzes, to which, in one of the ironies of history, he would owe his literary immortality.

The composer began work on the op. 52 *Liebeslieder* in the summer of 1868, shortly after completing the *Deutsches Requiem* and at about the same time he set his first solo songs to Daumer texts. He finished the collection of eighteen songs the next year.

The *Liebeslieder* do not constitute a classical song cycle, in which the order of the songs is critical to the telling of a story. Brahms is known to have tried many combinations himself and to have considered issuing the songs in as many as three separate collections. In the final arrangement that was used for the first printed edition Brahms seems to have been most concerned to have frequent changes of pace and character. Any rearrangement done by performers should probably be guided by the same principle.

---

[25]*Hafis: eine Sammlung persischer Gedichte nebst poetischen Zugaben aus verschiedenen Völkern und Ländern* (Hafis: a Collection of Persian Poetry along with Poetic Additions from Various Peoples and Lands), Daumer 1856. See the annotation to Robert Schumann's "Talismane," for additional information regarding the poetry of Hafis.

The question has been raised to what extent Daumer's "folk" poetry might possibly be something else—perhaps purloined art poetry or the product of his own pen. Since he provided no documentation of his work, an answer is unlikely to be forthcoming.

[26]These are admittedly inadequate renderings of terms that defy translation.

[27]Daumer's preface to "Russian-Polish miniatures" in *Polydora*, vol. 2, quoted in Kalbeck 1976, 2: 290.

Nänie, op. 82
Nenia
Friedrich Schiller

Auch das Schöne muß sterben!
Even the beautiful must die.

  Das Menschen und Götter bezwinget,
  What mortals and Gods subdues,

Nicht die eherne Brust
not the brazen breast

  rührt es des stygischen Zeus.
  touch it of the Stygian Zeus.

Einmal nur erweichte
Once only softened

  die Liebe den Schattenbeherrscher,
  — love the ruler of the shades,

Und an der Schwelle noch, streng,
and on the threshold yet, sternly

  rief er zurück sein Geschenk.
  called he back his gift.

Nicht stillt Aphrodite
Not soothes Aphrodite

  dem schönen Knaben die Wunde,
  of the beautiful boy the wounds,

Die in den zierlichen Leib
which into his delicate body

  grausam der Eber geritzt.
  cruelly the boar tore.

Nicht errettet den göttlichen Held
Not rescue the divine hero

  die unsterbliche Mutter,
  the immortal mother,

Wenn er, am skäischen Tor fallend,
when he, at the Scaean gate falling,

  sein Schicksal erfüllt.
  his destiny fulfills.

Aber sie steigt aus dem Meer
But she rises out of the sea

  mit allen Töchtern des Nereus,
  with all daughters of Nereus

Und die Klage hebt an
and the lament is raised

  um den verherrlichten Sohn.
  for the glorified son.

Siehe! Da weinen die Götter,
Behold, there weep the gods,

  es weinen die Göttinnen alle,
  — weep the goddesses all,

Daß das Schöne vergeht,
that the beautiful perishes,

  daß das Vollkommene stirbt.
  that the perfect dies.

Auch ein Klaglied zu sein im Mund
Even a lament to be in the mouth

  der Geliebten, ist herrlich,
  of the beloved is glorious,

Denn das Gemeine geht
for the common one goes

  klanglos zum Orkus hinab.
  silently to Orcus down.

Even the beautiful must die.
  That which subdues mortals and gods
does not touch the unyielding heart
  of the Stygian Zeus.

Only once did love soften
  the ruler of the shades,
and yet, at the threshhold, sternly
  he recalled his gift.

Aphrodite does not soothe the wounds
  of the beautiful boy
whose delicate body the boar
  cruelly tore.

The immortal mother does not rescue
  the divine hero,
when, at the Scaean gate, falling,
  he fulfills his destiny.

But she rises out of the sea
  with all the daughters of Nereus
and begins the lament
  for her glorified son.

Behold, the gods weep,
  all the goddesses weep,
because the beautiful perishes,
  the perfect dies.

Even to be a lament on the lips
  of a loved one is glorious,
for the common ones go down
  to Orcus unsung.

Source: Schiller 1867, 1: 274

*I*N ancient Rome, a death was often mourned by hiring women to sing a *nenie*, a poetic lament, in honor of the deceased. The motivation of Friedrich Schiller (1759–1805) in writing this lament from 1799 is unclear, and there is no evidence that it was meant to honor a particular individual. Brahms, however, conceived his composition (1880–1881) to memorialize a contemporary artist, Anselm Feuerbach (1829–1880), with whom he was unacquainted personally, but whose classically influenced paintings he admired.[28]

Schiller's poem is an elegy on the universality of death. It is written in "elegiac couplets" or "distichs," a form borrowed from Greek and Latin poetry. The first and last of the seven couplets (here stanzas) make general statements, while three examples from Greek mythology illustrate the theme in the intervening five couplets.

Brahms's choice of a text possessing classical form and content was probably suggested by Feuerbach's own works. Feuerbach had been schooled in Paris, where he developed a liking for classical subjects and presentation; this taste was intensified by sojourns in Rome (1855–1873) and later Venice. His large-scale paintings were, like those of the Frenchman Jean-Louis David and the English Pre-Raphaelites of the era, extremely detailed and almost photographic in quality. Feuerbach was appreciated by a relatively small group of educated aficionados (Brahms apparently among them) who understood the classical techniques and allusions in his works, but he failed to achieve a broad popularity, a fact he resented to his dying day. His posthumously published autobiography, *Ein Vermächtnis* (A Testament), is so ridden with self pity that the *Oxford Companion to Art* (Osborne 1970: 406) calls it "one of the most pathetic and repellent autobiographies ever written."

The allusions to Classical mythology in Schiller's poem might be clearer with some explanation:

Stanza 1. Euridice, Adonis, and Achilles, the three mythological personages mourned in the poem, were all examples of youth and beauty taken early from this life. Clearly, to Brahms Feuerbach must have been one of the "beautiful" as well. Zeus was the supreme God of the heavens, and Styx was the main river of the underworld, over which the shades of the dead were ferried on their way to Hades. Zeus's counterpart, therefore, was Hades or Pluto, the ruler of the underworld, the "Stygian Zeus."

Stanza 2. Hades, the "Ruler of the Shades," eventually takes all, irrevocably, into his kingdom. On a single occasion, however, the culmination of the greatest love story in mythology, he and his wife Persephone permitted the return to earth of one who had died. Orpheus was permitted to take back his beloved Euridice—on the condition that he not look at her until they had reached the world of light. Orpheus, however, succumbed to temptation and glanced back, whereupon Euridice was lost forever.

Stanza 3. This stanza refers to the love of Aphrodite (Venus), the goddess of love and beauty, for the beautiful young Adonis, who was killed by a wild boar during a hunt.

Stanzas 4–6. The most extended Classical allusion occupies the fourth through the sixth stanzas: the death of Achilles in the Trojan War, followed by the lament of his mother Thetis, a sea goddess, and her sisters. Thetis was one of the fifty Nereids, the daughters of the sea god Nereus. Their lament for Achilles is mentioned in Book xxiv of Homer's *Odyssey*, where the spirits of the Greek heroes of the Trojan War are depicted conversing with each other in the underworld.

Stanza 7. The closing couplet provides the reason for the *nenie*: If only for a moment, it raises its subject above the common folk, who descend to Orcus (the Roman term for "Hades") unnoticed.

---

[28]Kross (1958: 377–381) presents considerable material of interest regarding the dedication of "Nänie" to Feuerbach.

NEUE LIEBESLIEDER WALZER, op. 65
New Lovesong Waltzes

Georg Friedrich Daumer, trans; "In Conclusion" by Johann Wolfgang von Goethe

Verzicht', O Herz, auf Rettung, op. 65, no. 1 (satb)
Turkish

Verzicht', o Herz, auf Rettung,
Renounce, O heart, of rescue,

Dich wagend in der Liebe Meer!
— venturing on the love sea!

Denn tausend Nachen schwimmen
For thousand small boats drift,

Zertrümmert am Gestad' umher!
smashed on the coast all around!

Renounce, O heart, all hope of rescue,
venturing forth on love's sea!
For a thousand boats are drifting,
smashed and wrecked along the coast!

Source: Daumer 1855, 1: 248

Finstere Schatten der Nacht, op. 65, no. 2 (satb)
Hafis (Persian)

Finstere Schatten der Nacht,
Gloomy shadows of the night,

Wogen- und Wirbelgefahr!
billows' and whirls' dangers!

Sind wohl, die da gelind
Are [they] perhaps, who there gently

Rasten auf sicherem Lande,
rest upon secure land

Euch zu begreifen im Stande?
You to understand in that position?

Das ist der nur allein,
It is he only alone,

Welcher auf hoher See
who on high sea

Stürmischer Öde treibt,
stormy desolation drifts,

Meilenentfernt vom Strande.
Miles away from shore.

Gloomy shadows of the night,
dangerous billows and whirlpools!
Are they who gently
rest on secure land
able to understand you?
Only he alone understands,
he who drifts on the high sea's
stormy desolation,
miles away from shore.

Source: Daumer 1855, 1: 201
Variant: Line 7, hoher (high) = *wilder* (wild)

An jeder Hand die Finger, op. 65, no. 3 (s)
Latvian-Lithuanian

An jeder Hand die Finger
On each hand the fingers

Hatt' ich bedeckt mit Ringen,
had I covered with rings

Die mir geschenkt mein Bruder
that to me gave my brother

In seinem Liebessinn;
in his affection

Und einen nach dem andern
And one after the other

Gab ich dem schönen, aber
gave I to the handsome but

Unwürdigen Jüngling hin.
unworthy youth —.

On each hand my fingers
were covered with rings
that my brother gave to me
as tokens of his affection.
And one after the other
I gave them to the handsome but
unworthy youth.

Source: Daumer 1855, 2: 97

Ihr schwarzen Augen, op. 65, no. 4 (b)
Sicilian

Ihr schwarzen Augen,
You   black   eyes,

Ihr dürft nur winken—
you may only blink:

Paläste fallen
palaces   fall

Und Städte sinken.
and   cities crumble!

Wie   sollte stehn
How should stand

In solchem Strauß
in   such   strife,

Mein Herz, von Karten
my   heart, of   cards

Das schwache Haus!
the   feeble   house?

You black eyes,
you need only blink:
palaces fall
and cities crumble!

How should my heart
withstand such strife,
my heart, a feeble
house of cards?

Source: Daumer 1855, 2: 248
Variant: Line 5, stehn = *stehen*

Wahre, wahre deinen Sohn, op. 65, no. 5 (a)
Russian

Wahre, wahre deinen Sohn,
Guard, guard   your   son,

Nachbarin, vor Wehe,
neighbor, from sorrow,

Weil   ich ihn mit schwarzem Aug'
because I him with   black   eye

Zu bezaubern gehe.
to   enchant   go.

O   wie brennt das Auge mir;
Oh how   burns   –my eye–;

Das zu zünden fordert!
that to ignite requires!

Flammet ihm die Seele nicht—
Blazes   him the soul   not,

Deine Hütte   lodert.
your   house will burn.

Guard, guard your son
from sorrow, neighbor,
because I'm going to enchant him
with my black eyes.

Oh, how my eye burns;
it will enkindle him!
If his soul does not ignite,
your house will burn.

Source: Daumer 1855, 2: 34

Rosen steckt mir an die Mutter, op. 65, no. 6 (s)
Spanish

Rosen steckt   mir an die Mutter,
Roses pins on   me — the mother

Weil   ich gar so trübe bin.
because I — so   sad   am.

Sie hat recht. Die Rose sinket,
She is right. The rose wilts

So wie ich,   entblättert   hin.
so as I, stripped of leaves away.

My mother pinned roses on me
because I was so very sad.
She is right. The rose wilts
just like me, stripped of its leaves.

Source: Daumer 1855, 2: 250

Vom Gebirge Well' auf Well', op. 65, no. 7 (satb)
Russian-Polish Dance Song

Vom   Gebirge Well' auf Well',
From the mountains wave upon wave,

Kommen   Regengüsse,
come   rushing torrents,

Und ich   gäbe   dir so gern
And I would give you so willingly

Hunderttausend   Küsse.
hundred thousand   kisses.

From the mountains, wave upon wave,
come the rushing torrents!
And I would so willingly give you
a hundred thousand kisses.

Source: Daumer 1855, 2: 65

Weiche Gräser im Revier, op. 65, no. 8 (satb)
Russian-Polish Dance Song

Weiche Gräser im Revier,
Soft grasses on the hunting ground—

Schöne, stille Plätzchen—
lovely, quiet, little place!

O wie linde ruht es hier
Oh, how gently rests one here

Sich mit einem Schätzchen!
— with a sweetheart!

Soft grasses on the meadows—
such a lovely, quiet place!
How gently one rests here
with a sweetheart.

Source: Daumer 1855, 2: 67
Variants: Line 3, hier = *sich*
                    Line 4, sich = *hier*

Nagen am Herzen, op. 65, no. 9 (s)
Polish

Nagen am Herzen
Gnawing in heart

Fühl ich ein Gift mir.
feel I a poison —.

Kann sich ein Mädchen,
Can — a maiden,

Ohne zu fröhnen
without to indulge in

Zärtlichem Hang,
tender delights,

Fassen ein ganzes
conceive of an entire

Wonneberaubtes
bliss-robbed

Leben entlang?
life long?

I feel a poison
gnawing in my heart.
Can a maiden,
without indulging in tender delights,
conceive of being
robbed of bliss
her entire lifetime?

Source: Daumer 1855, 2: 63

Ich kose süß mit der und der, op. 65, no. 10 (t)
Malaysian

Ich kose süß mit der und der
I caress sweetly with one and another

Und werde still und kranke;
and become quiet and ill;

Denn ewig, ewig kehrt zu dir,
for always, always, returns to you,

O Nonna, mein Gedanke!
O Nonna, my thought!

I caress one maid and then another,
but then I become quiet and ill;
for always, always, O Nonna,
my thoughts return to you!

Source: Daumer 1855, 1: 192

Alles, alles in den Wind, op. 65, no. 11 (s)
Polish

Alles, alles in den Wind
All, all into the wind

Sagst du mir, du Schmeichler!
say you to me, you flatterer!

Allesamt verloren sind
Altogether lost are

Deine Müh'n, du Heuchler!
your efforts, you hypocrite!

All, all is spoken into the wind,
everything you say to me, you flatterer!
Altogether in vain are
your efforts, you hypocrite!

Einem andern Fang zu lieb
One   other victim to please

Stelle deine Falle!
set   your trap!

Denn du bist ein loser Dieb,
For you are a wanton thief;

Denn du buhlst um   alle.
for   you flirt around everyone.

For another victim's sake
set your trap!
You are nothing but a wanton thief;
you flirt around with everyone.

Source: Daumer 1855, 2: 60

Schwarzer Wald, dein Schatten ist so düster, op. 65, no. 12 (satb)
Serbian

Schwarzer Wald, dein Schatten ist so düster!
Dark   forest, your shadow is so gloomy!

Armes Herz, dein Leiden ist so drückend!
Poor   heart, your suffering is so heavy!

Was   dir einzig wert, es steht vor Augen;
What to you alone is worth, it stands before eyes;

Ewig   untersagt ist Huldvereinung.
forever forbidden is affection's-union.

Dark forest, your shadow is so gloomy!
Poor heart, your suffering is so great!
What you dearly prize is standing before
   your eyes;
forever forbidden is love's fulfillment.

Source: Daumer 1855, 2: 22

Nein, Geliebter, setze dich mir so nahe nicht!, op. 65, no. 13 (sa)
Russian

Nein, Geliebter, setze dich
No,   beloved, sit —

Mir   so nahe nicht!
to me so near not!

Starre nicht so brünstiglich
Gaze   not so   longingly

Mir   in's   Angesicht!
at me into the   face!

No, beloved, don't sit
so close to me.
Don't gaze so longingly
into my face!

Wie   es auch im   Busen   brennt,
How much it also in the bosom may burn,

Dämpfe deinen Trieb,
suppress your desire

Daß es nicht die Welt erkennt,
That it not the world know

Wie wir uns so lieb!
how we — so love!

No matter how much your heart burns,
suppress your desire
so that the world won't know
how much in love we are!

Source: Daumer 1855, 2: 38

Flammenauge, dunkles Haar, op. 65, no. 14 (satb)
Russian

Flammenauge, dunkles Haar,
Flaming eye,   dark   hair,

Knabe   wonnig und verwogen!
youth delightful and audacious:

Kummer ist durch dich hinein
grief   has owing to you into

In mein armes Herz   gezogen.
in my   poor   heart lodged.

Flaming eye, dark hair,
delightful and audacious youth:
because of you, misery
has lodged itself in my poor heart.

Kann in Eis der Sonne Brand,
Can into ice the sun's blaze?

Sich   in Nacht der Tag verkehren?
Itself into night the day   change?

Kann die heiße Menschenbrust
Can the burning human breast

Atmen ohne   Glutbegehren?
breathe without passionate desire?

Can the sun's blaze turn into ice?
Can the day change itself to night?
Can the ardent human heart
breathe without passionate desire?

Ist die Flur so voller Licht,
Is the field so full of light

Daß die Blum' im Dunkel stehe?
that the flower in darkness stands?

Ist die Welt so voller Lust,
Is the world so full of bliss

Daß das Herz in Qual vergehe?
that the heart in anguish passes away?

Is the field so full of light
that the flower stands in darkness?
Is the world so full of bliss
that the heart dies in anguish?

Source: Daumer 1855, 2: 41

Zum Schluß, op. 65, no. 15 (satb)
In Conclusion

Johann Wolfgang von Goethe

Nun, ihr Musen, genug!
Now, you muses, enough!

Vergebens strebt ihr zu schildern,
In vain strive you to describe

Wie sich Jammer und Glück wechseln
how — grief and happiness alternate

In liebender Brust.
in loving breast.

Now, you Muses, enough!
In vain you try to describe
how grief and happiness alternate
in a loving heart.

Heilen könnet die Wunden ihr nicht,
Heal can the wounds you not

Die Amor geschlagen;
that Cupid [has] inflicted,

Aber Linderung kommt einzig,
but relief comes solely,

Ihr Guten, von euch.
you good ones, from you.

You cannot heal the wounds
that Cupid has inflicted,
but relief comes solely,
dear Muses, from you.

Source: Goethe 1948–, 1: 190

*B*RAHMS wrote his popular *Liebeslieder* waltzes, op. 52,* in 1868–1869. Either the plan for a second set was gestating even then—he did sketches of "Wahre, wahre deinen Sohn" and "Vom Gebirge Well' auf Well'" at that time—or the success of opus 52 may have provided an impetus. Whatever the stimulus, Brahms composed a second collection of fifteen "Love-Song Waltzes" in 1874 and published them the next year as op. 65.

In their essence, the new verses are the same as those from the first set: epigrammatic love poems from a variety of cultures. For this reason, the reader is referred to the annotation for op. 52. There were differences, however. Whereas Brahms drew his entire opus 52 from volume 2 of Georg Friedrich Daumer's two-volume *Polydora* (1855), the *Neue Liebeslieder* included three poems of Turkish, Persian, and Malaysian origin from volume 1. Even the verses drawn from the second volume were more varied. In addition to the Russian, Polish and Russian-Polish songs that had dominated opus 52, here Brahms incorporated Sicilian, Spanish, Turkish, Persian, Latvian-Lithuanian, and Malaysian poetry. The result was a richer, more complex texture with a noticeably darker character.

Clearly Brahms was concerned about how to conclude the *Neue Liebeslieder*. *Polydora* apparently did not contain a poem that could adequately draw together and summarize the opus. To this end the composer turned to Johann Wolfgang von Goethe (1749–1832) and his closing lines to the elegy "Alexis and Dora," written in 1796. Goethe's words, which conclude that love is simply inexplicable to mere mortals, serve admirably as a postscript not just to the present work, but to both sets of *Liebeslieder*:

> Now, you Muses, enough!
> In vain you try to describe
> how grief and happiness alternate
> in a loving heart.
>
> You cannot heal the wounds
> that Cupid has inflicted;
> but relief comes solely,
> dear Muses, from you.

Rhapsodie, op. 53

[Alto] Rhapsody

Johann Wolfgang von Goethe

Aber abseits, wer ists?
But, apart, who is it?

Ins   Gebüsch verliert sich sein Pfad,
In the thicket loses — his path;

Hinter ihm schlagen
behind him close

Die Sträuche zusammen,
the bushes together;

Das Gras   steht   wieder auf,
the grass stands up again —;

Die Öde   verschlingt ihn.
the wasteland devours him.

But there, apart, who is it?
His path is lost in the thicket;
behind him the bushes
close together;
the grass rises again;
the wasteland devours him.

Ach, wer heilet die Schmerzen
Alas, who heals the pains

Des,   dem Balsam zu Gift   ward?
of him whom balsam to poison became?

Der sich Menschenhaß
who — human hatred

Aus der Fülle der Liebe trank!
from the fullness of love drank?

Erst verachtet, nun ein Verächter,
First despised, now a despiser,

Zehrt   er heimlich auf
consumes he secretly —

Seinen eignen Wert
his   own   worth

In ungnügender Selbstsucht.
in insatiable   vanity.

Alas, who will heal the pains of him
whose balsam turned to poison,
who drank his hatred of humankind
from the fullness of love?
First despised, now a despiser,
he secretly consumes
his own worth
in insatiable vanity.

Ist auf deinem Psalter,
Is on   your psaltery,

Vater der Liebe, ein Ton
Father of love, a tone

Seinem Ohre vernehmlich,
to his   ear   audible,

So erquicke sein Herz!
so restore his heart!

Öffne den umwölkten Blick
Open the   clouded view

über   die tausend Quellen
above the thousand springs

Neben dem Durstenden
next to the thirsting ones

In der Wüste!
in the desert.

If there be on your psaltery,
Father of love, a tone
that his ear can hear,
then restore his heart!
Open the clouded view
of the thousand springs
around him who thirsts
in the desert.

Source: Goethe 1948–, 1: 310

*B*ETWEEN November 27 and December 10, 1777 the young Johann Wolfgang von Goethe (1749–1832) made a journey through the Harz mountains, culminating with his scaling the Brocken, the highest peak in the range. At the end of the climactic day he wrote in awe of his experience:

What shall I say to the Lord with my pen, what sort of song shall I sing to him at this very moment, when all my prose turns to poetry and poetry to prose? It is simply impossible to say in speech what has happened to me; how shall I express it with a sharpened quill? . . . (Boyd 1949: 135, tr. ed.)

A poem entitled "Harzreise im Winter" (A Winter Journey through the Harz Mountains) was his answer.

According to James Boyd's *Notes to Goethe's Poems* (Boyd 1949, 1: 136), the trip was intended to kill three birds with one stone. The first two tasks were for others but the third was for the poet himself. Goethe, newly an administrative assistant to Duke Karl August of Saxe-Weimar, needed to inspect some mines in the Harz for his employer, and he was able to couple with this duty an unannounced and incognito visit to a troubled young man named Plessing who had bombarded the poet with depressive, hypochondriacal letters.[29] The third task, Goethe's own, was to climb the Brocken.

The visit with the disturbed Plessing and the ascent of the mountain profoundly affected the poet, whose thoughts on both are intertwined in "Harzreise im Winter," a work of eleven stanzas of varying length, from which Brahms selected nos. 5–7 for his "Rhapsody." The poem is a contemplation of man and fate that considers two types of men: those who accept fate and learn to live happily under its constraints, and those who "stand apart" in misery and internal conflict, "wishing to break from the bonds of the brazen thread which the shears, so bitter still, cut once alone."[30] (Goethe 1983: 67) Goethe often couches his thoughts in nature imagery, as in the first stanza of "Rhapsody" and the opening stanza of "Harzreise," in which he describes the joyous peace that comes from accepting fate:

> As a hawk aloft
> On heavy daybreak cloud
> With easy pinion rests
> Searching for prey,
> may my song hover.[31]
> (Goethe 1983: 67)

For his "Rhapsody" of 1881 Brahms selected three of Goethe's stanzas that deal with the "outsider," described in the first stanza of the "Rhapsody" as lost in this existence, "devoured" by the "wasteland." In this context it is not insignificant that he chose to use a single soloist. The next stanza asks how "the outsider" might be saved from his own vanity and poison, and the final verse prays for his deliverance from his self-imposed exile and anguish.[32]

The composer often said of himself, "alas, I am a poor outsider," referring to the opening line of the "Rhapsody" (Kross 1958: 284). Siegfried Kross, the author of *Die Chorwerke von Johannes Brahms* (Kross 1958) spends fully fourteen pages discussing why this might have been so. Among his observations, one is particularly resonant: Brahms's fateful decision to abandon the possibility of a more intimate relationship with Clara Schumann. Though he was to have many female friends throughout his life, he never was to duplicate the bonds that he had with Clara, the absence of which haunted him to the end of his days and may well have inspired much of his music.[33]

Brahms's confrontation with fate finds expression not only in the "Rhapsody," but in many other works as well, both sacred and secular. Of the former, the most obvious are the *Deutsches Requiem** and the motet "Warum ist das Licht gegeben."* Of the latter, two are particularly significant:, the "Gesang der Parzen"* (Song of the Fates), also to a poem by Goethe, and the "Schicksalslied"* (Song of Destiny) of Hölderlin. All three of these works share not only their topic but a scoring for large orchestra—an opportunity for Brahms to use the full palette of expression available to a musician in his time.

---

[29]Some sources, Boyd and Kross among them, suggest that Goethe's motivation to visit Plessing had originated from guilt or a sense of responsibility—Plessing had supposedly taken a turn for the worse upon reading Goethe's *Sorrows of the Young Werther*.

[30]The cutting of the thread refers to the three Fates of Classical mythology, one of whose tasks it was to cut the thread of life.

[31]Middleton translates the word "Geier" in the first line as "buzzard." This word choice casts a negative connotation (the buzzard is a carrion eater) on what is intended to be a noble, uplifting image.

[32]As is often the case in Romantic poetry, of which Goethe at this time was a precursor, the references to the Deity are rather secular or pantheistic, with "the god of love" in this stanza, and the reference to "a god" rather than "the God" in the first stanza of the poem.

[33]In the case of the present work, Kross (1958: 286) theorizes that the death the previous year of artist Anselm Feuerbach, who was Plessing's psychological sibling, might also have been among the stimuli behind Brahms's composition. See the discussion of "Nänie" for more information.

Schicksalslied, op. 54

Song of Destiny

Friedrich Hölderin

Ihr wandelt droben im Licht
You walk above in the light

Auf weichem Boden, selige Genien!
on soft ground, blessed spirits!

Glänzende Götterlüfte
Glistening divine airs

Rühren euch leicht,
touch you lightly,

Wie die Finger der Künstlerin
like the fingers of the [female] artist

Heilige Saiten.
holy strings.

Schicksallos, wie der schlafende
Fateless, like the sleeping

Säugling, atmen die Himmlischen;
suckling, breathe the celestials;

Keusch bewahrt
chastely protected

In bescheidener Knospe
in modest bud,

Blühet ewig
blooms eternally

Ihnen der Geist,
for them the spirit,

Und die seligen Augen
and the blessed eyes

Blicken in stiller
look in still,

Ewiger Klarheit.
eternal clarity.

Doch uns ist gegeben
Yet to us is given

Auf keiner Stätte zu ruhn,
— no place to rest;

Es schwinden, es fallen
— disappears, — falls

Die leidenden Menschen
the suffering people

Blindlings von einer
blindly from one

Stunde zur andern,
hour to the other,

Wie Wasser von Klippe
like water from cliff

Zu Klippe geworfen,
to cliff thrown,

Jahr lang ins Ungewisse hinab.
year long into the unknown down.

You walk above in the light
on soft ground, blessed spirits!
Glistening, divine breezes
touch you lightly,
just as the fingers of the fair artist
play the sacred harpstrings.

Free from fate, like the sleeping
infant, celestial spirits breathe;
chastely protected
in its modest bud,
their spirit
blooms forever,
and their blessed eyes
gaze in calm,
eternal clarity.

Yet we are given
no place to rest;
we suffering humans
vanish and fall
blindly from one hour
to the next,
like water flung
from cliff to cliff
endlessly down into the unknown.

Source: Hölderin 1990: 441

*F*EW if any of the texts that Brahms set to music affected him as deeply and immediately as the "Schicksalslied." Fortunately, the story of the composition's origins in the summer of 1868 is preserved in the memoirs of the Brahms's friend Albert Dietrich:

> In the summer Brahms came once again in order to attend some parties in the area along with the Reinthalers and us. One morning we journeyed together to Wilhelmshaven, as Brahms was interested in seeing the magnificent harbor, prepared for war.

While underway our friend [Brahms], normally so cheerful, was quiet and serious. He explained that on that morning . . . he had found Hölderlin's poems in a bookcase and that he was most deeply overcome by the "Song of Destiny." As we sat relaxing by the sea later that day after a long walk all around, and after having seen everything of interest, we soon discovered Brahms in the distance, sitting all alone and writing.

These were the first sketches of the "Schicksalslied" . . . . A previously planned party failed to take place. He rushed back to Hamburg to surrender himself to his work. (tr. ed.)[34]

The poem that so touched Brahms and inspired him to one of his most profound choral works came from the pen of the poet Friedrich Hölderlin (1770–1843) in 1799. Hölderlin, a native of the Stuttgart area, began to write poetry while in his mid teens. He studied theology at his mother's behest but his heart was not in it. In 1793 he took the first of what was to be a series of private tutorial positions.

He accepted new employment in Frankfurt in December, 1795 as tutor in the home of a banker named J.F. Gontard and his wife Susette, with whom Hölderlin reciprocally fell in love. While in their employment he began work on *Hyperion* (1797–1799), a novel set in contemporary Greece and written in the form of letters.[35] Hölderlin was expelled from the house in 1798 and saw Susette for the last time the following year. His love affair was strongly to color the second volume of *Hyperion,* in which the character Diotoma was a thinly veiled representation of Susette, who "became for him an embodiment of the Hellenic ideal." (Garland 1976: 398) Near the end Hyperion loses his will to live and writes to Diotoma that he is going to sacrifice himself in battle. He survives and becomes reconciled to life, only to find that Diotoma has died of heartsickness. "Hyperions Schicksalslied," the protagonist's response to the loss of his love, is "addressed by Hyperion to the 'blessed genii,' cosmic spirits who, unlike humans, enjoy communion with the gods." (Garland 1976: 757)

The first and second of the three strophes reveal an envy of the spirits, who are "free from fate" and glide undisturbed through their eternal existence. In the final strophe Hyperion contrasts their situation with the fate of mortals, whose life is spent in constant turmoil, like the waters that crash from rock to rock and descend inexorably and "endlessly down into the unknown."[36]

SECHS QUARTETTE, op. 112
Six Quartets

Sehnsucht, op. 112, no. 1
Yearning
Franz Kugler

Es rinnen die Wasser Tag und Nacht,
— **run the waters day and night,**

Deine Sehnsucht wacht.
your yearning awakes.

The waters run day and night;
your yearning awakes.

Du gedenkest der vergangenen Zeit,
You think of the past time,

Die liegt so weit.
which lies so far.

You think of times past,
now so far away.

Du siehst hinaus in den Morgenschein
You look out into the morning light

Und bist allein.
and are alone.

You gaze out into the morning light
and are alone.

Es rinnen die Wasser Tag und Nacht,
— **run the waters day and night;**

Deine Sehnsucht wacht.
your yearning is awake.

The waters run day and night;
your yearning awakes.

Source: Kugler 1840: 39

---

[34]Dietrich, Albert. *Erinnerungen an Johannes Brahms.* Leipzig, 1899: 65; quoted in Kross 1958: 304.

[35]This genre of novel, known as a *Briefroman* (letter-novel), was in fashion in late eighteenth-century Germany.

[36]Compare Goethe's similar treatment of the same subject in "Der Gesang der Geister über den Wassern"* (Schubert).

Nächtens, op. 112, no. 2
At Night
Franz Kugler

Nächtens wachen auf die irren,
At night awake — the deranged,

Lügenmächtgen Spukgestalten,
deceitful ghost figures,

Welche deinen Sinn verwirren.
who your mind bewilder.

At night the deranged,
deceitful specters awake
and perplex your mind.

Nächtens ist im Blumengarten
At night has in the flower garden

Reif gefallen, daß vergebens
hoarfrost fallen, so that in vain

Du der Blumen würdest warten.
you the flowers would await.

At night in the flower garden
hoarfrost has fallen; in vain
you would wait for the blossoms.

Nächtens haben Gram und Sorgen
At night have grief and sorrow

In dein Herz sich eingenistet,
in your heart –built their nest,–

Und auf Tränen blickt der Morgen.
and on tears looks the morning.

At night grief and sorrow
entrenched themselves in your heart,
and the morning looks upon tears.

Source: Kugler 1840: 7

Vier Zigeunerlieder, op. 112, no. 3
Four Gypsy Songs
Hugo Conrat, after Hungarian folk songs

Himmel strahlt so helle und klar
The Sky Beams so Bright and Clear

Himmel strahlt so helle und klar,
Sky shines so bright and clear,

Heller strahlt mir dein Augenpaar.
brighter shines for me your pair of eyes.

Du meine Rose, mir ins Auge blick,
You my rose, me into the eye look,

Daß ich dich segne in meinem Glück.
that I you bless in my happiness.

The sky beams so bright and clear,
but brighter beams your pair of eyes.
You, my rose, look into my eyes
so that I may bless you in my happiness.

Vögleins Lied so lieblich erklingt,
Little bird's song so lovely sounds;

Süßres Lied mir mein Liebchen singt.
sweeter song for me my beloved sings.

Du meine Rose, mir ins Auge blick,
You my rose, me into the eye look,

Daß ich dich segne in meinem Glück.
that I you bless in my happiness.

The little bird's song so sweetly rings;
sweeter still is the song my beloved sings.
You, my rose, look into my eyes
so that I may bless you in my happiness.

Sonne küßt das ganze Erdenrund,
Sun kisses the whole earth-round,

Heißer küßt mich dein Rosenmund.
hotter kisses me your rose mouth.

Du meine Rose, mir ins Auge blick,
You my rose, me into the eye look,

Daß ich dich segne in meinem Glück.
that I you bless in my happiness.

The sun kisses the entire globe;
hotter yet are the kisses from your rosy mouth.
You, my rose, look into my eyes
so that I may bless you in my happiness.

Rote Rosenknospen
Red Rosebuds

Rote Rosenknospen
Red   rose buds

Künden   schon des Lenzes Triebe.
announce already the spring's desire.

Rosenrote Wangen
Rose-red   cheeks

Deuten Mädchens erste Liebe.
indicate maiden's first love.

Kleiner roter Vogel,
Little   red   bird,

Flieg herab zur   roten Rose!
Fly down to the red   rose!

Bursche geht zum rosgen Mädchen kosen.
Lad   goes to the rosy   maiden to court.

Red rosebuds
already proclaim the stirring of spring.
Rose-red cheeks
betray the maiden's first love.
Little red bird,
fly down to the red rose.
The lad goes to court the rosy maiden.

Brennessel steht an Weges Rand
Stinging Nettles Stand at the Edge of the Path

Brennessel   steht an Weges Rand,
Stinging nettles stand at   path's edge,

Neider   und Feinde hab ich in Stadt und Land.
Envious ones and foes have I in town and country.

Neidet, haßt, verleumdet, doch das bringt mir keine Not.
Envy, hate, slander, but that brings me no distress.

Wenn mir nur mein süßes Liebchen treu   bleibt
If   me only my   sweet beloved faithful remains

bis   zum Tod.
until —   death.

Stinging nettles stand at the edge of the path;
Envious foes have I in town and country.
They envy, hate, and slander, but they bring me
    no distress.
If only my sweet love would remain faithful
    until death.

Liebe Schwalbe, kleine Schwalbe
Dear Swallow, Little Swallow

Liebe Schwalbe, kleine Schwalbe,
Dear swallow, little swallow,

Trage fort mein kleines Briefchen!
carry away my   little   letter!

Flieg zur   Höhe, fliege schnell aus,
Fly to the heights, fly   fast —,

Flieg hinein in Liebchens Haus!
Fly   in into belovéd's house!

Fragt man dich: woher   du kommest,
Asks one you: where from you come,

Wessen Bote   du   geworden,
whose messenger you have become,

Sag: du kommst vom   treusten Herzen,
say: you come from the most faithful heart,

Das   vergeht in Trennungsschmerzen.
which pines away in   separation pain.

Dear swallow, little swallow,
carry my little letter for me.
Fly high, fly quickly,
fly into my belovéd's house.

If anyone asks you where you come from,
whose messenger you are,
say that you come from the truest heart,
which languishes in the pain of being apart.

*T*HE poems of Franz Kugler (1808–1858) came to Brahms's attention almost by accident. In the summer of 1887 he was called on socially at his vacation house on Lake Thun in Switzerland by Professor Dr. Bernhard and Else Kugler from Tübingen. Brahms learned from Mrs. Kugler that her father-in-law Franz had left behind a manuscript collection of poetry, and he expressed an interest in seeing it. Later, when it was not forthcoming, he wrote requesting it again, and it was sent. This is the collection in which Brahms found "Sehnsucht" and "Nächtens."

Few poems can match the austere desolation of "Sehnsucht," a portrait of loneliness in which its subject, doubtless awake with his thoughts all night, looks out the window at dawn and cannot see the light for his tears. Brahms's setting, with its exquisitely beautiful piano part, synergistically elevates the poem. "Nächtens" begins as a Halloween nightmare set to music; the night, so often a symbol of tranquility, becomes the enemy. As the frost kills the flowers (stanza 2), so does the night kill happiness and peace, leaving nothing to do but weep (stanza 3). It may be more than just coincidence that both poems end with tears as the morning dawns; perhaps this fact played a role in the composer's decision to combine them in the same group.

Brahms found the four Gypsy Songs in the same collection by Hugo Conrat that had yielded the texts for the *Zigeunerlieder,** op. 103. He likely composed the settings of all the poems at about the same time in 1887, showing by his division of them into two groups that both *Zigeunerlieder* were intended to comprise integral sets, not just assemblages.

The pairing of these Germanized Hungarian folk/love-poems with the two melancholy verses by Kugler may not be as odd as it first seems. Brahms biographer Max Kalbeck suggests that the four *Zigeunerlieder* were intended to be a sort of relief from the intensity and dismal mood of the Kugler poems, implying that the entire group should be performed as a unit. (Kalbeck 1976, 4: 105)

VIER QUARTETTE, op. 92
Four Quartets

O schöne Nacht, op. 92, no. 1
Oh Lovely Night
Georg Friedrich Daumer

O schöne Nacht!
Oh lovely night!

Am Himmel märchenhaft
In the sky fairy tale-like

Erglänzt der Mond in seiner ganzen Pracht,
shines the moon in its full splendor;

Um ihn der kleinen Sterne liebliche Genossenschaft.
around it the little stars pleasant company.

Es schimmert hell der Tau
— glistens brightly the dew

Am grünen Halm; mit Macht
on the green stem; with power

Im Fliederbusche schlägt die Nachtigall;
in the lilac bush sings the nightingale;

Der Knabe schleicht zu seiner Liebsten sacht—
the youth sneaks to his beloved quietly.

O schöne Nacht!
Oh lovely night!

Oh lovely night!
In the sky, magically,
the moon shines in all its splendor;
around it is the pleasant company of little
  stars.

Dew glistens brightly on green stems;
in the lilac bush, the nightingale sings
  lustily.
The youth steals away quietly to his love.
Oh lovely night!

Source: Daumer 1855, 2: 129
Variants: (Brahms = roman, Daumer = *italics*)
  Stanza 2, line 4: Fliederbusche = *Fliederbaume*
  line 5: Liebsten = *Liebe*

*L*IKE the texts to the "Liebeslieder" waltzes, opp. 52 and 65, the poem "O schöne Nacht" was drawn from the *Polydora* of Georg Friedrich Daumer (1800–1875), which contained German translations of "folk" poetry, in this case from Hungary. (See the annotation to Brahms's *Liebeslieder*, op. 52, for additional information.) "O schöne Nacht," composed in 1877 at the latest, was the last piece from Daumer's anthology that Brahms set to music, the *Neue Liebeslieder* and "Fragen" (op. 64) having been composed in 1874.

Daumer's lyric is on its surface a lovely, innocent picture of a moonlit night, its silence broken only by the call of the nightingale. Only in the penultimate line, as the young man sneaks away quietly to his love, does it explicitly become a love poem.

In the Daumer *Polydora* "O schöne Nacht" directly follows "Am Donaustrande," which Brahms set as no. 9 in the op. 52 *Liebeslieder*. Brahms biographer Max Kalbeck points out that the former seems to be an "extension and conclusion" of the latter and he finds the artistic juxtaposition suspicious for what is supposed to be "folk" poetry. (Kalbeck 1976, 3: 512) He clearly believed that at least some of the poems were entirely of Daumer's authorship.

Brahms altered the poem twice, in both cases probably to intensify expression. The onomatopoeia of "fliederbu*sche schl*ägt" is certainly superior to "Fliederbaume schlägt," and having the youth steal away to his "most beloved" (*Liebsten*) is and sounds more intense than Daumer's "love" (*Liebe*).

Spätherbst, op. 92, no. 2
Late Autumn
Hermann Allmers

Der graue Nebel tropft so still
The gray mist drips so silently

Herab auf Feld und Wald und Heide,
down on field and forest and heath,

Als ob der Himmel weinen will
as if — heaven to weep wants

In übergroßem Leide.
in immense grief.

Die Blumen wollen nicht mehr blühn,
The flowers want no more to blossom;

Die Vöglein schweigen in den Hainen,
The little birds are silent in the groves.

Es starb sogar das letzte Grün,
— died even the last green,

Da mag er auch wohl weinen.
thus may he also well weep.

The gray mist drips so silently
down on field and forest and heath,
as if the heavens wished to weep
in overwhelming grief.

The flowers will bloom no more;
the little birds are silent in the groves.
Even the last green is dead—
thus the heavens may well weep.

Source: Allmers 1965: 343

Variants: (Brahms = roman, Allmers = *italic*)

Stanza 2, line 2: Vöglein = *Vögel*

line 4: Da mag er auch wohl weinen (thus the heavens may well weep) = *Was sollt er da nicht weinen* (why should the heavens not weep?)

*T*HIS poem by Hermann Allmers (1821–1902) provides the contrast within an otherwise rather light opus. While there is a reasonably positive tone to the other three songs, "Spätherbst" would not be out of place in the decidedly dark context of the opus 104 quartets such as "Letztes Glück"* (Last Happiness) and "Verlorene Jugend"* (Lost Youth).

Allmers was best known for longer prose and dramatic works; this is one of his only thirty-five poems. He was also a leader in what came to be known as *Heimatkunst* (art of the homeland), a mid-century movement to preserve the individuality of the many German regions against the equalizing pressures of industrial society. Local authors were encouraged to write about their own homeland and people, and thereby to carry forward their unique culture.

"Spätherbst" can be seen in this context as a description of the foggy, cold November typical of East Friesland, the north-German region of which Allmers was a native. On the other hand, it is not just a nature poem, but like so many romantic verses, it employs nature as a window on the human soul. In the first strophe the quiet of the fog elicits not a sense of serenity, but rather a sadness beyond expression. The reader hoping for relief in the second stanza will be disappointed as the silence of the first verse is understood as a death—of nature and the spirit—so profound that the heavens themselves will indeed weep.

Abendlied, op. 92, no. 3

Evening Song

Friedrich Hebbel

Friedlich   bekämpfen
Peacefully   struggle

Nacht sich und Tag.
night — and day.

Wie das zu dämpfen,
how that to soften,

Wie das zu lösen vermag!
how that to relieve is able!

In peaceful opposition
night struggles with the day.
What ability it has to soften,
what ability it has to relieve!

Der   mich bedrückte,
He who me   oppressed,

Schläfst du schon, Schmerz?
sleep   you already, sorrow?

Was mich beglückte,
What me made happy—

Sage, was wars doch, mein Herz?
say, what was it —,   my heart?

Sorrow that oppresses me,
are you already asleep?
That which made me happy—
say, my heart, what was it then?

Freude wie Kummer,
Joy   like   grief,

Fühl ich, zerrann,
feel   I, melt away,

Aber den Schlummer
but   the slumber

Führten sie leise heran.
bring they quietly to me.

Joy, like grief,
I feel, melts away;
but they bring me slumber
as they fade away.

Und im   Entschweben,
And in the floating away,

Immer empor,
always upward,

Kommt mir   das Leben
comes to me the   life

Ganz, wie ein Schlummerlied vor.
entire, like a slumbersong —.

And in the vanishing,
ever upward,
my entire life passes before me,
like a lullaby.

Source: Hebbel 1963–1967, 3: 47

*F*RIEDRICH Hebbel (1813–1863) composed his resigned meditation on life (day) and death (night) entitled "Abendgefühl" (Evening Feeling) in Munich on October 17, 1838 when he was only 25 years old. As he related in a letter of November 11 of the same year (no longer extant), he was moved to write it by the memorial service for a friend named Emil Rousseau, who had died on October 2. (Hebbel 1965, 3: 893) Hebbel was hit especially hard by this death, as it followed that of his mother by only a few weeks. In his diary, which he maintained from 1835 until his own passing, he wrote that he had been unable to make any entries for months because he would have had to face writing of these losses. (Hebbel 1965, 4: 236)

Warum?, op. 92, no. 4
Why?
Johann Wolfgang von Goethe

Warum doch erschallen
Why   then   resound

Himmelwärts die Lieder?
heavenwards   the   songs?

Zögen   gerne nieder Sterne,
Would draw gladly   down   stars

Die droben blinken und wallen,
that above   twinkle and sparkle;

Zögen   sich   Lunas lieblich Umarmen,
would draw to themselves Luna's lovely   embrace;

Zögen   die warmen, wonnigen Tage
would draw   the warm,   blissful   days

Seliger   Götter gern   uns   herab!
of blessed gods gladly upon us down!

Why then do songs
resound heavenwards?
They would fain draw down the stars
that twinkle and sparkle above;
they would draw to themselves
the moon's lovely embrace;
they would fain draw the warm, blissful days
of the blessed gods down upon us.

Source: Goethe 1948–, 3: 607

*T*HE opening of a new theater was a cause for celebration among actors and playwrights in Goethe's time, as it presented greater opportunities for their art. For the opening of a capacious new theater in Lauchstädt in the summer of 1802, Goethe wrote a *Vorspiel* (prologue) entitled "Was wir bringen" (What We Bring), from the tenth scene of which Brahms took the brief poem "Warum doch erschallen."

"Was wir bringen" was apparently intended as a good-natured spoof of the Weimar theatrical scene in Goethe's time. It is a pastiche of the many themes and conventions of Weimar theater at the beginning of the nineteenth century, all rolled into a single mini-play. It contains, to quote a review from the *Allgemeine Zeitung* of October 10, 1802, "burlesque, family drama, opera, tragedy, naïvete, as well as the mask" (Goethe 1948–, 3: 767), to which might be added magic and an omniscient narrator in the person of Mercury.

The Prologue looks in on the five residents of a peasant house in the country, parents and three daughters named Nymphe, Phone, and Pathos (!), who offer their hospitality to a well-dressed traveler—after he climbs into a window that opened inexplicably for him. He insinuates himself easily into their midst and identifies himself as a physicist (or is he perhaps a witch, as the mother believes?) who will use his talents to repay their kindness.

The traveler offers them a trip to a better place, for which they need not go out into the blizzard, as he will take them there on a magic carpet. The only carpet in the house is rolled up in the attic, however, and will take a couple of hours to bring down. This presents no problem to the traveler, who assures his hosts that if they just sing a short song, the carpet will come down by itself. The women sing the song, "Warum doch erschallen," the carpet makes its appearance, and all but the always-suspicious mother begin their journey, in which the modest house is transformed into a magnificent hall and the travelers find themselves dressed in elegant finery.

Waldesnacht, op. 62, no. 3

Forest Night

Paul Heyse

Waldesnacht du   wunderkühle,
Forest night you wonderful cool one

Die ich tausend   male grüß'
that I a thousand times greet

Nach dem lauten Weltgewühle
after the   loud world bustle,

O, wie ist dein Rauschen süß!
oh, how is your rustling sweet!

Träumerisch die müden Glieder
Dreamy   the   tired   limbs

Berg' ich weich   ins   Moos,
shelter I softly into the moss,

Und mir ist, als würd' ich wieder
and to me is, as if would I   again

All der   irren   Qualen los.
all of the insane torments rid.

Fernes Flötenlied, vertöne,
Distant flute song, die away,

Das ein weites Sehnen rührt,
which a   vast   longing stirs,

Die Gedanken in die schöne,
the thoughts into the beautiful

Ach! mißgönnte Ferne   führt.
alas,   envied distance carries.

Laß die Waldesnacht mich wiegen,
Let the forest night me   rock,

Stillen jede Pein!
soothe all pain,

Und ein seliges   Genügen
and a blessed contentment

Saug ich mit den Düften   ein.
inhale I with the fragrances —.

In den heimlich engen Kreisen
In the secret, narrow circles

Wird   dir wohl, du wildes Herz,
become you well, you wild heart,

Und ein Friede schwebt mit leisen
and a   peace floats with soft

Flügelschlägen niederwärts.
wing flaps   downward.

Singet, holde Vögellieder,
Sing, lovely bird songs,

Mich in Schlummer sacht!
me into slumber gently!

Irre   Qualen,   lös't euch wieder;
Insane torments, disappear again;

Wildes Herz, nun gute Nacht!
wild   heart, now "good night."

You wondrously cool forest night
that I greet a thousand times
after the loud bustle of the day,
oh, how sweet is your rustling!
Dreamily I sink my tired limbs
softly into the sheltering moss,
and I feel as if I would again
be rid of all of life's insane torments.

May the distant flute song,
which stirs a deep longing
and carries the thoughts into
the beautiful, alas, envied distance, die away.
Let the forest night cradle me
and soothe all my pain,
and a blessed contentment
shall I inhale with its fragrances.

In the secret, narrow circles
you become well, you wild heart,
and a peace floats down
with soft flutterings.
Dearest birdsongs,
sing me softly to sleep!
Insane torments, disappear again;
wild heart, now "good night."

Source: Heyse 1850: 35

*D*ER *Jungbrunnen* (The Fountain of Youth), an anthology of six original fairy tales, appeared in 1850, not long after the bloody and failed Prussian revolution of late 1848. In his introduction, Heyse felt it necessary to apologize for the appearance of a volume of humorous tales after the "Medusa of civil war had hardly lowered the glance with which she turned to stone the fear on all faces."

"Waldesnacht" is taken from a fairy tale entitled *Glückspilzchen* (Little Mushroom of Happiness). The main character, Hansel, an orphaned, fifteen-year-old cobbler's apprentice, grows tired of being beaten by his guardian and decides, after reading the book of Exodus, to travel to the "fleshpot of Egypt." Walking from his village toward Egypt with his accordion on his back, he meets a young poet and his little sister nicknamed "Glückspilzchen." At the end of the day they seek shelter and food at a solitary house and find themselves at a wedding, where the poet mesmerizes, Hansel entertains, and Glückpilzchen charms the guests. Just as a bed and a warm meal seem certain, the inebriated father of the bride boots them out. They have no choice but to spend the night in the forest, where they make beds on the grass, and the poet sings himself to sleep with *Waldesnacht*.

ZIGEUNERLIEDER, *op. 103*

Gypsy Songs

Hugo Conrat, trans.

He, Zigeuner, greife in die Saiten ein, op. 103, no. 1

He, Zigeuner, greife in die Saiten ein!
Hey, Gypsy,   strike on the strings —!

Spiel das Lied vom ungetreuen Mägdelein!
Play the song of the unfaithful maiden!

Laß die Saiten weinen, klagen, traurig bange,
Let the strings weep, lament, sadly tremble,

Bis   die heiße Tränen netzen diese Wange!
until the hot   tears moisten this cheek!

Hey, Gypsy, strike on your strings!
Play the song of the unfaithful maiden!
Let the strings weep, lament, and sadly tremble,
until hot tears moisten this cheek!

Hochgetürmte Rimaflut, wie bist du so trüb?, op. 103, no. 2

Hochgetürmte   Rimaflut, wie bist du so trüb,
High towering Rima flood, how are you so turbid!

An dem Ufer   klag ich laut nach dir, mein Lieb!
At the shore lament I loudly for you, my love!

Wellen fliehen, Wellen strömen,
Waves   flee, waves stream,

Rauschen an   den Strand heran zu mir;
rush   toward the shore   — to me;

An dem Rimaufer laßt mich ewig weinen nach ihr!
at the Rima shore let me forever weep for her!

High towering Rima waves, how turbid you are!
At the shore I cry loudly for you, my love!
Waves are rushing to and fro,
flooding towards me on the shore;
on Rima's banks let me forever weep for her!

Wißt ihr, wann mein Kindchen am allerschönsten ist?, op. 103, no. 3

Wißt ihr, wann mein Kindchen
Know you when my   darling

Am allerschönsten ist?
— most beautiful is?

Wenn ihr süßes Mündchen
When her sweet   mouth

Scherzt und lacht und küßt.
teases and laughs and kisses.

Mägdelein, du bist mein,
Maiden,   you are mine;

Inniglich küß ich dich,
fervently kiss I you.

Dich erschuf der liebe Himmel
You created the dear Heaven

Einzig nur für mich.
solely only for me.

[He:]
Do you know when my darling
is most beautiful?
When her sweet mouth
teases and laughs and kisses.
Maiden, you are mine;
fervently I kiss you.
Heaven created you
solely and only for me.

Wißt ihr, wann mein Liebster
Know you, when   my   love

Am besten mir gefällt?
—   best me pleases?

Wenn in seinen Armen
When in   his   arms

Er mich umschlungen hält.
he me   embraced holds.

Schätzelein,   du bist mein,
Sweetheart, you are mine;

Inniglich küß ich dich,
fervently kiss I you.

Dich erschuf der liebe Himmel
You created the dear Heaven

Einzig nur für mich!
solely only for me!

[She:]
Do you know when my love
pleases me most?
When he holds me
closely in his arms.
Sweetheart, you are mine;
fervently I kiss you.
Heaven created you
solely and only for me!

Lieber Gott, du weißt, wie oft bereut ich hab, op. 103, no. 4

Lieber Gott, du weißt, wie oft   bereut ich hab,
Dear   God, you know how often regretted I have

Daß ich meinem Liebsten einst ein Küßchen gab.
that I   my   belovéd once a small kiss gave.

Herz gebot, daß ich ihn küssen muß,
Heart bade, that I him   kiss   must;

Denk, so lang ich leb, an diesen ersten Kuß.
think, as long as I live, of   this   first kiss.

Lieber Gott, du weißt, wie   oft in stiller Nacht
Dear   God, you know how often in still night

Ich in Lust und Leid an meinen Schatz gedacht.
I in joy and sorrow of my   dearest thought.

Lieb ist süß, wenn bitter auch die   Reu,
Love is sweet, if   bitter also the remorse;

Armes Herze bleibt   ihm ewig, ewig treu.
poor   heart remains to him ever, ever faithful.

Dear God, you know how often I've regretted
that I once gave a small kiss to my belovéd.
My heart commanded that I should kiss him;
I shall think of that first kiss as long as I live.

Dear God, you know how often, in the still of night,
through joy and sorrow, I've thought of my dearest.
Love is sweet, even though remorse is bitter;
my poor heart will remain ever, ever true.

Brauner Bursche führt zum Tanze, op. 103, no. 5

Brauner Bursche führt zum Tanze
Brown   lad   leads to the dance

Sein blauäugig schönes Kind,
his blue-eyed beautiful child.

Schlägt   die Sporen keck zusammen,
[He] bangs the spurs boldly together,

Czardas–Melodie beginnt,
Czardas melody   begins,

Küßt und herzt   sein süßes Täubchen,
kisses and caresses his sweet little dove,

Dreht sie, führt sie, jauchzt und springt;
turns her, leads her, shouts and   leaps,

Wirft   drei blanke Silbergulden
throws three shiny silver guilders

Auf das Cimbal, daß es klingt.
on   the cymbal, that it rings.

The bronzed lad leads his lovely,
   blue-eyed sweetheart to the dance.
He kicks his spurs together boldly
   as the Czardas melody begins,
kisses and caresses his sweet little dove,
   whirls her, leads her, shouts and leaps for joy,
and throws three shiny silver guilders
   on the cymbal, making it ring.

Röslein dreie in der Reihe blühn so rot, op. 103, no. 6

Röslein   dreie in der Reihe blühn so rot,
Little roses three in the row bloom so red.

Daß der Bursch zum Mädel geht, ist kein Verbot!
That the lad   to the girl goes, is not forbidden!

Lieber Gott, wenn das   verboten wär,
Dear   God, if   that forbidden were,

Ständ   die schöne   weite Welt   schon
standing the beautiful, wide world already

   längst nicht mehr,
   long   no   more;

Ledig   bleiben Sünde wär!
Unmarried to remain sin   would be!

Schönstes   Städtchen in Alföld ist Ketschkemet.
Most beautiful town   in Alföld is Ketschkemet.

Dort gibt es gar viele   Mädchen schmuck und nett!
–There are a great many– girls   pretty and nice!

Freunde, sucht euch   dort ein Bräutchen aus,
Friends, seek for you there a little bride —;

Freit um ihre Hand und gründet euer Haus,
court for her hand and found your house;

Freudenbecher leeret aus!
joy-cup   empty out!

Three little roses all in a row bloom so red.
For the lad to visit his lass is not forbidden!
Dear God, if that were forbidden,
this beautiful, wide world would have
   perished long ago;
to remain unmarried would be a sin!

The most beautiful town in Alföld is Ketschkemet.
There are many girls there who are pretty and nice.
Friends, seek for yourself a little bride there;
ask for her hand and start a family;
empty the cup of joy!

Kommt dir manchmal in den Sinn, op. 103, no. 7

Kommt dir   manchmal in den Sinn,
Comes to you sometimes into the mind,

mein süßes Lieb,
my   sweet love,

Was   du einst mit heil'gem Eide
what you once with sacred   oath

mir   gelobt?
to me vowed?

Täusch mich nicht, verlaß mich nicht,
Deceive me   not, leave me   not;

Du weißt nicht, wie   lieb ich dich hab,
you know not, how dearly I   you have.

Lieb du mich, wie ich dich,
Love you me   as I   you;

Dann strömt Gottes Huld auf dich herab.
then streams God's grace on you down.

Do you sometimes remember, my sweet love,
what you once vowed to me with a sacred oath?
Deceive me not, leave me not;
you know not how dearly I love you.
Love me as I love you;
then God's grace will pour down on you.

Horch, der Wind klagt in den Zweigen, op. 103, no. 8

Horch, der Wind klagt in den Zweigen
Listen, the wind laments in the branches—

traurig sacht;
sadly, softly.

Süßes Lieb, wir müssen scheiden: gute Nacht!
Sweet love, we must   part: good night.

Ach, wie   gern in deinen Armen   ruhte   ich!
Ah, how gladly in your   arms would rest I,

Doch die Trennungsstunde naht, Gott schütze dich.
but the   parting hour nears; God protect you.

Dunkel ist die Nacht, kein Sternlein spendet Licht;
Dark   is the night; no little star gives light.

Süßes Lieb, vertrau auf Gott und weine nicht!
Sweet love, trust in God and weep not.

Führt der liebe Gott mich einst zu dir zurück,
Leads the dear God me   once to you back,

Bleiben wir vereint im   Liebesglück.
remain we united in love's happiness.

Listen: the wind moves in the branches—
sadly, softly.
Sweet love, we must part: "good night."
Ah, how gladly I would rest in your arms,
but the parting hour draws near; God protect you.

Dark is the night; not even a little star gives light.
Sweet love, trust in God and weep not.
If God leads me back to you one day,
we will remain united in love's happiness.

Weit und breit schaut niemand mich an, op. 103, no. 9

Weit und breit schaut niemand mich an,
Wide and far looks at nobody me —,

Und wenn sie mich hassen, was   liegt mir daran?
And if they me   hate, what   –do I care–?

Nur mein Schatz der soll mich lieben allezeit,
Only my darling he shall me   love always,

Soll mich küssen, umarmen und herzen in Ewigkeit.
shall me kiss, embrace, and caress eternally.

Kein Stern blickt in finsterer Nacht,
No   star shines in   dark   night,

Keine Blume   mir   strahlt in duftiger Pracht.
no   flower for me blooms in fragrant splendor.

Dein Augen sind mir Blumen Sternenschein,
Your eyes   are to me flowers, stars' light

Die mir leuchten so freundlich,
that me   shine   so kindly,

die blühen nur   mir   allein.
that bloom only for me alone.

Far and wide no one notices me,
and if they hate me, what do I care?
Only my darling shall love me always,
shall kiss me, embrace me, and caress me forever.

Not a single star shines in the dark night,
not a single flower blooms in fragrant splendor.
To me, your eyes are flowers and starlight
that shine so kindly on me and bloom for me alone.

Mond verhüllt sein Angesicht, op. 103, no. 10

Mond verhüllt sein Angesicht,
Moon   veils   his countenance,

Süßes Lieb, ich zürne   dir   nicht.
sweet love, I am angry with you not.

Wollt ich zürnend dich betrüben,
Wanted I angrily   you to distress,

Sprich, wie könnt ich dich dann lieben?
say   how could I   you then love?

Heiß für dich mein Herz   entbrennt,
Hotly for you my heart begins to burn.

Keine Zunge   dirs bekennt.
No   tongue to you it admits.

Bald   in Liebesrausch unsinnig,
Sometimes in love's intoxication mad,

Bald   wie Täubchen sanft und   innig.
sometimes like little dove gently and tenderly.

Even though the moon veils its face,
sweet love, I'm not angry with you.
If I were and wanted to distress you,
then how could I truly love you?

Fervently my heart begins to burn.
(No tongue admits it to you.)
Sometimes delirious from love's madness,
sometimes gently, tenderly—like a dove.

Rote Abendwolken ziehn am Firmament, op. 103, no. 11

Rote Abendwolken   ziehn
Red evening clouds move

Am   Firmament,
in the firmament;

Sehnsuchtsvoll nach dir, mein Lieb,
longing-full   for you, my love,

das Herze brennt;
the heart burns.

Himmel strahlt in glühnder Pracht
Heavens shine in glowing splendor,

Und ich träum   bei Tag und Nacht
and I dream during day and night

Nur allein von dem süßen Liebchen mein.
only solely of the sweet   love   mine.

Red clouds of evening drift across the sky;
full of longing for you, my love, my heart burns.
The heavens shine in glowing splendor,
and I dream by day and night
solely of my sweet love.

EUROPEANS in the romantic era were fascinated with people and places far removed in distance and time—the more remote and mysterious the better. This interest in the exotic manifested itself in many ways, from neo-classicism in literature and painting to pseudo-oriental art and poetry and even the advent of historical musicology.

Particularly intriguing to the romantics were the Gypsies, a people who originated in northwest India (a fact unknown at that time) and had been forced into Europe beginning in the eleventh century. Their mystique can be attributed to many factors—foreign appearance, quasi-nomadic lifestyle, incomprehensible language, and strange customs. Perhaps the most important element in their legend was their apartness; they were outcasts from most European society and over the centuries were subject to waves of repression that equalled or surpassed those experienced by the Jews during the same period. Although they were spread throughout the continent, they were especially concentrated in Hungary, a fact that led to most anything Hungarian being thought of as "Gypsy."

In 1887 Brahms first met the translator of the *Zigeunerlieder*, a Viennese businessman and amateur poet-musician named Hugo Conrat (dates unknown).[37] Conrat was one of three brothers, scions of a prosperous mercantile business, each of whom found recognition independently of the family enterprise, and each of

---

[37] In 1903 Conrat wrote a memoir of Brahms entitled "Brahms as I Knew Him" for the *Neue-Musik-Zeitung* of Cologne. (Conrat 1903: 1) In it he relates how he was befriended by the composer, who deliberately closed himself off from new friendships in the last decade of his life. It seems Conrat was an autograph collector and was particularly interested in "personal" items such as letters rather than receipts and other such "impersonal" material. He told Brahms that he had seen a letter of his being offered at auction in London, whereupon the composer became enraged at the intrusion into his privacy. Conrat arranged to purchase the letter at any price and had it sent to him under triple seal, so it would be clear that no one had read it. He then presented it to Brahms, who was touched and thereafter accepted Conrat into his social circle.

whom used different family names—perhaps to mask Jewish origins.[38] The best known of the three brothers was plant biologist Ferdinand Cohn (the only one to retain the family name); the other, Oskar Justinius, was a popular humorist and comedic poet.

Conrat had an interest in Hungarian folk song that he pursued with the help of his children's governess, a young woman named Witzl, who translated for him from a large collection of Hungarian folk songs. Conrat selected twenty-five of them and recast Fräulein Witzl's presumably non-literary German into poetry that fit the original melodies. These he then published as a collection, with accompaniments by Zoltán Nagy.[39] Showing his anthology to Brahms, the composer of the famous "Hungarian Dances" (no opus number, 1872 and 1869–1880), must have taken some courage but it was rewarded. Brahms was taken by the poems and chose eleven to set as one group (op. 103) and another four to set separately (op. 112). The opus 103 *Zigeunerlieder* followed shortly thereafter.

Brahms's delight with his compositions is clear in this excerpt from a letter by Marie Brüll, who was present at their first, private performance, and whose husband Ignaz accompanied the singers along with Brahms. As the singers sang, "All at once he [Brahms] ran as if shot by a cannon into our children's room and pulled our kind and modest Witzl out and brought her into the music room. As their 'creator' she was supposed to sit and listen to the quartet perform 'her' *Zigeunerlieder*." (Kalbeck 1976, 4: 95, tr. ed.)

The op. 103 "Gypsy Songs" were certainly intended to comprise a cycle, though not in the usual sense of a set of songs that tells a story. Rather, they represent eleven brief vignettes of "Gypsy" love—requited and unrequited, fierce and tender—arranged so as to create a constantly changing kaleidoscope of moods. Neither the poems nor the melodies had much to do with actual Gypsy culture, however. As noted earlier, Germans of that era associated anything Hungarian with Gypsies—particularly music and poetry.

Conrat and Brahms were to develop a friendship that lasted until Brahms's death a decade later. One of the most loving discussions of the composer is found in Conrat's memoir published in *La revue musicale* on November 1, 1904. Conrat concluded his tribute with a quotation from Goethe that Brahms would have appreciated: "Even the beautiful must die," the opening words of Brahms's lament "Nänie."* Even more enduring was the tribute from Conrat's daughter, the sculptor Ilse Conrat, who created the famous statue of Brahms that still stands in the central cemetery of Vienna.

ZWEI MOTETTEN, op. 29
Two Motets

Es ist das Heil uns kommen her, op. 29, no. 1
Salvation Has Come to Us

Paul Speratus

Es ist   das Heil   uns   kommen her
— has salvation to us   come   here

Von Gnad und lauter   Güte:
from grace and pure goodness.

Die Werke helfen nimmermehr,
The works help nevermore;

Sie mögen nicht behüten!
they may   not   protect!

Der Glaub   sieht   Jesum Christum an:
— faith looks at Jesus   Christ —

Der hat gnug für uns all getan,
he has enough for us all done.

Er ist der Mittler   worden.
He has the mediator   become.

Salvation has come to us
from grace and purest goodness.
Works and deeds help no more;
they will not protect us!

Faith sees that Jesus Christ
has done enough for all of us.
He has become our intercessor.

Source: Wackernagel 1964, 3: 31
Variants: (Brahms = roman, Wackernagel = *italics*)
line 3: Werke = *Werk die*
line 6: all = *alle*

𝔓̶̶̶̶̶̶̶̶̶̶̶̶̶̶̶̶̶̶̶

[38]The names "Cohn," "Cohen," "Kahane," and others similar have meaning in Judiasm as descendents of the original Temple priests. Kalbeck, the source for most of the information in this essay, calls attention to the discrepancy of names among the brothers but he does not imply that Conrat was Jewish. If he were, that might partially explain his interest in the Gypsies, another people "apart."

[39]The editors were unable to locate either a copy of this publication or specific bibliographic information.

AUL Speratus ("Hofer" or "Hoffer" in German), a priest in southern Germany and Salzburg, developed reformist thoughts at the same time as Luther. He courageously uttered them aloud, most notably in a sermon in defense of priestly marriage (he had already married in violation of Roman Catholic Church doctrine) in Vienna, January, 1522. This brought upon him the denunciation of the Viennese theology faculty, who had previously awarded Speratus the Doctor of Divinity degree. Thereafter he moved to the village of Iglau, Moravia, where he took up a pastorate as a reformist to the appreciation of his congregation. Nonetheless, his heretical views led to imprisonment, which but for a stroke of luck might well have ended with his burning at the stake. With Luther's support he was named court preacher to Duke Albrecht of Prussia in Königsberg, where in concert with Johann Gramman* he institutionalized the Reformation. From 1529 to his death he served as Lutheran bishop of Pomerania.

"Es ist das Heil" was probably composed during Speratus's 1523 imprisonment. It ultimately became what the *EKG* (section 3: 44) calls the "storm-song of the Reformation" in Heidelberg, Magdeburg, and other cities. Its message—Luther's principle of justification by faith—is proclaimed vigorously in the opening verse, which is based on Romans 3: 28: "For we hold that a man is justified by faith apart from works of law." Verses 2–10 constitute a comprehensive sermon on the subject, which is closed by a doxology in verse 11 and a versification of the Lord's Prayer in verse 12.

The first verse of the hymn provided the text for Brahms's motet of 1864. With two minor exceptions, he used the text as written by the hymnist three centuries before. This is interesting, in that a revised version of the hymn was to be found in at least some of the Lutheran hymnals of his time (e.g., *Gesangbuch* 1866: 313)

An unusual feature of the work is its repetition of the same text in two different compositional styles—first as an ornamented, note-against-note hymn, and then as a five-part, imitative motet. Brahms probably chose to repeat the opening text because of the nature of the Sparatus hymn itself. The first verse states the principle of justification by faith, and the following verses expound upon it. Whereas the first verse provides natural closure, the following verses, with the exception of the final verse, do not. The closing verse, however, is elided to the penultimate verse, and if Brahms had wanted to use it, he would have had to use both, which did not suit his design.

"Es ist das Heil" is found in the *EKG* as no. 242. It also appears in the *LBW* as no. 297 under the title "Salvation unto Us Has Come."

Schaffe in mir, Gott, ein rein Herz, op. 29, no. 2
Create in Me, O God, a Pure Heart
Psalm 51: 10–12

Schaffe in mir, Gott, ein rein Herz,
Create in me, God, a pure heart,

und gib mir einen neuen gewissen Geist.
and give me a new, confident spirit.

Verwirf mich nicht von deinem Angesicht,
Cast me not from your presence,

und nimm deinen heiligen Geist nicht von mir.
and take your holy Spirit not from me.

Tröste mich wieder mit deiner Hülfe,
Console me again with your support,

und der freudige Geist erhalte mich.
and the joyful spirit uphold me.

Create in me, O God, a pure heart,
and grant me a new, confident spirit.
Cast me not from your presence,
and take not your Holy Spirit from me.
May I be consoled again with your support,
and may the joyful spirit uphold me.

LIKE the "Geistliches Lied," op. 30, this work is among Brahms's earliest, from the period 1856–1858 when the young composer was engaged in the study of seventeenth- and eighteenth-century counterpoint. Siegfried Kross demonstrates that at least the first movement and possibly all three were finished in 1857. At the latest, the work was complete in 1860. (Kross 1958: 121–123)

The special quality of this motet lies in the density its counterpoint, which perhaps bespeaks its "student" origins. At the same time, the contrapuntal manipulation is so facile as to seem completely natural—as if the composer had no need to study a technique that he had already thoroughly mastered.

The reason for the choice of Psalm 51: 10–12 as the text for this work is unknown. It is also unknown whether Brahms planned the work from the beginning to be in three movements. If the second and third movements were afterthoughts, Brahms's use of verse 10 for the opening was fortuitous: Verses 11 and 12 are natural continuations and together with verse 10 form a logical unit. In addition, each verse has a different affect that invites individualized compositional treatment.

ZWEI MOTETTEN, op. 74
Two Motets

Warum ist das Licht gegeben?, op. 74. no. 1
Why Is Light Given?

1.
Job 3: 20–23

Warum ist das Licht gegeben dem Mühseligen,
Why   is — light given to the miserable,

und das Leben den betrübten Herzen
and   life   to the afflicted soul

(die   des Todes warten und kommt nicht,
(those — death wait for and it comes not;

und gruben ihn wohl aus dem Verborgenen,
and dig   it well   –out of the hidden–,

die sich fast freuen und sind fröhlich,
they — nearly rejoice and are glad

daß sie das Grab bekommen),
that they the grave obtain),

Und dem Manne, des Weg verborgen ist,
and to the man, whose way   hidden is

und Gott vor ihm denselben bedecket?
and God from him himself has hidden?

Why is light given to those in misery,
and life to afflicted souls
(to those who wait for death, and it comes not;
who dig for it in the void,
who nearly rejoice and are glad
that they have found the grave),
and to the one whose way is hidden
and from whom God has hidden himself?

2.
Lamentations 3: 41

Lasset uns unser Herz samt den Händen
Let   us   our heart with the hands

aufheben zu Gott im Himmel.
lift up   to God in heaven.

Let us lift up our hearts and our hands
to God in heaven.

3.
James 5: 11

Siehe, wir preisen selig,
Behold, we call   blessed,

die   erduldet haben.
those endured have.

Die Geduld Hiob habt ihr gehöret,
The patience of Job have you heard

und das Ende   des Herrn habt ihr gesehen;
and the purpose of the Lord have you seen;

denn der Herr ist   barmherzig,
for   the Lord is   compassionate,

und ein Erbarmer.
and a merciful God.

Behold, we call them blessed,
those who have endured.
You have heard of the patience of Job
and you have seen the purpose of the Lord;
for the Lord is compassionate,
and a merciful God.

4.

Martin Luther

Mit   Fried und Freud ich fahr dahin
With peace and   joy I go thither

In Gottes Willen;
in God's will;

Getrost   ist mir mein Herz und Sinn
comforted is — my heart and mind,

Sanft und stille.
calm, and still;

Wie Gott mir verheißen hat:
as   God me promised has,

Der Tod   ist   mir Schlaf worden.
— death has to me sleep become.

In peace and joy I now depart
according to God's will;
my heart and mind are comforted,
calm, and still;
as God has promised me,
death has become my sleep.

Source (chorale) Luther 1967: 31
Variant: (Brahms = roman, Luther = *italic*)
                      Line 6:   mir = *mein*

*L*IKE the *Deutsches Requiem** of 1857–1868, this motet from the year 1877 represents the composer's philosophical confrontation with death through texts that he in all likelihood chose himself. And also as in that work, both the Old and New Testaments supply the libretto, which Brahms concluded in this case with a hymn verse. Finally, like four of the movements from the *Requiem* (1, 3, 5, and 6), the motet first presents a situation of anguish, which it then answers with words of comfort.

Brahms begins with one of the most dismal texts from Job, the most dismal book of the Old Testament. It asks, for what purpose is life given to those for whom it is but misery? In the second section Brahms addresses the question—but does not answer it—with a verse from Lamentations. In his choice of text Brahms implies that the question cannot be answered by mortals, but only by the Almighty. And since we cannot know the answer, the Bible verse says, we can only put our trust in him and praise him.

For the third section, Brahms returns to James 5, which had provided the words for the second section of the *Deutsche Requiem's* second movement: *So seid nun geduldig* (So now be patient). Here he approaches an answer from another angle: we do not know why God does as he does, but he is compassionate and merciful, and those who endure are blessed.

The closing chorale summarizes the message of the motet, just as it did in Bach's cantatas, which Brahms owned, admired, and studied. He concludes with the opening verse of Martin Luther's 1524 chorale "Mit Fried und Freud ich fahr dahin,"* a four-stanza versification of the Song of Simeon from Luke 2: 29–32. Man does not need more of an answer to the question posed in Job; it suffices that it is God's will. With that knowledge we can leave this life, "in peace and joy."

O Heiland, reiß die Himmel auf, op. 74, no. 2
O Savior, Tear Open the Heavens
Friedrich Spee von Langenfeld, SJ

O Heiland, reiß die Himmel auf,
O Savior,   tear the heavens open,

Herab,   herauf vom Himmel lauf,
downward, upward from   heaven flow;

Reiß ab vom Himmel Tor und Tür,
tear off from heaven gate and door,

Reiß ab, was Schloß und Riegel   für.
tear off what   lock and bar [are] for.

O Savior, tear open the heavens,
flow down to us from heaven above;
tear off heaven's gate and door,
tear off every lock and bar.

145

O Gott, ein' Tau vom Himmel gieß,
O God,   a dew from heaven pour;

Im   Tau   herab   o Heiland fließ,
in the dew downward O Savior flow.

Ihr Wolken, brecht und regnet aus
You clouds break and rain   out

Den König über Jakobs   Haus.
the   king   over Jacob's house.

O earth, burst forth; burst forth, O earth,
so that mountain and valley all become green;
O earth, bring forth this little flower;
O Savior, spring forth out of the earth.

O Erd, schlag aus, schlag aus   o Erd,
O earth burst forth; burst forth O earth,

Daß   Berg   und   Tal   grün alles werd,
that mountain and valley green all   become;

O Erd, herfür dies   Blümlein   bring,
O earth, here this little flower bring,

O Heiland,   aus   der Erden spring.
O Savior, out of the earth spring.

O God, a dew from heaven pour;
in the dew, O Savior, downward flow.
Break, you clouds, and rain down
the king of Jacob's house.

Hie   leiden wir die   größte   Not,
Here suffer we the greatest distress;

Vor   Augen steht der bittre Tod,
before eyes stands — bitter death.

Ach komm, führ uns mit starker Hand
Ah, come, lead us with strong hand

Von   Elend zu dem Vaterland.
from misery to the fatherland.

Here we suffer the greatest distress;
before our eyes stands bitter death.
Ah, come lead us with your powerful hand
from this misery to our Father's land.

Da   wollen wir all danken   dir,
Therefore want   we all to thank you,

Unserm Erlöser   für und für,
our   redeemer, –for ever and ever–.

Da   wollen wir all   loben   dich,
Therefore want   we all   to praise you

Je allzeit   immer und ewiglich. Amen.
–all the time– always, and eternally. Amen.

Therefore we all want to thank you,
our redeemer, for ever and ever.
Therefore we also want to praise you
at all times, always, and forever. Amen.

Source: Härting 1979: 161

*T*HE text Brahms chose for his motet in the form of a set of chorale variations consists of verses 1–3 and 6–7 of a didactic hymn by Friedrich Spee (1591–1635), first published in 1622. (Regarding the author and the hymn, see "O Heiland, reiß die Himmel auf.")

Brahms's plan for the evolution of the piece from verse to verse seems to have been satisfied in five verses and might well have been too prolonged in seven. Since verses 1–3 go together with their direct address ("O - ") and the last two form a pair characterized by the tension in verse 6 and its resolution in verse 7, the omission of verses 4 and 5 was a natural choice.

Brahms mirrored the age of his text in an archaic, contrapuntal musical style, as well as in his dedication of the work to Philipp Spitta, the great nineteenth-century German scholar of the Baroque. Verse 1 is indistinguishable from a sixteenth-century chorale motet, complete with its notation in white notes, its F-Dorian modality, and the absence of expressive indications. Each of the following four verses contains progressively newer and more complex elements of style, though the music seldom leaves the Baroque period except in terms of a few harmonies.

Although the motet bears an opus number from the late 1870s, it was almost certainly the product of a period fully twenty years earlier, when the young Brahms was fascinated with and studying old counterpoint. (Kross 1958: 360–361)[40]

---

[40]Regarding the origins of this motet, Brahms biographer Max Kalbeck writes: "Brahms found the poem . . . in the winter of 1863/64 in the Vienna court library, in [David Gregor] Corner's large Catholic hymnal [1632]. The text and melody caught his eye and he took down both." (Kalbeck 1976, 3: 164, tr. ed.) Kross (1958: 362) points out, however, that "O Heiland reiß" is not found in that hymnal, and that the motet was certainly completed by 1860. In addition, Brahms needed to look no further than his own personal Lutheran songbook to find the complete hymn.

Dietrich Buxtehude

Alles was ihr tut, BuxWV 4
All that You Do
Librettist unknown

1. Sonata

2. Chorus
Colossians 3: 17

Alles was ihr tut,
All that you do,

mit Worten oder mit Werken,
with words or with deeds,

das tut alles im Namen Jesu
this do all in the name of Jesus

und danket Gott
and thank God

und dem Vater durch ihm.
and the Father through him.

All that you do,
with words or with deeds,
do all this in the name of Jesus
and give thanks to God
and the Father through him.

3. Sonata

4. Aria
Author unknown

Dir, Dir Höchster, Dir alleine
To you, to you Highest, to you alone,

Aller, Aller Höchster Dir,
Most, Most Highest, to you

Sinne, Kräfte und Begier
senses, strength, and desires

ich nur aufzuopfern meine.
I only to sacrifice intend.

Alles sei nach aller Pflicht,
Everything be according to all duty,

Nur zu deinem Preis gericht.
only for your praise directed.

To you, O Highest, to you alone
Most, Most High, to you only
do I want to sacrifice
my senses, strength, and desires.
May everything, in fulfillment of all duty,
be directed solely to your praise.

Helft mir spielen, jauchzen, singen,
Help me play, shout, sing;

hebt die Herzen himmelan,
lift the hearts heavenward,

jubele was jubeln kann;
rejoice who rejoice can,

lasst all Instrumenten klingen.
let all instruments sound.

Alles sei nach aller Pflicht,
Everything be according to all duty,

Nur zu deinem Preis gericht.
only for your praise directed.

Help me play, shout, and sing;
lift our hearts heavenward,
let them rejoice who can rejoice,
let all the instruments ring out.
May everything, in fulfillment of all duty,
be directed solely to your praise.

Vater, hilf um Jesu willen,
Father, help for Jesus' sake;

laß dies Loben löblich sein
let this praise worthy be

und zum Himmel dringen ein,
and into heaven penetrate —,

unser Wünschen zu erfüllen,
our desires to fulfill,

daß dein Herz nach Vaters Pflicht
that your heart, according to father's duty,

sei zu unserm Heil gericht.
might be to our salvation directed.

Father, help us for Jesus's sake;
let our praises be worthy
and penetrate into heaven
in order to fulfill our desires,
so that your heart, in accord with paternal duty,
might contribute to our salvation.

147

5. Arioso (bass)
Psalm 37: 4

Habe deine Lust   am Herrn,
Have your delight in the Lord,

der wird dir   geben,
who will to you   give

was dein Herz wünscht.
what your heart desires.

Delight in the Lord,
and he will give you
that which your heart desires.

6. Chorale (soprano)
Georg Niege

Gott will ich lassen raten,
God want I to let advise,

Der alle Ding vermag.
who all things can do.

Er segne meine Taten,
He bless my   deeds,

mein Vornehmen und Sach.
my   intentions and actions.

Denn ich   ihm heimgestellt
For   I   to him   entrusted:

mein Leib, mein Seel, mein Leben,
my body, my soul, my   life,

und was er mir sonst   geben;
and what he me otherwise has given;

er mach's, wie's ihm gefällt.
he do it, as it him pleases.

I want to let God, who can do
all things, counsel me.
May he bless my deeds,
my intentions, and my actions.
For I have entrusted to him
my body, my soul, my life,
and whatever else he has given me;
he will do with it as he pleases.

Darauf   so sprech' ich Amen
On that thus say   I "Amen"

und zweifle nicht daran:
and doubt   not   in it:

Gott wird uns all' zusammen
God will us all together

ihm   wohlgefallen lan.
to him   pleasing   let be.

Drauf   streck' ich aus mein Hand,
Thereupon stretch I out my hand,

greif   an das Werk mit Freuden,
undertake — the work with joy,

dazu   mich Gott bescheiden
for which me   God ordained

in meinem Beruf   und Stand.
in my   profession and class.

To that I say "Amen"
and I have no doubt:
God will let us all
be pleasing to him.
Therefore I reach out my hand
and joyfully set about the work
for which God has ordained me
in my profession and class.

7. Sonata

8. Chorus = Movement 2

Source (chorale): Wackernagel 1964, 5: 177
Variants: (Buxtehude = roman, Wackernagel = *italic*)
        Stanza 1, line 2: der alle (who all things) = *denn er all* (because he all things)
                line 4: Sach (actions) = *mein Sach* (my actions)

AS is the case with most of Buxtehude's cantatas, the name of the librettist of the present work has been lost to history. The textual structure represents the "modern" cantata of Buxtehude's time, in which Biblical verses (nos. 2, 5, and 8a) and hymn stanzas (no. 6) were united with contemporary poetry (no. 4). The opening movement, which is repeated at the end, is from Colossians 3: 17, part of the Epistle for the fifth Sunday after Epiphany, which is presumably the occasion for which the work was written.

The opening and closing Biblical verse commands the Christian to keep Jesus at the center of everything in life and to praise God through him. The aria, the only poetry in the cantata, represents the response of the individual Christian to that exhortation, with a declaration of readiness to do as commanded and a prayer for help in praising the Lord appropriately, so that he might assist in salvation. Psalm 37: 7, the text of the arioso that follows, confirms that the Lord will deliver the heart's desire—in this case, salvation—to those who "delight" in him. The final chorus is based on verses 6 and 7 of a hymn entitled "Aus meines Herzens Grunde" (From the Depths of My Heart) by Georg Niege (1525–1588), first published in 1592. Although it was customary to conclude sacred cantatas with chorales, it is unusual to find two verses set together. The verses chosen by the librettist fit the message of the cantata so perfectly, however, it is almost as if they were written for this purpose. The second verse is particularly convenient in that it begins with an "amen," saying "so be it" to all that has been sung previously. The text presented here is a modernized version of the original as given by Günter Graulich in the preface to the Hänssler edition (Buxtehude 1968a).

Georg Niege was a mercenary soldier and a civil official—hardly professions in which one would expect to find a poet. "Aus meines Herzens Grunde" is the only chorale by Niege to appear in any of the three editions of the German Lutheran hymnal in the twentieth century (*EKG*: 341). His memory survives not in hymnology, but rather in literature: He has the distinction of being the first person known to have written an autobiography in rhyming poetry. (See Bei der Wieden 1996.)

Das neugeborne Kindelein, BuxWV 13
The New-Born Child
Cyriakus Schneegaß

Das neugeborne Kindelein,
The newborn little child,

Das herzeliebe Jesulein
the dearly beloved Jesus-child,

Bringt abermal ein neues Jahr
brings again a new year

Der auserwählten Christenschar.
to the chosen Christian flock.

The newborn child,
the dearly beloved infant Jesus,
brings a new year once again
to the chosen Christian flock.

Des freuen sich die Engelein,
At this rejoice — the little angels,

Die gerne um und bei uns sein,
who gladly around and with us are

Und singen in den Lüften frei,
and sing in the air free

Daß Gott mit uns versöhnet sei.
that God with us reconciled is.

At this the angels rejoice
as they happily hover around us
and sing out in the open air
that God is reconciled to us.

Ist Gott versöhnt und unser Freund,
Is God reconciled and our friend,

Was kann uns tun der arge Feind?
what can to us do the evil foe?

Trotz Teufel, Welt und Höllen Pfort,
Despite devil, world, and hell's gate,

Das Jesulein ist unser Hort!
the little Jesus is our refuge!

If God is reconciled and is our friend,
what can the evil foe do to us?
Despite the devil, the world, and the gate of hell,
the infant Jesus is our refuge!

Es bringt das rechte Jubeljahr,
He brings the true jubilation-year;

Was trauern wir dann immerdar?
why mourn we then always?

Frisch auf, jetzt ist es Singens Zeit!
–Take heart– now is it singing time!

Das Jesulein wendt alles Leid!
the little Jesus averts all suffering!

He brings the true year of jubilation;
why then do we constantly mourn?
Take heart, it is now time to sing!
The infant Jesus averts all suffering!

Source: Wackernagel 1964, 5: 138
Variants: (Buxtehude = roman, Wackernagel = *italic*)
Stanza 2, line 3: und (and) = *sie* (they)
Stanza 3, line 2: kann (can) = *mag* (may)
       line 3: Teufel, Welt (devil, world) = *Türken, Papst* (Turks, Pope)
Stanza 4, line 3: jetzt ist es = *es ist itzt*

NONE of the seventy-three published hymns by Cyriakus Schneegaß (1546–1597) survives in the 1912 and 1953 German Lutheran hymnals, and only one is found in the hymnal of 1996. The present text, however, was immortalized in cantatas by both Buxtehude and J.S. Bach (BWV 122).

Schneegaß, born eight months after Luther's death, studied in Gotha with Cyriakus Lindemann, Luther's nephew, from whom he learned the basics of poetry. As a pastor in Thuringia he composed most of his hymns for the use of his own simple, rural congregation on the feast days of the church year—principally New Year and Christmas. Historian Eduard Emil Koch describes them as being products of "a heart filled with God's word and happy with his grace." (Koch 1973, 2: 253)

"The New-Born Child" is a hymn of celebration and praise—with gentle reminders in verses 2 and 3 of Jesus's role as the reconciler and refuge of humanity. Despite the joyous tone of the text, it is objective in the sense of avoiding the personal, first-person voice that distinguished the hymn style of the following century. While the hymn is not a Biblical paraphrase, verse 3 contains echoes of Paul's letter to the Romans 8: 31b–39:

> If God is for us, who is against us? . . . Who shall separate us from the love of Christ? Shall tribulation, or distress, or persecution, or famine, or nakedness, or peril, or sword? . . . No, through all these things we are more than conquerors through him who loved us. For I am sure that neither death, nor life, nor angels, nor principalities, nor things present, nor things to come, nor powers, nor height, nor depth, nor anything else in all creation, will be able to separate us from the love of God in Christ Jesus our Lord.

According to the Hänssler edition of this work (Buxtehude 1968b), "Das neugeborne Kindelein" first appeared in 1588 in a hymnal entitled *Sieben und zwentzigh neue Geistliche Gesenge*. The BuxWV (Karstadt 1985), however, dates the publication of the hymn from 1597, the last year of the author's life. Koch (1973) reports that it first appeared in the *Weihnachts und Neujahrs Gesäng* of 1595 (Erfurt: Baumann).

Erfreue dich, Erde, BuxWV 26
Rejoice, O Earth
Librettist unknown

1. Chorus

Erfreue dich, Erde, du Himmel, erschall! **Rejoice —, earth, you heaven, resound!**	Rejoice, O earth! You heavens, resound!
Ihr himmlischer Bürger, laßt eure beweglichsten **You heavenly inhabitants, let your most stirring**	You heavenly angels, let your most stirring voices ring!
Stimmen ertönen, **voices sound.**	May the earth resound with spirited singing and shouts of joy!
das Weltgebäu müße von mutigem Singen und **The earth may of spirited singing and**	Reply, you songs, to the joyous sound.
Jauchzen erdröhnen, **jubilation resound.**	
ihr Lieder erwidert den fröhlichen Hall. **You songs reply to the joyous sound.**	

2. Aria (soprano 1)

Freud ist die gewünschte Gabe, **Joy is the desired gift**	JOY is the desired gift
die der Heiland mit sich bringt, **that the Savior with himself brings**	that the Savior brings
wenn er kömmt zu euch hinabe **when he comes to you down**	when he descends to earth as a tender human child and
als ein zarter Menschenknabe, **as a tender human-boy**	puts pain and suffering aside!
leget Schmerz und Leiden abe. **puts pain and suffering aside.**	Both in heaven and here on earth there must now be JOY in abundance.
In dem Himmel und auf Erden **In — heaven and on earth**	
muss nun Freud die Fülle werden. **must now joy — abundance become.**	

3. Aria (soprano 2)

Fried macht alles voller Freuden,
Peace makes everything full of joy,

Friede, der um Gottes Thron
peace, which around God's throne

schwebet stets und was geschieden
hovers always and what is divided

neu vereinigt, weil aus beiden
newly unites, because from both

Mensch und Gott wird Gottes Sohn.
mortal and God becomes God's son.

In den Himmel und auf Erden
In the heaven and on earth

muss aus Friede Freude werden.
must from peace joy become.

PEACE fills everything full of JOY—
PEACE, which always hovers around God's throne
and unites anew that which is divided,
for God's son came
from both God and mortal.
Both in heaven and here on earth
PEACE must become JOY.

4. Aria (alto)

Gnade bringt den Fried zuwegen,
Grace –brings about peace–,

Gnade, die der Sohn erwirbt,
Grace, which the Son earns,

dadurch Heil und aller Segen
so that salvation and all blessings

euch Betrübten kommt entgegen,
you troubled ones –come to meet–,

Segen, der niemals verdirbt.
blessing, which never spoils.

In dem Himmel und auf Erden
In the heaven and on earth

soll euch alle Gnade werden.
shall to you all grace be.

GRACE causes this PEACE to be—
GRACE, which the Son earns,
so that salvation and every blessing
might come to you who are troubled,
blessings that never fade.
Both in heaven and here on earth,
shall all GRACE come to you.

5. Aria (bass)

Wahrheit, welche Gott geschworen
Truth, which God has promised

und darauf er treulich denkt,
and of which he faithfully thinks,

hat die Menschen, so verloren,
has the mortals, so lost,

jetzt zum Leben neu geboren
now to life newly born

und in Gottes Huld gesenkt.
and in God's favor placed.

In dem Himmel und auf Erden
In the heaven and on earth

soll Wahrheit gerühmet werden.
shall truth praised be.

The TRUTH that God has promised
and faithfully remembers
has given new life to mortals
who once were so forlorn
and placed them in God's favor.
Both in heaven and here on earth,
TRUTH shall be praised.

6. Chorus

So denket und danket der göttlichen Güte
So think and thank the divine goodness

mit freudigem Herzen und dankbarn Gemüte!
with joyful heart and grateful soul!

Die Freude bestehe, der Kummer vergehe,
The joy remain, the sorrow vanish,

die Feindschaft vergehe, der Friede bestehe;
the hatred vanish, the peace remain;

die Gnade vereinige Erden und Himmel,
the grace unite earth and heaven,

die Ungnad versinke zum Höllengetümmel;
the disgrace sink to hell's-turmoil;

Thus ponder and praise the divine goodness
with joyful heart and grateful soul!

May JOY endure and sorrow subside,
may hatred vanish and PEACE remain;
may GRACE unite the earth and heaven,
and disgrace sink to the turmoil of Hell;

151

die Klarheit der Wahrheit ermunter die Sinnen,
the clarity of truth inspire the senses

Gott freudig zu loben und Lieb zu gewinnen!
God joyfully to praise and love to earn.

Halleluja, lasset dem Höchsten zu Ehren
Hallelujah, let to the highest in honor,

mit Singen und Klingen in Ewigkeit hören.
with singing and ringing in eternity hear.

may the clarity of TRUTH inspire the senses
to joyfully praise God and earn his love.
Hallelujah! In honor of the highest,
let singing and ringing be heard evermore.

7. Chorus = 1. Chorus

*B*UXTEHUDE'S cantata started its life on March 14, 1681 as a wedding present for Dr. Joachim von Dalen, the Bürgermeister of Lübeck, under the title "Schlagt, Künstler die Pauken." Gustav Düben (1628–1690), a church musician and music collector in the German community of Stockholm, obtained or copied an exemplar, as he did for ninety-nine of Buxtehude's vocal works. Indeed, his collection is one of the three principal sources for Buxtehude's cantatas. Such an occasional piece could be used only once with the original text, and so someone made a second, more usable set of vocal parts, also preserved in Düben's collection, to a text for Christmas. The result was the parody cantata "Erfreue dich, Erde." The librettist is unknown for both versions of the work.

The opening chorus of "Schlagt, Künstler" exhorts the *Kapelle* to sound the trumpets and drums in celebration of "the marital feast." Four arias follow, each of which extols a single virtue "to which this lovely pair is devoted": love, beauty, youth, and virtue itself. In each successive aria, all the previous virtues are woven cumulatively into the narrative. The final movement (before the *da capo*) is a congratulatory chorus that wishes the "splendid pair" long life, love, happiness, prosperity, and children. A repeat of the opening chorus closes the cantata with pure jubilation.

In its sacred version the text has the same form: introductory and closing choruses framing four arias. Like the parallel movement in the wedding cantata, the opening chorus calls upon the musicians—here the angels—to rejoice and sing. The four arias, again like those of the wedding cantata, extol four virtues—in this case joy, peace, grace, and truth, all of which are linked here to the birth of Jesus Christ. The final movement calls upon the Christian to "ponder and praise the divine goodness" and prays for all four virtues to descend on mankind. The final line, "let singing and ringing be heard evermore," prepares a repeat of the festive opening movement.

Schlagt, Künstler, die Pauken, BuxWV 122
Musicians! Beat the Drums
Librettist unknown

1. Chorus

Schlagt, Künstler, die Pauken
Beat, artists, the drums

und Saiten aufs best!
and strings the best!

Stoßt eilend zusammen in eure
Blow quickly together into your

weltschallenden Silbertrompeten,
world-resounding silver trumpets;

vermischet das Trummeln auf kupfernen Trummeln
mix in the drumming on copper drums

mit klaren Klaretten.
with clear, high trumpets.

Heute feiren zwei Edle ihr ehliches Fest.
Today celebrate two nobles their marital feast.

Musicians! Beat the drums
and strike your strings the best you can!
Quickly! Blow your trumpets,
your loud, resounding silver trumpets;
join in the drumming on copper drums
with clear, high trumpets.
Today two nobles celebrate their marital feast.

2. Solo (soprano 1)

Lieben ist die Glut der Herzen,
To love is the glow of hearts

die von schönen Augen brennt,
that from beautiful eyes burns,

die man lauter süße Schmerzen,
that one only sweet pains,

Lieblichkeiten, Herzens scherzen
loveliness, heart's jesting,

und das holde Feuer nennt.
and the sweet fire calls.

Lieben ist das rechte Leben,
To love is the true life,

dem dies liebe Paar ergeben.
to which this lovely pair is devoted.

To LOVE the heart's glow
that burns from beautiful eyes,
the glow one calls pure, sweet pain,
loveliness, heart's jesting,
and sweet fire.
To LOVE is the true life
to which this lovely pair is devoted.

3. Solo (soprano 2)

Schönheit ist das Band der Seelen,
Beauty is the bond of souls

das mit Huld und Wonne bindt,
which with grace and delight unites,

das die Seelen zu vermählen
which the souls to wed,

und mit Anmut pflegt zu quälen,
and with sweetness tends to torment,

die der Geist allein empfindt.
that the spirit alone feels.

Schönheit ist der Liebe Leben,
Beauty is the love life,

dem dies schöne Paar ergeben.
to which this beautiful pair is devoted.

BEAUTY is the bond of souls
with which grace and delight unite,
to which the souls wed,
and which is wont to torment with a sweetness
that the soul alone feels.
BEAUTY is the life of LOVE
to which this beautiful pair is devoted.

4. Solo (alto)

Jugend ist der Leim der Liebe,
Youth is the glue of love,

der die Welt zusammenhält
that the world together holds.

wäre der nicht, ach, wo bliebe,
Were it not, ah, where would remain,

was uns zu der Liebe triebe
what us to — love drove

und durch Liebreiz mehrt die Welt.
and by love's-charm propagates the world.

Jugend ist der Schönheit Leben,
Youth is the beauty life,

dem dies frische Paar ergeben.
to which this youthful pair is devoted.

YOUTH is the glue of LOVE
that holds the world together.
Were it not, where would remain
that which drove us to the LOVE and which,
by love's charm, propagates the world?
YOUTH is the life of BEAUTY
to which this youthful pair is devoted.

153

5. Solo (bass)

Tugend über alles streichet
Virtue over all spreads

Balsam,   Bisam,   trinkbar Gold,
balsam, healing herbs, drinkable gold.

Jugend, Schönheit, Liebe weichet
youth,   beauty, love   yield

dieses edle Paar ihr gleichet
this   noble pair to it is equal

welchem Erd und Himmel hold.
which   earth and heaven pleases.

Tugend ist der Jugend leben,
Virtue is the youth life,

der   dies Tugend paar ergeben.
to which this virtuous pair is devoted.

VIRTUE covers everything with
balsam, healing herbs, and drinkable gold.
YOUTH, BEAUTY, and LOVE yield to it;
this noble pair personifies it,
and that pleases both earth and heaven.
VIRTUE is the life of YOUTH
to which this virtuous pair is devoted.

6. Chorus

So   liebet und lebet viel Zeiten zusammen,
Thus love and live many times together,

vortreffliche Beide in lieblichen Flammen!
splendid   both in lovely   flames!

Es müßen die Münde   wie Tauben sich küßen,
— must the mouths like doves –kiss each other–;

die Arme, die Arme wie Kletten umschließen;
the arms, the arms like burrs   embrace.

die Herbstzeit bringt Garben dem Sämann und Binder,
The autumn brings sheaves to sower and binder,

der Sommer die Rosen, der Winter die Kinder;
the summer the roses, the winter the children;

die Rosen den Gärten, die Kinder dem Freier,
the roses to the gardens, the children to the suitor,

es brenne   ohn Ende, ohn Ende, dies Feuer!
it may burn without end, without end, this fire!

Nie   hat es an Liebe und Früchten gefehlet,
Never has — in love and   fruits   lacked,

wo   Schönheit und Jugend und Tugend vermählet.
where beauty and youth and virtue   wed.

So love and live many years together,
you splendid pair, in lovely flames!
Your mouths must kiss like doves;
your arms must embrace like burrs.
Autumn brings sheaves to the sower and binder;
summer brings roses, winter brings children;
roses to the gardens, children to the suitor.
May this fire burn without end, without end!
Never have LOVE and progeny been lacking
when BEAUTY and YOUTH and VIRTUE have wed.

7. Chorus = 1. Chorus

For comments regarding the history of this cantata
see the annotation to Buxtehude's "Erfreue dich, Erde."

Johann Neopomuk David

Deutsche Messe, op. 42
German Mass

Der Bittruf (Das Kyrie)

The Call of Petition (The Kyrie)
Author unknown

Kyrie, Gott Vater in Ewigkeit,
Lord, God Father in eternity.

Groß ist dein' Barmherzigkeit,
great is your compassion;

aller Ding ein Schöpfer und Regierer,
of all things a creator and ruler,

eleison.
have mercy.

Kyrie, God the eternal Father,
great is your compassion;
O creator and ruler of all things,
eleison.

Christe, aller Welt Trost,
Christ, of all world consolation,

uns Sünder allein hast erlöst.
us sinners alone has redeemed.

O Jesu, Gottes Sohn,
O Jesu, God's Son,

unser Mittler bist in dem höchsten Thron,
our mediator, are on the highest throne,

zu dir schreien wir aus Herzensbegier:
to you cry we out of heart's-desire:

eleison.
have mercy.

Christe, consolation of all the world,
has alone redeemed us sinners.
O Jesu, Son of God,
our intercessor, who is at the highest throne,
to you we cry from longing hearts:
eleison.

Kyrie, Gott heliger Geist,
Lord, God Holy Spirit,

tröst, stärk uns im Glauben allermeist,
comfort, strengthen us, in the faith especially,

daß wir am letzten End
that we at the last end

fröhlich abscheiden aus diesem Elend,
joyful depart from this misery,

eleison.
have mercy.

Kyrie, God the Holy Spirit,
comfort and strengthen us, especially in the faith,
so that we, at the last hour,
might joyfully depart from this misery,
eleison.

Source: *EKG*: 130

Der Lobgesang (Das Gloria)

The Song of Praise (The Gloria)
Nicolaus Decius

Allein Gott in der Höh sei Ehr
Alone God in the highest be glory

und Dank für seine Gnade,
and thanks for his mercy.

Darum, daß nun und nimmermehr
Therefore, that now and nevermore

uns rühren kann kein Schade;
us touch can no harm.

Ein Wohlgefalln Gott an uns hat,
A pleasure God in us has,

nun ist groß Fried ohn Unterlass,
now is great peace unceasingly

all Fehd hat nun ein Ende.
all strife has now an end.

To God alone be glory in the highest
and gratitude for his mercy,
for nevermore
can harm come to us.
God has shown his pleasure in us;
now there is everlasting peace
and all strife has now ended.

Source: *EKG*: 131

155

Das Glaubensbekenntnis (Das Credo)

The Confession of Faith (The Credo)

Martin Luther

Wir glauben all an einen Gott,
We believe all in one God,

Schöpfer Himmels und der Erden,
creator of heaven and the earth,

der sich zum Vater geben hat,
who — to the father become has,

daß wir seine Kinder werden.
that we his children become.

Er will uns allzeit ernähren,
He wants us always to nourish,

Leib und Seele wohl bewahren;
Body and soul well to protect.

We all believe in one God,
creator of heaven and earth,
who became the father
that we might become his children.
He wants to nourish us always,
to protect our body and soul.

allem Unfall will er wehren,
All misfortune wants he to prevent,

kein Leid soll uns widerfahren;
no harm shall us befall.

Er sorget für uns, hüt' und wacht,
He cares for us, guards and watches.

es steht alles in seiner Macht.
— is all in his power.

He wants to prevent all misfortune;
no harm shall befall us.
He cares for us, guards us, and watches us.
Everything is in his power.

Wir glauben auch an Jesum Christ,
We believe also in Jesus Christ,

seinen Sohn und unsern Herren,
his son and our Lord,

der ewig bei dem Vater ist,
who eternally with the Father is,

gleicher Gott von Macht und Ehren;
equal God of power and glory.

We believe also in Jesus Christ,
his son and our Lord,
who is eternally with the Father,
a god of equal power and glory.

von Maria, der Jungfrauen,
Of Mary, the Virgin,

ist ein wahrer Mensch geboren
was a true mortal born

durch den Heilgen Geist im Glauben;
through the Holy Spirit in faith;

für uns, die wir warn verloren,
for us, who we were lost;

am Kreuz gestorben und vom Tod
on the cross died and from death

wieder auferstanden durch Gott.
again rose through God.

Of Mary, the Virgin,
a true mortal was born,
through the Holy Spirit in faith,
for us who were lost;
he died on the cross, and from death
rose again through God.

Wir glauben an den Heilgen Geist,
We believe in the Holy Spirit,

Gott mit Vater und dem Sohne,
God with Father and the Son,

der aller Blöden Tröster heißt
who of all the feeble comforter is called

und mit Gaben zieret schöne,
and with gifts adorns beautiful.

We believe in the Holy Spirit,
God with the Father and the Son,
who is called "the comforter of the weak"
and who adorns us with beautiful gifts.

die ganz Christenheit auf Erden
The whole Christendom on earth

hält in einem Sinn gar eben;
hold in one idea indeed :

hie all Sünd vergeben werden;
here all sins forgiven are;

All Christendom on earth
affirms with one accord:
here all sins are forgiven;

das Fleisch soll auch wieder leben.
the flesh shall also again live.

Nach diesem Elend ist bereit'
After this misery is prepared

uns ein Leben in Ewigkeit. Amen.
for us a life in eternity. Amen.

the flesh shall also live again.
After this misery, a life in eternity
has been prepared for us. Amen.

Source: Luther 1967: 37

Das Dreimal-Heilig (Das Sanctus)

The Three-Fold "Holy" (The Sanctus)

Martin Luther

Jesaja dem Propheten das geschah,
Isaiah the prophet that happened,

daß er im Geist den Herren sitzen sah
that he in the spirit the Lord sitting saw

auf einem hohen Thron in hellem Glanz,
on a high throne in bright splendor,

seines Kleides Saum den Chor füllet ganz.
his gown's seam of the chancel filled totally.

It came to pass that in a vision
Isaiah the prophet saw the Lord sitting
upon a high throne in bright splendor,
and the train of his robe filled the Temple.

Es stunden zween Seraph bei ihm daran;
— stood two seraphim with him thereon;

sechs Flügel sah er einen jeden han:
six wings saw he one each have.

mit zween verbargen sie ihr Antlitz klar,
With two hid they their face clear,

mit zween bedeckten sie die Füsse gar,
with two covered they the feet entirely,

und mit den andern zween sie flogen frei;
and with the other two they flew freely

gen ander riefen sie mit großem G'schrei:
to other cried out they with great cry:

There with him stood two seraphim,
and he saw that each one had six wings.
With two they veiled their faces,
with two they hid their feet,
and with the other two they flew freely
and cried to each other with a loud voice:

"Heilig ist Gott der Herre Zebaoth!
"Holy is God the Lord Sabaoth!

Heilig ist Gott der Herre Zebaoth!
Holy is God the Lord Sabaoth!

Heilig ist Gott der Herre Zebaoth,
Holy is God the Lord Sabaoth,

sein Ehr die ganze Welt erfüllet hat."
his glory the whole world filled has."

Von dem G'schrei zittert' Schwell und Balken gar,
From the screaming quaked doorstep and beam quite,

das Haus auch ganz voll Rauch und Nebel war.
the house also totally full smoke and mist was.

"Holy is God, the Lord God of Hosts!
Holy is God, the Lord God of Hosts!
Holy is God, the Lord God of Hosts;
his glory has filled all the earth!"
The beams and lintel trembled at the cry,
and the house was filled with smoke and
mist.

Source: Luther 1967: 39

Die Abendmahlsbitte (Das Agnus Dei)

The Communion Prayer (The Agnus Dei)

Author unknown

Christe, du Lamm Gottes,
Christ, you Lamb God's,

der du trägst die Sünd der Welt,
who you carry the sins of the world,

erbarm dich unser.
have mercy — on us.

Christe, du Lamm Gottes,
Christ, you Lamb God's,

der du trägst die Sünd der Welt,
who you carry the sins of the world,

erbarm dich unser.
have mercy — on us.

Christ, you Lamb of God,
who bears the sins of the world,
have mercy on us.

Christ, you Lamb of God,
who bears the sins of the world,
have mercy on us.

Christe, du Lamm Gottes,
Christ, you Lamb God's,

der du trägst die Sünd der Welt,
who you carry the sins of the world,

gib uns deinen Frieden. Amen.
give us your peace. Amen.

Christ, you Lamb of God,
who bears the sins of the world,
grant us your peace. Amen.

Source: *EKG*: 136

*T*HE term "Deutsche Messe" means simply "German Mass," and refers to a German version of the five movements of the Roman Catholic Mass Ordinary,[41] the portions of the Mass that remain the same throughout the church year. How they came into being requires a brief excursion into the history of the Lutheran Reformation.

When Luther posted his ninety-five theses on the door of the castle church in Wittenberg on October 31, 1517, he was attempting to initiate an academic debate on needed reforms in the Catholic Church, principally the sale of indulgences. The Wittenberg debate was never held, but the content of the Theses spread throughout Germany and stimulated a more widespread and spirited discussion than Luther could have imagined. He thus set in motion events that would lead to his excommunication (January 3, 1521) and to the formation of a new church that would bear his name.

After the excommunication, Pope Charles declared Luther "a heretic and outlaw who could be killed on sight" (Lueker 1975: 484). Luther was put into protective custody by the Prince of his region to protect him from being taken prisoner by representatives of Rome who would either kill him or ship him there for trial, the outcome of which certainly would have been grave. In March, 1522 Luther abandoned his protective custody and returned to Wittenberg, convinced that reform was impossible and that he had to begin a new church that followed the ideals of the early Christians and purged the corruption that had encrusted the Roman church over the centuries.

One of Luther's most basic arguments with the Roman church was over the sacraments and the role of the clergy. The established church held that the clergy were needed as intercessors between God and man, and that specific sacraments, which could be administered only by clergy, were required for salvation. Luther held, on the other hand, that salvation was a matter of God's grace, for which neither sacraments nor clergy were prerequisites. This concept moved the focus of his church and its worship from a passive congregation to an active one, and required that worship, scripture, and teaching be done in the vernacular rather than in Latin, a language the common man did not understand. Suddenly there was a pressing need for German-language scripture, liturgy, and hymns.

The next few years saw Luther at his most productive. In 1522 he translated the most urgently needed scripture, the New Testament. He then began a translation of the Old Testament that would take many years. In the meantime, by the end of 1524 he had produced twenty-four of his thirty-seven hymns, and a year later a new, German-language liturgy. His contributions to the German Mass also came from this period.

Luther's German-language liturgy was based directly on the Roman Catholic Mass after the excision of what he believed to be doctrinal corruption. In order to reach the congregant directly, Luther took the saying or singing of the Mass from the clergy and choir and gave it to the congregation, which he felt was best served by versified, poetic versions of the original prose texts.

The new German liturgy was first used in Wittenberg on October 29, 1525. It included an adaptation of the "Credo" to the words "Wir glauben all an einem Gott" (May/June, 1524) as well as a version of the "Sanctus" (without the "Benedictus") that began "Jesaia dem Propheten das geschah" (late 1525). Both of these texts are still in use today in the German Lutheran liturgy.

Over time, German versions of the other three movements of the Mass Ordinary were added to the service. Those still in current use all stem from the Reformation period. The Lutheran "Kyrie," to the text "Kyrie Gott Vater in Ewigkeit," was an adaptation of the Roman Catholic "Kyrie" trope "Kyrie fons bonitatis" and was first used in 1537. Nicolaus Decius (c. 1485–after 1546) was responsible for the German "Gloria," which begins "Allein Gott in der Höh sei Ehr." The "Agnus Dei," an anonymous translation of the Latin, was published in Low German in 1528 and in High German in 1540 as "Christe, du Lamm Gottes."

Johann Nepomuk David's "Deutsche Messe" follows the standard liturgical text without significant exception. He does, of course, divide the text and use repeats in ways that best suit his creative purposes. In the "Gloria" he also includes the *incipit* in Latin ("Gloria in excelsis Deo") in addition to the complete German text.

---

[41]For an introduction to the Latin Mass Ordinary and its history, see Jeffers 1988: 45–57.

Hugo Distler

Fürwahr, er trug unsere Krankheit, op. 12, No. 9
Truly, He Bore Our Affliction

1. Chorus
Isaiah 53: 4, 5a

Fürwahr, er trug unsere Krankheit,
Truly,   he bore our   affliction

und lud auf sich   unsere Schmerzen.
and loaded on himself our   sorrow.

Wir   aber   hielten   ihn für den,
We, however, considered him as the one

der geplagt von Gott geschlagen
who plagued by God   beaten

und gemartert wäre.
and tortured would be.

Aber um unserer Missetat willen
But for   our misdeed's sake

ward er verwundet,
was he wounded

und um unserer Sünde willen zerschlagen.
and for our   sin's sake   battered.

Die   Strafe   liegt auf ihm,
The punishment lies on him

auf daß wir Frieden   hätten.
so that we peace might have.

Truly, he bore our affliction
and carried our sorrow.
Yet we considered him to be the one
who would be plagued, beaten,
and tortured by God.

But he was wounded
for our transgressions
and he was battered for our sins.
The chastisement lies upon him
so that we might have peace.

2. Chorale
Paul Gerhardt

Ein Lämmlein geht und   trägt die Schuld
A small lamb goes and carries the guilt

Der   Welt und ihrer Kinder;
of the world and its   children;

Es geht und träget   mit Geduld
it goes and carries with patience

Die Sünden aller   Sünder;
the sins   of all sinners;

Es geht dahin,   wird   matt und krank,
it goes forth, becomes weak and ill,

Ergibt sich auf der   Würgebank,
yields itself on the slaughter-block,

Entzieht sich allen Freuden;
withdraws — from all joys.

Es nimmt auf sich Schmach, Hohn und Spott,
It takes upon itself shame, mockery, and derision,

Angst,   Wunden, Striemen, Kreuz und Tod
anguish, wounds, welts,   cross, and death,

und spricht: Ich will's gern   leiden.
and says: "I want it gladly to suffer."

A lamb goes forth and carries the guilt
of the world and its children;
it goes forth and patiently carries
the sins of all sinners;
it goes forth, becomes weak and ill,
surrenders itself on the slaughter block,
and withdraws from all joys.
It takes on shame, mockery, and derision,
anguish, wounds, stripes, the cross, and death,
and says: "All this I want to suffer."

Source (chorale): Gerhardt 1957: 30
Variants: (Distler = roman, Gerhardt = *italic*)
line 3: träget mit (carries with) = *büßet in* (repents in)
line 6: der = *die*
line 7: entzieht sich allen Freuden (withdraws from all joys) =
verzeiht sich aller Freuden (excuses himself from all joys)
line 8: es nimmt auf sich = *Es nimmet sie auf*

159

*T*HIS motet, no. 9 of twelve in Distler's *Geistliche Chormusik* (see also Distler's "Singet frisch und wohlge-mut"*), is the most tonally advanced and emotionally wrenching. The familiar Biblical text, the Messianic prophesy of Isaiah, with its unremitting images of pain and suffering, provided a perfect foundation for Distler's biting yet tonal harmonic language. For reasons unknown, Distler did not use one of the Luther Bibles of his own day, which differ somewhat from the wording of the motet. Instead his wording is identical to that of the 1545 *Biblia germanica* (Luther, 1545). (See "The Luther Bible.")

On one hand it would have been natural to close the motet with the remainder of Isaiah 5, the statement of faith "and with his stripes we are healed." But Distler had a different structure in mind, and the introduction of this triumphant phrase would have forced him into a premature resolution of the tension that he had carefully built. It also would have prevented him from repeating the entire opening section to close the movement. Finally, it would not have permitted him to end the first section with the phrase "so that we might have peace," which is what he provides in his serenely radiant setting of verse 1 from Paul Gerhardt's 1648 Passion chorale "Ein Lämmlein geht und trägt die Schuld der Welt" (*EKG*: 62). Gerhardt's chorale was, in a sense, a continuation of the passage from Isaiah, as it is based on Isaiah 53: 4–7 as well as John 1: 29.

Had the composer nonetheless continued with the text from Isaiah, in verse 6 he would have come to the words, familiar from Handel's *Messiah*, "all we like sheep are gone astray." The chorale provided him with a different symbolism of the lamb, the Lamb of God, sacrificed for mankind.

Singet frisch und wohlgemut, op. 12, no. 4
Sing Joyfully and Cheerfully
Johannes Geletzki (and Hugo Distler?)

1. Chorus

Singet frisch und wohlgemut,
Sing joyfully and cheerfully;

Lobet Gott das höchste Gut,
Praise God, the highest good,

Der so große Wunder tut
who such great wonders does

Und schickt uns seinen lieben Sohn
and sends us his dear son

Auf Erden,
to earth

Daß wir durch ihn sollen selig werden.
that we through him shall blessed become.

Eia, eia!
Hush, hush!

Eine Magd gebar uns Gott,
A maiden bore us God,

Wie es seine große Gnad
as it his great mercy

Gewollt hat.
willed has.

Heute uns erschienen ist
Today to us appeared has

Der Herre Christ,
the Lord Christ,

Immanuel!
Immanuel,

Der uns selig macht und führt
who us blessed makes and leads

aus Tod und Höll!
from death and hell!

Sing joyfully and cheerfully;
praise God, the highest good,
who performs such great miracles
and sends his son to us
on earth
so that we through him shall have salvation.
Eia, eia!
A maiden bore God for us,
as his great mercy
has willed it.
Today he has appeared to us,
Christ the Lord,
Immanuel,
who saves us and leads us
from death and hell!

2. Chorus

Kinder, singet alle gleich,
Children, sing all together;

Lobet Gott vom Himmelreich;
praise God from the heavenly kingdom;

Unser Not hat er erkannt
our need has he recognized

Und seinen lieben Sohn gesandt
and his dear son sent

Von oben,
from above

Daß wir ihn auf Erden sollen loben.
that we him on earth shall praise.

Eia, Eia!
Hush, Hush!

Loben wir mit Lieb und Dank,
Praise we with love and thanks,

Singen einen neuen Gesang
sing a new song

Dem Herren.
to the Lord.

Preisen ihn von Herzensgrund
Praise him from heart's-bottom

Mit gleichem Mund
with equal mouth,

Und hoffen frei,
and hope freely

Daß ihm unser Dienst ein Wohlgefallen sei.
that to him our service a pleasure might be.

Children, all of you sing together;
praise the God of heaven!
He has recognized our need
and sent his dear son
from above
so that we might praise him here on earth.
Eia, eia!
Let us praise him with love and gratitude,
let us sing a new song
to the Lord.
Let us praise him from the bottom of our hearts,
with one accord,
and freely hope
that our service might be pleasing to him.

3. Chorus

Schaut die lieben Engel an
Look at the dear angels —

Und tut, wie sie han getan,
and do as they have done:

Singt mit ihn'n das schöne Lied
sing with them the beautiful song

Von Gottes Gnad und neuem Fried
of God's grace and new peace

Mit Schallen,
with resonance,

Und habt dran ein herzlichs Wohlgefallen.
and have in it a heartfelt pleasure.

Eia, Eia!
Hush, Hush!

Wünschet Glück dem Christkindlein,
Wish happiness to the little Christ-child

Sprechet allzugleich in ein'm
speak all at once together

Mit Freuden:
with joy:

"Ehre sei Gott in der Höh,
"Glory be God in the highest,

Auf Erden Fried
on earth peace

Und große Freud
and great joy

Wiederfahre allen bis in Ewigkeit."
happen to all until eternity."

Observe the dear, sweet angels
and do as they have done:
sing with them the beautiful song
of God's grace and new peace
resoundingly,
and derive heartfelt pleasure from it.
Wish happiness to the infant Christ-child,
declare together now,
with joy:
"Glory be to God in the highest,
and on earth peace
and great joy
come to all for evermore."

161

Source: Wackernagel 1964, 4: 351
Variants: (Distler = roman, Wackernagel = *italic*)

      Stanza 1, line 4:   schickt uns = *schicket*
                  lines 8–14: see annotation
      Stanza 2, line 3:   unser Not hat er = *der unser Not hat*
      Stanza 3, line 12: große (great) = *sondre* (special)
                  line 13: wiederfahre (happen) = *sei unter uns* (be with us)

*H*UGO Distler took the text for this exquisite three-movement motet from a Christmas song by hymnist Johannes Geletzki (also Johann Geletzky, d. 1568), written in 1566. Geletzki was a member of the Protestant Bohemian Brethren (see the annotation to the Brahms "Begräbnisgesang"*) and the co-editor of the sect's 1566 hymnal, which contained some twenty-two of his own compositions. (Koch 1973, 2: 414)

As the heading in the hymn's first printing states, "Singet frisch" is "A song composed for the children." The central verse, which Distler sets as a *bicinium* for female (or children's) voices, addresses them directly: "Children, all of you sing together, praise the God of heaven!"

Distler followed the original, three-verse poem closely, except in the second half of verse 1, where his text of unknown origin is completely different. The original reads:

Eine Jungfrau keusch und rein,	A virgin chaste and pure,
welche Gottes Kraft umschein,	around whom God's power shines,
ward schwanger:	became with child.
Die hat nun in neuer Art	She has, in a new way
ganz rein und zart	so pure and tender,
den Sohn geborn,	given birth to the son
der uns all erlediget von Gottes Zorn.	who has relieved us all from God's wrath. (tr. ed.)

The idea of the new words—that the Virgin gave birth to the savior Christ—is the same as in Geletzki's original. Distler's emphasis is on the Christ-child, however, while Geletzki focuses on the Virgin Mary. The other changes shown under *Variants*, whatever their source, were favorable to Distler's setting. The addition of *uns* in verse 1, line 4 served to personalize the text: "God's dear son" was sent not just "to earth," but "to *us* on earth." The obsolete word *sondre* in the penultimate line meant "special," but could be easily confused with the more modern but still obsolete *sonder* (without); it was replaced by the modern *große* (great). The remaining two alterations served to "correct" the displaced accents of the original text, facilitating the musical setting of the words.

Distler's naturalness and sensitivity in setting this text are extraordinary—on a parallel with the exemplary text treatment of Heinrich Schütz (1585–1672), whose style was Distler's inspiration.

Geletzki wrote his poem to be sung to the melody of "Resonet in laudibus," one of the most popular and ancient of German carols. For additional information, see the annotation to the carol "Joseph, lieber Joseph mein,"* which is a variant of "Resonet in laudibus" in both text and melody.

Vorspruch, op. 19 [no. 1]
Prologue
Author unknown

Wer die Musik sich erkiest,
Who — music — chooses,

Hat ein himmlisch Gut bekommen,
has a heavenly good received,

Denn ihr erster Ursprung ist
for its first origin is

Von dem Himmel selbst genommen.
from — heaven itself taken,

Weil die Engel insgemein
because the angels usually

Selbsten Musikanten sein.
themselves musicians are.

Wenn einst in der letzten Zeit
When some day in the last time

Alle Ding' wie Rauch vergehen,
all things like smoke vanish,

Bleibet in der Ewigkeit
remains in — eternity

Doch die Musik noch bestehen.
yet — music still in existence

Weil die Engel insgemein
because the angels usually

Selbsten Musikanten sein.
themselves musicians are.

Those who choose music
have received a heavenly blessing,
for music's original source
is from heaven itself,
because the angels usually
are themselves musicians.

Some day, during the final hour,
when all things vanish like smoke,
music shall still persist
throughout eternity
because the angels usually
are themselves musicians.

Source: Mörike 1905, 3: 64

DISTLER accepted a faculty position at the Stuttgart Musikhochschule on April 1, 1937, and while living there had occasion to become acquainted with the works of the Swabian poet Eduard Mörike (1804–1875). He found in them a profound inspiration, and between September, 1938 and May, 1939 he composed a collection of forty-eight choral settings of thirty-nine Mörike poems, which he entitled the *Mörike Chorliederbuch* (Mörike Choral Songbook).

In the foreword to the *Chorliederbuch,* Distler stated that he had been drawn to Mörike by his "rhythmic strength and freedom of movement," "the objectified poetic content, reminiscent of old folk songs," and his "fervent subjectivity, independence, and individual character." (Rauchhaupt 1993: 2, tr. ed.)

Preceding the collection proper is a *Vorspruch,* or "prefatory aphorism," which was intended to be a motto for the entire collection. Distler wrote of his text's source:

> The poet writes a heading above this saying, which is preserved in Mörike's "mixed poems from the late years": "old verse, written in the sincere hand of a painter on the case of the organ in the church of Güglingen [a small town forty miles north-northwest of Stuttgart], which burned down twenty years ago."[42]

Among the eight editions of Mörike's works consulted by the editors, only one (Mörike 1905) contains the text to "Vorspruch"; it also has the heading as quoted above, suggesting that this is the edition used by Distler. The first two lines are occasionally to be found in various anthologies of quotations, ascribed either to Mörike or Martin Luther. (Lemmermann 1996: 26).

The poem is a simple and sincere song of praise for the divine blessing of music, which "when all things vanish like smoke . . . shall still persist throughout eternity because the angels usually are themselves musicians."

---

[42]Pontz, Stefan. "*Untersuchungen zum Mörike Chorliederbuch,* op. 19 von Hugo Distler." Master's Thesis, Munich, 1988. From the Hugo-Distler-Archiv, Lübeck. Cited in Lemmermann 1996: 26, tr. ed.

Hans Leo Hassler

Hassler's Secular Music and Texts

*T*HE explosions of poetic and musical creativity that were harnessed together in the sixteenth-century Italian madrigal unfortunately had no counterpart in German-speaking Europe. The first significant German-language collections of secular music did not even appear in print until late in the century, when the Italian madrigal was already running out of steam. Even then, the music was based on Italian models, as is illustrated in the four pieces we have selected for translation:

Ich weiß mir ein Meidlein is a short, simple, homophonic song, the opening rhythm of which (long-short-short) was the signature of the Italian *canzona*. Hassler likely would have classified it as a *canzonetta*.

Im kühlen Maien is a double-chorus piece written largely in block chords that are occasionally animated by quick rhythms. Hassler's debt to his eighteen months of study in Venice (1584–1585) in general and to his teacher Andrea Gabrieli in particular are easy to discern.

Ihr Musici, frisch auf is the most complex of the pieces in terms of texture, with several points of imitation. Among these four pieces, it is the closest relative to the Italian madrigal.

Tanzen und Springen is derivative in two ways. First, it owes a debt to the French dance masters (and their Italian followers) for its *galliard* rhythm. Second, it is written in the style of an Italian *balletto*, with its characteristic *fa-la* refrain.

The Italian madrigal composers of the sixteenth century drew their texts from both a centuries-old literary tradition and the works of many fine contemporary poets. The literary quality of the texts is thus one of the madrigal's most important characteristics. Neither the English nor the Germans possessed such literary traditions. The English managed nonetheless to create an extraordinary body of wonderful music, but the Germans failed to acquire the same momentum before the madrigal became passé.

Hassler produced over ninety secular songs, the great majority of which are settings of anonymous texts preserved solely in his music. This fact has led to the speculation that he may have written many of them himself. All four of the pieces discussed here are from his 1610 collection entitled *Lustgarten neuer teutscher Gesäng: Balletti, Galliarden und Intraden mit 4, 5, 6 and 8 Stimmen* (A Garden of Delights of New German Songs: *Balletts, Galliards,* and *Intradas* for 4, 5, 6, and 8 Voices).

Ich weiß mir ein Meidlein

I Know a Maiden

Author Unknown

Ich weiß mir ein Meidlein hübsch und fein,
I know — a maiden pretty and fine;

    Hüt du dich,
    protect — yourself.

Es kann wohl falsch und friendly sein,
She can perhaps deceitful and friendly be;

    Hüt du dich,
    protect — yourself,

Vertrau ihr nicht, sie narret dich,
Trust her not; she fools you—

    Hüt du dich!
    protect — yourself!

I know a maiden pretty and fine;
    be careful.
She may be deceitful and friendly;
    be careful.
Don't trust her; she fools you—
    be careful!

*T*HIS brief and simple text of unknown origin attained some popularity in the sixteenth century, with settings by Hassler, di Lasso, de Vento, and others. (Nearly three centuries later, Brahms set this poem as a soprano-alto duet under the title "Hüt du dich.") Perhaps of particular interest to Renaissance composers were the universal theme and the folk-song-like repetition of the warning "hüt du dich," which offered interesting compositional possibilities. The popularity of the text may have extended into the sacred realm, through a hymn entitled "Ich weiß mir ein Blümlein, hübsch und fein" (I Know a Flower), the first version of which hymnologist John Julian (1985, 1: 560) cites as appearing in print c. 1560 in Nuremberg, Hassler's native city. A version originally in eight stanzas dating from 1584 (Wackernagel 1964, 5: 10R) is found in some older English-language hymnals in Catherine Winkworth's translation as "I Know a Flower so Sweet and Fair."

164

Ihr Musici, frisch auf!
You Musicians, Refresh Yourselves
Author Unknown

Ihr   Musici,   frisch auf   und laßt doch hören,
You musicians,   refresh yourselves and let — hear;

Die   lieblich   Kunst
the   lovely   art

Tut   euch   zusammenkehren!
does yourselves gather together!

Ein   jeder   faß   sein Stimm   alsbald,
One each take his voice immediately,

Tenor und Baß, Diskant und Alt.
tenor and bass, descant and alto.

Singt   allerseits   zur rechten und   zur   linken.
Sing   everywhere, to the   right   and to the   left.

Denn   wer   nicht   singt,
Because who   not   sings,

der   soll   auch nicht   mittrinken.
he   shall   also   not   join in drinking.

You musicians, refresh yourselves
and let us hear you sing once more;
the lovely art
brings you together!
Each one take your part now:
tenor and bass, descant and alto.

Sing all around, to the right and to the left.
Because anyone who doesn't sing
shall also not join in drinking.

*T*HE "Wine, women, and song" character of the *Lustgarten* is nowhere more perfectly evidenced than in this song—except perhaps for the absence of the women. For the moment, at least, Hassler was content with just the song and the wine, the former being prerequisite to the latter, as we are told in the final couplet. Because Hassler chose a text with four verses to be sung to identical music, he was unable to wed the music to the words as closely as he did in "Im kühlen Maien." Verse 1 is presented here.

Im kühlen Maien
In the Cool Maytime
Author Unknown

Im   kühlen   Maien
In the   cool   Maytime

tun sich all   Ding   erfreuen,
— —   all   things take pleasure.

Die   Blümlein   auf dem Feld
The little flowers in   the   field

sich   auch   erneuen,
—   also   renew,

Und singen   d'Maidlein in ihren   Reihen:
And   sing   the maidens in their roundelays:

Willkommen   Maien!
"Welcome   Maytime!"

Zwei   liebe   Herzen
Two   dear   hearts

Sind voller Freud und Scherzen,
are full of   joy and   jest;

Im   Schatten kühl vergessen aller Schmerzen,
in the shade   cool,   forget   all   suffering.

Cupido blind,
Cupid   blind,

Das gar   listige   Kind,
the very cunning child,

Gsellt sich   dazu   mit seinem Pfeil geschwind,
joins —   thereto with his   arrow   swift.

Venus allwegen
Venus   always

Gibt   dazu ihren Segen,
gives   also her blessing

Auf daß zwei Herz' sich tun in Lieb bewegen.
so   that two hearts — —   to love are moved.

In the cool Maytime all things take pleasure.
Little flowers in the field also renew themselves,
and the maidens sing in their roundelays:
"Welcome Maytime!"

Two dear hearts
are full of joy and jest;
in the cool shade they forget all suffering.
Blind Cupid,
the very cunning child,
joins them together with his swift arrow.
Venus always
adds her blessing
so that two hearts are moved to love.

Wem nun dies Leben **To whom now this life**	Now those to whom this life gives good pleasure should without delay give love its measure, and sing with the maidens in the roundelay: "Welcome Maytime!"
tut wohlgefallen eben, **–gives pleasure– just,**	
Der soll sich ohn Verzug **He shall himself without delay**	
der Lieb ergeben, **to love yield,**	
Und mit den Maidlein singen im Reihen: **and with the maidens sing in the roundelay:**	
Willkommen Maien. **"Welcome Maytime."**	

*T*HIS text, with its light-hearted character, is typical of the texts Hassler chose (or wrote). The parallelism of the first and third stanzas certainly suggested musical parallels as well, and Hassler chose to set them identically. The central and somewhat longer stanza contains several images that inspired Hassler to madrigalesque word-painting—among them the "cool shade" in even, peaceful quarters; the "swift arrow" set to eighth notes; the name of Venus, which brings forth a grand climax; and the hearts being "moved to love" with sinuous, eighth-note melismas.

Tanzen und Springen
Dancing and Leaping
Author Unknown

Tanzen und springen, **Dancing and leaping,**	Dancing and leaping, singing and ringing, *fa la la . . .* Lutes and fiddles should also not be silent; to make music and celebrate is all that's on my mind. *fa la la . . .*
Singen und klingen, *fa la la . . .* **Singing and ringing,** *fa la la . . .*	
Lauten und Geigen **Lutes and fiddles**	
Soll'n auch nicht schweigen, **should also not be silent;**	
Zu musizieren **to make music**	
und jubilieren **and rejoice**	
Steht mir all mein Sinn. *fa la la . . .* **is to me all my mind.** *falala . . .*	
Schöne Jungfrauen **Beautiful maidens**	Beautiful maidens in the green meadows, *fa la la . . .* To stroll with them and to converse, to jest in friendly ways delights my heart more than silver and gold. *fa la la . . .*
In grünen Auen, *fa la la . . .* **in green meadows,** *falala . . .*	
Mit ihn'n spazieren **With them to stroll**	
Und konversieren, **and to converse,**	
Freundlich zu scherzen **friendly to jest**	
Freut mich im Herzen **delights me in the heart**	
Für Silber und Gold. *fa la la . . .* **for silver and gold.** *fa la la . . .*	

*T*HE source of the text is unknown, but as in the case for a number of texts from this collection, it may be by Hassler himself. The dance alluded to in the first line of the song is more than just theoretical: the rhythm of the piece is that of the *galliard*, a French dance popular in Germany at the turn of the seventeenth century, and the form of the piece is that of the Italian *balletto*, which was popularized by the Italian composer Giovanni Gastoldi (c. 1556–c. 1622).

Joseph Haydn

Three- and Four-Part Songs
[Aus des Ramlers *lyrischer Blumenlese*]

*I*N 1796, at the age of sixty two, Haydn began work on a set of German-language part songs—his first foray into this genre. This was a project close to Haydn's heart, as it was his and his alone. Georg August Griesinger, Haydn's friend and biographer, reported that "The songs were lovingly composed in carefree hours, without a commission."[43]

Haydn seems never to have found a sufficient number of suitable texts. In December, 1801 Griesinger wrote to the publishing firm of Breitkopf and Härtel, which in the previous year had begun the publication of Haydn's works, "He is finished with thirteen, which he has shown to me. The work is now going slowly, and he is lacking texts, for as he assures me, few poets write musically." Two weeks later he wrote to Breitkopf that the composer wanted twenty-five songs in the collection and suggested that "You could do Haydn a favor by providing texts, but nothing pretentious or with eccentric phrases." Whether Breitkopf ever responded we do not know, but Haydn wrote no more part songs.

The meaning of "nothing pretentious or with eccentric phrases" might be deduced from the texts that Haydn actually set. All are direct, simple, and succinct, and share a sincere but unsophisticated and almost folk-like character. Eight of the poems came from a single collection, the two-volume *Lyrische Blumenlese* (Bouquet of Lyrics) of the poet and literary scholar Karl Wilhelm Ramler (1774–1778).[44] Ramler provided succeeding generations with plenty of fodder for literary scholarship when he decided to publish all of the poems without attribution, "so that connoisseurs who judge a work's worth by the author's name might face a bit harder task."[45]

A number of the more than seventy poets represented in the *Blumenlese* were kindred spirits who have come to be known as "Anacreonites," after the Roman poet Anacreon, whose works they emulated.[46] Ramler himself translated and annotated a number of Anacreon's odes,[47] and all of the eighteenth-century writers chosen by Haydn except Gellert (Götz, Gleim, Lessing, Bürger, Ebert, and Weiße) wrote poetry based on Anacreon's light, wine-women-and-song model, as well as paeans to Anacreon and/or translations of his

---

[43]The limited information available on this collection is presented comprehensively in the foreword by Paul Mies to the edition within the *Joseph Haydn Werke* (*Mehrstimmige Gesänge*, Series xxx, Munich-Duisburg: G. Henle, 1958) and in the accompanying *Kritischer Bericht*. Unless otherwise indicated, all quotations have been taken from the foreword by Mies, pp. vi and vii, and have been translated by the editors.

[44]*Karl Wilhelm Ramlers lyrische Blumenlese*. Karlsruhe: Christian Gottlieb Schmieder, 1780. Ramler's collection was published in two volumes, as parts 102 and 103 of a series entitled *Sammlung der besten deutschen prosaischen Schriftsteller und Dichter* (Collection of the Best German Prose Writers and Poets), with the subtitle *Ramlers Schriften* (Ramler's Writings).

A note regarding the confusing "title" to Haydn's collection is in order. On the coversheet to his manuscript of the thirteen part songs, Haydn wrote:

Aus des Ramlers lyrischer Blumenlese.
in die Musik gesetzt
von Jos. Haydn 1796

From the Lyrische Blumenlese of Ramler.
set to music
by Jos. Haydn 1796

Since he was unable to find sufficient texts in this collection and had to go elsewhere, it seems likely that this was an early annotation based on his intentions; it certainly was not a title for the collection in its final form. The first edition, published under Haydn's supervision in 1803, bore the following inscription:

Three- and Four-Part
SONGS
with pianoforte accompaniment,
by Joseph Haydn

"Songs," or "Three- and Four-Part Songs" is thus as close as Haydn ever came to giving this collection a title.

[45]Ramler 1780, 1: x. The only poems for which Haydn provided attributions are the last five, by Gellert (4) and Anacreon (1), only the last of which is from the *Blumenlese*. Mies was unable to find the authors or translators of three of the eight remaining poems, nos. 1, 6, and 8. *The New Grove* (Larson 1980: 370) contains attributions for these, all but one of which the present editors verified by finding the poems in other publications. An independent source for no. 8 was not located.

[46]Over the centuries, hundreds of works and fragments have been attributed to Anacreon, but scholarship has discounted a great number of these as later imitations. In the final analysis, what came from the pen of Anacreon and what stemmed from others will never be fully known or agreed upon.

[47]Karl Wilhelm Ramler, trans. *Anakreons auserlesene Oden*. Berlin: Sander, 1801. The editor of this posthumous collection begins his foreword by saying that Ramler "did not want merely to be a precise translator of each ode that he selected, but rather much more a free imitator."

poetry. That they were well known to each other is evidenced by the copious correspondence among them and the numerous poems they wrote for and dedicated to each other.[48]

Johann Wilhelm Ludwig Gleim, the author of "Der Greis," began his 1744 collection of poems entitled *Versuch in scherzhaften Liedern* (An Essay in Humorous Poems and Songs) with a tribute to Anacreon that aptly illustrates his aesthetic:

Anacreon

Anacreon, my teacher,
Sings only of wine and love;
He soothes his face with salve,
And sings of wine and love;
He crowns his head with roses,
And sings of wine and love;
He makes love in the garden
And sings of wine and love;
He becomes a king through drink,
And sings of wine and love;
He plays with his gods,
He laughs with his friends,
Drives away grief and cares,
Rejects the wealthy rabble,
Spurns the praise of heroes,
And sings of wine and love.
Should then his faithful student
Sing of hate and water?
(Gleim 1964: 5, tr. ed.)

Of a more serious nature are the four "spiritual" poems of Christian Fürchtegott Gellert, which come at the end of the collection. The first is a reflection on death, and the remaining three are devotional prayers. These are the only verses Haydn set that are not included in the *Blumenlese* and were probably the last that he chose and set to music. Gellert, the devout son of a minister and a professor of "poetry, elocution, and morals" in Leipzig, inspired his student Goethe to describe his teachings on morality as "the foundation of German moral culture." All of the Gellert poems are from his *Geistliche Oden und Lieder* (Spiritual Odes and Songs) of 1757 and were intended to be set to music. Haydn would not have had to look far to find these texts, as they were widely known through countless editions and reprints and contained some of the most frequently set poems of the eighteenth century.

"An die Frauen" from the *Blumenlese* appears inexplicably in the middle of the Gellert poems.[49] While we have no knowledge of Haydn's motivation, he might well have seen this as a special and honorific place for Anacreon's "second ode," probably the most frequently translated and printed of the Anacreon poems.

While the texts are for the most part self explanatory and not particularly profound—as Haydn desired—some commentary on a few of the poems might raise some points of interest.

Die Harmonie in der Ehe. In this hymn of praise to matrimonial concord, the poet lists the husband's pleasures—each of which, he says in the same breath, the wife likes also. Haydn makes a little dramatic dialogue out of the poem, having the men of the chorus represent the husband and the women the wife. The women are given an active part, and in fact have the chance to chime in with "she" every time the men say "he." This is reflected in the present translation, in which the brackets represent Haydn's additions. On several occasions, particularly the ending, both parties speak at once, leaving the impression that neither is listening to the other.

Haydn's version might be read between the lines as the tongue-in-cheek complaint of a husband with a smothering wife, and one cannot help but consider the song in the light of Haydn's own joyless marriage. When his love Josepha Keller chose a convent over a wedding ring, he married her older sister Maria Anna Aloysia Appolonia out of a sense of duty to the father. Maria Anna had no interest in music and little interest in Haydn; indeed, Griesinger reports him as having said, "It's all the same to her if her husband is a cobbler or an artist." (Larson 1980: 332) Haydn's mistake haunted him for forty years.

---

[48]By way of example, Gleim's *Versuch in scherzhaften Liedern* contains poems—sometimes more than one each—to Ramler, Lessing, and Götz.

[49]On the basis of the paper and ink used, which does not match that of the Gellert settings, Mies suggests that this piece was composed earlier, perhaps at the same time as the other works with texts from Ramler.

Alles hat seine Zeit. This text is from *The Deipnosophists* (Athenaeus 1951) or "Banquet of the Learned," by Athenaeus of Naucratis, an Egyptian who likely lived in the mid third century A.D. *The Deipnosophists* is an epic, rambling work on gastronomy and the execution of banquets, along the copious observations on same in verse by Classical writers. No fewer than sixteen chapters in its fifteen books are devoted specifically to the art and pleasure of drinking. Athenaeus is less known for his own work than he is as the sole source for many quotations by authors of Classical Antiquity, both significant and obscure.

"Alles hat seine Zeit" is taken from book 15, chapter 15 of *The Deipnosophists*. It is no. 19 of 25 convivial songs or *scolia* sung at a banquet by the various guests in turn and transcribed without attribution by Athenaeus. In his explanation of the *scolia*, Athenaeus cites Anacreon as one of the great exponents of the form. (Athenaeus 1951, 7: 215)

The translator was a Hamburg poet named Johann Arnold Ebert, who provided several poems for the *Blumenlese*. In a footnote to a set of his poems from 1740, Ebert (1971: 237) offers indirect thanks to Ramler for publishing what he called his "first youthful experiments." "Alles hat seine Zeit" is found in his works from 1743, among thirteen drinking songs that he explains he translated from Greek. Ebert also thanks Hamburg poet Friedrich von Hagedorn for including some of his poems in one of his collections. One must wonder about the depth of Ebert's appreciation to both Ramler and Hagedorn: In the absence of copyright laws they both published his works without attribution. "Alles hat seine Zeit" appears in Hagedorn's *Abhandlungen von den Liedern der alten Griechen* (Treatise on the Songs of the Ancient Greeks) (Hagedorn 1968, part 3: 165) as an untitled example of a poem that "Athenaeus collected without naming the author."

A translation into English directly from the Greek differs in detail but not in substance from Ebert's version, except for the last line, which Ebert embellishes:

> "Drink with me, sport with me, love with me,
> wear wreaths with me,
> rage with me when I am raging,
> be sober when I am sober."

(Athenaeus 1951, 7: 227)

Die Beredsamkeit. The composer's footnote at the end of the composition merits quotation. The last measure contains the word *stumm* (mute) with no pitches in any voice. In his autograph Haydn explained as follows: "This final word, since it cannot be sung, must be spoken so softly that one can only perceive it from the opening of the mouth." (Haydn 1958, preface: 28)

Water, taken for granted in modern America as a healthy drink, was long considered an unpleasant and potentially dangerous fluid. European writings for two millennia have cautioned of the dangers of water, which was often polluted, and the virtues of wine, which was tasty and wholesome. Of course, wine also had the debatable "virtue" of promoting "eloquence." Among the interesting information offered by Athenaeus in *The Banquet of the Learned* (book 1, chapter 22) is the fact that Romans who wished to practice moderation mixed their wine with water in a 1:3 ratio. Horace (iii.19.11), however, suggests the reverse ratio for poets, as they are useless unless drunk.

Der Greis. Haydn must have been astounded and pleased to find a poem that fit his own biography. At sixty four, he felt his age and lamented his failing memory and intellect in a letter to his publisher Breitkopf and Härtel, dated June 12, 1799:

> Unfortunately, what I must do expands just as my years increase. And yet, it is as if my desire and passion for work grow as my mental faculties decline. . . . The world pays me many compliments every day, including those for the fire in my last compositions. But no one wants to believe the effort and strain that I must exert to produce them. On some days my poor memory and the weakening of my nerves just leave me exhausted, so that I fall into a depression and for many days am unable to conceive a single idea, until finally, encouraged by the prudence in my heart, I can sit once again at the piano and begin to hammer away. Then the ideas begin to come once again, thank God!

Haydn identified with this piece so closely that he had its opening measure ("Gone is all my strength") printed on his greeting card.

Daphnens einziger Fehler. Poets have long found it convenient to employ characters from Classical mythology because of the richness of allusion that attaches to them. While such allusions were meaningful to those of earlier ages who possessed classical educations, they are often lost on us today. Daphne was a mountain nymph beloved by Apollo. When she protested his advances, her father turned her into a laurel tree, which Apollo thereafter took as his symbol in her memory. Psyche was a beautiful mortal who fell in love with Cupid and achieved immortality when she married him. Hebe, the daughter of Zeus and the wife of Hercules, was the likewise comely goddess of eternal youth.

Haydn must not have wanted to set the neoclassic poetry that was in vogue in his day. Although the *Blumenlese* is packed with poetry that employs neoclassic subjects and characters, this is the only such poem that Haydn chose.

Die Warnung. Paul Mies, the editor of the part songs in the Haydn *Werke*, reports that the poet is unknown. Athenaeus and Ebert, respectively, are named as the author and translator in *The New Grove*, but this poem is absent from the only edition of Ebert's poetic works.[50] Like "Alles hat seine Zeit," this poem is from Athenaeus, book 15, chapter 15, where it has the same function and follows it directly as song no. 20. The only eighteenth-century source the editors could locate was Hagedorn's "Treatise on the Songs of the Ancient Greeks," (Hagedorn 1968, part 3: 147), in which it is printed as an example of the "moralistic poetry" of Athenaeus. In a translation directly from the Greek by Charles Gulick it is remarkably close to the German, even taking into account Ebert's use of rhyming verse:

> Under every stone, my friend,
> there lurks a scorpion.
> Have care that he does not sting you;
> for any kind of trickery may attend the unseen.
> (Athenaeus 1951, 7: 227)

Betrachtung des Todes. Gellert's poem of the same name is a fourteen-stanza reminder to Christians of their mortality and an admonition of their responsibility to keep Christ in their hearts. Haydn chose to set just the second verse, which can stand alone and has the character of a universal adage. Still, it is better understood in its Christian context, which the first, sixth, and fourteenth verses provide:

1. How securely lives man, a spot of dust!
    His life is but a fallen leaf;
    And he nonetheless enjoys flattering himself
    That the day of death lies far away.

6. Since your death is a daily threat,
    Be worthy and prepared;
    Examine your faith as a Christian,
    And whether Christ acts through your
        love.

14. Since I cry to you for grace,
    Always oppose my weakness,
    And in the strength of faith,
    Cry out with joy, "It is fulfilled!"
    (Gellert 1965: 305–307, tr. ed.)

Wider den Übermut. Haydn chose the first of the six stanzas of Gellert's poem of the same name. The theme of the poem, the need to be humble before God and thankful for his gifts, is introduced in the opening stanza. The next four stanzas pose "what if" questions for contemplation, and the final stanza provides the answer that was implied from the beginning:

> All prosperity comes from you,
> and every good gift from you,
> O highest good!
> Protect me, O God,
> from all that I have!
> From pride and arrogance.
> (Gellert 1965: 230, tr. ed.)

Aus dem Danklied zu Gott. The first of Gellert's thirteen stanzas supplied Haydn with his text. Each of the next six stanzas provides examples of God's grace, mercy, and assistance, and stanzas 8–11 thank the Lord for these "divine works." The final two stanzas bring the reader back to the theme of the first and summarize the poet's thoughts:

12. He helps. Lament persists in the evening
    and contentment in the morning.
    After a trial of but a few days
    He lifts salvation up to us.

13. Forget not your God, O soul!
    Forget not what he has done for you.
    Honor and observe his commandments
    And pray obediently to him.
    (Gellert 1965: 219, tr. ed.)

Haydn's awkward title ("From the Song of Thanksgiving to God") was never intended to be a title at all; it was merely a heading showing that the text was excerpted from a poem entitled "Danklied zu Gott"— which in fact appears in the original source under the title "Danklied."

---

[50]Ebert 1971. On the chance that Ramler himself was the translator, the editors surveyed his poetic works to locate this poem, but to no avail. (*Karl Wilhelm Ramlers poëtichen Werke.* 2 vols. Berlin: Johann Daniel Sander, 1800.)

Abendlied zu Gott. This poem of trust, faith, and humility before God, entitled simply "Abendlied," is in five stanzas, only the first of which Haydn set to music. As was the case with the other Gellert poems, the final stanza ties together those that preceded it. It likewise ties the Christian to his savior by using the final words of Jesus as the closing prayer:

> Clothed with your blessings,   My life and my end
> I hasten toward serenity;   Are yours; into your hands
> Your name be praised!   Father, I commend my spirit.
>
> (Gellert 1965: 288, tr. ed.)

DREI– UND VIERSTIMMIGE GESÄNGE
Hob. XXV, B 1–4, C 1–9
Three- and Four-Part Songs

1. Der Augenblick, Hob. xxv, C1
The Moment
Johann Nikolaus Götz

Inbrunst, Zärtlichkeit, Verstand,
Ardor,   tenderness, intellect,

Schmeicheleien, Sorgen, Tränen,
flattery,   sorrows, tears,

Zwingen nicht die Gunst der   Schönen,
force   not the favor of the beautiful one,

Schaffen uns nicht ihre Hand:
procure us not her hand;

Nur ein schwacher Augenblick,
only a   weak   moment

Fordert der Verliebten   Glück.
furthers the   lovers' happiness.

Ardor, tenderness, intellect,
flattery, sorrows, and tears
neither exact the favor of the beautiful one
nor obtain her hand;
only a weak moment
hastens the lovers' happiness.

Source: Götz 1817: 55; Ramler 1780, 2: 219
Variants: schwacher (Haydn) = *schwarzer* (black)
In the first edition, Haydn changed the final line to "bringt dem Liebenden sein Glück" (brings his happiness to the lover).

2. Die Harmonie in der Ehe, Hob. xxv, C2
Harmony in Marriage
Johann Nikolaus Götz

O wunderbare Harmonie,
O wonderful harmony:

Was er will,   will   auch sie,
what he wants, wants also she.

Er [sie] bechert gern, sie [er] auch,
He [she] drinks gladly; she [he] also.

Er [sie] lombert   gern, sie [er] auch,
He [she] plays omber gladly; she [he] also.

Er [sie] hat den Beutel gern,
He [she] likes the wallet —

Und spielet gern den Herrn,
and plays gladly the master.

Auch das ist ihr [sein] Gebrauch.
Also that is her [his] custom.

Oh wonderful harmony:
what he wants, so does she.
He [she] likes to drink; so does she [he].
He [she] likes to play cards; so does she [he].
He [she] likes to win the pot
and to be in control.
That's just what she [he] likes also.
Oh wonderful harmony:
what he wants, so does she.

Source: Götz 1817: 15; Ramler 1780, 2: 239

3. Alles hat seine Zeit, Hob. xxv, C3
Everything Has Its Time
Athenaeus of Naucratis, trans. J. A. Ebert

Lebe, liebe, trinke, lärme,
Live, love, drink, romp,

Kränze   dich mit mir,
put on wreaths — with me;

Schwärme mit mir wenn ich schwärme,
revel   with me when I   revel.

Ich bin wieder klug   mit dir.
I am again sensible with you.

Live, love, drink, romp,
put on wreaths with me;
revel with me when I revel.
Then I can be sensible again.

Source: Ebert 1971: 242; Ramler 1780, 2: 361

4. Die Beredsamkeit, Hob. xxv, C4
Eloquence
Gotthold Ephraim Lessing

Freunde, Wasser machet stumm,
Friends, water makes mute:

Lernet dieses an den Fischen,
learn this from the fish.

Doch beim Weine kehrt sich's um,
But with wine, turns — it around:

Dieses lernt an unsern Tischen.
this learn at our tables.

Was für Redner sind wir nicht,
What for orators are we indeed

Wenn der Rheinwein aus uns spricht,
when the Rhine wine from us speaks:

Wir ermahnen, streiten, lehren,
we admonish, argue, teach;

Keiner will den andern hören.
no one wants the other to hear.

Friends, water makes one mute:
learn this from the fish.
But with wine, it is the opposite:
learn this at our tables.
Oh, what orators we are
when the Rhine wine speaks through us:
we admonish, argue, and teach;
but no one wants to listen to anyone else!

Source: Lessing 1965, 1: 75; Ramler 1780, 2: 20

5. Der Greis, Hob. xxv, C5
The Old Man
Johann Ludwig Wilhelm Gleim

Hin ist alle meine Kraft,
Gone is all my strength.

Alt und schwach bin ich,
old and weak am I;

Wenig nur erquicket mich
little only refreshes me,

Scherz und Rebensaft.
joke and wine.

Gone is all my strength;
old and weak am I;
very little refreshes me,
only joking and wine.

Hin ist alle meine Kraft,
Gone is all my strength;

Meiner Wangen Rot
my cheeks' rosiness

Ist hinweg geflohn, der Tod
has away fled. — Death

Klopft an meiner Tür,
knocks at my door.

Gone is all my strength;
the color has fled
from my cheeks. Death
is knocking at my door.

Unerschreckt mach' ich ihm auf.
Unafraid make I to him open.

Himmel, habe Dank!
Heaven, have thanks!

Ein harmonischer Gesang
A harmonious song

War mein Lebenslauf.
was my life's journey.

Unafraid, I open it for him.
Heaven be praised!
My life's journey
was a harmonious song.

Source: Gleim 1811, 2: 321; Ramler 1780, 1: 416
Variant: Stanza 2: Kraft (Haydn) = *Zier* (airs)

6. An den Vetter, Hob. xxv, B1
To the Cousin
Christian Felix Weiße

Ja, Vetter, ja; ich fall' euch bei,
Yes, cousin, yes; I agree you —

Daß Lieb' und Torheit einerlei,
that love and folly the same,

Und ich ein Tor notwendig sei;
and I a fool necessary am.

Ich sei nun   aber,   was ich sei,
I am now nevertheless, what I am,

Ist Lieb' und Torheit einerlei.
is love and folly   the same.

So wißt! mir ist sehr wohl dabei.
Thus know: to me is very well with this!

Yes, cousin, yes! I agree with you
that love and folly are the same,
and that I am thus a fool.

I am, however, what I am
if love and folly are the same.
Please know that this is fine with me!

Source: Weiße 1772, 1: 41; Ramler 1780, 1: 362

7. Daphnens einziger Fehler, Hob. xxv, B2
Daphne's Only Fault
Johann Nikolaus Götz

Sie hat das Auge,
She has the eye,

die Hand,
the hand,

Den Mund
the mouth

der   schönen Pysche,
of the beautiful Psyche.

Sie hat den Wuchs,
She has the figure,

die Göttermiene,
the divine-look,

Das holde Lächeln
the lovely smile

der   jungen Hebe.
of the young Hebe.

Sie hat Geschmack
She has   taste

und   Weltmanieren,
and worldly-manners,

Und weiß zu reden,
and knows to talk

und weiß zu schweigen.
and knows to be quiet.

O   wüßte Daphne
Oh knew Daphne

nur noch zu lieben!
only also to love!

She has the eye,
the hand,
and the mouth
of the beautiful Psyche.

She has the figure,
the divine look,
and the lovely smile
of the young Hebe.

She has taste
and good manners,
and knows when to talk
and when to be quiet.
Oh, if only Daphne
also knew how to love!

Source: Götz 1817: 30; Ramler 1780, 1: 266

8. Die Warnung, Hob. xxv, C6
The Warning
Athenaeus of Naucratis, trans. J.A. Ebert

Freund! ich bitte, hüte dich,
Friend! I ask: protect yourself!

Skorpionen schleichen sich
Scorpions lurk —

Unter jeden Stein,
under every stone;

Und da, wo es dunkel ist,
and there, where it dark is,

Pflegt Betrügerei und List
usually deceit and cunning

Oft versteckt zu sein.
often hidden — are.

Friend! I implore you: protect yourself!
Scorpions lurk
under every stone;
and there, where it's dark,
deceit and cunning
are also wont to hide.

Source: Hagedorn 1968: 147

9. Betrachtung des Todes, Hob. xxv, B3
Reflection on Death
Christian Fürchtegott Gellert

Der Jüngling hofft des Greises Ziel,
The young man hopes the old man's goal,

Der Mann noch seiner Jahre viel,
the man still his years many,

Der Greis zu vielen noch ein Jahr,
the old man too many yet another year—

Und keiner nimmt den Irrtum wahr.
and no one takes the error true.

The young man hopes to become old,
the grown man hopes for many remaining years,
and the old man hopes for yet another year—
and not one realizes the error of his thinking.

Source: Gellert 1965: 305

10. Wider den Übermut, Hob. xxv, C7
Against Arrogance
Christian Fürchtegott Gellert

Was ist mein Stand, mein Glück,
What is my state, my happiness,

Und was ist jede gute Gabe?
and what is each good gift?

Ein unverdientes Gut;
An undeserved good.

Bewahre mich, o Gott!
Preserve me, O God,

Von dem ich alles habe,
from whom I everything have,

Vor Stolz und übermut.
from pride and arrogance.

What is my state, my happiness,
and each good gift?
An undeserved boon.
Preserve me, O God,
you who have given me everything,
from pride and arrogance.

Source: Gellert 1965: 229

11. An die Frauen, Hob. xxv, B4
To Women
Anacreon, trans. G.A. Bürger

Natur gab Stieren Hörner,
Nature gave steers horns;

Sie gab den Rossen Hufe,
she gave the horses hooves,

Den Hasen schnelle Füße,
the hares fast feet,

Den Löwen weite Rachen,
the lions wide jaws;

den Fischen gab sie Flossen,
the fishes gave she fins,

Und Fittige den Vögeln;
and wings to the birds.

Den Männern aber Weisheit.
To men, however, wisdom.

Den Männern! nicht den Weibern?
To men! not to women?

Was gab sie diesen? Schönheit,
What gave she to them? Beauty!

statt aller unsrer Spieße,
Instead of all our spears,

statt aller unsrer Schilde;
instead of all our shields,

Denn wider Weibesschönheit
because against women's-beauty

Besteht nicht Stahl, nicht Feuer.
persists not steel, not fire.

Nature gave steers horns;
she gave the horses hooves,
the hares fast feet,
the lions wide jaws;
to the fishes she gave fins,
and wings to the birds.
To men, however, she gave wisdom.

To men? Not to women?
What did she give to them? Beauty!
Instead of all our spears,
instead of all our shields,
because against women's beauty
neither steel nor fire can endure.

Source: Ramler 1780, 1: 312
Variants: Ramler's title is "Auf die Frauen."
The manuscript has the word *feuer*,
whereas the first edition reads *feu'r*.

12. Aus dem Danklied zu Gott, Hob. xxv, C8
From the Thanksgiving Song to God
Christian Fürchtegott Gellert

Du bist's, dem Ruhm und Ehre gebühret,
You are it, to whom praise and honor are due,

Und Ruhm und Ehre bring' ich dir.
and praise and honor bring I to you.

Du Herr! hast stets mein Schicksal regieret,
You, Lord, have always my fate ruled,

Und deine Hand war über mir.
and your hand was above me.

You are the one to whom praise and honor are due,
and praise and honor I bring to you.
You, Lord, always ruled my fate,
and your hand was always above me.

Source: Gellert 1965: 218

13. Abendlied zu Gott, Hob. xxv, C9
Evening Song to God
Christian Fürchtegott Gellert

Herr! der du mir das Leben,
Lord, who you me — life,

Bis diesen Tag gegeben,
until this day have given,

Dich bet' ich kindlich an;
you worship I child-like —.

Ich bin viel zu geringe,
I am much too unworthy

Der Treue, die ich singe,
of the loyalty which I sing,

Und die du heut' an mir getan.
and that you today for me have done.

Lord, you who have given me life
until this day—
I worship you like a child.
I am much too unworthy
of the loyalty of which I sing,
and that you have shown to me today.

Source: Gellert 1965: 288

DIE SCHÖPFUNG, Hob. XXI: 2

The Creation

"Lindley," after Milton's *Paradise Lost* and The Bible
trans. Gottfried van Swieten

No. 9 Recitative

Und die Himmlischen Heerschaaren verkündigten
And the heavenly hosts proclaimed

den dritten Tag, Gott preisend und sprechend:
the third day, God praising and saying:

And the heavenly hosts proclaimed
the third day, praising God and saying:

No. 10 Chorus

Stimmt an die Saiten, ergreift die Leier!
Start playing the strings, seize the lyre!

Laßt euren Lobgesang erschallen!
Let your praise-song resound!

Frohlocket dem Herrn, dem mächtigen Gott!
Rejoice to the Lord, the mighty God,

Denn er hat Himmel und Erde
for he has heaven and earth

bekleidet in herrlicher Pracht.
attired in magnificent splendor.

Strike up the strings, seize the lyre!
Let your song of praise resound!
Rejoice in the Lord, the almighty God,
for he has adorned heaven and earth
in glorious splendor!

No. 13 Chorus and Trio

Die Himmel erzählen die Ehre Gottes,
The heavens recount the glory of God,

und seiner Hände Werk zeigt an das Firmament.
and his hands' work displays the firmament.

Dem kommenden Tage sagt es der Tag;
To the coming day tells it the day;

die Nacht, die verschwand, der folgenden Nacht.
the night, that vanished to the following night.

Die Himmel erzählen die Ehre Gottes,
The heavens recount the glory of God,

und seiner Hände Werk zeigt an das Firmament.
and his hands' work displays the firmament.

In alle Welt ergeht das Wort,
Into all world goes the word,

jedem Ohre klingend,
to each ear sounding,

keiner Zunge fremd.
to no tongue foreign.

Die Himmel erzählen die Ehre Gottes,
The heavens recount the glory of God,

und seiner Hände Werk zeigt an das Firmament.
and his hands' work displays the firmament.

The heavens declare the glory of God,
and the firmament displays the work of his hands.

One day tells it to the next;
the vanished night tells the following night.

The heavens declare the glory of God,
and the firmament displays the work of his hands.

The word goes out to all the world,
sounding in every ear,
foreign to no tongue.

The heavens declare the glory of God,
and the firmament displays the work of his hands.

No. 25 Recitative

Und Gott sah jedes Ding, was er gemacht hatte;
And God saw every thing, that he made had,

und es war sehr gut: und der himmlische Chor
and it was very good. And the heavenly choir

feierte das Ende des sechsten Tages
celebrated the end of the sixth day

mit lautem Gesang.
with loud song.

And God saw every thing that he had made,
and it was very good. And the heavenly choir
celebrated the end of the sixth day
with sonorous song.

No. 26 Chorus

Vollendet ist das große Werk,
Completed is the great work;

der Schöpfer sieht's und freuet sich.
the creator sees it and rejoices — .

Auch unsre Freud' erschalle laut!
Also our joy may sound loudly;

Des Herren Lob sei unser Lied!
the Lord's praise be our song!

The great work is completed;
the Creator beholds it and rejoices.
May our joy also resound;
may the praise of the Lord be our song!

No. 27 Trio

Zu dir, o Herr, blickt Alles auf;
To you, O Lord, looks everything up.

um Speise fleht dich Alles an.
For food beseeches you all — .

Du öffnest deine Hand,
You open your hand,

gesättigt werden sie.
satisfied become they.

Du wendest ab dein Angesicht.
You turn away your countenance,

Da bebet alles und erstarrt.
then trembles all and is paralyzed.

Du nimmst den Odem weg;
You take the breath away,

in Staub zerfallen sie.
to dust disintegrate they.

Den Odem hauchst du wieder aus,
The breath breathe you again out,

und neues Leben sprosst hervor.
and new life sprouts forth.

Verjüngt ist die Gestalt der Erd'
Rejuvenated is the form of the earth

an Reiz und Kraft.
in charm and strength.

All things, O Lord, look up to you.
They beseech you for nourishment.
You open your hand,
and they become satisfied.

You turn away your face,
and all things tremble, terror-struck.
You inhale and take away their breath,
and they disintegrate into dust.

You breathe out again,
and new life sprouts forth.
The earth is rejuvenated;
its charm and vigor are restored.

No. 28 Chorus

Vollendet ist das große Werk,
Completed is the great work;

des Herren Lob sei unser Lied!
the Lord's praise be our song!

Alles lobe seinen Namen,
All things praise his name,

denn er allein ist hoch erhaben! Alleluja!
for he alone is high exalted! Alleluia!

The great work is completed!
Let the Lord's praise be our song!
Let all things praise his name,
for he alone is highly exalted! Alleluia!

No. 34 Chorus and Trio

Singt dem Herren, alle Stimmen!
Sing to the Lord, all voices!

Dankt ihm alle seine Werke!
Thank him all his works!

Lasst zu Ehren seines Namens
Let in honor of his name;

Lob im Wettgesang erschallen.
praise in the singing contest sound.

Des Herren Ruhm, er bleibt in Ewigkeit!
The Lord's glory, it remains in eternity!

Amen!
Amen!

Let every voice sing to the Lord!
Thank him for all his works!
In honor of his name,
let praises in contest sound!
The glory of the Lord endures forever!
Amen!

*T*HE origin of the libretto to *The Creation*, the fifth and penultimate oratorio by Joseph Haydn (1732–1809), is unknown. Haydn told his secretary and biographer Georg August Griesinger (1769–1845) that it was by one "Lindley," but historians have been unable to identify such an individual with any probability.[51]

The composer was given the libretto in 1795 by the German-born violinist and impresario Johann Peter Salomon (1745–1815), who had arranged Haydn's two triumphant sojourns in England (1791–1792 and 1794–1795). Haydn had been introduced to Handelian oratorio on those trips and saw in *The Creation* an opportunity to breathe new life into the genre that Handel had invented and popularized in the 1730s and 40s. In fact, the libretto had been intended for Handel, who never set it.

In addition to his own ideas and words, the author, whoever he was, made use of three pre-existent sources in constructing his libretto: the Creation narrative from Genesis, Milton's *Paradise Lost*, and the Book of Psalms. The verses from Genesis, both in quotation and paraphrase, provided the story line and much of the text for the recitatives, while the Psalms lent gravity and familiarity to many of the celebratory and laudatory choruses. *Paradise Lost* and "Lindley's" own creativity provided the framework for the arias as well as many of the recitatives that introduce them.

Haydn's own religiosity must have made the composition of a Biblical oratorio particularly attractive:

> Haydn was very religiously inclined, and a devout follower of the religion into which he grew up. . . . All his larger scores begin with the words "in Nomine Domini" and close with "Laus Deo" or "Soli Deo gloria."[52] "If, when I am composing, things don't go quite right," I heard him say, "I walk up and down the room with my rosary in my hand, say several Aves, and then the ideas come again. . . ." (Griesinger, quoted in Landon and Jones 1988: 299)

Haydn determined to set the oratorio both in the original English and in German. To this end he engaged the services of the Imperial librarian, Baron Gottfried van Swieten (1733–1803), to produce a German version. Van Swieten, who had already collaborated with Haydn on the *Seven Last Words* and probably *The Storm* as well, did a remarkable job of preserving both the meaning and the accentual pattern of the original. Inevitably, however, there were more syllables in some of the German sentences, which required rhythmic adjustments. Swieten also provided unsolicited advice and suggestions to Haydn as to how the texts might be set (see Landon 1977, volume 4: 350–353). The compositional process itself stretched from December, 1796 to perhaps as late as April, 1798. The work was given its premiere privately in April, 1798 and then publicly on March 19, 1799.

Griesinger's quotation of Haydn shows that this was a labor of faith as well as music:

> It was not till I completed half of my composition that I noticed that it had turned out very well; I was also never so devout as during that time when I was working on the Creation; every day I fell on my knees and asked God to give me strength to enable me to pursue the work to its successful conclusion. (Landon and Jones 1988: 304)

The selections translated here include some of the most popular choruses as well as their introductory recitatives, and all three of "Lindley's" sources are present. The "ritornello" in no. 13 (Peters numbering) is a close paraphrase of Psalm 19: 1, and the solo passages in the same movement are from verses 2 and 4. Genesis 1: 31 supplies the opening clause of recitative no. 25. The first stanza in no. 27 (the four lines beginning "All things, O Lord . . . .") is from Psalm 145: 15–16; its continuation and expansion, however, appear to be of the author's creation. Finally, Psalm 135: 13b provides the text for the last sentence of the final chorus, no. 34.

The role of *Paradise Lost* in the *Creation* libretto is a topic worthy of further investigation. While the non-Biblical characters, Raphael, Uriel, and Gabriel, are borrowed from Milton's work and there are similarities in tone, the editors were unable to locate quotations or paraphrases within the movements presented here. The closest yet admittedly tenuous parallel involves the second clause of recitative no. 25, which could possibly be a paraphrase of Milton's book 7, lines 558–568.

Followed with acclamation, and the sound
Symphonious of ten thousand harps, that tuned
Angelic harmonies: The earth, the air
Resounded, (thou rememberest, for thou heardst,)
The heavens and all the constellations rung, . . .

The great Creator from his work returned
Magnificent, his six days work, a World . . . .
And the heavenly choir in song divine
thus closed the sixth day.

---

[51]See Landon and Jones 1988: 316 for a discussion of the possible identities of "Lindley."

[52]J.S. Bach followed a similar practice, often beginning his works with "Jesu, juva me" and ending with "Soli Deo gloria."

Fanny Hensel

GARTENLIEDER, op. 3
Garden Songs

UNTIL recent years Fanny Hensel (1805–1847) was known principally for her diary and letters, which illuminate the biography of Felix Mendelssohn, her younger brother. She is now receiving long overdue recognition for her compositions. Hensel was a gifted pianist and composer, little of whose substantial body of work was published in her lifetime. Some of her early songs appeared under Felix's name as his opp. 2, 6, and 8, but the *Gartenlieder*, op. 3 were published as her own works by Bote and Bock of Berlin in 1846.

Nature was a source of great inspiration to the German romantic poets. The cycle of the seasons, the times of the day, the forests, and the waters supplied them with beautiful images—as well as analogies to the joys and travails of the human soul. More often than not, a "nature poem" was intended to be read on both of these levels. There existed, however, a body of nature poetry that was intentionally not overly burdened by Teutonic existential *Angst*, and that was meant to be read and heard for its beauty alone. Perhaps the best examples of such poems set to music are found in Felix Mendelssohn's opp. 41, 48, and 59, respectively subtitled "Im Freien zu singen" (To Be Sung in the Open Air), "Der erste Frühlingstag" (The First Day of Spring), and "Im Grünen" (In the Greenery). These three sets of songs were intended for social recreation rather than concert use; Mendelssohn himself led his singers in their performance during nature walks on the days following oratorio performances.

Hensel chose mostly poems of the same type. In this way they were appropriate as texts for *Gartenlieder*, songs to be sung in the outdoors. Her collection consists of six songs set to poems by four poets, Joseph Freiherr von Eichendorff (1788–1857), who was especially honored with three settings, Ludwig Uhland (1887–1862), Emanuel Geibel (1815–1884), and the composer's husband Wilhelm Hensel (1794–1861).

Prior to his beginning life-long work as a civil bureaucrat, Eichendorff was born into a noble family of means and was raised in a region of beautiful natural surroundings. His love of nature certainly stemmed from the experiences of his youth and was, along with his Catholic faith, a decisive influence on his poetic work. It is true, as editor René Strasser writes in the preface to Eichendorff's *Werke*, that the poet "has gone into the public consciousness as the singer of the German forests and as a poet of youthful wander-songs." (Eichendorff 1965, 1: 7, tr. ed.) The point of his subsequent paragraphs, however, is that this is an oversimplification of Eichendorff's significance. Yet it is precisely this type of poem that Hensel chose for the *Gartenlieder*—"simple" nature poetry characterized by beautiful images and exquisite use of German. Eichendorff scholar Egon Schwartz puts it eloquently:

> . . . Eichendorff's strength lies in his poems, but not so much in their subject matter or ideological content as in their rhythms and melodies, their ornaments and images; in other words: in exactly those features of language that are ultimately untranslatable. . . . They belong to a different tradition of poetry in which the musical, acoustic, and emotive faculties of language are exploited, often to the detriment of its semantic or thought properties. The German *Lied* is the glory of this lyric tradition, and Eichendorff figures prominently . . . . (Schwartz 1972: Preface, n.p.)

Perhaps because the poetry is so dependent on the original language, little of Eichendorff's work has been translated, and when it is wrought in another language it loses what endears it to German speakers.

Ludwig Uhland was born and spent most of his life in the southwest-German university city of Tübingen, where he followed in his grandfather's footsteps as a professor. In his student days he studied law and developed an interest in medieval literature. After an abortive stint as a civil servant he set up a private law practice and entered politics, through which he represented his region in various assemblies until 1849. Thereafter he turned his attention to the study of German literature, in which he was a pioneer. His creative energies were at their most intense in his youth: He wrote and published almost all of his poetry before the age of thirty.

If one were to read this volume cover to cover, it would be striking how many of the poets represented here were pastors, teachers, or civil servants whose work supported their extra-professional literary efforts. Emanuel Geibel—ironically not one of the greater poets—was an exception. He started writing poetry in his youth and through fortuitous contacts managed to receive a pension at the age of twenty seven from King Friedrich Wilhelm IV of Prussia, freeing himself of everyday financial burdens. He is best known among musicians for his poems in the *Spanisches Liederbuch*, published jointly with Paul Heyse, from which Hugo

Wolf set ten poems. Literary historians have not been kind to Geibel, in the hindsight of history finding his work lacking in originality.

Wilhelm Hensel married Fanny Mendelssohn after a courtship of six years when he was thirty four and she twenty three. The long delay was due to her parents' doubts as to his suitability for marriage in terms both of class and profession. Lea Mendelssohn, Fanny's mother, insisted that all letters from Hensel come to her, so that they might be censored before being read aloud to Fanny. Hensel is an unknown in German romantic literature; one will search in vain for biographical or analytical information in the usual reference sources. Some of his poetry has been preserved, however, through his wife's musical settings of it. Hensel was nonetheless somewhat of a celebrity in his time as a portraitist of royalty, the rich, and the famous. Of special interest to musicians are his portraits of the extended Mendelssohn family.

Hörst du nicht die Bäume rauschen, op. 3, no. 1
Don't You Hear the Trees Rustling?
Joseph von Eichendorff

Hörst du nicht die Bäume rauschen,
Hear you not the trees rustling,

Draußen durch die stille Rund'?
outside through the still surroundings?

Lockt's dich nicht, hinabzulauschen
Entices it you not, down-to-listen

Von dem Söller in den Grund,
from the loft to the ground,

Wo die vielen Bäche gehen,
where the many brooks go

Wunderbar im Mondenschein
wonderful in the moonlight,

Und die stillen Burgen sehen
and the silent castles look

In den Fluß vom hohen Stein?
into the river from the high rock?

Kennst du noch die süßen Lieder
Know you still the sweet songs

Aus der alten schönen Zeit?
from the old, beautiful time?

Sie erwachen alle wieder
They awaken all again

Nachts in Waldeseinsamkeit,
at night in forest-loneliness,

Wenn die Bäume träumend lauschen,
when the trees dreaming listen,

Und der Flieder duftet schwül
and the lilac smells so sweet,

Und im Fluß die Nixen lauschen,
and in the river the nymphs listen,

Komm herab, hier ist's so kühl.
come down, here it's so cool.

Don't you hear the trees rustling
through the stillness outside?
Doesn't it entice you to listen
from your height down to the depths,
where many brooks flow
so marvellously in the moonlight,
and the silent castles look down
into the river from the rocks above?

Do you still remember the sweet songs
from the old, wonderful time?
They all awaken again
at night in the solitude of the forest,
when the dreaming trees listen,
and the lilac smells so sweet,
and the nymphs listen in the river—
come down; it's so cool here.

Source: Eichendorff 1985, 1: 308
Variants: (Hensel = roman, Eichendorff = *italic*)
Line 7: Burgen (fortresses)= *Schlößer (palaces)*
Line 9: süßen (sweet) = *irren (confused)*
Line 15: lauschen (listen) = *rauschen (rustle)*

*T*HE first of the Eichendorff poems was originally named "Lockung" (Enticement) and is contained in a group to which the poet gave the heading "Sängerleben" (The Life of a Singer). The sweet night images of the poem provide two levels of enticement—in the first strophe "to listen from your height down to the depths," and in the second to dream of "old, wonderful" times past, figuratively following the invitation of the waiting nymphs. Eichendorff's words trip easily and naturally off the tongue, reinforcing the tranquility of the scene. The poet's attention to the sounds of his words is especially apparent in two examples, the first at the very beginning—the word *rauschen* is a lovely onomatopoeia for the rustling of the trees, which is prolonged by the next word, *draußen*. The second strophe also begins with and is imbued with character by another fortuitous choice of onomatopoetic words—*süßen* and *schönen*.

The first of Hensel's changes to Eichendorff's poem (see *Variants*) is innocent enough and does not change its meaning. The other two emendations, however, are significant. Hensel's replacement of *irren* (lost, confused) with *süßen* (sweet) eliminates the need for the listener to contemplate the unexplained darkness that *irren* introduces. Likewise, having the nymphs "listening" rather than "murmuring" disconnects the closing invitation ("come down; it's so cool here") from the inviters in the previous line. The sum of these changes is to neutralize the challenging elements of the poem and render it merely beautiful. The last of these changes must have been very important to Hensel, as the use of *lauschen* (listen) in the penultimate line forces an awkward rhyme with the same word two lines earlier.

Schöne Fremde, op. 3, no. 2
Beautiful Stranger
Joseph von Eichendorff

Es rauschen die Wipfel und schauern,
— **rustle the tree-tops and shudder**

Als hielten zu dieser Stund'
as if held at this hour

Um die halbverfallenen Mauern,
around the half-crumpled walls,

Die alten Götter die Rund'.
the old gods the circle.

Hier unter den Myrthenbäumen
Here under the myrtle-trees

In heimlich dämmernder Pracht,
in sweetly dawning splendor,

Was sprichst du wirr wie in Träumen
what say you confused like in dreams

Zu mir, phantastische Nacht?
to me, fantastic night?

Es funkeln mir zu alle Sterne
— **sparkle me at all stars**

Mit glühendem Liebesblick,
with glowing love-glance;

Es redet trunken die Ferne
— **speaks drunken the distance**

Von künftigem großem Glück!
of future great happiness!

The treetops rustle and shudder
as if, at this hour,
around the half-crumpled walls,
the old gods were gathering in a circle.

Here under the myrtle trees
in sweetly dawning splendor,
what are you saying to me, fantastic night,
confused, as in a dream?

All the stars twinkle at me
with a glowing, loving gaze;
the drunken distance speaks
of future, great happiness!

> **Source:** Eichendorff 1985, 1: 309
> **Variants:** (Hensel = roman, Eichendorff = *italic*)
> Line 2: hielten = *machten*
> Line 3: halbverfallenen = *halbversunkenen*
> Line 5: unter = *hinter*
> Line 9: mir zu = *auf mich*
> Line 12: von = *wie von*

EICHENDORFF'S "Schöne Fremde" comes from a group of his verses entitled "Wanderlieder" (Songs for Wandering). The pairing of this poem with the first is especially nice, given their common opening image of the rustling trees.

Again, Hensel's first, second, and fourth alterations must have been to satisfy her personal preference for sonance, as they do not change the original meanings, and the exchange of *unter* (under) for *hinter* (behind) is more idiomatic. The change in the last pair of lines—"the drunken distance speaks, *as if* of future, great happiness"—to merely "of future, great happiness" once again eliminates a twist that would require the listener to reflect on its meaning, and yields instead a simple, happy ending.

Im Herbste, op. 3, no. 3

In Autumn
Ludwig Uhland

Seid gegrüßt mit Frühlingswonne,
Be greeted with spring's bliss,

Blauer Himmel, goldne Sonne!
blue sky, golden sun!

Drüben auch aus Gartenhallen
Over there also from garden halls

Hör' ich frohe Saiten schallen.
hear I joyful strings sound.

Ahnest du, o Seele, wieder
Anticipate you, O soul, again

Sanfte, süße Frühlingslieder?
soft, sweet spring songs?

Sieh umher die falben Bäume!
See around the pale-yellow trees!

Ach, es waren holde Träume.
Oh, they were lovely dreams.

Be greeted with spring's delight,
blue sky, golden sun!
Over there, from the gardens,
I hear the sound of joyful strings.

Do you, O soul, again expect
the soft, sweet songs of spring?
See the pale-yellow trees all around!
Oh, they were lovely dreams.

Source: Uhland 1892: 17

*T*HE first verse of Ludwig Uhland's poem speaks of a spring day, which he paints eloquently in sound with pairs of voiced consonants (*Frühlingswonne, Himmel, Sonne, Gartenhallen, schallen*). In the second verse the listener is reminded that the fading of spring's beauty is mirrored by the fading of one's dreams. This darkening of mood is marked by the disappearance of the bright sonance of the text. Uhland's original text survived Hensel's pen without alteration.

Morgengruß, op. 3, no. 4

Morning's Greeting
Wilhelm Hensel

Schnell fliehen die Schatten der Nacht,
Quickly flee the shadows of the night;

Hell blühen die Matten in Pracht.
brightly blooms the meadows in splendor.

Hoch rauschet der Wald in dem Glanze,
High rustles the forest in the brilliance;

Still lauschet ihm heimlich die Pflanze.
silently listens to it secretly the plant.

Im Blütenverklärenden Tauen,
In the blossom-transfiguring dew,

Wie selig, den Morgen zu schauen.
how blessed, the morning to behold.

Was fehlt noch dem goldenen Raum?
What is missing yet to the golden place?

Komm, Liebchen, erfülle den Traum.
Come, sweetheart, fulfill the dream.

Mein Lied tönt in wonnigem Rauschen,
My song sounds in blissful murmurs,

O komm, wie die Blume zu lauschen.
Oh come, like the flower to listen.

Es will dich mein liebendes Sehnen
— wants you my loving longing

Betauen mit seligen Tränen.
bedew with happy tears.

The shadows of the night quickly flee;
the meadows bloom brightly in splendor.
High above, the forest rustles in the brilliance;
silently the plant secretly listens to it.
In the blossom-transfiguring dew,
how blessed it is to behold the morning.

What is still missing in this golden place?
Come, dearest, fulfill the dream.
My song murmurs blissfully;
Oh come, listen like the flower.
My loving longing wants to
bedew you with happy tears.

WILHELM Hensel's two–stanza poem contains no anguish and only the slightest hint of sadness. The first strophe pictures a glorious morning, and the second begins by questioning what could be wrong with the picture just painted. The answer is simple: the absence of the poet's beloved. The poem continues not with the lament that one might find in other works, but with a touching invitation to the beloved to come and share the beauty. The image of the morning dew in the first strophe is answered nicely by the "happy tears" in the second, and for the third time in the *Gartenlieder*, the forest is heard rustling.

The composer's manuscript differs from the first printed edition in line 5.[53] The manuscript's *glitzernden, blitzenden* (glistening, sparkling), challenging to the tongue and harsh to the ear, was replaced by *Blütenverklärenden* (blossom-transfiguring), which provides both a softer image and a gentler sound.

Abendlich schon rauscht der Wald, op. 3, no. 5
At Evening the Forest Already Murmurs
Joseph von Eichendorff

Abendlich   schon rauscht der Wald
In the evening already rustles the forest

Aus den tiefen Gründen,
from the deep valleys,

Droben wird der Herr nun bald
up there will the Lord now soon

An die Sterne zünden,
— the stars ignite;

Wie so stille in den Schlünden
How so still in the gorges

Abendlich   nur rauscht der Wald.
in the evening only rustles the forest.

Alles geht zu seiner Ruh',
All   goes to   its   rest,

Wie die Welt   verbrause.
as   the world calms down.

Schauernd hört der Wandrer zu,
trembling listens the wanderer —,

Sehnt sich tief nach Hause,
longs — deeply for home,

Hier in Waldes grüner Klause,
here in forest's green hermitage,

Herz, geh endlich auch zur Ruh!
heart, go at last also to rest!

At evening the forest already murmurs
from the deep valleys;
the Lord above will soon now
ignite the stars;
how so still in the steep canyons
at evening only the forest murmurs.
All goes to its rest
as the world calms down.
Trembling, the wanderer listens
and longs deeply for home.
Here in the forest's green cloister,
heart, go also at last to rest.

Source: Eichendorff, 1965, 1: 322
Variants: (Hensel = roman, Eichendorff = *italic*)
        Line 8:verbrause = *versausen*
        Line 10: tief = *recht*

JOSEPH von Eichendorff's poem welcomes the coming of the night and the peace it brings both to nature and to man's soul. The original title of the poem is "Abschied" (Farewell)—perhaps a "farewell" to the day. It is interesting that here, for the fourth time in this collection, this poem contains an image of the rustling (here translated as "murmuring") forest.

The composer altered the poem in two places. Eichendorff's "Wald und Welt versausen" (*versausen* likely being a verb of the poet's own creation) is transformed into "Wie die Welt verbrause."[54] Two lines later Hensel replaced *recht* with *tief*, which may have felt more musical to her.

---

[53]The editors are grateful to Barbara Gabler of Furore Verlag, Kassel, Germany, for providing information on the manuscript source, MA Ms 49: 55–57 from the Mendelssohn Archive of the Staatsbibliothek, Berlin, Preußischer Kulturbesitz.

[54]*Verbrause* would appear to be the subjunctive form of *verbrausen* (to settle down, calm down, subside), but such a form makes no sense in this context. It is a mystery why Hensel would change the perfectly clear original in favor of unnecessary ambiguity. The translation offered here, "as the world grows calm" (presumably after a hectic day), is one of several possibilities but it seems best to fit the context of the poem.

Im Wald, op. 3, no. 6

In the Forest
Emanuel Geibel

Im Wald, im hellen Sonnenschein,	In the forest, in the bright sunshine,
In the forest, in the bright sunshine,	when all the buds spring open—
	there I, in their midst, like
Wenn alle Knospen springen,	to sing a song.
when all buds burst—	
Da mag ich gerne mittendrein	
there like I — –in the middle–	
Eins singen.	
one [song] to sing.	

Wie mir zu Mut in Leid und Lust,	How I feel in suffering and joy,
How me to good cheer in suffering and joy,	in waking and in dreaming—
	I sing that song to the trees
Im Wachen und im Träumen,	at the top of my lungs.
in waking and in dreaming,	
Das stimm' ich an aus voller Brust	
that –I begin to sing– from full breast	
Den Bäumen.	
to the trees.	

Und sie verstehen mich gar fein,	And they understand me very well;
And they understand me very well;	the leaves all listen
	and join in at the right time
Die Blätter alle lauschen,	with rustling.
the leaves all listen	
Und fall'n am rechten Orte ein	
and join in at the right place —	
Mit Rauschen.	
with rustling.	

Und weiter wandelt Schall und Hall	And the sounds resound further
And further wander sound and echo	in treetops, rocks, and bushes.
	Mrs. Nightingale also warbles clearly
In Wipfeln, Fels und Büschen,	in their midst.
in treetops, rocks and bushes.	
Hell schmettert auch Frau Nachtigall	
Clearly warbles also madame Nightingale	
Dazwischen.	
in their midst.	

Da fühlt die Brust am eignen Klang,	There the heart feels from its own sound
There feels the heart from own sound	that it may venture something.
	O fresh joy! Song! Song
Sie darf sich was erkühnen—	in the greenery!
it may — something dare.	
O frische Lust: Gesang! Gesang	
O fresh joy! Song! Song	
Im Grünen!	
in the greenery!	

Source: Geibel 1893, 1: 48

*I*N contrast to "Im Herbste," but like "Morgengruß," Emanuel Geibel's "Im Wald" is completely joyous. The poet's greatest pleasure is being in the forest and singing to nature and to himself. Nature understands—the song echoes, the nightingale joins in, and for the fifth time in the collection, the trees rustle.

On May 14, 1847 Dr. Emanuel Klitzsch reviewed the *Gartenlieder* in the *Neue Zeitschrift für Musik*:

> The *Gartenlieder* of Fanny Hensel (born Mendelssohn-Bartholdy) stand out from the many others of this genre in terms of artistic conception, though we find in them less in the way of independent individuality and more of a predominant character of grace and friendliness, than a strong sentiment emanating from deep within the heart. The harmonic treatment is quite refined and makes one aware of an artistically tasteful hand. Above all of the songs hangs a gentle, poetic fragrance. This is true namely of no. 1, Eichendorff's "Hörst du nicht die Bäume rauschen?" and of no. 3, Uhland's "Im Herbste," in the latter of which the middle section, "Ahnest du, o Seele wieder," is particularly successful. (Klitzsch 1847: 1, tr. ed.)

Forty-one year old Fanny Hensel probably never saw these words of praise—she died the very same same day of a stroke.

Nachtreigen, op. 104, no. 2

Nocturnal Round Dance

Fanny Hensel / Wilhelm Hensel

Es rauschen die Bäume,
— **rustle the trees,**

Es wallen die Düfte
— **blow the fragrances,**

Und zärtliche Lüfte
and delicate winds

Umfangen die Träume
embrace the dreams

Mit bräutlichem Hauch.
with bride-like breath.

The trees rustle,
the fragrances waft,
and delicate breezes
embrace dreams
with bridal breath.

Wir wandeln und wallen
We wander and meander

Im trautem Umringen,
in intimate encircling;

Wir wallen und singen,
we wander and sing,

Und Echo tönt auch.
and Echo sounds also.

We wander and roam
in intimate encircling;
we roam and sing,
and Echo sings too.

Beseligend Schallen
Blissful sounding

Und Duften und Scheinen,
and sweet smelling and shining.

O heiliges Einen,
O holy uniting!

Schließt dichter den Kreis,
Close more tightly the circle,

Leis, leis.
quietly, quietly.

Blissful sounds
and fragrances and appearances.
O holy uniting!
Close the circle more tightly,
quietly, quietly.

Hallo! Hallo!
Hello! Hello!

So lustig schweift sich's durch Grün und Nacht.
So gaily roams — it through green and night,

Frisch wie die Luft der Gedanke,
fresh as the air [is] the thought,

Und froh mit dem singenden Vogel wacht
and happily, with the singing bird, wakes

Der Mensch, entronnen der Schranke.
the person, escaped the bounds.

Wie's scheinet und lacht.
How it shines and laughs!

Hello! Hello!
The greeting wafts gaily through the greenery
and the night.
The thought is as fresh as the air,
and happily, with the singing bird,
the mortal wakes who knows no bounds.
How the world shines and laughs!

Still! Still!
Still! Still!

Nicht die heil'ge Feier stören
Not the holy celebration disturb

Wollet mit dem lauten Ruf,
want you with the loud shout;

Lasset singen uns und hören,
let sing us and hear,

Schaffen, wie Natur erschuf.
create, like nature created.

Leise, weise,
Quietly, carefully,

Naht dem Kreise,
approach the circle—

Kommt!
Come!

Still! Still!
You don't want to disturb the holy celebration
with a loud shout;
let us sing and listen
and create, like nature created.
Quietly, carefully,
approach the circle—
Come!

Ja, wir kommen, überwunden
Yes, we are coming, overcome

Durch der Ruhe heil'ge Macht.
by the silence's holy might.

So bleibt friedlich uns verbunden,
Thus remain peacefully with us united,

Denn euch hat der Gott gebracht.
for you has — God brought.

Und gemeinsam sei empfunden,
And together be apprehended

Was der einzelne gedacht.
what the individual one thought.

Yes, we are coming, overcome
by the holy power of silence.
Thus remain peacefully united with us,
for God has brought you.
And may we together apprehend
what the one thought.

*A*S she had for the song "Morgengruß"* in the *Gartenleider,* Fanny Hensel (1805–1847) used a text from her artist husband Wilhelm (1794–1861) as the basis for this chorus. This is a rather pantheistic poem in which an undefined group communes with nature, finds individual spiritual enlightenment (stanza 4) and then, in imitation of nature's creative force (stanza 5), forges a unity, a oneness among themselves. This "holy uniting" (stanza 2) is symbolized by a round dance in which the circle becomes ever tighter and its members ever closer in their mystical harmony.

Fanny Hensel obviously saw compositional opportunities in the poem, with its constant progression toward unity. She set the text for a double chorus of women (chorus 1) and men (chorus 2), who first sing separately (women: stanzas 1–3; men: stanza 4; women: stanza 5), then in close alternation, and finally homophonically (stanza 6, lines 1–4). They are brought together simultaneously on the same text for the first time with the last two lines of the poem,

> And may we together apprehend
> what the one thought.

which Hensel sets as a fugue—symbolic of all parts thinking and becoming as one (each succeeding voice "apprehends" and sings what the first voice stated) and of the nocturnal round dance (the voices of the fugue follow one another just as the dancers would follow each other around the circle).

The variety of structures in the poem is interesting, with stanzas of four, five, and six lines (exclamations not included); three different poetic meters (1–3, 4, 5–6); and a different rhyme scheme in each stanza:

1	ABBAC
2	ABBC
3	ABBCC
4	ABABA
5	ABABCC
6	ABABAB

Of the rhymed poetry in this volume, no other example demonstrates such a free design. Perhaps this was one of the elements that particularly inspired Hensel, who composed her setting of the poem on June 29, 1829 as a birthday present for her husband-to-be. They married on October 3 of the same year and lived a life filled with artistic endeavors and mutual respect until Fanny's death of a stroke during a rehearsal on May 14, 1847.

Paul Hindemith

FÜNFSTIMMIGE MADRIGALE
NACH TEXTEN VON JOSEF WEINHEBER
Five-Part Madrigals
on texts by Josef Weinheber

OF all the poetry discussed in this volume, none is more challenging to translate and to understand than that of Josef Weinheber (1892–1944), whose extraordinary poetic skill[55] was matched only by the darkness of his outlook. Weinheber lost both parents as a child and was consigned to an orphanage, which he detested. He came to adulthood with the terror of WWI, lived through the economic disaster of the twenties, the ascent of Hitler and his National Socialist Party, and most of the war of the Third Reich against the rest of humanity. This was not a background conducive to optimism of world view, even in a man who nominally professed Christian faith—first Catholicism and after 1929, Lutheranism.

Weinheber's poetry and philosophy are complex and filled with internal contradictions. Nonetheless, ". . . the main impression of Weinheber's total output must be that of somber turbulence, of dark and tempestuous emotions. . . . It is evident that this poet envisages a victory of dark forces, which to him are very real. . . . (Hofrichter 1942: 66)

Within the limited confines of this essay, Weinheber's concept of reality is perhaps best seen through a series of quotations from Ruth Hofrichter (Hofrichter 1942), a perceptive critic who wrote at the beginning of WWII about Weinheber's philosophy and poetry:

> [To Weinheber] . . . the world of fragrance, color, and sound . . . is an illusion given to us by our senses in time and space and hides a deeper reality only disclosed to the searching soul. This "deeper reality" for Weinheber is "dark"—thus he qualifies the things that mean most to him, language and art. "And magnificent dark language goes down to be devoured by the day." Also "day" is the life of naïve unthinking multitudes: day and small happiness are their only reason for living. . . . The poet urges all brave men to plunge into the night. . . . "Night" appears often as the dangerous realm into which the hero plunges to prove his courage. It is the forbidden sphere of intoxication, of chaos; but there is also born the impulse to overcome the dark forces." (60)

> It is constantly evident that the poet is haunted by an apprehension of senselessness in life. Man is lost on a terrible sea, only dreaming of distant islands. Still, he must stand upright and prove his noble courage, even though he can see no goal in life. The world is lost, the sacrifice of Christ in vain. (56)

> "Things" seem dead to him. His secret love and longing, one would guess, belong to the urge for self-annihilation. . . . His conception of religion is hazy and confined to sentimental and nostalgic reminiscences of Francis of Assisi and Christ: in his scheme of things neither has to do with life on earth; both live in an undefined higher sphere. (57)

> For Weinheber, the lovely things of the earth, children and flowers, only intensify the grief caused by the senselessness of everything—the fact that he can find no essential meaning in life. (55)

> But his real home is the "strange world of art, which far away from the real one, and better than it, exists in the spirit." (46)

Weinheber's poems were often organized into cycles of astonishing length and complexity. Perhaps this is merely a reflection of the Teutonic tendency toward organization and pedantry—or perhaps it had to do as well with finding something over which the poet could exercise control in a world run amok, in which the individual was meaningless and powerless. For various reasons, Weinheber's work found a resonance within the National Socialist movement, and he was considered to be a poet of the Nazi Party, an association that he chose, whether out of convenience or conviction, not to disavow.

---

[55]Hofrichter wryly relates the following example of Weinheber's craft as demonstrated in a cycle of fifteen sonnets (Hofrichter 1942: 47):

> The scheme is transparent enough, and we recommend imitation to anyone wishing to submit to rigorous technical discipline: Write the last one of fifteen sonnets first, then use the first line to begin the first sonnet of your cycle, the second line to end it and begin sonnet number two. The third line of sonnet fifteen will become the last line of the second sonnet, as well as the first of number three, and so on. This exercise should greatly increase the neophyte's proficiency in use of the sonnet form.

The poet's conscious effort to find a philosophy of reality has a counterpart in Rosenberg's *Der Mythus des zwanzigten Jahrhunderts,* an account of the mythical conceptions underlying the National Socialist Weltanschauung [world view]. Here we read: The essence of the world revolution of today lies in the awakening of racial types. "The strongest personality in our day no longer aspires toward personality but toward the type."[56] Individualism and universalism are . . . philosophies of decadence."[57] "Today we know at last the forces of the racial soul awakening from a deep sleep."[58] All these utterances are death sentences pronounced on the individual, and the poet, half in terror, half in fascination, feels the forces at work. (Hofrichter 1942: 53)

Weinheber was ultimately as powerless to reconcile the conflicts within his spirit as he was to change the nightmarish world around him. As the Russians invaded Austria in 1944, Weinheber decided that the time had come to enter the darkness for eternity, which he did with an overdose of sleeping pills.

In 1938 Hindemith had fled the terror that ultimately took Weinheber's life, but he had lived under the Third Reich long enough to understand the existential questions that had beset Weinheber, whose poems must have spoken to him, as he chose a dozen of them for his *Twelve Madrigals* of 1958. They were culled from several collections; what they had in common was their challenge to the mind and spirit of the reader/listener. Even before leaving Germany as a cultural enemy of the Reich, Hindemith had committed himself to writing music for specific purposes, what he called *Sing- und Spielmusik* (music to sing and play) and has come to be known generally as *Gebrauchsmusik* (music for use). The madrigals fulfilled this purpose as music to bind a vocal ensemble together. In his program notes to the premiere performance on October 18, 1958 (which the composer used in part as his preface to the collection when it was published) Hindemith said of madrigals in general and of the Weinheber texts in particular:

> The texts [of madrigals] must give expression to what can move a small circle of participants to a feeling of unity. It seems to me that Weinheber's poems meet this standard at a high level, even with their generally pessimistic vein, which hardly gives rise to a sense of optimism within the group. . . . The twelve pieces are not thought of as a closed cycle. They may be performed in any assortment or order, but it is recommended to perform no. 12 ["Du Zweifel"] at the end if it is performed at all. . . . I am happy to be able to try out this attempt at a new/old a-cappella art here in Vienna, especially because . . . the Austrian, even Viennese tone of Weinheber's texts will be best understood and loved here, and like no other modern lyric poetry, Weinheber's is suited to the spirit of singing together. . . .[59]

It is not known how Hindemith came into contact with Weinheber's poems, or when the idea of writing a loose cycle of them came into his mind, but one experience may have been decisive:

> The dedication to the deceased Hedi Straumann only occurred to Hindemith while composition was already underway. As Hindemith told the editor of this volume personally, he was working on the madrigal "Trink aus!" when Gertrud Hindemith passed on the telephone message that the wife of his friend from Zurich, English teacher Heinrich Straumann, had died. On the left-hand page of his open volume of Weinheber's works Hindemith saw the poem "An eine Tote" (To One Dead) and he began immediately to set this poem to music. He dedicated the entire cycle to the deceased. (Rubeli 1989: 281, tr. ed.)

---

[56]Rosenberg 1935: 531. Alfred Rosenberg, a high official of the Nazi Party and its unofficial philosopher, was tried at Nuremberg by the Allies, and was convicted and executed in 1946 for crimes against humanity. Hitler's architect Albert Speer writes of this work:

> Rosenberg sold his seven-hundred page *Myth of the Twentieth Century* in editions of hundreds of thousands. The public regarded it as the standard text for party ideology, but Hitler . . . bluntly called it "stuff nobody can understand," written by "a narrow-minded Baltic German who thinks in horribly complicated terms." (Speer 1970: 115)

[57] *Ibid.*: 539.

[58] *Ibid.*: 564

[59]Rubeli 1989: unnumbered page preceding p. 49, tr. ed. The passage from " . . . I am happy" to the end of the quotation is excerpted from the portion of the program notes that Hindemith did not include in his preface to the madrigals when Schott published them as a set. This additional text is found in Rubeli 1989: 221.

Tauche deine Furcht
Plunge Your Fear
Josef Weinheber

Tauche deine Furcht in schwarzen Wein,
Plunge your fear into black wine,

Einsamer! Die dunklen Vögel ziehen.
lonely one! The dark birds are flying away.

Es wird eine lange Reise sein.
It will a long journey be.

Gott ist nah und raunt. Vergeblich fliehen
God is near and whispers. In vain flee

die Gedanken vor dem Blättertanz.
the thoughts from the leaves' dance.

Und zur Dämmrung ist der Tag gediehen.
And to dusk has the day progressed.

Auf ein leeres Grab fällt Sternenglanz ...
Upon an empty grave falls starlight ...

Tiefer mit dem letzten Mut zur Stille
deeper with the last courage for stillness,

drücke in die Stirn den welken Kranz!
press into the forehead the wilted wreath!

Plunge your fear into black wine,
lonely one! The dark birds are flying away.
It will be a long journey.

God is near and whispers. In vain
your thoughts flee from the dance of the leaves.
And the day has progressed to dusk.

Starlight falls onto an empty grave ...
Deeper, with the final courage for stillness,
press the wilted wreath into your forehead!

Source: Weinheber 1954, 1: 579

A brief collection from 1926 entitled *Boot in der Bucht* (The Boat in the Cove) is the source of this poem, which is untitled. It challenges humanity to set aside its fears and plunge into the darkness, "the deeper reality" of existence, even though "it will be a long journey." Perhaps the metaphor of the "black wine" represents just the darkness, but it also seems to suggest a Christian context—until the next line.

What God whispers in the second strophe is unknown, but it must contain a comfortless reminder of mortality, for humanity's thoughts immediately try to flee from that idea, the "dance of the leaves," as the sky inexorably blackens, leaving only starlight on an empty grave. But to whom does the grave belong? Once again, one could see this image through Christian eyes as a symbol of the risen Christ, but the lines that follow destroy that interpretation. The poem concludes with an exhortation to embrace the darkness and enter the grave[60]—an apparent incitement to suicide, which was how the poet himself resolved the conflicts of his life.

Judaskuß
The Judas Kiss
Josef Weinheber

Ihr seht nur das verfluchte Geld,
You see only the curséd money

das ich genommen hab.
that I taken have

Und schweigt davon, daß Er mir doch
and are silent — that he me indeed

beim Mahl den Bissen gab.
at the meal the bite gave.

Damit die Schrift erfüllet sei,
So that the scripture fulfilled be,

sollt es an mir geschehn.
had it to me to happen.

Er trug mir auf, es bald zu tun.
He ordered me —, it soon to do.

Und also mußt ich gehn
And therefore must I go

You see only the curséd money
that I have taken
and don't mention that He gave me
a bite of bread at the meal.

So that the scripture might be fulfilled,
it had to happen to me.
He ordered me to do it soon.
And therefore I had to go

---

[60]From Classical Antiquity until recently it was customary in some European cultures to display and bury corpses with a wreath upon the head as a final sign of respect. Wilhelm Hensel drew a picture of his wife, the composer Fanny Hensel,* lying in state wearing such a *Totenkranz*. (Hensel 1981: 29)

und ging und kam zurück und nahm
and went and came back and took

und hatte meinen Lohn.
and had my reward.

Doch jener, der am Kedron stand,
But that one, who at Kedron stood,

Er wußte alles schon,
He knew everything already;

und sah mich an und redete
and looked me at and spoke

und ließ mir keine Frist:
and permitted me no time:

"Mit einem Kuß verrätst du mich?"
"With a kiss betray you me?"

So hab ich ihn geküßt.
Thus have I him kissed.

Sie griffen Ihn und banden Ihn
They seized Him and bound Him

und schleppten Ihn davon.
and dragged Him away.

Und ob mir fast das Herz zerriß,
And even if me almost the heart tore,

ich hatte meinen Lohn.
I had my reward.

Du bittre Reue, Scham und Gram!
You bitter remorse, shame, and grief!

Er gab mir mein Geschick.
He gave me my fate.

Er starb für euch den Kreuzestod.
He died for you the cross's death.

Ich ging und nahm den Strick.
I went and took the rope.

and I went and came back and took
and had my reward.
But the one who stood on Kedron's banks
knew everything already;

and he looked at me and spoke
and allowed me no time to respond:
"With a kiss you betray me?"
Then I kissed him.

They seized Him and bound Him
and dragged Him away.
And even though my heart almost broke,
I had my reward.

O bitter remorse, shame, and grief!
He gave me my fate.
He died for you the death of the cross.
I went and took the rope.

Source: Weinheber 1954, 2: 279
Variants: (Hindemith = roman; Weinheber = *italic*)
Stanza 5, line 1: griffen = *ergriffen* in B
Stanza 6, line 1: Reue = *Reu* in T, B

*T*HE "Judaskuß" came from Weinheber's 1937 cycle entitled *O Mensch, gib Acht* (Beware, O Man), which the poet called "Ein erbauliches Kalendarbuch für Stadt- und Landleut" (An Edifying Calendar Book for City and Countryfolk). The introductory poem, *O Mensch, gib Acht*, serves as an inscription above the entire cycle. Then follow seven poems for each of the twelve months, in each case the first of which is titled with the month. Ruth Hofrichter says of this collection that "It gives homey advice in a 'folksy' style." (Hofrichter 1942: 59) If this is the case, "Judaskuß" (no. 5 of nine for the month of March) is a striking exception. The poem is structured in six strophes of four lines each, with rhymes between the second and fourth lines. The second, third, and fourth strophes constitute a single unit, however, with sentences—and thus thoughts—carried across their boundaries. Seldom in the poems presented in this volume does a poet make use of this "elision" technique.

The idea behind "Judaskuß" is powerful and thought-provoking. The poem considers the Passion from the standpoint of Judas Iscariot: Just as the Savior was fated to die, so was Judas inexorably fated to betray him. Given this premise, it is interesting that Judas accepts his guilt stoically rather than shifting responsibility to the Almighty. The reader traces the Passion through the disciple's eyes, as if he has walked this path countless times before and is condemned to walk it for eternity in his own personal hell. He knows what will happen, he knows that his betrayal is heinous, and yet he cannot stop himself from committing the ultimate evil—because God ordained his fate just as he did that of Jesus. The consummate irony is reached in the last two lines: The Savior gave the gift of life to mankind through his sacrifice. Among all of humanity Judas alone was ordained instead to receive thirty pieces of silver—"the curséd money"— and a rope.

Du Zweifel
You Doubt

Josef Weinheber

Du Zweifel an dem Sinn   der Welt!
You doubt about the meaning of the world!

Geschöpf, in diese Qual gestellt,
Creature, into this torment placed,

wer soll dir helfen tragen?
who shall you help to bear?

Dein Straucheln nennst du Menschlichsein,
Your stumbling call you being human;

in deine wilde Pein hinein
into your wild pain —

beginnst du wild zu fragen.
begin you wildly to question.

Was ist mit Wildheit schon getan?
What is with wildness after all done?

Das laute Wesen klagt, klagt an,
The loud creature laments, accuses,

doch klagt nur seine Schwäche.
however laments only his weakness.

Ach, eine Flöte, fern und schön,
Ah, a flute, distant and beautiful,

verklär mit fließendem Getön
transfigure with flowing tones

die Blut- und Tränenbäche.
the blood- and tear-stream.

Der Eine, der es alles lenkt,
The one who it all rules

die Stimmen ineinander mengt,
the voices into each other mixes

er wird auch dich erkennen.
he will also you recognize.

Auf daß du, hält er's an der Zeit,
So that you, considers he it –the right time–

nach Warten, Nacht und Einsamkeit
after waiting, night, and loneliness

ihn mögest Vater nennen.
him may Father call.

Source: Weinheber 1954, 2: 477

You—doubt about the meaning of the world!
Creature, thrust into this torment,
who shall help you carry on?
Your stumbling you call being human;
into your wild pain
you begin to question wildly.

What have we achieved with wildness?
The loud creature laments and accuses,
but it laments only its weakness.
Ah, a flute, distant and beautiful,
may transfigure with flowing tones
the streams of blood and tears.

The one who rules over all
and mixes the voices into each other
will recognize you as well.
So that when he thinks the time is right,
after waiting, darkness, and loneliness,
you may call him "Father."

---

*T*HE meaning of "Du Zweifel" is anything but clear, beginning with the first line, which addresses humanity as "doubt about the meaning of the world." What follows is as if spoken from the standpoint of a Classical deity, sitting in detachment above mankind and watching it vainly attempt to carry on in its mortal misery. Humanity, the "doubt," the "creature thrust into this torment" that is earthly life, is condemned to "carry on," stumbling through existence. But the pain brings "wild" questioning that the second strophe informs us is in vain, and we are left with only our weakness and the question posed in the first strophe: "Who shall help you?" In the second strophe an answer seems to come from the distance, the possibility of "transfiguration" achieved through "blood and tears." The Christian symbolism is palpable.

The last of the three strophes is the most perplexing. Until the final two lines it appears to be heading toward a confirmation of Christian salvation, and the poem can indeed be read that way—God will "recognize you" in his own time, after the "darkness and loneliness" of earthly life, and bring you to the joy of calling him "Father." But these lines could also be seen as a cynical detour: The Christian path is not a noble striving for union with God, but rather the Almighty's own perverse torment of his subjects before permitting them the "honor" of calling him "Father."

"Du Zweifel" is untitled, from a large collection entitled *Hier ist das Wort* (Here Is the Word, 1944), which is divided into nine sections of some three to fourteen poems each, with sectional subheadings relating to poetic composition and theory. Most of the poems, however, have little directly to do with the subject. The headings are "Here is the Word," "Form and Shape," "Melos," "Rhyme," "About Rhythm," "Declamation," "Regarding Forms," "Translations," and "Applied Poetry."

Heinrich Isaac

Innsbruck, ich muss dich lassen

Author unknown

Innsbruck, ich muss dich lassen,
Innsbruck, I must you leave;

Ich fahr dahin mein Straßen
I go there my roads

In fremde Land dahin.
in foreign lands there.

Mein Freud ist mir genommen,
My joy is from me taken;

Die ich nicht weiss bekommen,
it I not know to obtain

Wo ich im Elend bin.
since I in misery am.

Innsbruck, I must leave you;
I must travel my roads
to distant, foreign lands.
My joy has been taken from me;
I don't know how to regain it
since I am in such misery.

Groß Leid muss ich jetzt tragen,
Great sorrow must I now bear,

Daß ich allein tu klagen
that I alone do complain

Dem liebsten Buhlen mein.
to dearest sweetheart mine.

Ach Lieb, nun lass mich Armen
Ah love, now let me poor

Im Herzen dein erbarmen,
in heart your find pity

Daß ich muss von dannen sein!
because I must from that place be!

Great sorrow I now must bear,
so great that I will only complain
to my dearest sweetheart.
Ah love, let my destitution
find pity in your heart,
because I must leave!

Mein Trost ob allen Weiben,
My solace above all women,

Dein tu ich ewig bleiben,
yours do I forever remain,

Stet treu, der Ehren fromm.
constant, faithful to the honor pious.

Nun muss dich Gott bewahren,
Now must you God protect,

In aller Tugend sparen,
in all virtue preserve

Bis daß ich wieder komm!
until I again come!

My solace above all women,
yours I shall forever remain,
constant, faithful, committed to honor.
Now may God protect you
and preserve all your virtue
until I come again!

THE origin of Isaac's text has been lost to history but the music has seen countless incarnations—in the sixteenth century Isaac's melody was particularly favored for use as a secular *cantus firmus*. The song was so popular that it was transformed into a hymn that first appeared in 1506 under the incipit "O Welt, ich muß dich lassen." Wackernagel's first collection of early hymn texts contains the version below with no indication of its publication date. (Wackernagel 1841: 601, tr. ed.)

O Welt, ich muß dich lassen
und fahr dahin mein Strassen
ins Vaterland hinein!
Irdisch Freud ist mir gnommen,
die ich nicht mehr bger zu bekommen,
weil ich in Elend bin.

O world, I must leave you
and follow my path
into the fatherland!
From me has been taken earthly joy,
which I no longer yearn to receive
because I am in a woeful state.

Groß Leid muß ich jetzt tragen,
das ich allein tu klagen
dem liebsten Herren mein:
Ach Gott, nu laß mich armen
Im Herzen dein erbarmen,
Weil ich so arm muß sein!

I must now bear great sorrow,
which I alone bewail
to my dearest Lord:
O Lord, now permit miserable me
to receive your forgiveness in my heart,
since I must be so wretched!

Mein Trost ist allem Leiden,	My consolation is suffering to all;
Von dir soll mich nicht scheiden	No anguish in this world shall
Kein Not in dieser Welt.	separate me from you.
Kein Armut sein zu schwere,	No poverty is too severe;
Mein Sinn und all mein bgere	My mind and all my desire
Zu dir allein habe gstellt!	I have placed solely in you.

The *EKG* (312) provides another version that differs completely from the one above except for the opening three lines; it gives the source of that text as "Nuremberg, 1555."

Felix Mendelssohn

Denn er hat seinen Engeln befohlen über dir
(from Elijah, op. 70)
For He Has Commanded His Angels to Watch over You
Psalm 91: 11, 12

Denn er hat seinen Engeln
For He has his angels

befohlen über dir,
commanded over you,

daß sie dich hüten
that they you protect

auf allen deinen Wegen,
on all your paths,

daß sie dich auf den Händen tragen,
that they you on the hands carry

und du deinen Fuß
and you your foot

nicht an einen Stein stoßest.
not on a stone hit.

For He has commanded his angels
to watch over you,
to protect you
on all your paths,
and to uphold you with their hands
lest you dash your foot
on a stone.

ON May 22, 1836 Mendelssohn's first oratorio, *St. Paul*, was presented to spectacular success at the Rhine Music Festival in Düsseldorf, a triumph repeated at the British premiere in Liverpool several months later. When he decided to follow up on his first success with a second oratorio, the composer could have had no inkling that the process would consume ten years, and that the libretto would be his greatest challenge.

After determining that he wanted to set the story of the prophet Elijah, Mendelssohn passed over the librettist for *St. Paul*, a pastor from Dessau named Julius Schubring, in favor of an old friend named Karl Klingemann, at that time resident in London. Klingemann ignored at least three entreaties to take up the work and was persuaded only by a visit from Mendelssohn, at which some progress was made. Nonetheless, after Mendelssohn left he ceased work and ultimately returned everything to the composer. Mendelssohn, who must have been terribly embarrassed, then approached Schubring, who agreed to take over where Klingemann had left off. Differences of opinion surfaced almost immediately. Schubring wanted Jesus to appear to Elijah, reversing of the vision of the Transfiguration in Matthew 17: 2 and Mark 9: 2. This did not sit well to Mendelssohn, who also wanted a more dramatic work than Schubring seemed prepared to write. Further negotiations deepened the differences between the men, which could not have been lessened by Schubring knowing that he had been the second choice for the task, and that Mendelssohn intended to retain most of the work that Klingemann had done on part one of the oratorio. Progress came to a standstill in February, 1839 when Schubring wrote that he was giving up the project.

An invitation in June, 1845 to take over direction of the Birmingham, England Music Festival (which Mendelssohn declined) and to compose a new oratorio for the August, 1846 festival (which he accepted) led to renewed cooperation with Schubring, now under extreme time pressure. Mendelssohn and Schubring collaborated on the libretto via mail, sending material back and forth for each other's suggestions and criticism. Correspondence indicates that at least two other men were involved in the preparation of the libretto during this period, and it is not known who produced what.

The completion of the German libretto did not end Mendelssohn's headaches, as the premiere was to be in English. The translation was done by a Mr. Bartholomew of London, who had served Mendelssohn in this capacity previously and was recommended by him to the festival organizers in Birmingham. It required yet more time and necessitated musical adjustments that Mendelssohn completed only a couple of weeks before the performance on August 26, 1846.

"Denn er hat seinen Engeln" was a pre-existent, unaccompanied composition from 1844 that Mendelssohn had written in thanks for the escape of Prussian King Friedrich Wilhelm IV from an assassination attempt. He even sent a manuscript to the King himself. (Bolin 1995: 31) For the oratorio Mendelssohn added an orchestral accompaniment and used the chorus as no. 7 in part one, immediately after the angel's command that Elijah depart eastward and "hide" by "Cherith's brook." After the chorus sings of Elijah's angelic protection on his journey, Elijah performs a miracle, raising a boy from the dead.

Die Nachtigall, op. 59, no. 4
The Nightingale
Johann Wolfgang von Goethe

Die Nachtigall, sie war entfernt,
The nightingale, she was far away,

Der Frühling lockt sie wieder,
the springtime attracts her again.

Was neues hat sie nicht gelernt,
What new [songs] has she not learned?

Singt alte liebe Lieder.
[She] sings old, beloved songs.

The nightingale was far away,
but springtime is drawing her back again.
Hasn't she learned anything new?
She still sings the old, cherished songs.

Source: Goethe 1948–, 1: 386

GOETHE'S simple, four-line poem, originally titled "Ländlich" (Rustic), was a product of his old age. In 1824 or 1825 he translated it, more or less, from a poem contained in an anthology called *Popular Songs of Modern Greece*, in which the Greek texts were offered along with French translations by the editor, C.C. Fauriel. (Goethe 1961–1964, 1: 714)

When Goethe first published the poem in 1827, it was contained in a section entitled "From Foreign Languages," grouped with other poems under the heading "New Greek Love-Scolia."[61] In a subsequent publication he did not label it as a translation; "for him it probably thus belonged to what he occasionally called 'angeeignetes'; i.e., he had the sense that these verses were fully in his own, personal style." (Goethe 1961–1964, 1: 714).

Heilig
Holy
Isaiah 6: 3b; Matthew 21: 9b

Heilig, heilig, heilig
Holy, holy, holy

ist Gott der Herr Zebaoth,
is God, the Lord Sabaoth!

alle Lande sind seiner Ehre voll!
All nations are of his glory full!

Hosianna in der Höh!
Hosanna in the highest!

Gelobt sei, der da kommt
Blessed be he who comes

im Namen des Herrn!
in the name of the Lord!

Hosianna in der Höh!
Hosanna in the highest!

Holy, holy, holy
is God, the Lord of hosts!
All nations are full of his glory!
Hosanna in the highest!

Blessed be he who comes
in the name of the Lord!
Hosanna in the highest!

THE "Sanctus" of the Roman Catholic Mass, including the "Benedictus" and the "Osanna," provided Mendelssohn with the text for this double-chorus motet.

---

[61]The *scolia* was a simple, convivial poem, usually centered on wine, women, and song. Its prime exponent in the Classical literature was Anacreon.* Joseph Haydn* sought such poems for his part songs and based two of them on poems thought to be by Anacreon. (See the annotation to Haydn's "Three- and Four-Part Songs.")

Mitten wir im Leben sind, op. 23, no. 3
In the Midst of Life

Martin Luther

See Hymns, "Mitten wir im Leben sind."

Richte mich, Gott, op. 78
Judge Me, O God

Psalm 43

Richte mich, Gott, und führe meine Sache
Judge me, God, and lead my cause

wider das unheilige Volk und errette mich
against the unholy nation, and deliver me

von den falschen und bösen Leuten!
from the false and malicious people!

Denn du bist der Gott meiner Stärke;
For you are the God of my strength.

warum verstößest du mich?
Why cast away you me?

Warum lässet du mich so traurig gehn,
Why let you me so sorrowfully go

wenn mein Feind mich drängt?
when my foe me oppresses?

Sende dein Licht und deine Wahrheit,
Send your light and your truth,

daß sie mich leiten
that they me lead

und bringen zu deinem heiligen Berge
and bring to your holy mountain

und zu deiner Wohnung,
and to your dwelling,

daß ich hineingehe zum Altar Gottes,
that I go in to the altar of God,

zu dem Gott, der meine Freude und Wonne ist,
to the God, who my joy and delight is,

und dir, Gott, auf der Harfe danke, mein Gott.
and you, God, on the harp thank, my God.

Was betrübst du dich, meine Seele,
Why trouble you —, my soul,

und bist so unruhig in mir?
and are so restless in me?

Harre auf Gott!
Hope in God!

denn ich werde ihm noch danken,
for I will him still thank,

daß er meines Angesichts Hülfe
that he my countenance's help

und mein Gott ist.
and my God is.

Judge me, O God, and lead my cause
against the unholy nation, and deliver me
from the deceitful and malicious people!
For you are the God of my strength.
Why do you cast me away?
Why do you let me be so sorrowful
when my foe oppresses me?
Send your light and your truth,
that they might lead me
and bring me to your holy mountain
and to your dwelling,

that I might enter unto the altar of God,
to the God who is my joy and my delight,
and give thanks to you, my God, on the harp.

Why are you so troubled, my soul,
and why are you so restless within me?
Hope in God!
For I will still give thanks to him,
because he is the salvation of my countenance
and my God.

Wolfgang Amadeus Mozart

Eine kleine Freimaurer-Kantate, K. 623
A Short Masonic Cantata
Emanuel Schikaneder

1. Chorus (ttb chorus and soli)

Laut   verkünde unsre Freude
Loudly announce our   delight,

Froher   Instrumentenschall,
joyful sound of instruments;

Jedes Bruders Herz empfinde
every brother's heart   feel

Dieser Mauern Widerhall.
of these walls reverberation.

Denn wir   weihen   diese Stätte
For   we consecrate this site

Durch die goldne   Bruderkette
by   the golden chain of brotherhood

Und den echten Herzverein
and the   true heart's union

Heut' zu unserm Tempel ein.
today to   our   temple — .

Loudly proclaim our delight,
you joyful-sounding instruments;
may every brother's heart feel
the reverberation of these walls.

For today we consecrate this site
to be our temple
by the golden chain of brotherhood
and the true union of hearts.

2. Recitative (tenor)

Zum   ersten Male, edle Brüder,
For the first time, noble brothers,

schließt uns dieser neue Sitz
surrounds us   this new abode

der Weisheit und der Tugend ein.
of   wisdom and of virtue —.

Wir   weihen diesen Ort
We consecrate this place

zum   Heiligtum unserer Arbeit,
to the sanctuary of our work,

die   uns das große Geheimnis entziffern soll.
which for us the great mystery   decipher shall.

Süß   ist die Empfindung des Maurers
Sweet is the   feeling   of the Mason

an so einem festlichen Tage,
on such a   festive   day,

der die   Bruderkette
which the chain of brotherhood

neu   und enger schließt;
again and tighter closes;

süß   der Gedanke, daß nun die Menschheit
sweet the thought that now — humanity

wieder einen Platz unter Menschen gewann;
again   a   place among humans   won;

For the first time, noble brothers,
we are surrounded by this new abode
of wisdom and virtue.
We consecrate this place
to be the sanctuary of our work,
which shall decipher the great mystery for us.

Sweet is the feeling of the Mason
on such a festive day,
which closes the chain of brotherhood
even tighter once again.
Sweet is the thought that humanity
has again won a place among humans;

süß   die Erinnerung an die Stätte,
sweet the memory   of the place

wo   jedes Bruderherz ihm,
where every brother's heart him,

was er war, und was er ist,
what he was, and what he is,

und was er werden kann,
and what he become can,

so   ganz   bestimmt,
so completely determines;

wo   Beispiel ihn belehrt,
where example him teaches,

wo   echte Bruderliebe seiner pflegt
where true brother-love   him nurtures,

und wo   aller Tugenden heiligste,
and where of all   virtues the holiest,

erste, aller Tugenden Königin,
first of all virtues   queen,

Wohltätigkeit in stillem Glanze   thront.
charity   in quiet splendor reigns.

sweet is the memory of the place
where every brother's heart
determines so completely
what he was, what he is,
and what he can become;
where he learns from example,
where true brotherly love nurtures him,
and where charity, the holiest of all virtues,
the first and queen of all virtues,
in silent splendor reigns.

3. Aria (tenor)

Dieser Gottheit Allmacht   ruhet
Of this divinity omnipotence is based

Nicht auf Lärmen, Pracht und   Saus,
not   on uproar, luxury and bluster.

Nein, im Stillen   wiegt   und spendet
No,   in silence is cradled and   gives

Sie der Menschheit Segen aus.
it   to humanity blessing —.

Stille Gottheit, deinem Bilde
Silent divinity, to your image

Huldigt   ganz des Maurers Brust,
pays homage totally of the Mason breast,

Denn   du wärmst mit   Sonnenmilde,
because you warm with sun-mellowness

Stets   sein Herz in süßer   Lust.
always his heart in sweet delight.

The omnipotence of this divinity is not based
on uproar, luxury, and bluster.
No, this divinity silently cradles humanity
and bestows its blessing upon it.

Silent divinity, to your image
the Mason's heart pays full homage,
because you always warm his heart
with the gentle sunshine of sweet delight.

4. Recitative (tenor/bass)

Wohlan   ihr Brüder, überlaßt euch   ganz
Now then, you brothers, abandon yourself totally

der Seligkeit eurer Empfindungen,
to the bliss of your   feelings,

da   ihr nie, daß ihr Maurer seid, vergeßt.
because you never, that you Masons are, forget.

Diese heut'ge   Feier   sei ein Denkmal
This of today celebration be a monument

des wieder neu und   fest geschloßen Bunds.
of the again new and tightly closed   union.

Verbannet sei auf immer Neid, Habsucht
Banished be for ever envy,   greed,

und Verleumdung aus unsrer Maurerbrust,
and defamation from our Mason breast,

und Eintracht knüpfe fest   das   teure Band,
and harmony   unite strongly the precious bond

das reine Bruderliebe   webte.
that pure brotherly love wove.

Now then, my brothers, abandon yourself totally
to the bliss of your feelings,
because you will never forget that you are Masons.
This celebration today should be a monument
of the renewed and very exclusive union.
May envy, greed, and defamation be banished forever
from every Mason's heart,
and harmony unite the precious bond
that wove pure brotherly love.

5. Duet (tenor/bass)

Lange sollen diese Mauern
Long   shall   these   walls

Zeuge   unsrer Arbeit sein,
witness of our   work   be,

Und damit sie ewig daure,
and so that it forever lasts,

Weiht   sie heute Eintracht ein.
consecrates it today harmony —.

Laßt uns teilen jede Bürde
Let   us   share every burden

Mit der Liebe Vollgewicht,
with   love's   full weight;

Dann empfangen wir mit Würde
then   receive   we with dignity

Hier aus Osten wahres Licht.
here from East   true   light.

Diesen Vorteil zu erlangen,
This   benefit to   attain,

Fanget froh   die Arbeit an.
begin happily the work —.

Und auch der   schon angefangen,
And also the one already   begun

Fange heute wieder an.
begin today again —.

Haben wir an diesem Orte
Have   we   at this   place

Unser Herz und unsre Worte
our   heart and our words

An die Tugend ganz   gewöhnt,
to —   virtue totally accustomed,

O dann ist der Neid gestillet,
Oh then is — envy stilled,

Und der Wunsch so   ganz   erfüllet,
and the desire so completely fulfilled

Welcher unsre Hoffnung krönt.
that   our   hope   crowns.

Long shall these walls
be a witness to our work,
and so that it might last forever,
harmony consecrates it today.

Let us share every burden
with the full weight of love;
then we will receive with dignity
the true light from the East.

To attain this benefit,
happily begin the work.
And may those who have already begun
begin anew today.

When we here in this place
have totally accustomed
our hearts and our words to virtue,
then envy is quelled,
and the wish that crowns our hope
is completely fulfilled.

6. Chorus = 1. Chorus

*E*MANUEL Johann Jakob Schikaneder (1751–1812), a Viennese actor, singer, theater superintendent, impresario, and writer, first met Mozart in 1780 in Salzburg. Eleven years later, when both men were living in Vienna and Mozart had but months to live, they collaborated on Mozart's last opera, *The Magic Flute* (K. 620). Schikaneder, like Mozart a member of the Fraternal Order of the Free and Accepted Masons, wrote the libretto, which was filled with Masonic symbolism. When the opera premiered on September 5, 1791, the librettist was also featured in the starring role of Papageno.

Mozart's fellow Mason also provided the text to the present cantata, written for the dedication of the lodge "Zur neu gekrönten Hoffnung" (of newly crowned hope), of which Mozart was a member. As would be expected of such an occasional work, the text directly expresses the principles of Freemasonry, which hold that all men are brothers and children of the same God, who is best worshipped through service to others. Harmony, friendship, and charity are thus the guiding ideas of Freemasonry, all of which are extolled in Schikaneder's libretto. Like *The Magic Flute*, it contains references to Masonic symbols, such as "the golden chain" (no. 1), "the great mystery" (no. 2), and "the true light from the east" (no. 5).

Mozart conducted the performance of the cantata at the lodge dedication just nineteen days before his death, a time when he was quite ill and must have been working on the *Requiem*. The cantata is the last entry he made in his *Werkeverzeichnis*, his personal list of his works.

Johann Pachelbel

Nun danket alle Gott
Let All Give Thanks to God
Ecclesiasticus 50: 22–24, Martin Rinckart

Nun danket alle Gott
Now thank all God

der große Dinge tut
who great things does

an allen Enden;
at all ends;

der uns von Mutter Leibe
who us from mother's womb

an lebendig erhält,
on living keeps

und tut uns alles Guts.
and does us all good.

Let all give thanks to God,
to him who does great things
here and everywhere;
who preserves and sustains us
from the beginning of life
and grants us every good.

Er gebe uns ein fröhlich Herz,
He give us a joyful heart,

und verleihe immerdar Friede
and grant forever peace

zu unsern Zeiten in Israel,
at our times in Israel,

und daß seine Gnade
and that his grace

stets bei uns bleibe,
always with us remain

und erlöse uns solange wir leben.
and redeem us as long as we live.

May he give us a joyful heart,
and grant us peace forever,
peace at our time in Israel,
and may his grace
always abide with us
and deliver us as long as we live.

Nun danket alle Gott
Now thank all God

mit Herzen, Mund, und Händen,
with heart, mouth, and hands,

der große Dinge tut
who great things does

an uns und allen Enden;
by us and all ends;

der uns von Mutterleib
who us from womb

und Kindesbeinen an
and infancy on

unzählig viel zugut
innumerably much benefit,

und noch jetzund getan.
and still now has done.

Let all give thanks to God
with heart, voice, and deeds,
to the one who achieves great things
for us and in all ways;
who from the womb
and early childhood on
has done us incalculable good,
and does so even now.

Source (chorale): Neumann 1974: 184

JOHANN Pachelbel (1653–1706) chose the text for this delightful double-chorus concerto from the apocryphal book of Jesus Sirach (Ecclesiasticus) 50: 22–24. The first section provides a song of thanks, and the second offers a prayer for joy and peace. The closing section is the first verse of Martin Rinckart's hymn "Nun danket alle Gott,"* based on the scripture that has just been sung. Pachelbel distinguishes it from the opening section and clarifies the text by giving the chorale melody to the soprano as a *cantus firmus*.

199

Max Reger

DREI FÜNFSTIMMIGE MOTETTEN, op. 110

Three Five-Voice Motets

Mein Odem ist schwach op. 110, no. 1

My Breath Is Weak

Job 17: 1–3; 26: 2, 3; 19: 25

Mein Odem ist schwach,
My breath is weak,

und meine Tage sind abgekürzt;
and my days are shortened;

das Grab ist da.
the grave is there.

Fürwahr, Gespött umgibt mich,
Indeed, mockers surround me,

und auf ihrem Hadern
and upon their discord

muß mein Auge weilen,
must my eye abide,

muß mein Auge ruhen.
must my eye rest.

Sei du selbst mein Bürge bei dir;
Be you yourself my guarantor with you:

wer will mich sonst vertreten?
who wants me else to represent?

Wie stehest du dem bei,
How stand you him by,

der keine Kraft hat,
who no power has

hilfst dem, der keine Stärke
help him, who no strength

in den Armen hat!
in the arms has!

Wie gibst du den Rat dem,
How give you — counsel to him

der keine Weisheit hat,
who no wisdom has

und tust kund Verstandes die Fülle!
and make known understanding the fullness!

Aber ich weiß, daß mein Erlöser lebet;
But I know, that my redeemer lives,

und er wird mich hernach
and he will me hereafter

aus der Erde aufwecken.
from the earth awaken.

My breath is weak
and my days are shortened;
the grave is ready.
Indeed, mockers surround me,
and upon their discord
my eye must abide,
my eye must rest.
Lord, may you be my guarantor:
who wants to represent me otherwise?

How you stand by
those who have no power
and help those who have no strength
in their arms!
How you give counsel to one
who has no wisdom
and reveal the fullness of understanding!

For I know that my redeemer lives,
and that he will hereafter
awaken me from the earth.

Ach, Herr, strafe mich nicht, op. 110, no. 2
Ah, Lord, Rebuke Me Not
Psalm 6: 1, 2; 4: 1, 8; 6: 6a; 7: 10; 18: 1; 16: 11

Ach, Herr, strafe mich nicht in deinem Zorn,
Ah, Lord, rebuke me not in your anger

und züchtige mich nicht in deinem Grimm!
and chastise me not in your wrath!

Herr, sei mir gnädig, denn ich bin schwach.
Lord, be to me merciful, for I am weak.

Ah, Lord, rebuke me not in your anger
and chastise me not in your wrath!
Lord, be merciful to me, for I am weak.

Erhöre mich, wenn ich rufe,
Hear me when I call,

Gott meiner Gerechtigkeit,
God of my righteousness;

der du mich tröstet in Angst;
who you me comfort in fear,

sei mir gnädig und erhöre mein Gebet!
be to me merciful and hear my prayer.

Ich liege und schlafe ganz in Frieden,
I lie down and sleep wholly in peace,

denn allein du, Herr, hilfst mir,
for alone you, Lord, help me

daß ich sicher wohne.
that I safely dwell.

Hear me when I call,
God of my righteousness;
you who comfort me in fear,
be merciful to me and hear my prayer.
I lie down and sleep in perfect peace,
for you alone, Lord, help me
dwell in safety.

Ich bin so müd' von seufzen.
I am so tired from sighing.

I am so weary from groaning.

Mein Schild ist bei Gott,
My shield is with God,

der den frommen Herzen hilft.
who the devout hearts helps.

My defense is with God,
who preserves the upright of heart.

Herzlich lieb habe ich dich,
With-all-my-heart love have I you,

Herr, meine Stärke!
Lord, my strength.

With all my heart I love you,
O Lord, my strength.

Du tust mir kund den Weg zum Leben;
You –make known to me– the way to life;

vor dir ist Freude die Fülle
before you is joy plentiful,

und liebliches Wesen zu deiner Rechten ewiglich.
and delightful reality at your right eternally.

Vor dir ist Freude ewiglich.
Before you is joy eternally.

You show me the path of life;
with you joy is plentiful,
and delights exist at your right hand eternally.
With you there is joy forever.

O Tod, wie bitter bist du, op. 110. no. 3

O Death, How Bitter You Are

Ecclesiasticus 41: 1, 2

O Tod,   wie   bitter bist du,
O death, how bitter are you

wenn an dich gedenket ein Mensch,
when on you   thinks a person,

der gute Tage und genug hat
who good days and enough has

und ohne   Sorgen lebet;
and without worries lives;

und dem es wohl geht in allen Dingen
and who --lives well- in all   things

und wohl noch essen mag!
and well also eat may!

O Tod,   wie wohl tust du   dem Dürftigen,
O death, how good do you to the needy,

der da schwach und alt ist,
who — weak and old is,

der in allen Sorgen steckt
who in all worries is stuck,

und nichts Besseres zu hoffen
and nothing better to hope for

noch zu erwarten hat!
nor to expect has!

O death, how bitter you are
when one thinks about you,
one who has good days and sufficient goods
and lives without worries,
one who is prosperous in all things
and also able to eat well.

O death, how soothing you are to one in need,
one who is weak and old,
who is stuck in constant worries,
and has nothing better to hope for
nor to wait for.

*L*ATE in his brief life of forty-three years, Max Reger (1873–1916) composed three unrelated German motets that he drew together into opus 110. Reger was a devout Catholic, yet none of the motets was suitable for the Mass—they were in German rather than Latin, all were long and difficult, and they had librettos drawn from Biblical but non-liturgical texts.

Reger wrote no. 3 in the set, "O Tod, wie bitter bist du," in memory of Lili Wach, the daughter of Felix Mendelssohn, in a mere five hours on July 23, 1912. The motet is in several ways a cousin to Brahms's op. 74, no. 1, "Warum ist das Licht gegeben dem Mühseligen."* Reger would certainly have been complimented by this comparison, as he greatly admired the music of his older contemporary.

The most obvious similarity is the conclusion of both works with emulations of a Bach chorale. More pertinent to the present discussion, however, is the similarity between the texts. Both motets begin with expressions of anguish and pain, which is transfigured in the chorale—by Brahms into a radiant statement of faith and trust in God, and by Reger into a welcoming of death's peace. To create this effect, Brahms had to pick and choose disparate texts from three different books of the Bible and from Luther. Reger, on the other hand, set a single passage from the Apocryphal book of Ecclesiasticus that presents this transformation in two successive verses—in the first death is cursed as the spoiler of life, and in the second it is welcomed as the final release from pain.

In "Mein Odem is schwach" (no. 1, 1909) the misery of too long a life is similarly transformed into confidence in God's grace. The Bible did not present the text as conveniently as it had for no. 3, however, and to achieve the same effect Reger had to combine out-of-sequence portions from the book of Job.

"Ach Herr, straf mich nicht" (no. 2, 1911) is remarkable for its even more synthetic Biblical libretto, the romantic personalization of which is matched in this volume only by Georg Schumann's "Herr, erhöre meine Worte,"* written at about the same time. Reger draws his words from Psalms 6, 4, and 8, returns to Psalm 6, and then finishes with excerpts from Psalms 7, 18, and 16. This selectivity gave him a text that was Biblical yet of his own creation.

In terms of music, the work is structured in three sections, the first and last of which are further divided in two. The first section is an austere yet sometimes demanding prayer for mercy, while the second, a pseudo-chorale, expresses confidence and trust in God's help. The third and final section is a song of praise expressed in two elaborate and densely chromatic fugues.

1a   Ah, Lord, . . . Hear me when I call.
1b   God of my righteousness . . . . help me dwell in safety.
2   I lie down and sleep . . . . the upright of heart.
3a   With all my heart . . . . path of life;
3b   with you joy is plentiful . . . . there is joy forever.

Johann Hermann Schein

Die mit Tränen säen
Those Who Sow with Tears
Psalm 126: 5, 6

Die mit Tränen säen,
Who with tears sow

werden mit Freuden ernten.
will with joy reap.

Sie gehen hin und weinen
They go forth and weep,

und tragen edlen Samen
and bear precious seed,

und kommen mit Freuden
and come with joy,

und bringen ihre Garben.
and bring their sheaves.

Those who sow with tears
shall reap with joy.
They go forth and weep,
bearing precious seed,
and return with joy,
bringing their sheaves.

THE close juxtaposition of highly contrasting affects contained in these two verses from Psalm 126 appealed to a number of Baroque composers, including Heinrich Schütz and his exact contemporary and friend Johann Hermann Schein (1586–1630). Schein, who preceded J.S. Bach by a century as the Cantor of the St. Thomas School in Leipzig, utilized some of the most picturesque word-painting of his era in his madrigalistic setting of this text.

Arnold Schönberg

Dreimal tausend Jahre, op. 50a
Three Times a Thousand Years
Dagobert D. Runes

Dreimal tausend Jahre
Three times thousand years

Seit ich Dich gesehn,
since I you [have] seen

Tempel in Jerusalem,
Temple in Jerusalem,

Tempel meiner Wehn.
Temple of my woes!

Three times a thousand years
since I have seen you,
Temple in Jerusalem,
temple of my woes!

Und ihr Jordanwellen—
And you Jordan's waves,

Silbern Wüstenband;
silver desert band,

Gärten und Gelände
gardens and countryside

Grünen, neues Uferland.
green, new shoreland.

And you, waves of Jordan,
silver strip of desert,
gardens and countryside
are greening, a new shore.

Und man hört es klingen
And one hears it sound

Leise von den Bergen her,
softly from the mountains —

Deine altverschollnen Lieder
Your long-forgotten songs

Künden Gottes Wiederkehr.
announce God's return.

And softly, from the mountains,
one hears
your long-forgotten songs
announce God's return.

Source: Runes 1948: 1
Variants: (Schönberg = roman, Runes = *italic*)
Stanza 2, line 1:   Und man hört es klingen (And one hears them sounding) =
Und mir ists als rauschten (And it is to me as if murmured)
line 4:   künden (announce) = *flüsternd* (whispering)

*T*HE Jewish *Seder* meal, part of the observance of *Pesach* (Passover), ends with the words, "next year in Jerusalem," a prayer for the return of the Jewish people to the Holy Land after millennia of exile. On May 14, 1948 the dream of generations of Jews came true with the establishment of the state of Israel.[62]

Arnold Schönberg had been born a Jew but had converted to Christianity in 1898, apparently more as a matter of convenience than as an act of faith. His experiences with anti-semitism during and after WWI, however, led him to Zionism and to the belief in the establishment of a Jewish state—through military means, if necessary. Shortly after the creation of Israel and a few years before his death, Schönberg turned back to his roots and for the first time since 1915 wrote compositions inspired directly by his Jewish heritage, the present piece among them. It was at this time that Schönberg became acquainted with the extraordinary man who was to provide the text for his "Dreimal tausend Jahre," Dagobert David Runes (1902–1982).[63]

Runes, a Vienna-educated Romanian historian, philosopher, and scholar of Judaism, came to New York in the 1920s. Like all immigrants, he needed a means of support, which he found in publishing. A man of great intellectual breadth, he began with magazines ranging in subject from model airplanes to philosophy, the latter being his passion and the subject of his Ph.D. After establishing a sound financial base through his magazines, he founded the Philosophical Library, a publishing house dedicated to philosophy and ideas. His authors included many of the great minds of the century,[64] a large number of whom were fellow Jews who emigrated to the United States in flight from the Nazi terror—among them Arnold Schönberg.

In 1948 Runes published an abridged English translation of Schönberg's 1910 *Harmonielehre* entitled *The Theory of Harmony*, and in 1950 a set of fifteen essays entitled *Style and Idea*. As the two men got to know each other during the preparation of the first book, Schönberg read a set of twenty-seven German poems by Runes entitled *Jordan Lieder*, which Runes had published in 1948, likely in honor of the creation of Israel.[65] The first of these, a poem entitled "Gottes Wiederkehr" (God's Return) particularly impressed the composer, and he asked permission to set it to music. The result was "Dreimal tausend Jahre," written in 1949.

Schönberg made two minor changes to the Runes poem, both in the final strophe. He apparently wanted both to generalize the poem's message and to strengthen it. He thus changed the focus from the first to the third person and had the "old, lost songs" "announce" the return of God rather than "whispering" it:

Runes	**Schönberg**
And it is to me as if,	And one hears them sounding
softly, down from the mountains,	softly, down from the mountains—
your old, lost songs murmured,	your old, lost songs
whispering the return of God.	announce the return of God.

---

[62]Jerusalem itself, however, was to remain a part of Jordan for another nineteen years, until the Israeli victory in the Six-Day War of 1967 and the subsequent annexation of the West Bank.

[63]The editors are grateful to Dr. Runes's daughter, Nageen Runes Najar, the present head of the Philosophical Library, for providing information on her father not available elsewhere (Najar 1999).

[64]Among them, for example, H.G. Wells, Leon Trotsky, Albert Einstein, and Albert Camus.

[65]Mrs. Najar stated that her father, while not a Zionist militant, was nonetheless a "philosophical Zionist."

Friede auf Erden, op. 13

Peace on Earth

Conrad Ferdinand Meyer

Da die Hirten ihre Herde
When the shepherds their herds

Ließen und des Engels Worte
left and the angel's words

Trugen durch die niedre Pforte
carried through the lowly portal

Zu der Mutter mit dem Kind,
to the mother with the child,

Fuhr das himmlische Gesind
Came the heavenly servants

Fort im Sternenraum zu singen,
forth in the star-space to sing,

Fuhr der Himmel fort zu klingen:
came — heaven forth to sound:

"Friede, Friede auf der Erde!"
"Peace, peace on — earth!"

When the shepherds left their flocks
and carried the angel's words
through the lowly doorway
to the mother with the child,
the heavenly hosts came forth
to sing in the starry expanse,
and heaven resounded with the words:
"Peace, peace on earth!"

Seit die Engel so geraten,
Since the angels thus appeared,

o wie viele blut'ge Taten
oh how many bloody deeds

Hat der Streit auf wildem Pferde,
has — strife on wild horse,

Der geharnischte, vollbracht!
the armored, accomplished!

In wie mancher heil'gen Nacht
In –many a– –Christmas eve–

Sang der Chor der Geister zagend,
sang the choir of spirits timidly,

Dringlich flehend, leis verklagend:
urgently imploring, quietly accusing:

"Friede, Friede auf der Erde!"
"Peace, peace on — earth!"

Since the angels thus appeared,
oh how many bloody deeds has
strife, the armored one, committed
while riding his wild horse!
On many a Christmas eve
the choir of spirits has sung timidly,
urgently imploring, quietly accusing:
"Peace, peace on earth!"

Doch es ist ein ew'ger Glaube,
Yet it is an eternal belief

Daß der Schwache nicht zum Raube
that the weak not to robbery

Jeder frechen Mordgebärde
to every insolent murder-gesture

Werde fallen allezeit:
will fall always:

Etwas wie Gerechtigkeit
Something like justice

Webt und wirkt in Mord und Grauen
weaves and works in murder and horror

Und ein Reich will sich erbauen,
and a kingdom wants — to build

Das den Frieden sucht der Erde.
that — peace seeks for the earth.

Yet it is an eternal belief
that the weak will not always fall prey
to insolent, murderous conduct.
Something like justice
weaves and works amid murder and horror
and wants to build a kingdom
that seeks peace for the earth.

Mählich wird es sich gestalten, **Gradually will it — be formed,**	Gradually it will be formed and carry out its holy duty;
Seines heil'gen Amtes walten, **its holy office carry out;**	weapons will be forged without danger, and flaming swords for justice,
Waffen schmieden ohne Fährde, **weapons be forged without danger,**	and a royal race will blossom forth with strong sons
Flammenschwerter für das Recht, **flaming swords for the right,**	whose ringing trumpets will proclaim: "Peace, peace on earth!"
Und ein königlich Geschlecht **and a royal race**	
Wird erblühn mit starken Söhnen, **will blossom with strong sons**	
Dessen helle Tuben dröhnen: **whose ringing trumpets roar:**	
"Friede, Friede auf der Erde! " **"Peace, peace on — earth!"**	

Source: Meyer 1892: 255

CONRAD Ferdinand Meyer (1825–1898) was perhaps the most significant Swiss poet of the latter half of the nineteenth century. He suffered under mental illness for his entire life and produced most of his work during a period of remission from 1870 to 1887. "Friede auf Erden" is from the very end of this period and looks forward to a world of peace—a striking contrast to the lack of same in the poet's own mind.

The poem was commissioned by the editor of *Schorer's Wochenschrift* (Schorer's Weekly), Franz Hirsch, on September 29, 1886. He requested of Meyer a "moving poem for Christmas." Meyer consented on October 19 and was given a deadline of precisely one week, which he met. (Meyer 1975, 4: 352)

Meyer took the words of Luke 2: 13, 14 as the starting point for his poem: "And suddenly there was with the angel a multitude of the heavenly host praising God and saying, 'Glory to God in the highest, and on earth peace among men in whom he is well pleased.'" The poet then turned his attention away from the nativity to the question of peace, which is seen in the second strophe as a timid and forlorn cry from the spirits in the face of the "many bloody deeds" over the centuries. The third and fourth strophes proclaim optimistically that the innocent will not always suffer, that "something like justice" will eventually prevail in glory.

The poet was connected with the peace movement of his day, and the present poem is particularly meaningful within that context. The founder and president of the movement, Bertha von Suttner, claimed in her memoirs to have had a correspondence with Meyer lasting from 1885 to at least 1891, represented today in only one surviving document, in which Meyer says that "I declare myself out of the deepest conviction to be in agreement with the goals of every peace organization, in obedient reverence for our exalted master from Nazareth." (Meyer 1975, 4: 355, tr. ed.) On March 4, 1891 Meyer completed a questionnaire from the peace organization on which was asked, "Do you believe that one day there will be no war?" He answered, "In truth, it appears to me not to be impossible." (Meyer 1975, 4: 355, tr. ed.)

In his early years Schönberg also believed in the possibility of peace, and this may have been what drew him to the poem, which he set in 1907. The composer's optimism was crushed, however, by the Great War. On June 23, 1923 he wrote of his disappointment to conductor Hermann Scherchen, an artistic supporter and friend. Scherchen had been rehearsing "Friede auf Erden," and the choir had written "kind words" to Schönberg about the experience. The composer requested that Scherchen

Tell them that my chorus "Peace on Earth" is an illusion for mixed choir, and illusion, as I know today, having believed in 1906 (?), when I composed it, that this pure harmony among human beings was conceivable, and more than that: [I] would not have thought it possible to exist without perpetual insistence on the required elevation of tone. Since then I have perforce learnt to yield, and have learnt that peace on earth is possible only if there is the most intense vigilance as to harmony, in a word; not without accompaniment. If human beings are ever to reach the stage of singing peace at sight, without rehearsal, each individual will first have to be immune to the temptation to sink. (Schönberg 1964: 96)

We do not know how the poem came to Schönberg's attention, but it is known that he took the text from the 1892 edition of Meyer's poems cited in the *References*; his otherwise mysterious annotation of the number "255" on his manuscript turns out to be the page on which the poem appears in that publication.

Franz Schubert

Begräbnislied, D. 168

Funeral Song

Friedrich Gottlieb Klopstock

Begrabt den Leib in seiner Gruft,
Bury   the body in   its   grave

Bis   ihn des Richters Stimme ruft!
until him the   judge's voice calls!

Wir säen ihn; einst   blüht er auf
We sow it, some day blooms it —

Und steigt   verklärt   zu Gott hinauf.
and ascends, transfigured, to God up.

Bury the body in its grave
until the judge's voice calls!
We sow it, and it will bloom some day
and ascend, transfigured, unto God.

Grabt mein verwesliches Gebein
Bury my   perishable   bones,

O ihr noch Sterblichen nur ein!
O you still   mortals only —!

Es bleibt, es bleibt   im   Grabe nicht:
It remains, it remains in the grave not,

Denn Jesus kommt und hält   Gericht.
for   Jesus comes and holds judgment.

Bury my perishable bones,
O you who are still merely mortal!
They will not remain in the grave,
for Jesus will come and hold judgment.

Ach, Gott Geopferter, dein Tod
O   God sacrificed, your death

Stärk'   uns in unsrer letzten Not!
strengthens us in   our   last misery!

Laß' unsre ganze Seele dein
Let   our   whole soul yours

Und freudig unser Ende sein!
and joyful   our   end be!

O sacrificial Lamb! May your death
strengthen us in our last misery!
Let our entire soul be yours
and let our end be joyful!

Source:	Klopstock 1854, 5: 189
Variants:	(Schubert = roman, Klopstock = *italic*)
	Stanza 1, line 1: seiner = *seine*
	line 2: ihn = *ihm*
	Stanza 2, line 2: Sterblichen = *Sterbliche*

SCHUBERT excerpted his text from a poem by Friedrich Gottlieb Klopstock (1724–1803), one of the great literary figures of eighteenth-century Germany. The poem is a "revision" of the 1531 hymn "Nun lasst uns den Leib begraben" (Now Let Us Bury the Body) by Michael Weiße (c. 1488–1534). (See the "Begräbnisgesang" of Johannes Brahms for text and discussion.)

Klopstock wrote a number of "sacred songs" himself, but more interesting are his twenty-nine "revised hymns," the revision of which he claimed to have undertaken not to make them more religiously orthodox, but rather to improve them from the literary standpoint and to modernize their "severe" language. He found over half a dozen hymns by Luther to be in need of his attention, as well as "Wie schön leuchtet der Morgenstern"* and "Wachet auf"* of Philipp Nicolai, among others. He explains that:

> A hymn is a prayer. After good deeds, the Christian can do nothing greater than to pray. How marvelous it is to speak with God! And should we not employ all of our energies to do so to some extent in a worthy manner . . . ? These hymns do not cease thereby [i.e., as a result of Klopstock's revisions] to be the property of their authors. With the exception of but a few strophes, I have only changed them and not reworked them. . . . The principal rules that I followed were these: I had to seek out the principal message [*Hauptton*] of the hymn, and then pursue that message with every word that I wrote. As soon as the author deviated from his principal message, I had to bring him back to it. (Klopstock 1854: 158–159, tr. ed.)

Despite Klopstock's protestation to the contrary, he did radical surgery to Weiße's hymn, expanding it from seven to thirteen verses and leaving not a single sentence, clause, or even phrase of Weiße's chorale intact. Klopstock seems to have found the austerity and objectivity of sixteenth-century diction impossibly archaic for his age; his revisions invariably made the hymns more personal and subjective. Schubert employed Klopstock's first two verses, which roughly paraphrase the opening two verses from Weiße, and Klopstock's thirteenth, a direct appeal to God, which makes sense as a conclusion to the hymn, but nonetheless has no parallel in Weiße's original.

Chor der Engel, D. 440
Chorus of the Angels
Johann Wolfgang von Goethe

Christ ist erstanden!
Christ has arisen!

Freude dem Sterblichen,
Joy to the mortal one,

Den die verderblichen,
whom the pernicious,

Schleichenden, erblichen
insidious, hereditary

Mängel umwanden.
imperfections imprisons.

Christ has arisen!
Joy to the mortal one,
who is imprisoned by
pernicious, insidious,
hereditary imperfections.

Source: Goethe 1948–, 5: 166, lines 738–742

JOHANN Wolfgang von Goethe (1749–1832) was engaged in the composition of *Faust: A Tragedy* over some sixty years—his entire adult life. Like life, it is filled with contradictions and quandaries that are explored profoundly and originally, yet most are never resolved. The work thus reflects in a very real sense Goethe's personal confrontation with the purpose of earthly existence as well as his romantic response to the question.

The "Chor der Engel" or "Chorus of the Angels" set by Schubert is the first of three angel choruses from part 1, act 1, scene 1 ("Night") of *Faust*. In this scene, which takes place on Easter eve, the night before the resurrection of the Savior and the redemption of the world, Faust broods on his classical education, from which he realizes he has learned little of meaning about the world, and he ponders the thirst for experience that consumes him.

He is forced to face these thoughts even more directly through conversations with the earth spirit, whom he conjures up, and his student Wagner, in whom he sees his own past. In his first soliloquy, Faust reflects aloud and concludes that a vial of poison is perhaps the best solution for his tortured soul:

> Now is the time, through deeds, to show that mortals
> The calm sublimity of gods can feel;
> To shudder not at yonder dark abyss . . . .
> Let this last draught, the product of my skill,
> My own free choice, be quaff'd with resolute will,
> A solemn festive greeting, to the coming day! (Goethe 1882: 43)

Just as he is about to drink, the first "Chorus of the Angels" is heard, beginning with the words of a medieval Easter hymn, "Christ ist erstanden."* Thereafter, however, the angels' words take a rather non-Christian direction and lead Faust to reconsider emptying his glass.

> Christ has arisen!
> Joy to the mortal one,
> who is imprisoned by
> pernicious, insidious,
> hereditary imperfections. (tr. ed.)

The "Chor der Engel" is thus a pivotal point in the drama, for without it Goethe would have had to kill off his protagonist—making for a short and unsatisfactory play—or find another means to save him.

What inspired Schubert to compose the "Chorus of the Angels" is not known, but the impetus may well have been *Faust* itself. Schubert first set a *Faust* text, the haunting song "Gretchen am Spinnrade" (D. 118), in October, 1814 at the age of seventeen, when it is likely that the work was new to him. *Faust* clearly lingered in his mind, as he composed "Chor der Engel" (June, 1816) and three other *Faust* songs (D. 126, 367, and 564) over the next three years, the last (unfinished) in May, 1817. Thereafter his interest turned elsewhere and he never came back to *Faust*.

Coronach, D. 836
A Scottish Funeral Song
Sir Walter Scott, trans. Adam Storck

Er ist   uns geschieden vom   Berg   und vom Walde
He has from us parted   from mountain and from forest

Wie versiegte Quelle   als   Not uns bedrängte.
like dried-up spring when need us   beset.

Die Quelle wird fliessen genährt von dem Regen,
The spring will   flow, nourished by the   rain;

Uns scheint nie mehr Freude, dem Duncan kein Morgen!
to us appears never more joy,   to Duncan no tomorrow!

He is gone on the mountain,
　He is lost to the forest,
Like a summer-dried fountain,
　When our need was the sorest.
The font, reappearing,
　From the raindrops shall borrow,
But to us comes no cheering,
　To Duncan no morrow!

Die Hand   des Schnitters nimmt reife Ähren,
The hand of the   reaper   takes ripe ears [of corn];

Unser Trauergesang   klagt   bluhende Jugend.
our   mourning song laments flowering youth.

Der Herbstwind   treibt Blätter die gelben, die welken,
The autumn wind blows leaves, the yellow, the wilted;

Es   blüht' unsre Blume als Mehltau sie welkte.
— blossoms our flower as mildew it wilted.

The hand of the reaper
　Takes the ears that are hoary,
But the voice of the weeper
　Wails manhood in glory.
The autumn winds rushing
　Waft the leaves that are searest,[†]
But our flower was in flushing
　When blighting was nearest.

Ihr flüchtigen Füße, du   Rat   in Bedrängnis,
You fleet   feet, you counsel in   distress,

Du Arm im Streite, wie tief ist dein Schlummer.
you arm in conflict, how deep is your   slumber.

Wie Tau auf den Bergen, wie Schaum auf dem Bache,
Like dew on the mountains, like foam on the brook,

Wie Blas' auf der Welle   bist ewig geschieden.
Like bubbles on the wave [you] are forever   gone.

Fleet foot on the correi,[†]
　Sage counsel in cumber,[†]
Red hand[†] in the foray,
　How sound is thy slumber!
Like the dew on the mountain,
　Like the foam on the river,
Like the bubble on the fountain,
　Thou art gone, and forever!

Sir Walter Scott

Source:　Scott 1900: 177

SCHUBERT'S "Coronach" is taken from the historical romance "The Lady of the Lake," written in 1810 by Sir Walter Scott (1771–1832), one of the most prominent Scottish poets of his century. The writings of James Macpherson, passed off nearly seventy years earlier as the work of a third-century Gaelic poet named "Ossian," had stimulated in many writers an interest in the romance of the ancient Scottish people, and Scott was among those affected, a fact that he himself acknowledged. (Scott 1900: 153). (For a discussion of Ossian, see the annotation to "Darthula's Grabesgesang" by Brahms.)

Scott's romance takes place over a period of six days, on the third of which one of the protagonists, a "valiant warrior" named Duncan, is killed. His death is mourned in a *coronach*, an old Scottish funeral practice that Scott himself describes a follows:

> The coronach of the Highlanders . . . was a wild expression of lamentation, poured forth by the mourners over the body of a departed friend. When the words of it were articulate, they expressed the praises of the deceased, and the loss the clan would sustain by his death. (Scott 1900: 544)

Schubert took his text from a prose translation of "The Lady of the Lake" by a professor from Bremen named Philipp Adam Storck (1780–1822). Although the meter of the original was lost, Storck preserved Scott's meaning almost literally.[66] Scott's romance particularly appealed to Schubert; in 1825 and early 1826 he wrote seven songs (D. 831, 837–839, 843, 844, and 907) and two part songs (D. 835 and 836) to excerpts from Scott's poem.

[†]*searest* = withered; *correi* = a hollow in a hillside where game take refuge; *cumber* = trouble, time of trouble; *red hand* = bloody, not afraid of battle.

[66]*The New Grove* (Brown 1980: 765) states that "Schubert hoped that the addition of Scott's original text, when the songs were published, would help to make his name known in England." It is difficult to imagine how Scott's original text could have been fit to Schubert's music, which was written to Storck's non-metrical prose translation.

Der 23. Psalm, D. 706

Psalm 23

trans. Moses Mendelsohn

Gott ist mein Hirt,
God is my shepherd;

mir wird nichts mangeln,
for me will nothing be wanting.

er lagert mich auf grüne Weide;
He lays me on green pastures,

er leitet mich an stillen Bächen:
he leads me by quiet brooks,

er labt mein schmachtendes Gemüt,
he restores my languishing spirit;

er führt mich auf gerechtem Steige,
he leads me on right path

zu seines Namens Ruhm.
for his name's honor.

God is my shepherd;
I will want for nothing more.
He lays me down on green pasture,
he leads me by quiet brooks,
he restores my languishing spirit;
he leads me on the right path
for the honor of his name.

Und wall' ich auch im Todesschatten Thale;
And wander I also in the death's shadow valley,

so wall' ich ohne Furcht:
thus go I without fear:

denn du beschützest mich.
for you protect me;

dein Stab und deine Stütze
your rod and your staff

sind mir immerdar mein Trost.
are to me evermore my comfort.

And if I wander in the valley of death's
shadow,
thus I will go without fear:
for you protect me;
your rod and your staff
are my comfort for evermore.

Du richtest mir ein Freudenmahl
You prepare for me a joyous meal

im Angesicht der Feinde zu:
in th presence of the foes —;

du salbst mein Haupt mit Oele,
you anoint my head with oil

und schenkst mir volle Becher ein.
and pour me full cup —.

Mir folget Heil und Seligkeit
Me follow health and happiness

in diesem Leben nach.
in this life after.

Einst ruh' ich ewge Zeit,
One day rest I for eternity,

dort in des Ew'gen Haus.
there, in his eternal house.

You prepare a joyous meal for me
in the presence of my foes;
you anoint my head with oil
and fill my cup.
Health and happiness will follow me
the rest of this life.
Some day I will rest for eternity,
there, in his eternal home.

Source: Mendelsohn 1783: 47
Variants: (Schubert = roman, Mendelsohn = *italic*)
          Line 6: er führt mich (he leads me) = *und führt mich* (and leads me)
          Line 10: beschützest (protect) = *begleitest* (accompany)
          Line 12: *mir* is not in Mendelsohn's original

SCHUBERT'S text is interesting in that it is one of only three Biblical quotations[67] that he set to music, and the only one in German. It was also from an unusual source. Since the official Catholic Bible, the *Vulgata*, was in Latin, Catholic composers seldom had occasion to set Biblical texts in German. When they did use a German text, they did not have an official denominational Bible from which to take it, as did the Lutherans. Instead of using a Protestant Bible or one of the many Catholic translations, Schubert chose the translation of a Jew, Moses Mendelsohn (1729–1786), the grandfather of composer Felix Mendelssohn.

---

[67]The others are the *Magnificat*, D. 486, in Latin, and Psalm 92, D. 953, in Hebrew.

Moses Mendelsohn was a great intellect of his day and a prolific writer in the fields of philosophy and aesthetics. The last decade of his life, however, saw a turn toward his Jewish heritage in his thinking and writing. In 1780 he published a new translation of the *Torah*, the first five books of the Judeo-Christian Old Testament, and three years later a translation of the Psalter, from which Schubert took his text. It was dedicated to Karl Wilhelm Ramler* (1725–1798) the poet and anthologist who had assembled the collection from which Haydn took many of his part song texts, and Mendelsohn's trusted mentor in matters poetic.

In his preface "to the reader," Mendelsohn explains that he consulted the translations of a number of writers, but that he found the work of Martin Luther the most helpful:

> Regarding language, I have held more closely to Dr. Luther than to later translators. Where his translation is accurate, I find his German to be excellent and graceful. And I have not shied away from the Hebrew manner of expression that is found in Luther, even if it is not the best German. (Mendelsohn 1783: xi, tr. ed.)

His approach to the Psalms probably would have delighted their ancient authors:

> Here I pass on to the reader the fruits of more than a decade of work, which during this time has given me many comfortable hours and has sweetened many a travail. I translated the Psalms not in order, one after another; instead I chose a Psalm that appealed to me, that was in tune with the time and my mood, and that stimulated me either through its difficulty or its beauty. I then carried it about in my mind, through a variety of activities, until I believed that I was as attuned to my poet as I could be, given my abilities. The writing down of the text was then but a minor task. (Mendelsohn 1783: ix, tr. ed.)

Schubert altered Mendelsohn's translation unnecessarily in three places. In the first case, changing "and" to "he" makes for four lines in a row beginning with "he," an awkwardness that Mendelsohn had avoided. The second instance, the change of the verb "accompany" to "protect," made the implication of the former explicit, but unnecessarily and non Biblically. In the last case, Schubert added a redundant *mir* (to me) to line 12. The reasons for these alterations are uncertain; it is entirely possible that Schubert, who was notoriously careless, simply copied the text incorrectly.

Der Gondelfahrer, D. 809
The Gondolier
Johann Mayrhofer

Es tanzen Mond und Sterne
— **dance moon and stars**

Den flüchtigen Geisterreihen.
the fleeting, ghost-round-dance.

Wer wird von Erdensorgen
Who will by earthly sorrows

Befangen immer sein?
overcome always be?

The moon and stars dance
their fleeting, ghostly roundelay.
Who will always be overcome
by earthly sorrows?

Du kannst in Mondesstrahlen
You can in moonbeams

Nun, meine Barke, wallen,
now, my small boat, bobble,

Und aller Schranken los
and of all limitations free,

Wiegt dich des Meeres Schoß.
rocks you the sea's bosom.

You can bobble in the moonbeams
now, my little boat,
and, free of all constraints,
the sea's bosom rocks you.

Von Markusturme tönte
From Marco's tower sounded

Der Spruch der Mitternacht,
the saying of midnight.

Sie schlummern friedlich alle,
They slumber peacefully all,

Und nur der Schiffer wacht.
and only the boatman is awake.

The tower of San Marco
proclaims the midnight hour.
Everyone sleeps peacefully;
only the gondolier is awake.

*J*OHANN Mayrhofer (1787–1836) served by day as a low-level government censor, but when at leisure he was a member of Schubert's extended and somewhat libertine social circle of would-be poets, artists, and musicians. Of his poetic abilities, Dietrich Fischer-Dieskau writes: "We should consider Mayrhofer to be by far the best among [Schubert's] dilettantish poet friends, a man who fit the common concept of the 'Romantic character' all too well." (Fischer-Dieskau 1996: 57) Schubert set nearly fifty songs to texts by Mayrhofer, with whom he lived for two years from November 1818 to the end of 1820, at which time they became estranged for unknown reasons. Mayrhofer was a hypochondriac with a strong depressive tendency; he attempted suicide in 1830 and finally succeeded at same in 1836, when he leapt from his third-story office window rather than risk infection in a cholera epidemic.

"Der Gondelfahrer" was written in March, 1823 and was published in 1824 in a collection of Mayrhofer's poetry. It was the last of Mayrhofer's texts that Schubert set to music. The three stanzas of the poem paint a picture of Venice at night, peacefully sleeping under the moon- and starlight. The final stanza begins with the words "The tower of San Marco proclaims the midnight hour," which Schubert sets as an onomatopoetic imitation of the basilica's bells.

Der Tanz, D. 826
The Dance
"Schnitzer"

Es redet und träumet die Jugend so viel,
— talks and dreams — youth so much,

Von Tanzen, Galloppen, Gelagen,
of dancing, galloping, feasting;

Auf einmal erreicht sie ein trügliches Ziel,
at once achieves it a treacherous goal,

Da hört man sie seufzen und klagen.
then hears one it sigh and complain.

The young talk and dream so much
of dancing, horse-back riding, and feasting;
all at once they reach a treacherous goal,
then they start to sigh and complain.

Bald schmerzet der Hals, und bald schmerzet die Brust,
Soon hurts the throat, and soon hurts the chest—

Verschwunden ist alle die himmlische Lust.
disappeared is all the heavenly joy.

"Nur diesmal noch kehr' mir Gesundheit zurück!"
"Only this time yet return to me health again!"

so flehet vom Himmel der hoffende Blick!
Thus implores from heaven the hopeful glance!

Soon the throat hurts, and then the chest—
gone is all the heavenly joy.
"If only my health would return once more!"
Thus the hopeful glance implores from heaven!

Source: Deutsch 1964: 323

*S*CHUBERT composed songs for all sorts of occasions, but the circumstances surrounding "Der Tanz" may have been among the more unusual. The explanation of Otto Erich Deutsch is that a fourteen-year-old acquaintance of Schubert's named Irene von Kiesewetter (1811–1872), a pianist who accompanied Schubert from time to time, had alarmed her father with her inordinate passion for dancing. He is supposed to have been the source of an 1825 commission to Schubert and the poet "Schnitzer"[68] to produce a song meant to suppress her enthusiasm. (Deutsch 1947: 473)

Dietrich Berke, the editor of this work in the *Neue-Schubert-Ausgabe*, casts doubt on Deutsch's story, placing the composition of the work in three years later, in 1828, and suggesting that it was for a different purpose. He believes that the song was composed for a celebration of Miss Kiesewetter's recovery from an illness, an occasion for which Schubert wrote another work, "Al par del ruscelletto," D. 936. (Berke 1996: xx) This would explain the references to ill health in the second verse, which are difficult to understand in Deutsch's scenario. Verse 3, lacking in the Breitkopf edition of Schubert's works, is given in Deutsch 1964.

Next to nothing is known of the author. Deutsch says, "The writer is probably identical with K.A.F. Schnitzer, a translator from the French and Greek, or with the amateur musician Kolumban Schnitzer, later von Meerau (possibly one and the same person in any case)." (Deutsch 1947: 473) Kolumban Schnitzer appeared frequently in the concert halls of Vienna in the late 1820s, from time to time singing tenor in works by Schubert. He and Schubert were well enough acquainted that Schubert noted only his last name as author of this text. Schnitzer was among the 158 individuals who subscribed to a special first edition of Schubert's *Schwanengesang*, which was ultimately issued after the composer's death.

---

[68]*The New Grove's* attribution to "K. Schnitzer von *Mecrau*" in the list of Schubert works is presumably a typographical error.

Deutsche Messe, D. 872[69]

German Mass

Johann Philipp Neumann

Zum Eingang

For the Introit

Wohin soll ich mich wenden,
Where shall I — turn

Wenn Gram und Schmerz mich drücken?
when grief und pain me oppress?

Wem künd' ich mein Entzücken,
to whom announce I my delight

Wenn freudig pocht mein Herz?
when joyfully beats my heart?

Zu Dir, zu Dir, o Vater,
To you, to you, O Father,

Komm' ich in Freud' und Leiden,
come I in joy and suffering:

Du sendest ja die Freuden,
you send — the joys;

Du heilest jeden Schmerz.
you heal every pain.

Where shall I turn
when grief and pain oppress me?
To whom shall I announce my delight
when my heart beats joyfully?
To you, to you, O Father,
I come in times of joy and suffering:
you are the one who sends the joy;
you heal every pain.

Zum Gloria

At the Gloria

Ehre sei Gott in der Höhe!
Glory be to God in the highest!

Singet der Himmlischen selige Schar.
sings the heavenly blessed flock.

Ehre sei Gott in der Höhe!
Glory be to God in the highest!

Stammeln auch wir, die Erde gebar.
stammer also we, who earth bore.

Staunen nur kann ich
Marvel only can I

Und staunend mich freu'n;
and marveling — rejoice,

Vater der Welten!
Father of the worlds!

Doch stimm' ich mit ein:
— -I join in singing-:

Ehre sei Gott in der Höhe!
Glory be to God in the highest!

"Glory be to God in the highest!"
sings the blesséd heavenly flock.
"Glory be to God in the highest!"
stammer we earthlings below.
I can only marvel
and, in marveling, rejoice,
Father of the universe!
I join in the singing also:
"Glory be to God in the highest!"

Zum Evangelium und Credo

At the Gospel and Credo

Noch lag die Schöpfung formlos da,
Still lay — creation formless there,

Nach heiligem Bericht;
according to holy report;

Da sprach der Herr: Es werd Licht.
Then spoke the Lord: It [shall] become light.

Er sprach's, und es ward Licht.
He spoke it, and it became light.

All creation lay there without form,
according to the Holy Word;
then the Lord spoke: "It shall become light."
Thus he spoke, and it became light.

---

[69]*Gesänge zur Feier des heiligen Opfers der Messe, nebst einem Anhange: Das Gebet des Herrn.* (Songs for the Celebration of the Holy Sacrifice of the Mass, with an Appendix: The Lord's Prayer)

Und Leben regt, und reget sich,
And life stirs, and stirs —,

Und Ordnung tritt hervor.
and order comes forth.

Und überall, all überall
And everywhere, — everywhere

Tönt Preis und Dank empor.
sounds praise and thanks upward.

And life stirs and moves about,
and an order evolves.
Every creature, everywhere
sends up praise and thanks.

Zum Offertorium

At the Offertory

Du gabst, o Herr, mir Sein und Leben,
You gave, O Lord, to me being and life

Und Deiner Lehre himmlisch Licht.
and your teaching's heavenly light.

Was kann dafür, ich Staub, Dir geben?
What can for that, I dust, to you give?

Nur danken kann ich, mehr doch nicht.
Only thank can I, more surely not.

You gave me, O Lord, my being and life
and the heavenly light of your teaching.
What can I, mere dust, give you in return?
I can only thank you, nothing more.

Zum Sanctus

At the Sanctus

Heilig, heilig, heilig ist der Herr!
Holy, holy, holy is the Lord!

Heilig, heilig, heilig ist nur Er!
Holy, holy, holy is only he!

Er, der nie begonnen, Er, der immer war,
He who never began, he who always was,

Ewig ist und waltet, sein wird immer dar.
eternally is, and rules, be will evermore —.

Allmacht Wunder, Liebe, alles ringsumher!
Almighty wonder, love all around!

Heilig, heilig, heilig ist der Herr!
Holy, holy, holy is the Lord!

Holy, holy, holy is the Lord!
Holy, holy, only he is holy!
He who had no beginning, he who always was,
eternally is, and reigns, and will be evermore.
Almighty wonder, omnipresent love!
Holy, holy, holy is the Lord!

Nach Wandlung

After the Transubstantiation

Betrachend Deine Huld und Güte,
Contemplating your graciousness and goodness,

O mein Erlöser, gegen mich
O my redeemer, towards me

Seh' ich beim letzten Abendmahle
see I at the last supper

Im Kreise Deiner Teuren Dich.
in the circle of your faithful ones you.

Du brichst das Brot, du reichst den Becher.
You break the bread, you pass the cup.

Du sprichst: Dies ist mein Leib, mein Blut,
You say: This is my body, my blood;

Nehmt hin und denket meiner Liebe,
take — and think of my love

Wenn opfernd ihr ein Gleiches tut.
when sacrificing you the same do.

Contemplating your graciousness and goodness
towards me, my redeemer,
I see you at the Last Supper
in the company of your faithful disciples.
You break the bread, you pass the cup.
You say: "This is my body and my blood;
take it and remember my love
when you perform the same sacrifice."

Agnus Dei
Lamb of God

Mein Heiland, Herr und Meister!
My savior, Lord and master!

Dein Mund so segensreich,
Your mouth so blessing-rich,

Sprach einst das Wort des Heiles:
spoke once the word of salvation:

"Der Friede sei mit Euch."
" — peace be with you."

O Lamm, das opfernd tilgte
O Lamb, which sacrificing atoned

Der Menschheit schwere Schuld,
— humanity's heavy guilt,

Send' uns auch Deinen Frieden
send us also your peace

Durch Deine Gnad' und Huld.
through your grace and kindness.

My savior, Lord, and master!
Your mouth, so full of blessings,
once spoke the words of salvation:
"Peace be with you."
O Lamb, whose sacrifice atoned
for humanity's heavy guilt,
send your peace to us also
through your grace and kindness.

Benediction
Benediction

Herr, Du hast mein Fleh'n vernommen,
Lord, you have my supplication heard;

Selig pocht's in meiner Brust,
happily beats it in my breast.

In die Welt hinaus, in's Leben
Into the world out, into life,

Folgt mir nun des Himmels Lust.
follows me now — heaven's delight.

Dort auch bist ja Du mir nahe,
There also are indeed you to me near,

überall und jederzeit,
everywhere and always;

Aller Orten ist Dein Tempel
at all locations is your temple

Wo das Herz sich fromm Dir weiht.
where the heart itself devoutly to you devotes.

Segne, Herr, mich und die Meinen,
Bless, Lord, me and mine,

Segne unsern Lebensgang!
bless our life's course!

Alles unser Tun und Wirken
All our doing and working

Sei ein frommer Lobgesang.
be a pious praise-song.

Lord, you have heard my supplication;
it beats happily in my breast.
Out into the world, into life,
heaven's delight follows me.
There you indeed are close to me,
everywhere and at all times;
your temple is everywhere
the heart devoutly dedicates itself to you.
Lord, may you bless me and mine;
may you bless our life's course!
May all our deeds and works
be a devout song of praise.

Anhang. Das Gebet des Herrn
Appendix. The Prayer of the Lord

Anbetend Deine Macht und Größe
Adoring your might and greatness,

Versinkt in Nichts mein bebend Ich.
sinks into nothing my trembling I.

Mit welchem Namen, Deiner würdig,
With what name, of you worthy,

Du Unnennbarer, preis' ich Dich?
you Unnameable, praise I you?

Adoring your might and greatness,
my trembling being sinks into nothingness.
With what name worthy of you
may I praise you, Unnameable One?

Wohl mir!   ich darf Dich Vater nennen,
–I am blessed–! I may you Father call,

Nach   Deines Sohnes Unterricht;
according to   your   son's instruction;

So   sprech' ich denn zu Dir, mein Schöpfer!
thus speak   I   then to you, my   creator

Mit   kindlich froher Zuversicht.
with child-like, happy confidence.

I am blessed! I may call you "Father,"
according to your son's instruction;
thus, then, I speak to you, my creator,
with happy, child-like confidence.

O Vater, der Du bist im Himmel
O Father, who you are in heaven

Und   überall   zu jeder Zeit,
and everywhere at any time,

Zu preisen deinen Vaternamen
to praise   your father's name

Sei jedem Herzen   Seligkeit!
be to each heart blessedness!

O lass, durch Deine   Huld   und Liebe,
O let, through your graciousness and love,

Erscheinen uns Dein Gnadenreich,
appear   to us your grace-kingdom,

Und treues Tun   nach   Deinem Willen
and faithful acting according to your   will

Mach'   auch die Erde Himmelgleich!
shall make also the earth heaven's equal!

O Father, you who are in heaven
and everywhere at any time,
the praising of your name
shall be each heart's bliss!
Through your graciousness and love
let your kingdom of grace appear to us,
and faithful living according to your will
shall make the earth heaven's equal!

Herr, der Du nährst die jungen Raben,
Lord, who you nourish the young raven,

Du kennst auch Deiner Kinder Not.
you know also your children's need,

Nicht ist vergebens unser   Flehen:
not is in vain   our supplication:

Gib uns auch täglich unser Brod!
give us also daily our bread!

Vergib uns, was wir irrend fehlten,
Forgive us what we errantly failed

Wenn wir die Schuld vor Dir bereu'n,
when we — guilt before you repent,

Wie wir, auf Dein   Gebot,   den Brüdern,
as we upon your commandment, the brothers,

Wie wir den Feinden auch verzeih'n.
as we the foes   also forgive.

Lord, you who nourish the young raven,
you know also the need of your children,
our supplication is not in vain:
give us also our daily bread!
Forgive our errant failures
when we repent our guilt before you,
as we also forgive, as you commanded,
our brothers and our foes.

Will   die Versuchung uns verlocken,
Wants — temptation us   entice,

Gib Kraft, O Herr, zum Widerstand!
give strength, O Lord, to resistance!

So   vor der Seele höchstem Übel,
Thus from the soul's highest   evil,

Vor Sünde schütz' uns Deine Hand!
from sin   protect us your hand!

Send' uns Geduld und Trost in Leiden!
Send us patience and comfort in sorrow!

Und kann's zu unser'm Heil   gescheh'n,
And can it for   our   salvation happen,

So lass, durch Deine   Vatergüte,
so let, through your father-goodness,

Den bittern Kelch vorübergeh'n!
the bitter cup   pass over!

If temptation tries to entice us,
give us the strength, O Lord, to resist!
May your hand protect us
from sin and the highest evil.
Send us patience and comfort in times of sorrow.
And, if our salvation can come to pass,
so then, through your fatherly goodness,
let the bitter cup pass over us!

A professor of physics at the Vienna Polytechnic Institute by profession and a writer by avocation, Johann Philipp Neumann (1774–1849) commissioned this composition from Schubert, paying him 100 Florin upon receipt of the completed manuscript in October, 1827. Neumann had written the text himself, most likely with the intention of having it sung by Catholic congregations. On October 24, 1827, Neumann petitioned the ecclesiastical censor of Vienna for permission to have the text used in the city's Catholic church services. The petition was unsuccessful, and "the work was admitted for use only in the second half of the nineteenth century."[70]

Neumann's texts appear to consist of generalized substitutes for the Ordinary and Proper of the Mass, though the "Kyrie," "Credo," "Benedictus," "Osanna," and some sections of the Proper are missing. Most striking is the personal tone of the text, with frequent references to the first-person singular, as in the "Offertory":

> You gave me, O Lord, my being and life
> and the heavenly light of your teaching.
> What can I, mere dust, give you in return?
> I can only thank you, nothing more.

The "Appendix," "Das Gebet des Herrn," is an elaborate trope of the liturgical Lord's Prayer, which Neumann organizes and expresses as follows:

	Neumann	Lord's Prayer
Stanza 1:	. . . With what name worthy of you may praise you . . . ? I may call you Father. . . .	Our Father who art in heaven, hallowed be thy name.
Stanza 2:	O Father, you who are in heaven . . . , let your kingdom of grace appear to us, and faithful living according to your will	Thy kingdom come, thy will be done, on earth as it is in heaven.
Stanza 3:	Lord, you who nourish the young raven . . . , give us also our daily bread! Forgive our errant failures . . . as we also forgive . . . our brothers and our foes.	Give us this day our daily bread, and forgive us our trespasses as we forgive those who trespass against us.
Stanza 4:	If temptation tries to entice us, give us strength, O Lord, to resist! May your hand protect us from sin and the highest evil	And lead us not into temptation, but deliver us from evil.

It is interesting to compare Neumann's expansion of the Lord's Prayer with that of Martin Luther ("Vater unser im Himmelreich"*), whose trope takes fully ten stanzas but is truer to the original.

Die Geselligkeit, D. 609

Life's Joy

Johann Karl Unger

Wer Lebenslust fühlet, der bleibt nicht allein,
Who life's joy feels, — remains not alone.

Allein sein ist öde, wer kann sich da freu'n?
Alone to be is dull; who can himself then enjoy?

Im traulichen Kreise, beim herzlichen Kuß,
In the intimate circle, with the heart-felt kiss,

Beisammen zu leben, ist Seelengenuß!
together to live, is soul's delight!

Das lehrt uns der Tauber, für Liebe und Lust
— teaches us the dove: for love and desire

Erhebt sich dem Täubchen die seidene Brust,
expands — to the sweetheart the silky breast;

Es girret für Wonne, es lehret im Kuß,
he coos in bliss, he teaches through the kiss,

Beisamen zu leben, ist [sop. = *sei*] Herzensgenuß.
together to live is [to be] heart's-pleasure.

Those who experience life's joy do not remain alone.
To be alone is so dull; who can possibly enjoy that?
In an intimate circle of friends, with a heart-felt kiss,
to live together is the soul's delight!

The dove teaches us: for love and desire
he expands his silky breast to his sweetheart;
he coos in bliss and teaches through kisses
that to live together is the heart's pleasure.

---

[70]Deutsch 1947: 683. The texts of the relevant documents and Deutsch's commentary, upon both of which this essay is based, are given in Deutsch 1947: 681–683.

| Geselligkeit | fessel | die ganze Natur, | Good fellowship binds together all creation |
| **Good fellowship binds** | **–all of Nature–,** | | in the air, in the waters, and in the laughing meadow. |

Im Lüften, im Wasser, auf lächender Flur,
in the air, in the waters, in laughing meadow.

The one who created all commanded it:
to live together is the duty of all humankind.

Er selber gebot es, der alles erschuf:
He himself commanded it, who all created:

Beisammen zu leben ist Menschenberuf.
together to live is humanity's duty.

Dem folget, ihr Guten, und singet nicht mehr:
It follow, you good ones, and sing no more:

Obey the command, good people, and sing no more:
solitude would indeed be dreary and empty.
Living alone brings only longing and pain,
but living together satisfies the heart.

die Einsamkeit wäre nicht öde nicht leer,
— solitude would be indeed dreary and empty.

Allein sein erzeuget nur Sehnsucht und Schmerz,
Alone to be produces only longing and pain,

Beisammen zu leben befriedigt das Herz.
together to live satisfies the heart.

*S*CHUBERT'S simple paean to the joy of friendship is based on a poem entitled "Die Geselligkeit" (Good Fellowship) by Johann Karl Unger (1771–after 1836) that appeared in the *Österreichischen Tagebuch für das Jahr 1804*. Schubert entitled his setting "Quartetto," perhaps ignorant of the actual title. "Lebenslust," the title given in the old Breitkopf Schubert edition, appears to have been assigned by the editor of the first Schubert thematic catalogue. The identity of the poet was lost until the 1960s and may not even have been known to Schubert, though the two were acquainted.[71] Schubert may have taken a particular liking to the text—his entire artistic career and personal life were built on an extended network of friends, many of whom were his librettists, performers, and muses.

Otto Erich Deutsch, the great Schubert scholar of the first half of the twentieth century, describes the author Johann Karl Unger as follows:

> Unger . . . had been a theological student, then studied law and became professor of natural history at the Theresian Academy of Knights in Vienna, later tutor in the household of Ignaz, Freiherr [Baron] von Forgács, and in 1810 councillor of domestic economy to Josef, Freiherr von Hackelberg-Landau. He was also a writer and poet, an editor of almanacs, and a member of the Philharmonic Society as an amateur singer. (Schubert 1947: 91)

Unger and Schubert met in 1818 at the latest, when Unger introduced the composer to Count Johann Karl Esterházy and recommended him to tutor the Count's two daughters. How Unger came to write "Die Geselligkeit" and how it came into Schubert's hands is unknown, but it was not unusual for Schubert's acquaintances to grace him with their own literary efforts. In many cases the author was rewarded with a song.

Unger and Schubert had another connection, Unger's daughter Karoline (1803–1877), whose singing Schubert greatly admired. Karoline became one of the great singers in the first half of her century, and was the alto for the premiere of Beethoven's ninth symphony on May 7, 1824. It was she who complained about the range of her part, only to be told by Beethoven to practice harder.

The *Neue-Schubert-Ausgabe* (Berke 1996: xvi) has significantly revised the history of this song, beginning with much of the information in the opening paragraph to this essay. In addition, Berke reveals that the work actually has four verses, the last three of which did not see print until their publication in the *NSA*.

---

[71]It was Schubert's custom to note the name of the poet on his scores, but no name appears in this case.

Gesang der Geister über den Wassern, D. 704, 705, 714
Song of the Spirits upon the Waters
Johann Wolfgang von Goethe

Des Menschen Seele
The human soul

Gleicht dem Wasser:
resembles the water:

Vom Himmel kommt es,
from heaven comes it,

Zum Himmel steigt es,
to heaven ascends it,

Und wieder nieder
and again down

Zur Erde muß es,
to earth must it [go],

Ewig wechselnd.
forever changing.

The human soul
is like water:
from heaven it comes,
to heaven it ascends,
and down again
to earth it must return,
forever changing.

Strömt von der hohen,
Streams from the high,

Steilen Felswand
steep rock wall

Der reine Strahl,
the pure jet,

Dann stäubt er lieblich
then turns to mist it lovely

In Wolkenwellen
in cloud waves

Zum glatten Fels,
to the smooth rock,

Und leicht empfangen
and lightly received,

Wallt er verschleiernd,
flows it veiling,

Leisrauschend
softly rustling,

Zur Tiefe nieder.
to the depths down.

The pure jet
rushes down from the
high, steep rockface,
then turns to mist in cloud-waves
of sweet spray
against the smooth rock
and, kindly welcomed,
it flows on, veil-like,
softly murmuring,
to the depths below.

Ragen Klippen
Rise cliffs

Dem Sturz entgegen,
the fall against,

Schäumt er unmutig
foams it angrily,

Stufenweise,
step by step,

Zum Abgrund.
to the abyss.

If cliffs rise up
against its fall,
it foams angrily,
step by step,
to the abyss.

Im flachen Bette
In the flat bed

Schleichet er das Wiesenthal hin,
sneaks it the meadow valley toward,

Und in dem glatten See
and in the smooth lake

Weiden ihr Antlitz
graze their countenance

Alle Gestirne.
all stars.

In its level bed
it steals toward the meadowy vale,
and in the glassy lake
all the stars
gaze at their faces.

Wind ist der Welle **Wind is the wave's**	Wind is the wave's sweet lover; wind stirs up foaming billows from the deep.
Lieblicher Buhler; **sweet lover;**	
Wind mischt von Grund aus **wind mixes from the deep —**	
schäumende Wogen. **foaming waves.**	
Seele des Menschen, **Soul of humanity,**	Soul of mortals, how like water you are! Fate of mortals, how like the wind.
Wie gleichst du dem Wasser! **how resemble you the water!**	
Schicksal des Menschen, **Fate of humanity,**	
wie gleichst du dem Wind! **how resemble you the wind.**	

Source:	Goethe 1948–, 1: 306
Variants:	(Schubert = roman, Goethe = *italic*)
	Stanza 4, line 2: schleichet = *schleicht*
	Stanza 6, line 3: von = *vom*

WOLFGANG von Goethe (1749–1832) composed the "Song of the Spirits upon the Waters" from October 9 to 11, 1779, after seeing the waterfall at Stuppach, Switzerland. The poem imaginatively and pictorially compares the human soul to water: It begins and ends its journey in the heavens, in the meantime traversing all manner of earthly barriers and obeying the whims of fate. While the poem was admired from the beginning, the same was not true of Schubert's musical rendering of it.

Schubert confronted this text on five occasions and must have found it difficult. His first, never-completed setting was for solo voice (D. 484, September, 1816). This was followed by D. 538 (1817) for TTBB chorus a cappella, which apparently still did not have the dramatic effect he sought. He thereafter developed a more elaborate setting for eight-voice male choir and low strings, in which form he completed his final version (D. 714b) in February, 1821. It was first performed on March 7 in Vienna's Kärntnertortheater as the third selection in a program that began with "Erlkönig," Schubert's great hit of that period.

According to all reports, the performance was a disaster, and the music utterly puzzled the audience. Schubert's radical harmonic shifts and his similarly radical changes of style from section to section—occasioned by the contrasts in the text—were simply too much for the listeners, who had probably come to hear the less-challenging "Erlkönig." History has been kinder, seeing in "Gesang der Geister" one of Schubert's most imaginative and original compositions.

Schubert was apparently occupied with thoughts about the meaning of life as he worked on his first version of the "Gesang der Geister" in September, 1816. His diary from September 8 reveals some of his own musings:

Man resembles a ball, to be played with by chance and passion. This sentence seems extraordinarily true to me.

I have often read authors to the effect that the world is like a stage on which every human being plays a part. Applause and censure follow in the next world.—But as the stage part is assigned, so is our part assigned to us, and who is to say whether he has played it well or ill?—It is a bad producer who gives his actors parts they cannot play. (Deutsch 1947: 70)

Gott in der Natur, D. 757

God in Nature

Ewald Christian von Kleist

Groß ist der Herr! Die Himmel ohne Zahl
Great is the Lord! The heavens without number

Sind Säle seiner Burg,
are halls of his fortress;

Sein Wagen Sturm und donnerndes Gewölk'
his chariot storm and thundering clouds

Und Blitze sein Gespann.
and lightning his carriage horses.

Die Morgenröth' ist nur ein Wiederschein
The dawn is only a reflection

Von seines Kleides Saum,
of his gown's seam,

Und gegen seinen Glanz ist Dämmerung
and against his radiance is twilight

Der Sonne flammend Licht.
of the sun flaming light.

Er sieht mit gnäd'gem Blick zur Erd' herab,
He looks with merciful eye to the earth down

Sie grünet, blüht und lacht.
it grows green, blooms, and laughs.

Er schilt, es fähret Feuer vom Felsen auf,
He scolds, — rises fire from the rock —,

Und Meer und Himmel bebt!
and sea and heaven quakes!

Lobt den Gewaltigen, den großen Herrn,
Praise the mighty one, the great Lord,

Ihr Lichter seiner Burg,
you lights of his fortress,

Ihr Sonnenheere! flammt zu seinem Ruhm!
you sun-armies! Blaze for his glory!

Ihr Erden singt sein Lob.
You earth sing his praise.

Great is the Lord! Firmaments without number
are the halls of his fortress;
his chariot is the storm, and thundering clouds
and lightning are his team of harses.

The dawn is only a reflection
of the hem of his gown,
and compared to his radiance,
the sun's blazing light is as twilight.

When he casts a merciful eye upon the earth
it becomes green, blooms, and laughs.
When he scolds, fire flames forth from the rocks,
and the sea and heavens quake!

Praise the great and almighty Lord,
you lights of his fortress,
you hosts of suns! Blaze for his glory!
Earth, sing his praise.

Source: Kleist 1766, 1: 2
Variants: (Schubert = roman, Kleist = *italacs*)

Stanza 1: Sind Säle seiner Burg (are rooms in his fortress) =
Sind seine Wohnungen (are his dwellings)

Stanza 2: Dämmerung der Sonne flammend Licht (twilight of the sun flaming light) =
alles Licht der Sonne, Dämmerung (all the light of the sun, twilight)

Stanza 3: zur Erd' herab, Sie grünet, blüht, und lacht (upon the earth, it becomes green,
blooms, and laughs) = *von seiner Höh zur Erd herab; sie lacht* (from its heights
down to the earth, it laughs)

Stanza 3: Und Meer und Himmel bebt! (and heaven and earth quake) =
Des Erdballs Axe bebt! (the globe's axis quakes)

Stanza 4: großen Herrn (great Lord) = *gnädgen Herrn* (merciful Lord)

S CHUBERT chose as his text for this vivacious piece for women's chorus an ode of Ewald Christian von
Kleist (1715–1759). It is the second poem in a set of seven odes, and was originally entitled "Hymne." The
poem consists of seventeen stanzas, of which Schubert used the first four, with considerable alteration.

The changes to Kleist's text were all apparently designed to increase its strength, directness, or drama.
For example, Kleist's "dwelling" in stanza 1 pales in comparison to Schubert's image of the "fortress," and
the "great Lord" of the last stanza is a more powerful image than the "merciful Lord." The use of *groß* (great)
might also have had its origins in an attempt to round the form of the poem, which begins with the same
adjective.

If these revisions stemmed from Schubert, it is clear that the composer did not hold his text sacrosanct. On the other hand, perhaps he received it in manuscript form, with the changes already made. Whoever adapted the poem was aided indirectly by the poet himself, who facilitated tampering by writing without rhyme. Schubert could not even recall the poet's name when he wrote his score—it erroneously bears the inscription "Gleim," apparently referring to Johann Ludwig Wilhelm Gleim* (1719–1803), a poet unknown anywhere else in Schubert's song output.

Ewald Christian von Kleist has an interesting biography for a poet. Even though he disliked the daily grind of military life, he was a lifelong professional soldier, first for Denmark and then Prussia. He used his stationing in various cities as an opportunity to become acquainted with the local literati, including Lessing in Leipzig. Kleist died in battle at the age of forty four.

"Gott In der Natur" (1822), the only text by Kleist that Schubert set to music, is a joyous "hymn" of praise to the all-powerful God, whose manifestations in nature provide the subjects of the poet's imagery. The piece was the last work of Schubert's presented by the Vienna Philharmonic Society (February 28, 1828) prior to his death.

Nachtgesang im Walde, D. 913
Night Song in the Forest
Johann Gabriel Seidl

Sei uns   stets gegrüßt, o Nacht!
Be by us always greeted, O night!

We always welcome you, O night!
but doubly so here in the forest,
where your eye laughs more furtively,
where your footsteps echo more quietly.

Aber doppelt hier im Wald,
but   doubly here in the forest,

Wo   dein Aug' verstohlner lacht,
where your eye more furtively laughs,

Wo   dein Fußtritt   leiser   hallt!
where your footstep more quietly resounds.

Auf der Zweige   Laubpokale
On the branches' leaf-goblets

On the branches' leafy goblets
you pour out your silver;
you hang out the moon and its beams
as a lamp for us in this house of leaves.

Gießest du dein Silber aus,
pour   you your silver out;

Hängst   den Mond mit seinem Strahle
you hang the moon with its   beam

Uns   als Lamp' in's   Blätterhaus.
for us as lamp in the leaf-house.

Säusende Lüftchen sind deine Reden,
Rustling breezes are your words;

Rustling breezes are your words;
spinning rays are your threads.
Whatever your mouth has soothingly touched,
lowers its eyelids and sinks into sleep.

Spinnende Strahlen sind deine Fäden;
spinning   rays   are your threads.

Was nur dein Mund beschwichtigend traf,
What only your mouth   soothingly   touched,

Senket das Aug' und sinket in Schlaf.
lowers the eye and sinks into sleep.

Und doch— es ist zum Schlafen zu schön:
And yet— it is for sleeping too beautiful:

And yet—it's too beautiful for sleeping:
So, arise! and, with the sound of horns,
with crashing waves of brighter sounds,
wake those who early lay in torpid slumber.

D'rum auf! und weckt mit Hörnergetön,
So,   arise! and wake with horn-tones,

Mit hellerer Klänge Wellenschlag,
with brighter sounds wave-dashing,

Was frühbetäubt im Schlummer lag.
what early dazed in   slumber lay.

Auf! Auf!—
Up! Up!

Arise! Arise!
The forest foliage
is already astir;
the little birds think
the night has fled,

Es regt   in den Lauben
— is moving in the leaves

Des Waldes sich schon,
of the forest — already;

Die Vöglein,   sie glauben,
the little birds, they believe

Die Nacht sei entflohn,
the night has   fled,

222

Die wandernden Rehe
the wandering deer

Verlieren sich zag,
disperse — timidly;

Sie wähnen, es gehe
they think it would go

Schon bald an den Tag.
already soon toward the day.

and the wandering deer
disperse timidly;
they think the day
will soon begin.

Die Wipfel des Waldes
The tops of the forest

Erbrausen mit Macht;
begin to shake with might;

Vom Quell her erschallt es,
from the spring — sounds it

Als wär' er erwacht!
as if had it awakened!

The forest treetops
begin shaking mightily;
the spring sounds
as if the forest had awakened!

Und rufen wir im Sange:
And call we in song:

"Die Nacht ist im Walde daheim,"
" — night is in the forest at home."

So ruft auch Echo lange;
Then calls also Echo for a long time:

"Sie ist im Wald daheim— daheim!"
"It is in the forest at home— at home!

And we call out in song:
"Night is at home in the forest!"
Then Echo calls out again and again:
"It is at home in the forest— at home!"

D'rum sei uns doppelt hier im Wald
So be by us twice here in the forest

Gegrüßt, o holde Nacht!
greeted, O lovely night!

Wo alles, was dich schön uns malt,
where all that you beautifully for us paints,

Uns noch weit schöner lacht!
for us even much more beautifully laughs.

So be twice as welcome here in the forest,
O sweet, sweet night,
where everything that makes you beautiful
becomes, for us, even more beautiful!

Source: Seidl 1877, 1: 81

AUSTRIAN poet Johann Gabriel Seidl (1804–1875) provided the text for Schubert's "Night Song in the Forest" for male chorus and four horns. Night- and nature-poems by Seidl's contemporaries in the romantic period often used nature as a metaphor for the human soul and thus frequently had a darker side. Not so with this poem, a joyous admiration of the peace—and life—of the forest night, which here brings wonder rather than fear.

The first three stanzas describe the night amidst the trees, with its amplification of the softest whisper, its dewy leaves, and its softness that lulls to sleep those it has kissed. Stanza 4 provides a pivot to the second half of the poem, in which we become aware of the activity of the moonlit forest and hold it in the same awe as the forest's peace. It is indeed "too beautiful for sleeping." The poet ends stanza 4 in peace, but Schubert proceeds immediately to the "Arise! Arise!" that begins stanza 5.

Seidl intensifies his expression in the next three stanzas through a compression of structure: He changes his rhyme scheme from AABB to ABAB and cuts the length of his lines in half. A final touch is his elision of stanzas 5 and 6. The concluding two stanzas return to longer lines but retain the immediately preceding rhyme scheme. Here the poet rounds the form of his poem through a return to ideas from the beginning, the image of the "double welcome" and the personification of the laughing forest.

The echo of the final stanza is particularly intriguing: The poet calls out *Night* is at home in the forest," but the echo returns "*It* is at home on the forest." This "inaccurate" response (and Seidl's omission of the article *das* preceding *Echo*) must mean that the response is from Echo, the mountain nymph of Greek mythology who was condemned to repeat the words of others. Schubert cleverly and humorously underlines Seidl's trick by having the echo sung in augmentation.

Nachthelle, D. 892
Bright Night
Johann Gabriel Seidl

Die Nacht ist heiter und ist rein,
The night is clear and is pure,

Im allerhellsten Glanz:
in the brightest splendor:

Die Häuser schau'n verwundert drein,
the houses look amazed —,

Steh'n übersilbert ganz.
stand covered with silver totally.

The night is clear and pure,
in the brightest splendor:
the houses, bathed in silver light,
behold it in amazement.

In mir ist's hell so wunderbar,
In me is it bright so wonderful,

So voll und übervoll,
so full and over full;

Und waltet drinnen frei und klar,
and prevails within freely and clearly

Ganz ohne Leid und Groll.
wholly without pain and resentment.

Inside me it's so wonderfully bright,
so full and overflowing;
all within me is free and clear,
wholly without pain or resentment.

Ich fass' in meinem Herzenshaus
I contain in my heart's house

Nicht all' das reiche Licht:
not all the rich light.

Es will hinaus, es muß hinaus—
it wants out, it must out;

Die letzte Schranke bricht!
the last barrier is breaking!

I cannot contain within my heart
all of the rich light.
It wants out, it must come out;
the last barrier is breaking!

Source: Seidl 1877, 1: 38
Variant: (Schubert = roman, Seidl = *italic*)
Stanza 2, line 3:   Und waltet drinnen frei und klar =
Und innen waltet frei und klar

SCHUBERT'S text is from the pen of Johann Gabriel Seidl (1804–1875), a fellow native Austrian whose poems provided texts for fifteen of his part songs and solo *Lieder*. Seidl's poem is brief—just three stanzas of four lines—but highly expressive. Stanza 1 paints a wondrous picture of a crystalline night bathed in brilliant moon- and star-light. The second stanza extends the image to the spirit of the poet, which is just as wondrously bathed in an internal light of joy that cannot be contained and breaks out in all its radiance in the final stanza.

Sehnsucht, D. 656
Longing
Johann Wolfgang von Goethe

Nur wer die Sehnsucht kennt,
Only who — longing knows,

Weiß, was ich leide!
knows what I suffer!

Allein und abgetrennt
Alone and separated

Von aller Freude,
from all joy,

Only one who knows longing
understands what I suffer!
Alone and separated
from every joy,

Seh' ich ans Firmament
Look I at the firmament

Nach jener Seite.
to the other side.

Ach! der mich liebt und kennt,
Ah! he me loves and knows

Ist in der Weite.
is in the distance.

I gaze at the firmament
toward the other side.
Alas, he who loves and knows me
is so far away.

224

Es schwindelt mir, es brennt
It is dizzy to me, it burns

Mein Eingeweide.
my innards.

Nur wer die Sehnsucht kennt,
Only who — longing knows,

Weiß, was ich leide!
knows what I suffer!

Source: Goethe 1948–, 7: 258

I am reeling;
my insides are burning.
Only one who knows longing
understands what I suffer!

SCHUBERT'S part song is based on the poem that closes the fourth chapter of the novel *Wilhelm Meisters Lehrjahre* (Wilhelm Meister's Years of Apprenticeship) by Johann Wolfgang von Goethe (1749–1832), written in spurts over a period of eighteen years, from 1777 to 1795. It is an early example of a German literary genre popular in the nineteenth century called the *Bildungsroman*, a novel that tells the story of the development and self-realization of its protagonist. Goethe's subject is a well-to-do young man who becomes enamored of and swept up in the theater, and whose life is molded and changed by the people he meets through it—especially the women.

As book 4, chapter 11 ends, Wilhelm is recovering from an attack on his troupe by highwaymen and is dreaming of the attractive, mysterious woman who cared for him and then disappeared without giving her name. Her handwriting resembles that of the beautiful Countess at whose home his company had performed just before the attack, and his mind turns to her as well. "He fell into a dreamy yearning. And how in tune with his feelings was the song that Mignon and the harpist [two members of the company] began to sing just then with the most heartfelt expression as a rowdy duet." (Goethe 1948–, 7: 257, tr. ed.) The song is "Sehnsucht," a song of longing for a distant love.

The editors of the *Oxford Companion to German Literature* (Garland 1976: 946) are of the opinion that "The novel contains eight of Goethe's finest songs," including "Kennst du das Land." Schubert apparently agreed: He set to music no fewer than seven of the eight poems.

Ständchen, D. 920, 921
Serenade
Franz Grillparzer

Zögernd leise,
Hesitantly, quietly,

In des Dunkels nächt'ger Stille,
in the darkness's nocturnal stillness,

Sind wir hier.
are we here.

Und den Finger sanft gekrümmt,
And the finger gently bent,

Leise, leise
lightly, lightly

Pochen wir
knock we

An des Liebchens Kammerthür.
at — sweetheart's chamber door.

Doch nun steigend,
But now increasing,

Schwellend, hebend,
swelling, rising,

Mit vereinter Stimme laut
with united voice loudly,

Rufen aus wir hochvertraut:
call out we confidently:

Schlaf du nicht,
sleep you not

Wenn der Neigung Stimme spricht!
when — affection's voice speaks!

Hesitantly, quietly,
in the dark's nocturnal stillness,
we are here.
And with fingers gently bent,
lightly, lightly
we knock
at our sweetheart's chamber door.

But now increasing,
swelling, rising,
with a loud, united voice,
we call out confidently:
"Sleep not
when the voice of affection speaks!"

Sucht' ein Weiser nah und ferne, **Searched a wise man near and far,**	Once a wise man with a lantern searched far and near for friends. How much rarer than gold are people who are gracious and kind. So, when friendship or love speaks, friend, sweetheart, do not sleep!
Menschen einst mit der Laterne; **people once with the lantern.**	
Wie viel seltner dann als Gold **How much rarer then than gold**	
Menschen uns geneigt und hold. **people to us gracious and kind.**	
Drum, wenn Freundschaft, Liebe spricht, **So, when friendship, love speaks,**	
Freundin, Liebchen, schlaf du nicht! **friend, sweetheart, sleep you not!**	

Aber was in allen Reichen **But what in all empires**	But what in all the world would be comparable to sleep? So, instead of words and gifts, you shall now also have rest.
Wär' dem Schlummer zu vergleichen? **would to slumber to compare?**	
Drum, statt Worten und statt Gaben, **So, instead of words and instead of gifts,**	
Sollst du nun auch Ruhe haben. **shall you now also rest have.**	

Noch ein Grüßchen, noch ein Wort! **Again one little greeting, again one word!**	One more little greeting, one more word! The joyful melody becomes silent; quietly, quietly, again we steal away.
Es verstummt die frohe Weise; **it grows silent the joyful melody;**	
Leise, leise, **quietly, quietly,**	
Schleichen wir uns wieder fort. **sneak we — again away.**	

Source: Grillparzer 1952: 203

Variants: (Schubert = roman, Grillparzer = *italics*)
- Stanza 1, line 1:   leise = *stille*
- line 2:   Stille = *Hülle*
- line 4:   sanft = *leicht*
- Stanza 2, line 2:   schwellend, hebend = *hebend, schwellend*
- line 3:   mit vereinter Stimme, laut = *stark und stärker, lauter, laut*
- Stanza 4, original lines 3 and 4 omitted:
  - *Was du weißt und hast und bist, / Zahlt nicht was der Schlaf vergißt.*
  - (What you know and have and are / does not atone for what sleep forgets.)
- line 3:   Drum, statt Worten und statt gaben =
  - *Drum, statt aller Freundschaftsgaben.*
- Stanza 5, line 2:   verstummt die frohe Weise = *verstummet unsre Weise*

FRANZ Grillparzer (1791–1872), known to literary history primarily for his dramatic works and short novels, was an important figure in the artistic milieu of Vienna at the time of Schubert's residence there. The two were acquainted, and Schubert set three of Grillparzer's poems, two for chorus and one for solo voice. They both were among the torchbearers for Beethoven's funeral on March 29, 1827, and Grillparzer was the writer of an oration for the occasion.

"Ständchen," titled *Notturno* (Nocturne) in Grillparzer's collected poems, describes the furtive nighttime visit of a lover to his lady. In the first section he quietly approaches and attempts to wake her, in the second he muses on the joys of love and friendship, and in the final section he decides she needs her sleep more than his amorous advances.

The story of this poem and the composition of Schubert's setting is best told by Gerhard von Breuning, who claimed to have commissioned both:

> Whenever a name day or birthday approached for [Louise] Gosmar, later Mrs. L. Sonnleitner,[72] I would
> go to Grillparzer and request him to write something for the occasion. This I did once again as her birthday

---

[72]In the nine-year period from 1815 to 1824, many of Schubert's songs and ensemble vocal works were composed for and introduced at musical evenings held in the Vienna home of Grillparzer's uncle, Ignaz von Sonnleitner (also "Sonnleithner"). Sonnleitner, a physician, was the principal bass for the concerts of the Gesellschaft der Musikfreunde, of which his father Joseph was one of the founders (1812). Ignaz's son Leopold, a close friend of both Schubert and the Fröhlich sisters, was later to marry Louise Gosmar.

[July or beginning of August, 1827] neared. I said to him, "Dear Grillparzer, I cannot help you, but you really should write me a poem for Gosmar's birthday." He answered, "Well yes, if something comes to me." I countered, "Well, be sure that something comes to you." A few days later he gave me "Ständchen": "Leis klopf ich mit gekrümmten Finger. . . . " [Zögernd leise. . . .] And then when Schubert soon came over I said to him, "Dear Schubert, you must set this to music." He said, "well, let me have it." He put it on the piano and read it through repeatedly, crying out over and over, "This really is beautiful; it is beautiful!" He stared at the page for a while and finally said, "O.K., it is done; I have it." And sure enough, three days later he brought it to me completed, set for mezzo soprano (specifically, for Pepi) and for four male voices. I said to him, "No Schubert, I can't use it, as this is supposed to be a celebration for Gosmar's female friends. You have to make the chorus for women's voices." I know precisely how I said this to him, with him sitting there at the window. Soon he brought it to me, set for Pepi and women's voices, just as it is now.[73] (tr. ed.)

The alto soloist "Pepi" was Josefine Fröhlich, the sister of Grillparzer's fiancée of six years Kathi Fröhlich. The performance took place on August 11 (or possibly August 28), 1827 at the Gosmar house, where Beethoven happened to have resided in 1815. A piano was secretly moved into the garden under Miss Gosmar's window, where her friends delivered their serenade. The vision of a female ensemble serenading a girlfriend with a poem written from a male standpoint must have been a bit strange and certainly humorous. Schubert, who was to be present, did not witness the performance, however; not always the greatest model of responsibility, he forgot to show up. (Yates 1972: 15)

The poem as published in Grillparzer's collected poems differs from the version preserved in Schubert's composition, the latter omitting two lines and on several occasions substituting or reversing words. Whether Schubert modified Grillparzer's original or the poet later edited his earlier version is not known.

The special circumstances surrounding the composition of "Ständchen" explain the incongruity that the poem treats the serenader in the plural. In the version from the Grillparzer collected poems, this can be read as a formal expression of the singular. (As Queen Victoria supposedly was wont to say, "we are [i.e., I am] not amused.") Schubert's version, however, clearly refers to more than one person when he says in stanza 2, "Now increasing, swelling, rising, with *unified voice* ("vereinter Stimme"). If this was in fact the original version, it is understandable that Grillparzer would later omit the unambiguously plural reference, changing the line to read "strong and stronger, louder, loud."

The reference to the wise man with the lantern searching for friends hearkens back to classical Greece. The philosopher Diogenes of Sinope (d. c. 320 B.C.), known for his idiosyncratic protests against societal corruption, is supposed to have walked the streets of Athens with a lantern in the light of day, looking, always vainly, for an honest man. Grillparzer transforms this story into a search for friendship.

Unendliche Freude, D. 51, 54
Never-ending Joy
Friedrich Schiller

Unendliche   Freude
Never-ending joy

Durchwallet   das Herz.
rushes through the heart.

Hier   mangelt der Name dem trauernden Leide
Here is lacking the name of the mournful suffering,

Sanftes Entzücken nur   heißet man Schmerz.
gentle   delight merely calls one   pain.

Never-ending joy
rushes through my heart.
Here there is no word for mournful suffering,
mere gentle delight is what one calls "pain."

Source: Schiller 1960, 1: 103
Variant: (Schubert = roman, Schiller = *italic*)
Line 4:   man (one) = *hier* (here)

SCHUBERT'S text is from a six-stanza poem by Johann Friedrich Schiller (1759–1805) called "Elysium," written in 1782 and first published in 1800. Schiller's words paint a thoroughly romantic, secular picture of heaven, in which God appears to be conveniently absent—at least he is never mentioned—but the residents nonetheless enjoy eternal happiness. The first stanza sets the stage for the rest of the poem:

---

[73]Excerpt from "Aus Grillparzers Wohnung" (From Grillparzer's Home) by Gerhard von Breuning, 1884, in *Grillparzers Gespräche und die Charakteristiken seiner Persönlichkeit durch die Zeitgenossen*, ed. A. Sauer, Vienna, 1904–1941, 1: 19. Quoted in Grillparzer 1969–1970, 4: 926–927, tr. ed. Deutsch 1947: 657 cites Anna Fröhlich, the third Fröhlich sister and the music teacher of Louise Gosmar and her friends, as the commissioner of the poem. The editor of this work in the *Neue-Schubert-Ausgabe*, Dietrich Berke, says that Anna Fröhlich delivered her commission using Breuning as a middle man.

ELYSIUM
Eine Kantate [A Cantata]

Chor [Chorus]

Vorüber die stöhnende Klage!	Gone are the groaning laments!
Elysiums Freudengelage	Elysium's revels of joy
Ersaufen jegliches Ach—	drown every "alas."
Elysiums Leben	Elysium's life—
Ewige Wonne, ewiges Schweben,	Eternal bliss, eternal soaring—
Durch lachende Fluren ein flötender Bach.	Through laughing fields a sweetly piping stream. (tr. ed.)

Each successive stanza discusses a different aspect of the Elysian joys. The third, the one used by Schubert, makes one simple point in its four lines: The joys of heaven are so great that anything but utter bliss seems like pain.

In the first editions of Schiller's poems (1800 and 1803) these verses appear under the heading "cantata," and each stanza after the first is assigned to a different "voice" (stanza 2 = "first voice," stanza 3 = "second voice," etc.). These designations disappeared in the 1805 edition of his works. (Schiller 1960 1: 871)

Widerspruch, D. 865
Contradiction
Johann Gabriel Seidl

Wenn ich durch Busch und Zweig **When I through bush and branch**	When I break through bush and branch on a narrow trail,
Brech auf beschränktem Steig: **break on narrow trail,**	I become so boundless, so free, my heart wants to break in two.
Wird mir so weit, so frei, **becomes to me so wide, so free,**	
Will mir das Herz entzwei. **wants me the heart break in two.**	
Rings dann im Waldeshaus **Around then in the forest-house**	Then all around me the walls of the forest house push outward;
Rücken die Wänd' hinaus, **move the walls out;**	the leafy chamber arches high above, a roof of dizzying height.
Wölbt sich das Laubgemach **arch — the leaf room**	
Hoch mir zum Schwindeldach, **high for me into a dizziness-roof.**	
Webt sich der Blätter schier **Weaves itself of the leaves almost**	Nearly every leaf weaves itself into wings for me,
Jedes zur Schwinge mir, **each into wings for me,**	so that my boundless heart longs for infinity.
Daß sich mein Herz, so weit, **that — my heart so vast**	
Sehnt nach Unendlichkeit! **longs for infinity.**	
Doch wann im weiten Raum, **But when in the vast space**	But when I stand in the vast expanse at the rim of the mountain range,
Hoch am Gebirgessaum **high at the mountain range's edge**	high above the valley, when I look down to the valley,
Über dem Tal' ich steh', **above the valley I stand,**	
Nieder zum Tale seh', **down to the valley look,**	

Ach, wie beschränkt, wie eng
alas, how restricted, how confined

Wird mir's im Luftgedräng!
becomes to me it in the air-crowding;

Rings auf mein Haupt, so schwer,
around on my head, so heavy,

Nicken die Wolken her,
nod the clouds to me,

alas, how restricted, how confined
and crowded the air becomes;
the clouds around my head
nod so heavily toward me,

Niederzustürzen droht
to crash down threatens

Rngs mir das Abendrot,
around me the sunset,

Und in ein Kämmerlein
and into a little chamber

Sehnt sich mein Herz hinein!
longs — my heart —.

the sunset threatens
to crash down around me,
and my heart longs to withdraw
into a cozy little room.

Source: Seidl 1877, 1: 179

*J*OHANN Gabriel Seidl's "Widerspruch" (Contradiction) employs the imagery of nature to describe the poet's spiritual conflict: The freer he is, the more constrained he feels, and vice versa. Perhaps the underlying subject is love, as it often is in romantic poetry, or perhaps the poem was meant to be read in terms of a less specific spiritual conflict. The poet gives no hint, but the quandary is the same in either case.

As the poem begins the poet feels freedom and joy when hiking through the dense brush; the walls of the "forest house" arch outward in his mind, liberating his soul though his body is confined. Yet as he stands on a mountain crest, as free as one can be, anxiety enters his heart and he longs to be enclosed again.

This "contradiction" lies at the heart of much artistic creation. As expressed by Igor Stravinsky in his *Poetics of Music*:

> The creator's function is to sift through the elements he receives from her [the imagination], for human activity must impose limits upon itself. The more art is controlled, limited, worked over, the more it is free. . . .

> As for myself, I experience a sort of terror when at the moment of setting to work and finding myself before the infinitude of possibilities that present themselves, I have the feeling that everything is permissible to me. If everything is permissible to me, the best and the worst; if nothing offers me any resistance, then any effort is inconceivable . . . . I shall go even further: my freedom will be so much the greater and more meaningful the more narrowly I surround myself with obstacles. Whatever diminishes constraint, diminishes strength. The more constraints one imposes, the more one frees one's self of the chains that shackle the spirit. (Stravinsky 1970: 63–65)

Seidl (1804–1875), like Eichendorff, Goethe, and several other poets represented in this volume, made a career as a civil bureaucrat. He began his professional life as a schoolteacher but left that job at the age of thirty six to become what Deutsch describes as "custodian of the collection of coins and antiques in Vienna, and also a censor." (Deutsch 1947: 958) Schubert, unknowingly nearing the end of his life, and Seidl, just beginning his, likely made contact in 1826; thirteen of Schubert's fifteen compositions to Seidl's poems stem from that year, the others being from 1827 and 1828.

The poem as presented here and in Seidl 1877 is in three stanzas of four, eight, and twelve lines, respectively, which correspond to the three sections of the poem. Later editions divide the work into six stanzas of four lines, with stanzas 4 through 6 elided (i.e., no terminal punctuation after stanzas 4 and 5), distorting the original structure.

Seidl was one of the few nineteenth-century poets to attempt the creation of a literature in Low German, in his case the lower-Austrian dialect of the countryfolk in his homeland of Styria. A full volume of his complete works (Seidl 1877) consists of poetry in this dialect, a curious amalgam of German and Hungarian.

Clara Schumann

DREI GEMISCHTE CHÖRE

Three Mixed Choruses

*F*OR her trio of mixed choruses Clara Schumann (1819–1896) chose three poems by Emanuel Geibel (1815–1884), who was considered in her day to be a "poet of refinement and an apostle of beauty." (Garland 1976: 268) Unlike most romantic poets, for whom writing was an avocation beside their more pedestrian, everyday employment (Eichendorff and Goethe among them), Geibel could put all of his energies into literature, owing to a pension (an ongoing grant) that he received at age twenty seven from King Friedrich Wilhelm IV of Prussia. He spent much of his creative life in Munich, where he was considered a leader in the literary community.

Geibel was less comfortable confronting existential dilemmas in his poetry than he was in creating images of beauty and sensitivity. That tendency is clear in the present poems, which form a nicely balanced trio with two placid night poems flanking a vigorous appeal to strive "forward" throughout life.

The "celebration" in "Evening Celebration in Venice" does not refer to a secular festival, but rather to a Mass, apparently being celebrated outdoors under the colorful, darkening sky. In the first strophe the poet is taken with the atmosphere of the moment, in which the beauty of the coming night blends with the devotions to create an ethereal spiritual experience. The second strophe turns more introspective, but not seriously so. God's power and might are not the subject of the poet's thoughts, but rather the "soft trembling" that "penetrates every heart" through the beauty and joy of the moment.

"Vorwärts" provides a complete contrast. Geibel does not waste time in getting to his point: Strive in life, "untiringly press forward!" The second and third strophes comprise a warning not to let the grass grow under your feet. Good fortune is not a signal to become complacent, but rather to redouble your efforts in joy and a song of celebration for your good fortune, until God shines his "golden beam" upon you and calls you home. In the casket, with the funeral wreath about your head (see the footnote to Hindemith's "Tauche deine Furcht"), then may you rest. Geibel would have agreed with Pablo Casals, who according to legend was once asked why he worked so furiously at his advanced age. He is supposed to have said, "I have eternity to rest."

Schumann returns to the city of San Marco with "The Gondolier." The atmosphere is reminiscent of "Evening Celebration in Venice," but dusk has turned to night and God the Father fades from memory as the god of the stars ascends in the heavens. What is now being celebrated is love.

While Schumann's three songs certainly can be performed separately, the structure of this triptych, with its connections between the outer poems, and the contrasting lyric between them, suggests the virtue of performing them as a set.

1. Abendfeier in Venedig
Evening Celebration in Venice
Emanuel Geibel

Ave Maria!
Hail Mary!

Meer und Himmel ruhn,
Ocean and heaven rest,

Von allen Türmen hallt der Glockenton,
from all towers rings the bell tone,

Ave Maria! Laßt vom ird'schen Tun,
Hail Mary! Desist from worldly ways,

Zur Jungfrau betet, zu der Jungfrau Sohn!
to the Virgin pray, to the Virgin's son!

Des Himmels Scharen selber knieen nun
The heavens flocks themselves kneel now

Mit Lilienstäben vor des Vaters Thron,
with lily rods before the Father's throne,

Und durch die Rosenwolken wehn die Lieder
and through the rose-clouds waft the songs

Der sel'gen Geister feierlich hernieder.
of the blessed spirits solemnly down.

Ave Maria!
Ocean and heaven rest,
and from all the towers the bells ring,
"Ave Maria!" Desist from worldly ways,
pray to the Virgin, to the Virgin's son!
Now heaven's flocks kneel
with long-stemmed lilies before the Father's throne,
and through the rosy clouds the songs
of the blessed spirits waft solemnly down.

O heil'ge Andacht, welche jedes Herz
Oh holy devotion, which every heart

Mit leisen Schauern   wunderbar durchdringt!
with soft trembling wonderfully penetrates!

O sel'ger Glaube, der   sich himmelwärts
Oh blessed faith, which — heavenward

Auf des Gebetes weißem Fittig schwingt!
on the prayer's white wing swings!

In milde Tränen   löst   sich da der Schmerz,
In gentle tears dissolves — — the pain,

Indes der Freude Jubel   sanfter   klingt!
while   joy's   exultation more softly sounds!

Ave Maria! Erd' und Himmel scheinen
Hail Mary! Earth and heaven   appear

Bei diesem Laut sich liebend zu vereinen.
at   this   sound — lovingly to   unite.

O holy devotion, which penetrates every heart
so wonderfully with its soft trembling!
O blessed faith, which swings heavenward
on the white wing of prayer!
Pain dissolves in gentle tears,
while joy's exultation rings more softly.
Ave Maria! Earth and heaven appear
to unite lovingly at this sound.

Source: Geibel 1906, 1: 63
Variants: (Schumann = roman, Geibel = *italic*)
Stanza 1, line 2: Glockenton = *Glocketon*
Stanza 2, lines 7, 8: Erd' und Himmel scheinen / bei diesem Laut sich liebend zu vereinen
=*Wenn die Glocke tönet,/so lachen Erd' und Himmel mild versöhnet.*
(When the bell rings, / earth and heaven laugh, gently reconciled.)

2. Vorwärts

Forward

Emanuel Geibel

Laß das Träumen! laß das Zagen!
Stop the dreaming, stop the wavering!

Unermüdet wandre fort!
Unfatigued   press onward!

Will   die   Kraft   dir schier versagen,
Wants the strength you nearly   fail,

Vorwärts ist das rechte Wort.
forward is   the right word.

Stop the dreaming, stop the wavering!
Untiringly press onward!
When your strength seems about to fail,
"forward" is the right word.

Darfst   nicht weilen, wenn die Stunde
[You] may not   linger, when the hour

Rosen   dir   entgegen bringt,
roses to you   brings,

Wenn dir   aus des Meeres Grunde
when to you from the ocean's depths

Die Sirene   lockend   singt.
the siren enticingly sings.

You can't linger when life
brings you roses,
when, from the ocean's depths,
the siren sings enticingly to you.

Vorwärts! vorwärts! im Gesange
Forward, forward! In   song,

Ringe   mit dem Schmerz der   Welt,
struggle with the   pain of the world

Bis   auf deine heiße Wange
until upon your   hot   cheek

Goldner Strahl von   oben fällt;
golden beam from above falls,

Forward, forward! In song,
struggle with the pain of the world
until a golden beam
falls from above on your hot cheek,

231

Bis der Kranz, der dichtbelaubte,
until the wreath, the dense, leafy one,

Schattig deine Stirn umwebt,
shade your forehead weaves around,

Bis verklärend überm Haupte
until radiantly above the head

Dir des Geistes Flamme schwebt.
for you the spirit's flame hovers.

until the leafy wreath
weaves around your forehead,
until the spirit's flame
hovers radiantly above your head.

Vorwärts drum durch Feindes Zinnen,
Forward therefore through enemies' battlements,

Vorwärts durch des Todes Pein;
forward through death's pain;

Wer den Himmel will gewinnen,
who — heaven wants to gain,

Muß ein rechter Kämpfer sein.
must a real fighter be.

Forward, therefore, through the enemy's battlements,
forward through the pain of death!
The one who would gain heaven
must be a real warrior.

Source: Geibel 1893, 1: 113

3. Gondoliera
The Gondolier
Emanuel Geibel

O komm zu mir, wenn durch die Nacht
Oh come to me, when through the night

Wandelt das Sternenherr!
wanders the lord of the stars!

Dann schwebt mit uns in Mondespracht
then floats with us in moon-splendor

Die Gondel übers Meer.
the gondola over the sea.

Die Luft ist weich, wie Liebesscherz,
The air is gentle, like love's banter,

Sanft spielt der goldne Schein,
softly plays the golden light,

Die Zither klingt, und zieht dein Herz
the zither sounds, and pulls your heart

Mit in die Lust hinein.
along into — pleasure — .

Oh come to me when the lord of the stars
wanders through the night!
Then the gondola floats with us
over the sea, resplendent in the moonlight.
The air is gentle, like love's banter,
the golden light sparkles softly,
and the zither plays and draws your heart
along into the pleasure.

Das ist für Liebende die Stund',
That is for lovers the hour,

Liebchen, wie ich und du,
sweetheart, like me and you;

So friedlich blaut des Himmels Rund,
so peacefully becomes blue the sky's circle,

Es schläft das Meer in Ruh.
— is sleeping the sea in peace.

Und wie es schläft, da sagt der Blick,
And as it is sleeping, — says the eye

Was nie die Zunge spricht,
what never the tongue speaks;

Die Lippe zieht sich nicht zurück
the lip draws — not back

Und wehrt dem Kuße nicht.
and resists the kiss not.

That, sweetheart, is the hour
for lovers like you and me;
the encircling sky becomes so peacefully blue,
and the sea is calmly sleeping.
And, as it sleeps, the eye says
what is unspoken by the tongue;
the lip does not draw back
and does not resist the kiss.

Source: Geibel 1906, 1: 62

Georg Schumann

DREI MOTETTEN, op. 52
Three Motets

Komm, heil'ger Geist, op. 52, no. 1
Come, Holy Spirit

Martin Luther; Unknown

Komm, heil'ger Geist,
Come, Holy Spirit,

erfülle die Herzen deiner Gläubigen,
fill the hearts of your faithful.

entzünde in ihnen das Feuer
Kindle in them the fire

deiner göttlichen Liebe.
of your divine love.

Come, Holy Spirit,
fill the hearts of your faithful.
Kindle in them the fire
of your divine love.

Komm, heil'ger Geist,
Come, Holy Spirit,

erleuchte uns, daß wir
enlighten us, that we

erkennen all unsre Sünde
recognize all our sins

und dem Tod entrinnen.
and — death escape from.

Come, Holy Spirit,
enlighten us, that we
may recognize all our sins
and escape from death.

Komm, heil'ger Geist,
Come, Holy Spirit,

und stärke die Deinen,
and strengthen — yours,

schenke Frieden und Trost.
grant peace and comfort.

Come, Holy Spirit,
and strengthen your people;
grant them peace and comfort.

GEORG Alfred Schumann (1866–1952) was a German composer, organist, violinist, and choral conductor who conducted the Berlin Singakademie (Singing Academy) for fifty years and also served as president of the Berlin Akademie der Künste (Academy of the Arts).

The first half of Schumann's motet (mm. 1–22) sets the opening sentence of the Lutheran hymn *Komm, Heiliger Geist** (*EKG*: 124), which is Martin Luther's verbatim translation of *Veni Sancte Spiritus*, a medieval Antiphon for Pentecost. Presumably for musical reasons, Schumann made slight changes, expanding contracted words (*erfülle* and *entzünde*) and contracting the adjective *heiliger*. The remainder of the text echoes images from the Sequence *Veni Creator Spiritus* and the hymn *Veni Sancte Spiritus*, both of which also belong to the Feast of Pentecost. The editors were unable to locate a source for the second and third verses.

Schumann clearly saw interesting compositional possibilities in the word *komm*, as one can see from the serene, suspended atmosphere of the opening. He consequently repeated the word and its musical material at every opportunity, i.e., before every verb. The Holy Spirit is thus entreated to "come" and to "fill," "kindle," "enlighten," and "strengthen" his people. In addition, the composer added the appeal *komm* to the end of each of the two major sections of the motet, intensifying the request and creating a natural rounding of both the textual and musical structures. When one omits the repeats of the word *komm*, the text has a three-strophe structure, which is how it is presented here.

Das ist ein köstliches Ding, op. 52, no.2

It Is A Precious Thing

Psalm 92: 1–5

Das ist ein köstliches Ding, dem Herrn danken
It is a precious thing to the Lord to give thanks

und lobsingen deinem Namen, du Höchster,
and sing praises to your name, you high one;

des Morgens deine Gnade,
in the morning your grace;

des Abends deine Güte,
in the evening your goodness;

des Nachts deine Wahrheit verkündigen.
at night your truth to proclaim.

It is a precious thing to give thanks to the Lord
and sing praises to your name, O Most High;
to proclaim your grace in the morning;
in the evening, your goodness;
and, at night, your truth.

Denn, Herr, du lässest mich
For, Lord, you let me

fröhlich singen von deinen Werken,
joyfully sing of your works.

ich rühme die Geschäfte deiner Hände.
I praise the accomplishments of your hands;

Herr, wie groß sind deine Werke.
Lord, how great are your works!

For, Lord, you let me
sing joyfully of your works.
I praise your handiwork;
O Lord, how great are your works!

Der Gerechte wird grünen wie ein Palmenbaum,
The righteous will flourish like a palm tree;

er wird wachsen wie eine Zeder auf Libanon.
he will thrive like a cedar in Lebanon.

Und wenn sie gleich alt werden,
And when they alike old become,

werden sie dennoch blühen und grünen
will they still bloom and flourish

und verkündigen deine Güte.
and proclaim your goodness.

The righteous will flourish like a palm tree;
they will thrive like a cedar in Lebanon.
And when they become old like those trees,
they will still bloom and flourish
and proclaim your goodness.

Ich will singen dir, du treuer Gott.
I want to sing to you, you faithful God.

Das ist ein köstliches Ding dir danken mein Gott.
It is a precious thing you to thank, my God.

I want to sing to you, you faithful God.
It is a precious thing to thank you, my God.

Herr, erhöre meine Worte, op. 52, no. 3

Lord, Hear My Words

Psalm 5: 1, 2; 6: 2a, 3a, 4a, 7, 6a, 6b

Herr, erhöre meine Worte, **Lord, hear my words,**	Lord, hear my words, hear my supplication, and attend to what I say.
erhöre mein Flehn, **hear my supplication,**	
und merke auf meine Rede. **and notice my words.**	
Vernimm mein Schrein, **Hearken to my cry,**	Hearken to my cry, my King and my God; I want to pray before you.
mein König und mein Gott; **my king and my God;**	
ich will beten vor dir. **I want to pray before you.**	
Herr, sei gnädig und geduldig, **Lord, be merciful and patient,**	Lord, be merciful and patient, for I am miserable and weak.
denn ich bin elend und bin schwach; **for I am miserable and am weak.**	
Meine Seele ist erschrocken, **my soul is frightened;**	My soul is frightened;
wende dich und errette mich. **turn yourself and save me.**	turn to me and save me.
Meine Gestalt ist verfallen vor Trauern, **My body is weak from grieving;**	My body is weak from grieving; I have become old because I have become afraid everywhere.
ich bin alt geworden, **I have old become**	
da ich allenthalben geängstiget werde. **because I everywhere afraid become.**	
Ich bin so müde vom Seufzen **I am so tired of sighing**	I am so tired of sighing and at night I moisten my bed with tears.
und netze des Nachts mein Lager mit Thränen. **and moisten at night my bed with tears.**	
Höre mein Weinen, **Hear my weeping,**	Hear my weeping, hear my supplication, O Lord!
erhöre mein Flehn, ach, Herr! **hear my supplication, O Lord!**	

SELDOM in the entirety of choral literature and only twice in this volume will the reader find a Biblical text reinterpreted in such a personal fashion as this.[74] Composers such as Bach and Brahms often combined verses from various books of the Bible, but it is rare to see a single Biblical text that has been so shredded, personalized, and thereby romanticized as these verses from the Psalms.

Psalms 5 and 6 provided Schumann with the ideas he wanted, expressed for the most part as he wanted. The problems appear to have been that the Biblical material was not in the order the composer desired, and that it contained "extra" phrases that he did not want to set (see italics, left column). Schumann's solution was to reorder and rewrite his Bible verses, adding a phrase in one case (see italics, right column) and deleting several others. All in all, he cut some 30% of the Biblical text:

---

[74]See "Ach Herr, straf mich nicht in deinem Zorn"* by Max Reger.

Verses	*Die Bibel* (1885)	Verses	Schumann
5: 2a 5: 2b	Herr, höre meine Worte, merke auf meine Rede!	5: 2a 5: 2b	Herr, erhöre meine Worte, *erhöre mein Flehn,* und merke auf meine Rede.
5: 3	Vernimm mein Schreien, mein König und mein Gott; denn ich will vor dir beten.	5: 3	Vernimm mein Schrein, mein König und mein Gott; ich will beten vor dir.
6: 3a 6: 3b	Herr, sei mir gnädig, denn ich bin schwach; *heile mich, Herr,* *denn meine Gebeine sind erschrocken*	6: 3a 6: 3b	Herr, sei gnädig und geduldig, denn ich bin elend und bin schwach;
6: 4a 6: 4b	und meine Seele ist sehr geschrocken. *Ach du, Herr, wie lange!*	6: 4a	meine Seele ist erschrocken,
6: 5a 6: 5b	Wende dich, Herr, und errette meine Seele, *hilf mir um deiner Güte willen.*	6: 5a	wende dich und errette mich.
6: 7a 6: 7b 6: 7c	Ich bin so müde vom Seufzen; *ich schwemme mein Bette* die ganze Nacht, und netze mit meinen Tränen mein Lager.	6: 8	Meine Gestalt ist verfallen vor Trauern, ich bin alt geworden, da ich allenthaben geängstiget werde.
6: 8	Meine Gestalt ist verfallen vor Trauern, Und ist alt geworden, denn ich allenthaben geängstiget werde.	6: 7a 6: 7c	Ich bin so müde vom Seufzen und netze des Nachts mein Lager mit Tränen.
6: 9a 6: 9b	*Weichet von mir, alle Übeltäter;* denn der Herr hört mein Weinen,	6: 9b	Höre mein Weinen,
6: 10a 6: 10b	Der Herr höret mein Flehen; *mein Gebet nimmt der Herr an.*	6: 10a 6: 4b	erhöre mein Flehn, ach, Herr!

The adaptation begins with the second word, *erhöre*, a verb form the editors were unable to find in any of the Luther Bibles consulted. One can only speculate about why Schumann did what he did, but the results suggest some explanations. For example, the addition of *erhöre mein Flehn* to verse 5: 2 may have been intended to create parallelism with the last three lines of the motet. The three omissions that follow, from verses 3–5, serve to condense the text into a single sentence, which begins and ends with an appeal to God and in the middle explains why the Lord's help is needed. Schumann reversed the order of verses 6 and 7, probably so that the litany of woes would be stated as a unit, and its consequence—thrashing in bed through the night—would come at the end. Finally, the cuts from verses 9 and 10, aided by the additional and romantic *ach Herr!* at the end (possibly derived from the *Ach Herr* Schumann deleted from verse 6: 4b), serve to make the appeal of the last three lines parallel to that of the first three lines, providing a rounding of the text and its message.

Robert Schumann

Am Bodensee, op. 59, no. 2

On Lake Constance

Hallermunde August, Graf von Platen

I

Schwelle die Segel, günstiger Wind!
Swell the sails, favorable wind!

Trage mein Schiff an das Ufer der Ferne;
Carry my ship to the shore of the distant land;

Scheiden muß ich, so scheid' ich gerne.
depart must I, so depart I gladly.

Schwelle die Segel, günstiger Wind!
Swell the sails, favorable wind!

Schwelle die Segel, günstiger Wind!
Swell the sails, favorable wind!

Daß ich den Boden, den heimischen, schaue,
that I the ground, the native, behold.

Fahre du wohl, Helvetiens Aue.
fare you well, Switzerland's meadow.

Schwelle die Segel, günstiger Wind!
Swell the sails, favorable wind!

Schwelle die Segel, günstiger Wind!
Swell the sails, favorable wind!

Wenn ich auch hier im Entzücken verweile,
Even if I — here in delight linger,

Drüben knüpfen mich liebende Seile.
over there bind me loving ropes.

Schwelle die Segel, günstiger Wind!
Swell the sails, favorable wind!

Swell the sails, favorable wind!
Carry my ship to the distant shore;
I must depart, so I depart gladly.
Swell the sails, favorable wind!

Swell the sails, favorable wind,
so that I may behold my native soil.
Farewell, Swiss meadows.
Swell the sails, favorable wind!

Swell the sails, favorable wind!
Even if I linger here in delight,
over there loving ties bind me.
Swell the sails, favorable wind!

II

Wiederkehrend nach dem Vaterlande
Returning to the fatherland,

Hofft ich deine Lilienhand zu drücken,
hoped I your lily-white hand to clasp.

Trautre Bande
More intimate bonds

Würden uns, so hofft' ich, dann beglücken,
would us, so hoped I, then bless,

Wiederkehrend nach dem Vaterlande!
returning to the fatherland!

Wehe mir, du bist vorangegangen
–Oh woe– you have gone ahead

Nach viel bess'rem Vaterlande, wehe mir!
to much better fatherland, –Oh woe–!

Welch Verlangen,
What desire,

Daß auch ich bald meinen Nachen steure
that also I soon my boat steer

Nach viel bess'rem Vaterland, O Teure!
to much better fatherland, O beloved!

Returning to the fatherland,
I hoped to hold your lily-white hand.
Then more intimate bonds would bless us—
so I hoped, returning to the fatherland!

Oh woe! You have gone on ahead
to a much better fatherland. Oh woe!
Such is my desire
that soon I will also steer my boat
to a better fatherland, O beloved!

Source: Platen 1969, 5: 174, 115
Variant: (Schumann = roman, Platen = *italic*)
Stanza 5, line 2: Vaterlande, wehe mir! (fatherland, oh woe) =
Vaterland, o Teure! (fatherland, O beloved!)

*K*ARL August Georg Maximilian, Graf von Platen-Hallermünde—Platen for short—was a man of modest means despite his title. At age eighteen he entered the army, an occupation for which he was poorly suited. Although he enlisted during a war, he was blessed with a comfortable, non-combatant posting in Munich. That job left generous time for travel and poetry, including the composition of the poems Schumann chose for his composition.

A poem entitled "Am Bodensee" provided stanzas 1–3 of Schumann's text; another, untitled poem supplied stanzas 4 and 5. The latter, "Wiederkehrend. . . ," was the earlier of the two, written on August 17, 1815. A year later, on August 2, 1816, Platen wrote *his* "Am Bodensee" ("Schwelle die Segel . . . .") while spending time on Lake Constance (= Bodensee), between Germany and Switzerland.

Schumann's combination of the poems elevates both of them. The first three stanzas paint a carefree picture with both the words and the sing-song poetic meter. The picture darkens with the fourth stanza's "return to the Fatherland," which the listener gradually realizes to be a metaphor for death.

Der Schmied, op. 145, no. 1
The Blacksmith
Ludwig Uhland

Ich hör' meinen Schatz,
I hear my sweetheart,

den Hammer er schwinget;
the hammer he swings;

das rauschet, das klinget,
that thunders, that rings,

das dringt in die Weite
that pierces in the distance

wie Glockengeläute
like bell ringing

durch Gassen und Platz.
through streets and squares.

Am schwarzen Kamin,
At the black furnace

da stehet mein Lieber,
there stands my loved one;

doch, geh' ich vorüber,
but go I past,

die Bälge dann sausen,
the bellows then roar;

die Flamme aufbrausen
the flames flare up

und lodern um ihn.
and blaze around him.

I hear my sweetheart
swinging his hammer;
it thunders, it rings,
and pierces through the air
like a bell ringing
through streets and square.

At the black furnace
my loved one stands;
but if I walk by,
the bellows roar;
flames flare up
and blaze around him.

Source: Uhland 1892: 27
Variant: (Schumann = roman, Uhland = *italic*)
Stanza 2, line 2: stehet (stands) = *sitzet* (sits)

*L*UDWIG Uhland's poem is similar in character to those chosen by Johannes Brahms for his *Liebeslieder* Waltzes opp. 52 and 65: simple, to the point, and filled with passion. The scene is a blacksmith's shop; a girl passes by her love as he toils at the fire and anvil, and her heart is enflamed by the sight of his strength and masculinity. In his choice of words, particularly in the first strophe, Uhland (1787–1862) underlines the image he creates with the sounds of his words; the verbs in particular—*schwinget, rauschet, klinget*, and *dringt*—are nicely onomatopoetic. In the second strophe one gets the impression that the blacksmith's world is a male realm that a woman may never enter—"the flames flare up and blaze around him" when she comes near. Perhaps this draws her heart even closer.

Die Rose stand im Tau, op. 65, no. 5
The Rose Stood in the Dew
Friedrich Rückert

Die Rose stand im Tau,
The rose stood in the dew,

Es waren Perlen grau.
they were pearls gray.

Als Sonne sie beschienen,
As the sun them shone on,

Wurden sie zu Rubinen.
became they — rubies.

The rose stood in the dew,
covered with gray pearls.
As the sun shone on them,
they became rubies.

Source: Rückert 1897: 48

OF all the poems in this volume, "Die Rose stand im Tau" is perhaps the simplest. Friedrich Rückert (1787–1862) was capable of poetry of depth and intensity, but here his goal is simply the creation of a beautiful image. The picture is of the dawn and the transformation of the dewy roses in the first light. As the day's earliest ray strikes the dewdrops, they appear transformed into rubies. The imagery may be clearer when one understands that German for "dawn" is "Morgenrot"—morning red. Thus the word itself in German conveys a picture in color that does not survive translation into English.

Gute Nacht, op. 59, no. 4
Good Night
Friedrich Rückert

Die gute Nacht, die ich dir sage,
The good night that I to you say,

Freund, hörest du;
friend, hear you.

Ein Engel, der die Botschaft trage,
An angel, who the message may carry,

Geht ab und zu.
goes now and then.

Er bringt sie dir, und hat mir wieder
He brings it to you, and has to me again

Den Gruß gebracht:
the greeting brought;

Dir sagen auch des Freundes Lieder
to you say also the friend's songs,

Jetzt gute Nacht!
now good night!

You hear the "good night"
that I say to you, my friend.
An angel who may carry the message
leaves now and then.

He brings it to you, and again he has brought
your greeting back to me.
Your friend's songs also say to you,
"now good night!"

Source: Rückert 1979, 2: 186
Variant: (Schumann = roman, Rückert = *italic*)
Stanza 2, line 4: jetzt = *nun*

RÜCKERT'S "Gute Nacht" (originally untitled) is almost a lullaby. The words are spoken or thought by one who imagines that his gentle thoughts of "good night" are carried to his friend by an angel, who serves as a tender and willing messenger. The image of the angel is peaceful and almost whimsical, and the reader perhaps expects that the poem will unfold as love song. Perhaps it is, but the masculine gender of the word *Freund* (friend) means that the recipient of the angel's message is a man, while its sender could be of either gender. While there is tenderness in the words, they avoid any direct expression of love.

VIER DOPPELCHÖRIGE GESÄNGE, op. 141
Four Double-Choir Songs

*W*HY Schumann chose the texts he did for opus 141 is uncertain, but it is known why he composed these settings. In December, 1847 he had organized a choir in Dresden under the name *Verein für Chorgesang* (Society for Choral Song) that grew quickly in membership to sixty or seventy singers. Schumann wrote to his friend Ferdinand Hiller in April of 1849 that "My *Verein* is a source of much joy, for I can try out, to my great delight, all the music I love."[75] Among the music that he "tried out" were many of his own compositions that probably would not have come into being otherwise, including the present works for double choir.

An die Sterne, op. 141, no. 1
To the Stars
Friedrich Rückert

Sterne,
Stars,

In des Himmels Ferne!
in the sky's distance,

Die mit Strahlen beßrer Welt
which with rays of a better world

Ihr die Erdendämmrung hellt;
for her the earth's dusk brighten,

Schaun nicht Geisteraugen
look — spirit's eyes

Von euch erdenwärts,
from you earthward,

Daß sie Frieden hauchen
so that they peace breathe

Ins umwölkte Herz!
into the clouded heart?

Sterne,
Stars,

In des Himmels Ferne!
in the sky's distance,

Träumt sich auch in jenem Raum
dreams — also in that space

Eines Lebens flücht'ger Traum?
a life's fleeting dream?

Hebt Entzücken, Wonne,
lift delight, bliss,

Trauer, Wehmut, Schmerz,
sorrow, sadness, pain,

Jenseit unsrer Sonne
beyond our sun

Auch ein fühlend Herz!
also a feeling heart?

Sterne,
Stars,

In des Himmels Ferne!
in the sky's distance,

Stars
in the distant sky,
you who brighten earth's twilight
with rays from a better world,
do you gaze earthward
with your spirit's eyes
so that they might breathe peace
into the clouded heart?

Stars
in the distant sky,
is life's fleeting dream
also dreamed where you are?
Can a sensitive heart
elevate its delight, bliss,
sorrow, sadness, and pain
beyond our sun?

Stars
in the distant sky,

---

[75]Schumann *Briefe*, Neue Folge: 302, quoted in Daverio 1997: 398.

240

Winkt ihr nicht schon   Himmelsruh'
signal you not already heavenly peace

Mir   aus euren Fernen zu?
to me from your distance — ?

Wird nicht einst dem Müden
Will   not once for the weary

Auf den goldnen   Aun
in   the golden pastures

Ungetrübter Frieden
unclouded   peace

In   die Seele taun!
into the soul   melt?

are you not already showing me signs
of heavenly peace from your distant places?
Won't untroubled peace
some day melt
into the weary soul
in paradise?

Sterne,
Stars,

In des Himmels   Ferne!
in the   sky's   distance!

Bis   mein Geist den Fittig hebt,
Until my spirit the wing lifts

Und zu eurem Frieden schwebt,
and to your   peace   soars,

Hang' an euch mein Sehnen,
hangs on you my longing,

Hoffend, glaubevoll!
hoping,   full of faith!

O ihr holden, schönen,
Oh you lovely, beautiful—

Könnt ihr täuschen wohl?
could you deceive, maybe?

Stars
in the distant sky!
Until my spirit takes wing
and soars up to your peace,
my longing clings to you,
hoping, and full of faith!
O you lovely, beautiful ones—
could you perhaps be deceiving me?

Source: Rückert 1979, 7: 92

*R*ÜCKERT'S stars are symbols of peace, of a "better world" (stanza 1) for which the poet dreams. The first three stanzas gently contrast that peace with earthly emotions and cares, and the poet wonders whether they will melt away in the distant paradise. In the final stanza he declares that he will hold fast to his faith in the better world the stars seem to promise, but at the last moment he wonders whether it is all just deception.

Ungewisses Licht, op. 141, no. 2
Uncertain Light
Johann Christian, Freiherr von Zedlitz

Bahnlos und pfadlos, Felsen hinan
Pathless and trail-less, cliffs   up

Stürmet der Mensch, ein Wandersmann:
storms the mortal, a   wanderer;

Stürzende Bäche, wogender Fluß,
plunging brooks, surging   river,

Brausender Wald,   nichts hemmet den Fuß!
stormy   woods, nothing stops the foot!

Without a path or trail, up the cliffs
storms the mortal, the wanderer;
plunging brooks, a surging river,
stormy woods—nothing breaks the stride!

Dunkel im   Kampfe über ihn hin,
Dark   in the struggle over him —,

Jagend   im   Heere die Wolken zieh'n;
chasing in an army the clouds move;

Rollender Donner, strömender   Guß;
rolling   thunder, streaming downpour,

Sternlose Nacht— nichts hemmet den Fuß!
starless night— nothing stops the foot!

Dark clouds billow in battle above,
pursuing the wanderer like an army;
rolling thunder, a streaming downpour,
a starless night—nothing breaks the stride!

Endlich, ha! endlich schimmert's von fern!
At last, ha! at last glitters it from afar!

Ist es ein Irrlicht, ist es ein Stern?
Is it a will-o'-the-wisp, is it a star?

Ha, wie der Schimmer so freundlich blinkt,
Ha, how the glimmer so friendly twinkles,

Wie er mich locket, wie er mir winkt!
how it me entices, how it me signals!

Rascher durcheilet der Wandrer die Nacht,
Faster hurries through the wanderer the night,

Hin nach dem Lichte zieht's ihn mit Macht!
toward to the light draws it him with force!

Sprecht wie, sind's Flammen, ist's Morgenrot?
Speak how, is it flames, is it sunrise?

Ist es die Liebe— ist es der Tod?
Is it — love— is it — death?

At last, ha, at last it glitters from afar!
Is it a will-o'-the-wisp, is it a star?
Ha, how friendly is its twinkle,
how it entices me, how it beckons!

Even faster the wanderer hurries through the night,
drawn forcefully toward the light!
Tell me: is it fire, is it the sunrise?
Is it love—is it death?

Source: Zedlitz 1879: 244

*T*HE tranquility of "An die Sterne" is shattered by the "Uncertain Light" of Zedlitz (1790–1862), in which the mortal fearlessly traverses mountains, rivers, and stormy woods in search of we know not what. Schumann's disjointed melodies underline the roughness and danger of the journey, which is of course a symbol for a spiritual quest. (Compare "Gesang der Geister"* by Schubert, with text by Goethe.) A distant glimmer of beckoning light is seen for the first time in stanza three. We still cannot make out what it is but are drawn inexorably toward it, wondering if it is the light of love—or of death. The last-minute twist of this poem resembles that of "An die Sterne" and raises the question whether this might have been a factor in Schumann's decision to pair them together.

Zuversicht, op. 141, no. 3
Assurance
Johann Christian, Freiherr von Zedlitz

Nach oben mußt Du blicken,
Upward must you look,

Gedrücktes, wundes Herz,
oppressed, wounded heart;

Dann wandelt in Entzücken
then changes to delight

Sich bald dein tiefster Schmerz.
— soon your deepest pain.

"Froh darfst Du Hoffnung fassen,
"Gladly may you hope seize,

Wie hoch die Flut auch treibt;
how high the flood ever rises;

Wie wärst Du denn verlassen,
how would you after all be forsaken,

Wenn dir die Liebe bleibt?"
if for you — love remains?"

You must look upward,
oppressed, wounded heart;
then your deepest pain
will soon change to delight.

"You may gladly cling to hope
no matter how high the flood rises.
How can you be forsaken
if love still remains?"

Source: Zedlitz 1879: 246

*T*HE questions asked in the first two pieces receive an answer of sorts in Zedlitz's "Assurance," which tells man that peace is found in faith, hope, and love. It is interesting that the question/answer structure and the message of Brahms's motet "Warum ist das Licht gegeben" (Why Is Light Given to Those in Misery), op. 74, are the same, but in a secular context in Schumann and a Christian context in Brahms.

The poet's title for this poem was "Der Blick gen Himmel" (The Gaze toward Heaven). Zedlitz's original was seven stanzas long, from which Schumann borrowed stanzas 6 and 7.

Talismane, op. 141, no. 4
Talismans
Johann Wolfgang von Goethe

Gottes ist der Orient!
God's is the orient!

Gottes ist der Okzident!
God's is the occident!

Nord- und südliches Gelände
Northern and southern terrain

Ruht im Frieden seiner Hände.
rests in the peace of his hands.

Er, der einzige Gerechte,
He, the only just one,

Will für jedermann das Rechte.
wants for everyone the right thing.

Sei, von seinen hundert Namen,
Be of his hundred names,

Dieser hochgelobet! Amen.
this one highly praised! Amen.

Mich verwirren will des Irren;
Me to confuse wants the erring,

Doch du weißt mich zu entwirren.
but you know me to disentangle.

Wenn ich handle, wenn ich dichte,
When I act, when I write,

Gib du meinem Weg die Richte.
give you my way — direction.

Gottes ist der Orient!
God's is the orient!

Gottes ist der Okzident!
God's is the occident!

Amen.
Amen.

The East is God's!
The West is God's!
Northern and southern lands
rest in the peace of his hands.

He who alone is just
wants what is right for everyone.
Of his hundred names,
may this one be highly praised! Amen.

Error tries to confuse me,
but you know how to extricate me.
When I act, when I write,
give my path direction.

The East is God's!
The West is God's!
Amen.

Source: Goethe 1948–, 3: 290

*T*HE final piece in this opus is a succinctly joyous celebration of God's power and grace, and a prayer for his guidance. It also has an interesting textual history. The poet, Johann Wolfgang von Goethe (1749–1832), was always interested in pithy, proverb-like poems, especially in his later years. He was particularly fascinated by examples from Islamic culture, in which proverbs are an integral part of both poetic art and everyday speech. Records of his library loans show that he checked out numerous books of middle-eastern poetry and literature, and it is known that he turned to such sources again and again for inspiration. (Mommsen 1988: 595)

In 1814 Goethe read a German translation of works by the Persian poet Hafiz (also "Hafis," 1320–1389). Hafiz is remembered in the history of literature for his often melancholic poems of distant and unrequited love called *ghazals*, which before him existed in two, parallel but different styles: the earthly or secular, and the mystical.

> In the 14th c. the two streams of the *ghazal* began to merge, a movement which culminated in the poetry of Hafiz of Shiraz (d. 1389–90). Using language in a way unparalleled in the Persian tradition, Hafiz extended and combined the imagery of secular and mystical poetry and created *ghazals* with multiple levels of meaning, all simultaneously present and inseparable. Read wherever Persian culture was influential, Hafiz's *ghazals* made a profound impression in Europe . . . . (Preminger and Brogan 1993: 898)

The elegance, succinctness, and subtlety of the Hafiz poems strongly affected Goethe and moved him to write his own poems in free emulation of the Hafiz style. He assembled them into twelve "books," each of which received both Persian and German titles. Ultimately the collection as a whole was entitled *West-östliche Divan*, or "West-East Anthology of Oriental Poetry."[76] Hafiz was not Goethe's only inspiration: At the time he

---

[76]The term *Divan* (*Diwan* in Germanic sources) denotes a collection of "oriental" poetry, or a "council" or "a parliament." A number of English-language secondary sources and translations choose the second meaning of the term rather than the first in the present context. For example, Christoph Middleton (Goethe 1983) translates the title in question as "The Parliament of West and East."

was smitten by Marianne von Willemer, a young married woman who is known to have been the subject of many of the poems. Several verses by von Willemer herself are included in the collection.

Goethe wrote that he intended to "strew talismans throughout the book" (Mommsen 1988: 595, 597) and indeed he did; it is filled with poems that convey "truths," prayers, and words of comfort and divine praise in the most concise fashion. Goethe explicitly labels one set of five poems in the first of the twelve *Divan* books (*Moganni Nameh*, the "Book of the Singer"), *Talismane*, or "Talismans," and it was from these five poems that Schumann derived the text for this composition. The opening poem is Goethe's adaptation of the Koran, Sure (chapter) 2: 142b: "The East and West belong only to Allah. He guides whom he likes to the right path." The second poem praises God (in this case Allah of "a hundred names") for his justice, and the third prays for guidance in times of trouble and confusion.

Schumann personalized Goethe's poems through repetition and his combination of three independent poems into one. After presenting the first two verses he repeated the opening two lines ("The East is God's! The West is God's"), which he followed with the third poem. He then rounded off the composition with a repeat of the entire opening poem and concluded with an "amen." Schumann's concept of his "motet"—and that is what it most closely resembles, with its quasi-religious tone and final, elaborate "amen"—eliminated the last two of Goethe's five "talismans," which are perhaps the most interesting:

Ob ich irdisches denk und sinne,	Were I to think and speculate about earthly things,
Das gereicht zu höherem Gewinne.	It would contribute to a greater good.
Mit dem Staube nicht der Geist zerstoben,	The spirit is not scattered with the dust;
Dringet, in sich selbst gedrängt, nach oben	freed from its material existence, it surges upward.
Im Atemholen sind zweierlei Gnaden:	There are two graces in breathing:
Die Luft entziehn, sich ihrer entladen;	inhaling the air and exhaling it.
Jenes bedrängt, dieses erfrischt;	The former constrains; the latter refreshes.
So wunderbar ist das Leben gemischt.	Life is mixed just as wonderfully.
Du danke Gott, wenn er dich preßt,	Thank God when he puts pressure on you
Und dank ihm, wenn er dich wieder entläßt.	and thank him when he lets you go. (tr. ed.)

Zigeunerleben, op.29, no. 3
Gypsy Life
Emanuel Geibel

Im Schatten des Waldes, im Buchengezweig,
In the shadows of the forest, in the beech branches,

da regt's sich und raschelt und flüstert zugleich;
there stirs it — and rustles and whispers together.

Es flackern die Flammen, es gaukelt der Schein
— flares the flames, — flutters the light

um bunte Gestalten, um Laub und Gestein.
around many-colored figures, around leaves and rocks.

In the forest shadows, among the beech branches,
something stirs and rustles and whispers.
The flames flare and the light flutters around
the colorful figures and leaves and rocks.

Da ist der Zigeuner bewegliche Schaar,
There is the Gypsy wandering band

mit blitzendem Aug' und mit wallendem Haar,
with lightning-like eyes and with wild, flowing hair,

gesäugt an des Niles geheiligter Flut,
nursed at the Nile's sacred flow,

gebräunt von Hispaniens südlicher Glut.
burned from Spain's southern warmth.

It is the wandering gypsy band
with lightning-like eyes and wild, flowing hair,
nursed at the Nile's sacred stream,
burned by Spain's southern warmth.

Um's lodernde Feuer, in schwellendem Grün,
Around the blazing fire, in swelling greenery,

da lagern die Männer verwildert und kühn,
there lie the men wild and bold;

da kauern die Weiber und rüsten das Mahl,
there crouch the women and prepare the meal,

und füllen geschäftig den alten Pokal.
and fill busily the old goblet.

Around the blazing fire, in the swelling grass,
lie the men, wild and bold;
the women crouch and prepare the meal,
and busily fill the old goblet.

Und Sagen und Lieder ertönen im Rund,
And legends and songs resound in the circle,

wie Spaniens Gärten so blühend und bunt,
of Spanish gardens so florid and colorful,

und magische Sprüche für Not und Gefahr
and magic sayings for need and danger

verkündet die Alte der horchenden Schaar.
proclaims the old woman to the attentive band.

Legends and songs are heard around the circle,
as florid and colorful as the gardens of Spain,
and magic sayings to ward off misery and danger
are told by the old woman to the attentive band.

Schwarzäugige Mädchen beginnen den Tanz;
Black-eyed maidens begin the dance.

Da sprühen die Fackeln im rötlichen Glanz,
There spark the torches in the reddish glow.

Es lockt die Gitarre, die Cymbal klingt,
— beckons the guitar, the cymbal rings,

Wie wild und wilder der Reigen sich schlingt.
As wild and wilder the round dance itself weaves.

Black-eyed maidens begin the dance.
The torches sparkle in the red glow.
The guitar beckons, the cymbal rings,
as the dance becomes wild and wilder.

Dann ruhen sie ermüdet vom nächtlichen Reih'n;
Then rest they weary from the nocturnal dance,

Es rauschen die Buchen im Schlummer sie ein,
— rustle the beech trees, in sleep they are

Und die aus der glücklichen Heimat verbannt,
And they from the happy homeland banned,

sie schauen im Traume das glückliche Land.
they see in a dream the happy land.

Then they rest, weary from the nocturnal dance,
lulled to sleep by the beech trees' rustling,
and, banished from their homeland,
they see this happy land in their dreams.

Doch wie nun im Osten der Morgen erwacht,
But as now in the east the morning awakes,

verlöschen die schönen Gebilde der Nacht;
vanish the beautiful images of the night,

es scharret das Maultier bei Tagesbeginn,
— paws the mule with day's beginning,

fort ziehn die Gestalten. Wer sagt dir wohin?
away draw the figures— who says to you whither?

But now in the east, as the morning awakes,
the beautiful images of the night vanish;
the mule paws the ground as the day begins,
and the figures steal away—who can say whither?

Source: Geibel 1906, 1: 4
Variants: (Schumann = roman, Geibel = *italics*)

Stanza 1,	line 2:	regt's sich und raschelt = *regt sich's und raschelts*
Stanza 2,	line 1:	da = *das*
Stanza 3,	line 1:	schwellendem = *schwellenden*
Stanza 5,	line 3:	es lockt = *heiß lockt*
	line 4:	wie wild = *wilder*
Stanza 6,	line 1:	ruhen = *ruhn*
	line 2:	Buchen = *Wipfel*
	line 3:	glücklichen (happy) = *sonnigen* (sunny)
	line 4:	glückliche (happy) = *gesegnete* (blessed)

GERMAN romantic poets and composers were attracted to the exotic, and few things triggered their imaginations more than the enigmatic Gypsies. (See the annotation to Brahms's *Zigeunerlieder*.*) A largely nomadic people, the Gypsies roamed eastern Europe, particularly Hungary, inspiring legends with their strange language and customs. But their mystique arose mostly from their apartness from the rest of society, which spurned them at it same time it exalted them in romantic fascination.

The "Zigeunerleben" of Emanuel Geibel (1815–1884) describes a night in a Gypsy camp. The Gypsy band, "nursed at the Nile's sacred stream and burned by Spain's southern warmth," gathers for dinner, stirred in its pot by an old hag (perhaps a witch?), after which they join in drink, dance, song, and love. The reverie goes deep into the night, but at dawn they set out again, mysteriously as always, for places unknown.

Geibel created an atmosphere of mystery by his choice of viewpoint and words. To begin with, the night setting in the dark forest is "apart" from normal experience, as the Gypsies are a people apart. And one must wonder whether the "stirring," "rustling," and "whispering" of stanza 1 is the Gypsies or the observers making noise as they spy in fascination from the bushes. In the last stanza Geibel refers to the *Gestalten* or "forms" of the Gypsies stealing away, *Gestalt* being a word also used in conjunction with supernatural apparitions.

Each of the six stanzas of the poem has an individual character that must have appealed to Schumann, as he followed the poet's lead in differentiating them strongly. Throughout the poem Geibel was particularly helpful to the composer in his choice of onomatopoetic words, such as *raschelt* and *flüstert* in stanza 2, which depict the rustling and whispering.

The number of changes Schumann made to the poem—nine in all—is surprising. Several (da/*daß*, es lockt/*heiß lockt*, Buchen/*Wipfel*) were probably matters of personal preference in sound. Others served musical purposes, such as the rewording in stanza 1, which is easier to articulate than Geibel's original, and the change of *wilder* to *wie wild* in stanza 5, which gave Schumann an anacrusis that he needed at the beginning of the line. The change from *ruhn* to *ruhen* in stanza 6 seems inexplicable, as it destroys the parallelism of meter with the following line while adding nothing. It is especially strange when one considers that Schumann altered the last line of the same stanza to create the same parallelism he destroyed in line 1.

"Zigeunerleben" was one of the first pieces Schumann composed following his marriage to Clara Wieck on September 12, 1840. It was published with two solo songs as op. 29, a fact that has caused it often to be included awkwardly in bibliographies under "songs," as in *The New Grove*. All that it has in common with its fellows in op. 29 is that its text is by Geibel.

Heinrich Schütz

Ach Herr, du Schöpfer aller Ding, SWV 450
O Lord, Creator of All Things
Martin Luther

Ach Herr, du Schöpfer aller Ding, **O Lord, you creator of all things,**	O Lord, creator of all things, how did you become so tiny that you lie there on the hard grass that the cow and donkey eat?
Wie bist du worden so gering **how did you become so small**	
Daß du da liegst auf dürrem Gras, **that you there lie on hard grass**	
Davon ein Rind und Esel aß. **of which a cow and donkey ate?**	

Source: Luther 1967: 44

SCHÜTZ chose verse 9 of the Christmas hymn "Vom himmel hoch"* by Martin Luther (1483–1546) as the text for this brief yet amazing motet. Like the text of Tomas Luis de Victoria's "O magnum mysterium," Schütz's text concentrates on only one, narrow aspect of the Christmas story, the humble of circumstances of God's incarnation as man. Like that motet as well, but more obviously, Schütz uses his music to connect the birth with the Passion, the event without which the incarnation is meaningless to Christians.[77] The composition contains a nearly continuous string of suspensions that creates a sense of mystery and reminds the Christian again and again, through their dissonance, of the pain and redemptive death for which the little child in the manger was destined.

---

[77]References to the Passion in Christmas music are not rare and make sense in Christian theology. "O magnum mysterium" would have been sung on January 1, the Feast of the Circumcision. This feast and the Passion are the two observances of the shedding of Christ's blood, a fact that may also have occasioned musical references to the Passion. The middle section of "O magnum mysterium" begins with a bright, D-major evocation of the Virgin Mary. Almost immediately, however, the harmonies revert to minor, and the somber, upper-neighbor motive with which Victoria had begun the motet returns. Here the composer refers again to the Passion: in his motet for Maundy Thursday entitled "Vere languores" (from the same 1572 publication), he used precisely the same music for the words *sustinere regem*; "Gentle cross and gentle nails that bore so sweet a burden; you alone were *worthy of bearing* the King of Heaven and the Lord." The two ideas are theologically complementary: The Virgin's womb alone *was worthy to bear* the Christ child, and the cross alone *was worthy to bear* the King of Heaven. (Adapted from Paine 1989: 55, 61)

Also hat Gott die Welt geliebt, SWV 380
For God so Loved the World
John 3: 16

Also hat Gott die Welt geliebt,
So did God the world love

daß er seinen eingebornen Sohn gab,
that he his only-begotten son gave,

auf daß alle, die an ihn glauben,
so that all who in him believe

nicht verloren werden,
not lost become,

sondern das ewige Leben haben.
but — eternal life have.

For God so loved the world
that he gave his only-begotten son,
so that all who believe in him
would not be forsaken,
but would have everlasting life.

Der Herr ist mein Hirt, SWV 33
The Lord Is My Shepherd
Psalm 23

Der Herr ist mein Hirt;
The Lord is my shepherd;

mir wird nichts mangeln.
to me will be nothing wanting.

Er weidet mich auf einer grünen Aue
He grazes me on a green meadow

und führet mich zum frischen Wasser.
and leads me to fresh water.

The Lord is my shepherd;
I will want for nothing.
He feeds me on a green pasture
and leads me to fresh water.

Er erquicket meine Seele;
He refreshes my soul;

er führet mich auf rechter Straße
he leads me on right path

um seines Namens willen.
for his name's sake.

He refreshes my soul;
he leads me on the proper path
for his name's sake.

Und ob ich schon wandert
And though I already wandered

im finsteren Tal des Todes,
in the dark valley of death,

fürcht ich kein Unglück;
fear I no misfortune,

denn du bist bei mir,
for you are with me;

dein Stecken und Stab trösten mich.
your rod and staff comfort me.

And although I wander
through the dark valley of death,
I fear no misfortune,
for you are with me;
your rod and staff comfort me.

Du bereitest vor mir einen Tisch
You prepare before me a table

gegen meine Feinde.
across from my foes;

Du salbest mein Haupt mit öle
You anoint my head with oils

und schenkest mir voll ein.
and pour me full —.

You prepare a table before me
in the presence of my foes;
you anoint my head with oils
and fill my cup.

Gutes und Barmherzigkeit werden mir folgen
Goodness and mercy will me follow

mein Leben lang, und werde bleiben
my life long, and [I] will remain

im Haus des Herren immerdar.
in the house of the Lord forever.

Goodness and mercy will follow me
all my life, and I will remain
in the house of the Lord forever.

Deutsches Magnificat, SWV 494

German Magnificat

Luke 1: 46–49, 51–55, doxology

Meine Seele erhebt den Herren,
My   soul exalts the   Lord,

und mein Geist   freuet   sich Gottes
and my spirit rejoices — in God

meines Heilandes;
my   savior.

denn er hat die Niedrigkeit
For he has the lowliness

seiner   Magd   angesehen.
of his handmaiden regarded.

Siehe,   von nun an
Behold, from now on

werden mich seligpreisen alle Kindeskind.
will   me blessed call   all generations.

My soul magnifies the Lord,
and my spirit rejoices in God
my savior.
For he has regarded the lowliness
of his handmaiden.
Behold, from henceforth
all generations will call me blessed.

Denn er hat große Ding an mir getan,
For   he has great things to me done,

der da   mächtig ist
who that mighty is

und   des Name heilig ist.
and whose name holy is.

Er   übet Gewalt mit seinem Arm
He shows power with his   arm

und zerstreuet die hoffärtig sind
and   scatters who arrogant are

in ihres Herzens   Sinn.
in their hearts' imagination.

Er   stößet die Gewaltigen vom Stuhl
He thrusts the mighty   from the seat

und erhöhet die Niedrigen.
and exalts the   lowly.

For he has done great things to me,
he who is mighty
and whose name is holy.
He shows power with his arm
and scatters those with arrogance
in their hearts.
He thrusts the mighty from their thrones
and exalts the lowly.

Die Hungerigen füllet er mit   Gütern
The hungry   fills he with good things

und lässet die Reichen leer.
and lets go the rich   empty.

Er   denket   der Barmherzigkeit
He remembers the   mercy

und hilft seinem Diener Israel auf,
and helps his   servant Israel —,

wie er geredt hat unseren Vätern,
as he spoken has to our   fathers,

Abraham und seinem Samen ewiglich.
Abraham, and his   seed eternally.

The hungry he fills with good things
and the rich he sends away empty.
He remembers his mercy
and helps his servant Israel,
as he spoke to our fathers,
to Abraham, and to his seed forever.

Ehre sei dem Vater und dem Sohn
Glory be to the Father and to the Son

und auch dem Heiligen Geiste,
and also to the Holy   Spirit,

wie es war im   Anfang, jetzt und immerdar
as it was in the beginning, now, and evermore,

und von Ewigkeit zu Ewigkeit. Amen.
and from eternity to eternity. Amen.

Glory be to the Father and to the Son
and also to the Holy Spirit,
as it was in the beginning, is now and evermore,
world without end. Amen.

GABRIEL the Archangel appeared to the Virgin Mary in Luke 1: 26–38 to reveal that she had been selected to bear the Messiah and that her aged kinswoman Elizabeth would also bear a child. Following this annunciation scene, Mary went to visit Elizabeth (verses 39–45), who greeted her with the words, "blessed are you among women, and blessed is the fruit of your womb" (the Roman Catholic *Ave Maria*). Mary's eloquent response in verses 46–55 constitutes what is known as the "Canticle of the Blessed Virgin Mary," or the *Magnificat*, after its opening word in Latin. Mary "sings praise to God her savior (verses 46–50), recalls the mercies shown to Israel (verses 51–53), and sings of the Incarnation's fulfillment of God's ancient promise to Abraham (verses 54–55)." (Jeffers 1988: 155) In the Roman Catholic Church the *Magnificat* was the climax of the daily Office of Vespers and was also an important text in other Marian contexts.

Schütz set the German *Magnificat* text three times; the present composition is not only the last of them, but the last work in his final collection, the so-called *Schwanengesang* (Swan Song). The text follows that of the Luther Bible but for the curious omission of verse 50:

Und seine Barmherzigkeit währet immer
für und für bei denen, die ihn fürchten.

And his mercy is on those who fear
him from generation to generation.

Schütz's German "Magnificat" (SWV 426) from the *Zwölf geistliche Gesänge* (1657) uses the complete *Magnificat* text, but the setting from the *Symphoniae sacrae II* (SWV 344, 1647) omits verse 49. Hans Joachim Moser rejects the theory that Schütz had doctrinal problems with verses 49 and 50 and suggests that the omissions were "for structural reasons." (Moser 1959: 552–553) Readers familiar with the King James and Revised Standard versions of the *Magnificat* will note that Luther's translation retained the present tense for many clauses that appear in the past tense in the English Bibles.

Ehre sei dir, Christe
(from St. Matthew Passion, SWV 479)
Glory Be to You, Christ
Author unknown

Ehre sei dir, Christe,
Glory be to you, Christ,

der du littest Not
who you suffered pain

an dem Stamm des Kreuzes,
on the stem of the cross

für uns den bittern Tod,
for us — bitter death

und herrschest mit dem Vater
and rule with the Father

dort in Ewigkeit:
there in eternity.

hilf uns armen Sündern
Help us poor sinners

zu der Seligkeit.
to — salvation.

Kyrie eleison,
Lord, have mercy,

Christe eleison,
Christ, have mercy,

Kyrie eleison.
Lord, have mercy.

Glory be to you, Christ,
you who suffered pain
on the stem of the cross,
who suffered bitter death for us
and reign with the Father
there in eternity.
Help us poor sinners
attain salvation.

Kyrie eleison,
Christe eleison,
Kyrie eleison.

HEINRICH Schütz (1585–1672) wrote his three settings of the Passion in his old age, beginning with the St. Luke at about age 68 (c. 1653) and concluding with the St. John and St. Matthew at age 81 (1666). Each begins with an introductory chorus and closes with another chorus that summarizes the message of the Passion. "Ehre sei dir, Christe" fulfills the latter function in the *St. Matthew Passion*.

Schütz chose as his text the seventh verse of a chorale entitled "O wir armen Sünder" (O We Poor Sinners), a hymn by a Luther student from Osnabrück named Hermann Bonn or Bonnus (1504–1548). Based on pre-existing material probably in Latin, Bonn's six-verse chorale first appeared in print in 1542. The seventh verse, published without attribution in 1560, is an extended trope of the words *Laus tibi, Christe* (Glory to you, O Christ), which are sung in the Roman Church as a response following the reading of the Gospel.

Schütz would have been hard pressed to find a more suitable closing for his Passion, or one that offered more musical possibilities. Contrasting images follow one another line by line (glory, pain, bitter death, reign, poor sinners, salvation), suggesting the different musical treatments that Schütz exploited. The prayer for mercy (*Kyrie eleison*) with which the text closes is a feature of each verse of the hymn.

"O wir armen Sünder" appears as a Passion hymn in *EKG*: 57, where the present verse is identical to the version set by Schütz. It was translated into English in 1567–1568 and then again in 1860 as "'Twas Our Great Transgression."

Ein Kind ist uns geboren, SWV 384
A Child Is Born to Us
Isaiah 9: 6, 7

Ein Kind ist uns geboren,
A child is to us born.

ein Sohn ist uns gegeben,
A son is to us given

welches Herrschaft ist auf seiner Schulter;
whose government is on his shoulder;

und er heisst: Wunderbar, Rat, Kraft,
and he is called Wonderful, Counselor, Mighty,

Held, Ewig Vater, Friedefürst.
Hero, Eternal Father, Peace-Prince.

Auf daß seine Herrschaft groß werde,
So that his reign great becomes

und des Friedes kein Ende,
and of peace no end

auf dem Stuhle David,
on the seat of David

und seinem Königreiche;
and his kingdom;

daß ers zurichte und stärke
that he it [might] prepare and strengthen

mit Gericht und Gerechtigkeit
with judgment and justice.

von nun an bis in Ewigkeit.
from now on until eternity.

Solches wird tun der Eifer
Such will do the zeal

des Herren Zebaoth.
of the Lord Sabaoth.

A child is born to us.
A son is given to us
whose government is on his shoulder;
and he is called "Wonderful, Counselor, Mighty, Hero, Eternal Father, Prince of Peace."

So that his reign might become great
and his peace unending,
on the throne of David,
and upon his kingdom;
so that he might prepare and strengthen it
with judgment and justice
from henceforth until eternity.
Such will the zeal
of the Lord of Hosts accomplish.

Herr, nun lässest du deinen Diener, SWV 281
(Canticum Simeonis)
Lord, Now Let Your Servant
(The Song of Simeon)

Chorus 1 (aattb)
Luke 2: 29–32

Herr, nun lässest du deinen Diener
Lord, now let you your servant

in Friede fahren, wie du gesagt hast.
in peace depart, as you said have.

Denn meine Augen haben deinen Heiland gesehen,
For my eyes have your savior seen

welchen du bereitet hast für allen Völkern,
whom you prepared have for all peoples,

ein Licht, zu erleuchten die Heiden,
a light to enlighten the heathen

und zum Preis deines Volks Israel.
and as the glory of your people Israel.

Lord, now let your servant
depart in peace, as you have spoken.
For my eyes have seen your savior
whom you have prepared for all peoples,
a light to enlighten the Gentiles
and the glory of your people Israel.

Chorus 2 (ssb)
Revelation 14: 13; Wisdom of Solomon 3: 1

Selig   sind die Toten,
Blessed are the dead,

die in dem Herren sterben,
who in the Lord   die;

sie ruhen von ihrer Arbeit,
they rest from their toil,

und ihre Werke folgen ihnen nach.
and their works follow them after.

Sie sind in der Hand des   Herren,
They are in the hand of the   Lord,

und keine Qual rühret sie.
and no torment touches them.

"Blessed are the dead
who die in the Lord;
they rest from their labor,
and their works follow after them."

They are in the hands of the Lord,
and no torment touches them.

SCHÜTZ used these two Biblical excerpts for the closing movement of his *Musikalische Exequien* of 1636, written for the funeral of Prince Heinrich Posthumus of Reuss (d. 1635), who chose the words himself in preparation for his death. The chorus is assigned the Song of Simeon from Luke, the words of an old man whose life was fulfilled by seeing the Christ-child before his death. (See the annotation to Luther's hymn "Mit Fried und Freud ich fahr dahin" for further discussion.) The words from Revelation, familiar from the closing movement to the Brahms *Requiem*, are given to three soloists representing the seraphim, who call blessings upon the dead from the heavens. Schütz distinguishes these singers from the rest of the ensemble and underlines their "heavenly" role by having them sing in a high register and by removing the support of the five viols given to the main ensemble. He would also have wanted the two ensembles distinctly separated.

Herr, wenn ich nur dich habe, SWV 280
Lord, if I Have Only You
Psalm 73: 25, 26

Herr, wenn ich nur dich habe,
Lord, if I only you have,

so frage ich nichts nach Himmel und Erden.
then ask I nothing of   heaven and earth.

Wenn   mir gleich Leib und Seele verschmacht,
Although to me   — body and soul   languish,

so bist du doch, Gott,
so are you —   God,

allezeit meines Herzens   Trost   und mein Teil.
always my   heart's consolation and my portion.

Lord, if I have only you,
then I desire nothing of heaven and earth.
Although my body and soul languish,
you, O God, are always
my heart's consolation and my portion.

Ich weiß, daß mein Erlöser lebt, SWV 393
I Know that My Redeemer Lives
Job 19: 25–27

Ich weiß daß mein Erlöser lebt;
I   know that my redeemer lives,

und er wird mich hernach
and he will me hereafter

aus der Erden   auferwecken,
from the earth raise from the dead,

und werde mit dieser meiner Haut umgeben werden,
and will with this   my   skin clothed become,

und werde in meinem Fleisch Gott sehen.
and will in   my   flesh God see.

Denselben werde ich mir   sehen,
The same   will I myself   see,

und meine Augen werden ihn schauen,
and my   eyes will   him behold,

und kein Fremder.
and no stranger.

I know that my redeemer lives,
and that hereafter he will
raise me from the dead,
and I will become clothed with my skin,
and in my flesh I will see God.
The same will I see for myself;
my eyes will behold him,
and not through the eyes of a stranger.

Jauchzet dem Herren, SWV 36
Shout to the Lord
Psalm 100, doxology

Jauchzet dem Herren alle Welt!
Shout for joy to the Lord all world!

Dienet dem Herrn mit Freuden;
Serve the Lord with gladness;

kommt vor dein Angesicht mit Frohlocken!
come before his presence with rejoicing!

Erkennet, daß der Herre Gott ist.
Know that the Lord God is.

Er hat uns gemacht— und nicht wir selbst—
He has us made, and not we ourselves,

zu seinem Volk und zu Schafen seiner Weide.
to his people and to sheep of his pasture.

Gehet zu seinen Toren ein mit Danken,
Go in to his gates — with thanksgiving

zu seinen Vorhörfen mit Loben;
to his courts with praise.

danket ihm, lobet seinen Namen!
Give thanks to him; praise his name!

Denn der Herr ist freundlich,
For the Lord is kind,

und seine Gnade währet ewig
and his mercy lasts eternally,

und seine Wahrheit für und für.
and his truth –for ever and ever–.

Ehre sei dem Vater und dem Sohn
Glory be to the Father and to the Son

und auch dem heilgen Geiste
and also to the Holy Spirit

wie es war im Anfang, jetzt und immerdar
as it was in the beginning, now and always,

und von Ewigkeit zu Ewigkeit. Amen.
and from eternity to eternity. Amen.

Shout for joy to the Lord, all the earth!
Serve the Lord with gladness;
come before his presence with rejoicing!
Know that the Lord is God.
He has made us, and not we ourselves,
to be his people and the sheep of his pasture.
Enter into his gates with thanksgiving
and into his courts with praise.
Give thanks to him; praise his name!
For the Lord is kind,
and his mercy is everlasting,
and his truth endures for ever and ever.

Glory be to the Father and to the Son
and also to the Holy Spirit
as it was in the beginning, is now and always,
world without end. Amen.

Selig sind die Toten, SWV 391
Blessed are the Dead
Revelation 14: 13

Selig sind die Toten,
Blessed are the dead,

die in dem Herren sterben
who in the Lord die

von nun an.
from now on.

Ja, der Geist spricht:
Yes, the Spirit speaks:

sie ruhen von ihrer Arbeit,
they rest from their toil,

und ihre Werke folgen ihnen nach.
and their works follow them after.

"Blessed are the dead
who die in the Lord
from now on."
Yea, the Spirit speaks:
"they rest from their labor,
and their works follow after them."

Vater unser, SWV 411
Our Father (The Lord's Prayer)
Matthew 6: 9–13

Vater unser, der du bist im Himmel,
Father our, who you are in heaven,

geheiliget werde dein Name,
hallowed become your name;

zukomm dein Reich.
come to your kingdom.

Dein Will gescheh, wie im Himmel,
Your will be done, as in heaven,

also auch auf Erden.
so also on earth.

Unser täglich Brot gib uns heute,
Our daily bread give us today;

vergib uns unser Schulde,
forgive us our offenses

als wir vergeben unsern Schuldigern,
as we forgive our offenders.

führe uns nicht in Versuchung,
Lead us not into temptation,

sondern erlöse uns von dem Übel!
but deliver us from — evil.

Denn dein ist das Reich, und die Kraft,
For yours is the kingdom, and the power,

und die Herrlichkeit in Ewigkeit. Amen.
and the glory in eternity. Amen.

Our Father, you who are in heaven,
may your name become hallowed;
may your kingdom come.
Your will be done, as in heaven,
so also here on earth.
Give us today our daily bread;
forgive our offenses
as we forgive those who offend us.
Lead us not into temptation,
but deliver us from evil.
For yours is the kingdom, and the power,
and the glory for all eternity. Amen.

U NLIKE Luther's well-known trope on the Lord's Prayer, "Vater unser im Himmelreich,"* the present text is an accurate rendering of the Biblical prayer. It nonetheless differs substantially from the Luther Bibles consulted by the editors.

Wie lieblich sind deine Wohnungen, SWV 29
How Lovely Are Your Dwellings
Psalm 84

Wie lieblich sind deine Wohnungen, Herre Zebaoth!
How lovely are your dwellings, Lord Sabaoth!

Mein Seel verlanget und sehnet sich
My soul desires and longs —

nach den Vorhöfen des Herren;
for the courts of the Lord;

mein Leib und Seele freuet sich
my body and soul rejoice —

in dem lebendigen Gott.
in the living God.

Denn der Vogel hat ein Haus funden
For the bird has a house found

und die Schwalbe ihr Nest,
and the swallow her nest

daß sie Junge hecken:
that they young ones hatch:

nämlich deine Altar, Herre Zebaoth,
namely your altars, Lord Sabaoth,

mein König und mein Gott.
my king and my God.

How lovely are your dwellings, O Lord of Hosts!
My soul desires and longs for
the courts of the Lord;
my body and soul rejoice
in the living God.

For the bird has found a house
and the swallow her nest
where she may raise her young:
namely your altars, O Lord of Hosts,
my king and my God.

Wohl   denen, die in deinem Hause wohnen;
Well-being to those, who in your house dwell;

die   loben dich immerdar. Sela.
they praise you forever. Selah.

Wohl   den Menschen,
Well-being to the   people,

die dich für ihre Stärke halten
who you as their strength consider

und von Herzen dir nachwandeln,
and from heart you follow after,

die durch das Jammertal gehen
who through the vale of tears go

und graben daselbst Brunnen.
and dig   there   wells.

Blessed are those who dwell in your house;
they praise you forever. Selah.
Blessed are the people
who deem you to be their strength
and follow after you from their hearts,
who pass through the vale of tears
and dig wells there.

Und die Lehrer   werden mit viel Segen geschmücket.
And the teachers will be with many blessings adorned.

Sie   erhalten einen Sieg nach dem andern,
They receive one victory after the other,

daß man sehen muß,
that one see must,

der rechte Gott sei zu Zion.
the true God be in Zion.

Herr Gott Zebaoth, höre mein Gebet;
Lord God Sabaoth, hear my prayer;

vernimms, Gott Jakobs! Sela.
hearken,   God of Jacob! Selah.

And the teachers will be adorned with many blessin[g]
They receive one triumph after another,
so that one must see
that the true God dwells in Zion!
Lord God of Hosts, hear my prayer;
hearken, O God of Jacob! Selah.

Gott, unser Schild, schau doch;
God, our shield, behold —,

siehe an das Reich   deines   Gesalbten!
look at the kingdom of your anointed one!

Denn ein Tag in deinen Vorhöfen
For one day in your   courts

ist besser denn sonst   tausend.
is better than elsewhere a thousand.

Ich will   lieber der Tür hüten
I want to rather the door guard

in meines Gottes Hause
in my   God's house

denn lange wohnen in der Gottlosen Hütten.
than long dwell in the godless's tents.

Behold, O God our shield,
look on the kingdom of your annointed one!
For one day in your courts
is better than a thousand elsewhere.
I would rather guard the door
in my God's house
than dwell for long in the tents of the ungodly.

Denn Gott der Herr ist Sonn und Schild;
For   God the Lord is sun and shield;

Der Herr gibt Gnad und Ehre;
the Lord gives grace and glory.

er wird kein Gutes mangeln lassen den Frommen.
He will nothing good   lack   let to the pious.

Herr Zebaoth,   wohl   dem Menschen,
Lord Sabaoth, well-being to the   one

der sich auf dich verlässt!
who — in you trusts!

For God the Lord is sun and shield;
the Lord gives grace and glory.
He will withhold nothing good from the pious.
O Lord of Hosts, blessed are those
who trust in you!

Richard Strauss

Deutsche Motette, op. 62

German Motet

Friedrich Rückert

Die Schöpfung ist zur Ruh' gegangen, O wach in mir!
— **creation has to rest gone, O wake in me!**

Es will der Schlaf auch mich umfangen, O wach in mir!
— **wants — sleep also me to embrace, O wake in me!**

Du Auge, das am Himmel wachet mit Sternenblick,
You eye, which in the heavens watches with star gaze,

Wenn mir die Augen zugegangen, O wach in mir!
when –my– eyes have closed, O wake in me!

Du Licht, im äther höher strahlend als Sonn' und Mond;
You light, in the ether higher shining than sun and moon,

Wenn Sonn' und Mond ist aufgegangen, O wach in mir!
When sun and moon have risen, O wake in me!

Wenn sich der Sinne Tor geschlossen der Außenwelt,
When — the sense's door closed to the outer world,

So laß die Seel' in sich nicht bangen, O wach in mir!
So let the soul — — not fear, O wake in me!

Laß nicht die Macht der Finsternisse, das Grau'n der Nacht
Let not the power of darkness, the horror of the night,

Sieg übers innre Licht erlangen, O wach in mir!
victory over the inner light gain, O wake in me!

O laß im feuchten Hauch der Nächte, im Schattenduft
O let in the moist breath of the nights in the shadow-aroma

Nicht sprossen sündiges Verlangen, O wach in mir!
not sprout sinful desire, O wake in me!

Laß aus dem Duft von Edens zweigen in meinem Traum
Let from the fragrance of Eden's branches in my dream

Die Frucht des Lebens niederhängen, O wach in mir!
th fruit of life hang down, O wake in me!

O zeige mir, mich zu erquicken, im Traum das Werk
Oh show me, myself to refreshen, in the dream the work

Vollendet, das ich angefangen, O wach in mir!
completed, that I began, O wake in me!

In deinem Schoße will ich schlummern, bis neu mich weckt
In your womb want I to slumber, until newly me awakens

Die Morgenröte deiner Wangen; O wach in mir!
the morning-redness of your cheeks; O wake in me!

All creation has gone to rest: O wake in me!
Sleep also wants to embrace me: O wake in me!

You eye, in the heavens watching with starry gaze, when my eyes have closed: O wake in me!

You light in the ether, shining brighter than sun or moon, when the sun and moon have risen: O wake in me!

When the gates of the senses have closed to the outer world, let my soul be not afraid: O wake in me!

Let not the power of darkness, the horror of the night, gain victory over the inner light: O wake in me!

O let sinful desire not grow in the moist breath of night, in the fragrance of the shadows. In my dream, out of the fragrance, let the fruit of life hang down from Eden's branches: O wake in me!

In my dream, to refresh me, show me the work completed that I once began: O wake in me!

I want to sleep in your womb until the blush of your cheeks newly awakens me—O wake in me!

Source: Rückert 1897, 1: 322
Variants: (Strauss = roman, Rückert = *italics*)
line 2: umfangen = *befangen*
line 6: aufgegangen = *ausgegangen*
line 16: vollendet = *geendet*

*T*HROUGHOUT history, the line between sacred and secular has evaded anyone who has tried to draw it. The Song of Solomon, for example, is earthy love poetry, yet it is also sacred scripture. In our modern, "secular" age we would recoil at selling chickens and beer in churches, yet such "secular" use of "sacred" buildings was common until recent centuries.

Like much romantic poetry, Friedrich Rückert's "German Motet" straddles the terrain between sacred and secular—between a prayer to the Divine and a sensuous, romantic "night poem." On one hand, it has the appearance of a liturgical litany, with its repeated plea, "O wake in me." On the other hand, in a litany one would expect the plea to be "O Lord . . . ," and in the Rückert poem it is never clear who is being addressed or what "wake in me" actually means. And while the petitions of the text are often similar to those of a prayer (e.g., freedom from fear and temptation), the lush sensuality of the imagery (e.g., "fragrance of the shadows," "blush of your cheeks") is more reminiscent of a romantic love poem.

The poet's word and phrase order also blur his meaning. The order of elements in a German sentence is considerably more flexible than in English, but in this poem Rückert's sentence structure sometimes forces even the German reader to wonder about its meaning:

Laß	Let
aus dem Duft	out of the fragrance
von Edens zweigen	of Eden's branches
in meinem Traum	in my dream
die Frucht des Lebens niederhängen.	the fruit of life hang down.

Any of several arrangements of these five lines yields a grammatically plausible sentence in both languages. Our choice for English would be:

> In my dream,
> out of the fragrance,
> let
> the fruit of life hang down
> from Eden's branches.

Even if the grammar is clarified, the meaning is not. Rückert may well have taken delight in such ambiguity, but it did not serve Strauss well. He set Rückert's words to music in 1913, on the eve of the First World War. A lifelong political naïf, he apparently did not realize that his text could be taken as a hymn to nascent German nationalism, which it was by many. Two decades later his music was to be embraced and then shunned by the Nazis, clouding with political strife the last years of an artist who wanted from life only the unfettered opportunity to compose.

DREI MÄNNERCHÖRE, o op. A.V. 123
Three Male Choruses

RÜCKERT'S trio of poems in this opus forms a set with sharply differing emotional colors, from the dejection of no. 1 to the light-hearted dance of no. 3. Strauss begins with "Vor den Türen," a poem of suicidal depression, in which Rückert's continually unanswered door symbolizes the failures of life. The image is most effective, emphasizing the passivity of the speaker. Wealth, honor, and love evaded him; work provided no joy, and he never found contentment. All that remains is to knock on the door of death, where peace is guaranteed.

The tranquillity of "Traumlicht" could hardly provide a greater contrast to the dejection of "Vor den Türen." As in that poem, the speaker yearns to close his eyes, but for a different reason: When he does he dreams of his love (or of God?), the dream symbolized here by the star, the light. The night and sleep are thus blissful experiences, as are the daydreams in which the light comes as well. Nonetheless, the poet gives no hint of who comes in the light, leaving the reader to ponder its meaning.

"Fröhlich im Maien" is a gay May dance at which the old sit to the side watching, admiring, and envying their children and grandchildren, who now dance as they themselves once did. But the May dance is also the dance of courtship, and the elders advise the boys in the last stanza to pair off before the best girls are taken and their chance is lost. Rückert even made the words themselves dance with his choice of a poetic meter that invites a musical setting in triple meter.

Strauss's choral music is almost never heard in concert, perhaps owing to its difficulty and to the fact that it is simply unknown. Michael Kennedy's article on Richard Strauss in *The New Grove* says of his choral music that "If only a comparatively small percentage of Strauss's 200 or more songs is well known, the plight or his choral works is worse." (Kennedy 1980: 233) Having said this he then provides two column inches on the choral music and a full page on the songs.

Vor den Türen, o op. A.V. 123, no. 1
At the Doors
Friedrich Rückert

Ich habe geklopft an des Reichtums Haus;
I have knocked on — wealth's house;

Man reicht mir 'nen Pfennig zum Fenster heraus.
someone handed me a penny through window —.

Ich habe geklopft an der Liebe Tür;
I have knocked on — love's door;

Da standen schon fünfzehn andre dafür.
there stood already fifteen other in front.

Ich klopfte leis' an der Ehre Schloß;
I knocked softly on — honor's castle;

Hier tut man nur auf dem Ritter zu Roß.
here opens one only — for the knight on horseback.

Ich habe gesucht der Arbeit Dach;
I have sought — labor's roof;

Da hört' ich drinnen nur Weh und Ach!
there heard I inside only woe and grief!

Ich suchte das Haus der Zufriedenheit;
I sought the house of contentment;

Es kannt' es niemand weit und breit.
— knew it no one far and wide.

Nun weiß ich noch ein Häuslein still,
Now know I -another- little house quiet,

Wo ich zuletzt anklopfen will.
where I at last knock want to.

Zwar wohnt darin schon mancher Gast,
True, lives in it already some guests,

Doch ist für viele im Grab noch Rast.
yet is for many in the grave still rest.

Source: Rückert 1897, 1: 225

I knocked on the house of wealth;
someone handed me a penny through the window.
I knocked on love's door;
fifteen others were already standing there.
I knocked softly on the castle of honor;
here one opens only for a knight on horseback.
I have sought the shelter of labor;
inside I heard only woe and grief.
I sought the house of contentment;
no one knew it far and wide.
Now I know another quiet, little house
where I want to knock one last time.
True, some guests live in it already,
but there is still rest for many in the grave.

Traumlicht, o op. A.V. 123, no. 2
Dream Light
Friedrich Rückert

Ein Licht im Traum hat mich besucht,
A light in the dream has me visited;

Es nahte kaum und nahm die Flucht.
It came near barely and took — flight.

Der Blick ist tief hier eingesenkt,
The glance is deeply here sunk in,

Den, als ich schlief, du mir geschenkt.
which, while I slept, you me gave.

Hell dämmert mild am Tage wach,
Brightly dawns mildly during the day awake,

O Nachtgebild', dein Glanz mir nach.
O night image, your glimmer -upon me-.

Komm oft, o Stern, in meiner Ruh'!
Come often, O star, in my rest!

Dir schließ' ich gern die Augen zu.
For you close I gladly the eyes —.

Hell dämmert mild ein Licht
Brightly dawns mildly a light

Im Traum am Tage mir nach.
in the dream during the day -upon me-.

Komm oft, o Stern, in meiner Ruh'!
Come often, O star, in my rest!

Dir schließ' ich gern die Augen zu.
For you close I gladly the eyes —.

Source: Rückert 1979, 3: 128

A light visited me in my dream;
it hardly came near, and then took flight.
The glance you bestowed on me
while I slept has penetrated deeply.
O image of the night, your glimmer
shines brightly on me during the day.
Come often, O star, during my rest!
For you I gladly close my eyes.
A bright and gentle light flickers
in my dream during the day.
Come often, O star, during my rest!
For you I gladly close my eyes.

Fröhlich im Maien, o op. A.V. 123, no. 3
Gaily in May
Friedrich Rückert

Blühende Frauen,
Blossoming ladies,

lasset euch schauen
let yourselves be seen

fröhlich im Tanze
gaily in the dance

unter dem Kranze!
under the wreath!

Tanzet *zu zweien*
Dance two by two

unter Schalmeien,
under shawms,

tanzet am Reihen
dance in a roundelay,

fröhlich im Maien!
gaily in May!

Prüfende Kenner
Scrutinizing connoisseurs!

kommet, ihr Männer,
Come, you men,

sehet die klaren
see the bright

Bilder sich paaren,
figures — form pairs.

Refrain

Freuet euch, ihr Alten,
Rejoice — , you old ones,

junger Gestalten!
young figures!

Wie ihr gesprungen,
As you did jump,

springen die Jungen!
jump the young!

Refrain

Junge und schöne
Young and beautiful

Töchter und Söhne,
daughters and sons,

Enkel nicht minder
grandchildren no less

reizend als Kinder.
delightful than children.

Refrain

Junges Gelichter,
Young ones,

ihr seid nicht Richter;
you are not judges;

Jünglinge, wählet,
lads, choose,

eh' es euch fehlet!
before it to you is missing!

Refrain

Budding young women,
let yourselves be seen
dancing gaily
under the wreath!
Dance two by two
to the sound of the shawms;
dance in a roundelay,
gaily in May.

Come, you men,
you scrutinizing connoisseurs!
See the bright figures
form into pairs.
Refrain

Rejoice, you old ones,
in the figures of the young!
As you once leaped,
now leap the young!
Refrain

Young and beautiful
daughters and sons,
and grandchildren no less
delightful than children.
Refrain

You young ones,
you're not judges;
choose, lads,
before you miss out!
Refrain

Source: Rückert 1868–1869, 2: 359

Anton Webern

Entflieht auf leichten Kähnen, op. 2
Flee in Light Boats
Stefan George

Entflieht auf leichten Kähnen
Flee in light boats

Berauschten Sonnenwelten
intoxicated sun-worlds,

Daß immer mildre Tränen
that always milder tears

Euch eure Flucht entgelten.
you your flight reward.

Flee in light boats
from intoxicated worlds of light,
that milder tears might always
reward you for your flight.

Seht diesen Taumel blonder,
Watch this frenzy of blond,

Lichtblauer Traumgewalten
light-blue dream powers

Und trunkner Wonnen sonder
and drunken delights without

Verzückung sich entfalten.
ecstasy — unfold.

Watch this frenzy of blond,
light-blue visions
and drunken delights unfold,
devoid of ecstasy.

Daß nicht der süße Schauer
That not the sweet shudder

In neues Leid euch hülle—
in new suffering you envelop,

Es sei die stille Trauer
it be the silent sorrow

Die diesen Frühling fülle.
that this spring fills.

So that the sweet shudders
might not envelop you in new suffering,
may it be silent sorrow
that fills this spring.

Source: George 1958, 1: 161

*T*HE life and poetry of Stefan George (1868–1933) straddled two centuries and in a sense, two worlds. The decades before his birth witnessed the breakdown of traditional society as a consequence of wars and the industrial revolution. At his birth, Germany was still a confederation of princedoms as it had been for centuries; by the time George was three years old it had become a modern nation-state. German poetry had yet to fully confront the new realities and indeed provided an insulation and isolation from them in its continued romanticism.

Germany had been yet more radically transformed when George reached his fiftieth birthday. Its population had doubled over his lifetime, traditional class structures had disintegrated, and WWI had shattered its economy and whatever optimism remained in its people. The poetry of the day, commonly called "expressionistic," reflected the roughness of this world in the rawness of its subjects and language, and in its intentional turning away from the poetic heritage of the romantics. The expressionist poets were interested in real rather than objectified emotions and in the impact rather than the beauty of their language.

Stefan George provided a sort of link between the romantic and expressionistic movements while considering himself a part of neither.[78] His poetry attempted to deal with genuine human emotions and conflicts while still holding the beauty of language and poetic expression sacrosanct. He became known for this "Third Humanism" and attracted a small but intensely loyal circle of disciples, the *George-Kreis*, many of whom remained with him for decades and became his emotional support in his later years. By the third

---

[78]Perhaps as a symbol of the "apartness" of his work, he avoided normal punctuation and did not capitalize common nouns, as is customary in German. In this sense he is to German as e.e. cummings is to English.

decade of the twentieth century George, who had previously spent many years in literary obscurity, was generally considered Germany's greatest living poet.[79]

In 1928 George published a poetic cycle called *Das neue Reich* (The New Empire), which was venerated by the National Socialist movement. In that collection George had attempted, as always, to confront the humanistic issues of concern to him in poetry of beauty; it was an unfortunate accident of history that his work was perverted by others. The Nazis attempted to get him to accept one honor after another, including the establishment of a poetry prize in his name. George resisted every overture and died on December 3, 1933 after having lived for only eleven months of Hitler's Third Reich.

Nearly all of George's poetry belongs to massive, complex cycles, assembled and organized with the same meticulous care the poet put into his words. "Entflieht auf leichten Kähnen" is one of ninety-eight poems in *Das Jahr der Seele* (The Year of the Soul), dating from (perhaps not just coincidentally) 1898. Michael and Erika Metzger offer the following description of the cycle, from which the present editors have removed the German titles for the sake of brevity:

> The book contains ninety-eight poems symmetrically divided into three sections. The first part, to which the title of the volume most directly applies, consists of three sections: "After the Vintage," "Pilgrims in the Snow," and "Summer's Triumph." The second part, "Inscriptions and Dedications," contains the "Aphorisms for the Guests in T," and the brief tributes to George's friends, who are . . . identified by their initials. The closing section of thirty-two poems is entitled "Mournful Dances." (Metzger 1972: 87)

The absence of spring from the cycle of the seasons in the first section is striking, as is the serious, even depressive tone of many of the poems, which are nonetheless expressed in language of great craft and beauty that belies its content. In 1896 George had ended a relationship with a woman named Ida Coblenz, and it has been theorized that much of *Das Jahr der Seele* relates to the death of that relationship. (Metzger 1972: 87)

The poem is not subject to easy interpretation, but it seems that the poet is withdrawing from the world of intense emotion and perhaps love, the "intoxicated worlds of light," that he has found "devoid of ecstasy" despite their "drunken delights." The "blond, light-blue visions" are indeed attractive, but they ultimately "envelop you in new suffering," to which "silent sorrow" filling the spring is preferable.

It is apparently unknown how Webern came upon the poem or why he decided to set it to music in 1908. The dreamlike images must have appealed to him, though, as a parallel in words to the musical language that he was formulating for himself, a language that was beginning to show the influence of his studies with Schönberg in the period 1904–1908.

Kantate I, op. 29

Cantata No. 1

Hildegard Jone

I

Zündender Lichtblitz des Lebens	The kindling lightning of life
Kindling lightning of life	struck from the cloud of the word.
	Thunder, the heartbeat, follows,
schlug ein aus der Wolke des Wortes.	until it dies away in peace.
struck — from the cloud of the word.	
Donner, der Herzschlag, folgt nach,	
Thunder, the heartbeat, follows —,	
bis er in Frieden verebbt.	
until it in peace dies away.	

---

[79]George's thought and thus his poetry were profoundly affected by a two-year mentoring relationship he had with a boy named Maximilian Kronberger ("Maximin"), which ended with the young man's death from meningitis at the age of sixteen in 1904. The effect on George of the boy's passing was so great that in the literature his work is referred to as "pre-" or "post-Maximin." Since the poem under consideration was written before this experience, it will not be discussed further.

II

Kleiner Flügel Ahornsamen, schwebst in Winde!
Little   wing   maple seed,   hover   in wind!

Mußt doch in der Erde   Dunkel sinken.
Must — into the earth's darkness sink.

Aber du wirst auferstehn dem Tage,
But you will   arise   to the day,

all den   Düften   und der Frühlingszeit;
all to the fragrances and the springtime;

wirst aus Wurzeln in das Helle steigen,
will from roots into the light climb,

bald im Himmel auch verwurzelt sein.
soon in heaven also   rooted   be.

Wieder wirst aus dir du kleine Flügel senden,
Again   will from you you little wings send,

die in sich   schon tragen deine ganze
which in themselves already carry your entire

schweigend Leben sagende Gestalt.
silent   life-telling   form.

Little wingéd maple seed, you hover in the wind!
You must sink into earth's darkness.
But you will arise to the day,
to all the fragrances and the springtime;
you will climb from roots into the light,
and soon you will also be rooted in heaven.
Again you will send out your little wings,
which already bear silently within themselves
the story of your entire life.

III

Tönen   die seligen Saiten   Apolls,
Resound the blessed strings of Apollo,

wer nennt   sie Chariten?
who calls them Graces?

Spielt er sein Lied durch den wachsenden Abend,
Plays he his song through the lengthening evening,

wer   denket Apollon?
who   thinks of Apollo?

Sind doch im   Klange die früheren Namen alle
Have yet in the sound the earlier names all

verklungen?
faded?

sind doch im   Worte die schwächeren Worte
Have yet in the word the   weaker   words

lange   gestorben?
long ago   died?

und auch die blasseren Bilder   zum Siegel
And also the paler   images to the seal

des   Spektrums   geschmolzen.
of the spectrum   melted.

Charis,   die Gabe des Höchsten:
Charis,   the gift of the highest

die Anmut der Gnade erglänzet!
the loveliness of   grace shines forth!

Schenkt sich im Dunkel   dem werdenden Herzen
Gives   itself in darkness to the ripening   heart

als Tau der Vollendung.
as dew of   perfection.

When Apollo's blessed strings resound,
who calls them "Graces?"
When he plays his song throughout the
   lengthening evening,
who gives thought to Apollo?

Have not the older names faded into the sound?
Have not the weaker words died in the word long
   ago?
And the paler images have also melted to become
   the seal of the spectrum.
Charis, the gift of the highest:
the loveliness of her grace shines forth!
It bestows itself in darkness on the ripening
   heart
as the dew of perfection.

Source: Webern 1957

*I*N 1926 composer Anton von Webern first met Hildegard Jone (1891–1963), a Viennese poet and painter, and her husband Josef Humplik, a sculptor. The trio—especially Webern and Jone—immediately felt a profound artistic and personal kinship that was to build in intensity over the years. For Webern, the artistic connection was so visceral that he set to music some seventeen of Jone's poems and never again set the work of another poet.

It is unfortunate that only Webern's contribution to the Jone-Humplik/Webern correspondence has survived, and this only in part. Nonetheless, Webern's letters say a great deal about his artistic thinking, particularly with regard to "Cantata 1," which was inspired by and set to three of Jone's verses. When Jone sent the poems to Webern is unknown, but his first comment on them is in a letter of July 10, 1938, in which he reports a conception for a large-scale work based on the poem that was to become the second movement of the "Cantata."

> I am now composing "Kleiner Flügel Ahornsamen schwebst im Winde . . . ." [Little, winged maple seeds, you float in the wind]. It shall be the key to a grand symphonic cycle for solo, chorus, and orchestra, in which other of your works will also appear—a sort of symphony with vocal sections. (Webern 1959: letter 83, tr. ed.)

On January 24, 1939 Webern sent a full score to the Humpliks, along with an enthusiastic discussion of his reaction to the poem.

> I am convinced that you will be able to derive everything from the "drawing" that arises from the notes themselves. [Neither Jone nor Humplik was a musician.] But what seems so freely to float about ("float in the wind") . . . is the result of a rigid structure (the "tiny wings," "they already carry in themselves"—in fact, not merely symbolically—the "entire . . . form." Just as your words say!) the like of which has probably never to this time been used as the basis for a musical conception. But how these words have spoken to me! (Webern 1959: letter 86, tr. ed.)

Webern next turned to the poem that was to become the first movement of the cantata, reporting to Jone on May 14 that he was finishing the production of the full score, in which he "did not employ the entire text as originally envisioned, for the musical form required quite otherwise." On August 12 he wrote that he was at work on a third movement that he called the "Chariten,"[80] and on December 2 he wrote that this too was finished. His effusive discussion of the wedding of words and music is most telling, as are his thoughts on the order of movements, on which he was not yet settled:

> I think that, for both musical and textual reasons, the "Chariten" must become the first movement. Do not the "tiny wings" and "lightning and thunder" give answer to the question of the "Chariten" strophe, my dear Hildegard? Do they not say what is meant by "sound," "word," and "seal of the spectrum"?

> Of course, the "Chariten" were also composed based on the same twelve-tone row as the other two movements. As I have already said, the individual characteristic of this row is that the last six tones are written as the retrograde inversion of the first six, so that each series of six tones always leads back to the beginning. It is always the same, whether the "blessed strings," the "charm of grace," the "tiny wings," the "lightning-stroke of life," or "thunder, the heartbeat. . . . " And yet, it is completely different each time! (Webern 1959: letter 92, tr. ed.)

In the month that followed, Webern reconsidered the order of movements. In December it had seemed to him that the "Chariten" had to open the cantata. In his letter of January 16, however, he was equally convinced that it belonged at the end and had apparently forgotten his previous certainty as to its placement elsewhere.

> I have completed the full score of my "Cantata"—that is, the last section on which I have been working. How I wish to show it to you: how your marvelous words, dear Hildegard, have been transformed into music. . . . Now I have placed this movement at the end of the cantata. Musically, it must be the conclusion. I had planned to put it there and that has now transpired. There is in this piece no single climax. The harmonic construction (as a result of the voices) is such that everything remains floating. (Webern 1959: letter 94, tr. ed.)

Even today, audiences still find Webern's music to be a challenge to the ears and mind. Jone, who considered it to be a reflection of the same universal art that she and her husband served, saw it as a most beautiful reflection of the soul:

> What is expressed in Anton Webern's music is not just description or representation, but rather a moving radiance of the heart. . . . The existence of people like Anton Webern renders life so much friendlier and full of joy. (Webern 1959: letter 70, tr. ed.)

Webern began his composition with the second movement, "Little, winged maple seeds," and only later saw that the other two poems made the most sense as a frame around it. As he says in his own words above, all three movements are based on the same tone row, the second half of which is a retrograde inversion of the first. Thus all the movements are different but sprout from the same seed, which "bears within itself" the story of the "entire life" of the composition. He was absolutely delighted to find an exact musical parallel to Jone's words.

The idea of the renewal of life through death, the subject of "Little, winged maple seed," finds different and more complex expression in the surrounding movements. In the first movement the transitory nature of

---

[80]In Greek mythology, "The Graces," the three sister goddesses of beauty in the retinue of Aphrodite: *Aglaia* (brilliance or radiance of beauty), *Euphrosyne* (joy), and *Thalia* (the flowering of beauty). Earlier there were thought to be only two Graces, one of whom was named "Charis."

life is symbolized in lightning and thunder, the most powerful and yet among the most fleeting manifestations of the God's creative energy (= the "cloud of the word"?).

Movement 3, with its fragmentary grammar, its allusions to Greek mythology (Apollo, the Chariten, and Charis), and its strange imagery, is difficult to grasp and presents severe challenges for a translator. Its essence seems to echo the opening of Schiller's "Nänie":* "Even the beautiful must perish" and perish in an instant. Apollo, second only to Zeus among the Gods in the Greek pantheon, is forgotten even as he plays his songs, and words, far more enduring than flesh, inevitably and inexorably fade away into the background noise of history. Yet through it all, Charis, the goddess of beauty and one of the Graces referred to in line 2, continues to bestow her grace and beauty on all life, both that of the flesh and that of the word.

As Webern composed his cantata and took such inspiration from and delight in Jone's poems, the lightning of war was preparing to strike Europe. Both Jone and Webern survived the six years of conflict, but in one of the ironies of history, Webern was cut down accidentally by the bullet of an American serviceman four months after the hostilities ended.

Hugo Wolf

Der Feuerreiter
The Fire-Rider
Eduard Mörike

Sehet ihr am Fensterlein
See you at the little window

Dort die rote Mütze wieder?
there the red cap again?

Nicht geheuer muß es sein,
–eerie– must it be,

Denn er geht schon auf und nieder.
for he is going already up and down.

Und auf einmal, welch Gewühle
And –suddenly– what throng

Bei der Brücke, nach dem Feld!
at the bridge, toward the field!

Horch! das Feuerglöcklein gellt:
Hark! the little firebell shrieks:

Hinterm the Berg,
Behind the hill,

Hinterm the Berg,
Behind the hill,

Brennt es in der Mühle!
is burning it in the mill!

Schaut! da sprengt er wütend schier
Look! There gallops he furiously nearly

Durch das Tor, der Feuerreiter,
through the gate, the fire-rider,

Auf dem rippendürren Tier,
on the rib-thin animal,

Als auf einer Feuerleiter!
as if on a fire ladder!

Querfeldein! Durch Qualm und Schwüle
Across the field! Through smoke and heat

Rennt er schon und ist am Ort!
races he already and is at the place!

Drüben schallt es fort und fort:
over there sounds it on and on:

Hinterm the Berg,
Behind the hill,

Hinterm the Berg,
Behind the hill,

Brennt es in der Mühle!
is burning it in the mill!

Do you see—at the little window
there—the red cap again?
There must be something weird going on,
because he's already pacing up and down.
And suddenly a great throng
is at the bridge; now off to the field!
Hark! the firebell is shrieking:
    behind the hill,
    behind the hill
there's a fire in the mill!

Look! there, galloping almost madly,
through the gate: the fire-rider
on his skeletal steed,
as if on a fire ladder!
Across the field! Through the smoke and
stifling heat he races, and now he's there!
The distant bell shrieks on and on:
    behind the hill,
    behind the hill
there's a fire in the mill!

263

Der so oft den roten Hahn
He so often the fire

Meilenweit von fern gerochen,
for miles from afar has scented,

Mit des heil'gen Kreuzes Span
with the holy cross's splinter

Freventlich die Glut besprochen—
sacrilegious the flames conjured—

Weh! dir grinst vom Dachgestühle
Woe! At you is grinning from the rafters

Dort der Feind im Höllenschein.
there the devil in hell's fire.

Gnade Gott der Seele dein!
Have mercy God on the soul yours!

    Hinterm the Berg,
    Behind the hill,

    Hinterm the Berg,
    Behind the hill,

Rast er in die Mühle!
reges he in the mill!

You who have so often smelled fire
from many miles away,
who with the True Cross's splinter
blasphemously conjured away the flames—
Beware! Over there the devil is grinning
from the rafters, in the fires of hell.
God have mercy on your soul!
    Behind the hill,
    behind the hill
he's raging in the mill!

Keine Stunde hielt es an,
No hour lasted it —,

Bis die Mühle borst in Trümmer;
until the mill burst in ruins;

Doch den kecken Reitersmann
yet the reckless horseman

Sah man von der Stunde nimmer.
saw one from that hour never.

Volk und Wagen im Gewühle
People and carriages in the throng

Kehren heim von all dem Graus;
return home from all the horror;

Auch das Glöcklein klinget aus:
also the little bell stops ringing:

    Hinterm the Berg,
    Behind the hill,

    Hinterm the Berg,
    Behind the hill,

Brennts! —
it's burning!

It was less than an hour
until the mill burst into ruins,
yet the reckless rider
was never seen from that hour on.
People and carriages in the throng
return home from the horror;
the bell also dies away:
    behind the hill,
    behind the hill
it's burning!

Nach der Zeit ein Müller fand
After the time a miller found

Ein Gerippe samt der Mützen
a skeleton together with the cap

Aufrecht an der Kellerwand
upright on the cellar wall

Auf der beinern' Mähre sitzen:
on the bones of the mare sitting:

Feuerreiter, wie so kühle
Fire-rider, how so coolly

Reitest du in deinem Grab!
are riding you in your tomb!

Husch! da fällts in Asche ab.
Hush! there falls away in ashes —.

    Ruhe wohl,
    Rest well,

    Ruhe wohl
    rest well

Drunten in der Mühle!
down there in the mill!

Sometime afterwards a miller found
a skeleton along with the cap
sitting upright against the cellar wall
on top of the bones of a mare:
Fire-rider, how very coolly
you are riding in your tomb!
Hush! They're crumbling into ashes.
    Rest well,
    rest well
down there in the mill!

    Source: Mörike 1905, 1: 54

*F*EW poems have as long and complicated a history as this folk legend set to verse by Eduard Mörike (1804–1875), one of the greatest German romantic poets, at the age of twenty. Most literature on Mörike repeats the common wisdom that there are two versions, the draft of 1824 and a second and final version with an added stanza from 1841. A comprehensive source study by Rainer Pohl (Pohl 1975) provides evidence, however, that the poet revised and polished "Der Feuerreiter" at nearly every opportunity over a period of four decades. The poem is known through Wolf's solo and choral settings, both of which have as their text the last of the versions printed during Mörike's lifetime.

"The Fire-rider" has its origins in Swabian[81] folk legend. As related by Mörike in a preface to the version of 1824:

> From an unfinished novel. There the story is told: In a certain old town there lived under the gables of an otherwise abandoned house a young man of strange, emaciated appearance about whose daily life no one knew anything because he never permitted himself to be seen, except, so the legend goes, each time just before a fire would break out. Then he would be seen pacing back and forth in front of a window wearing a scarlet hood—a sure sign of impending disaster. At the first sound of the fire bell he would spring out of a stall on a skinny old nag, and with the speed of an arrow would unfailingly advance toward the scene of the blaze.[82] (tr. ed.)

The preface is helpful to the reader, as the poem begins without introduction of the main character, and the action is so fast that it is over before one grasps what has happened. As the poem begins, people on the street are anxiously watching a red-capped young man pacing behind his window, and then chaos—screaming citizens and clanging bells—explodes. Only in the second stanza do we learn who is wearing the red cap: the fire-rider, who by that time is riding furiously toward the burning mill. Mörike wastes no time with narrative; one moment the fire-rider is seen dashing across the field and the next he is already at the blazing mill. Such compressed action is a key to the intensity of the poem, as is the folk song-like refrain.

In early versions the third strophe as shown here did not exist, and the poem continued with the fourth strophe. There it is clear that time has passed and the action is over. The mill has burned down, the alarm bells have died away (note the truncated last line of the refrain), and the fire-rider is no more to be seen.

The final strophe introduces a mysterious element of the supernatural. Inside the mill the miller finds the red cap, miraculously unburned, sitting atop the skeleton of the fire-rider, who is still on his horse, which has also been reduced to bones. Then, suddenly and inexplicably, the bones collapse into dust. The poet closes by wishing the fire-rider a peaceful rest for eternity, and the reader is left wondering what the poem means. Did the fire-rider set the fire himself? Was he an incarnation of the fire demon, with whom he was united in death?

Mörike included the poem in his 1832 novel *Maler Nolten*—the "unfinished novel" of the quotation above—in which he transformed the preface into a story told by one of his characters. (Mörike 1967–1970, 1: 31) At this time he also made several subtle changes of wording. In 1841 he made further revisions, the most significant of which was the addition of a new strophe that had the fire-rider using a splinter of the True Cross to conjure away the blaze, which presumably had been set by the devil. At this time Mörike, who believed that he personally experienced spiritual apparitions (Pohl 1975: 342), was interested in such things and was a reader of *Magicon* (1840–1853), a magazine on the supernatural and occult published by his friend and fellow-poet Justinus Kerner. (Sams 1983: 131)

With the added strophe Mörike transformed the poem from a folk legend into a Christian allegory. But was the devil victorious because he was more powerful than the relic, or was the blasphemous use of the cross repaid by a divinely ordained fiery death, which the devil merely observed with delight from his perch in the rafters? Mörike is silent on these questions, but they have kept literary commentators busy for well over a century. Pohl theorizes that the poet, a Lutheran minister, indeed intended to transform the poem into a Christian fable, and he presents evidence that the poet was "concerned at the time of revision with literary examples of naive Christian piety . . . [and] Christian folk ideas." (Pohl 1975: 147, tr. ed.)

Even the 1841 version of the poem was not yet its final form. Mörike continued to make changes to "Der Feuerreiter" as late as the publication of the fourth edition of his poems in 1867—forty-three years after he had first composed it.

---

[81]Swabia is a region in southwestern Germany roughly congruent to the current state of Baden-Württemberg, with its capital city of Stuttgart.

[82]LBS, cod. poet. quart. 144; pp. 22–24, commonly known as the "green volume." Quoted in Pohl 1975: 337, tr. ed. Pohl provides no location for the manuscript, but it is presumably housed in the Württembergische Landesbibliothek, Stuttgart.

Hugo Wolf found the poem fascinating and worked especially hard to understand it:

> Wolf would not rest until he had mastered the background detail and studied the relevant issues of *Magicon*, where Mörike too had found the inspiration of the idea for the third verse, about mastering fires by the use of black magic and the inevitable penalty to be paid. Thus the imagination of both poet and composer was fired and fused from the same sources into music of nerve-flaying intensity; and the song rivets attention and compels acceptance with a force that all but outmatches the poem.[83]

SECHS GEISTLICHE LIEDER
SIX SACRED SONGS

ROMANTIC poetry tended to deal superficially with religion. Religious imagery is frequently found, but more often than not the context is actually secular. Issues of the spirit are most often treated obliquely, through analogies to nature, and the motive force of the poems is often pantheistic rather than Christian.

It is thus particularly interesting to encounter the spiritual and religious poetry of Joseph von Eichendorff (1788–1857), a devout Catholic whose poetic work—and not just that of an explicitly religious character—is permeated by his faith. Egon Schwartz encapsulates the tensions in Eichendorff's poetry most perceptively. He begins by looking at other romantics:

> They are either esoteric youths alternating between ecstatic and angelic states of mind, and destined to die an early death . . . or the anti-bourgeois and utterly Bohemian types with torn souls . . . whose own lives seem to have been the foremost models for their artistic creations. In contrast to this, Eichendorff seems to have been an armchair romantic whose civilian existence [as a government bureaucrat] was strangely dissociated from the figments of his imagination.
>
> . . . [T]here exist undeniable tensions between Eichendorff's conception of poetry and his religious faith. What is more these tensions lend his creative work a vibrating energy without which it would be lacking an important dimension. Reduced to the simplest terms, the reason for the lack of total compatibility between his two formative influences [poetry and religion] lies in the role played by "nature" in each of them. For the poet, nature, objectified in the forests, streams, and mountains, but also in man's inner impulses broadly defined as erotic, is a vital force of inspiration. . . . In the Christian world view nature is a danger and a threat. Man is not only a vegetative but also a moral being, with a soul and an inborn quest for immortality. By giving in to his longing for union with nature, without which the poet can neither live nor create, he falls under its spell and becomes himself subject to its endless rhythms of blooming and wilting, alertness and torpor, revival and death. Only religion can interrupt the cycle and give life an aim and a purpose; only the Christian faith promises immortality. (Schwartz 1972: 13–15)

The six Eichendorff poems that Wolf selected to set to music were taken from the poet's eighty-two works that he labeled *geistliche Gedichte* (spiritual poetry). They embody the "tension" and "vibrating energy" described by Schwartz—especially when viewed as a whole. Wolf renamed the three to which the poet had given his own titles, and then named the three that were originally untitled. At first this seems odd, but considered in terms of the set as a poetic-musical whole it makes perfect sense. The editor of these pieces in the Wolf collected works, Hans Jancik, explains:

> Decsey[84] points out that the six choruses form a logically connected sequence, and the reason why Wolf later altered the titles of some of the poems was that it was not until after the fourth chorus that he perceived the idea of a "programme" linking the individual poems. Originally, the first three settings were given the same titles as the poems, but later Wolf altered both the order and the titles, and the titles of numbers 4–6 were adapted to his concept of a "programme." The occasion of their composition was perhaps the recent break with Vally Franck [his first love and at that time fiancée] by which Wolf was profoundly distressed. (Jancik 1974: Foreword)

---

[83]Sams 1983: 131. The song to which Sams refers is the solo setting, but his comments are just as applicable to the choral version.

[84]Decsy, Ernst. *Hugo Wolf*. Leipzig and Berlin: Schuster and Loeffler, 1903–1906.

In summary:

No.	Year of poem	Eichendorff Title		Wolf Title	
1	1837	*Mittag*	(Noon)	*Aufblick*	(Upward Glance)
2	1837	*Nachtgruß*	(Night Greeting)	*Einklang*	(Harmony [unison])
3	1835	*Der Einsiedler*	(The Hermit)	*Resignation*	(Resignation)
4	1837	*Der Pilger (5)*	(The Pilgrim, 5)	*Letzte Bitte*	(Last Request)
5	1837	*Der Pilger (2)*	(The Pilgrim, 2)	*Ergebung*	(Submission)
6	1837	*Der Pilger (4)*	(The Pilgrim, 4)	*Erhebung*	(Exaltation)

Wolf's titles capture the nature of the spiritual progression of the poems, from a glance upward to the heavens for help, through the turmoil of life, to submission to the Divine, and the ultimate exaltation brought by that submission.

1. Aufblick
Upward Glance
Joseph von Eichendorff

Vergeht mir der Himmel
Disappears to me the sky

Vor Staube schier,
because of dust sheer,

Herr, im Getümmel
Lord, in this turmoil

Zeig Dein Panier!
show your banner!

Wie schwank ich sündlich,
As falter I sinfully

Läßt Du von mir;
depart You from me;

Unüberwindlich
Invincible

Bin ich mit Dir!
am I with You!

Should the sky disappear,
clouded by sheer dust,
Lord, in this turmoil
show me your banner!

How I sinfully falter
when you depart from me;
I'm invincible
when I am with you.

  Source: Eichendorff 1955: 251

*T*HE first of Eichendorff's poems, the shortest and most direct of the six, paints a picture of humanity lost in the cloud of "sheer dust," through which it cries to God in heaven (the "upward glance" of the title) for strength and guidance. "Mittag" (noon) was the original title, which further intensifies the image: The cloud obscuring the Divine is so thick that it blocks the light even at midday.

2. Einklang
Harmony
Joseph von Eichendorff

Weil jetzo alles stille ist
Since now all quiet is

Und alle Menschen schlafen,
and all people sleep,

Mein Seel das ewge Licht begrüßt,
my soul the eternal light greets,

Ruht wie ein Schiff im Hafen.
rests like a ship in the harbor.

Since all is quiet now
and everyone is asleep,
my soul greets the eternal light
and rests like a ship in the harbor.

Der falsche Fleiß,   die Eitelkeit,
The false diligence, the vanity,

Was keinen mag erlaben,
that no one may restore,

Darin   der Tag das Herz zerstreut,
wherein the day the heart scatters,

Liegt   alles   tief begraben.
lies everything deeply buried.

The false diligence, the vanity
that can restore no one—
where the day scatters the heart,
everything lies deeply buried.

Ein andrer König wundergleich
A different king wonderful-same

Mit königliche Sinnen,
with royal sense,

Zieht herrlich ein im stillen Reich,
moves gloriously — in the quiet kingdom

Besteigt die ewgen Zinnen.
climbs the eternal pinnacles.

Another king, just as wonderful
and of royal disposition,
moves gloriously in his quiet kingdom
and scales the eternal ramparts.

Source: Eichendorff 1955: 252

*O*RIGINALLY entitled "Nachtgruß" (Night Greeting), the second poem seems to begin as a run-of-the-mill romantic paean to the peace of the night. A moral tone appears in the second stanza, however—the night does not just bring peace but freedom from worldly vanities as well. The religious underpinning of the poem becomes explicit in the third stanza, and the poet, rather than yearning for his distant love, contemplates the omnipresence of the King of Heaven, in harmony (*Einklang*) with the divine universe.

3. Resignation
Resignation
Joseph von Eichendorff

Komm, Trost der Welt, du stille Nacht!
Come, comfort of the world, you peaceful night!

Wie steigst du von den Bergen sacht,
How descend you from the mountains quietly.

Die Lüfte alle schlafen,
The winds all sleep;

Ein Schiffer nur noch,   wandermüd,
a boatsman only yet, tired of wandering,

Singt   übers Meer sein Abendlied
sings over the sea his evening song

Zu Gottes Lob im Hafen.
to God's praise in the harbor.

Come, comfort of the world, you peaceful night!
How quietly you descend from the mountains.
The winds are all asleep;
only a sailor in the harbor, weary of wandering,
sings out over the sea
his evening song of praise to God.

Die Jahre wie die Wolken gehn
The years like the clouds go

Und lassen mich hier einsam stehn,
and let me here lonely stand;

Die Welt hat mich vergessen,
the world has me forgotten.

Da   tratst du wunderbar zu mir,
Then stepped you wonderfully to me

Als ich beim Waldesrauschen hier
when I by forest-rustling here

Gedankenvoll   gesessen.
full of thoughts sat.

The years pass like the clouds
and leave me here all alone;
the world has forgotten me.
Then you miraculously came to me
as I sat here in the forest,
engrossed in thought.

O Trost der Welt, du stille Nacht!
O comfort of the world, you peaceful night!

Der Tag hat mich so müd gemacht,
The day has me so tired made;

Das weite Meer schon dunkelt,
the wide sea already darkens.

Laß ausruhn mich von Lust und Not,
let rest me from desire and need

Bis einst das ewge Morgenrot
until some day the eternal dawn

Den stillen Wald durchfunkelt.
the silent forest shines through.

O comfort of the world, you peaceful night!
The day has made me so tired;
the vast sea already darkens.
Let me rest from desire and need
until the day when the eternal dawn
shines through the silent forest.

Source: Eichendorff 1955: 265

THE mood of "Resignation," originally entitled "The Hermit,"[85] seems to begin where "Einklang" left off— even to the image in the first stanza of the sailor in the harbor, a symbol for the soul at peace. But the focus immediately turns to resignation to this life and years of loneliness and pain, which are relieved by God's visit to the poet as he sits alone in the forest. In the third stanza he looks forward with faith to the day of "eternal dawn" when the "night" will be banished forever.

4. Letzte Bitte

Last Request

Joseph von Eichendorff

Wie ein todeswunder Streiter,
Like a mortally wounded warrior,

Der den Weg verloren hat,
who the way lost has,

Schwank ich nun und kann nicht weiter,
stagger I now and can not go on,

Von dem Leben sterbensmatt.
from the life tired to death.

Nacht schon decket alle Müden
Night already covers all tired ones,

Und so still ists um mich her,
and so still is it around me —,

Herr, auch mir gib endlich Frieden,
Lord, also me give finally peace;

Denn ich wünsch und hoff nichts mehr.
then I wish and hope nothing more.

Like a mortally wounded warrior
who has lost his way,
I stagger now and can't go on,
tired to death from life.
Night already covers the weary,
and it's so silent all around me.
Lord, grant me also peace at the last;
I wish and hope for nothing more.

Source: Eichendorff 1955: 263

THIS poem, no. 5 from Eichendorff's brief cycle entitled *The Pilgrim*, is an extension and intensification of "Resignation." Here the poet has fought the battle valiantly and entreats God for the same relief from life's trials that has already been granted to those around him ("the weary" covered by the night). His "Last Request" is to be granted "peace at the last."

---

[85]"Der Einsiedler" bears a resemblance to the "Song of the Hermit" in H.J.G. von Grimmelshausen's novel *Der abendteuerliche Simplicissimus* (The Adventerous Simpleton), which begins "Komm Trost der Nacht, o Nachtigall." (Eichendorff 1977: 985)

5. Ergebung
Submission
Joseph von Eichendorff

Dein Wille, Herr, geschehe!
Your will, Lord, be done!

Verdunkelt schweigt das Land,
Darkened   is silent the land.

Im   Zug   der Wetter sehe
In the passage of the storm, see

Ich schauernd Deine Hand.
I   in awe   Your hand.

O   mit uns Sündern gehe
O with us   sinners go

Erbarmend   ins   Gericht!
mercifully   into the judgment!

Ich beug im tiefsten Wehe,
I   bow in deepest woe

Zum Staub mein Angesicht,
to the dust   my   face;

Dein Wille, Herr, geschehe!
Your will, Lord, be done!

Your will, O Lord, be done!
The darkened land is silent;
in the passage of the storm,
awestruck, I see your hand.
O Lord, go with us sinners
mercifully into the judgment!
In deepest woe I bow
my face to the dust;
your will, O Lord, be done!

Source: Eichendorff 1955: 262

NOW the poet ceases his struggle and "bows his face into the dust" in "submission" to divine will. He places his faith in God and his fate in God's hands and humbly asks that the Lord be with him in death and at his judgment. "Submission" is no. 2 from *The Pilgrim*.

6. Erhebung
Exaltation
Joseph von Eichendorff

So   laß herein nun brechen
Thus let   in   now rush in

Die Brandung, wie sie will,
the   surf,   as it wants,

Du darfst ein Wort nur sprechen,
You may one word only   speak,

So   wird   der Abgrund still;
then becomes the   abyss   silent.

Und bricht die letzte Brücke,
And breaks the last bridge,

Zu Dir, der   treulich   steht,
to You, who faithfully stands,

Hebt über Not und Glücke
lifts above need and happiness

Mich einsam das Gebet.
me   lonely the prayer.

Thus let the surf rush in,
breaking as it desires;
If you speak but one word,
the abyss will become silent.
And when the last bridge crumbles,
I will lift up my solitary prayer
above need and happiness
to you, who wait faithfully.

Source: Eichendorff 1955: 263

HAVING taken the journey through the five previous stages of life and faith, the poet is now possessed by the "exaltation" of faith in the all-powerful God, who can stop the ocean waves with but a word. That exaltation fortifies him to bear the trials of life with supreme confidence of God's power and presence. Number 4 from *The Pilgrim*, "Exaltation" brings to completion the spiritual journey Wolf began five poems earlier.

Hymns

Aus tiefer Not schrei ich zu dir

In Deep Distress I Cry to You

Martin Luther

Aus tiefer Not schrei ich zu dir,
From deep distress cry I to you:

Herr Gott, erhör mein Rufen;
Lord God, hear my cries;

dein gnädig Ohren kehr zu mir
your gracious ears incline to me

und meiner Bitt sie öffen!
and my request them hear!

Denn so du willst das sehen an,
For as you want that to consider —,

was Sünd und Unrecht ist getan,
what sin and injustice have done,

wer kann, Herr, vor dir bleiben?
who can, Lord, before you remain?

Bei dir gilt nichts denn Gnad und Gunst,
With you matters nothing but grace and favor

die Sünde zu vergeben;
— sin to forgive.

Es ist doch unser Tun umsonst
It is only our doing in vain

auch in dem besten Leben.
even in the best life.

Vor dir niemand sich rühmen kann;
Before you no one –be boastful– can;

des muß dich fürchten jedermann
— must you fear everyone

und deiner Gnade leben.
and your grace live [by].

Darum auf Gott will hoffen ich,
Therefore on God want to rely I,

auf mein Verdienst nicht bauen;
on my merit not build;

auf ihn mein Herz soll lassen sich
on him my heart shall rely —

und seiner Güte trauen,
and his goodness trust,

die mir zusagt sein wertes Wort;
which me promises his valued word.

das ist mein Trost und treuer Hort,
That is my comfort and faithful refuge;

des will ich allzeit harren.
that want I always to trust.

In deep distress I cry to you:
Lord God, hear my cries;
incline your gracious ears to me
and open them to my request!
For if you choose to consider
what sin and injustice have done,
Lord, who can withstand your scrutiny?

With you nothing matters but grace and favor
to forgive sin.
Our doing is only in vain,
even in the best life.
Before you no one can be boastful;
therefore everyone must fear you
and live by your grace.

Therefore I want to trust in God
and not build on my own merit;
my heart shall rely on him
and trust in his goodness,
which his precious word promises.
His word is my comfort and reliable refuge;
I always want to trust his word.

Und ob es währt bis in die Nacht
And if it lasts until into the night

und wieder an den Morgen,
and again into the morning,

doch soll mein Herz an Gottes Macht
still shall my heart in God's might

verzweifeln nicht noch sorgen.
abandon hope not nor be troubled.

So tu' Israel rechter Art,
So treat Israel right way,

der aus dem Geist erzeuget ward,
he from the spirit begotten was,

und seines Gotts erharre.
and his God wait for.

And even if it lasts into the night
and again into the morning,
still my heart shall not abandon hope
in God's might, nor be troubled.
So act justly toward Israel,
which is begotten of the spirit
and wait for its God.

Ob bei uns ist der Sünden viel,
Although with us is — sins much,

bei Gott ist viel mehr Gnade;
with God is much more grace;

sein Hand zu helfen hat kein Ziel,
his hand to help has no end,

wie groß auch sei der Schade.
how great ever be the wrong.

Er ist allein der gute Hirt,
He is alone the good shepherd

der Israel erlösen wird
who Israel save will

aus seinen Sünden allen.
from its sins all.

Although with us are many sins,
with God there is much more grace;
his helping hand has no limit,
however great the wrong.
He alone is the good shepherd
who will save Israel
from all its sins.

Source: Luther 1967: 4

*P*SALM 130 was a favorite of Luther's, and he used it as the basis for this, one of his most moving hymns. In its original form, published as an individual print in 1523 and in a hymnal in 1524, the eight verses of the Psalm were paraphrased in four stanzas. But perhaps even before this version was printed, Luther expanded the second verse into two, lengthening the hymn into the five verses that appear in the modern *EKG*. This final version was also published in 1524 and has appeared in nearly every Lutheran hymnal since.

One of the doctrines that distinguished Luther from his Roman Catholic contemporaries was salvation by grace—the concept that God's mercy rather than earthly good works was the basis for salvation. Luther took pains to express this doctrine whenever possible. His expansion of this hymn gave him both an opportunity to do so and the chance to give it pride of place at the center of the hymn:

Psalm 130		Aus tiefer Not
verses 1–3	=	v. 1 (prayer for divine help)
verse 4	=	v. 2 (forgiveness)
–	=	**v. 3 (salvation by grace)**
verses 5–6	=	v. 4 (waiting for the Lord)
verses 7–8	=	v. 5 (hope in the Lord)

"Aus tiefer Not" has been a comfort in times of trouble ever since it was written:

> The hymn was sung, May 9, 1525, at the funeral of Elector Friedrich the Wise in the court church at Wittenberg; by the weeping multitude at Halle, when on Feb. 20, 1546, Luther's body was being taken to its last resting place at Wittenberg; and again as the last hymn in the Cathedral at Strasburg before the city was captured by the French in 1681. (Julian 1985: 96)

"Aus tiefer Not" appears in the *EKG* as no. 195. It is found in the *LBW* under the title "Out of the Depths I Cry to You" as no. 295.

Christ ist erstanden

Christ Has Arisen

Author unknown, 12th & 15th centuries

Christ ist erstanden
Christ has   arisen

von der Marter   alle;
from the torment all;

des   solln wir alle froh sein,
of that should we all joyful be.

Christ   will   unser Trost sein.
Christ wants to our   comfort be.

Kyrieleis.
Lord, have mercy.

Christ has arisen
from all his agony;
for that we should all be joyful.
Christ wants to be our consolation.
Kyrieleis.

Wär   er nicht erstanden,
Were he not   arisen,

so wär   die Welt vergangen;
so would be the world   lost;

seit daß er erstanden ist,
since   he arisen   has,

so   loben wir den Vater Jesus Christ.
thus praise we the Father Jesus Christ.

Kyrieleis.
Lord, have mercy.

Were he not arisen,
the world would have been lost;
since he has arisen,
we praise the Father Jesus Christ.
Kyrieleis.

Halleluja,   halleluja,   halleluja!
Hallelujah, hallelujah, hallelujah!

Des   solln wir alle froh sein,
Of that should we all joyful be;

Christ will   unser Trost sein.
Christ wants to our   comfort be.

Kyrieleis.
Lord, have mercy.

Hallelujah, hallelujah, hallelujah!
For that we should all be joyful;
Christ wants to be our consolation.
Kyrieleis.

*M*ARTIN Luther expressed great appreciation for this, one of the oldest German-language hymns: "After a time one tires of singing all other hymns, but the 'Christ ist erstanden' one can always sing again." (Julian 1985: 225)

The folk origins of the hymn are reflected in the numerous versions that were in circulation during the pre-Reformation period as well as in the hymn's irregularities of accent and meter. Like many texts of folk origin, "Christ ist erstanden" combines elements from various eras. The first verse is from the twelfth century. It shares musical elements with the Sequence for Easter, "Victimae paschali laudes," but there are no textual parallels.[86] According to the *EKG*, verses 2 and 3 as presented here stem from the fifteenth century. They share the same types of structural irregularities described above.

"Christ ist erstanden" appears as no. 75 in the *EKG* (from which the present text was taken) and as no. 136 in the *LBW*, under the title "Christ Is Arisen."

---

[86]Stulken (1981: 234) and others state that the hymn text was "based on" the Sequence. Little congruence will be found, however, between the texts. The reader can compare the two by consulting the annotation to the hymn "Christ lag in Todesbanden," where they are printed in parallel columns. For a detailed discussion of the Sequence, see Jeffers 1988: 243.

Christ lag in Todesbanden

Christ Lay in Death's Bonds

Martin Luther

Christ lag in Todesbanden
Christ lay in death's bonds,

Für unsre Sünd gegeben,
for our sins given.

Er ist wieder erstanden
He has again risen

Und hat uns bracht das Leben.
and has us brought — life.

Des wir sollen fröhlich sein,
for this we shall joyful be,

Gott loben und ihm dankbar sein
God praise, and to him thankful be,

Und singen Halleluja.
and sing Hallelujah.

Christ lay in death's bonds,
sacrificed for our sins.
He has risen again
and brought us life.
Therefore we shall be joyful,
praise God, and be thankful to him,
and sing Hallelujah.

Den Tod niemand zwingen kunnt
— death no one subdue could

Bei allen Menschenkindern;
among all humans.

Das macht' alles unsre Sünd,
This does all our sin;

Kein Unschuld war zu finden.
no innocence was to be found.

Davon kam der Tod so bald
Therefore came — death so soon,

Und nahm über uns Gewalt,
and seized over us power,

Hielt uns in seinem Reich gefangen.
held us in his realm captive.

No one among all mortals
could conquer death.
Our sin causes all this;
no innocence was to be found.
Therefore death came so soon,
seized power over us, and
held us captive in his realm.

Jesus Christus, Gottes Sohn,
Jesus Christ, God's son,

An unser Statt ist kommen
in our stead has come

Und hat die Sünde abgetan,
and has — sin taken away.

Damit dem Tod genommen
Thereby — death taken

All sein Recht und sein Gewalt;
all his privilege and his power.

Da bleibet nichts denn Tods Gestalt,
There remains nothing but death's image;

Den Stachl hat er verloren.
the sting has it lost.

Jesus Christ, the Son of God,
has come in our stead
and taken away our sin.
Thereby he has taken from death
all its dominion and power.
Nothing remains but death's mere form;
it has lost its sting.

Es war ein wunderlich Krieg,
It was a strange war

Da Tod und Leben rungen,
when death and life wrestled:

Das Leben behielt den Sieg,
— life retained the victory;

Es hat den Tod verschlungen.
it has — death devoured.

Die Schrift hat verkündigt das,
The scripture has made known this,

Wie ein Tod den andern fraß;
how one death the other consumed;

Ein Spott aus dem Tod ist worden.
a mockery of — death has become.

It was a strange war
when life and death struggled:
life retained the victory;
it has devoured death.
The scripture has proclaimed this,
how one death consumed the other;
death has become a mockery.

Hier ist das rechte Osterlamm,
Here is the true Paschal Lamb

Davon hat Gott geboten;
which has God offered;

Das ist an des Kreuzes Stamm
that has on the cross's stem,

In heißer Lieb gebraten.
in hot love roasted.

Das Blut zeichnet unsre Tür,
The blood marks our door,

Das hält der Glaub dem Tode für,
that holds — faith — death before;

Der Würger kann uns nicht rühren.
the slayer can us no touch.

Here is the true Paschal Lamb
whom God has offered;
he is high on the stem of the cross,
roasted in burning love.
His blood marks our door, and
faith holds this up before death;
the slayer can not touch us.

So feiern wir dies' hoh' Fest
Therefore celebrate we this high feast

Mit Herzensfreud und Wonne,
with heart's joy and delight

Das uns der Herre scheinen läßt.
that to us the Lord shine lets.

Er ist selber die Sonne,
He is himself the sun,

Der durch seiner Gnade Glanz
who through his grace's splendor

Erleuchtet' unsre Herzen ganz,
illuminates our hearts wholly;

Der Sünden Nacht ist vergangen.
the sin's night has past.

Therefore we celebrate this high feast
with joyous heart and great delight
that the Lord allows to shine upon us.
He is himself the sun,
who through the splendor of his grace
wholly illumines our hearts;
the night of sin has past.

Wir essen und wir leben wohl
We eat and we live well

In rechten Osterfladen;
on the true Passover bread;

Der alte Sauerteig nicht soll
the old sourdough not shall

Sein bei dem Wort der Gnaden,
exist beside the word of grace.

Christus will die Koste sein
Christ wants to the food be

Und speisen die Seel allein,
and feed the soul alone;

Der Glaub will keins andern leben.
— faith wants to no other live.

We eat and live well
on the true Passover bread;
the old leaven shall not exist
beside the word of grace.
Christ desires to be the food
that alone will feed the soul;
faith wants to live on no other.

Source: Luther 1967: 14

*L*UTHER'S first chorales, "Christ lag in Todesbanden" among them, saw publication in 1524. The roots of this hymn go back much further, however. Luther drew inspiration as well as several phrases of text from the eleventh-century Latin Sequence for Easter, "Victimae paschali laudes." He likewise borrowed from a twelfth-century[87] Easter folk song entitled "Christ ist erstanden."* It is interesting to see how Luther borrowed and paraphrased from both:

---

[87]Verses 2 and 3 are from the fifteenth century. See the previous footnote regarding the connection —or lack of it—between "Victimae paschali" and "Christ ist erstanden."

Christ ist erstanden	*Hymn*	Victimae paschali laudes[88]	*Hymn*
Christ has arisen from all of his agony.	v. 1	To the Paschal Victim let Christians *offer their*	v. 1
For this we shall be joyful;	v. 1	*praises.*	v. 5
Christ shall be our comfort.		*The Lamb has redeemed the sheep: Christ, the sinless one,*	
Lord have mercy.		*has reconciled sinners to the Father.*	v. 4
		Death and Life have engaged in a wondrous conflict: the	
Had He not arisen		*slain leader of life reigns alive.*	
the world would have been lost.		Tell us Mary, what did you see on your way?	
Since He has arisen		I saw the sepulchre of the living Christ and the	
we praise the Father, Jesus Christ.		glory of Him rising:	
		I saw the angelic witnesses, the napkin, and the	
Lord have mercy.		linen clothes.	
Halleluja, halleluja, halleluja!	vv. 1–7	Christ my hope has risen: he shall go into Galilee.	v. 1
For this we shall be joyful;	v. 1	We know that *Christ has truly risen from the dead.* O	
Christ shall be our comfort.		thou, Victor, King, have mercy upon us.	
Lord have mercy.			

It was remarked in the essay on "The Luther Bible"* that Luther was a master of German language and rhetoric. Nowhere in his hymns is that more true than here. His language engages the listener with an ascetic ecstasy that is reinforced by the austerity of his melody. At the same time, he saturates the text with Biblical allusions, making the hymn a complete sermon on the crucifixion and resurrection.[89]

Verse 1 is a straightforward exposition of the thesis on which the rest of the hymn builds: Christ died for sinful mankind, and through his death and resurrection brought salvation. In verse 2 we learn that "no innocence was to be found among men," whose sins gave death its universal power. In the next verse, however, innocence is found in Jesus, the "lamb without blemish" (Exodus 12: 5), whose sacrifice took the sting from death as was prophesied in 1 Corinthians 15: 54–55. The term "high feast" in verse 3 normally refers to the celebration of the Passover, which here is transformed into Easter. The metaphor is extended further in later verses.

The imagery of the "strange war" in verse 4 comes directly from "Victimae paschali laudes," while the idea of one death (that of Jesus) consuming or swallowing the other (that of humanity) is found both in the Old and New Testaments (Isaiah 25: 8–9 and 1 Corinthians 15: 54–55). Luther's choice of verb, *fraß* (infinitive *fressen*) is particularly pungent: It is normally used to characterize eating by animals or uncouth gorging by people.

This chorale is unusual among Easter hymns in looking back to the Passover for many of the rich allusions in verses 5–7. There the death of Jesus for the salvation of mankind is compared to the Jewish sacrifice and roasting of a lamb in observance of Passover. Jesus, however, is "roasted in burning love." The blood of Jesus figuratively marks the door of the Christian and protects him from Satan ("the slayer"), just as the blood of the sacrificial lambs protected the Jews from the Passover, the last of God's plagues on Egypt, in which he killed the first-born of both man and animal (Exodus 12).

The image in verse 6 of the sun as representative of the Savior and his salvation has both New- and Old-Testament roots. Isaiah 16: 20 says that "Thy sun shall no more go down; neither shall thy moon withdraw itself: but the Lord shall be thine everlasting light, and the days of thy mourning shall be ended." Revelation 21: 23 offers a similar image of holy light: "And the city had no need of the sun, neither of the moon, to shine in it: for the glory of God did lighten it, and the Lamb is the light thereof."

In the final verse Jesus is compared to the Passover bread, representing the New Covenant. The "old leaven," the leavened bread that is still uneaten on Passover eve, is ceremonially burned by Jews to mark the beginning of the holiday. In Luther's allegory it represents the Old Covenant, which itself was ceremonially destroyed through the sacrifice on the cross.

In this hymn and others, Luther's verbal and musical phrases are not always congruent, a fact that can lead to misunderstanding the text. Verse 6, for example, consists of two clauses, the first of three lines, the second of four. The music, however, is organized in phrases of 2 + 2 + 3 lines, leading the listener to expect the end of the first sentence one line later than it actually occurs. Heard in this way, the apparent second sentence ("Der durch seiner Gnaden Glanz . . . .") appears confused, as it lacks a subject, and its actual subject ("[Er ist selber] die Sonne") appears to be elided to the preceding sentence.

---

[88]Translation from Jeffers 1988: 243–245.

[89]For a detailed listing of related Biblical citations, see Unger 1996: 11–14.

Ein feste Burg ist unser Gott

A Mighty Fortress Is Our God

Martin Luther

Ein feste Burg   ist unser Gott,
A firm fortress is our God,

Ein gute Wehr   und Waffen;
a good bulwark and weapon;

Er hilft uns frei aus aller Not,
he helps us free from all misery

Die uns jetzt hat betroffen.
that us now has affected.

Der alte böse Feind,
The old evil foe:

Mit   Ernst   er's jetzt meint,
with seriousness he it now intends.

Groß Macht und viel   List
Great power and much cunning

Sein grausam Rüstung ist,
his   cruel armament is;

Auf Erd ist nicht seinsgleichen.
on earth is not   his equal.

A mighty fortress is our God,
a strong bulwark and weapon;
he sets us free from all the misery
that has now beset us.
The ancient, evil foe:
grave is his intent.
Vast power and cunning
are his cruel weapons;
on earth he has no equal.

Mit unsrer Macht ist nichts getan,
With our power is nothing done;

Wir sind gar bald verloren.
we are very soon   lost.

Es streit' vor uns der rechte Mann,
— fights for us the just man,

Den   Gott selbst   hat erkoren.
whom God himself has chosen.

Fragst du, wer er ist?
Ask   you, who he is?

Er heißt   Jesus Christ,
He is called Jesus Christ,

Der Herre Zebaoth,
the Lord Sabaoth,

Und ist kein andrer Gott,
and is no other God;

Das Feld muß er behalten.
the field must he retain.

With our own power, nothing is accomplished;
we will very soon be lost.
The just man fights for us,
the one whom God himself has chosen.
Do you ask who he is?
His name is Jesus Christ,
the Lord of Sabaoth,
and if there is no other God;
master of all he must remain.

Und wenn die Welt voll Teufel   wär
And   if the world full of devils were

Und wollten   uns verschlingen,
and wanted to us   devour,

So fürchten wir uns nicht so sehr,
so fear   we — not so much,

Es soll uns doch gelingen.
–we shall still succeed– .

Der Fürst dieser Welt,
The prince of this world,

Wie   saur   er sich stellt,
how difficult he — poses,

Tut er uns doch nicht,
does he to us —   not.

Das macht, er ist gericht',
That means, he is judged;

Ein Wörtchen kann ihn fällen.
a   little word can him fell.

And if the world were full of devils
who wanted to devour us,
we would not be too frightened,
for we shall still succeed.
The prince of this world,
however troublesome he seems,
does us no harm.
That means he is doomed;
a mere word can fell him.

Das Wort sie sollen lassen stahn	They must allow the word to stand
The word they shall let stand	and not be concerned about it.
	He is surely with us on the field of battle,
Und kein' Dank dazu haben.	along with his Spirit and its gifts.
and no thanks in addition have.	If they take from us our body,
	goods, honor, child, and wife,
Er ist bei uns wohl auf dem Plan	let them go;
He is with us surely on the battlefield,	they gain no victory from that,
	for the kingdom is ours forever.
Mit seinem Geist und Gaben.	
with his spirit and gifts.	

Nehmen sie uns den Leib,
Take they from us the body,

Gut, Ehr, Kind und Weib,
goods, honor, child, and wife,

Laß fahren dahin,
let go thither;

Sie habens kein' Gewinn;
they have no gain.

Das Reich muß uns doch bleiben.
The kingdom must for us — remain.

Source: Luther 1967: 39

*T*HIS, Luther's best known chorale, has one of the murkiest histories. Stulken (1981: 307) and Julian (1985, 1: 322) present arguments in support of dates ranging from 1521 to 1530. And the story related by the poet Heinrich Heine is fanciful and romantic although light on historical accuracy:

> A battle hymn was this defiant song, with which he [Luther] and his comrades entered Worms [April 16, 1521]. The old cathedral trembled at these new notes, and the ravens were startled in their hidden nests in the towers.[90]

Such an early date is unlikely, as it was Luther's practice to publish his hymns shortly after their composition, but the earliest source, which apparently still survived when Julian wrote a century ago but is now lost, is from 1529. Luther scholar Johannes Ficker states that:

> Ein feste Burg was written in the late autumn of 1529, influenced by the liberation of Vienna, as a confessional hymn to the Christian God who revealed himself in the Christ. The text cannot be shown to have appeared before the end of 1529. It was doubtless to be found in the (now lost) Wittenberg hymnal [pub. Kluge] of 1529. (Schröder 1953–1973, 1: 89)

Stulken (1981: 307) reports that "Julian and Ronander and Porter give as a possible inspiration the Diet of Speyer (Spires) in 1529 at which German princes protested against the revocation of their liberties, giving rise to the term 'Protestant.'" Finally, Gerhard Hahn, the editor of the collected hymns of Luther (Luther, 1967), lists the period of composition as 1526 to mid 1528.

The first two lines of the opening verse are based on Psalm 46: 1. Thereafter, however, Luther diverges from the Psalm. The first verse raises the specter of Satan, "the ancient, evil foe," who has no equal on earth. The beginning of the second verse expresses the powerlessness of man, raising the question of who is to stand for us against the devil. The second half answers: "His name is Jesus Christ." With these words Luther changes the focus of the hymn from the Old Testament to the New. Verse 3 expresses the confidence of the Christian in Christ's power over evil, a thought continued and expanded in the fourth and final verse.

Although Heinrich Heine (quotation above) may have had his history wrong, he was certainly right in calling this chorale the "battle hymn" of the Reformation. Luther trusted not only in God, but in the power of music as well. "The devil, the originator of sorrowful anxieties and restless troubles, flees before the sound of music almost as much as before the word of God." (Osbeck 1982: 14) "Ein feste Burg" possessed a second level of meaning during the Reformation, with Satan being understood as the established church. The words "If they take from us the body, goods, honor, child, and wife" were to be taken literally, as all of these penalties were likely to be exacted of the Protestant who had the ill fortune to be called to answer for heresy. "Ein feste Burg" doubtless provided solace to many as they mounted the scaffold. Luther avoided this fate himself, but the opening line appears on his tombstone to accompany and comfort him through eternity.

This chorale is no. 201 in the *EKG*, and no. 228 in the *LBW*, with the title "A Mighty Fortress Is Our God."

---

[90]Heinrich Heine, quoted in Julian 1985, 1: 323.

Es ist ein' Ros' entsprungen

A Rose Has Come Forth

Author of verses 1–2 unknown; verse 3, Friedrich Layriz

Es ist ein' Ros' entsprungen
— is a rose come forth

Aus einer Wurzel zart,
from a root tender,

Wie uns die Alten sungen;
as to us the old sang.

von Jesse kam die Art
From Isaiah came the lineage

Und hat ein Blümlein bracht
and has a little flower brought

Mitten im kalten Winter,
middle in the cold winter,

Wohl zu der halben Nacht.
right at the half night.

A rose has come forth
from a tender root,
as the prophets of old sang to us.
From Isaiah came the lineage,
and it has brought us a flower
in the cold midwinter,
right at the midnight hour.

Das Röslein, das ich meine,
The little rose that I mean,

Davon Jesaja sagt,
about which Isaiah spoke,

Hat uns gebracht alleine
has to us brought alone

Marie, die reine Magd;
Mary, the pure maiden.

Aus Gottes ewgem Rat
From God's eternal counsel,

Hat sie ein Kind geboren,
has she a child borne

Bleibend ein reine Magd.
remaining a pure maiden.

The little rose that I mean,
about which Isaiah spoke,
has been brought to us by
Mary, the pure virgin.
Fulfilling God's eternal counsel,
she has borne a child
and yet remained a virgin.

Das Blümelein so kleine,
The little flower so small

Das duftet uns so süß;
that smells to us so sweet;

Mit seinem hellen Scheine
with his bright light

Vertreibts die Finsternis:
he dispels the darkness.

Wahr' Mensch und wahrer Gott,
True human and true God,

Hilft uns aus allem Leide,
help us out of all suffering;

Rettet von Sünd und Tod.
deliver from sin and death.

The tiny little flower
smells so sweet to us;
with his bright light
he dispels the darkness.
True human and true God,
help us out of all our suffering;
deliver us from sin and death.

*T*HE simplest and most familiar of texts sometimes has a most involved history. That is certainly true of the "Es ist ein' Ros' entsprungen." Scholarship on the song places its roots most likely in the late fifteenth or early sixteenth century. The earliest surviving source, however, is a manuscript from the medieval city of Trier in Germany's Rhineland containing sixteen verses and dating from ca. 1582–1588. "Es ist ein' Ros'" was first published in 1599 in a Catholic hymnal (*Alte katholische geistliche Kirchengeseng*, Cologne) that provided twenty-three verses. These comprise an anthology of images from Luke 1 and 2 and Matthew 2 dealing with the Annunciation, the Conception, the Visitation, the birth, the shepherds, and the Magi. This eclectic structure suggests that the text started off simply and accrued new verses on new topics over time. Yet more verses have arisen since the sixteenth century; the third of the three in the *EKG*, for example, is by Friedrich Layriz (also Layritz) (1808–1859).

The basis for the opening two verses is Isaiah 11: 1, the beginning of his Messianic prophesy:

(*Die Bibel*, 1975)	Translation
Und es wird ein Reis hervorgehen aus dem Stamm Isais und ein Zweig aus seiner Wurzel Frucht bringen.	And a shoot shall come forth from the stem [family] of Isaiah and a branch from his root shall bring forth fruit. (tr. ed.)

The hymn text builds on this image of Isaiah's family tree, with David the root, Isaiah the stem, Mary a rose, and Jesus a diminutive rose. This hierarchy becomes confused in some English versions, which mingle the separate references to Jesus and Mary. Compare the German text with the rhyming rendition of Dr. Theodore Baker (1851–1934), the most familiar English version:

German (*EKG*: 23)	Translation (ed.)	Theodore Baker
Es ist ein' Ros' entsprungen	A rose has come forth	Lo! how a rose e'er blooming,
aus einer Wurzel zart,	from a tender root,	From Jesse's stem hath sprung,
wie uns die Alten sungen;	As the ancients sang to us;	Of Jesse's lineage coming
von Jesse kam die Art	From Isaiah came the lineage	As seers of old have sung;
Und hat ein Blümlein bracht	*And brought us a little flower*	*It came a blossom bright,*
mitten im kalten Winter	in the midst of the cold winter,	Amid the cold of winter
wohl zu der halben Nacht.	right at the midnight hour.	When half-spent was the night.
Das Röslein, das ich meine,	The little rose that I mean,	Isaiah 'twas foretold it,
davon Jesaja sagt,	about which Isaiah spoke,	The rose I have in mind;
hat uns gebracht alleine	*Mary alone, the pure virgin*	*With Mary we behold it,*
Marie, die reine Magd;	*has brought to us;*	*The Virgin Mother kind:*
Aus Gottes ewgem Rat	from God's eternal counsel	To show God's love aright
hat sie ein Kind geboren	she has given birth to a child,	She bore to us a savior
bleibend ein reine Magd.[91]	remaining a pure virgin.	When half-spent was the night.

In the German it is clear that the rose in verse 1, line 1 must be the Virgin Mary, as the rose brings forth the "little flower" and the "little rose" (verse 2) that must be the Christ-child. This distinction is lost in the Baker translation, which refers to Jesus in both cases. The German syntax in verse 2, lines 3 and 4 has also led to misunderstanding. Read literally (and nonsensically), the little rose brought the Virgin Mary to us. The German is poetic, however, with the subject (*Marie*) following the verb (*hat gebracht*). Reversing the two lines in translation, as above, renders the meaning as intended.

Adding to the confusion in one sense but clearing it up in another is the fact that some sources substitute *Reis* ("branch," as in the earlier quotation from Isaiah) for *Ros'* and *Reislein* (twig) for *Röslein*:

German (Keyte and Parrott 1992: 218)	Translation (ed.)
Es ist ein Reis entsprungen	A branch has come forth
aus einer Wurzel zart,	from a tender root,
Wie uns die Alten sungen;	As the ancients sang to us;
Von Jesse kam die Art	From Isaiah came the lineage
Und hat ein Blümlein bracht	And brought us a little flower
mitten im kalten Winter	in the midst of the cold winter,
wohl zu der halben Nacht.	right at the midnight hour.
Das Reislein, das ich meine,	The twig that I mean
So uns das Blümlein bringt,	brings to us the little flower;
Maria ists, die reine,	It [the twig] is Mary, the pure,
Von der Jesias sagt.	of whom Isaiah spoke.
Aus Gottes ewgem Rat	From God's eternal counsel
hat sie ein Kind geboren	she has given birth to a child,
und bleibt doch reine Magd.	and yet remains a pure virgin.

In this version, with different text in verse 2, lines 2–4, the family tree is much more distinct: Mary is the branch (verse 1) and the twig (verse 2, *Reislein* = diminutive of *Reis*) from whom the "little flower" (Jesus) in both verses springs.

---

[91]This line is shown as it appeared in an early version of the hymn (Keyte and Parrott 1992: 217), before Michael Praetorius deleted it in favor of a repetition of the end of verse 1. See the explanation in the penultimate paragraph of this essay.

Lutherans embraced this hymn early on; the famous setting ascribed to Michael Praetorius (1571–1621) that appears in many modern hymnals was published in 1609 but probably existed even before his birth.[92] The Catholic roots of the hymn and its emphasis on Mary may not have set well with some of them, Praetorius included. The second reference to the Virgin Birth, at the end of verse 2, appears to have been more than Praetorius could bear, as he omitted it, substituting a repetition of the last line of verse 1. This curious alteration has been carried over into English translations including that of Dr. Baker (see above), and even into the *EKG*.

"Es ist ein Ros'" is found in the Christmas section of the *EKG* as no. 23 (the source of the text given here, with the last line of verse 2 restored) and in the *LBW* as no. 58 under the title "Lo How a Rose Is Growing."

Jesu, meine Freude
Jesu, My Joy
Johann Franck

Jesu, meine Freude,
Jesu, my joy,

Meines Herzens Weide,
my heart's pasture,

Jesu, meine Zier,
Jesu, my adornment,

Ach, wie lang, ach lange
Ah, how long, ah long

Ist dem Herzen bange
is the heart anxious

Und verlangt nach dir!
and longs after you!

Gottes Lamm, mein Bräutigam,
God's lamb, my bridegroom,

Außer dir soll mir auf Erden
besides you shall to me on earth

Nichts sonst Liebers werden.
nothing else dearer become.

Jesu, my joy,
my heart's delight,
Jesu, my treasure,
how long, ah, how long
my heart is troubled
and longs for you!
God's lamb, my bridegroom,
besides you, nothing else on earth
shall become dearer to me.

Unter deinem Schirmen
Under your protection

Bin ich vor den Stürmen
am I from the storms

Aller Feinde frei.
of all foes free.

Laß den Satan wettern,
Let — Satan curse,

Laß die Welt erzittern,
Let the world tremble,

Mir steht Jesus bei.
me stands Jesus by.

Ob es jetzt gleich kracht und blitzt,
If it now instantly crashes and flashes,

Ob gleich Sünd und Hölle schrecken,
if instantly sin and hell frighten,

Jesus will mich decken.
Jesus wants me to protect.

Under your protection
I am free from the storms
of all my foes.
Let Satan curse and swear,
let the world tremble,
Jesus stands by me.
If a storm suddenly crashes and flashes,
if sin and hell suddenly frighten me,
Jesu wants to protect me.

---

[92]Keyte and Parrott 1992: 222. *The New Oxford Book of Carols* contains additional prespectives on the text to this hymn, which interested readers will want to consult—particularly regarding the *Ros/Reis* question and the use by Praetorius of *Roess* (= abbreviation of *Röslein*) in the place of *Ros.'*

Trotz dem alten Drachen,
Despite the old dragon,

Trotz des Todesrachen,
despite — death's jaws,

Trotz der Furcht dazu!
despite — fear in addition,

Tobe Welt und springe:
Rage, world, and burst,

Ich steh' hier und singe,
I stand here and sing

In gar sichrer Ruh.
in such secure peace.

Gottes Macht hält mich in acht;
God's might holds me in awe;

Erd und Abgrund muß verstummen,
earth and abyss must become silent,

Ob sie noch so brummen.
though they still so grumble.

Despite the old dragon,
despite death's jaws,
and despite fears as well,
even though the world rage and burst,
I stand here and sing,
in such secure peace.
God's might holds me in awe;
earth and abyss must become silent,
even though they still grumble.

Weg mit allen Schätzen!
Away with all treasures!

Du bist mein Ergötzen,
You are my delight,

Jesu, meine Lust.
Jesu, my pleasure.

Weg, ihr eitlen Ehren,
Away, you vain honors,

Ich mag euch nicht hören,
I want you not to hear;

Bleibt mir unbewußt!
remain to me unknown!

Elend, Not, Kreuz, Schmach und Tod
Misery, distress, cross, shame, and death

Soll mich, ob ich viel muß leiden,
shall me, though I much must suffer,

Nicht von Jesu scheiden.
not from Jesu separate.

Away with all treasures!
You are my delight,
Jesu, my pleasure.
Away, you vain honors,
I do not want to hear you;
remain unknown to me!
Misery, distress, cross, shame, and death
shall not, though I must suffer greatly,
separate me from Jesu.

Gute Nacht, o Wesen,
Good night, O existence

Das die Welt erlesen,
that the world [has] chosen;

Mir gefällst du nicht!
me please you not!

Gute Nacht, ihr Sünden,
Good night, you sins.

Bleibet weit dahinten,
Stay far away behind;

Kommt nicht mehr ans Licht;
come not more into light!

Gute Nacht, du Stolz und Pracht!
Good night, you pride and pomp;

Dir sei ganz, du Lasterleben,
to you be utterly, you life of iniquity,

Gute Nacht gegeben!
good night given!

Farewell, O life
that the world has chosen;
you please me not!
Farewell you sins.
Stay far behind me;
come no more into the light!
Farewell pride and pomp;
to you, life of iniquity,
a final farewell be bidden.

Weicht, ihr Trauergeister!
Yield,   you   grief-spirits!

Denn mein Freudenmeister,
for   my   joy master,

Jesus,   tritt herein.
Jesus, enters in.

Denen, die Gott lieben,
Those who God love,

Muß auch ihr Betrüben
must even their sorrows

Lauter Freude sein.
pure   joy   be.

Duld' ich schon hier Spott   und Hohn,
Endure I even here mockery and scorn,

Dennoch bleibst du auch im   Leide,
yet   remain you even in suffering,

Jesu, meine Freude.
Jesu, my   joy.

Give way, you spirits of grief!
for my lord of joy,
Jesus, enters in.
For those who love God,
even their sorrows
must be pure joy.
Even if I must endure mockery and scorn,
you still remain, even in suffering,
Jesu, my joy!

Source: Franck 1674: 191
Variants: (*EKG* = roman, Franck = *italics*)

Verse 2,	line 4:	wettern = *wüttern*
	line 5:	erzittern = *erschüttern*
Verse 4,	line 8:	ob ich viel muß = *muß ich gleich viel*
Verse 5,	lines 7, 8:	du = *o*
Verse 6,	line 6:	Freude (joy) = *Zucker* (sugar, sweetness)

*T*HIS hymn, which achieved special renown through J.S. Bach's motet setting, is the work of Johann Franck (1618–1677), a lawyer and civic leader from the east German city of Guben. Franck had studied poetry and elocution with Simon Dach, also a hymnist, in Königsberg, East Prussia. His training manifested itself in numerous hymns, four of which are still in use in Germany and appear in the *EKG*. Franck was a friend of Johann Crüger and Paul Gerhardt,* two of the greatest hymn writers of his day; many of his hymns appeared in Gerhardt's publications, and Crüger was the author of the melody to the present hymn. It was first published in Crüger's *Praxis pietatis melis* of 1653.[93]

> As a hymn writer he holds a high rank and is distinguished for unfeigned and firm faith, deep earnestness, finished form, and noble, pithy simplicity of expression. In his hymns we miss the objectivity and congregational character of the older German hymns, and notice a more personal, individual tone; especially in the longing for the inward and mystical union of Christ with the soul as in his "Jesu meine Freude." (Julian 1985, 1: 386)

Verses 1–3 speak of the many facets of Jesus: (verse 1) delight, treasure, sacrificial lamb, and bridegroom to the Christian;[94] (verse 2) protector; and (verse 3) savior. Verses 4 and 5 exhort the Christian to cast off the trappings of this world (verse 4) and bid it farewell (verse 5). The preparation for union with Christ now complete, the final verse welcomes Jesus as he enters the Christian's heart.

In the *EKG* (293) "Jesu, meine Freude" is classified as a hymn for general use. The latter verses, in which the burdens of this life are tossed off in favor of union with Christ, suggest its use as a funeral chorale. "Jesu, meine Freude" is found in the *LBW* as no. 457 under the title "Jesus, Priceless Treasure." The hymn is presented here as it appears in the *EKG*.

---

[93]Julian (1985, 1: 59) states that the first publication was two years later.

[94]Regarding the symbolism of the lamb, see the annotation to cantata BWV 4, "Christ lag in Todes Banden." The symbolism of the bridegroom is discussed in the annotation to cantata BWV 140, "Wachet auf."

Komm, Heiliger Geist, Herre Gott

Come, Holy Spirit, Lord God

Author of verse 1 unknown; verses 2–3, Martin Luther

Komm, Heiliger Geist, Herre Gott,
Come, Holy Spirit, Lord God,

erfüll mit deiner Gnaden Gut
fill with your grace's good

deiner Gläubgen Herz, Mut und Sinn,
your believers' heart, courage, and sense;

dein brünstig Lieb entzünd in ihn'.
your fervent love ignite in them.

O Herr, durch deines Lichtes Glanz
O Lord, through your light's brightness

zu dem Glauben versammelt hast
to the faith gathered have

das Volk aus aller Welt Zungen.
the people from all the world's tongues.

Das sei dir, Herr, zu Lob gesungen.
That be to you, Lord, in praise sung.

Alleluia, Alleluia.
Alleluia, Alleluia.

Come, Holy Spirit, Lord God,
and with the blessing of your grace
fill your believers' heart, courage, and mind;
ignite your fervent love in them.
O Lord, through the brightness of your light
you have gathered people to the faith
from all the world's tongues.
For this, O Lord, your praise be sung.
Alleluia, Alleluia.

Du heilges Licht, edler Hort,
You holy light, precious sanctuary,

laß uns leuchten des Lebens Wort
let for us shine — life's word

und lehr uns Gott recht erkennen,
and teach us God correctly to recognize,

von Herzen Vater ihn nennen.
–from our hearts– Father him to call.

O Herr, behüt vor fremder Lehr,
O Lord, protect from foreign teachings,

daß wir nicht Meister suchen mehr
that we not masters seek more

denn Jesum mit rechtem Glauben
except Jesus with true faith

und ihm aus ganzer Macht vertrauen.
and him from all might trust.

Alleluia, Alleluia.
Alleluia, Alleluia.

You holy light and precious sanctuary,
let life's word shine for us
and teach us to recognize God truly
and to call him "Father" with all our hearts.
O Lord, protect us from the teachings of others,
so that we, with true faith,
seek no other masters than Jesus
and trust him with all our might.
Alleluia, Alleluia.

Du heilige Brunst, süßer Trost,
You holy fire, sweet consolation,

Nun hilf uns, fröhlich und getrost
now help us, joyful and consoled,

In deim Dienst beständig bleiben,
in your service steadfast to remain;

Die Trübsal uns nicht abtreiben.
the affliction us not drive away.

O Herr, durch dein Kraft uns bereit
O Lord, by your power us prepare

Und stärk des Fleisches Blödigkeit,
and strengthen the flesh's timidity,

Daß wir hie ritterlich ringen,
that we here gallantly struggle

Durch Tod und Leben zu dir dringen.
through death and life to you reach.

Alleluia, Alleluia.
Alleluia, Alleluia.

You holy fire, sweet consolation,
now help us, joyful and consoled,
to remain steadfast in your service;
let affliction not drive us away.
O Lord, prepare us by your power
and strengthen our feeble flesh,
so that we here may gallantly struggle
through death and life to reach you.
Alleluia, Alleluia.

Source: Luther 1967: 2

*P*ENTECOST is the third major feast of the Lutheran church year, after the feasts of Easter and Christmas. A commemoration of the descent of the Holy Spirit upon the disciples (Acts 2), Pentecost began to be observed as a festival among Christians in the third century. In the Roman Catholic Church, several texts beginning with the words *Veni Sancte Spiritus* (Come, Holy Spirit) and *Veni creator Spiritus* (Come, Creator Spirit) were associated with this day. (See Jeffers 1988: 231–241.) Among these was an eleventh-century Antiphon, the text to which is as follows:[95]

Veni Sancte Spiritus reple tuorum corda fidelium,	Come, Holy Spirit, fill the heart of your faithful
et tui amoris in eis ignem accende:	one and kindle in him the fire of your love,
qui per diversitatem linguarum cunctarum,	you who through the diversity of all languages
gentes in unitate fidei congregasti.	has brought nations together in the unity of faith.
Alleluia.	Alleluja. (tr. ed.)

Three fifteenth-century manuscripts as well as another from 1514 contain a German version of this text. "It was well known in Luther's day. Luther was fond of it, and in his table talks spoke of both the words and music as having been composed by the Holy Ghost himself." (Stulken 1981: 254) Luther created the principal Pentecost hymn of the Lutheran church, "Komm, Heiliger Geist, Herre Gott," by adding two verses to the German "Veni Sancte Spiritus," which he adopted nearly verbatim. It was written around Pentecost, 1524 and was published in the same year.

The images of fire and tongues are closely associated with Pentecost, as the Holy Spirit is said to have descended upon the disciples as a "tongue of fire" (Acts 2: 3), which bestowed on them the ability to be understood by people speaking other languages or tongues.

Luther's hymn is found in the *EKG* as no. 98. The English version is contained in the *LBW* as "Come Holy Ghost, God and Lord," no. 163.

Lobe den Herren, den mächtigen König der Ehren
Praise to the Lord, the Mighty King of Glory
Joachim Neander

Lobe   den Herren, den mächtigen König der Ehren,
Praise to the Lord,   the mighty   king of glory;

Meine geliebete Seele, das ist mein Begehren.
my   beloved soul, that is my   desire.

Kommet   zuhauf,
Come   together;

Psalter   und Harfe, wacht auf,
psaltery and harp,   awake!

Lasset   die Musicam hören!
Let [us] the   music   hear!

Praise to the Lord, the mighty king of glory;
my beloved soul, that is my desire.
Come together;
psaltery and harp, awake!
Let the music be heard!

Lobe   den Herren, der alles so herrlich   regieret,
Praise to the Lord, who all so gloriously rules,

Der dich auf Adelers Fittichen sicher geführet,
who you on   eagle's   wings   safely has led,

Der dich   erhält,
who you preserves,

Wie es dir   selber   gefällt;
as it   you   yourself pleases;

Hast   du nicht dieses   verspüret?
have you not   this   perceived?

Praise to the Lord, who rules so gloriously over all,
who has led you safely on eagle's wings,
who preserves you,
as it pleases you.
Have you not perceived this?

---

[95]The better-known "Veni Sancte Spiritus et emitte. . . ." is the Sequence for Pentecost, and the text "Veni creator Spiritus mentes tuorum visita. . . ." is a hymn.

Lobe den Herren, der künstlich und fein dich bereitet,
Praise the Lord, who artfully and finely you prepares,

Der dir Gesundheit verliehen, dich freundlich geleitet.
who to you health has given, you kindly led.

In wieviel Not
In how much distress

Hat nicht der gnädige Gott
has indeed the merciful God

über dir Flügel gebreitet!
over you wings spread!

Praise to the Lord, who artfully and finely
  prepares you,
who has given you health and kindly led you.
In how many times of distress
has the merciful God indeed
spread his wings over you!

Lobe den Herren, der deinen Stand sichtbar gesegnet,
Praise to the Lord, who your state visibly blessed,

Der aus dem Himmel mit Strömen der Liebe geregnet.
who from the heaven with streams of love rained.

Denke daran,
Think of that,

Was der Allmächtige kann,
what the Almighty can do,

Der dir mit Liebe begegnet.
who you with love meets.

Praise to the Lord, who has visibly
  blessed your state,
who has rained streams of love from the heavens.
Consider
what the Almighty can do,
he who meets you with such love.

Lobe den Herren; was in mir ist, lobe den Namen.
Praise to the Lord; what in me is, praise the name.

Alles, was Odem hat, lobe mit Abrahams Samen.
All that breath has, praise with Abraham's seed.

Er ist dein Licht,
He is your light;

Seele, vergiß es ja nicht;
soul, forget it — not!

Lob ihn und schließe mit Amen!
Praise him and conclude with Amen!

Praise to the Lord; all within me praise his name.
All that has breath, praise with Abraham's seed.
He is your light;
O soul, forget it not!
Praise him and close with Amen!

Source: Neander 1700: 42
Variants: (*EKG* = roman, Neander = *italics*)
          Verse 5, line 5: Lob ihn und (praise him and) = *Lobende* (those who praise)

*T*HIS five-verse hymn by Joachim Neander (1789–1850) is worthy of an honored place among the great psalms of praise. In contrast to many of the chorales treated in this volume, most of which are from the Reformation period in the sixteenth century, "Lobe den Herren" dates from 1680. Whereas the literary style of the early chorale was rather objective and tended to speak for humanity in general rather than the individual, the hymns of the seventeenth century became more personal in focus. Such is the case with "Lobe den Herren," in which opening and closing verses of praise frame three verses that address the reasons why *individuals* owe thanks and praise to the Lord.

Those familiar with the Book of Psalms will hear echoes of at least two of them here—specifically, Psalm 103: 1–6 and Psalm 150, both of which contributed directly to the poet's language and images.

"Lobe den Herren" appears in the *EKG* as no. 234; it is also included in the *LBW* (no. 543) under the title "Praise to the Lord, the Almighty." The hymn appears here as presented in the *EKG*.

Mit Fried und Freud ich fahr dahin

In Peace and Joy I now Depart

Martin Luther

Mit Fried und Freud ich fahr dahin
With peace and joy I go thither

In Gottes Wille;
in God's will;

Getrost ist mir mein Herz und Sinn,
consoled is — my heart and mind,

Sanft und stille;
calm, and still;

Wie Gott mir verheißen hat,
as God me promised has,

Der Tod ist mein Schlaf worden.
— death has my sleep become.

In peace and joy I now depart
according to God's will;
my heart and mind are comforted,
calm, and still;
as God has promised me,
death has become my sleep.

Das macht Christus, wahr Gottes Sohn,
That does Christ, truly God's son,

Der treu Heiland,
the faithful Savior,

Den du mich, Herr, hast sehen lan
whom you me, Lord, have seen let

Und macht bekannt,
and made known,

Daß er sei das Leben und Heil
so that he might be — life and salvation

In Not und Sterben.
in distress and dying.

This Christ has done, God's true son,
the faithful Savior,
whom you, Lord, have let me see
and made known to me,
so that he might be my life and salvation
in distress and dying.

Den hast du allen vorgestellt
Him have you to all presented

Mit groß Gnaden,
with great grace,

Zu seinem Reich die ganze Welt
to his kingdom the whole world

Heißen laden
summon

Durch dein teuer heilsams Wort,
through your dear, healing word

An allem Ort erschollen.
in all places sounded.

You have presented him to all
with abundant grace
and summoned the entire world
to his kingdom,
through your precious, healing word,
which has resounded in all places.

Er ist das Heil und selig Licht
He is the salvation and blessed light

Für die Heiden,
for the Gentiles,

Zu erleuchten, die dich kennen nicht,
to enlighten those you know not,

Und zu weiden.
and to nurture.

Er ist deins Volks Israel
He is your people's Israel

Der Preis, Ehr, Freud und Wonne.
the reward, glory, joy, and bliss.

He is the salvation and blessed light
for the Gentiles,
to enlighten those who know you not
and to nurture them.
He is, to your people Israel,
the reward, glory, joy, and bliss.

Source: Luther 1967: 31

*T*HIS hymn is among the thirteen in which Luther paraphrased scripture into verse—a technique known as "versification." Here the text involved is Luke 2: 29–32, part of the story of the circumcision of Jesus and his presentation in the Temple. These events were important because they signified that Jesus had been born "under the Law" and by being circumcised, he was ceremonially bound to keep the Law as a Jew. Even as his obedience to the Law was being symbolically sealed, a prophecy of his Messianic future came forth from a witness named Simeon. As related in Luke 2: 25–32:

Now there was a man in Jerusalem, whose name was Simeon, and this man was righteous and devout, looking for the consolation of Israel, and the Holy Spirit was upon him. And it had been revealed to him by the Holy Spirit that he should not see death before he had seen the Lord's Christ. And inspired by the Spirit he came into the temple; and when the parents brought in the child Jesus, to do for him according to the custom of the law, he took him up in his arms and blessed God and said, *"Lord, now lettest thou thy servant depart in peace, according to thy word; for mine eyes have seen thy salvation, which thou hast prepared in the presence of all peoples, a light for revelation to the Gentiles, and for glory to thy people Israel."*

Simeon's prophecy of Jesus as the Messiah for both Jews and Gentiles is one of the most touching moments in the New Testament and has served as the basis for many musical compositions. The Latin form of this text is known as the "Nunc dimittis," or "Canticum Simeonis"—in English, the "Song of Simeon," and in German "Simeons Lobgesang." In the Roman Catholic Church it is one of several "Canticles," texts similar in structure to the Psalms that have always been considered Biblical "songs" and have many liturgical uses— in this case principally the Feast of the Purification of Mary.

Luther versified the complete words of Simeon, each Biblical verse becoming a stanza of the hymn:

Luke 2:	Standard Revised Version	Mit Fried und Freud
29	Lord, now lettest thou thy servant	stanza 1
30	for mine eyes have seen thy salvation	stanza 2
31	which thou hast prepared	stanza 3
32	a light for revelation to the Gentiles	stanza 4

"Mit Fried und Freud" was written in the first quarter of 1524, during Luther's most intense period of hymn composition. It has remained popular to the present day among German-speaking congregations and is included in the *EKG* as no. 310. Its fortunes have not been as good in English, and it has failed to retain a foothold among English-speaking Lutherans; it is not included in the *LBW*.

Mitten wir im Leben sind

In the Midst of Life
Martin Luther

Mitten wir im Leben sind
Middle we in life are

mit dem Tod umfangen.
with — death surrounded.

Wen suchen wir, der Hilfe tu,
Whom seek we, who help does

daß wir Gnad erlangen?
that we grace obtain?

Das bist du, Herr, alleine.
That are you, Lord, alone.

Uns reuet unsre Missetat,
To us is regrettable our misdeed,

die dich Herr, erzürnet hat.
that you, Lord, angered has.

Heiliger Herre Gott,
Holy Lord God,

heiliger starker Gott,
holy strong God,

heiliger barmherziger Heiland,
holy merciful savior,

du ewiger Gott,
you eternal God,

laß uns nicht versinken
let us not sink

in des bittern Todes Not.
in — bitter death's distress.

Kyrieleison.
Lord, have mercy.

In the midst of life we are
surrounded by death.
Whom shall we seek
who can help us obtain grace?
You alone, Lord, are the one.
We regret our transgressions,
Lord, that have angered you.
Holy Lord God,
holy and mighty God,
holy, merciful savior,
you eternal God,
let us not drown
in death's bitter distress.
Kyrieleison.

Mitten in dem Tod anficht
Middle in — death assail

uns der Höllen Rachen.
us — hell's jaws.

Wer will uns aus solcher Not
Who wants to us from such distress

frei und ledig machen?
free and unburdened make?

Das tust du, Herr, alleine.
That do you, Lord, alone.

Es jammert dein Barmherzigkeit
— pities your compassion

unsre Sünd und großes Leid.
our sin and great suffering.

Heiliger Herre Gott, heiliger starker Gott,
heiliger barmherziger Heiland, du ewiger Gott,

laß uns nicht versagen
let us not fail

vor der tiefen Höllen Glut.
before — deep hell's fires.

Kyrieleison.
Lord, have mercy.

Mitten in der Höllen Angst
Middle in — hell's anguish

unsre Sünd uns treiben.
our sins us drive.

Wo solln wir denn fliehen hin,
Where shall we then flee to

da wir mögen bleiben?
where we want to remain?

Zu dir, Herr Christ, alleine.
To you, Lord Christ, alone.

Vergossen ist dein teures Blut,
Spilled is your dear blood,

das gnug für die Sünde tut.
which enough for the sin does.

Heiliger Herre Gott, heiliger starker Gott,
heiliger barmherziger Heiland, du ewiger Gott,

laß uns nicht entfallen
let us not fall away

von des rechten Glaubens Trost.
from the true faith's consolation.

Kyrieleison.
Lord, have mercy.

In the midst of death
the jaws of hell assail us.
Who wants to make us free
and unburdened from such distress?
You alone, Lord, are the one.
Your merciful compassion pities
our sin and great suffering.

Holy Lord God,
holy and mighty God,
holy, merciful savior,
you eternal God,
let us not wither
before the deep fires of hell.
Kyrieleison.

Into the midst of hell's anguish
our sins drive us.
Whither shall we flee
where we would want to stay?
To you, Lord Christ, alone.
Your precious blood is spilled,
and this atones our sin.

Holy Lord God,
holy and mighty God,
holy, merciful savior,
you eternal God,
let us not forsake
the consolation of true faith.
Kyrieleison.

Source: Luther 1967: 3

*A*MONG Luther's chorales are eleven in which at least the opening verse is a translation or paraphrase of a hymn, Antiphon, or other sacred text of Roman Catholic origin. "Mitten wir im Leben sind" is one of these, the first verse having been adapted from the Latin Antiphon "Media vita in morte sumus." Traditionally and probably wrongly ascribed to Notker Balbulus (d. 910), it first appeared in two eleventh-century manuscripts (Stulken 1981: 401). Julian (1985: 720) cites its presence in a Sarum (the rite of Salisbury, England) Breviary of 1531, in which it is given as the Antiphon to the "Nunc dimittis"* for fifteen days in Lent. The Antiphon does not appear, however, in Antiphonales from the immediate pre-Vatican II period.

Several German versions were in existence by the fifteenth century. In his rendition, Martin Luther altered the character of the hymn from an almost frantic cry for help to a positive statement of faith, and added two stanzas of his own. This text first appears in the Erfurt *Enchiridia*, 1524, and has long held a foremost place among German hymns for the dying. (Stulken 1981: 401)

Each of the three verses has the same structure, providing the hymn with unusual unity and clarity:

Section		Verse 1 (example)
(1) 2 lines	Thesis:	In the midst of life we are surrounded by death.
(2) 5 lines	Question:	Who . . . can help us obtain grace?
	Answer:	You alone, Lord.
(3) 4 lines	*Trisagion* (doxology)	Holy Lord God, holy and mighty God, holy, merciful savior.
(4) 3 lines	Prayer, ending with "Kyrie eleison"	Let us not drown in death's bitter distress.

(1) The "thesis" that begins each verse establishes the condition of the Christian, surrounded in this life by death, the wrath of hell, and the fear of both.

(2) The "question" each time, born of the Christian's fears, is essentially "Who is to help us?" The answer is predictably and consolingly unchanging: "the Lord alone."

(3) Then follows a *Trisagion*, a doxology of fifth-century Greek origin characterized by a three-fold "holy"—in this case, "Holy Lord God, holy and mighty God, holy, merciful savior."

(4) Having established that the Lord in all his splendor and might is the omnipresent help in time of distress, each verse concludes with a prayer for his help, ending with the traditional appeal for mercy that begins the Roman Catholic Mass Ordinary: "Kyrie eleison" (Lord, have mercy).

"Mitten wir im Leben sind" is no. 309 in the *EKG,* under the heading "Death and Eternity." It is included in the *LBW* as no. 350 with the title "Even as We Live each Day."

Nun danket alle Gott
Let All Give Thanks to God
Martin Rinckart

Nun danket alle Gott
Now thank all God

Mit Herzen, Mund und Händen,
with heart, mouth, and hands,

Der große Dinge tut
who great things does

An uns und allen Enden,
at us and all ends;

Der uns von Mutterleib
who us from womb

Und Kindesbeinen an
and infancy on

Unzählig viel zugut,
innumerably much benefit

Bis hierher hat getan.
until now has done.

Let all give thanks to God
with heart, voice, and deeds,
to the one who achieves great things
for us and in all ways;
who from the womb
and childhood on
has done us incalculable good
and does so even now.

Der ewig reiche Gott
The eternally rich God

Woll uns bei unserm Leben
may to us in our life

Ein immer fröhlich Herz
an always joyful heart

Und edlen Frieden geben
and genuine peace give

Und uns in seiner Gnad
and us in his grace

Erhalten fort und fort
preserve forever

Und uns aus aller Not
and us from all distress

Erlösen hier und dort.
deliver here and there.

May the ever-bounteous God
give us throughout our life
an ever-joyful heart
and genuine peace,
and in his grace
preserve us forever and ever,
and from all distress
deliver us here and there.

Lob, Ehr und Preis sei Gott,	Praise, honor, and glory be to God,
Praise, honor and glory be to God,	to the Father, and to the Son,
	and to him who is the same as both
Dem Vater und dem Sohne	on heaven's high throne,
to the father and to the son	to God the Three-in-One,
	as it was in the beginning
Und dem, der beiden gleich	and is and shall be
and to him, who both the same	now and evermore.
Im hohen Himmelsthrone,	
on the high heavenly throne,	
Dem dreimal einen Gott,	
to the three-fold, one God,	
Wie es ursprünglich war	
as it originally was	
Und ist und bleiben wird	
and is and remain will	
Jetzund und immerdar.	
now and evermore.	

*T*HE earliest surviving source for this popular hymn dates from 1647. It was included in the second edition of Rinckart's *Jesu Heartz-Büchlein* from 1663, and almost certainly in the first edition of 1636, now lost. It is therefore likely that the hymn dates from 1636 or before.

Martin Rinckart (1586–1649) lived a hard life, the last thirty-two years of it as Lutheran Archdeacon of Eilenburg, a walled city in northern Germany. His tenure began just before and ended just after the Thirty Years War, which brought Swedish occupation and the miseries of war to his city. It also brought the plague, which took his wife and his Lutheran colleagues of the cloth, leaving him alone to preside over as many as fifty funerals a day. Such tribulations among hymn writers often brought forth chorales of great joy and thanksgiving,[96] as they did here.

The first two stanzas are versifications of chapter 50, verses 22–24 of the book of Ecclesiasticus from the Apocrypha (see "The Luther Bible"*). Note that the imperative of the opening words is lost in the usual translation, "Now thank we all our God."

22: And now bless the God of all, who in every way does great things; who exalts our days from birth, and deals with us according to his mercy.
23: May he give us gladness of heart, and grant that peace may be in our days in Israel, as in the days of old.
24: May he entrust to us his mercy! And let him deliver us in our days!

The plea for peace in verse 23 may well have figured in Rinckart's choice of text, given the omnipresence of war around him. The closing verse is an imaginative and vigorous doxology.

"Nun danket alle Gott" appears in the *EKG* as no. 228 and in the *LBW* as no. 533, under the title "Now Thank We All Our God." The version presented here, from the *EKG*, is identical to that set by Bach in BWV 192,* but for the last line of verse 1 and a couple of minor changes to verse 3.

Nun komm, der Heiden Heiland
Now Come, the Heathens' Savior
Martin Luther

Nun komm, der Heiden Heiland,	Now come, savior of the Gentiles,
Now come, the Gentile's savior,	you who are known as the Virgin's child,
	so that the whole world marvels
Der Jungfrauen Kind erkannt,	that God ordained for him such a birth.
of the Virgin child recognized,	
Daß sich wundert alle Welt,	
so that — marvels all world	
Gott solch Geburt ihm bestellt.	
God such birth for him ordained.	

---

[96]Philipp Nicolai, the composer of "Wie schön"* and "Wachet auf"* and also a Lutheran pastor, wrote his hymns during a similarly tragic plague epidemic forty-eight years earlier.

Nicht von Manns Blut noch von Fleisch,
Not from man's blood nor from flesh,

Allein von dem Heilgen Geist
alone from the Holy Spirit

Ist Gotts Wort worden ein Mensch,
is God's word become a human

Und   blüht   ein Frucht Weibes   Fleisch.
and flourishes a fruit of woman's flesh.

Not through man's blood nor his flesh,
but only through the Holy Spirit
has God's word become a human being
and flourishes as a fruit of woman's flesh.

Der Jungfrau Leib schwanger ward,
The virgin's body pregnant became,

Doch blieb   Keuschheit rein bewahrt,
yet remained virginity pure preserved.

Leucht herfür manch Tugend schon,
Shines   forth many a virtue already;

Gott   da   war in seinem Thron.
God there was in his   throne.

The Virgin became pregnant,
yet her virginity was preserved and pure.
Many a virtue shines forth already;
God was there on his throne.

Er ging aus der Kammer sein,
He went from the chamber his,

Dem Königlichen Saal so rein,
to the   royal   hall so clean—

Gott von Art   und Mensch, ein Held;
God in nature and human, a hero;

Sein' Weg er zu laufen   eilt.
his   way he to walk hurries.

He went forth from his chamber
and the clean and chaste royal hall—
A God by nature, and human, a hero;
he hastens to traverse his path.

Sein Lauf kam vom Vater her,
His course came from father to here,

Und kehrt wieder zum Vater,
and returns again to the father;

Fuhr hinunter zu der Höll
went down to — hell

Und wieder zu Gottes Stuhl.
and   again   to God's throne.

His course came from the Father
and returns again to the Father;
he went down to hell
and returned again to God's throne.

Der du bist dem Vater gleich,
Who you are to the father equal,

Führ hinaus den Sieg   im Fleisch,
lead   forth the victory in the flesh,

Daß dein ewig Gotts Gewalt
that your eternal God's power

In uns das krank Fleisch enthalt.
in us the sick   flesh include.

You who are equal to the Father,
lead the victory in the flesh,
so that your eternal God's power
might be embodied in our mortal flesh.

Dein Krippen glänzt   hell   und klar,
Your manger shines brightly and clearly;

Die Nacht gibt ein neu Licht dar.
the night gives a new light —.

Dunkel   muß nicht kommen drein,
Darkness must not   come therein;

Der Glaub bleibt immer im   Schein.
— faith remains always in the radiance.

Your manger shines bright and clear;
the night emits a new light.
Darkness must not enter therein;
faith endures forever in the radiance.

Lob   sei Gott, dem Vater, ton,
Praise be God, the Father given,

Lob   sei Gott, sein'm eingen Sohn,
Praise be God,   his   only son,

Lob   sei Gott, dem Heilgen Geist,
Praise be God, the Holy   Spirit,

Immer und in Ewigkeit!
always and in eternity!

Praise be given to God the Father,
praise be to God, his only son,
praise be to God, the Holy Spirit,
always and eternally!

Source: Luther 1967: 23

292

*T*HE roots of this Advent chorale reach back to the fourth-century Latin hymn "Veni redemptor gentium," attributed to St. Ambrose of Milan (340–397), the "father of Latin hymnody" (Stulken 1981: 127):

Veni redemptor gentium,	Come, thou savior of the Gentiles;
Ostende partum virginis,	make manifest thy Virgin Birth.
Miretur omne saeculum,	May all time marvel at it,
Talis decet partus Deum.	for such birth is fitting for God.

Twelve hymns likely to be by Ambrose survive, as well as some ninety "Ambrosian" hymns in imitation of his style. Despite the centuries separating them, Ambrose's hymns and those of Luther share a crucial characteristic: they were meant to be sung by the congregation. Luther's nearly literal translation of Ambrose in his first verse dates from 1523, placing "Nun komm, der Heiden Heiland" among his earliest chorales.

Luther wrote seven verses, only five of which appear in the *EKG*, his verses 2 and 3 being omitted. The chorale begins with an invitation for the Savior to come. The next two verses reflect on the wonder of the Virgin Birth, and verses 4 and 5 remind the listener that Jesus was God in the flesh. Verse 6 looks back to the birth in Bethlehem and likens the radiance from the manger to the light of faith and salvation, while the final verse provides a simple doxology.

Advent, the period of preparation for the coming of the Lord, should not be thought of merely as preparation for Christmas. While it is indeed a ritual of preparation for the observance of Jesus's birth, more importantly, it looks toward the Second Coming. This is clear in Luther's chorale through his use of the past tense—the Savior has already been here, has died on the cross, descended into hell, and arisen into heaven.

"Nun komm der Heiden Heiland" has pride of place in the *EKG* as hymn no. 1; it appears in the *LBW* as no. 28, under the title "Savior of the Nations, Come."

O Haupt voll Blut und Wunden
O Head Full of Blood and Wounds
Paul Gerhardt

O Haupt voll Blut und Wunden,
O head full of blood and wounds,

Voll Schmerz und voller Hohn,
full of pain and full of scorn,

O Haupt, zum Spott gebunden
O head, for mockery bound

Mit einer Dornenkron,
with a thorn-crown,

O Haupt, sonst schön gezieret
O head, at other times beautifully adorned

Mit höchster Ehr und Zier,
with highest honor and adornment,

Jetzt aber hoch schimpfieret:
now however highly reviled:

Gegrüßet seist Du mir!
greeted be you by me!

O head full of blood and wounds,
full of pain and full of scorn,
O head mockingly bound
with a crown of thorns,
O head, at other times beautifully adorned
with highest honor and adornment,
but now, however, highly reviled:
I greet you!

Du   edles   Angesichte,
You   noble   countenance,

Davor   sonst   schrickt   und scheut
before which otherwise shrinks away and fears

Das große Weltgewichte.
the   great   universe,

Wie bist du so bespeit,
how are you so spat at;

Wie bist du so erbleichet!
how are you so   paled!

Wer hat dein Augenlicht,
Who has   your   eye's light,

Dem   sonst   kein Licht nicht gleichet,
which otherwise no   light not resembles,

So schändlich   zugericht?
so shamefully [been] battered?

You noble countenance,
before which the endless universe
otherwise shrinks in fear,
how you are spat upon;
how pale you have become!
How has the light of your eyes,
which is like no other light,
been battered so shamefully?

Die Farbe deiner Wangen,
The color of your cheeks,

Der roten Lippen   Pracht
the   red   lips' splendor

Ist hin und   ganz   vergangen;
is away and completely gone;

Des   blassen Todes Macht
Of the   pale   death's power

Hat alles hingenommen,
has all   taken away,

Hat alles hingerafft,
has all snatched up:

und daher   bist du kommen
and therefore have you   come

von deines Leibes   Kraft.
from your   body's power.

The color of your cheeks,
the magnificence of your red lips
is gone and has utterly disappeared;
death's pale power
has taken all away,
has stolen everything:
and thus have you lost
the strength of your mortal flesh.

Nun, was   du, Herr, erduldet,
Well, what you, Lord, suffered,

Ist alles meine   Last;
is   all   my   burden.

Ich hab es selbst verschuldet,
I have it myself   caused

Was du getragen hast.
what you borne   have!

Schau her, hier steh ich Armer,
Look here, here stand I poor man

Der Zorn   verdienet hat;
who anger deserved has.

Gib   mir, o mein Erbarmer,
Give me, O my merciful one,

Den Anblick deiner Gnad!
the   sight of your grace!

What you have suffered, Lord,
is all my burden.
I myself have caused
what you have borne!
Behold—here I stand, a poor sinner
who has deserved anger.
Grant me, merciful one,
the sight of your grace!

Erkenne   mich, mein Hüter,
Recognize me,   my guardian;

Mein Hirte, nimm mich an.
my shepherd, accept me —.

Von dir, Quell aller Güter,
From you, source of all goods,

Ist mir   viel Gut's getan:
is to me much good done:

Dein Mund hat mich gelabet
your mouth has me refreshed

Mit Milch und süßer Kost,
with milk and sweet food;

Dein Geist hat mich begabet
your spirit has me bestowed

Mit mancher Himmelslust.
with many a heavenly joy.

Recognize me, my guardian;
my shepherd, accept me.
From you, source of all good things,
much good is done for me:
your mouth has refreshed me
with milk and sweet food;
your spirit has bestowed on me
many a heavenly joy.

Ich will   hier bei dir stehen;
I want to here with you stand;

Verachte mich doch nicht!
despise me — not!

Von dir will ich nicht gehen,
From you want I not to go

Wenn dir dein Herze bricht;
when — your heart breaks.

Wenn dein Haupt wird erblassen
When your head becomes pale

Im   letzten Todesstoß,
in the last death blow,

Alsdann will ich dich fassen
then   want I you to hold

In meinen Arm und Schoß.
in my arms and bosom.

I want to stand here with you;
despise me not!
I do not want to part from you
when your heart breaks.
When your face becomes pale
at the last death blow,
then I want to hold you
in my arms and bosom.

Es dient zu meinen Freuden
It serves — my   joys

Und kommt mir herzlich wohl,
and does me heartily well

Wenn ich in deinem Leiden,
when I, in your suffering,

Mein Heil,   mich finden soll.
my salvation me find shall.

Ach möcht ich, o mein Leben,
Oh could I, O my life,

An deinem Kreuze hier
on your cross here

Mein Leben von mir geben,
my life from me give—

Wie wohl   geschähe   mir!
how well would happen to me!

It brings me much joy
and does my heart good
when I, in your suffering,
shall find my salvation.
O my life and my Lord,
I desire to offer up my life
here, on your cross;
how good it would be for me!

Ich danke dir   von Herzen,
I   thank you from   heart,

O Jesu, liebster Freund,
O Jesus, dearest   friend,

Für deines Todes Schmerzen,
for   your death's   pains,

Da   du's so gut gemeint.
since you it so well   meant.

Ach   gib,   daß   ich mich halte
Alas grant, that   I   —   hold

Zu   dir und deiner   Treu
on to you and   your faithfulness,

Und, wenn ich nun   erkalte,
and   when I   now become cold,

In dir   mein Ende sei.
in you   my   end   be.

I thank you from my heart,
O Jesus, dearest friend,
for your death's pains,
since you meant so well.
Alas, grant that I might hold on
to you and your faithfulness,
and when I become cold,
may my end be in you.

Wenn ich einmal soll scheiden,
When   I   once shall depart,

So scheide nicht von mir;
so depart not   from me.

Wenn ich den Tod   soll leiden,
When I   — death shall suffer,

So tritt du   dann herfür;
so step you then   out.

Wenn   mir   am allerbängsten
When to me   –most fearful–

Wird   um   das Herze sein,
will   around the heart   be,

So reiß mich aus   den Ängsten
so tear me out of   the   fears

Kraft   deiner Angst   und Pein.
by strength of your anguish and pain.

When I depart one day,
depart not from me.
When I suffer death,
then come forth.
When the most horrible fears
fill my anguished heart,
release me from my fears
by the strength of your anguish and pain.

Erscheine mir   zum Schilde,
Appear   to me as a   shield,

Zum   Trost   in meinem Tod
as consolation in   my   death,

Und laß mich sehn dein Bilde
and let me   see your image

In deiner   Kreuzesnot.
in your cross-distress.

Da   will ich nach dir blicken,
There want I   to   you look,

Da   will ich glaubensvoll
there want I   full of faith

Dich fest an mein Herz drücken.
you firmly to my   heart to press.

Wer   so stirbt, der stirbt wohl.
Who thus dies, he   dies   well.

Appear as my shield,
as consolation in my death,
and let me see the image of
your distress on the cross.
Then will I want to gaze upon you,
and, filled with faith, will I want
to press you firmly to my heart!
Who so dies, dies well.

Source: Gerhardt 1974: 31

---

*P*AUL Gerhardt's Passion hymn "O Haupt voll Blut und Wunden" is a German adaptation of the Latin "Salve, caput cruentatum," formerly attributed to Bernard de Clairveaux (1091–1153) but more likely by Arnulf von Löwen (ca. 1195–1250).

Bernard de Clairveaux was one of the most influential political figures in the Church of his time. He was instrumental in the selection of Pope Innocent II, as well as in the ascent of one of the monks (a relative no less) from the abbey he established at Clairveaux to become Pope Eugene III. He was also the prosecutor at the heresy trial of theologian Peter Abelard (1140) and was involved in the organization of the Second Crusade (1147), the failure of which was blamed largely on him. Arnulf von Löwen was a relatively anonymous Cistercian monk and Abbot of Villiers in Brabant, France.

Whoever its author, "Salve, caput cruentatum" was taken from an extraordinary and much longer work of 350 lines entitled "Salve mundi salutari." This was a Passion devotional in seven sections of fifty lines, each of which addressed a different part of the body of the crucified Christ (feet, knees, hands, side, breast, heart, and head). (Stulken 1981: 215)

Gerhardt's hymn, first published in 1656 by fellow-hymnist Johann Crüger, was an adaptation of the last of these seven sections, extended to ten verses of eight lines each. The first three verses are spoken as if by a loved one preparing the battered body for burial and asking, "Why did this happen?" Verse 4 answers, "What you suffered, Lord, is all my burden. I myself have caused what you have borne!" Thus the recognition of original sin. The remainder of the hymn prays personally for the forgiveness of that sin and expresses the sinner's yearning for union with Christ.

Paul Gerhardt (1607–1676) was born near Wittenberg, the home city of Luther's adulthood, a century and a quarter after the great reformer. The *EKG* (part 3: 16) calls him "after Luther, the greatest hymn poet of German Protestantism." He is not known to have composed a single secular text, and his hymns number approximately 130, of which thirty-eight are in the *EKG*—more than any other author, and more than Luther composed in his entire lifetime.

"O Haupt voll Blut und Wunden" is no. 63 in the *EKG* and no. 116 in the *LBW*, there with the title "O Sacred Head, Now Wounded." The text presented here is the version of the *EKG*, which differs insignificantly from Gerhardt's original. In part through J.S. Bach's use of it five times in his *St. Matthew Passion*, this hymn has become one of the most recognized and popular of Lutheran chorales.

O Heiland, reiß die Himmel auf

O Savior, Tear open the Heavens

Friedrich Spee von Langenfeld, SJ

O Heiland, reiß die Himmel auf,
O Savior, tear the heavens open,

Herab, herauf vom Himmel lauf,
downward, upward from heaven flow;

Reiß ab vom Himmel Tor und Tür,
tear off from heaven gate and door,

Reiß ab, was Schloß und Riegel für.
tear off what lock and bar [are] for.

O Savior, tear open the heavens,
flow down to us from heaven above;
tear off heaven's gate and door,
tear off every lock and bar.

O Gott, ein' Tau vom Himmel gieß,
O God, a dew from heaven pour;

Im Tau herab o Heiland fließ,
in the dew downward O Savior flow;

Ihr Wolken, brecht und regnet aus
You clouds break and rain out

Den König über Jakobs Haus.
the king over Jacob's house.

O God, a dew from heaven pour;
in the dew, O Savior, downward flow.
Break, you clouds, and rain down
the king of Jacob's house.

O Erd, schlag aus, schlag aus o Erd,
O earth, burst forth; burst forth, O earth,

Daß Berg und Tal grün alles werd,
that mountain and valley green all become;

O Erd, herfür dies Blümlein bring,
O earth here this little flower bring,

O Heiland, aus der Erden spring.
O Savior out of the earth spring.

O earth, burst forth; burst forth, O earth,
so that mountain and valley all become green;
O earth, bring forth this little flower;
O Savior, spring forth out of the earth.

Wo bleibst du, Trost der ganzen Welt,
Where remain you, comfort of the whole world,

Darauf sie all ihr Hoffnung stellt?
upon whom all its hope places?

O komm, ach komm vom höchsten Saal,
O come, O come from the highest hall;

Komm, tröst uns hier im Jammertal!
come, comfort us here in the vale of tears.

Where are you, comforter of the world,
you in whom the world places all its hope?
O come, please come from the highest hall;
come, console us here in this vale of tears.

O klare Sonn, du schöner Stern,
O clear sun, you beautiful star,

Dich wollten wir anschauen gern;
you would like we look upon gladly.

O Sonn, geh auf, ohn deinen Schein
O sun, arise, without your light

In Finsternis wir alle sein.
in darkness we all be.

O clear sun, beautiful star,
how we want to look upon you.
O sun, arise, for without your light
we would all be in darkness.

Hie leiden wir die größte Not,
Here suffer we the greatest distress;

Vor Augen steht der bittre Tod,
before eyes stands — bitter death.

Ach komm, führ uns mit starker Hand
Ah, come, lead us with strong hand

Von Elend zu dem Vaterland.
from misery to the fatherland.

Here we suffer the greatest distress;
before our eyes stands bitter death.
Ah, come lead us with your powerful hand
from this misery to our Father's land.

Da wollen wir all danken dir,
Therefore want we all to thank you,

Unserm Erlöser für und für,
our redeemer, –for ever and ever–.

Da wollen wir all loben dich,
Therefore want we all to praise you

Je allzeit immer und ewiglich. Amen.
–all the time– always, and eternally. Amen.

Therefore we all want to thank you,
our redeemer, for ever and ever.
Therefore we also want to praise you
at all times, always, and forever. Amen.

Source: Härting 1979: 161

*L*UTHERAN hymnists of the Reformation era met the need for German hymn texts by writing new ones from scratch, adapting secular songs into sacred, and translating many texts used in the Roman Church. Later hymnists could also avail themselves of a small body of sacred poetry written by Catholics in German instead of Latin. "O Heiland, reiß der Himmel auf" is of such origin.

Friedrich Spee (1591–1635) was a Jesuit priest in northwestern Germany during a particularly difficult period. He and his brothers worked toward the reinstitution of Catholicism in their region, facing opposition that included an assassination attempt on Spee in 1629. He served his fellow man through his devotional writings and his pastoral care, which included the preparation of convicted witches for execution and the care of the ill. The latter cost him his life in the plague epidemic of 1635.

Spee's writings are remarkably free of the literary conventions and restraints that had originated and been perpetuated in the writings of contemporary Lutherans. His religious poetry was truly, as Spee himself described it, of a type "never before seen in the German language in true poetic form." (Spee 1985: 1') They are also possessed of a universality that is expressed in the dedication of his *Trutz-Nachtigal* of 1634: "To all spiritual, God-loving souls, and especially those admirers educated in the art of poetry, for their edification." (Spee 1985: 1', tr. ed.)

Verse 1 has its origins in Isaiah 64: 1. The following two verses appear to have been inspired by the "Rorate coeli," the Roman Catholic Introit for the fourth Sunday of Advent, which itself is an abbreviated paraphrase of Isaiah 45: 8:

Rorate coeli desuper, et nubes pluant justum:
aperiatur terra et germinet salvatorem.

Let the heavens drop dew and clouds rain the just:
Let the earth open to bud forth a savior.

"O Heiland reiß" does not appear in the Spee complete-works edition (Spee 1985), most likely because it was among a number of his early poems published anonymously before 1625 and never included in later works published under his name.[97] The poem was first printed in a collection entitled *Psalm XLIV. . . ,*

---

[97]The principal source for the information on this hymn (Härting 1979) involved the editor of the Spee edition, Theo G.M. van Oorschot, as a collaborator. In complete-works editions it is common for unattributed works to be printed last, and a fourth and final volume in the set therefore may be forthcoming. On the other hand, Härting 1979 is itself a critical edition and a duplication of it in the Spee complete works may not be necessary.

published in Würzburg in 1622,[98] which was structured as a series of five lessons in song on knowing "wer der Messias ist" (who the Messiah is). "O Heiland, reiß" is the first poem in the first lesson, which deals with "how greatly the holy patriarchs and prophets yearned for the Messiah; what Isaiah prophesied; what is foreseen about him through metaphors in the Old Testament. . . ." (Spee's Foreword, Härting 1979: 160, tr. ed.) The lessons that follow trace the story of the Messiah from Old Testament prophecy through the birth of Jesus.

In its original form the hymn is in six verses; the seventh verse was added, presumably by Spee, in 1631. With the exception of changes in spelling and punctuation, the hymn remains the same in the *EKG*, where it is in the Advent section as no. 5. It also appears in the *LBW* as no. 38, "O Savior, Rend the Heavens Wide."

Vater unser im Himmelreich
Our Father in the Kingdom of Heaven
Martin Luther

Vater unser im Himmelreich,
Father our in the heaven-kingdom,

Der du uns alle heißest gleich
who you us all command equally

Brüder sein und dich rufen an,
brothers to be and you to call upon,

Und willst das Beten von uns han,
and you want — praying from us have:

Gib, daß nicht bet allein der Mund,
give, that not pray alone the mouth,

Hilf, daß es geh von Herzensgrund.
help, that it comes from heart's–depth.

Our Father in the kingdom of heaven,
who commands us all equally
to be brothers and to call upon you,
and who wants us to pray to you:
grant that we not pray only with our mouths,
but help us, so that it may also come
from the depths of our hearts.

Geheiliget werd der Name dein,
Hallowed be — name your.

Dein Wort bei uns hilf halten rein,
Your word with us help keep pure,

Daß auch wir leben heiliglich,
that also we live saintly

Nach deinem Namen würdiglich.
according to your name worthily.

Behüt uns, Herr, vor falcher Lehr,
Protect us, Lord, from false teaching;

Der arm, verführet Volk bekehr.
the poor, misled people convert.

Hallowed be your name.
May your word help keep us pure,
so that our lives may also be saintly
and worthy of your name.
Protect us, Lord, from false doctrine;
convert the poor, misled people.

Es komm dein Reich zu dieser Zeit
— come your kingdom at this time

Und dort hernach in Ewigkeit.
and there hereafter in eternity.

Der heilig Geist uns wohne bei
The holy spirit us dwell with

Mit seinen Gaben mancherlei;
with his gifts various;

Des Satans Zorn und groß Gewalt
— Satan's wrath and great strength

Zerbrich, vor ihm dein Kirch erhalt.
shatter, against him your church preserve.

May your kingdom come in our time
and hereafter in eternity.
May the Holy Spirit dwell with us
with his various gifts.
Shatter Satan's wrath and great power;
preserve your church against him.

---

[98]A number of older sources show the first publication of the poem to have occurred in 1631. This was the state of knowledge until the discovery of earlier sources in the mid twentieth century.

Dein Will gescheh, Herr Gott, zugleich
Your will be done, Lord God, just as

Auf Erden wie im Himmelreich.
on earth as in the heaven-kingdom.

Gib uns Geduld in Leidenszeit,
Give us patience in sorrow-time,

Gehorsam sein in Lieb und Leid;
obedient be in love and sorrow;

Wehr und steur allem Fleisch und Blut,
defend and guide all flesh and blood,

Das wider deinen Willen tut.
that against your will act.

Gib uns heut unser täglich Brot
Give us today our daily bread

Und was man b'darf zur Leibesnot;
and what one requires for the body's need;

Behüt uns Herr vor Unfried und Streit,
protect us Lord from strife and quarrel,

Vor Seuchen und vor teurer Zeit,
from plagues and from hard times,

Daß wir in gutem Frieden stehn,
that we in good peace stand,

Der Sorg und Geizes müßig gehn.
of the grief and avarice vain go.

All unser Schuld vergib uns, Herr,
All our offenses forgive us, Lord,

Daß sie uns nicht betrüben mehr,
that they us not distress more,

Wie wir auch unsern Schuldigern
as we also our offenders

Ihr Schuld und Fehl vergeben gern.
their offenses and faults forgive gladly.

Zu dienen mach uns all bereit
To serve make us all ready

In rechter Lieb und Einigkeit.
in true love and harmony.

Führ uns, Herr, in Versuchung nicht;
Lead us, Lord, into temptation not,

Wenn uns der böse Geist anficht
when us the evil spirit challenges;

Zur linken und zur rechten Hand,
on the left and on the right hand

Hilf uns tun starken Widerstand,
help us give strong resistance,

Im Glauben fest und wohlgerüst'
in faith firm and well-prepared

Und durch des heilgen Geistes Trost.
and through the holy spirit's consolation.

Von allem Übel uns erlös;
From all evil us deliver,

Es sind die Zeit' und Tage bös.
— are the time and days wicked.

Erlös uns vom ewigen Tod
Deliver us from eternal death

Und tröst uns in der letzten Not;
and comfort us in the last distress.

Bescher uns auch ein seligs End,
Bestow on us also a blissful end;

Nimm unsre Seel in deine Händ.
take our soul into your hands.

Your will be done, Lord God,
on earth as it is in the kingdom of heaven.
Give us patience in times of sorrow,
obedience in love and sorrow;
defend and guide all flesh and blood
that act against your will.

Give us today our daily bread
and whatever else our bodies need.
Protect us from quarrels and strife,
from plagues and from difficult times,
so that we might live in good peace,
and vain grief and avarice might depart.

Forgive us all our offenses, Lord,
so that they will not distress us further,
as we also gladly forgive others
their offenses and faults.
Make us all ready to serve
in true love and harmony.

Lead us, Lord, not into temptation
when the evil spirit challenges us;
on both the left and the right hand
help us give strong resistance, and to
be firm in our faith, well-prepared,
and mindful of the Holy Spirit's consolation.

Deliver us from all evil
for our time and these days are wicked.
Deliver us from eternal death
and comfort us in our final distress.
Grant us also a blissful end;
take our soul into your hands.

Amen, das ist: es werde wahr!
Amen, that is: it become true!

Stärk   unsern Glauben immerdar,
Strengthen   our   faith   evermore,

Auf daß wir ja nicht zweifeln dran,
so   that we — not   doubt   that,

Was wir hiermit gebeten han.
what we   herewith   prayed have.

Auf   dein Wort, in dem Namen dein.
Upon your word in — name   your,

So sprechen wir das Amen   fein.
So   say   we the Amen grand.

Amen. That is to say: may it become true!
Strengthen our faith evermore,
so that we never, ever doubt
what we have herewith prayed.
Upon your word and in your name,
we say this grand "Amen."

Source: Luther 1967: 47

*L*UTHER wrote this expanded version of the Lord's Prayer in 1538 or early 1539, describing it as a "brief interpretation, composed to be sung." The first line or two of each stanza constitutes a phrase or clause from the Lord's Prayer (Matthew 6: 9–13), which is then elaborated upon in the subsequent lines. By Luther's time this process, known as "troping," had a long history. In the Middle Ages it was common to trope many sacred texts—particularly the Kyries of Masses (e.g., "Kyrie, fons bonitatis," "Kyrie, virginitatis amator," "Kyrie, magne deus potentie"). The early Lutheran church adopted a number of tropes from the Roman Catholic liturgy, translating the Latin into German (e.g., "Kyrie, Gott Vater in Ewigkeit"). Luther's trope of the Lord's Prayer thus represented the continuation of a venerable tradition.

Most hymns can be abbreviated by the selective omission of verses; the present text, however, makes sense only if all ten verses are sung. It is likely for this reason that it is not commonly used in worship, despite its beauty and theological virtues. "Vater unser im Himmelreich" appears in the *EKG* as no. 241; it is not found, however, in the *LBW*.

Verleih uns Frieden

Grant Us Peace

Verse 1: Martin Luther; verse 2: Johann Walter

Verleih uns Frieden gnädiglich,
Grant   us peace mercifully,

Herr Gott, zu unsern Zeiten.
Lord God, at   our   times.

Es   ist doch ja kein andrer nicht,
There is indeed   no   other indeed

der für uns könnte streiten,
who for us could   fight

denn du, unser Gott alleine.
than you,   our   God, alone.

Mercifully grant us peace,
Lord God, during our life on earth.
There is indeed no other
who could fight for us
than you, our God, alone.

Gib   unsern Fürsten und aller Obrigkeit
Give   our   princes and all   authorities

Fried und gut Regiment,
peace and good government,

daß wir unter ihnen
that   we under them

ein geruhig und stilles Leben führen mögen
a   calm and quiet life   lead   may

in aller Gottseligkeit und   Ehrbarkeit. Amen.
in   all   devotion   and worthiness. Amen.

Give our princes and authorities
peace and good government,
so that under them we
may lead a calm and quiet life
in all devotion and worthiness. Amen.

Source: Luther 1967: 41

*T*HE history of this brief hymn stretches from the Middle Ages to the mid sixteenth century. In 1528 Martin Luther published verse 1, a rhyming, poetic translation of the sixth- or seventh-century Latin prayer for peace "Da pacem Domine," which had been used in Catholic churches preceding the "Agnus Dei" since 1279:

Da pacem Domine in diebus nostris: quia non est alius qui pugnet pro nobis, nisi cu Deus noster.

Lord, grant us peace in our time: for there is no other who could struggle for us than you, our God.

The book of 2 Chronicles, chapter 20, especially verses 12–15, relates a story of impending war that was the principal basis for the Latin hymn. Luther's motivation in writing the first verse may have been the advance of the Turks, "who threatened all of Christendom by moving unhindered as close as Vienna. Luther called upon young and old to overcome the enemy with prayer." (Stulken 1981: 494). Johann Walter, the hymnist of the early Lutheran movement, penned the second verse in prose in 1566.

Verse 1, line 3 presents one of the more confusing constructions found in this volume. Translated literally, this line appears to present a nonsensical double negative:

Es   ist   doch   ja   kein andrer nicht.
There is, to be sure, indeed, none other   not.

The word *nicht,* today used exclusively for negation, used to be employed poetically in the opposite sense as an affirmation, and that is the intent here. Luther must have wanted to make his point emphatically, since three of his seven words in this clause are words of emphasis:

Es   ist   *doch*   *ja*   kein andrer *nicht.*
There is, to be sure, indeed, none other indeed.

"Verleih uns Frieden" appears in the *EKG* as no. 139 and in the *LBW* as no. 471 ("Grant Peace, We Pray, in Mercy, Lord"). The hymn is used in German Lutheran churches to close the worship service. Luther's text is unaltered in the *EKG,* but Walter's now-anachronistic *Fürsten* (princes) in verse 2 is replaced by *Volke* (people).

Vom Himmel hoch
From Heaven on High

Martin Luther
(Verses 1–4, 7, 13, 15)

Vom Himmel hoch, da komm ich her,
From heaven high there come I hither;

Ich bring euch gute neue Mär;
I bring to you good new tidings!

Der guten Mär bring ich so viel,
the good tidings bring I so many

Davon ich singen und sagen will.
of which I sing and speak want to.

From heaven on high I come to you;
I bring you good new tidings!
I bring you so many good tidings
of which I want to sing and speak.

Euch ist ein Kindlein heut geborn
To you is a little child today born

Von einer Jungfrau auserkorn,
from a virgin chosen;

Ein Kindelein so zart und fein,
a little child so gentle and delicate,

Das soll eur Freud und Wonne sein.
who shall our joy and delight be.

To you this day a tiny child is born
of a chosen virgin;
a child so gentle and delicate
who shall be your joy and delight.

Es ist der Herr Christ, unser Gott,
It is the Lord Christ, our God.

Der will euch führn aus aller Not,
He wants to you lead out of all misery;

Er will eur Heiland selber sein,
He wants to your savior himself be,

Von allen Sünden machen rein.
from all sins to make pure.

It is the Lord Jesus Christ, our God.
He wants to lead you out of all misery;
he wants to be your savior,
to make you pure and free from sin.

Er bringt euch alle Seligkeit,
He brings you all salvation,

Die Gott der Vater hat bereit',
which God the Father has prepared

Daß ihr mit uns im Himmelreich,
that you with us in the heavenly kingdom,

Sollt leben nun und ewiglich.
shall live now and forever.

He brings you all salvation,
which God the Father has prepared
so that you shall live with us in the
kingdom of heaven, now and forevermore.

Merk auf, mein Herz, und siehe dorthin:
Attend —, my heart, and behold there:

was liegt doch in dem Krippelein?
what lies — in the little crib?

Wes ist das schöne Kindelein?
Who is the beautiful little child?

Es ist das liebe Jesulein.
It is the dear little Jesus.

Give heed, my heart, and look over there:
what is lying in the little crib?
Who is the beautiful little child?
It is the dear infant Jesus.

Ach mein herzliebes Jesulein,
Ah my dearly beloved little Jesus,

Mach dir ein rein, sanft Bettelein,
make you a clean, soft little bed

Zu ruhen in meins Herzens Schrein
to rest in my heart's shrine

Daß ich nimmer vergesse dein.
that I never forget you.

Ah, my belovéd infant Jesus,
make a clean, soft little bed
to rest in the shrine of my heart
so that I may never forget you.

Lob, Ehr sei Gott im höchstem Thron,
Praise, honor be to God on the highest throne,

Der uns schenkt seinen ein'gen Sohn;
who to us gives his only son,

des freuen sich der Engel Schar'
about which rejoices — the angel host

Und singen uns solch neues Jahr.
and sing to us such new year.

Praise and honor be to God on the highest throne,
who gives to us his only son,
about which the host of angels rejoices
and sings to us of such a new year.

Source: Luther 1967: 44

*W*ITH fifteen verses, not all of which are presented here, this Christmas hymn is the longest of Luther's chorales. The first verse was derived from a "garland song" of his time:

Aus fremden Landen komm ich her
und bring euch viel der neuen Mär,
der guten Mär bring ich so viel,
mehr den ich euch hie sagen will.

I come here from foreign lands
and bring you much good news;
so much good news I bring—
more than I want to tell you now. (tr. ed.

In a popular singing game of Luther's day, a young man would sing this refrain and then give out a riddle to one of the girls in the circle. If she could not solve the riddle she had to give the singer her wreath or garland. (Stulken 1981: 153)

The chorale constitutes an extended trope of or elaboration on the familiar passage from Luke 2: 10–12, in which the angel appears to the shepherds to announce the birth of Jesus. Verses 1, 5, 7, and 15 are derived directly from this text:

And the angel said unto them, "Be not afraid; for behold, I bring you good news of a great joy which shall come to all people; for unto you is born this day in the city of David a Savior, who is Christ the Lord. And this shall be a sign for you: you will find a babe wrapped in swaddling clothes and lying in a manger." And suddenly there was with the angel a multitude of the heavenly host praising God and saying, "Glory to God in the highest, and on earth peace among those with whom he is pleased!"

The angel speaks in verses 1–5, and the Christian reacts in the remaining stanzas. It is interesting that this hymn is the most personal and perhaps subjective of Luther's chorales, with no fewer than six uses of the first-person singular. Julian offers an explanation:[99]

---

[99]Julian 1985: 1227, quoting Richard Lauxmann in Koch 1973, 7: 21.

Luther was accustomed every year to prepare for his family a Christmas Eve's entertainment . . . and for this festival of his children he wrote this Christmas hymn. . . . It is said that Luther celebrated the festival in his own house in this original fashion. By his orders the first seven verses of this hymn were sung by a man dressed as an angel whom the children greeted with the eighth and following verses.

"Vom Himmel hoch" was likely written near the Christmas season in the period 1533–1535 and was published in 1535. All fifteen verses appear in the *EKG* as no. 16; the *LBW* presents the hymn as no. 51 under the title "From Heaven above." Verse 9, omitted here, will be found under the entry for "Ach Herr, du Schöpfer aller Ding" by Schütz.

Wachet auf, ruft uns die Stimme
"Awake," Call the Voices
Philipp Nicolai

"Wachet auf," ruft uns die Stimme
Wake   up,   call to us the voices

Der   Wächter   sehr hoch auf der   Zinne,
of the watchmen very high on the battlement.

"Wacht auf, du Stadt Jerusalem!
Wake up, you city Jerusalem.

Mitternacht heißt   diese Stunde!"
Midnight   is called this   hour!"

Sie rufen uns, mit hellem Munde:
They call us, with bright voices:

"Wo   seid ihr klugen Jungfrauen?
where are you   wise   virgins?

Wohl auf, der Bräutgam   kömmt;
Cheer up, the bridegroom is coming.

Steht auf, die Lampen nehmt!
Get   up, the lamps   take!

Hallelujah!
Hallelujah!

Macht   euch   bereit
Make yourself ready

Zu der Hochzeit,
for the wedding;

Ihr müsset ihm entgegen gehn!"
you must   him –go to meet– !"

"Awake," call the voices of the watchmen
from the high battle tower.
"Awake, you city of Jerusalem!
This is the midnight hour!"
They call to us, with ringing voices:
"Where are you, wise virgins?
Cheer up; the bridegroom is coming.
Rise up; take your lamps!
Hallelujah!
Prepare yourself
for the wedding;
you must go to meet him!"

Zion hört die Wächter singen;
Zion hears the watchmen singing;

Das Herz tut ihr vor Freuden springen,
the heart does her for joy   leap;

Sie wachet und steht eilend auf.
she awakens and gets hurriedly up.

Ihr Freund kommt vom Himmel prächtig,
Her friend comes from heaven glorious,

Von Gnaden stark, von Wahrheit mächtig;
of   grace strong, of   truth mighty;

Ihr Licht   wird   hell, ihr Stern geht auf.
her light becomes bright, her star   rises.

Nun komm, du werte   Kron,
Now come, you worthy crown,

Herr Jesu, Gottes Sohn!
Lord Jesus, God's son!

Hosianna!
Hosanna!

Wir folgen all
We   follow all

Zum Freudensaal
to the   hall of joy

Und halten mit das Abendmahl.
and –partake of– the communion.

Zion hears the watchmen singing;
her heart leaps for joy;
she awakens and quickly rises.
Her friend comes from heaven's glory,
strong in grace, mighty in truth;
her light brightens, her star rises.
Now come, you worthy crown,
Lord Jesus, God's son!
Hosanna!
We all will follow
to the banquet hall
and take communion together.

Gloria sei dir gesungen
Glory be to you sung

Mit Menschen- und englischen Zungen,
with mortal and angelic tongues,

Mit Harfen und Zimbeln schön.
with harps and cymbals beautiful.

Von zwölf Perlen sind die Pforten,
Of twelve pearls are the portals;

An deiner Stadt sind wir Konsorten
in your city are we consorts

Der Engel hoch um deinen Thron.
of the angels high around your throne.

Kein Aug hat je gespürt,
No eye has ever perceived,

Kein Ohr hat je gehört
no ear has ever heard

Solche Freude.
such joy.

Des sind wir froh,
Of that are we glad,

Io! io!
io! io!

Ewig *in dulci jubilo.*
Eternally with sweet rejoicing.

Glory be sung to you
with mortal and angelic voices, and
with beautiful harps and cymbals.
Your gates are made of twelve pearls;
in your city we are consorts
of the angels high around your throne.
No eye has ever seen,
no ear has ever heard
such joy.
Therefore we are glad,
io! io!
Ever *in dulci jubilo.*

Source: Nicolai 1963: 412

*P*HILIPP Nicolai (1556–1608) wrote only four hymns. Yet remarkably, two—the present chorale and "Wie schön leuchtet der Morgenstern"*—are recognized as among the greatest chorales in the literature. They were likely the products of a most extreme testing of the spirit. In 1597 Nicolai was the pastor of a Lutheran congregation in the city of Unna, Westphalia, when one of the dreaded, periodic waves of the plague arrived. His parsonage looked out upon the cemetery, where up to thirty parishioners would be laid to rest daily. In his preface to his 1599 *Freudenspiegel* (Mirror of Joy), which contains "Wachet auf," Nicolai recalled how he dealt spiritually with the carnage:

> There seemed to me nothing more sweet than the contemplation of the noble, sublime doctrine of Eternal Life obtained through the blood of Christ. This I allowed to dwell in my heart day and night. Then day by day I wrote out my meditations, found myself, thank God! wonderfully well, comforted in heart, joyful in spirit, and truly content; gave to my manuscript the name and title of a *Mirror of Joy*, and took this so-composed *Frewden-Spiegel* to leave behind me . . . as a token of my peaceful, joyful, Christian departure, or (if God should spare me in health) to comfort other sufferers whom he should also visit with the pestilence. . . .[100]

On its surface, the present chorale reveals no trace of its origin. The hymn appears to be a simple and joyous allegorical look toward Advent, the time of preparation for the coming of Jesus, the bridegroom, who will wed his bride, the faithful Christian. The more serious underlying message, regarding another type of preparation, is revealed in the scriptures upon which the chorale is based, principal among them the parable of the ten virgins from Matthew 25: 1–13.[101] At night ten virgins went with their oil lamps to meet a bridegroom and escort him to the wedding feast. Five of them were wise and brought extra oil, not knowing when he would come. The other five were foolish and came unprepared. When the bridegroom was delayed, the foolish ones were out of oil and had to seek out a dealer to provide it. In the meantime the wise virgins with their full lamps took the bridegroom to the feast. The doors were locked after them, excluding those who stupidly had run out of oil.

The moral, as expressed in Matthew 25: 13: "Watch, therefore, for you know neither the day nor the hour" of your death or of the coming of the Lord. Those who are unprepared will be locked out of the Kingdom of Heaven.

The image of the watchman high on his tower, calling to those below, has origins in the genre of the medieval "morning songs": "The secular morning-song had usually concerned two lovers parting at the

---

[100]Quoted from Julian 1985: 805. Julian notes on the same page that one scholar maintains "Wachet auf" was written before the plague period, in 1596.

[101]Further Biblical sources for this chorale: Revelation 19: 6, 21: 21; 1 Corinthians 2: 9; Ezekiel 3: 17; and Isaiah 52: 8.

break of day, with a garrulous and sententious watchman moralizing over their predicament." (Day 1966: 26) The relationship between this tradition and Nicolai's hymn is but one of many examples of how secular and sacred ideas, literature, and images were freely traded from one realm to the other at this time.

The first letters of the three verses (WZG) comprise a retrograde acrostic for **Graf zu Waldeck**, the title of a former student whom Nicolai had tutored for many years, and who lost his life to the plague. The relationship must have been profound, as Nicolai memorialized him similarly in "Wie schön leuchtet der Morgenstern."*

Nicolai's hymn remains in use today in both Germany (*EKG*: 121) and this country (*LBW*: 31: "Wake, Awake, for Night Is Flying") as a chorale for the closing of the church year. Verse 3 of the current German version has been edited heavily to modernize the language.

Wie schön leuchtet der Morgenstern
How Beautifully Shines the Morning Star
Philipp Nicolai

Wie schön leuchtet der Morgenstern
How beautifully shines the morning star

Voll Gnad und Wahrheit von dem Herrn,
full of grace and truth from the Lord,

Die süße Wurzel Jesse!
the sweet root [of] Isaiah.

Du Sohn Davids aus Jakobs Stamm,
You son of David from Jacob's stem,

Mein König und mein Bräutigam,
my king and my bridgroom,

Hast mir mein Herz besessen,
has me my heart possessed—

Lieblich, freundlich,
lovely, friendly,

Schön und herrlich, groß und ehrlich,
beautiful and glorious, great and honest,

Reich von Gaben,
Rich in gifts,

Hoch und sehr prächtig erhaben.
highly and very splendidly exalted.

How beautifully shines the morning star,
full of grace and truth from the Lord,
the sweet root of Isaiah.
You, David's son from Jacob's lineage,
my king and my bridegroom,
you have possessed my heart—
lovely, friendly,
beautiful and glorious, great and righteous,
rich in blessings,
high and magnificently exalted.

Ei, mein Perle, du werte Kron,
Ah, my pearl, you worthy crown,

Wahr' Gottes und Marien Sohn,
truly God's and Mary's son,

Ein hochgeborner König!
a high-born king!

Mein Herz heißt dich ein Lilium;
My heart calls you a lily;

Dein süßes Evangelium
your sweet Gospel

Ist lauter Milch und Honig.
is pure milk and honey.

Ei, mein Blümlein,
Ah, my dearest flower:

Hosianna, Himmlisch' Manna,
Hosanna, heavenly manna

Das wir essen,
that we eat,

Deiner kann ich nicht vergessen.
you can I not forget.

Ah, my pearl, you worthy crown,
true son of God and Mary,
a high-born king!
My heart calls you a lily;
your sweet Gospel
is pure milk and honey.
Ah, my dearest flower:
Hosanna, heavenly manna
that we eat,
I cannot forget you.

Gieß sehr tief in das Herz hinein,
Pour very deep into the heart —,

Du heller Jaspis und Rubin,
you bright jasper and ruby,

Die Flamme deiner Liebe,
the flame of your love,

Und erfreu' mich, daß ich doch bleib'
and delight me, that I — remain

An deinem auserwählten Leib
in your chosen body

Ein lebendige Rippe!
a living rib.

Nach dir ist mir,
After you –I long–,

Gratiosa coeli rosa,
favorite heavenly rose;

Krank und glimmend,
sick and glowing,

Mein Herz mit Liebe verwundet.
my heart with love [is] wounded.

Pour very deeply into my heart,
you bright jasper and ruby,
the flame of your love,
and delight me, so that I might remain
in your chosen body
a living rib.
For you I long,
beloved, heavenly rose;
sick and glowing,
my heart is wounded by love.

Von Gott kommt mir ein Freudenschein,
From God comes to me a joy-radiance,

wenn du mich mit deinen Äugelein
when you me with your eyes

gar freundlich tust anblicken.
very friendly do look at.

O Herr Jesu! mein trautes Gut,
O Lord Jesus, my beloved treasure,

dein Wort, dein Geist, dein Leib und Blut
your word, your spirit, your body and blood

mich innerlich erquicken.
me spiritually refresh.

Nimm mich freundlich
Take me kindly

in dein' Arme, daß ich warme
into your arms, that I warm

werd von Gnaden;
become from grace;

auf dein Wort komm ich geladen.
by your word come I invited.

From God a joyous radiance comes to me,
when you look at me
with your friendly eyes.
O Lord Jesus, my beloved treasure,
your word, your spirit, your body and blood
refresh me spiritually.
Take me kindly
in your arms, so that your grace
might warm me;
invited by your word, I come.

Herr Gott, Vater, mein starker Held!
Lord God, Father, my strong hero,

Du hast mich ewig vor der Welt
you have me eternally for the world

In deinem Sohn geliebet.
in your son loved.

Dein Sohn hat mich ihm selbst vertraut,
Your son has me to him himself betrothed;

Er ist mein Schatz, ich bin sein' Braut,
he is my beloved, I am his bride,

Sehr hoch in ihm erfreuet.
Very highly in Him delighted.

Eia, eia,
Ah, ah,

Himmlisch Leben wird er geben
heavenly life will he give

Mir dort oben;
to me there above;

Ewig soll mein Herz ihn loben.
eternally shall my heart him praise.

Lord God, Father, my strong hero,
For the world you have had me
fall in love with your son.
Your son has betrothed himself to me;
he is my beloved, I am his bride,
greatly delighted in him.
Ah, ah,
heavenly life he will give me
there above;
my heart shall praise him forever.

Zwingt die Saiten in Cythara
Compel the strings –of the Kithera–

Und laßt die süße Musica
and let the sweet music

Ganz freudenreich erschallen,
totally joyfully sound,

Daß ich möge mit Jesulein,
that I may with dear Jesus,

Dem wunderschönen Bräut'gam mein,
the very beautiful bridegroom my

In steter Liebe wallen.
in constant love wander.

Singet, springet,
Sing, leap,

Jubilieret, triumphieret,
rejoice, exult,

Dankt dem Herren!
thank the Lord!

Groß ist der König der Ehren.
Great is the king of glory!

Tune the strings of the zither
and let the sweet music
joyfully resound,
so that I may wander with my dearest Jesus,
my wonderfully beautiful bridegroom,
in steadfast love.
Sing, leap for joy,
rejoice, exult,
thank the Lord!
Great is the King of Glory!

Wie bin ich doch so herzlich froh,
How am I — so sincerely glad

Daß mein Schatz ist das A und O,
that my beloved is the A[lpha] and O[mega],

Der Anfang und das Ende!
the beginning and the end.

Er wird mich doch zu seinem Preis
He will me — as his prize

Aufnehmen in das Paradeis,
take into — paradise,

Des klopf ich in die Hände.
about which clap I –my hands–.

Amen! Amen!
Amen! Amen!

Komm, du schöne Freudenkrone!
Come you beautiful joy crown;

Bleib nicht lange,
remain not long.

Deiner wart ich mit Verlangen.
You await I with longing.

I am so sincerely glad
that my beloved is the A and O,
the beginning and the end!
He will, to his praise,
accept me into Paradise;
for this, I clap my hands.
Amen! Amen!
Come, you beautiful crown of joy;
tarry not too long.
I await you with longing.

Source: Nicolai 1963: 409

*T*HE present hymn is the fraternal twin to "Wachet auf, ruft uns die Stimme."* Both were written at the same time under the same affliction, they also share the symbolism of Christ as the bridegroom to the faithful Christian, and they were first published in the same collection. Last but not least, they are among the most beloved of chorales.

Author Philipp Nicolai (1556–1608) made clear the purpose and source of his hymn in his subtitle, "A Spiritual Bridal Song of the Beloved Soul concerning Jesus Christ, her Heavenly Bridegroom, founded on the 45th Psalm of the Prophet David."

> This Psalm . . . was written for the wedding of a king, possibly Solomon, and contains the real or imagined songs of the procession of the groom and (from the words "Hearken O daughter") of the bride's party which awaits him. (Keyte and Parrott 1992: 237)

Psalm 45 is seen by scholars as a Psalm of Messianic prophesy:

> The Davidic kings, "sitting on the throne of the Kingdom of the Lord" (1 Chronicles 28: 4–7; 29: 23), were chosen not only to establish the kingdom of God in their day, but also to let their reign foreshadow the fulfillment of the divine plan of salvation unfolding in Israel's history and culminating in the Messiah. (Roehrs and Franzmann 1979: 362)

Though Nicolai's two great chorales share their wedding imagery, their messages are quite different. While "Wachet auf" admonishes the Christian symbolically to be prepared for the Second Coming of the Christ, "Wie schön leuchtet" is an ecstatically joyful song of love and praise for the Messiah, the "morning star," the "sun of righteousness" (Micah 4: 2). The tone is extraordinarily personal and intimate, with every verse containing first-person references. Many of these are possessive—the Savior is "my king and bridegroom," "my pearl," whose father is beseeched to "revive me" through his son, who will "take me as his prize into Paradise."

In the *EKG* this hymn appears in the Epiphany section. It is, however, sometimes taken for a Christmas or Advent song because of its apparent Christmas references. The "morning star" in verse 1 refers not to the star of Bethlehem, but rather to the Savior, the "light for the revelation to the Gentiles" (or any of a dozen other Biblical "light" references). The repeated exclamation *eia* in verse 5, a staple of Christmas carols, here relates to the peace accompanying contemplation of the "heavenly life." And finally, the diminutive *Jesulein* (little Jesus) in verse 6 refers not to size, but to the affection of the Christian for the Christ-child.

Like "Wachet auf," the first letters of the seven verses (WEGUHZW) form an acrostic in homage to **W**ilhelm **E**rnst, **G**raf **u**nd **H**err **z**u **W**aldeck, a beloved former student of Nicolai's who was taken by the plague epidemic that had spared Nicolai and had moved him to write his hymns.

Of all the hymns discussed in this volume, "Wie schön leuchtet" has been most subject to revision. The version presented here is as originally published by Nicolai in his *Freudenspiegel* of 1599. (See the annotation to "Wachet auf, ruft uns die Stimme.") In the seventeenth and eighteenth centuries it remained reasonably intact, but in the last century it disappeared from many hymnals. The hymn reappeared in the Lutheran hymnal of 1912 and remained in the subsequent editions of 1953 and 1996, but with considerable modernization as well as editing to replace Latin with German, to omit extra syllables, and to improve congruence of musical and textual accent.

"Wie schön leuchtet der Morgenstern" appears as no. 48 in the *EKG*. In the *LBW* it is no. 76, "O Morning Star, How Fair and Bright."

Carols

Dort oben vom Berge
From the Mountain above

Dort oben vom Berge da wehet der Wind,
There above from the mountain — blows the wind;

Da sitzet Maria und wieget ihr Kind;
there sits Mary and rocks her child.

Sie wiegt es mit ihrer schneeweißen Hand,
She rocks it with her snow-white hand,

Drum braucht sie ja nimmer zum Wiegen ein Band.
thus needs she — never for the cradle a string.

Down from the mountain top blows the wind;
Mary sits there and rocks her child.
She rocks him with her snow-white hand,
and she never needs to use a rocking-string.

Es kommen die Englein und sehen ihr zu
— come the angels and watch her —

Und schützen dem schlummernden Kindlein die Ruh',
and guard of the slumbering child the peace;

Sie bringen ihr Blumen vom Paradies,
they bring their flowers from paradise,

drum schläft auch das Kindlein so ruhig und süß.
thus sleeps — the child so peacefully and sweetly

Now come the angels and watch over her
and guard the peace of the slumbering child;
they bring their flowers from paradise,
and thus the child sleeps so peacefully and sweetly.

Die Vögel umsingen die Mutter gar fein
The birds sing around the mother very fine

und gucken zum Kindlein in die Wiege hinein.
and peer at the child in the cradle —.

Sie fliegen hinzu und fliegen empor
They fly to him and fly above

und singen dann fröhlicher als zuvor.
and sing more joyously than before.

The birds surround the mother with beautiful song
and look into the manger at the child.
They fly to him and soar aloft
and sing yet more joyously than before.

Source: Weber-Kellerman 1982: 46

ACCORDING to Hugh Keyte and Andrew Parrott, the editors of the *New Oxford Book of Carols*, the use of cradles and cradle-songs in Christmas worship services was established in Germany well before the Lutheran schism from the Roman Catholic Church in the early sixteenth century.[102]

> By the late Middle Ages cradles were being enthusiastically rocked at Christmas vespers and matins throughout Germany and the Low Countries. Typically, the cradle would stand before the altar, with the brightly coloured Christ-child visible within, and the priest would rock it in time to the triple-time music of the appropriate Wiegenlied (cradle-song) carol, with the lullaby refrain "Eia! Eia!" and sometimes "Susani! susani! . . ." Cradles were also carried about the streets by groups of carol-singing children, who would rock them in a similar manner while singing cradle-songs. (Keyte and Parrott 1992: 182)

The cradle-song or lullaby-carol often featured the visit of the shepherds, who might play their rustic instruments for the new-born Savior. In this carol the shepherds are absent, but the Christ-child is nonetheless watched over (or threatened?) by the wind (verse 1), and comforted by the angels (verse 2) and the singing birds (verse 3). The text is self explanatory but for the last line of the first stanza. A cradle could be rocked in two ways: either directly by hand or from a distance by the use of a string. The carol seems to suggest that the Virgin Mother attended closely to the Christ-child, rocking him by hand.

Because of their age, little if any information survives about the origins of individual lullaby carols.[103] Such is the case with the present song, about which apparently nothing is known other than its probable place of origin in the Bohemian forest. "Dort oben vom Berge" survives in a number of versions, among them "Auf dem Berge, da gehet der Wind" and "Da droben vom Berge," a fact suggestive of its evolution over an extended period of time.

---

[102]*Das Buch der Weihnachtslieder* (Weber-Kellermann 1983: 53) places the beginning of the custom much later: "Only in the late sixteenth century did cribs come to Germany from Italy via the Jesuits as part of a spiritual-education program for the common people." Later, however, the author states in apparent contradiction, "It was thus that nearly all of the shepherd- and crib-songs originated in the Middle Ages or early modern era. . . ." (tr. ed.)

[103]Other cradle-songs in this volume are "Still, still, still," "O Jesulein zart," Joseph, lieber Joseph mein," and "Singet frisch und wohlgemut."

In dulci jubilo

With Sweet Rejoicing

Verses 1, 2, 4, Anonymous 14th century; verse 3, Valentin Triller

In dulci jubilo
With sweet rejoicing

Nun singet und seid froh!
now sing and be joyful!

Unsers Herzen Wonne
Our hearts' delight

Leit *in praesepio*
lies in manger

Und leuchtet als die Sonne
and shines as the sun

Matris in gremio.
of mother in lap.

Alpha es et O.
Alpha are and O[mega].

With sweet rejoicing
now sing and be joyful!
Our hearts' delight
lies in a manger
and shines like the sun
on the mother's lap.
You are Alpha and O.

O Jesu parvule,
O Jesu infant,

Nach dir ist mir so weh.
for you is me such woe.

Tröst mir mein Gemüte,
Comfort me my soul

O Puer optime;
O boy finest;

durch alle deine Güte,
by means of all your goodness,

O Princeps Gloriae,
O Prince of Glory,

Trahe me post te!
Draw me after you [to heaven].

O infant Jesus,
my heart aches for you.
Comfort my soul
with all your goodness,
O finest of boys;
by your great goodness,
O Prince of Glory,
take me to heaven.

O Patris caritas!
O of father love!

O Nati lenitas!
O of son mercy!

Wir wärn all' verloren
We would all be lost

Per nostra crimina;
through our sins,

So hat er uns erworben
but has he us obtained

Coelorum gaudia;
of heaven joys.

Eia, wärn wir da!
Ah, would be we there!

Oh love of the Father!
Oh mercy of the Son!
We would all be lost
because of our sins,
but he has obtained for us
the joys of heaven.
Oh, that we were there!

Ubi sunt gaudia?
Where are joys?

Nirgends mehr denn da,
Nowhere more than there,

Da die Engel singen
there the angels sing

Nova cantica,
new songs

Und die Schellen klingen
and the bells ring

In Regis curia.
in King's courts.

Eia, wärn wir da!
Ah, would be we there!

Where are the joys?
Nowhere more than there,
where the angels sing
new songs
and the bells ring
in the courts of the King.
Oh, that we were there!

Source: Keyte and Parrott 1992: 195

*T*HIS beloved carol may be the earliest preserved German macaronic song. It is first mentioned in a vision of the mystic Heinrich Suso (c. 1295–1366), who wrote that it had been sung by angels who drew him into an ecstatic, "heavenly" dance in order to free him from his woes, which it did. (Keyte and Parrott 1992: 197) Over the next centuries it appeared in numerous versions in both High and Low German, of which Wackernagel 1964, a comprehensive, five-volume anthology of German hymnody, contains no fewer than nine.

The earliest surviving source is a Leipzig University manuscript of ca. 1400, the same source that preserves "Joseph, lieber Joseph mein." Both carols were almost certainly intended for dancing, which was common in medieval German churches, especially in connection with Christmas. Particularly interesting about the macaronic structure of the carol, which implies alternating performance by choir and congregation, is the way that the two languages are seamlessly joined into a single text rather than divided into longer sections in a single language.

In the sixteenth and seventeenth centuries "In dulci jubilo" appeared in numerous hymnbooks, both Catholic and Protestant. The preponderance of Latin and the Marian focus of the fourth and last verse ("Mater et filia ist Jungfrau Maria . . . ."; The Virgin Mary is both mother and daughter . . . .) gave pause to some Lutherans. In his 1545 Leipzig hymnal, Valentin Triller (d. 1573) dropped the Marian reference and substituted "O patris caritas! O nati lenitas! (Oh love of the father! Oh mercy of the son!)" He completed his revision by exchanging verses 3 and 4, the result being the version presented here.

Latin was removed from "In dulci jubilo" at a later date to make it more palatable for Lutheran hymnals, and it was fundamentally rewritten. The resultant all-German form first appeared in print in Hanover (1646) and it continues to be used in German Lutheran churches today (*EKG*: 26). It exchanges the first and second lines of the original and is thus entitled "Nun singet und seid froh."

Joseph, lieber Joseph mein
Joseph, My Dear Joseph
Author unknown, 15th century

Joseph, lieber Joseph mein,
Joseph, dear Joseph my,

hilf mir wiegen mein Kindelein,
help me rock my little child,

Gott, der wird mein Lohner sein
God, who will my rewarder be

im Himmelreich, der Jungfrau Sohn Maria.
in heaven, the Virgin's son Mary.

Joseph, my dear Joseph,
help me rock my little child,
God, who will be my rewarder
in heaven, the Virgin Mary's son.

Gerne, liebe Muhme mein,
Gladly, dear cousin my,

helf' ich dir wiegen dein Kindelein,
help I you rock your little child,

Gott, der wird mein Lohner sein
God, who will my rewarder be

im Himmelreich, der Jungfrau Kind Maria.
in heaven, the Virgin's child Mary.

Gladly, my dear lady,
I will help you rock your little child,
God, who will be my rewarder
in heaven, the Virgin Mary's child.

Freu' dich nun, du christlich' Schar!
Rejoice — now, you Christian flock!

Gott, der Himmelskönig klar,
God, the heavenly king radiant,

macht uns Menschen offenbar
made to us mortals revelation

der uns gebar die reine Magd Maria.
who for us bore the pure maiden Mary.

Now rejoice, you Christians all!
God, the radiant, heavenly king,
reveals to us mortals
who the pure maiden Mary bore for us.

Alle Menschen sollen gar
All humanity shall —

ganz in Freuden kommen dar,
totally in joy come —,

daß ein jeder recht erfahr',
that –each– truly meet

den uns gebar die reine Magd Maria.
whom for us bore the pure maiden Mary.

All humanity shall come
in complete and total joy,
so that each may truly meet the one
whom the pure maiden Mary bore for us.

Uns erschien Emanuel,
To us appeared Emanuel,

wie uns verkündet Gabriel,
as to us announced Gabriel

und bezeugt Ezechiel:
and prophesied Ezekiel:

Du Mensch ohn' Fehl', dich hat gebor'n Maria!
You person without fault, you has borne Mary!

To us appeared Emanuel,
as announced to us by Gabriel
and prophesied by Ezekiel:
You without fault, Mary has borne you!

Ew'gen Vaters ew'ges Wort,
Eternal Father's eternal word,

wahrer Gott, der Tugend Hort,
true God, –virtue's– refuge,

irdisch hier, im Himmel dort
on earth here, in heaven there

der Seelen Pfort', die uns gebar Maria.
the souls' gate, which for us bore Mary.

Eternal Father's eternal word,
true God, virtue's refuge,
here on earth, there in heaven,
the souls' portal, which Mary bore for us.

Süßer Jesu, auserkorn,
Sweet Jesus, chosen one,

weißt wohl, daß wir war'n verlorn:
know well, that we were lost:

Stille deines Vaters Zorn.
Still your father's wrath.

Dich hat geborn die reine Magd Maria.
You has borne the pure maiden Mary.

Sweet Jesus, chosen one,
you know well that we were lost:
still your father's wrath.
The pure maiden Mary has borne you.

Himmlisch' Kind, o großer Gott,
Heavenly child, O great God,

leidest in der Krippen Not.
suffer in the manger's misery.

Machst die Sünder frei vom Tod,
Make the sinners free of death,

du englisch' Brot, das uns gebar Maria.
you angelic bread that for us bore Mary.

Heavenly child, great God,
you suffer misery in the manger.
You make us sinners free of death,
you angelic bread that Mary bore for us.

Er ist erschienen am heutigen Tag in Israel:
He has appeared –today– in Israel,

der Maria verkügdigt ist durch Gabriel.
— Mary foretold was by Gabriel.

Eia! Eia!
Eia! Eia!

Jesum Christ hat uns gebor'n Maria.
Jesus Christ has for us borne Mary:

von Maria ist das Heil ersprossen in alle Welt.
from Mary has — salvation bloomed in all earth.

Magnum nomen Domini Emanuel,
Great name of Lord Emanuel,

Quod annunciatus ist per Gabriel.
as announced was by Gabriel.

He has appeared today in Israel,
as foretold to Mary by Gabriel.
Eia! Eia!
Mary has given birth to Jesus Christ for us:
from Mary has salvation bloomed across the
whole earth.
Great is the name of the Lord, Emanuel,
as foretold by Gabriel.

Source: Keyte and Parrott 1992: 178

314

*O*NE of the oldest of German carols, "Joseph, lieber Joseph mein" originated at least as early as 1400, around which time the earliest known source was set to paper. That source, a manuscript from Leipzig University, preserves eight verses and a refrain, presented here in highly modernized form.[104]

The history, text, and music of this carol are intertwined with those of another work, "Resonet in laudibus," also likely of fourteenth-century origin. Both share the same melody, which exists in various versions, both have refrains with many common elements, and both were performed in the German *Wechselgesang* tradition of the Reformation and post-Reformation periods.

> The roots of the Wechselgesang tradition are in pre-Reformation Bohemia, from where it was adopted and brought to its fullest flowering by German Lutherans in their Christmas Night ante-communion services which replaced the former masses at midnight and dawn. Its essence was the alternation or "exchange" (*Wechsel*) of whole sections of extended songs between different groups of voices and instruments placed strategically around the church: clergy, the unison *chorus choralis* and congregation, polyphonic *chorus musicus*, organ, and often other groups such as boys in high galleries . . . or singing actors . . . . (Keyte and Parrott 1992: 182)

The carol has seen so many variants that it is impossible to speak of an "original" or "correct" version. In *Wechselgesang* performance, for example, "Joseph, lieber Joseph mein" was often elaborately interwoven with "Resonet in laudibus" and related texts. The refrain given in the *New Oxford Book of Carols* (but not in Weber-Kellerman 1982, which is otherwise identical) and shown in the translation above was found in no setting of the carol located by the editors. Another refrain, entirely in Latin and set to a melodic variant, is frequently seen, however:

Virgo Deum genuit,	God has been born of a virgin
Quem divina voluit clementia.	as ordained by heaven's grace.
Omnes nunc concinite,	Everyone join together now,
Nato regi psallite,	sing praises to the new-born king and
Voce pia dicite:	proclaim with a pious voice:
Sit gloria Christo nato infantulo.	"Glory be to the new-born Christ!"
Hodie apparuit in Israel,	Today has appeared in Israel
Quem praedixit Gabriel, est natus rex.	the one foretold by Gabriel; the king is born!

In the first verse, Mary sings to Joseph, who answers in the second. The six verses that follow provide commentary from attendants or onlookers. "Joseph, lieber Joseph mein" is thus perfectly suited to a dramatic performance (which was common in both Catholic and Lutheran churches until the early eighteenth century), and may well have been designed for such. The simplest form of dramatic performance would have been the singing of the carol while a cradle at the front of the church was rocked by the Priest/pastor or congregants. This custom was associated with an entire genre of carols, the "cradle-songs" or lullabies, of which several are presented in this volume. See the annotation to "Dort oben vom Berge" for additional discussion of this form.

---

[104]See Keyte and Parrott 1992: 177.

Maria durch ein' Dornwald ging
Mary Walked through a Thorn-Wood
Author unknown, 15th century

Maria durch ein' Dornwald ging,
Maria through a thorn-wood went,

Kyrieleison!
Lord, have mercy!

Maria durch ein' Dornwald ging,
Maria through a thorn-wood went;

der hatte in sieben Jahren kein Laub getragen,
it had in seven years no leaves borne,

Jesus und Maria.
Jesus and Mary!

Was trug Maria unter ihrem Herzen?
What carried Maria below her heart?

Kyrieleison!
Lord, have mercy!

Ein kleines Kindlein ohne Schmerzen,
a small little child without suffering,

das trug Maria unter ihrem Herzen!
that carried Maria below her heart,

Jesus und Maria.
Jesus and Mary!

Da haben die Dornen Rosen getragen,
There have the thorns roses borne,

Kyrieleison!
Lord, have mercy!

Als das Kindlein durch den Wald getragen,
As the little child through the wood [was] carried,

da haben die Dornen Rosen getragen,
there have the thorns roses borne,

Jesus und Maria.
Jesus and Mary!

Mary walked through a thorn-wood,
Kyrieleison!
Mary walked through a thorn-wood;
it had not born leaves for seven years,
Jesus and Mary!

What did Mary carry below her heart?
Kyrieleison!
An innocent little child,
that's what Mary carried below her heart,
Jesus and Mary!

Roses on the thorns appeared,
Kyrieleison!
As the child was carried through the wood,
roses on the thorns appeared,
Jesus and Mary!

Source: Keyte and Parrott 1992: 584

*K*EYTE and Parrott, the editors of the *New Oxford Book of Carols*, state that this song of seven verses "has many of the characteristics of a fifteenth-century German folk carol." (1992: 585) Its earliest printed ancestor, however, is in the *Andernacher Gesangbuch* of 1608. The song appears to have passed into oral tradition until the mid nineteenth century. In 1850 it was first printed in its modern form. "Maria" was especially popular among German Lutheran young people during the German "youth movements" of the years surrounding the turn of the twentieth century, and later in the period immediately following WWII:

> It stood in stark contrast to the mindless children's songs of their fathers' generation. . . . Unlike the taboos of the late Victorian era, these old songs spoke in an open and direct language that touched the youth more than the song repertoire of the past. (Weber-Kellermann 1982: 211, tr. ed.)

The austere imagery may have appealed as well. Mary is portrayed in the opening verse as walking through a forest of thorn bushes that had not borne flowers in seven years—a symbol of the sinful, pre-redemption world. In the second and third verses she carries the Jesus-child through the forest, which miraculously blooms with roses—symbolic of the Savior's coming and his ultimate blood sacrifice.[105] The subsequent verses (not given here) deal with the child's name (verse 4), his baptism (verse 5), and the gifts he will receive (i.e., heaven and earth, verse 6). The seventh and final verse catechistically asks, "Who alone redeemed the world?" and answers, "That is what the Christ-child did; he alone redeemed the world."

---

[105]The connection of Jesus with the rose has a very long history. See the annotation to the hymn "Es ist ein' Ros' entsprungen," p. 279, for another example of the rose as symbolic of Christ's coming. "Exite Sion filiae" by Hildegard von Bingen (1098–1179) provides a yet earlier example of rose imagery, here in symbolism of the Passion:

> His bloodied head is disheveled with hair rent by thorns . . . . What field uncrossed by furrows, bristling with briars and brambles brought this grievous harvest? . . . The thorn, reddening with the blood of Christ, changes its spines into roses and, surpassing the palm-frond, is made a more fitting sign of triumphs." (Czerny 1998)

O du fröhliche

O You Merry

Author unknown

O du fröhliche,
O you merry,

O du selige,
O you blessed,

Gnadenbringende Weihnachtszeit!
grace-bringing   Christmas time!

Welt   ging verloren,
World was   lost,

Christ ward geboren.
Christ was   born.

Freue,   freue dich, o Christenheit!
Rejoice, rejoice —, O Christendom!

O you merry,
O you blessed,
grace-bestowing Christmas time!
The world was lost,
then Christ was born.
Rejoice, rejoice, O Christendom!

O du fröhliche,
O you merry,

O du selige,
O you blessed,

Gnadenbringende Weihnachtszeit!
grace-bringing   Christmas time!

Christ ist erschienen,
Christ has appeared,

Uns zu versühnen.
us   to reconcile.

Freue,   freue dich, o Christenheit!
Rejoice, rejoice —, O Christendom!

O you merry,
O you blessed,
grace-bestowing Christmas time!
Christ has appeared
to reconcile us.
Rejoice, rejoice, O Christendom!

O du fröhliche,
O you merry,

O du selige,
O you blessed,

Gnadenbringende Weihnachtszeit!
grace-bringing   Christmas time!

Himmlische Heere,
Heavenly   hosts,

Jauchzen dir   Ehre.
shout   to you praises.

Freue,   freue dich, o Christenheit!
Rejoice, rejoice —, O Christendom!

O you merry,
O you blessed,
grace-bestowing Christmas time!
Heavenly hosts
shout your praises.
Rejoice, rejoice, O Christendom!

Source: Weber-Kellerman 1982: 158

JOHANNES Falk (1768–1826) served in the early nineteenth century as the warden (superintendent) of the Lutherhaus, a Lutheran orphanage in the east German city of Weimar. In 1819 he produced a Christmas pageant for his charges to perform, entitled "Dr. Martin Luther and the Reformation in Folk Songs." One of the songs in the pageant was a Catholic hymn, "O sanctissima! O piissima!" set to German words for Christmas, the first verse by Falk and the second two by another employee of the Lutherhaus, Heinrich Holzschuher. Thus was the carol "O du fröhliche" born.

"O du fröhliche" became popular with its publication in 1830 and has remained so; it appears in all three twentieth-century editions of the German Lutheran hymnal cited in *References*. Its origin as a carol for children can be seen in its simplicity, with four of its six lines repeated in each verse. The two lines that change from verse to verse carry a simple message divided into three parts: The world was lost until Jesus was born; / he came to redeem humanity, / and the angels sing his praises. Whether by chance or design, the messages of the last two verses are identical to those of the parallel verses in the carol "In dulci jubilo."*

"O du fröhliche" appears in the *EKG* as no. 406. It also appears in sundry English-language carol collections but is not in the *LBW*. Its melody is used in the LBW, however, in a hymn for the closing of the service.

O Jesulein zart

O Tender Infant Jesus

Author unknown

O   Jesulein   zart,
O infant Jesus tender,

Dein Kripplein ist hart.
your little crib is hard.

O   Jesulein   zart,
O infant Jesus tender,

Wie liegst du so   hart.
how lie you so roughly.

Ach schlaf, ach tu
Oh   sleep, oh close

Dein Äugelein zu.
your little eyes — .

Schlaf und gib uns
Sleep and give us

Die ewige   Ruh.
— eternal peace.

O   Jesulein   zart,
O infant Jesus tender,

Wie liegst du so   hart.
how lie you so roughly.

O   Jesulein   zart,
O infant Jesus tender,

Das Kripplein ist hart.
the little crib is hard.

O tender infant Jesus,
your little crib is hard.
O tender infant Jesus,
how uncomfortably you lie.
O sleep, O close
your little eyes.
Sleep, and give us
eternal peace.
O tender infant Jesus,
how uncomfortably you lie.
O tender infant Jesus,
the little crib is hard.

Seid stille, ihr Wind,
Be   still, you wind,

Laßt schlafen das Kind.
let   sleep   the child.

All Brausen sei   fern,
All uproar be distant;

Es ruhen will   gern.
it   rest wants to much.

Schlaf, Kind, und tu
Sleep, child, and close

Dein Äugelein zu,
the   little eyes — .

Schlaf und gib uns
Sleep and give us

Die ewige   Ruh.
— eternal peace!

Ihr Stürme, halt' ein,
You storms, be calm,

Das Rauschen laßt sein.
the howling let cease.

Seid stille, ihr Wind,
Be   still, you wind,

Laßt schlafen das Kind.
let   sleep   the child.

Be still, you wind,
let the child sleep.
All tumult be gone;
the child wants to rest.
Sleep, child, and close
your little eyes.
Sleep, and give us
eternal peace!
You storms, be calm,
cease your howling.
Be still, you wind,
let the child sleep.

Nichts   mehr sich bewegt,
Nothing   more — moves,

Kein   Mäuslein sich regt.
no   little mouse — stirs.

Zu schlafen beginnt
to   sleep   begins

Das herzige Kind.
the   dear   child.

Schlaf denn und tu
Sleep   then   and   close

Dein Äugelein zu.
your little eyes — .

Schlaf und gib uns
Sleep and give us

Die ewige Ruh.
— eternal rest.

Nichts   mehr mann dann singt,
Nothing more man then sings,

Kein Stimmlein erklingt:
no   little voice sounds.

Schalf, Jesulein zart
Sleep, Jesus   tender

Von göttlicher Art.
of   divine nature!

Nothing else moves,
no little mouse stirs.
The dear child
begins to sleep.
Sleep then, and close
your little eyes.
Sleep, and give us
eternal rest.
Nothing more is sung,
no little voice sounds.
Sleep, tender Jesus;
sleep, divine child!

Source: Zimmer 1981: 104

*L*ITTLE is known about this tender carol except that it was first printed in the hymnal of Peter von Brachel, published in Cologne in 1623, and was set by a several seventeenth-century composers, including Samuel Scheidt. Verses 1, 4, and 5 of five are presented here. Verses 2 and 3 present two manger scenes, the first that of the ox, ass, and sheep, and the second that of the angels, the cherubim, and the seraphim.

Like a number of other early carols, including "Still, still, still,"* "O Jesulein zart" features textual repeats at the ends of verses. The inconsistency of the repeats is notable: the first four lines are repeated in the first verse (the last two lines reversed), the first two lines in the second verse (also inverted), the third and fourth in the third verse, and the first two lines, without inversion, in verse 4. While there is no exact repeat in the last verse, at the end it does recall the opening reference to "Jesulein zart," thus rounding the form of the poem.

O Tannenbaum

O Evergreen

Verse 1 Author unknown; verses 2–3 Ernst Anschütz

O Tannenbaum, o Tannenbaum,
O evergreen,   O evergreen,

wie grün sind deine Blätter!
how green are your leaves!

Du grünst nicht nur zur Sommerszeit,
You green not only in the summertime,

nein, auch im Winter, wenn es schneit.
no,   also in the winter, when it snows.

O Tannenbaum, o Tannenbaum,
O evergreen,   O evergreen,

wie grün sind deine Blätter!
how green are your leaves!

O evergreen, O evergreen,
how green are your leaves!
You are green not only in summer,
but also in winter, when it snows.
O evergreen, O evergreen,
how green are your leaves!

O Tannenbaum, o Tannenbaum,
O evergreen,   O evergreen,

du kannst mir sehr   gefallen.
you can me very much please.

Wie oft hat doch zur Weihnachtszeit
How often has — at Christmas-tide

ein Baum von dir mich hocherfreut.
a   tree of yours me   delighted.

O Tannenbaum, o Tannenbaum,
O evergreen,   O evergreen,

du kannst mir sehr   gefallen.
you can me very much please.

O evergreen, O evergreen,
you can please me very much.
How often at Christmastide has
a tree of your kind delighted me.
O evergreen, O evergreen,
you can please me very much.

O Tannenbaum, o Tannenbaum,
O evergreen,   O evergreen,

dein Kleid kann mich was   lehren:
your garb can   me something teach:

Die Hoffnung und Beständigkeit
—   hope   and constancy

gibt Trost und Kraft zu jeder Zeit.
give comfort and strength at any   time.

O Tannenbaum, o Tannenbaum,
O evergreen,   O evergreen,

dein Kleid kann mich was   lehren.
your garb can   me something teach.

O evergreen, O evergreen,
your foliage can teach me something:
that hope and constancy
give comfort and strength at any time.
O evergreen, O evergreen,
your foliage can teach me something.

Source: Weber-Kellermann 1982: 160

*E*VERGREENS, which "green not only in summer, but also in winter, when it snows," were a pre-Christian symbol of "the continuing life-force at the winter solstice." (Keyte and Parrott 1992: 600) The tree first became a symbol of Christ's renewal of life in the Rhineland during the late Middle Ages. The use of Christmas trees apparently took considerable time to spread eastward, as it may have been relatively new in eastern Germany in the early nineteenth century, when the present carol first appeared. (Weber-Kellermann 1982: 161) Even so, the tradition was so ingrained in the later nineteenth century that many Lutherans thought it to have stemmed from Martin Luther himself. Given the long history of the evergreen as a Christmas symbol, it is remarkable that "O Tannenbaum" was the first carol in which it appeared as such. (Weber-Kellermann 1982: 161)

The first verse, which has nothing explicitly to do with Christmas, was published by August Zarnack in his *Weisenbuch zu den Volksliedern für Volksschulen* (Folk Song Tunebook for Public Schools) of 1810, set to the familiar "O Tannenbaum" melody, which had previously seen service as a student song.[106] Four years later a Leipzig schoolteacher named Ernst Anschütz (1780–1861?) wrote two additional and intentionally didactic verses for his pupils. It is in this form that the carol is known today.

---

[106]Zarnack's verse may not have been entirely original. It resembles a much older song entitled "O Dannebom" that was well known at that time and with which he may have been familiar.

Psallite
Sing!
Author unknown

Psallite ungenito Christo Dei Filio!
Sing to only begotten Christ of God son!

Psallite Redemptori Domino,
Sing to redeemer Lord,

puerulo, jacenti in praesepio.
child, lying in manger.

Ein kleines Kindelein liegt in dem Krippelein;
A small tiny child lies in the little crib;

Alle liebe Engelein dienen dem Kindelein,
all lovely little angels serve the little child

und singen ihm fein.
and sing to him sweetly.

Sing to Christ, the only-begotten son of God!
Sing to the redeemer, our Lord,
the child, lying in the manger.
A tiny child lies in the little crib;
all the lovely angels serve the little child
and sing sweetly to him.

Singt und klingt
Sing and play:

Jesu, Gottes Kind
Jesu, God's child

und Marien Söhnelein,
and Mary's little son,

Unserm lieben Jesulein,
our dear little Jesus

im Krippelein
in the little crib

beim Öchse und beim Eselein!
beside the oxen and beside the little ass!

Sing and play:
Jesus, God's son
and the son of Mary,
our beloved Jesus-child
in the manger
beside the ox and ass.

Source: Keyte and Parrott 1992: 161

*H*ISTORY has not preserved the name of the author of this carol text, popularized by Michael Praetorius, but it was certainly written prior to 1599, when another setting, in triple meter, was published in the *Alte catholische geistliche Gesangbuch*. The bilingualism of "Psallite" is an extension of the medieval practice of writing macaronic texts, in which Latin and the vernacular were mixed, usually in alternate lines, as is the case here. The carol is a simple call to praise the Christ-child, who is idyllically pictured lying in the manger, surrounded by the animals. According to Keyte and Parrott (1992: 162), the music is not by Praetorius, but is instead an anonymous French chanson entitled "Ho la hé, par la vertu goi," first published in 1530.

In German-speaking countries "Psallite" is also known by the opening words of a German version, "Singt und klingt," which is first found in Catholic hymnals of the early seventeenth century. Although those publications retained the Latin text for the opening "Psallite" section, they provided German for the repeat. Modern German editions, however, often provide the German text throughout as shown above.

Still, Still, Still

Still, Still, Still

Author unknown

Still, still, still,
Still, still, still,

Weil's   Kindlein schlafen will!
because the little child sleep wants to!

Maria tut es niedersingen,
Maria does it down-sing

Ihre keusche Brust darbringen.
her pure breast offers.

Still, still, still,
Still, still, still,

Weil's   Kindlein schlafen will!
because the little child sleep wants to!

Still, still, still,
the little child wants to sleep!
Mary sings him down to sleep
and offers her pure breast.
Still, still, still,
the little child wants to sleep!

Schlaf, schlaf, schlaf,
Sleep, sleep, sleep,

Mein liebes Kindlein, schlaf!
my dear little child, sleep!

Die Engel tun schön musizieren,
The angels do beautifully make music;

Vor dem Kindlein jubilieren.
before the little child rejoice.

Schlaf, schlaf, schlaf,
Mein liebes Kindlein schlaf!

Sleep, sleep, sleep,
my dear little child, sleep.
The angels make music so beautifully;
they rejoice before the child.
Sleep, sleep, sleep,
my dear little child, sleep.

Groß, groß, groß,
Great, great, great,

Die Lieb' ist übergroß!
the love is very great!

Gott hat den Himmelsthron verlassen
God has the heaven-throne left

Und muß reisen auf der Straßen.
and must travel on the streets.

Groß, groß, groß,
Die Lieb ist übergroß!

Great, great, great,
the love is very great!
God has left his heavenly throne
and now must travel on the streets.
Great, great, great,
the love is very great!

Auf, auf, auf,
Up up, up,

Ihr Adamskinder, auf!
you Adam's children, up!

Fallet Jesum all' zu Füßen,
Fall Jesus all at feet,

Weil   er für uns d'Sünd tut büßen!
because he for us the sin does atone!

Auf, auf, auf,
Ihr Adamskinder, auf!

Up, up, up,
you children of Adam, up!
Fall down at Jesu's feet,
because he atones for our sins!
Up, up, up,
you children of Adam, up!

Wir, wir, wir,
We, we, we,

Wir rufen all zu dir:
we call all to you:

Tu uns des Himmels Reich aufschließen,
make for us the heaven's kingdom open,

Wenn wir einmal sterben müssen.
when we one day die must.

Wir, wir, wir,
Wir rufen all zu dir!

We, we, we,
we all call to you:
open the kingdom of heaven for us
when we one day must die!
We, we, we,
we all call to you.

Source: Weber-Kellerman 1982: 90

322

THIS carol had probably been preserved by oral tradition for a long time before it was first committed to paper around 1800 in the Salzkammergut, a lake district in Austria. Another version of the carol, to a different melody, stems from the village of Lothringen. The structure and meter of the present carol also characterize the four verses of the Lothringen carol, "Still, still, still, wer Gott erkennen will" (Zimmer 1981: 111), the first verse of which reads:

Still, still, still, wer Gott erkennen will.
Ein Kind, geboren in einer Nacht,
hat uns das Heil der Welt gebracht:
still, still still, wer Gott erkennen will.

Still, still, still, you who wish to recognize God.
A child born in the night
brought salvation to the world:
still, still, still, you who wish to recognize God. (tr. ed.)

Stille Nacht! heilige Nacht!
Silent Night, Holy Night!
Joseph Mohr

Stille Nacht! heilige Nacht!
Silent night, holy night!

Alles schläft, einsam wacht
All is sleeping, lonely is awake

Nur das traute hochheilige Paar.
only the beloved highly holy pair.

Holder Knabe im lockigen Haar,
Lovely boy in the curly hair,

Schlaf in himmlischer Ruh'.
sleep in heavenly peace.

Silent night, holy night!
All is sleeping; only the lonely couple,
the beloved, most holy pair, is awake.
O lovely boy with curly hair,
sleep in heavenly peace.

Stille Nacht! heilige Nacht!
Silent night, holy night,

Gottes Sohn, o, wie lacht
God's son, oh, how laughs

Lieb' aus deinem göttlichen Mund,
love from your divine mouth,

Da uns schlägt die rettende Stund',
as for us strikes the saving hour,

Christ, in deiner Geburt.
Christ, in your birth.

Silent night, holy night!
Son of God, oh how love radiates
from your divine mouth,
as our salvation's hour strikes,
O Christ, with your birth.

Stille Nacht! heilige Nacht!
Silent night, holy night,

Die der Welt Heil gebracht
which to the world salvation brought

Aus des Himmels goldenen Höhn.
from heaven's golden heights.

Uns der Gnade Fülle läßt sehn:
Us the grace's abundance lets see

Jesum in Menschengestalt.
Jesus in human form.

Silent night, holy night,
which brought salvation to the world
from heaven's golden heights.
The abundance of grace lets us see
Jesus in human form.

Stille Nacht! heilige Nacht!
Silent night, holy night,

Wo sich heut' alle Macht
where — today all power

Väterlicher Liebe ergoß,
of fatherly love poured out,

Und als Bruder huldvoll umschloß
and as brother graciously embraced

Jesus die Völker der Welt.
Jesus the peoples of the world.

Silent night, holy night,
where today all the power
of fatherly love poured out,
and Jesus was embraced as a brother
by all the peoples of the world.

Stille Nacht! heilige Nacht!
Silent night, holy night,

Lange schon uns bedacht,
long already by us pondered,

Als der Herr, vom Grimme befreit,
when the Lord, from wrath freed,

In der Väter urgrauer Zeit
in the father's ancient-gray time

Aller Welt Schonung verhieß.
to all world mercy promised.

Silent night, holy night,
that we have long pondered,
when the Lord, freed from rage,
promised mercy to all the world
in the ancient, grey days of our ancestors.

Stille Nacht! heilige Nacht!
Silent night, holy night,

Hirten erst kundgemacht.
[to] shepherds first known made

Durch der Engel Hallelujah
through the angels' Hallelujah,

Tönt es laut von fern und nah:
sounds it loudly from far and near:

Christ, der Retter, ist da!
Christ the savior is here!

Silent night, holy night,
first made known to the shepherds
through the angels' "Hallelujah,"
it sounds loudly from far and near:
"Christ the savior is here!"

Source: Weber-Kellerman 1982: 164

*I*N both German- and English-speaking lands, no Christmas song exceeds the popularity of "Silent Night." It is one of the few carols the origins of which are documented with some precision, thanks to the efforts of folk-song scholar Franz Magnus Böhme (1827–1898)[107] and the composer himself.

The text came from the pen of Joseph Mohr (1792–1848), the assistant pastor of the St. Nicola-Kirche in Oberndorf (near Laufen on the Salzach River) in the Austrian (now German) Alps. As reported by Böhme, on Christmas Eve day 1818 Mohr presented a new song of six verses to the church organist, Franz Gruber (1787–1863), with the request to set it to music for choir, two soloists, and guitar (an instrument unknown to his rural congregants and initially mistaken by them for an insect trap). Gruber did so, and the song was first heard in the midnight service that night. Böhme says that guitar was chosen as accompaniment to avoid the "miserable organ"; other reports say that the organ was broken, a proposition Keyte and Parrott (1992: 304) hold to be romantic legend. The organ aside, it is agreed among the sources consulted that the yearly composition of such folk-like Christmas songs was an established tradition in the churches of this area.

Mohr's text appears likely to have been a reworking of a three-verse Latin antecedent that begins "Alma nox, tacita nox" (Tender Night, Silent Night) that was found on the organ platform of a village church in the Bavarian woods. The beginnings are obviously related, the meter of both is the same, and they share many of the same images and ideas. "Stille Nacht" first appeared in a reasonably critical edition in the *Musikalischen Hausschatz der Deutschen* (Gottfried Wilhelm Fink, ed.) of 1843, but labeled as a Tyrolian folk song and lacking any mention of the poet. Incorrect attribution or lack of same followed the carol until 1854, when Gruber formally documented its origins.

The universality of "Stille Nacht" invited its use as the basis for variants unrelated to Christmas. Early in the twentieth century the hymn became the basis for a number of worker protest songs, the texts of which bespeak the strong class divisions of the age. (Weber-Kellermann 1982: 167)

---

[107]The German text of Böhme's narrative is contained in Weber-Kellermann 1982: 165, as are the full text of the hymn "Alma nox" (164), and a facsimile score with the text of "Stille Nacht" written out by Franz Gruber in 1855 (166).

Canons

Auf den Erfinder des Metronoms

To the Inventor of the Metronome

(Ludwig van Beethoven) a 4

Author probably Ludwig van Beethoven

Ta ta ta ta ta ta ta ta   lieber Mälzel,
Ta ta ta ta ta ta ta ta   dear Mälzel,

lebet wohl, sehr wohl.
live well, very well.

Banner der Zeit, großer Metronom!
Banner of time, great metronome!

Ta ta ta ta ta ta ta ta dear Mälzel,
fare well, very well!
Banner of time: the great metronome!

AROUND the year 1200 an otherwise anonymous Arab astronomer named Ibn Unis discovered that a pendulum of given length swayed back and forth at a constant rate. This knowledge, lost for nearly 400 years, was rediscovered by the Italian astronomer Galileo Galilei c. 1589 and was later put to practical use in the first pendulum-driven clock (1656). Over the next two centuries it occurred to many musicians that pendulums of different lengths could be used to determine musical tempo. The American composer William Billings, for example, described tempos in terms of pendulum length in three of his publications, beginning with *The New England Psalm Singer* of 1770.

In the first decade of the nineteenth century, a Dutchman named Dietrich Nikolaus Winkel devised a "musical chronometer" with a pendulum of adjustable length. According to *The New Grove* (Richardson 1980: 223), the inventor Johann Nepomuk Mälzel (1772–1838) saw the Winkel device on a visit to Amsterdam in 1815. He miniaturized and patented it, and just a year later brought it to market. Thus, for better or worse, Mälzel has received the credit for the invention of the metronome, and his name is enshrined for posterity in the abbreviation "M.M." (= Mälzel's metronome).

The present canon and its text have an unclear history. Beethoven had known Mälzel at least as early as 1813 as the inventor of a mechanical instrument called the "panharmonicon," for which he wrote his *Wellington's Victory* (op. 91). The editor of the Beethoven *Werke-Verzeichnis*, Anthony von Hoboken, states that the canon was likely written for a farewell dinner (presumably farewell to Mälzel) a year earlier, in the spring of 1812. He dates the version of the text given here from late 1817 at the earliest, and states that it was supposed to have been written down by Beethoven in 1820 at the request of Anton Schindler, his secretary. As Hoboken notes, the text must have been different in 1812, since (according to Gustav Nottebohm, who assembled the first thematic catalogue of Beethoven's works) the term "metronome" was not in use until 1815. *The New Grove* questions the authenticity of the canon, which could not be genuine if it had been written on the subject of Mälzel's metronome in 1812, three years before Mälzel even saw the Winkel "chronometer."

Aus tiefer Not

From Deep Distress

(Martin Agricola) a 2

Martin Luther

Aus tiefer Not schrei ich zu dir,
From deep distress cry I to you:

Herr Gott, erhör mein Rufen;
Lord God, hear my cries;

dein gnädig Ohr neig her zu mir
your gracious ear bend over to me

und meiner Bitt sie öffne!
and to my prayer it open.

Denn so du willt das sehen an,
For as you want to it look at —

was Sünd und Unrecht ist getan,
what sin and injustice has been done,

wer kann, Herr, vor dir bleiben?
who can, Lord, before you remain?

In deep distress I cry to you:
Lord God, hear my cries;
incline your gracious ear to me
and listen to my prayer.

For if you choose to consider
what sin and injustice has been done,
Lord, who can withstand your scrutiny?

VERSE 1 of Luther's chorale of the same name* (with minor modernizations in lines 2, 3, and 4) provides the text for this sixteenth-century canon.

Die Musici

The Musicians

(Traditional) a 2

Himmel und Erde müssen vergehn,	Heaven and earth must pass away,
Heaven and earth must pass away,	but musicians endure forever.
Aber die Musici bleiben bestehn.	
but the musicians remain enduring.	

*T*HE sentiments of this canon should warm the hearts of all musicians. The anonymous author appears to have paraphrased Luke 21: 33, "Himmel und Erde vergehen, aber meine Wort vergehet nicht." (Heaven and earth will pass away, but my words will not pass away.)

Die Nachtigall, K. 382a

The Nightingale

{Wolfgang Amadeus Mozart) a 3

Ludwig Christoph Heinrich Hölty

Sie, sie ist dahin, dahin,	She, she is gone, gone,
She, she is gone, gone,	the songstress, who sang the May-songs!
	She, who made the grove more beautiful
Die Sängerin, die Maienlieder tönte!	with her song,
the songstress, who May-songs sounded!	she is gone, alas, she is gone!
	The songstress, whose song resounded
Sie, die durch ihr Lied den Hain verschönte,	throughout the grove,
She, who by her song the grove made beautiful,	whose song beautified the entire grove,
	she is gone! The songstress is gone!
Sie ist dahin, ach, sie ist dahin!	
she is gone, ah, she is gone!	
Die Sängerin, deren Lied durch den Hain ertönte,	
The songstress, whose song through the grove resounded,	
Deren Lied den ganzen Hain verschönte,	
whose song the whole grove beautified,	
Sie ist dahin! Die Sängerin, sie ist dahin!	
She is gone! The songstress, she is gone!	

*A*CCORDING to Köchel (1951) what has become known as "Die Nachtigall," a canon for three voices by Mozart, was originally (c. 1781–1783) untexted and likely written for the enjoyment and intellectual exercise of the composer. When Breitkopf and Härtel published the *Oeuvres* (works) of Mozart c. 1804, they apparently felt the need to add a text so that the canon could be performed vocally. They chose a poem by Ludwig Christoph Heinrich Hölty* (1748–1776) entitled "Auf den Tod einer Nachtigall" (On the Death of a Nightingale). With forty-seven measures, "Die Nachtigall" is by far the longest of Mozart's approximately forty canons, a fact that probably facilitated finding a suitable text.

Ein feste Burg ist unser Gott
A Mighty Fortress Is Our God
(Johann Friedrich) a 4

Martin Luther

Ein feste   Burg ist unser Gott,
A firm fortress is   our God,

Ein gute   Wehr   und Waffen;
a   good bulwark and weapon.

Er hilft uns frei aus aller Not,
He helps us free from all misery

Die uns itzt hat betroffen.
that us now has affected.

Der alte böse Feind,
The old evil   foe:

Mit   Ernst   er's jetzt meint,
with seriousness he it now intends.

Groß Macht und viel   List
Great power and much cunning

Sein grausam Rüstung ist,
his   cruel armament is;

Auf Erd ist nicht seinsgleichen.
on earth is   not   his equal.

A mighty fortress is our God,
a strong bulwark and weapon.
He sets us free from all the misery
that has now beset us.

The ancient, evil foe:
grave is his intent.
Vast power and cunning
are his cruel weapons;
on earth he has no equal.

*F*RIEDRICH chose for his text the first verse of the Luther's chorale "Ein feste Burg ist unser Gott,"* which he set without alteration.

Es ist ein' Ros' entsprungen
A Rose Has Come Forth
(Melchior Vulpius) a 4

Author unknown

Es ist ein' Ros' entsprungen
— is a rose come forth

aus einer Wurzel zart,
from a   root tender.

Wie uns   die Alten sungen,
As   to us the old   sang,

von   Jesse kam die Art.
from Isaiah came the breed.

A rose has come forth
from a tender root.
As prophets of old sang to us,
from Isaiah came the lineage.

*V*ULPIUS'S canon is a setting of the first four lines of the seven that comprise verse 1 of the anonymous chorale of the same name.*

Herr, wie lange
Lord, How Long?
(Georg Phillipp Telemann) a 2

Psalm 13: 1

Herr, wie lange willst du mein
Lord, how long will you me

so   gar   vergessen,
so totally   forget?

wie lange verbirgest du
How long   hide   you

dein Antlitz vor mir?
your face from me?

Lord, how long will you
so completely forget me?
How long will you hide
your face from me?

Meister Jakob
Master Jacob
(Traditional) a 4

Meister Jakob, schläfst du noch?
Master Jacob, sleep you still?

Hörst du nicht die Glocken:
Hear you not the bells:

bim bam, bim bam.
bim bam, bim bam.

Master Jacob, are you still asleep?
Don't you hear the bells:
"bim bam, bim bam."

*I*N both text and melody, "Meister Jakob" is an adaptation of the French childrens' canon known in its original language as "Frère Jacques."

Musikantenkanon
Musicians' Canon
(Jens Rohwer) a 3

Author Unknown

Fa la la la la *musica,*
Fa la la la la music

artium suprema est!
of arts supreme is!

Hundertfach geschwungen,
Hundred times swung,

gehupft wie gesprungen,
skipped as well as jumped,

jeder Ton ein Fest!
every tone a feast!

Munter, munter!
Lively, lively!

Kunterbunter Kontrapunkt, doch ah!
Multi-colored counterpoint, — ah!

die Einigkeit ist doch da,
the unity is — there,

die *harmonia,* die Harmonie— ja!
the harmony, the harmony— yes!

Fa la la la la, *musica*
artium suprema est!
A hundred times whirled about,
skipped, and jumped,
every tone a feast!
Multi-colored counterpoint—ah!
The unity is truly there!
and *harmonia,* the harmony!—yes!

Nachtigallenkanon
Nightingale Canon
(Joseph Haydn) a 3

Author unknown

Alles schweiget, Nachtigallen
All is silent; nightingales

locken mit süßen Melodien
bring with sweet melodies

Tränen ins Auge,
tears into the eye,

Schwermut ins Herz.
sadness into the heart.

All is silent; nightingales
with their sweet melodies
bring tears to the eye,
sadness to the heart.

*T*HE Haydn *Werke* (Haydn, 1959, Reihe xxxi, ed. Otto Erich Deutsch) contains some forty-seven secular canons, the "Nachtigallenkanon" not among them. This work is among the large number of spurious or questionable compositions attributed to Haydn after his death, and is far enough removed from him not even to merit a mention in the otherwise copious listings of spurious and doubtful works in *The New Grove.* The source of the text is not known.

Selig sind die Toten
Blessed Are the Dead
(Heinrich Spitta) a 3

From Revelation 14: 13

Selig sind die Toten;
Blessed are the dead;

sie ruhen von ihrer Arbeit!
they rest from their labor!

Blessed are the dead;
they rest from their labor.

Trinkkanon, K. 559a
Drinking Canon
(Wolfgang Amadeus Mozart) a 4

Author unknown

Freunde, lasset uns beim Zechen
Friends, let us during drinking

wacker eine Lanze brechen!
lustily a lance break!

Es leb' der Wein, die Liebste mein!
— live the wine, — most beloved my!

Drauf leer' sein Gläschen jeder aus.
To that empty out his glass everyone —.

Friends, while we're drinking,
let's have a hearty joust!
May the wine live, my most favorite!
To the wine! Everyone empty out his glass!

Mit euch ist gar nichts anzufangen,
With you is nothing to be done;

da sitzt ihr still wie Hopfenstangen.
there sit you silent like hops-stalks.

Sie lebe hoch! So schreiet doch!
She lives high! So shout —!

Seid ihr wie Stockfisch denn geworden stumm?
Have you like dried cod then become mute?

There is nothing to be done with you;
you sit there as silent as hops stalks.
May she prosper! Shout it out!
Have you become mute like dried fish?

So schreit, ihr Esel, doch, seid nicht so dumm!
So shout, you donkeys, — be not so stupid!

Es leb' die Liebe und der Wein!
— live — love and the wine!

Vivat, vivat, vivat!
Live, live, live!

Was könnt' auf Erden schönres sein?
What could on earth more beautiful be?

Vivat, vivat, vivat, sie lebe hoch!
Live, live, live, she live high!

Then shout, you donkeys, don't be so stupid!
Long live love and wine!
Vivat, vivat, vivat!
What on earth could be more beautiful?
Vivat, vivat, vivat—may she live well!

MOZART enjoyed playing with rhymes, puns, and double-entendres, and found an outlet for his sense of humor in writing canons to earthy texts unburdened by the culture that saturated his world as a composer. In 1788 he wrote an elaborate canon to a scatological text, the beginning and tamest portion of which is as follows:

O du eselhafter Martin,
o du martinischer Esel,
du bist also faul
als wie ein Gaul.

O you ass, Martin,
O you martinine ass,
You are as lazy
As an old nag horse.

The unremitting coarseness of the words made the original canon unsuitable for public performance, condemning the music to oblivion. At a later time, however, an unknown author composed a second, more acceptable text for the canon, the convivial drinking song presented here.

Vater unser

Our Father

(Adam Gumpelzhaimer) a 2

Martin Luther

Vater unser im Himmelreich,
Father our in the heaven-kingdom,

Der du uns alle heißest gleich
who you us all command equally

Brüder sein und dich rufen an,
brothers to be and you to call upon,

Und willst das Beten von uns han,
and you want — praying from us have:

Gib, daß nicht bet allein der Mund,
give, that not pray alone the mouth,

Hilf, daß es geh von Herzensgrund.
help, that it comes from heart's–depth.

Our Father in the kingdom of heaven,
who commands us all equally
to be brothers and to call upon you,
and who wants us to pray to you:
grant that we not pray only with our mouths,
but help us, so that it may also come
from the depths of our hearts.

*M*ARTIN Luther's meditation on the Lord's Prayer, verse 1, supplied Gumpelzhaimer with his text. See the annotation to the hymn "Vater unser im Himmelreich" for additional information.

Vom Himmel hoch

From Heaven on High

(Johann Friedrich) a 4

Martin Luther

Vom Himmel hoch da komm ich her,
From heaven high there come I hither,

ich bring euch gute neue Mär;
I bring you good new tidings;

der guten Mär bring ich so viel,
the good tidings bring I so many,

davon ich singn und sagen will.
of which I sing and speak want to.

From heaven on high I come to you;
I bring you good new tidings!
I bring you so many good tidings
of which I want to sing and speak.

*V*ERSE 1 of Martin Luther's beloved Christmas chorale "Vom Himmel hoch, da komm ich her"* provides the text for this seventeenth-century canon.

Willkommen, lieber schöner Mai, D. 224

Welcome, Dear Beautiful May

(Franz Schubert) a 3

Ludwig Heinrich Christoph Hölty

Willkommen, lieber schöner Mai,	Welcome, dear, beautiful May;
Welcome, **dear beautiful May;**	to you the birds sing their hymn of praise.
dir tönt der Vögel Lobgesang.	
to you sounds the birds' praise-song.	

Source: Hölty n.d.: 107

*L*UDWIG Heinrich Christoph Hölty (1748–1776) was particularly fond of seasonal poems, especially for spring. He wrote at least seven verses entitled either "Mailied" as in this case, or "Maigesang," one of which provided Schubert with the text for his canon.[108] Schubert, wanting a very brief text, combined the opening lines of the first two verses to create a complete thought in just nine words:

Willkommen, lieber schöner Mai,	Welcome, beloved, beautiful May,
Der unsre Flur verjüngt,	who rejuvenates our meadows,
Daß ringsum Laub und Blume neu	so that everywhere leaves and flowers
Aus vollen knospen bringt.	spring anew from ripe buds.
Dir tönt der Vögel Lobgesang;	The birds' hymn of praise sounds for you;
Der ganze Buchenhain	the entire beech grove
Am Blumental ist Silberklang,	in the flowered valley is a silvery sound,
Und Bäche murmeln drein.	and brooks murmur therein.
Rot stehn die Blumen, weiß und blau,	The flowers stand in red, white, and blue,
Und Mädchen pflücken sie,	and girls pick them
Und tanzen auf der grünen au':	and dance in the green meadow:
Ahi, herr Mai, Ahi!	"Hello, Mr. May, Hello!"
Ihr Busen ist von Blümchen bunt;	Their bosoms are bright with flowers;
Von schöner Melodie	Their rosy mouths sing beautiful melodies
Ertönt, und lacht ihr Rosenmund;	and laugh :
Ahi, herr Mai, ahi!	"Hello, Mr. May, Hello!" (tr. ed.)

The rosy character with which Hölty endowed this spring poem from 1773 was not shared by them all. In many others omens of death are seen in the mirror of spring's short life.[109] Hölty's own destiny is reflected in these poems: he died of tuberculosis at the youthful age of 27.

Schubert wrote two versions of his canon (1815), one in A major and the other in F-sharp minor, thus embodying in music the same contrast of character found among Hölty's *Mailieder*. He set the complete Hölty poem as a vocal duet in the same year (or possibly in 1813).

---

[108]Another version of "Mailied," dated January 31, 1773, appears in Hölty 1869: 145. Likewise in four stanzas of four lines each, this poem shares the refrains at the end of the last two stanzas; it also contains five additional lines from the poem shown above. The word "ahi" is an untranslatable exclamation of joy that seemed best treated as "hello" in a poem of greeting.

[109]A good example is the poem to which Brahms composed "Die Mainacht," op. 43, no. 2.

Appendices

ABBREVIATIONS

BuxWV   Karstadt, Georg. *Thematisch-systematisches Verzeichnis der musikalischen Werke von Dietrich Buxtehude* (BuxWV) 2^d exp. and rev. ed. Wiesbaden: Breitkopf and Hartel, 1985.

> Thematic catalogue to the works of Buxtehude. Organization is by genre rather than chronology, which is in large part unknown.

BWV   Schmieder, Wolfgang. *Thematisch-systematisches Verzeichnis der musikalischen Werke von Johann Sebastian Bach.* 2^d ed. Leipzig: Breitkopf and Hartel, 1958.

> Thematic catalogue to the works of J.S. Bach. Numbering of the vocal works has to do with the order of their publication in the Breitkopf and Härtel complete works edition rather than chronology of composition.

D.   Deutsch, Otto Erich. *Schubert; Thematic Catalogue of All His Works in Chronological Order.* New York: W.W. Norton, 1951.

EKG   *Evangelisches Kirchen Gesangbuch.* Stuttgart: Verlag des Evangelischen Gesangbuchs, 1953.

> Hymnbook of the German Lutheran Church.

Hob.   Hoboken, Anthony van. *Joseph Haydn; thematisch-bibliographisches Werkverzeichnis.* Mainz: B. Schott's Söhne, 1957-1978.

> Thematic catalogue to the works of Haydn. Numbering of individual works is by genre ("Series") rather than chronology.

K.   Köchel, Ludwig, Ritter von. *Chronologisch-thematisches Verzeichnis sämtlicher Tonwerke Wolfgang Amadeus Mozarts.* 6th ed. Wiesbaden: Breitkopf and Hartel, 1964.

> Thematic catalogue to the works of Mozart, organized chronologically.

LBW   *Lutheran Book of Worship.* Prepared by the churches participating in the Inter-Lutheran Commission on Worship. Minneapolis: Augsburg Publishing House, 1978.

> The hymnal in current use by all three branches of the Lutheran church in the United States.

o op.   "Werk ohne Opus-Zahl"

> Designates "works without opus number."

SWV   *Schütz-Werke-Vezeichnis,* kleine Ausgabe. Werner Bittinger, ed. Kassel: Bärenreiter, 1960.

> Thematic catalogue to the works of Schütz.
> Organization chronological.
>> SWV 1–435 = printed works.
>> SWV 436–494 = works in manuscript only.

*
(asterisk)   An asterisk indicates a work translated and annotated in this volume as well as a composer or poet who has at least one work represented here.

REFERENCES

Works Cited

Allmers, Hermann. 1965. *Werke*. Kurd Schulz, ed. Göttingen: Sachse and Pohl.

Athenaeus, of Naucratis. 1951. *The Deipnosophists*. Charles Burton Gulick, trans. 7 vols. Cambridge, MA: Harvard University Press.

Bach, Johann Sebastian. 1988. "Ich lasse dich nicht," BWV Anh. 159. Daniel Melamed, ed. Neuhausen-Stuttgart: Hänssler Verlag.

Beckler, Heinz. 1980. "Brahms, Johannes." *The New Grove Dictionary of Music and Musicians*. Stanley Sadie, ed. Macmillan.

Beethoven, Ludwig van. 1966. *Fantasien [sic], Piano, Mixed Voices, Orchestra, op. 80*. Introduction by Willy Hess. London, New York: Ernst Eulenberg.

Bei der Weiden, Brage. 1996. *Leben im 16. Jahrhundert: Lebenslauf und Lieder des Hauptmanns Georg Niege*. Berlin: Akademie Verlag.

Berke, Dietrich, ed. 1996. *Gesänge für gemischte Stimmen*. Teil A. Neue-Schubert-Ausgabe. Serie III: Mehrstimmige Gesänge. Band 2.

Bittinger, Werner. 1960. *Schütz-Werke-Vezeichnis*, kleine Ausgabe. Kassel: Bärenreiter.

Bolin, Norbert. 1995. "Menschensohn und Gottesknecht: Der Prophet Elias." Notes to Hänssler Classic CD 98.928, Mendelssohn: *Elias*.

Boyd, James. 1949. *Notes to Goethe's Poems*. Blackwell's German Texts. 2 vols. Oxford: Basil Blackwell.

Brentano, Clemens. 1963–1968. *Werke. [von] Clemens Brentano*. Friedheim Kemp, ed. 4 vols. Munich: Hanser.

Brown, Maurice J.E. 1980. "Schubert, Franz." *The New Grove Dictionary of Music and Musicians*. Stanley Sadie, ed. Macmillan.

Buxtehude, Dietrich. 1968a. *Alles was ihr tut*. Günter Graulich, ed. Stuttgart: Hänssler Verlag.

Buxtehude, Dietrich. 1968b. *Das neugeborne Kindelein*. Günter Graulich, ed. Stuttgart: Hänssler Verlag.

Conrat, Hugo. 1903. "Brahms, wie ich ihn kannte." *Neue-Musik-Zeitung* 24, no. 1 (November, 1903): 1.

Czerny, Carl. 1988. *Exite Sion filiae*. Martin Banner, ed. John P. Dyson, trans. Chapel Hill, NC: Treble Clef.

Daumer, Georg Friedrich. 1855. *Polydora; ein weltpoetisches Liederbuch*. 2 vols. Frankfurt am Main: Literarisches Anstalt.

Daumer, Georg Friedrich. 1856. *Hafis: eine Sammlung persischer Gedichte nebst poetischen Zugaben aus verschiedenen Völkern und Ländern*. Hamburg: Hoffman and Campe.

Daverio, John. 1997. *Robert Schumann: Herald of a "New Poetic Age."* New York and Oxford: Oxford University Press.

Day, James. 1966. *The Literary Background to Bach's Cantatas*. New York: Dover.

deGaetano, Paul J. 1989. *James Macpherson*. Boston: Twayne Publishers.

Deutsch, Otto Erich, ed. 1964. *Schubert. Die Dokumente seines Lebens*. Neue-Schubert-Ausgabe. Serie viii supplement, Band 5. Kassel: Bärenreiter.

Deutsch, Otto Erich, ed. 1947. *The Schubert Reader: a Life of Franz Schubert in Letters and Documents*. Eric Blom, trans. New York, W.W. Norton.

Deutsch, Otto Erich. 1951. *Schubert: Thematic Catalogue of All His Works in Chronological Order*. New York: W.W. Norton.

Dürr, Alfred. 1971. *Die Kantaten von Johann Sebastian Bach*. 2 vols. Kassel: Bärenreiter.

Ebert, Johann Arnold. 1971. *Johann Arnold Eberts Episteln und vermischte Gedichte*. Hamburg: Bohn, 1789; facsimile reprint. Bern: Herbert Lang.

Eichendorff, Joseph, Freiherr von. 1955. *Werke in einem Band*. Wolfdietrich Rasch, ed. Munich: C. Hanser.

Eichendorff, Joseph, Freiherr von. 1958. *Neue Gesamtausgabe der Werke und Schriften, [von] Joseph Freiherr von Eichendorff*. Gerhart Baumann and Siegfried Grosse, eds. 4 vols. Stuttgart: Cotta.

Eichendorff, Joseph, Freiherr von. 1977. *Werke in einem Band*. Wolfdietrich Rasch, ed. Munich: C. Hanser.

Eichendorff, Joseph, Freiherr von. 1965. *Werke in vier Bänden*. Ludwig Krähe and René Strasser. Zürich: Frankfurt, Innsbruck, Paris, Brussels, Lausanne: Stauffacher-Verlag.

Eichendorff, Joseph, Freiherr von. 1985–. *Werke in sechs Bänden*. Hartwig Schultz, ed. Frankfurt am Main: Deutscher Klassiker Verlag.

EKG. 1953. *Evangelisches Kirchen Gesangbuch*. Ausgabe für die evangelische Landeskirche in Württemberg. Stuttgart: Verlag des evangelischen Gesangbuchs Stuttgart.

Fischer-Dieskau, Dietrich. 1996. *Schubert und seine Lieder*. Stuttgart: Deutsche Verlags-Anstalt.

Fleming, Paul. 1965. *Paul Flemings deutsche Gedichte*. Stuttgart: Anton Hiersemann, 1865; facsimile reprint. Darmstadt: Wissenschaftliche Buchgesellschaft.

Franck, Johann. 1674. *Johann Franckens geistliches Sion*. . . . Guben: C. Gruber.

Franck, Salomo. 1715. *Evangelisches Andachts-Opfer*. . . . Weimar.

Garland, Henry and Mary. 1976. *The Oxford Companion to German Literature*. Oxford: Clarendon Press.

Geibel, Emanuel. 1893. *Gesammelte Werke*. 3. Auflage. 8 vols. in 4. Stuttgart, Cotta.

Geibel, Emanuel. 1906. *Emanuel Geibels gesammelte Werke in acht Bänden*. 4th ed. Stuttgart and Berlin: Cotta.

Gellert, Christian Fürchtegott. 1965. *Sämtliche Fabeln und Erzählungen. Geistliche Oden und Lieder*. Munich: Winkler.

George, Stefan. 1958. *Stefan George Werke*. 2d ed. Munich: H. Kupper.

Gerhardt, Paul. 1957. *Dichtungen und Schriften*. Eberhard von Cranach-Sichart, ed. Munich: Paul Müller.

Gesangbuch für die evangelische Kirche in Württemberg. 1866. Stuttgart: Verlags-Comptoir des neuen evangelischen Gesangbuchs.

Gleim, Johann Wilhelm Ludwig. 1811. *Sämmtliche Werke*. Wilhelm Korte, ed. Halberstadt: Bureau für Literatur und Kunst.

Gleim, Johann Wilhelm Ludwig. 1965. *Versuch in scherzhaften Liedern und Lieder*, Alfred Anger, ed. Tübingen: Max Niemeyer.

Goethe, Johann Wolfgang von. 1948–. *Gedenkausgabe der Werke, Briefe und Gespräche*. Ernst Beutler, ed. 27 vols. Zurich, Artemis-Verlag.

Goethe, Johann Wolfgang von. 1961–1964. *Goethe's Werke*. Erich Trunz, et al., eds. 14 vols. Hamburg: Christian Wegner.

Goethe, Johann Wolfgang von. 1983. *Selected Poems*. Christopher Middleton, ed. Goethe Edition, vol. 1. Boston: Suhrkamp/Insel Publishers.

Goethe, Johann Wolfgang von. 1882. *Goethe's Faust, in Two Parts*. Anna Swanwick, trans. New York: Hurst.

Götz, Johann Nikolaus. 1817. *Vermischte Gedichte*. Vienna: Bauer.

Graulich, Günther, ed. 1968. Preface to Dietrich Buxtehude. *Das neugeborne Kindelein*. Neuhausen-Stuttgart: Hänssler Verlag.

Grillparzer, Franz. 1952. *Franz Grillparzer, Gedichte und Erzählungen*. Reinhold Backmann, ed. Vienna: Bergland Verlag.

Grillparzer, Franz. 1969–1970. *Sämtliche Werke . . . Franz Grillparzer*. Peter Frank and Karl Pörnbacher, eds. 2d rev. ed. Munich: C. Hanser.

Groth, Klaus. 1956–1960. *Sämtliche Werke [von] Klaus Groth*. Ivo Braak and Richard Mehlem, eds. 5 vols. Flensburg: C. Wolff.

Guthrie, D., et. al. 1970. *New Bible Commentary*. 3d ed. Grand Rapids: William B. Eerdmans.

Hagedorn, Friedrich von. 1968. *Herrn Friedrichs von Hagedorn sämmtliche poetische Werke, in dreien Teilen*. Hamburg: Johann Carl Bohn, 1757; facsmile reprint. Bern: Herbert Lang.

Härting, Michael. 1979. *Friedrich Spee: die anonymen geistlichen Lieder vor 1623*. Philologische Studien und Quellen, vol. 65. Berlin: Erich Schmidt Verlag.

Haydn, Joseph. 1958. *Joseph Haydn: mehrstimmige Gesänge*. Paul Mies, ed. *Joseph Haydn Werke*, Series xxx. Munich-Duisburg: G. Henle.

Haydn, Joseph. 1959. *Joseph Haydn: Kanons*. Otto Erich Deutsch, ed. *Joseph Haydn Werke*, Series xxxi. Munich-Duisburg: G. Henle.

Hebbel, Friedrich. 1963–1967. *Werke*. Gerhard Fricke, Werner Keller, and Karl Pörnbacher, eds. 5 vols. Munich: Hanser.

Hensel, Wilhelm. 1981. *Preussische Bildnisse des 19. Jahrhunderts: Zeichnungen von Wilhelm Hensel*. Berlin: Nationalgalerie Berlin, Staatliche Museen Preussischer Kulturbesitz.

Herder, Johann Gottfried. 1967–1968. *Sämtliche Werke [von] Johann Gottfried Herder*. Bernhard Suphan, ed. Berlin: Weidmann, 1877–1913; facsimile reprint. Hildesheim: Georg Olms.

Herder, Johann Gottfried. 1975. *Stimmen der Völker in Liedern*. 1778, 1779; reprint. Stuttgart: Reclam.

Herzogenberg, Heinrich von. 1994. "Die Nacht," op. 22, no. 2. Richard Bloesch, ed. Houston, TX: Alliance Music Publications.

Heyse, Paul. 1850. *Die Jungbrunnen: neue Märchen von einem fahrenden Schüler*. Berlin: Alexander Düncker.

Hoboken, Anthony van. 1957–1978. *Joseph Haydn; thematisch-bibliographisches Werkverzeichnis*. Mainz: B. Schotts Söhne.

Hofrichter, Ruth J. 1942. *Three Poets and Reality: Study of a German, an Austrian, and a Swiss Contemporary Lyricist*. New Haven: Yale University Press.

Hölderlin, Friedrich. 1990. *Werke in einem Band*. Munich: Carl Hanser Verlag.

Hölty, Ludwig Heinrich Christoph. 1869. *Gedichte von Ludewig [sic] Heinrich Christoph Hölty*. Karl Halm, ed. Leipzig: Brockhaus.

Hölty, Ludwig Heinrich Christoph. n.d. *Hölty's Gedichte*. Leipzig: Wilhelm Engelmann.

Jancik, Hans. 1974. Foreword to *Hugo Wolf. Sämtliche Werke*. vol. 10, *Kleine Chöre a cappella oder mit Klavierbegleitung*. Vienna: Musikwissenschaftlicher Verlag.

Jeffers, Ron, ed. 1988. *Translations and Annotations of Choral Repertoire. Vol. 1, Sacred Latin Texts*. Corvallis, OR: earthsongs.

Julian, John. 1985. *Dictionary of Hymnology: Origin and History of Christian Hymns and Hymnwriters of All Ages and Nations*. J. Murray, 1908; facsimile reprint. Grand Rapids: Kregel Publications.

Kalbeck, Max. 1976. *Johannes Brahms*. 4 vols. Berlin: Deutsche Brahms-Gesellschaft, 1915; facsimile reprint. Tutzing: Hans Schneider.

Karstadt, Georg. 1985. *Thematisch-systematisches Verzeichnis der musikalischen Werke von Dietrich Buxtehude*. 2^d exp. and rev. ed. Wiesbaden: Breitkopf and Härtel.

Kennedy, Michael. 1980. "Strauss, Richard." *The New Grove Dictionary of Music and Musicians*. Stanley Sadie, ed. Macmillan.

Kerman, Joseph and Alan Tyson. 1980. "Beethoven, Ludwig van." *The New Grove Dictionary of Music and Musicians*. Stanley Sadie, ed. Macmillan.

Keyte, Hugh and Andrew Parrott, eds. 1992. *The New Oxford Book of Carols*. Oxford: Oxtord University Press.

Kinsky, Georg. 1955. *Das Werk Beethovens: thematisch-bibliographisches Verzeichnis seiner sämtlichen vollendeten Kompositionen*. Munich: G. Henle Verlag.

Kleist, Ewald Christian von. 1766. *Des Herrn Christian Ewald von Kleist sämtliche Werke*. 2 vols. in 1. Berlin: C.F. Voss.

Klitzsch, Dr. Emanuel. 1847. "Mehrstimminge Gesänge." [review of collections of choral songs] *Neue Zeitschrift für Musik* 26, no. 40 (May 14, 1847): 1.

Klopstock, Johann Gottlieb. 1854. *Klopstocks sämtliche Werke*. 10 vols. Leipzig: Göschen.

Koch, Eduard Emil. 1973. *Geschichte des Kirchenlieds und Kirchengesangs der christlichen, inbesondere deutschen evangelischen Kirche*. Completed by Adolf Wilhelm Koch after the death of the author. 3^d ed., revised and improved. Stuttgart: 1866-77; reprint. Hildesheim, New York: G. Olms Verlag.

Köchel, Ludwig, Ritter von. 1964. *Chronologisch-thematisches Verzeichnis sämtlicher Tonwerke Wolfgang Amade Mozarts*. 6th ed. Wiesbaden: Breitkopf and Härtel.

Kross, Siegfried. 1958. *Die Chorwerke von Johannes Brahms*. Berlin-Halensee: Max Hesses Verlag.

Kugler, Kranz. 1840. *Gedichte von Franz Kugler*. Stuttgart and Tübingen: Cotta.

Landon, H. C. Robbins and David Wyn Jones. 1988. *Haydn: His Life and Music*. London: Thames and Hudson.

Landon, H. C. Robbins. 1977. Haydn: *Chronicle and Works*. 5 vols. vol. 4. *Haydn: The Years of "The Creation."* Bloomington: Indiana University Press.

Larsen, Jens Peter. 1980. "Haydn, Joseph." *The New Grove Dictionary of Music and Musicians*. Stanley Sadie, ed. Macmillan.

LBW. 1978. *Lutheran Book of Worship*. Prepared by the churches participating in the Inter-Lutheran Commission on Worship. Minneapolis: Augsburg Publishing House.

Lemmermann, Dirk. 1996. *Studien zum weltlichen Vokalwerk Hugo Distlers: analytische, ästhetische und rezeptionsgeschichtliche Untersuchungen unter besonderer Berücksichtigung des Mörike-Chorliederbuches*. European University Studies. Series XXXVI. Frankfurt am Main, New York: P. Lang.

Lessing, Gotthold Ephraim. 1965. *Gotthold Ephraim Lessing: Werke in sechs Bänden*. Julius Petersen, Waldemar von Olshausen, and Fritz Fischer, eds. Zurich: Stauffacher.

Lueker, Erwin L. 1975. *Lutheran Cyclopedia*. Rev. ed. St. Louis: Concordia Pub. House.

Luther, Martin, trans. 1545. *Biblia* [germanica]. Wittenberg: Hans Lufft; facsimile reprint. Stuttgart: Württembergische Bibelanstalt, n.d.

Luther, Martin, trans. 1975. *Die Bibel*. Stuttgart: Deutsche Bibelstiftung.

Luther, Martin. 1909. *Dr. Martin Luthers Werke*. Weimar: Hermann Boehlaus Nachfolger.

Luther, Martin. 1967. *Martin Luther: Die deutschen geistlichen Lieder*. Gerhard Hahn, ed. Tübingen: Niemeyer.

Macpherson, James. 1926. *The Poems of Ossian, Translated by James Macpherson, with Notes, and with an Introduction by William Sharp*. Edinburgh: John Grant.

Melamed, Daniel R. 1988. "The Authorship of the Motet 'Ich lasse dich nicht' (BWV Anh. 159)." *Journal of the American Musicological Society* 41: 491–526.

Mendelsohn, Moses, trans. 1783. *Die Psalmen*. Berlin: Friedrich Maurer.

Metzger, Michael M. and Erika. 1972. *Stefan George*. New York: Twayne Publishers.

Meyer, Conrad Ferdinand. 1892. *Gedichte*. 5th ed. Leipzig: H. Haessel.

Meyer, Conrad Ferdinand. 1975. *Sämtliche Werke*. Hans Zeller and Alfred Zäch, eds. Bern: Benteli Verlag.

Mommsen, Katherina. 1988. *Goethe und die arabische Welt*. Frankfurt am Main: Insel Verlag.

Mörike, Eduard. 1905. *Sämtliche Werke in sechs Bänden*. Rudolf Krauß, ed. Leipzig: Max Hesses Verlag.

Mörike, Eduard Friedrich. 1967–1970. *Sämtliche Werke*. Munich: Winckler.

Moser, Hans Joachim. 1959. *Heinrich Schütz: His Life and Work*. Carl Pfatteicher, trans. St. Louis: Concordia Publishing House.

Müller, Wilhelm, ed. 1838. *Volksharfe: Sammlung der schönsten Volkslieder aller Nationen*. In 6 parts, constituting section 8 of the series Bibliothek des Frohsinns. J.M. Braun, ed. Stuttgart: Franz Köhler.

Najar, Nageen Runes. 1999. Telephone interview with Gordon Paine. November 10, 1999.

Neander, Joachim. 1700. *Vermehrte Glaub- und Liebes-Übung, auffgemuntert durch einfältige Bundes-Lieder und Danck-Psalmen. . . .* Frankfurt and Leipzig: Johann Philipp Andre.

Neander, Joachim. 1984. *Bundeslieder und Dankpsalmen von 1680*. Oskar Gottlieb Blarr, ed. Cologne: Rheinland-Verlag.

Neumann, Werner, ed. 1974. *Sämtliche von Johann Sebastian Bach vertonte Texte*. Leipzig: VEB deutscher Verlag für Musik.

Neumeister, Erdmann. 1717. *Fünffache Kirchen-Andachten*. Leipzig: Johann Großens Erben.

Nicolai, Philipp. 1963. *Freudenspiegel des ewigen Lebens*. Frankfurt am Main, 1599; facsimile reprint. Soest: Mocker and Jahn.

Ophüls Gustav, ed. 1983. *Brahms-Texte: sämtliche von Johannes Brahms vertonten und bearbeiteten Texte*. Completed and newly edited by Kristian Wachinger. Ebenhausen bei München: Langwiesche-Brandt.

Osbeck, Kenneth W. 1982. *Singing with Understanding, Including 101 Favorite Hymn Backgrounds*. Grand Rapids: Kregel Publications.

Osborne, Harold, ed. 1970. *The Oxford Companion to Art*. Oxford: Clarendon Press.

Paine, Gordon. 1989. "Score Selection, Study, and Interpretation." In *Up Front!: Becoming the Complete Choral Director*. Boston: E.C. Schirmer.

Platen, August Graf von. 1969. *Sämtliche Werke*. Max Koch and Erich Petzet, eds. 12 parts in 6 vols. 1910; facsimile reprint. 6 vols. in 3. Hildesheim: Georg Olms.

Pohl, Rainer. 1975. "Zur Textgeschichte von Mörikes "Feuerreiter." In *Eduard Mörike*. Victor G. Doerksen, ed. Wege der Forschung, vol. 446. Darmstadt: Wissenschaftliche Buchgesellschaft.

Preminger, Alex and T.V.F. Brogan, eds. 1993. *The New Princeton Encyclopaedia of Poetry and Poetics*. Princeton: Princeton University Press.

Price, Percival. 1983. *Bells and Man*. Oxford: Oxford University Press.

Ramler, Karl, ed. 1780. *Karl Wilhelm Ramlers lyrische Blumenlese*. Sammlung der besten deutschen prosaischen Schriftsteller und Dichter, parts 102 and 103. Karlsruhe: Christian Gottlieb Schmieder.

Rauchhaupt, Ursula von. 1993. Distler, Hugo. Notes to *Mörike-Chorliederbuch. Selections*. Compact disc. Kassel: Musicaphon. (Musicaphon BM 56820)

Reisiger, Hans. 1970. *Johann Gottfried Herder; sein Leben in Selbstzeugnissen, Briefen und Berichten*. Berlin: Propyläen, 1942; facsimile reprint. Hildesheim: Georg Olms.

Richardson, E.C. 1980. "Metronome." *The New Grove Dictionary of Music and Musicians*. Stanley Sadie, ed. Macmillan.

Rilling, Helmuth. 1985. "Bach's Significance." *Bach: Journal of the Riemenschneider Bach Institute*, July, 1985.

Roehrs, Walter R. and Martin Franzmann. 1979. *Concordia Self-Study Commentary: an Authoritative In-Home Resource for Students of the Bible*. St. Louis: Concordia Publishing House.

Rosenberg, Alfred. 1935. *Der Mythus des zwanzigsten Jahrhunderts*. Munich: Hoheneichen Verlag.

Rubeli, Alfred, ed. 1989. Hindemith, Paul. *Sämtliche Werke* vii/5. *Chorwerke a cappella*. Mainz: B. Schott's Söhne.

Rückert, Friedrich. 1868–1869. *Gesammelte poetische Werke in 12 Banden*. 12 v. in 10. Frankfurt am Main: Sauerländer.

Rückert, Friedrich. 1897. *Rückerts Werke*. Georg Ellinger, ed. Meyers Klassiker-Ausgaben. Leipzig and Vienna: Bibliographisches Institut.

Rückert, Friedrich. 1979. *Rückerts Werke: Auswahl in acht Teilen*. Edgar Groß and Elsa Hertzer, eds. 3 vols. Berlin: Bong and Co., 1910; facsimile reprint. Hildesheim: Georg Olms.

Runes, Dagobert David. 1948. *Jordan Lieder: frühe Gedichte*. New York: Philosophical Library.

Sams. Eric. 1983. *The Songs of Hugo Wolf*. London: Eulenburg Books.

Scheide, William H. 1982. "'Nun ist das Heil und die Kraft' (BWV 50): Doppelchörigkeit, Datierung und Bestimmung." *Bach-Jahrbuch* 68 (1982): 81.

Schiller, Friedrich. 1867. *Schillers sämtliche Werke in zwölf Bänden*. Stuttgart: Cotta.

Schiller, Friedrich. 1960. *Sämtliche Werke*. 2[d] ed. 5 vols. Munich: Carl Hanser Verlag.

Schmieder, Wolfgang. 1958. *Thematisch-systematisches Verzeichnis der musikalischen Werke von Johann Sebastian Bach*. 2[d] ed. Leipzig: Breitkopf and Hartel.

Schönberg, Arnold. 1964. *Arnold Schönberg Letters*. Selected and edited by Erwin Stein; translated by Eithne Wilkins and Ernest Kaiser. London: Faber and Faber.

Schroeder, Otto, ed. 1953–1973. Editorial notes to Walter, Johann. *Sämtliche Werke, [von] Johann Walter*. 3 vols. Kassel: Bärenreiter; St. Louis, Concordia Pub. House.

Schwarz, Egon. 1972. *Joseph von Eichendorff*. New York: Twayne.

Scott, Walter, Sir. 1900. *The Complete Poetical Works of Sir Walter Scott*. Cambridge Edition. Boston: Houghton, Mifflin.

Seidl, Johann Gabriel. 1877. *Johann Gabriel Seidls gesammelte Schriften*. Hans Max, ed. Vienna: Wilhelm Braumüller.

Shakespeare, William. 1986. *William Shakespeare: the Complete Works*. Stanley Wells *et al.*, eds. Oxford [Oxfordshire]: Clarendon Press; New York: Oxford University Press.

Shakir, M.H. trans. 1982. *Holy Qur'an* = [al-Qur'an al-hakim]. First U.S. ed. Elmhurst, NY: Tahrike Tarsile Qur'an.

Snyder, Kerala Johnson. 1980. "Neumeister, Erdmann." *The New Grove Dictionary of Music and Musicians*. Stanley Sadie, ed. Macmillan.

Spee, Friedrich [von] 1985–. *Sämtliche Schriften*. ed. Theo G.M. von Oorschot. 3 vols. Bern: A Francke.

Speer, Albert. 1970. *Inside the Third Reich*. New York: Macmillan.

Stapel, Wilhelm. 1950. *Luthers Lieder und Gedichte*. Stuttgart: Evangelisches Verlagswerk Stuttgart.

Stravinsky, Igor. 1970. *Poetics of Music in the Form of Six Lessons*. Arthur Knodel and Ingolf Dahl, trans. Cambridge, MA: Harvard University Press.

Stulken, Mary Kay. 1981. *Hymnal Companion to the Lutheran Book of Worship*. Philadelphia: Fortress Press.

Uhland, Ludwig. 1892. *Gedichte von Ludwig Uhland*. Friedrich Brandes, ed. Leipzig: Reclam.

Unger, Melvin. 1996. *Handbook to Bach's Sacred Cantata Texts*. Lanham, MD: Scarecrow Press.

Wackernagel, Philipp. 1841. *Das deutsche Kirchenlied von Martin Luther bis auf Nicolaus Herman und Ambrosius Plaurer*. Stuttgart: Leisching.

Wackernagel, Philipp. 1964. *Das deutsche Kirchenlied von der ältesten Zeit bis zu Anfang des 17. Jahrhunderts. Mit Berücksichtigung der deutschen kirchlichen Liederdichtung im weiteren Sinne und der lateinischen von Hilarius bis Georg Fabricius und Wolfgang Ammonius*. Leipzig, 1864–77; facsimile ed. 5 vols. Hildesheim: G. Olms.

Wagner, Paul, ed. 1697. *Andächter Seelen geistliches Brand- und Gantzopfer . . . Gesangbuch*. Leipzig: Andreas Seidlern.

Weber-Kellermann, Ingeborg. 1982. *Das Buch der Weihnachtslieder: 151 deutsche Advents- und Weihnachtslieder, Kulturgeschichte, Noten, Texte, Bilder, mit Klavier- und Orgel-Begleitung*. Mainz and New York: Schott.

Webern, Anton. 1957. *I. Kantate für Sopran-Solo, gemischten Chor und Orchester, op. 29*. Vienna: Universal Edition (UE 12485).

Webern, Anton. 1959. *Briefe an Hildegard Jone und Josef Humplik*. Josef Polnauer, ed. Vienna: Universal Edition.

Weinheber, Josef. 1954. *Josef Weinheber: sämtliche Werke*, Joseph Nadler and Hedwig Weinheber, eds. Salzburg: Otto Müller.

Weiße [Weisse], Christian Felix. 1772. *Kleine lyrische Gedichte*. 3 vols. Leipzig: Weidmann.

Weiße, Michael. 1957. *Ein new Gesang Buchlen (Gesangbuch der Böhmischen Brüder)*. Jungbunzlau, Bohemia: Georg Wylmschwerer, 1531; facsimile reprint. Konrad Ameln, ed. Kassel: Bärenreiter.

Wenzig, Josef. 1830. *Slawische Volkslieder, übersetzt von Joseph Wenzig*. Halle: Renger.

Whittaker, W. Gillies. 1959. *The Cantatas of J.S. Bach: Sacred and Secular*. 2 vols. London: Oxford University Press.

Wolff, Christoph and Hans-Joachim Schulze. 1985–. *Bach Compendium: analytisch-bibliographisches Repertorium der Werke Johann Sebastian Bachs*. Frankfurt and New York: C.F. Peters. Vol. 1. Vokalwerke (4 parts).

Yates, W.E. 1972. *Grillparzer: a Critical Introduction*. Cambridge, UK: Cambridge University Press.

Young, W. Murray. 1989. *The Cantatas of J.S. Bach: an Analytical Guide*. Jefferson, NC and London: McFarland and Co.

Zedlitz, Johann Christian von. 1879. *Gedichte von J. Chr. Freiherrn von Zedlitz*. Stuttgart: Cotta.

Ziegler, Christiane Mariane von. 1728. *Versuch in gebundener Schreib-Art*. Teil 1. Leipzig: Johann Friedrich Braun.

Zimmer, Ulrich, ed. 1981. *Es ist ein Ros': deutsche Weihnachtslieder aus sechs Jahrhunderten*. Kassel: Bärenreiter.

Other Bibliography

Bibles

Bibell. . . . [Catholic translation]. Cologne: Arnold Quentel, 1601.

Biblia [germanica]. Martin Luther, trans. Wittenberg: Hans Lufft, 1545.; facsimile reprint. Stuttgart: Württembergische Bibelanstalt, n.d.

Biblia pentapla. . . . Martin Luther, trans. 2 vols. [Wandesbeck bei Hamburg]: Hermann Heinrich Holle, 1711.

Biblia sacra . . . . Martin Luther, trans. Frankfurt am Main: Balthasar Christoph Wust [the elder], 1660.

Biblia sacra. . . . Martin Luther, trans. Kassel: Wilhelm Wessel, 1601.

Biblia. . . . Martin Luther, trans. Annotations by Daniel Cramer. Strassburg: Lazar Zeißner, 1625.

Biblia. . . . Martin Luther, trans. Annotations by Paul Tossani. Basel: Turneisen, 1729.

Biblia. . . . Martin Luther, trans. Büdingen: Johann Friedrich Stöhr, 1780.

Biblia. . . . Martin Luther, trans. Tübingen: J.C. Cotta, 1739.

Die Bibel. . . . Martin Luther, trans. Basel: Turneisen, 1814.

Die Bibel. Martin Luther, trans. Cologne: Britische und ausländische Bibelgesellschaft, 1885.

Die Bibel. Martin Luther, trans. Stuttgart: Deutsche Bibelstiftung, 1975.

Die Bibel. Martin Luther, trans. Stuttgart: Privilegierte Württembergische Bibelanstalt, 1912.

Die Gantze heilige Schrift. . . . Martin Luther, trans. Basel: Turneisen, 1720.

Die heilige Schrift neuen Testaments. . . . Martin Luther, trans. Commentary by Johann Christian Klemmen. Tübingen: J.C. and C.G. Cotta, 1729.

Die Heilige Schrift. . . . Martin Luther, trans., ed. J.F. Haug et. al. Parts 1–8. Bad Berlenburg: 1726–1742.

Hymnals

Evangelisches Gesangbuch. Stuttgart: Gesangbuchverlag Stuttgart, 1996.

Geistriches Gesangbuch. Johann Anastasio Freylinghausen, ed. Halle, 1713.

Gerhardt, Paul. *Paulus Gerhardts geistliche Lieder getreu nach der bei seinen Lebzeiten erschienen Ausgabe wiederabgedrückt.* Stuttgart; Leisching, 1853; facsimile reprint. Bern: Herbert Lang, 1974.

Gesangbuch für die evangelische Kirche in Württemberg. Stuttgart: Verlagskontor des evangelischen Gesangbuchs, 1912.

Gesangbuch für die evangelischen Kirchen und Schulen des Königreichs Württemberg. Stuttgart: Metzler, 1832.

Geystliche gesangk Buchleyn (Das geistliche Gesangbüchlein). Johann Walter, ed. Wittenberg, 1525; facsimile reprint (second printing, Worms, 1525). Kassel: Bärenreiter, 1979. Documenta musicologica. 1. Reihe, Druckschriften-Faksimiles, no. 33.

Additional Sources

Allen, Roy F. *German Expressionist Poetry.* Boston: Twayne Publishers, 1979.

Ambrose, Philip. *Texte zu den Kirchenkantaten von Johann Sebastian Bach.* Neuhausen-Stuttgart: Hänssler Verlag, 1984.

Athenaeus, of Naucratis. *The Deipnosophists; or, Banquet of the Learned.* Yonge, C. D., trans. 3 vols. London: H.G. Bohn, 1854.

Billings, William. *The Continental Harmony.* Boston: Isaiah Thomas and Ebenezer T. Andrews, 1794; facsimile reprint. Hans Nathan, ed. Cambridge, MA: The Belknap Press of Harvard University Press, 1961.

Billings, William. *The New England Psalm Singer*. The Complete Works of William Billings. Karl Kroeger, ed. vol. 1. [no place]: The American Musicological Society and The Colonial Society of Massachusetts, 1981.

Brahms, Johannes. *Geistliche Chormusik*. Günter Graulich, ed. [Stuttgart]: Carus-Verlag, [1983?].

Brahms, Johannes. *Johannes Brahms: Life and Letters*. Selected and annotated by Styra Avins. Josef Eisinger and Styra Avins, trans. Oxford, New York: Oxford University Press, 1997.

Brahms, Johannes. *Zigeunerlieder*, op. 103. Sergej Rogowoj, ed. Stuttgart: Carus Verlag, 1998.

Buxtehude, Dietrich. *Alles, was ihr tut mit Worten oder mit Werken*. Eugen Klause, ed. Berlin: Verlag Merseburger, [1947?].

Buxtehude, Dietrich. *Every Word and Thought [Alles, was ihr tut mit Worten oder mit Werken]*. Paul Bunjes, ed. St. Louis: Concordia, 1957.

Buxtehude, Dietrich. *Schlagt, Künstler, die Pauken*. Dietrich Kilian, ed. Berlin: Merseburger, 1958.

Buxtehude, Dietrich. *Schlagt, Künstler, die Pauken*. Dietrich Kilian and Fritz Oberdoerffer, eds. New York: C.F. Peters, 1965.

Buxtehude, Dietrich. *Werke*. 8 vols. Klecken: Ugrino Verlag, 1925–.

Closs, A. *The Genius of the German Lyric: an Historical Survey of its Formal and Metaphysical Values*. London: The Cresset Press, 1962.

Conrat, Hugo. "Johannes Brahms (Souvenirs Personnels)." *La Revue Musicale*. Year 4, no. 21 (November, 1904): 514.

Deutsch, Otto Erich, ed. *Franz Schubert: Briefe und Schriften*. 4th ed. Vienna: Verlag Brüder Hollinek, 1954.

Deutsch, Otto Erich. *Schubert: Memoirs by his Friends*. London: Adam and Charles Black, 1958.

Distler, Hugo. *Geistliche Chormusik, op. 12*. Kassel: Bärenreiter, 1993.

Edwards, Frederick George. *The History of Mendelssohn's Oratorio "Elijah."* London, 1896.

Einstein, Alfred. *Schubert: a Musical Portrait*. New York: Oxford University Press, 1951.

Ellison, Ross Wesley. "Mendelssohn's Elijah: Dramatic Climax of a Creative Career." *American Choral Review* (January 1980): 3.

Finscher, Ludwig, ed. *"Harfen." Die Musik in Gesichichte und Gegenwart*. 2d rev. ed. Sachteil 4. Kassel: Bärenreiter, 1994–1998.

Götz, Johann Nikolaus. *Die Gedichte Anakreons und der Oden Sappho*. Karlsruhe: Michael Macklot, 1760; reprint. Stuttgart: Metzler, 1970.

Hassler, Hans Leo. *Lustgarten neuer teutscher Gesäng*. . . . [2d ed.] Nüremberg: Kaufmann, 1610.

Hassler, Hans Leo. *Sämtliche Werke*. C. Russell Crosby, ed. vol. 9: *Lustgarten neuer teutscher Gesäng (1610)*. Wiesbaden: Breitkopf and Härtel, 1968.

Hebbel, Friedrich. *Samtliche werke*. Richard Maria Werne, ed. 24 vols. in 15. Berlin: B. Behr, [1901?–07?].

Hensel, Fanny Mendelssohn. *Gartenlieder*. Berlin: Bote und Bock, 1846. Score and voice parts.

Hensel, Fanny Mendelssohn. *Gartenlieder*. Kassel: Furore Edition, 1988; reprint. Bryn Mawr, PA: Hildegard Publishing Co., 1997.

Hensel, Fanny. "Nachtreigen." Ulrike Schadl, ed. Stuttgart: Carus Verlag, 1994.

Herz, Gerhard, ed. *Bach Cantata No. 4*. Norton Critical Score Series. New York: W.W. Norton, 1967.

Hough, Robbin R. *Concordance to Hymn Texts Lutheran Book of Worship*. Minneapolis: Augsburg Pub. House, 1985.

Kohl, Katrin M. *Rhetoric, the Bible, and the Origins of Free Verse: the Early Hymns of Friedrich Gottlieb Klopstock*. Berlin: Walter de Greyter, 1990.

"Kranz." Brockhaus Enzyklopädie. 7th ed. 20 vols. Wiesbaden: F.A. Brockhaus.

Landon, H. C. Robbins. *Haydn, a Documentary Study*. New York: Rizzoli, 1981.

Larkin, Rochelle. "Philosophical Library Redux." *Publisher's Weekly* 232 (August 21, 1987): 26.

Lassus, Orlandus. *Neue teutsche Lieder*. . . . Munich: Berg, 1583.

Luther, Martin. *Luther's Works.* Ulrich S. Leupold, ed. Philadelphia: Fortress Press, 1965.

Mäckelmann, Michael. *Arnold Schoenberg und das Judentum.* Hamburger Beiträge zur Musikwissenschaft, vol. 28. Hamburg: Karl Dietmar Wagner, 1984.

Mare, Margaret. *Eduard Mörike: The Man and the Poet.* London: Methuen, 1957.

McCorkle, Margit. *Johannes Brahms: thematisch-bibliographisches Werkverzeichnis.* Munich: G. Henle, 1984.

Mörike, Eduard Friedrich. *Werke in drei Bänden [von] Eduard Mörike.* August Leffson and Gisela Spiekerkötter, eds. Zurich: Stauffacher-Verlag, 1965.

Mörike, Eduard. *Sämtliche Werke.* Munich: Carl Hanser Verlag, 1964.

Nettl, Paul. *Beethoven Cyclopedia.* New York: Philosophical Library, 1956.

Oglesby, Donald. *Bach Cantata Database.* Self published, 1996.

Pachelbel, Johann. *Nun danket alle Gott.* Hans Heinrich Eggebrecht, ed. Basel; Bärenreiter Verlag; St. Louis: Concordia, [1955?].

Ramler, Karl Wilhelm, trans. *Anakreons auserlesene Oden.* Berlin: Sander, 1801.

Ramler, Karl Wilhelm. *Karl Wilhelm Ramlers poëtichen Werke.* 2 vols. Berlin: Johann Daniel Sander, 1800.

Schiff, David. "Jewish and Musical Tradition in the Music of Mahler and Schoenberg." *Journal of the Arnold Schoenberg Institute* 9, no. 2 (November, 1986): 217.

Schiller, Friedrich. *Schillers Werke.* 4 vols. Frankfurt am Main: Insel Verlag, 1966.

Schiller, Friedrich. *Schillers Werke.* Nationalausgabe. Julius Petersen and Gerhard Fricke, eds. Weimar: H. Böhlaus Nachfolger, 1943.

Schlegel, August Wilhelm von. *Sämmtliche Werke.* Eduard Böcking, ed. Leipzig: Weidmann'sche Buchhandlung, 1846–1847; facsimile reprint. 12 v. in 7. Hildesheim, New York: G. Olms, 1971–1972.

Seidl, Johann Gabriel. 1905. *Johann Gabriel Seidls ausgewählte Werke.* Wolfgang von Wurzbach, ed. 4 vols in 1. Leipzig: Max Hesse.

Shakespeare, William. *The Complete Works of Shakespeare.* Irving Ribner and George Lyman Kittredge, eds. Waltham, Mass: Ginn, 1971.

Slessarev, Helga. *Eduard Mörike.* New York: Twayne Publishers, 1970.

Spee, Friedrich von. *Samtliche Schriften; historisch-kritischeAusgabe in drei Banden.* Emmy Rosenfeld, ed. Munich: Kosel-Verlag, 1967–.

Stöcklein, Paul. *Joseph von Eichendorff in Selbstzeugnissen und Bilddokumenten.* Reinbek bei Hamburg: Rowohlt, 1963.

Storz, Gerhard. *Eduard Mörike.* Stuttgart: Klett Verlag, 1967.

Strand, Kenneth A. *German Bibles before Martin Luther.* Grand Rapids: Wm. B. Eerdmans, 1966.

Tombo, Rudolf. *Ossian in Gemany.* New York: Columbia University Press, 1901; facsimile reprint. New York: AMS Press, 1966.

Trenner, Franz. *Richard Strauss: Werkverzeichnis.* Vienna: Doblinger, 1985.

Vliegenthardt, Frits. Notes to Globe CD GLO 5147, *Robert Schumann, Vier Gesänge, Op. 141.*

Von Wiese, Benno. *Eduard Mörike.* Tübingen and Stuttgart: Rainer Wunderlich Verlag, 1950.

Webern, Anton. *Entflieht auf leichten Kahnen,* op. 2. Vienna: Universal-Edition, 1948.

Weiße, Christian Felix. *Scherzhafte Lieder.* Leipzig: 1758; facsimile reprint. Stuttgart, Metzler, [1965].

Wolters, Gottfried. 1956. *Mozart-Kanons im Urtext.* Wolfenbüttel: Möseler Verlag.

Youens, Susan. *Schubert's Poets and the Making of Lieder.* Cambridge: Cambridge University Press, 1996.

GERMAN MUSICAL VOCABULARY

Gemischter Chor – Mixed Choir	Kleine Trommel – Snare Drum
zweistimmiger Chor – 2-part Choir	Große Trommel – Bass Drum
drei gemischte Stimmen – 3 Mixed Voices	Becken – Cymbals
5 bis 8 stimmigen Chor – 5- to 8-part Choir	Holzkaste – Woodblock
Frauenchor – Women's Choir	Schellen – Sleighbells
Männerchor – Men's Choir	
Kinderchor – Children's Choir	Klavier – Piano
Chorstimme – Voice Part	Orgel – Organ
Chorpartitur – Choral Score	Positiv – Positiv Organ
Klavierauszug – Piano/Vocal Score	Cembalo – Harpsichord
Studienpartitur – Study (Miniature) Score	Generalbaß – continuo
	Harfe – Harp
Holzbläser – Woodwinds	Laute – Lute
Kleine Flöte – Piccolo	
Flöte – Flute	Streichinstrumente – Strings
Blockflöte – Recorder	Violine – Violin
Oboe – Oboe	Geige – Violin
Oboe d'amore – Oboe d'amore	Bratsche – Viola
Oboe da caccia – Oboe da caccia	Violoncell – Cello
Englisch Horn – English Horn	Kontrabaß – Contrabass
Klarinette – Clarinet	
Baß Klarinette – Bass Clarinet	C-Dur – C major
Fagott – Bassoon	Cis-Dur – C-sharp major
Kontrafagott – Contrabassoon	c-Moll – C minor
	cis-Moll – C-sharp minor
Blechinstrumente – Brass	Es-Dur – E-flat major
Trompete – Trumpet	As-Dur – A-flat major
Posaune – Trombone	b-Moll – B-flat minor
Tuba – Tuba	H-Dur – B major
	h-Moll – B minor
Schlagzeug – Percussion	4/4 Takt – 4/4 time
Pauken – Timpani	25 Takte – 25 measures

abdämpfen – to mute
aber – but
abnehmend – decreasing, *diminuendo*
Abschlag, der – downbeat, cut-off
abschlagen – to cut off
abschwellen – to decrease
absolutes Gehör – absolute pitch
absteigen – to descend
abwechseln – to alternate
accentuiert – accented
Akkord, der – chord
Akzent, der – accent
akzentuieren – to accent
alle – *tutti*
allein – solo
allmählich – gradually
Alt, der – alto
Analyse, die – analysis
andächtig – with devotion
Anfang, der – beginning
anfangs, wie – as at the beginning
angeben (Ton) – to give (the pitch)
anmutig – gracefully
anschwellen – to grow louder, *crescendo*
Ansingen, das – attack
Anspielen, das – attack
ansteigen – to ascend
antizipieren – to anticipate
anwachsend – *crescendo*
Arie, die – aria
Auffassung, die – interpretation
aufführen – to perform
Aufführung, die – performance
Aufgabe, die – exercise, task

Aufschlag, der – upbeat
Auftakt, der – upbeat
aus der Ferne – from a distance
Ausdruck, der – expression
Ausdruck, mit – with expression
ausdrucksvoll – *molto espressivo*

Ausgabe, die – edition
ausgeziert – embellished, ornate
aushalten – to sustain
äußerst – extremely, exceedingly
aussetzen – to realize (figured bass)
Aussprache, die – enunciation, pronunciation
Auswahl, die – selection
auswendig – by memory, by heart
Auszug, der – arrangement, adaptation

Ballade, die – ballad
Ballett, das – ballet
Baß, der – bass
Bassetthorn, das – tenor clarinet
Bebung, die – vibrato
bezifferter Baß – figured bass
Bearbeitung, die – arrangement
Becken, das/die – cymbal(s)
bedächtig – unhurried, steady
begleiten – to accompany
Begleitung, die – accompaniment
besetzen – to score for, cast
Besetzung, die – performing forces
betonen – to accent, stress
betont – *marcato*
betrübt – sadly
beweglich – nimbly, agilely

bewegt – with movement
bis – until, to
blasen – to blow
Bogen, der – the bow
breit – broad(ly)
Bühne, die – stage

Celeste, die – celeste
Cembalo, das – harpsichord
Chor, der – choir, chorus
Choral, der – chorale, anthem, hymn, chant
Chorführer, der – choir director
Chorgesang, der – chorus, anthem
Chorist, der – member of the chorus
Chorknabe, der – choir boy, chorister
Chorsatz – setting for choir
chorweise – in chorus, tutti

dämpfen – to mute or muffle, damp(en)
Dämpfer, mit – with mute
Dämpfer, ohne – without mute
deutlich – clear, distinct
Deutsche Messe – German Mass
Deutung, die – interpretation
Dichter, der – poet
Dichtung, die – text, lyrics, poetry
Dirigent, der – conductor
dirigieren – to conduct
Diskant, der – descant
Dissonanz, die – dissonance
doppel.... – double....
Doppelchörig – double choir
drängend – *stringendo*
dreifach – divisi a 3, threefold
Dreiklang, der – triad
Duett, das – duet
duftig – *dolce*
Dur – major
Durchführung – development, exposition
durchsingen/spielen – to sing/play through

Einklang, der – unison
Einleitung, die – introduction
Einsatz, der – entrance, cue
einsetzen – to enter
einstimmig – unison
Empfindung, die – feeling
ernsthaft – seriously
erst – first
etwas – somewhat
Exposition, die – exposition

Falsett, das – falsetto
feierlich – solemnly
Fermate(a), die – fermata
Ferne, aus der – from a distance
festlich – festively
feurig – passionately, fervently
flehend – entreatingly
fließend – flowingly, fluently
folgend – following
Form, die – form, shape, design
Fortschreitung, die – progression
Frauenchor, der – female choir
frei – freely
Freitag, das Stiller – Good Friday
freudig – joyous(ly)
frisch – fresh(ly)
fröhlich – merrily
Frosch, am – at the frog (str)
Fuge, die – fugue

ganz, gänzlich – completely

ganz leise – pianissimo
Ganzton, der – whole tone
gedämpft – muted
gedeckt – covered
gedeckter Stimme, mit – *sotto voce*
Gefühl, das – feeling
gehalten – sustained
gehaucht – whispered
geheimnisvoll – mysteriously
geistlich – spiritual, sacred
geistliche Chormusik – sacred choral music
Gemeinde, die – congregation
gemessen – moderato
gemischt – mixed
gemischter Chor – mixed chorus
Gesamtausgabe, die – complete edition
Gesang, der – singing, voice, song
Gesangbuch, das – hymn–book, song–book
Gesänge, geistliche – sacred songs
Gesangverein, der – choral society
geschwind – nimbly
gestopft – muted (horn)
geteilt – divided
getragen – sustained
gewöhnlich – *modo ordinario*
glänzend – brilliantly
gleich – similarly, at once
gleichmäßig – even(ly), equal
Glocke, die – bell
Glockenspiel, das – glockenspiel, carillon
Griffbrett, am – over the fingerboard (str)
Gründonnerstag – Maundy Thursday

Halbchor – half chorus
Hammerklavier, das – (early) pianoforte
Handschrift, die – manuscript
Harmonie, die – harmony
Harmonik, die – harmonic structure, overtone
hastig – hastily
Heiliger Abend – Christmas Eve
heiter – cheerfully
hervorheben – to bring out
hinauszögern – delay, *ritard*
Holz, mit – with the wood, *col legno*
Hymne, die – hymn
Hymnus, der – hymn

immer – continually, *sempre*
Improvisation, die – improvisation
improvisieren – to improvise
Inhalt, der – contents
Inhaltsangabe, die – table of contents
Inhaltsverzeichnis, das – index
innig – with deep, genuine feeling
Instrument, das – instrument
Interval, das – interval

Jahrkreis, der – church year

Kadenz, die – cadence
Kammerchor – chamber choir
Kanon, der – canon
Kantate, die – cantata
Kantorei, die – choral-instrumental ensemble
Kapelle, die – chapel, orch, band, ensemble
Karfreitag, der – Good Friday
Karwoche, die – Holy Week, Passion Week
Kirche, die – church
Kirchenjahr, das – ecclesiastical year
Kirchenlied, das – chorale, hymn
Klage, die – lamentation
Klang, der – sound, sonority, tone
klingen – to sound

klingend – resonant
Knabenchor, der – boys choir
Koda, die – coda
Koloratur, die – coloratura
komponieren – to compose
Komponist, der – composer
Komposition, die – composition
Kontrapunkt, der – counterpoint
Konzert, das – concert, recital, concerto
kräftig – strongly, vigorously, robustly
Kreis, der – cycle, circle
Kritik, die – criticism, critique
Krummhorn, das – crumhorn
Kunstlied, das – art song

Ländler, der – forerunner of the waltz
langsam – slow, *lento*
laut – loud, *forte*
lebhaft – lively, *vivace, animato*
leicht – lightly, *leggiero*
leidenschaftlich – passionately
leise – soft, *piano*
Leitung, die – direction
lieblich – sweetly, *dolce*

Lied, das – song, tune, air
Liederabend, der – song recital
Lobgesang, der – hymn of praise
lustig – merrily

Madrigal, das – madrigal
Männerchor, der – male choir
massig – heavily, *pesante*
mäßig – moderate, *moderato, andante*
mehrchörig – polychoral
mehrstimmig – polyphonic
Melodie, die – melody
Messe, die – Roman Catholic Mass
mit – with
　　freiem Vortag – *ad lib.*
　　gedeckter Stimme – *sotto voce*
　　großem Ausdruck – great expression
　　voller Stimme – full voice
Modulation, die – modulation, inflection
Moll – minor
Motette, die – motet
munter – lively, bright, *allegro*
Musik, die – music
musikalisch – musical

nach und nach – *poco a poco*
Nachschlag – grace note
Nachspiel, das – postlude, epilogue
natürlich – in the usual manner, *ordinario*
nicht – not, *non*
nicht zu – not too, *non troppo*
nimmt (piccolo) – take (piccolo)
Notation, die – notation
Note, die – note
Noten, die – sheet music
Notensystem, das – brace, staff

Oberton, der – harmonic, overtone
offen – open
ohne – without
Oktett, das – octet
Oper, die – opera or opera house
Operette, die – operetta
Oratorium, das – oratorio
Orchester, das – orchestra
Orgel, die – organ
Orgelmesse, die – organ Mass
Oster(n), die – Easter, Passover

Oster(sonn)tag, der – Easter Sunday
Osterwoche, die – Easter week
Ouvertüre, die – overture

Partie, die – part, passage
Partitur, die – (full) score
Pause, die – rest, intermission
Phrasierung, die – phrasing
plötzlich – suddenly, *subito*
Polyphonie, die – polyphony
Posaune, die – trombone
Postludium, das – postlude
Praeludium, das – prelude
Probe, die – rehearsal
Program, das – program
Pult, das – desk, stand
Pult, erstes – first desk
Punkt, der – dot
punktiert – dotted

Quartett, das – quartet
Quintett, das – quintet

rasch – fast, *allegro*
recht – very, quite
Register, das – register, stop (organ), index
Requiem, das – Requiem Mass
Rezitativ, das – recitative
Rhythmik, die – rhythmic structure
Rhythmus, das – rhythm
ruhig – calmly, *tranquillo*
ruhevoll – peacefully

Saite, die – string
Sämtliche Werke – collected works
sanft – gently, smoothly
Satz, der – movement, musical setting
Schalltrichter auf – bells in the air
scherzhaft – jokingly
Schlag, der – stroke, blow, beat
Schlaginstrumente, die – percussion
Schlagzeug, das – percussion or drums
schleppen – drag
schleppen, nicht – do not drag
Schlüssel, der – clef
schmerzlich – sadly, grievously
schmetternd – resounding, blaring, brassy
schnell – fast, *allegro*
Schnelligkeit, die – speed, tempo
schrittweise – step by step
schwächer – weaker, fainter
schwermütig – melancholy
sehnsuchtsvoll – wistfully
sehr – very
Seite, die – page
Seite, auf – on page (10)
Silbe, die – syllable
Sinfonie, die – symphonia, symphony
singen – to sing
Solist, der/Solisten, die – soloist/soloists
Sonate, die – sonata
Sopran, der – treble, soprano
spielen – to play
Spielanweisung, die – direction for playing
Spitze, am – at the point of the bow (str)
Ständchen – serenade
stark/stärker – loud/louder
Steg, am – near the bridge (str)
stets – steadily, continuously, *sempre*
Stichnoten, die – small notes, cue notes
Stichwort, das – cue
Stil, der – style
Stimmbildung, die – vocal training

Stimme, die – voice, part
Stimme, mit halber – sing with half voice
Stimme, mit voller – sing with full voice
stimmen – to tune
Stimmung, die – mood, tuning
strahlend – shining, radiantly
Streicher, die – strings (section)
Strich, der – bowing
stürmisch – stormy, impetuous(ly)
summen – to hum
Symphonie, die – symphony
synkopieren – syncopate
System, das (Noten) – brace, staff

Takt, der – time, meter, measure, bar
   der Dreiertakt – triple time
   Dreivierteltakt – 3/4 time
   Takt halten – keep time
   Takt schlagen – beat time
   Viervierteltakt – 4/4 time
Taktart, die – meter
Taktmesser, der – metronome
Taktstock, der – baton
Taktstrich, der – bar
Taktzahl, die – measure number
Tamburin, das – tamborine
Tamtam, das – gong, tam tam
Tanz, der – dance
tänzerisch – dancelike
Teil, der – part, section (of a composition)
Tempo, das – tempo
Tempo, im – *a tempo*
Tenor, der – tenor
Terzett, das – trio
Text, der – text
Textdichter, der – author, poet
Themenaufstellung – exposition
Themendurchführung – development
tief – low, deep, flat
Ton, der – tone, note, sound
Tonalität, die – tonality
Tonart, die – key, mode
Tonhöhe, die – pitch
Tonleiter, die – scale
Tonsatz, der – musical composition
Tonwechsel, der – key change
tragen – to sustain, carry
transponieren – transpose
Transposition, die – transposition
träumerisch – dreamingly
Tremolo, das – tremolo
Triller, der – trill
Trinklied, das – drinking song
Trommel, die – drum
Trompete, die – trumpet

üben – to practice, exercise
Übergang, der – transition
übermässig – augmented
Übersetzung, die – translation
Übung, die – practice, excercise
umsetzen – transpose
Umsetzung, die – transposition
unbetont – unaccented
ungeduldig – impatiently
Unterricht, der – instruction, teaching; lesson
Uraufführung, die – first performance
Urtext, der – original version

Variation, die – variation
Varlängerung, die – lengthening
Vergrösserung – augmentation
verhalten – sustain, *sostenuto*

Verkleinerung, die – diminution
Verkürzung, die – reduction (of note values)
verlangsamen – make broader, slower
verlöschend – dying away
verschieben – to syncopate
verschoben – syncopated
versetzen – to transpose
Versetzung, die – transposition
verstimmt – out of tune
verweilend – *rallentando*
verzögern – delay, *ritard*
viel – very
vokal – vocal
Vokal, der – vowel
vokalisieren – vocalize
voll – full
Volkslied, das – folk song
von – from
Vorausnahme, die – anticipation
vorbereiten – prepare
Vorhang, der – curtain
Vorhang fällt – the curtain falls
Vorhang geht auf – the curtain rises
vorher, wie – as before
Vorschlag, der – grace note, anacrusis
Vorsingen, das – audition
Vorspiel, das – overture, prelude, audition
Vortrag, der – interpretation
Vortrag, mit freiem – *ad lib.*
Vortragsbezeichnung, die – expression mark
Vorzeichen, das – accidental

wachsend – increasing, *crescendo*
Waldhorn, das – french horn
Walzer, der – waltz
Wärme, mit – with warmth
Wechsel, der – change, alternation
wechseln – to change, alternate
weich – mellow, soft, piano
Weihnacht(en), die – Christmas
Weihnachtsabend, der – Christmas Eve
Weihnachtslied, das – Christmas carol
Weise, die – tune, melody
weltlich – secular
weltliches Chormusik – secular choral music
wenig – a little, *poco*
wie zuvor – as before
wieder – again
wiederholen – repeat
Wiederholung, die – repetition
Wiederholungszeichen, das – repeat sign
würdevoll – majestic, *maestoso*
würdig – with dignity

zart – tender, gentle, *dolce*
zärtlich – fondly, affectionately
Zäsur, die – break, *caesura*
Zeichen, das – mark, sign
Zeile, die – line
Zeitmaß, das – time unit, tempo
ziemlich – somewhat, fairly, moderately
zögern – to hesitate, *ritard*
Zuhörer, der – listener, (plural) audience
zu 2 – a 2
zurückhalten – to *ritard; mezza voce*
zusammen (einfach) – together, unison
Zwei Chöre – double choir
Zwölftonmusik, die – 12- tone music
Zyklus, der – cycle

SELECTED SETTINGS OF GERMAN TEXTS

This listing provides information about the variety of composers and voicings associated with each of the translated texts. Performers are first encouraged to check the thorough listings in Musicdata's *Sacred Choral Music in Print* (Master Index, 1992) and *Secular Choral Music in Print* (Master Index, 1993; Supplement, 1996) for available editions and prices. In addition, consult the complete works and the listings of specific composers in *The New Grove Dictionary of Music and Musicians* (1980) as well as publishers' catalogs. Electronic databases like *Musica* and *Worldcat* are also very helpful. If you still have questions, contact the publisher of this book and we will provide what information we have. Some of these listings are only as good as our sources and, although considerable discretion has been exercised, it has not been possible to verify the accuracy and authenticity of each entry. We apologize for any spurious listings and any inconvenience this may occasion.

Abbreviations:	satb/satb	double chorus
	satb (ttbb)	optional voicing written by the composer
	satb; org (2vn)	optional instruments
	(2) satb	two different settings for satb
	T, ssa	Tenor solo, ssa chorus

A, a	alto	hp	harp	str	strings
B, b	bass	hpsd	harpsichord	T, t	tenor
bc	basso continuo	hrn	horn	tmp	timpani
br	brass	inst	instruments	trb	trombone
bsn	bassoon	ob	oboe	trp	trumpet
cb	contrabass	orch	orchestra	va	viola
cel	celesta	org	organ	vc	violoncello
cl	clarinet	perc	percussion	vg	viola da gamba
eh	english horn	pno	piano	vib	vibraphone
eq	equal voices	rec	recorder	vn	violin
fl	flute	S, s	soprano	vv	voices

Abendfeier in Venedig
Schumann, C. — satb

Abendlich schon rauscht die Welt
Hensel, F. — satb
Reger, M. — tttbbb

Abendlied
Brahms, J. — satb, pno

Abendlied zu Gott (*Herr, der du mir das Leben*)
Haydn, J. — satb, hpsd
Reger, M. — satb

Abendständchen
Brahms, J. — ssattb (pno)
Reger, M. — Bar, ttbb

Ach, arme Welt
Brahms, J. — satb

Ach, Herr, du Schöpfer aller Ding
Schütz, H. — sattb, bc

Ach, Herr, strafe mich nicht
Knüpfer, S. — ssatb, 2 trp, tmp, str, bc
Reger, M. — ssatb
Telemann, G.P. — canon a 2

Alles hat seine Zeit
Haydn, J. — satb, pno

Alles was ihr tut
Buxtehude, D. — SB, satb, str, bc
Dedekind, C.C. — sa

Also hat Gott die Welt geliebt
Bach, J.S. (BWV 68) — SB, satb, orch

(Also hat Gott die Welt geliebt)
Distler, H. — sab
Franck, M. — satb
Graun, C.H. — satb
Graupner, C. — SB, satb, str, bc
Gregor, C. — sstb, str
Hammerschmidt, A. — ssattb, (bc)
Herbst, J. — ssab, str
Praetorius, M. — ssattb
Riemann, A. — 8 vv
Schütz, H. — sattb
Telemann, G.P. — sa(b), bc

Am Bodensee
Schumann, R. — satb

An den Vetter
Haydn, J. — sat, pno

An die Frauen
Haydn, J. — ttb, hpsd

An die Heimat
Brahms, J. — satb, pno

An die Sterne
Schumann, R. — satb / satb

Auf den Erfinder des Metronoms
Beethoven [?] — canon a 4

Aufblick
Wolf, H.   satb

Aus dem Danklied zu Gott
Haydn, J.   satb, hpsd

Aus der Tiefen rufe ich
Bach, J.S. (BWV 131)   SATB, satb, orch
Fortner, W.   sa
Graun, C.H.   satb
Graupner, C.   SATB, satb, 3 trp, tmp, 2 ob, str, bc
Schütz, H.   satb/satb, bc

Aus tiefer Not
Agricola, M.   canon a 2
Bach, J.S. (BWV 38)   SATB, satb, orch
Distler, H.   ssatb
Erbe, E.I.   satb
Franck, M.   satb
Franck, M.   sattb
Hassler, H.L.   satb
Lassus, O.   satb
Lechner, L.   sattb
Mendelssohn, A.   S, chorus, org, orch
Mendelssohn, F.   ATB, satb, org
Praetorius, M.   sat
Praetorius, M.   satb/satb
Praetorius, M.   12 vv
Reda, S.   ssatb
Scheidt, S.   (2) stb, bc
Schein, J.H.   SS, bc
Schein, J.H.   satb, bc
Schütz, H.   satb

Begräbnisgesang
Brahms, J.   satbb, orch (org)

Begräbnislied
Schubert, F.   satb, pno

Betrachtung des Todes
Haydn, J.   stb, pno

Brennessel steht an Weges Rand
Brahms, J.   satb, pno

Chor der Engel
Liszt, F.   mixed vv, hp/pno
Schubert, F.   satb

Christ ist erstanden
David, J.N.   sab, org
Eccard, J.   sattb, (bc)
Hassler, H.L.   satb
Heiller, A.   satb
Isaac, H.   4 vv
Lasso, O.   satb
Lechner, L.   satb
Pepping, E.   ssatb
Praetorius, M.   ssb
Praetorius, M.   (3) 4 vv
Praetorius, M.   5 vv
Praetorius, M.   21 vv
Reger, M.   ssaattb
Scheidt, S.   stb, bc
Schein, J.H.   satb, bc
Schubert, F.   satb

Schütz, H.   SAT, satb/satb, 4 va, 4 trb, bc
Senfl, L.   satttb
Senfl, L.   sattbb
Vulpius, M.   satb
Vulpius, M.   satb/satb

Christ lag in Todesbanden
Bach, J.S. (BWV 4)   SATB, satb, (3 trb), str, bc
Bach, J.S.   (3) satb
Eccard, J.   sattb, (bc)
Hassler, H.L.   satb
Pachelbel, J.   SATB, satb, 2 vln, 3 va, bsn, bc
Praetorius, M.   ssattb
Praetorius, M.   stt
Praetorius, M.   (2) 4 vv
Praetorius, M.   (2) 5 vv
Praetorius, M.   8 vv
Reda, S.   5 vv
Scheidt, S.   satb/satb, bc
Schein, J.H.   satb, bc
Schein, J.H.   ssatb, bc
Telemann, G.P.   satb

Coronach
Schubert, F.   ssa, pno

Daphnens einziger Fehler
Haydn, J.   ttb, pno

Darthulas Grabesgesang
Brahms, J. (Macpherson)   saatbb, (pno)
Schoenberg, A. (Goethe) (fragment)   14 vv

Das ist ein köstliches Ding (see: Es ist ein köstliches...)
Schumann, G.   ssatbb
Telemann, G.P.   satb, str, bc

Das neugeborne Kindelein
Bach, J.S. (BWV 122)   SATB, satb, orch
Buxtehude, D.   satb, 3 vn, bc
Vulpius, M.   satb

Dem dunkeln Schoß
Brahms, J.   satb

Denn Er hat seinen Engeln
Mendelssohn, F.   ssaattbb

Der 13. Psalm (see: Herr, wie lange)
Brahms, J.   ssa, org

Der 23. Psalm (see: Der Herr ist mein Hirt)
Liszt, F.   T/S, (male vv) hp/pno, org/harm
Pepping, E.   mixed vv
Schubert, F.   ssaa, pno

Der Abend
Brahms, J.   satb, pno
Orff, C.   sprechchor
Strauss, R.   16 vv

Der Augenblick
Haydn, J.   satb, pno

Der Feuerreiter
Distler, H.   ssaatb
Wolf, H.   ssaattbb, orch

Der Gang zu Liebchen
Brahms, J.   satb, pno

Der Gärtner
Brahms, J.	ssa, 2 hrn, hp / pno
Mendelssohn, F.	ss, pno

Der Geist hilft unser Schwachheit auf
Bach, J.S.	satb / satb, (2ob, bsn, str, bc)
Geisler, J.C.	ssab, str

Der Gondelfahrer
Schubert, F.	ttbb, pno

Der Greis
Haydn, J.	satb, pno

Der Herr ist mein Hirt
Bach, J.S.	satb
Bach, J.S. (BWV 112)	SATB, satb, orch
Calvisius, S.	sab
Franck, M.	satb
Gregor, C.	ssab
Hammerschmidt, A.	ssb, bc
Hammerschmidt, A.	8 vv
Hassler, H.L.	(2) satb
Homilius, G.A.	satb
Michael,T.	ssatb / ssatb, bc
Pepping, E.	satb
Praetorius, M.	sat
Praetorius, M.	satb
Schreck,G.	satb
Schubert, F.	ssaa, pno
Schütz, H.	ssat / satb / ssat, bc
Schütz, H.	sat / satb, 2 vn, bc
Telemann, G.P.	ss(b), bc
Vulpius, M.	4 vv
Zimmerman, H.W.	satb, cb, org

Der Schmied
Schumann, R.	satb

Der Tanz
Schubert, F.	satb, pno

Deutsche Messe
Biebl, F.	mixed vv
David, J.N.	4–8 vv
Distler, H.	ssatbb
Fortner, W	mixed vv
Heiller, A.	satb, org
Krenek, E.	satb, cl, tpt, 2 tbn, tmp, org
Mendelssohn, A.	8 vv
Mendelssohn, F.	8 vv
Pepping, E.	(2) ssatbb
Poos, H.	satb / ssatbb
Praetorius, M.	6 vv
Schubert, F.	satb, orch (org)
Schütz, H.	satb, bc
Spitta, H.	mixed vv

Deutsche Motette
Strauss, R.	SATB, ssssaaaattttbbbb

Deutsches Magnificat (see: **Meine Seele erhebt...**)
Haydn, M.	SS, ss, 2 hrn, cb, org
Scheidt, S.	satb, bc
Schütz, H.	satb / satb, (bc)

Die Beredsamkeit
Haydn, J.	satb, pno

Die Geselligkeit (*Lebenslust*)
Schubert, F.	satb, pno

Die Harmonie in der Ehe
Haydn, J.	satb, pno

Die Himmel erzählen die Ehre Gottes
Bach, J.S. (BWV 76)	SATB, satb, orch
Haydn, J.	STB, satb, orch
Mendelssohn, F.	5 vv
Schütz, H.	ssattb

Die mit Tränen säen
Antes, J.	satb, str
Bach, J.L.	SATB, satb, str, bc
Gambold, J.	ssab, bc
Gambold, J.	S, ssab, str
Geisler, J.C.	ssab, 2 fl, str
Jäschke, C.	satb, str
Krenek, E.	satb, org / pno
Maler, W.	canon a 3
Peter, J.F.	satb(ssab), fl, bsn, str, bc
Schein, J.H.	ssatb, (bc)
Schütz, H.	satbb / satbb, (inst, bc)
Schütz, H.	ssatb, (bc)

Die Musici
Anonymous	canon a 2

Die Nachtigall
Mendelssohn, F.	satb
Mozart, W.A.	canon a 3

Die Rose stand im Tau
Schumann, R.	ttbbb

Die Schöpfung
Haydn, J.	STB, ssatb, orch

Die Warnung
Haydn, J.	satb,pno

Dort oben vom Berge
Biebl, F.	SA, mixed vv

Dreimal tausend Jahre
Schönberg, A.	satb

Du Zweifel
Hindemith, P.	ssatb

Ehre sei dir, Christe
Distler, H.	satb
Schütz, H.	satb

Ein deutsches Requiem
Brahms, J.	SB, satb, orch
Schubert, F.	SATB, satb, org

Ein feste Burg ist unser Gott
Bach, J.S. (BWV 80)	SATB, satb, orch
Bach, J.S.	(2) satb
Beethoven, L.	canon a 2
Crüger, J.	satb, (2 inst, org)
Franck, M.	satb
Friederich, J.	canon a 4
Hassler, H.L.	(2) satb
Herbst, J.	SSATB, ssatb, 2 vn, 2 va, bc
Krieger, J.P.	satb, str, bc
Praetorius, M.	sat
Praetorius, M.	ttbbb, bc

Scheidt, S.	satb / atbb
Schein, J.H.	SS, bc
Schein, J.H.	satb, bc
Schütz, H.	satb
Telemann, G.P.	satb, bc
Vulpius, M.	sat / sab

Ein Kind ist uns geboren (see: Uns ist ein Kind geboren)
Biebl, F.	male vv
Franck, M.	satb / satb
Scheidt, S.	ssattb, bc
Schütz, H.	satb, bc
Schütz, H.	ssattb, bc

Einklang
| Wolf, H. | satb |

Elegischer Gesang
| Beethoven, L. | satb, str qt / pno |

Entflieht auf leichten Kähnen
| Webern, A. | satb |

Erfreue dich, Erde
| Buxtehude | SSAB, ssab, 2 trp, timp, 2 vn, vc, bc |

Ergebung (Dein Wille, Herr)
| Reger, M. | S, pno / org / harmonium |
| Wolf, H. | satb |

Erhebung
| Wolf, H. | satb |

Es ist das Heil
Bach, J.S. (BWV 9)	SATB, satb, fl, ob, str, bc
Brahms, J.	satbb
Distler, H.	satb
Hassler, H.L.	satb
Pepping, E.	satb
Praetorius, M.	sab
Praetorius, M.	satb / satb
Schein, J.H.	satb, (bc)
Vulpius, M.	satb

Es ist ein köstliches Ding
Bach, J.S. (BWV 176)	SAB, satb, 2 ob, eh, str, bc
Distler, H.	unis, org
Gesius, B.	ssatb
Gregor, C.	sstb, str
Herbst, J.	ssab, str
Peter, J.F.	ST, satb, str
Poos, H.	ssaa / sa
Schein, J.H.	satb, (bc)
Schumann, G.	saatbb
Schütz, H.	satb

Es ist ein' Ros' entsprungen
Distler, H.	satb
Distler, H.	S, satb
Praetorius, M.	satb
Vulpius, M.	satb
Vulpius, M.	canon a 4

Es tönt ein voller Harfenklang
| Brahms, J. | ssa, 2 hrn, hp / pno |

Fantasie
| Beethoven, L. | piano, chorus, orch |

Fest– und Gedenksprüche
| Brahms, J. | satb / satb |

Fragen
| Brahms, J. | satb, pno |

Freude, schöner Götterfunken
Beethoven, L.	SATB, satb, orch
Haydn, J.M.	sssb
Schubert, F.	S/T, unison chorus, pno

Freunde, lasset uns beim Zechen
| Mozart, W.A. | canon a 4 |

Friede auf Erden
| Schönberg, A. | ssaattbb (8 inst) |

Fröhlich im Maien
| Strauss, R. | ttbb |

Fürchte dich nicht
Bach, J.C.	sattb, (bc)
Bach, J.S.	satb / satb, (bc)
Geisler, J.C.	ssab, str

Fürwahr, er trug unsere Krankheit
Buxtehude, D.	SB, ssatb, 5 str, bc
Distler, H.	satb
Erbe, E.I.	satb
Franck, M.	satb
Graun, K.H.	satb
Gregor, C.	ssab, bc
Herbst, J.	ssab / ssab, str
Herbst, J.	satb, str
Herbst, J.	(2) sstb (ssab), str

Gartenlieder
| Hensel, F. | satb |

Geistliches Lied (Lass dich nur nichts nicht dauern)
| Brahms, J. | satb, org (pno) |
| Hensel, F. | satb |

Gesang aus Fingal
| Brahms, J. | ssa, 2 hrn, hp / pno |

Gesang der Geister über dem Wassern
| Schubert, F. | ttbb, pno |
| Schubert, F. | ttttbbbb, 2 va, 2 vc, cb |

Gesang der Parzen
| Brahms, J. | saatbb, orch |

Gesänge für Frauenchor
| Brahms, J. | ssa, 2 hrn, hp / pno |

Gondoliera
| Schumann, C. | satb |

Gott der Herr ist Sonn und Schild
| Bach, J.S. (BWV 79) | SAB, satb, orch |

Gott in der Natur
| Schubert, F. | ssaa, pno |

Gott ist mein Hirt
| Schubert, F. | ssaa, pno |

Gottes Zeit ist die allerbeste Zeit
| Bach, J.S. (BWV 106) | SATB, satb, 2 rec, 2 vg, bc |

Gute Nacht
| Schumann, R. | satb |

Heilig

Bach, C.P.E.	satb/satb, orch
Bach, J.S.	satb
Bach, W.F.E.,	4 vv, instr
Caldara, A.	canon a 3
Hammerschmidt, A.	ssatb, 2 obl, bc
Lonas, H.	satb, br
Mendelssohn, F.	satb/satb
Naumann, J.G.	satb, 2 hrn, str/SS, 2 fl, bsn
Praetorius, M.	5 vv
Schubert, F.	satb, orch/org

Herr, erhöre meine Worte

Schumann, G.	ssaattbb
Schütz, H.	satb, satb, bc

Herr, nun lässest du deinen Diener

Bach, J.C.	satb/satb, (bc)
Franck, M.	satb
Franck, M.	ssab/attb
Mendelssohn, F.	SATB, satb
Praetorius, M.	satb
Riemann, A.	Bar, ssaattbb, bfl
Schein, J.H.	satb, (bc)
Schütz, H.	(2) ssattb, (bc)
Schütz, H.	aattb/ssb
Zimmerman, H.W.	satb, vib, cb, org

Herr, wenn ich nur dich habe

Bach, J.M.	sattb, (bc)
Schütz, H.	satb/satb, (bc)

Herr, wie lange

Brahms, J.	ssa, org
Hammerschmidt, A.	ssatb
Hassler, H.L.	satb
Lasso, O.	satb
Liszt, F.	T, satb, orch
Scheidt, S.	ssat/atbb
Schumann, G.	mixed vv
Schütz, H.	ssattb, 2 vn, bc
Telemann, G.P.	canon a 2
Zimmerman, H.W.	satb, cb, org

Himmel strahlt so helle und klar

Brahms, J.	satb, pno

Hörst du nicht die Bäume rauschen? *(Lockung)*

Hensel, F.	satb
Rheinberger, J.	satb, pno

Ich aber bin elend

Brahms, J.	satb/satb
Telemann, G.P.	ss(b), bc

Ich lasse dich nicht

Bach, J.S.	satb/satb
Bach, J.S. (BWV 157)	TB, satb, fl, ob, va, bc
Buxtehude, D.	TB, 5 str, 2 trb, bc
Herbst, J.	ssab, str
Schein, J.H.	ssatb, bc

Ich weiß mir ein Meidlein

Brahms, J.	SA, pno
David, J.N.	satb
de Vento, I.	5 vv
Hassler, H.L.	satb
Lasso, O.	satb

Scheidt, S.	satb, bc
Schein, J.H.	(2) satb, (bc)

Ich weiß, daß mein Erlöser lebt

Bach, J.M.	sattb
Fabricius, A.	sattb
Franck, M.	satbb
Geisler, J.C.	ss/ssab, str
Praetorius, M.	satb
Schein, J.H.	satb, bc
Schütz, H.	ssaatbb
Schütz, H.	ssattb

Ihr Musici frisch auf

Hassler, H.L.	ssatbb

Im Herbst

Brahms, J.	satb

Im Herbste

Hensel, F.	satb

Im kühlen Maien

Hassler, H.L.	satb/satb

Im Wald

Biebl, F.	mixed vv
Hensel, F.	satb

In dulci jubilo

Bach, J.S.	satb
Biebl, F.	mixed vv
Buxtehude, D.	ssb, 2 vn, bc
Eccard, J.	sattb, (bc)
Hassler, H.L.	satb
Praetorius, M.	(2) satb
Praetorius, M.	sat
Praetorius, M.	ssat
Praetorius, M.	satb/satb
Praetorius, M.	20 vv
Reger, M.	ssatbb
Scheidt, S.	ssat/atbb, (2 inst)
Scheidt, S.	satb, (bc)
Schein, J.H.	satb, (bc)
Telemann, G.P.	ATB, satb, 2 hrn, str, bc

In stiller Nacht

Brahms, J.	satbb

Innsbruck, ich muss dich lassen

Isaac, H.	satb

Jauchzet dem Herren

Bach, J.S.	satb/satb, bc
Fortner, W.	5 vv, 3 hrn, 2 trp, 2 trb
Graun, K.H.	ssab
Hammerschmidt, A.	ssattb, (bc)
Homilius, G.A.	satb/satb, (bc)
Mendelssohn, F.	ssaattbb
Mendelssohn, F.	(2) satb
Pachelbel, J.	satb, 2 ob, 2 vn, 3 va, vc, bc
Pachelbel, J.	5 vv, 4 trp, tmp, str, bsn, bc
Reger, M.	satb, org, orch
Scheidt, S.	ssatb, bc
Schütz, H.	(2) satb/satb, bc
Schütz, H.	satb/satb/satb, bc
Schütz, H.	ssatb/ssat/st/ssatb
Telemann, G.P.	stb, 2 fl, str, bc

Zimmerman, H.W.   S, satb / satb, sm.orch
Zimmerman, H.W.   satb, cb, org

Jesu, meine Freude
Bach, J.S.   ssatb, (bc)
Buxtehude, D.   SSB, ssb, 2 vn, bsn, bc
Crüger, J.   satb
Hammerschmidt, A.   5 vv
Mendelssohn, F.   satb / satb, str
Telemann, G.P.   SB, satb, 2 ob, str, bc

Joseph, lieber Joseph mein
Calvisius, S.   ssattb
Handl, J.   satb
Lasso, O.   satb
Praetorius, M.   3 vv
Praetorius, M.   5 vv
Scheidt, S.   satb, bc

Judaskuß
Hindemith, P.   ssatb
Hindemith, P. (Das verfluchte Geld)   ttbb

Kantate I
Webern, A.   S, satb, orch

Komm, Heiliger Geist, Herre Gott
Bach, J.S.   (3) satb
David, J.N.   2 choruses, orch
Distler, H.   satb
Eccard, J.   sattb, (bc)
Hassler, H.L.   satb
Haydn, J.M.   ssb, 2 hrn, 3 trb, org
Poos, H.   sa / ttbb / unison
Praetorius, M.   sat
Praetorius, M.   (2) 4 vv
Praetorius, M.   5 vv
Praetorius, M.   6 vv
Praetorius, M.   satb / satb
Praetorius, M.   11 vv
Reda, S.   satb
Reger, M.   satb
Scheidt, S.   satb / satb
Scheidt, S.   ssatb, bc
Scheidt, S.   ss, 2 trb, bc
Schein, J.H.   satb, (bc)
Schein, J.H.   ssatb, (bc)
Schumann, G.   ssaattbb
Schütz, H.   sattbb, bc
Telemann, G.P.   (2) satb, (bc)
Telemann, G.P.   satb, 3 trp, tmp, str, bc

Komm, Jesu, komm
Bach, J.S.   satb / satb, (bc)

Lass dich nur nichts nicht dauern
Brahms, J.   satb, org (pno)
Hensel, F.   satb
Reger, M.   S, pno / org / harmonium

Laut verkünde unsre Freude
Mozart, W.A.   TTB, ttbb, orch

Lebenslust (Die Geselligkeit)
Schubert, F.   satb, pno

Letze Bitte
Wolf, H.   satb

Letztes Glück
Brahms, J.   saatbb

Liebe Schwalbe, kleine Schwalbe
Brahms, J.   satb, pno

Liebeslieder
Brahms, J.   SATB, satb, pno (4-hands)
Brahms, J. (O wie sanft   canon a 4 (ssaa)

Lied von Shakespeare
Brahms, J.   ssa, 2 hrn, hp / pno

Lobe den Herren, den mächtigen König
Anonymous   canon a 4
Bach, J.S.   satb
Bach, J.S. (BWV 137)   SATB, satb, orch
Distler, H.   satb

Lobet den Herrn, alle Heiden
Bach, J.S.   satb, bc
Franck, M.   ssatb
Herbst, J.   satb, 2 fl (ob), 2 hrn, str
Lasso, O.   ssatb
Sartorius, E.   canon a 4
Scheidt, S.   ssattb, bc
Schütz, H.   ATB, 2 vn, bc
Telemann, G.P.   sa, bc
Telemann, G.P.   sa, 2 vn, bc
Telemann, G.P.   satb, str, bc
Telemann, G.P.   ss(b), (3 trp, tmp), str
Vulpius, M.   satb

Maria durch ein' Dornwald ging
David, J.N.   satbb
Distler, H.   sab

Mein Odem ist schwach
Reger, M.   ssatb

Meine Seele erhebt den Herren (see: D. Magnificat)
Bach, J.S. (BWV 10)   SATB, satb, orch
Crüger, J.   ST, satb, vn, bc
Eccard, J.   sattb, (bc)
Franck, M.   satb
Gregor, C.   ssab, bc
Hammerschmidt, A.   ssattb, bc
Herbst, J.   ssab / ssab, str
Mendelssohn, F.   SATB, satb
Praetorius, M.   4 vv
Praetorius, M.   5 vv
Praetorius, M.   3-6 vv
Praetorius, M.   8 vv
Praetorius, M.   satb / satb / satb
Praetorius, M.   19 vv
Scheidt, S.   satb, bc
Schein, J.H.   satb, (bc)
Schütz, H.   satb / satb
Telemann, G.P.   ssb, bc
Telemann, G.P.   SATB, satb, ww, str, bc
Viadana, L.   satb
Zimmerman, H.W.   ssatb, vib, hpsd, cb

Meister Jakob
Traditional German   canon a 4

Mit Fried und Freud ich fahr dahin

Agricola, M.	attb
Bach, J.S.	satb
Bach, J.S. (BWV 125)	ATB, satb, orch
Eccard, J.	sattb, (bc)
Gesius, B.	satb
Praetorius, M.	stb (sab)
Praetorius, M.	satb / satb
Praetorius, M.	13 vv
Reger, M.	satb
Scheidt, S.	satb, 2 vn, bc
Schein, J.H.	SS, bc
Schein, J.H.	satb, (bc)
Schumann, G.	S, ssaattbb, br, (org)

Mitten wir im Leben sind

Bach, J.S.	satb
Mendelssohn, F.	ssaattbb
Pepping, E.	male vv
Praetorius, M.	2 vv
Praetorius, M.	3 vv
Reger, M.	sattb
Schein, J.H.	satb, (bc)

Morgengruß

Hensel, F.	satb

Musikantenkanon

Rohwer, J.	canon a 3

Nach dir, Herr, verlanget mich

Bach, J.S. (BWV 150)	SATB, satb, bsn, 2 vn, bc
Schein, J.H.	satb, bc

Nächtens

Brahms, J.	satb, pno

Nachtgesang im Walde

Schubert, F.	ttbb, 4 hrn

Nachthelle

Schubert, F.	T, ttbb, pno

Nachtigallenkanon

Haydn, J.	canon a 3

Nachtreigen

Hensel, F.	ssaattbb

Nachtwache I (*Leise Töne der Brust*)

Brahms, J.	saatbb
Brahms, J.	canon a 4

Nachtwache II (*Ruhn sie?*)

Brahms, J.	saatbb

Nänie

Brahms, J.	satb, orch / pno

Neckereien

Brahms, J.	satb, pno

Neue Liebeslieder

Brahms, J.	SATB, satb, pno (4-hands)

Nun danket alle Gott

Bach, J.S. (BWV 192)	SB, satb, 2 fl, 2 ob, str, bc
Bach, J.S.	(2) satb

Buxtehude, D.	ssatb, 4 br, 3 str, bsn, bc
Crüger, J.	satb
Geisler, J.C.	ssab, str
Liszt, F.	male / mixed, br, (tmp), org
Liszt, F.	chorus / pno
Mendelssohn, F.	org, (ssattbb, br, tmp)
Pachelbel, J.	satb / satb, bc
Poos, H.	ssattb
Praetorius, M.	satb
Scheidt, S.	ssat / satb / ttbb, bc
Scheidt, S.	ssatb / ssatb
Scheidt, S.	12, 17, or 23 vv, bc
Schein, J.H.	ssattb, bc
Schütz, H.	ssattb, bc

Nun ist das Heil

Bach, J.S. (BWV 50)	satb / satb, orch
Schein, J.H.	ssaatb, 2 trp, 3 trb, bc

Nun komm, der Heiden Heiland

Bach, J.S. (BWV 60)	STB, satb, orch
Bach, J.S. (BWV 61)	SATB, satb, orch
Crüger, J.	satb, (2 inst, org)
David, J.N.	sab, org
Distler, H.	sab
Eccard, J.	sattb, (bc)
Hassler, H.L.	satb
Praetorius, M.	sat
Praetorius, M.	satb
Praetorius, M.	satb / satb
Praetorius, M.	ssattb
Praetorius, M.	12 vv
Reda, S.	sab
Scheidt, S.	satb / satb
Schein, J.H.	satb, bc
Schein, J.H.	ssatb, bc
Telemann, G.P.	SATB, satb, 2 ob, str, bc
Vulpius, M.	satb

O du fröhliche

Biebl, F.	mixed vv

O Freunde, nicht diese Töne

Beethoven, L.	SATB, satb, orch

O Haupt voll Blut und Wunden

Bach, J.S.	satb
Hassler, H.L.	sattb
Herbst, J.	ssab, str, bc
Kellner, J.P.	ssab, fl, bsn, str
Liszt, F.	chorus, pno
Mendelssohn, F.	1 v, pno
Mendelssohn, F.	satb, org / pno
Mendelssohn, F.	B, satb, orch
Pepping, E.	A / Bar, orch
Reger, M.	AT, satb, ob, vn, org

O Heiland, reiß die Himmel auf

Brahms, J.	satb
David, J.N.	3 vv
Distler, H.	satb

O Jesulein zart

Bach, J.S.	satb
Reger, M.	satb
Scheidt, S.	satb

O schöne Nacht
Brahms, J.   satb, pno

O Tannenbaum
Marx, K.   satb, ob, 3 vn

O Tod, wie bitter bist du
Reger, M.   ssatb

Psallite
Praetorius, M.   satb
Scheidt, S.   satb, bc
Scheidt, S.   satb / satb

Resignation (*Der Einsiedler*)
Reger, M.   Bar, ssattbb, orch
Wolf, H.   satb

Rhapsodie
Brahms, J.   A, ttbb, orch

Richte mich, Gott
Friderici, D.   canon a 2
Mendelssohn, F.   satb / satb
Scheidt, S.   ssat / atbb

Rote Rosenknopsen künden
Brahms, J.   satb, pno

Schaffe in mir, Gott
Brahms, J.   ssatbb
Buxtehude, D.   S, 2 vn, vc, bc
Hammerschmidt, A.   ssatbb

Schicksalslied
Brahms, J.   satb, orch

Schlagt, Künstler, die Pauken
Buxtehude.   AB,ssab, 2 trp, tmp, 2 vn, vc, bc

Schöne Fremde
Hensel, F.   satb

Sehnsucht (*Es rinnen die Wasser*)
Brahms, J.   satb, pno

Sehnsucht (*Nur wer die Sehnsucht kennt*)
Schubert, F.   ttbbb

Selig sind die Toten
Brahms, J.   satb, orch
Distler, H.   sab
Graun, C.H.   satb
Homilius, G.A.   satb
Mendelssohn, F.   TTBB, ttbb
Rheinberger, J.   satb
Schütz, H.   ssattb, bc
Schütz, H.   aattb / ssb
Spitta, H.   canon a 3
Telemann, G.P.   satb, bc
Telemann, G.P.   satb, str, bc

Singet dem Herrn ein neues Lied
Bach, J.S. (BWV 190)   ATB, satb, orch
Bach, J.S.   satb / satb, (bc)
Distler, H.   satb
Freydt, J.L.   ssab, str
Freydt, J.L.   ssab / ssab, 2 hrn, str
Geisler, J.   ssab / ssab, 2 hrn, str
Hammerschmidt, A.   sttb (satb), bc
Hammerschmidt, A.   8 vv, 4 br

Hassler, H.L.   satb
Herbst, J.   satb, 2 hrn, str
Mendelssohn, F.   SATB, satb / satb, orch
Naumann, J.G.   sstb, 2 fl, bsn, str
Pachelbel, J.   satb / satb, bc
Poos, H.   ttbb
Schütz, H.   (2) satb
Schütz, H.   satb / satb, bc
Telemann, G.P.   SATB, satb, (2 ob), str, bc
Zimmermann, H.W.   ssatb, cb

Singet frisch und wohlgemut
Distler, H.   satb

Singt dem Herren, alle Stimmen!
Haydn, J.   SATB, satb, orch

Spätherbst
Brahms, J.   satb, pno

Ständchen
Liszt, F.   T, ttbb
Schubert, F.   A, ssaa, pno
Schubert, F.   A, ttbb, pno

Stille Nacht
Grüber, F.   SA, satb, gtr

Stimmt an die Saiten
Haydn, J.   satb, orch

Talismane
Barthe, E.   canon a 5
Schumann, R.   satb / satb

Tanzen und springen
Biebl, F.   male vv
Hassler, H.L.   ssatb

Tauche deine Furcht
Hindemith, P.   ssatb

Traumlicht
Strauss, R.   ttbbb

Unendliche Freude
Schubert, F.   ttb
Schubert, F.   canon a 3

Ungewisses Licht
Schumann, R.   satb / satb

Uns ist ein Kind geboren (see: **Ein Kind ist uns geb.**)
Bach, J.S.   satb
Dedekind, C.C.   sa(b), bc
Franck, M.   (2) satb, bc
Geisler, J.C.   ssb / ssb, 2 fl, str
Herbst, J.   ssab, str
Kuhnau, J.   ATB, satb, 2 fl, 2 ob, str, bc
Pepping, E.   mixed vv
Peter, J.F.   ssab, str, bc
Peter, J.F.   satb, 2 fl, bsn, 2 hrn, str
Poos, H.   sat / sab (inst)
Telemann, G.P. ATB, satb, 2 fl, 2 ob, str, bc
Verbeek, J.R.   satb, 2 fl (hrn), str, bc
Vulpius, M.   ssatb
Zimmermann, H.W. ssatb, vib, hpsd, cb, (perc)
Zimmermann, H.W.   ssatb, cb

Unsere Väter hofften auf dich
Brahms, J.   satb / satb

Vater unser im Himmelreich
Bach, J.S. satb
Eccard, J. sattb/saatb
Eccard, J. satb
Franck, M. satb
Hassler, H.L. satb
Heiler, A. women's vv
Lasso, O. 5 vv
Praetorius, M. sat
Praetorius, M. 8 vv
Praetorius, M. 12 vv
Praetorius, M. 18 vv
Scheidt, S. satb/satb
Schein, J.H. satb, bc

Vater unser, der du bist im Himmel
Bach, W.F.E. TB, satb, orch
Gumpelzhaimer, A. canon a 2
Hammerschmidt, A. ssatb/satb
Hassler, H.L. (2) satb
Liszt, F. Bar, ssaattbb, (org)
Praetorius, M. (3) 3 vv
Reger, M. satb/satb/satb
Rheinberger, J. satb/satb
Schein, J.H. AT, ssatb, bc
Schein, J.H. ssatb, 2 trp, 2 trb, bc
Schein, J.H. satb
Schütz, H. SSTTB/satb, 2 vn, bc
Zimmermann, H.W. ssaatbb, cb

Verleih uns Frieden
Distler, H. satbb
Eccard, J. sattb, (bc)
Hammerschmidt, A. 9 vv
Hassler, H.L. satb
Mendelssohn, F. satb, orch (org)
Mendelssohn, F. satb
Praetorius, M. sat
Praetorius, M. satb/attb
Schein, J.H. satb, bc
Schütz, H. 2 S/T, 2 vn, bc
Schütz, H. ssatb, (bc)

Verlorene Jugend
Brahms, J. saatbb

Vineta
Brahms, J. saatbb, (pno)

Vollendet ist das große Werk
Haydn, J. STB, satb, orch

Vom Himmel hoch
Bach, J.S. (2) satb
Calvisius, S. ssattb
Crüger, J. [ba 0594]
Distler, H. 4 vv
Eccard, J. ssatb, (bc)
Friederich, J. canon a 4
Gumpelzhaimer, A. satb
Hammerschmidt, A. 5 vv
Hassler, H.L. satb
Mendelssohn, F. SB, ssatb, orch
Mendelssohn, F. satb
Praetorius, M. sab

Praetorius, M. satb
Praetorius, M. ssatb
Praetorius, M. satb/satb
Praetorius, M. 12 vv
Reger, M. satb
Reger, M. SATB, ssaa, cong, 2 vn, org
Schein, J.H. ssatb, bc
Schein, J.H. satb, bc
Stravinsky, I. satb, inst

Vor der Türen
Strauss, R. ttbb

Vorspruch (*Wer die Musik sich erkiest*)
Distler, H. satbb
Hindemith, P. canon a 2 s, 4 inst
Jeffers, R. ssaa
Lau, H. ttb (ssa) (unis)
Micheelsen, H.F. ttbb, br, str
Micheelsen, H.F. canon a 4 (satb)
Mittergradnegger, G. ttbb
Pappert, R. women's vv
Rein, W. ssa/ttbb
Schrey, W. satb (ssa)(ttbb)
Spitta, H.A.T. mixed vv (ttbb)
Strohbach, S. bar, satb, orch/pno

Vorwärts
Schumann, C. satb

Wachet auf, ruft uns die Stimme
Bach, J.C.F. satb
Bach, J.S. (BWV 140) STB, satb, orch
Bach, J.S. satb
Buxtehude, D. SB, ssb, 4 vn, bc
Buxtehude, D. ATB, 2 vn, bc
Distler, H. SS, ssatb
Praetorius, M. 2 vv
Praetorius, M. (5) 3 vv
Praetorius, M. sst/attb (satb)
Praetorius, M. 17 vv
Spitta, H. canon a 3
Spitta, H. canon a 4
Zimmermann, H.W. ssatbb

Waldesnacht
Brahms, J. satbb

Warum?
Brahms, J. satb, pno

Warum ist das Licht gegeben?
Brahms, J. ssatbb

Wechsellied zum Tanze
Brahms, J. satb, pno

Wenn ein starker Gewappneter
Brahms, J. satb, pno

Wenn wir in höchsten Nöten sein
Brahms, J. satb/satb
Gesius, B ssatb/ssatb
Lechner, L. ssat
Praetorius, M. 2 vv, bc
Praetorius, M. ttb
Praetorius, M. satb/satb
Praetorius, M. 9vv

Praetorius, M.	21 vv
Scheidt, S.	stb, bc
Schein, J.H.	satb

Wider den Übermut

Haydn, J.	satb, hpsd

Widerspruch

Schubert, F.	ttbb, pno

Wie lieblich sind deine Wohnungen

Brahms, J.	satb, orch
Geisler, J.C.	ssab, str
Geisler, J.C.	ssab/ssab, 2 fl, 2 hrn, str
Hammerschmid	ssatb, (bc)
Rheinberger, J.	ssaa, hp (pno/org)
Schein, J.H.	satb, bc
Schütz, H.	ssab/ttbb, bc
Telemann, G.P.	sab, bc
Telemann, G.P.	AB, satb, 2 ob, bsn, str, bc
Telemann, G.P.	satb, fl, 3 ob, bsn, 2 trp, str, bc

Wie schön leuchtet der Morgenstern

Bach, J.S. (BWV 1)	STB, satb, orch
Bach, J.S.	satb
Bach, W.F.E.	4 vv, instr
Distler, H.	satb
Graupner, C.	satb, str, bc
Kuhnau, J.	SST, satb, orch

Kuhnau, J.	ssatb, 2 hrn, str, bc
Mendelssohn, F.	satb (4 inst)
Praetorius, M.	sab
Praetorius, M.	ssatb
Praetorius, M.	13 vv
Reda, S.	satb
Scheidt, S.	8 vv
Schein, J.H.	satb, bc

Willkommen, lieber schöner Mai

Biebl, F.	mixed vv
Mendelssohn, F.	mixed vv
Schubert, F.	(2) canon a 3

Wo ist ein so herrlich Volk

Brahms, J.	satb/satb

Zigeunerleben

Schumann, R.	satb, pno, (perc)

Zigeunerlieder

Brahms, J., op. 103, no. 1–11	satb, pno
Brahms, J., op. 112, no. 3: 1–4	satb, pno

Zündender Lichtblitz

Webern, A.	S, satb, orch

Zuversicht

Schumann, R.	satb/satb

AUTHOR INDEX

TITLE & FIRST LINE INDEX

**So eine Arbeit wird eigentlich nie fertig, man muß sie für fertig erklären,
wenn man nach Zeit und Umständen das Mögliche daran getan hat.**

Such a task is actually never finished, but one must declare it so when one has done
with it what is possible within the given time and circumstances.

Goethe: *Italienische Reise*